T0271205

International Perspectives on Consumers' Access to Justice

Consumer protection law in the age of globalisation poses new challenges for policy-makers. This book highlights the difficulties of framing regulatory responses to the problem of consumers' access to justice in the new international economy. The growth of international consumer transactions in the wake of technological change and the globalisation of markets suggests that governments can no longer develop consumer protection law in isolation from the international legal arena.

Leading scholars consider the broader theme of access to justice from both a socio-legal and a law and economics perspective, as well as addressing specific topics such as standard form contracts, the legal challenges posed by mass infections (such as mad cow disease and CJD), ombudsman schemes, class actions, alternative dispute resolution, consumer bankruptcy, conflict of laws, and cross-border transactions. This book demonstrates that advancing and achieving access to justice for consumers proves to be a challenging, and sometimes elusive, task.

CHARLES E. F. RICKETT has been Professor of Commercial Law in the University of Auckland since 1994, which is a chair held jointly in the Schools of Law and of Business and Economics. He is also Director of the University's Research Centre for Business Law. He has been involved in a consulting capacity in a range of major equitable and restitutionary commercial litigation in New Zeland. In 2001 he was appointed a Professorial Fellow at the University of Melbourne.

THOMAS G. W. TELFER is Associate Professor of Law and Director of the Area of Concentration in Business Law at the University of Western Ontario. He joined the Western Faculty of Law in 2002 from the University of Auckland where he was an active participant in the work of the Research Centre for Business Law and a member of the Council of the Legal Research Foundation. He has acted as a consultant to the New Zealand Ministry of Economic Development on insolvency law reform and was for several years the sole academic member of the New Zealand Joint Insolvency Committee.

International Perspectives on Consumers' Access to Justice

edited by
CHARLES E. F. RICKETT
and
THOMAS G. W. TELFER

CAMBRIDGE
UNIVERSITY PRESS

CAMBRIDGE UNIVERSITY PRESS
Cambridge, New York, Melbourne, Madrid, Cape Town, Singapore, São Paulo

Cambridge University Press
The Edinburgh Building, Cambridge CB2 2RU, UK

Published in the United States of America by Cambridge University Press, New York

www.cambridge.org
Information on this title: www.cambridge.org/9780521824323

First published 2003

A catalogue record for this publication is available from the British Library

Library of Congress Cataloguing in Publication data

International perspectives on consumers' access to justice / edited by Charles E. F. Rickett
and Thomas G. W. Telfer.
    p.   cm.
Includes bibliographical references and index.
ISBN 0 521 82432 X
1. Consumer protection – Law and legislation. 2. Conflict of laws – Consumer protection.
3. Commercial law. 4. Dispute resolution (Law) I. Rickett, C. E. F. II. Telfer, Thomas G. W.
K3842.I584   2003   343.07′1 – dc21   2002031456

ISBN-13 978-0-521-82432-3 hardback
ISBN-10 0-521-82432-X hardback

Transferred to digital printing 2006

Contents

Contributors

ANTHONY DUGGAN Professor of Law, University of Toronto; Professorial Fellow, University of Melbourne

RICHARD FAULK Chairman of the Environmental Practice Group of Gardere Wynne Sewell, LLP, in Houston, Texas

LORNA GILLIES Lecturer in Law, University of Leicester

AXEL HALFMEIER Academic Assistant, University of Bremen

JENNY HAMILTON Senior Lecturer in Law, University of Strathclyde

RHODA JAMES Senior Lecturer in Law, University of Sheffield

PHILIP MORRIS Senior Lecturer in Business Law, University of Stirling

LEONE NIGLIA Lecturer in Law, University of Sheffield

IAIN RAMSAY Professor of Law – Osgoode Hall Law School, York University, Toronto

CHARLES RICKETT Professor of Commercial Law, University of Auckland; Professorial Fellow, University of Melbourne

JANE STAPLETON Research Professor, Law Program, Research School of Social Sciences, Australian National University; Statutory Visiting Professor, University of Oxford (2000–3); Ernest E. Smith Professor of Law, University of Texas (2002–)

CHARLES TABB Alice Curtis Campbell Professor of Law, University of Illinois College of Law

THOMAS TELFER Associate Professor of Law, University of Western Ontario

ELIZABETH THORNBURG Professor of Law, Southern Methodist University, Texas

MICHAEL J. TREBILCOCK Professor of Law and Director of the Law and Economics Program, University of Toronto

THOMAS WILHELMSSON Professor of Civil and Commercial Law, University of Helsinki; Vice-Rector of the University of Helsinki

MIK WISNIEWSKI Senior Research Fellow, Business School, University of Strathclyde

Preface

The Eighth International Consumer Law Conference was held in Auckland, New Zealand, from 9–11 April 2001. John Skinnon of the Open Polytechnic of New Zealand was instrumental in ensuring that the Conference came to New Zealand on behalf of the International Association for Consumer Law, where it was jointly hosted by the Open Polytechnic and the Research Centre for Business Law at The University of Auckland. It was in large part made possible because of the generous sponsorship of the New Zealand Ministry of Consumer Affairs, the Emily Carpenter Consumer Charitable Trust, Butterworths (NZ), CCH (NZ) and the Open Polytechnic. Over 120 delegates attended from numerous countries, including Argentina, Australia, Belgium, Brazil, Britain, Canada, China, Denmark, Finland, Germany, India, Indonesia, Israel, Italy, Japan, Korea, Macau, Malta, New Zealand, Portugal, Singapore, South Africa, Sweden, Turkey and the United States.

The theme was 'Consumers' Access to Justice'. The essays collected in this volume were chosen from among the sixty papers presented. We thank the authors for their willingness to have their contributions included, and for the enormous patience they have shown during a lengthy editing and pre-publication period. We hope the quality of the final product convinces them that the wait was worthwhile!

Words of appreciation only inadequately compensate other people who worked with us on this project. First, Thierry Bourgoignie, President of the International Association for Consumer Law, was most gracious in all his contacts with those who organised and hosted the Conference, and was very helpful throughout. Secondly, in the staging of the Conference itself, the contributions of John Skinnon, John McDermott, Ross Grantham, Jane Needham and Bruna Correa were both vital and enormous. Thirdly, Jane Stapleton, John Skinnon, Paul Myburgh and John McDermott aided us in the process of refereeing the papers and determining which would be included in the book. In fact, more papers were initially chosen than could ultimately be accommodated in the book. Those additional papers were published in two issues of the *New Zealand Business Law Quarterly* in August and September 2002. Fourthly, Barnaby Stewart worked tirelessly on editing and reference checking, and Anne Russell proved to be a marvellous proofreader. Their work enabled a particularly clean and complete manuscript to be delivered to the publisher. Fifthly, we must acknowledge the financial contribution of the Research Centre for Business Law at The University of Auckland to the expenses incurred in the preparation of this book. Finally, we express our indebtedness to Finola O'Sullivan, at Cambridge University Press, for her wise advice, enthusiasm and commitment to bringing this project to fruition, and to those others at the Press who worked on this project.

Charles Rickett and Thomas Telfer

Anzac Day, 2002

Table of cases

Australia

Canada

European Court of Human Rights

European Union

France

Germany

The Netherlands

United Kingdom

United States

World Intellectual Property Office (WIPO)

Table of statutes and other instruments

European Union

Conventions

Directives

Regulations

Treaties

Finland

Germany

The Netherlands

United Kingdom

United States

1   Consumers' access to justice: an introduction

CHARLES E. F. RICKETT AND THOMAS G. W. TELFER

Introduction

Consumer protection law in the age of globalisation poses new challenges for policy-makers. The legislative and regulatory framework developed to undergird consumer protection law in the 1960s and 1970s has come under pressure, 'spurred', as Michael Trebilcock suggests in his essay in this volume, 'both by the changes in the nature of modern industrial economies and the evolution of economic theories'. Trebilcock argues that consumer protection law at the beginning of the new millennium 'is a much messier and more complex affair' than it was some thirty or forty years ago. The changes he describes include 'rapidity of technological change, deregulation of hitherto monopolised industries, globalisation of markets' and the 'increasing sophistication in economic theories that evaluate market structure, conduct and performance'.

Governments can no longer develop domestic consumer protection law in isolation from international developments. Iain Ramsay argues herein that globalisation has 'increased the international dimensions of access to justice and consumer protection as developments in communication technology facilitate the possibility of cross-border frauds'. Consumer law in the twenty-first century must become what he calls 'applied comparative law'.

The growth of international consumer transactions and the emergence of a new conception of the role of the state have led to a proliferation of consumer protection models all designed with the idea of improving access to justice. As Ramsay demonstrates in his essay, consumer protection and access to justice have traditionally been linked. Legislators often view the improvement of access to justice as one of the overarching goals of any new consumer protection legislation. However, not all legislative and regulatory schemes achieve that goal. The aim of the essays collected for this book is essentially to highlight some of the difficulties in framing regulatory responses to the problem of consumers' access to justice and to illustrate how governments and industry have responded to some of the new international problems that have arisen in the global economy.

The essays in the volume, which were originally delivered at the Eighth International Consumer Law Conference at Auckland, New Zealand, in April 2001, examine traditional private law mechanisms, such as judicial scrutiny of exclusion

1

clauses, as well as newer forms of protection, such as ombudsman schemes, class actions and schemes designed to deal with cross-border transactions. In some instances, new initiatives derogate from more traditional rights and erode consumers' rights to redress or remedies. The growth of private dispute mechanisms on the Internet which limit a consumer's right of redress, and the restrictions on the consumer bankruptcy discharge in North America, are two examples which are examined in this volume. As the essays demonstrate, the achievement of access to justice for consumers proves to be a challenging and sometimes elusive task.

Perspectives on consumers' access to justice

The volume begins with three essays that introduce the general theme of access to justice for consumers. Each of the contributors offers a different perspective or approach to the issue. Iain Ramsay's essay adopts a socio-legal approach. He urges that the 'study of consumer law and policy should be contextual and informed by an understanding of the role of law in society'. Ramsay notes that there has always been a tension between narrow and broad concepts of access to justice. 'The narrow dimension equates access to justice with access to legal institutions whereas a broader approach is concerned with the general conditions of justice in society.'

Ramsay's essay challenges its readers to take a much broader view of access to justice.While he notes that access to justice and consumer protection share common goals and appear to have the 'redistributional potential' for the protection of the poor and disadvantaged, his essay disputes this notion. He suggests that individualised redress procedures 'may have a distributional tilt against lower-income consumers and disadvantaged groups'. He points out the problems faced by consumers in lower-income markets and concludes that 'complaint as a problem-solving mechanism' is likely to be less effective in those lower-income markets than in the consumer market of the middle class.

Beyond the distributional aspects of dispute resolution mechanisms, Ramsay also identifies intermediaries and small claims courts as two institutions that have a significant impact upon access to justice. Intermediaries such as lawyers, social workers, debt counsellors and consumer advisors have significant power by virtue of their 'discretionary decisions', which may ultimately affect a consumer's choice of remedy. Ramsay's study of intermediaries also has implications for future reforms. He notes that the privatisation of services, which is often heralded as allowing greater consumer choice, may ultimately result in professional domination of consumer choice. To avoid this domination, he suggests the need for bright line rules that reduce the need for intermediaries. Bright line rules provide a universal and uniform approach and reduce the possibilities for the exercise of discretion.

Ramsay suggests that the concept of self-enforcing consumer laws merits further study particularly in an era of a shrinking public sector.

Whereas Ramsay offers a socio-legal analysis of the problem, Anthony Duggan examines the issue of access to justice from a law and economics perspective. According to Duggan, 'civil justice is a valuable commodity'. It not only benefits the parties themselves, but it has a wider social benefit in that adjudication lowers the social costs of disputes by providing orderly dispute resolution. Thus, adjudication performs a corrective justice role by avoiding the costs of disorder. Duggan also argues that the civil justice system works to avoid disputes in the future by generating 'judge-made rules to guide future behaviour'. Civil justice thus operates as a deterrent, by encouraging parties to 'take cost effective preventive measures to avoid liability in future cases'.

In designing a civil justice regime, the goal or economic objective is, according to Duggan, to 'achieve equilibrium in the market for consumer justice'. Duggan concludes that the cost of the civil justice system discourages people from litigating too much. Thus, possible problems of overinvesting in litigation at the expense of other methods of dispute resolution are controlled by the costs of bringing a claim. The problem, however, is that the legal cost burden discourages parties from litigating often enough to achieve equilibrium in the market for consumer justice. Market failure on both the demand and supply side discourages litigation. On the demand side, the high fixed component of the legal costs regime (parties must pay a set cost regardless of the amount at stake) discourages 'all but relatively large claims'. Conventional methods of pricing legal services 'discriminate systemically in favour of large claims and against small claims'. The costs regime also favours repeat players who may achieve economies of scale by spreading costs over a large number of claims, whereas 'one-shotters', typically consumers, are worse off. Similarly, on the supply side, the indirect costs of litigation, which include information costs, opportunity costs and emotional costs, work to discourage litigation.

Duggan suggests that there are two possible methods of resolving the problem of the cost burden. The consumer's costs must either be spread or avoided. His essay examines a variety of cost-spreading and cost-avoidance mechanisms. Cost-spreading solutions include legal aid, contingent fees, and class actions. Cost-spreading techniques facilitate access to ordinary courts. In other words, cost-spreading measures aim to give the consumer at least some of the firm's advantages so that the consumer can 'fight the case up at [the firm's] level'.

Cost avoidance techniques include small claims tribunals, mediation by consumer agencies, and industry-specific dispute resolution schemes such as tribunals, ombudsmen or compensation funds. Cost-avoidance measures typically involve 'forms of alternative dispute resolution. They involve substitutes for ordinary courts.' These alternative dispute mechanisms involve the firm fighting the case 'down at [the consumer's] level'.

Duggan concludes that 'no one measure is a complete solution. Each has its costs and benefits.' He recommends that 'there should be a mix of cost spreading and cost avoidance measures to secure the benefits of both traditional litigation and alternative dispute resolution'. His essay offers recommendations on how each of the cost spreading or cost avoidance mechanisms might be better tailored to specific types of claims. The essay offers a valuable method by which to assess each of the more specific mechanisms discussed in the essays in the later sections of the volume.

Finally in the first section, in a wide-ranging essay, Michael Trebilcock develops principles for an information-based approach to consumer protection policy and evaluates a number of institutional options for the provision of civil justice. Trebilcock argues that the true focus of consumer protection policy is 'the quality and cost of consumer information'. He begins with what he terms 'an information-based model of a consumer transaction' which analyses a consumer's decision on how many resources to expend on information about a particular transaction. His model isolates two important characteristics of the market setting: (1) the value of the information to the consumer; and (2) the cost of the information. He concludes that consumers are less likely to be in need of consumer protection where the cost of the information is low relative to the value of the information. Consumer protection problems occur, according to Trebilcock, where information costs are relatively high or the value of information is perceived to be relatively low.

Trebilcock's essay demonstrates that policy-makers are faced with a number of choices at many different levels. The essay provides both a framework for determining whether or not regulation is necessary, and a feasible response to the consumer protection problem. He urges that policy-makers must 'identify the policy objectives to be served by state involvement or intervention with maximum clarity and precision'. Beyond the decision whether to regulate or not, policy-makers must choose a relevant policy instrument to serve the particular objectives. These policy instruments must be evaluated and re-evaluated in light of comparative, historical and empirical evidence. Trebilcock examines a variety of policy instruments, including warnings, bans, information intermediaries, experience ratings and standardised contract terms.

Legislators also face the task of choosing an administrative or institutional forum that will have the responsibility for administering the chosen policy instruments. Trebilcock's essay provides a decision-tree framework for evaluating institutional options for the provision of civil justice, and analyses a variety of institutional mechanisms including public or private enforcement, public education, informal dispute resolution, no fault liability regimes, and small claims courts. Trebilcock also makes several suggestions for reforming the formal adjudication process, including possible roles for class actions, legal insurance, contingent fees and punitive damages. His essay concludes with a detailed discussion of judicial policing of standard form contracts.

Issues in contract and tort

Standard form contracts are the focus of the first of two essays in this section. Leone Niglia questions the widely accepted view that terms in standard form contracts that shift to consumers as many of the risks of the transaction as possible should be regarded as unquestionably 'unfair'. Niglia argues that the unquestionably unfair viewpoint was conceived and sustained by a socio-legal analysis that understood standard form contracts as the exercise of unjust firm power over consumers, such power emanating either from the monopoly position of or the institutional structure of the firm. The accuracy, and hence pre-eminence of this socio-legal analysis, has in the last twenty years or so been challenged as a part of the emergence of law and economics scholarship, whereby standard form contracts are not *per se* unfair, but are unfair only where the high transaction costs involved mean they do not reflect the parties' actual preferences.

Niglia demonstrates, however, that the law and economics analysis has 'left largely unaffected the belief that certain standardised terms are unquestionably unfair'. Although the victimised-consumer model is rejected, the imposition of compulsory terms – which 'would save the customer from the transaction costs of acquiring information and the seller those of disclosing information' – is widely seen as the best solution.

Niglia's thesis is that both the socio-legal and efficiency-oriented analyses are 'too concerned with preserving the unfairness belief'. His ultimate concern is that both the striking down of unfair terms and the imposition of compulsory terms are too costly for society. In the first case, the decision-maker uses 'fairness' or 'unfairness' as a proxy for the decision-maker's own 'choice on how to allocate costs that society ought to bear in the face of the materialisation of the contractual risk contemplated in the term under consideration'. In the second case, the decision-maker 'will allocate the relevant costs to the drafter [of the standard form contract], but this is not necessarily convenient for society', since the costs might be wrongly allocated.

The resulting challenge for consumer law scholarship in the context of maximising protection of consumers transacting by standard form contracts (or indeed preserving their access to meaningful justice) is, as Niglia suggests, the stark choice – *either* to admit that the notion of unquestionable unfairness is wrong, *or* to sustain the noble purpose of protecting the weak against abuse of private power but to admit at the same time that the application of the noble purpose 'merely generat[es] unintended perverse effects'.

Concentration, in the context of consumers' access to justice, on processes by which consumers' rights are more efficiently vindicated is important, but it must not be overlooked that the provision of effective liability rules, determining such rights, is just as vital a part of modern consumer law. Mass infections of product sectors is an area of particular importance and difficulty in this respect. The second essay in this section, by Jane Stapleton, is part of her ongoing research on the challenges that this area throws out to product liability regimes around the world. The essay concentrates on the manner in which the US *Restatement (Third) of Torts: Product Liability* (1998) deals with those challenges. Stapleton's particular focus is on how the *Restatement* will cope with cases of BSE/CJD ('mad cow disease'). Her argument is that the fragmented approach that the *Restatement*'s structure mandates means that 'the treatment of BSE/CJD cases . . . would be highly fractured'. More particularly, this fractured approach 'does not', as the *Restatement*'s Reporters claim, 'immediately seem to be the most effective way of addressing the "conceptual difficulties in trying to respond to products liability claims rationally, consistently, and fairly"'. In fact, Stapleton argues, the US regime 'is incoherent in its approach to infection cases'. There would be no redress for infections contracted from human blood or tissue; there might be recovery if contracted from food, or from leather/woollen clothing; and 'the US regime might provide recovery only on the basis that the product condition was to be classed as a design case . . .'

Stapleton contrasts the unsatisfactory response of the *Restatement* with the response offered by the 1985 European Directive on Product Liability and its various clones. She suggests that, although the existing case law is thin and mixed in its application to infected products, the Directive's avoidance of the fragmented approach of the *Restatement* might have offered hope of producing a better model for dealing with mass infection cases. Interestingly, however, Stapleton suggests that 'despite all the energy thrown into the Directive and *Third Restatement*, the law of negligence may continue to provide citizens with a more flexible and coherent cause of action'. 'Traditional general causes of action, such as negligence and warranty, also provide a clearer forum for courts to enunciate the complex moral and policy dilemmas that characterise generic mass infections of essential product sectors.'

Stapleton also makes passing reference to the artificial distinction often made between products and services. Delivery of essential products to consumers in truth contemplates the delivery of a service to those consumers. In such circumstances, the point is well taken that liability regimes should accordingly encompass both products *and* services.

Services and the consumer

Consumers of course come into contact with a variety of service industries, where the focus is principally on the service rendered rather than a product, and the challenge for policy-makers is to determine whether to and how best to regulate particular services as they intersect with the interests of consumers. Thomas Wilhelmsson examines the implications of the privatisation of publicly provided services and asks whether European principles of private law may play a role in assisting consumers. The two papers that follow in this section examine specific reform programmes in respect of United Kingdom financial services and banking. Rhoda James and Philip Morris explore the implications of the new Financial Ombudsman Service, while Jenny Hamilton and Mik Wisniewski examine the new Financial Services Authority and question whether the introduction of a cost–benefit analysis regime protects the interests of consumers.

The supply of services is an area where consumers suffer from acute information asymmetries. Consumers are often unable to make informed evaluations of the quality of service providers. Governments may respond by instituting general minimum service guarantees that might be implied into all service contracts or by adopting industry-specific regulation that might impose service standards, disclosure requirements or mandatory rules governing the form and content of the service provider's contract.

In his essay, Wilhelmsson adopts a 'more principled approach' and examines the opportunities for developing private law responses to the issue of the shrinking public state and the deregulation movement. He asks 'what new private law means are to be envisaged when public services are, to an increasing extent, performed on the basis of market rationality'. His analysis begins with the premise that private law has the potential to assist consumers when dealing with privatised service industries. However, he also extends his examination to include other services that fulfil the needs of citizens. In this category he includes financial services and information society services. He argues that such services are 'central to the infrastructure of society, and the consumer cannot reasonably be expected to live without them'. Aspects of financial and information services 'can be treated as social rights in the same way that services provided by "traditional" public utilities are'. New principles of private law that are developing in response to the privatisation of public utilities might 'infect' (or provide what Wilhelmsson calls the 'Trojan horse effect') service providers such as banks that have traditionally operated in the realm of the private sector.

Wilhelmsson argues that access to services has become more important than before with the 'privatisation of public functions, as well as the increased role of private actors with social functions such as banks and financial institutions'. Here he develops a principle of non-discrimination that would focus not simply on racial and gender discrimination but also on economic discrimination. He argues that 'when public supervision and control become more lenient' service providers should be required to 'adhere to certain fundamental principles, namely, access to the service, equal treatment of the consumers, and transparency in relation to the consumers'.

In addition, Wilhelmsson explores the additional principle of social *force majeure*. A society has a responsibility to ensure that more 'unfortunate members also have ongoing access to services that the fulfilment of our basic needs require'. Social *force majeure* operates in favour of a consumer who is affected by some unforeseeable unfortunate circumstance (such as a change in health, employment or family circumstances). Various legal consequences might be attached to the principle. The service provider might lose certain rights against the consumer and be prevented, for example, from terminating the contract and cutting off the supply of services.

James and Morris argue that the financial services industry poses particular challenges for consumers. In that industry there is 'characteristically an acute inequality of bargaining power between the product provider and the purchaser coupled with, perhaps most notoriously in the insurance sector, a body of legal doctrine heavily weighted against the consumer'. Their essay evaluates the new Financial Ombudsman Service (FOS) in the United Kingdom and evaluates the new statutory scheme against the existing 'fragmented patchwork quilt' of largely voluntary complaint redress mechanisms.

As noted earlier, Duggan suggests that an ombudsman scheme represents one of the many possible techniques of cost avoidance in the civil justice scheme. The FOS represents part of the British New Labour Government's larger effort to reform access to civil justice. Government discussion papers have emphasised a shift towards alternative dispute resolution and a civil justice system 'where courts are a forum of last resort'. Ombudsman schemes feature in the Government's plans as 'exemplars of decision-making bodies providing "alternative adjudication"'. The new FOS brings together eight existing complaints schemes and provides a single 'one-stop' organisation for consumers.

James and Morris argue that one of the advantages of an ombudsman technique is that it has the 'capacity to transcend strict legal rules and draw upon a range of extra-legal standards in a manner that usually operates to the benefit of consumers'. Their essay provides a detailed analysis of the FOS and evaluates the effectiveness of the regime on a number of different fronts, including accessibility, procedure, jurisdiction, remedies and the performance of a quality control function.

The FOS is part of a larger reform of the financial services industry in the United Kingdom with the adoption of the Financial Services and Markets Act 2000 and the creation of a new 'super regulator', the Financial Services Authority (FSA). Hamilton and Wisniewski examine the FSA, and, in particular, the statutory requirement that the regulator conduct a cost–benefit analysis (CBA) of any proposed new regulation. Their essay evaluates the CBA process and its potential impact upon consumers. While the FSA was hailed by the British Government as the introduction of a protection measure for consumers, the authors argue that the regime does not offer a strong commitment to 'public interest' regulation but rather at its heart the regime is a 'strong affirmation of market efficiency, individual responsibility, and the need for regulatory efficiency'.

The essay includes a discussion of: (1) the reasons for introducing CBA; (2) an overview of the CBA process, including its origins and how a CBA is undertaken; (3) a description of the specific CBA process undertaken by the FSA with respect to the possible regulation of mortgage advice; and (4) a critique of the CBA undertaken by the FSA.

CBA is often presented as a value-neutral way in which regulators or government officials may determine the fundamental question of whether or not to regulate. While Hamilton and Wisniewski focus on the specific FSA statutory requirement to conduct a CBA, their essay has broader application and points out the more general problems with a CBA and draws upon the work of cultural theorists to suggest ways in which consumers might have more of a voice in the design of policy parameters and in identifying values. Rather than merely commenting on or choosing between policy choices designed by experts in a 'top-down' approach, consumer input should take place at an earlier stage. The authors conclude that 'once the science has been "done" and presented to the consumer a particular cultural view about what is important and what is valuable already dominates. It is too late for other voices to be heard.'

Consumer bankruptcy law

The two essays in this section highlight recent reforms and proposed reforms to consumer bankruptcy law in North America. Thomas Telfer and Charles Tabb examine American and Canadian bankruptcy law reforms that significantly affect the ability of a consumer to obtain access to the bankruptcy law discharge. Although there are major historical differences between the evolution of Canadian and American bankruptcy law, nevertheless both jurisdictions have provided in some form a means for a debtor to obtain a fresh start through the bankruptcy discharge. With the rapid expansion of consumer debt, consumer bankruptcies have increased in both Canada and the United States. Both essays illustrate a common trend by the two jurisdictions to curtail the number of consumer bankruptcies by channelling or encouraging debtors into proposal or repayment schemes.

Telfer's essay traces consumer bankruptcy reform efforts in Canada and provides a historical perspective on the issue. He argues that there has been a reconceptualisation of the role of the discharge in bankruptcy law and a new view of debtor rehabilitation has emerged. The 1997 amendments to the Canadian Bankruptcy and Insolvency Act have significantly restricted access to the bankruptcy discharge. The new regime encourages debtors into repayment plans and discourages debtors from filing for straight bankruptcy. Debtors in Canada who opt for straight bankruptcy are scrutinised and if surplus income is found mandatory payments to the trustee are required. The new regime presumes that many debtors have the ability to pay creditors from surplus income and sets out new mandatory repayment levels. Telfer argues that 'whereas traditional bankruptcy discharge policy referred to the rehabilitation of the debtor, Parliament now asks debtors to rehabilitate their debts by making payments out of surplus income'.

Telfer's essay concludes with a historical discussion of the evolution of the bankruptcy discharge in Canadian law dating back to the nineteenth century. His paper illustrates that the 1997 reforms are not the first time Canada has restricted access to the discharge and that for a period in its history Canada operated without any bankruptcy law after Parliament decided to repeal the bankruptcy statute in the nineteenth century. Repeal however was a policy failure and a significant creditor interest group sought and obtained in 1919 a bankruptcy law that featured a discharge. Telfer's essay challenges its readers to review the current debates over the 'evils' of the rising number of bankruptcies and the legislative restrictions as part of the legislative pendulum that has over time swung routinely in favour of increasing restrictions on the discharge.

Tabb demonstrates how the bankruptcy reform bills of the Senate and the House of Representatives would 'reshape radically the contours of the United States consumer bankruptcy laws in favour of financial institutions and to the detriment of needy individual debtors'. The traditional promise of a fresh start for consumer debtors would become a 'cruel and ephemeral illusion'. The bankruptcy reform bills, according to Tabb, will have a 'draconian' effect for those debtors most in need of bankruptcy relief, while at the same time the bills offer substantial 'succour to wealthier debtors' in the form of exemptions.

Procedure and process issues

The contributors in this section consider two further methods or techniques to best achieve consumers' access to justice. The two essays provide an interesting contrast between the cost-avoidance and cost-spreading techniques identified by Duggan. Alternative dispute resolution is an example of cost-avoidance, while the class action is a mechanism to spread costs among a large number of parties. The essays provide concrete examples of some of the potential problems with each of these policy choices. Elizabeth Thornburg's essay examines the growth of private dispute resolution mechanisms in the context of Internet commerce and raises concerns about the increasing role that such private mechanisms are playing in the market place. Richard Faulk's essay considers the abuse of American class actions in international disputes.

Thornburg begins by acknowledging that alternative dispute procedures are typically faster and cheaper than court-based resolution. However, she claims that 'faster is not always better. Cheap is not always fair or accurate.' The essay explores 'three worlds of privatised dispute resolution': (1) the domain name dispute policy of the Internet Corporation for Assigned Names and Numbers; (2) the use by copyright owners of digital rights management technology to provide computer-activated self-help automatically to enforce contract terms even at variance with 'real world substantive law'; and (3) contractual shrinkwrap or clickwrap clauses which mandate binding arbitration in consumer transactions.

Thornburg argues that the growth of these technological and Internet-based dispute resolution mechanisms will have several important consequences for access to justice. First, the regimes will result in privatised justice with little or no input from government actors. Secondly, the resolution mechanisms shift procedural advantage to powerful players. Thirdly, the privatised regimes do not meet the traditional requirements of due process, such as 'affordable access to justice, discovery, collective action, live hearings, confrontation of witnesses, a neutral decision-maker and a transparent process'. Finally, Thornburg claims that by eliminating the courts as the arbiters of disputes, 'these processes decrease the power of the government to shape and enforce substantive law'. Thornburg challenges the notion that dispute resolution as an alternative to litigation is meant to reduce costs. She argues that 'the cost of making a claim and the burden of uncertainty' are shifted onto the less powerful claimant. Further, she illustrates that in some instances shrinkwrap or clickwrap contractual provisions, which mandate arbitration, preclude the alternative cost-spreading technique of class actions. According to Thornburg, 'privately chosen rules are being substituted for public law'.

As Faulk's essay demonstrates, class actions were originally allowed in American law on the basis that 'wrongdoers should not be allowed to reap unscrupulous gains from multitudes of victims who, without the class device, would probably forgo claims for relief in court because their losses were relatively small'. Faulk's essay, however, addresses a more recent phenomenon, the use of international class actions in the context of human rights violations in countries outside the United States. Faulk, who focuses on mass tort claims in international disputes, such as slave labour and Holocaust victims' class actions against German companies and Swiss banks, argues that the procedure is open to abuse and is critical of proposals that would seek to expand the use of the device internationally, or that would allow international enforcement of class action judgments by treaty. He notes that settlements in these cases occurred in the absence of any rulings on the merits of the case, and, in relation to the German claims, despite favourable rulings holding that the matters were not justiciable in United States courts. Further, settlements occurred before classes were certified, which according to Faulk demonstrates 'the coercive effects of class allegations'.

Globalism in this context is disturbing when 'procedural devices that are not yet recognised internationally are used to resolve claims arising from conduct that occurs beyond the forum state's borders'. Faulk's essay thus addresses the broader issue of the merits of transplanting legal rules and procedures from one legal culture to another. In our increasingly shrinking world, can American class action rules and procedures be effectively utilised to resolve international disputes? The differences between the American legal system and the civil law traditions make the 'American paradigm . . . clearly unsuitable for wholesale export to foreign legal systems'.

While class actions may have been designed to allow claims to be pursued that would not otherwise have been initiated, Faulk argues that 'the goal of promoting increased "access to justice" is not achieved by promoting access alone'. A system of collective litigation must also ensure 'the reliable and efficient dispensation of justice to all participating parties'.

Conflict of laws issues

The book concludes with two essays that raise conflict of laws issues. As noted in the opening paragraph of this introduction, the age of globalisation brings special challenges to consumer law. One particular challenge is that offered by the increasing practice of concluding electronic consumer contracts between parties in different states. Lorna Gillies, in the first of the two essays, argues that the harmonisation of private international law rules is essential if the use of electronic consumer contracting is to be facilitated and thereby encouraged and if, at the same time, efficient access for consumers to justice in connection with such activity is to be achieved. Her position is that 'access to justice will not benefit if different national (i.e., international private) laws' procedures regulate electronic commerce'.

Her paper examines, first, the initiatives of the European Union in promoting a regional adaptation of private international law rules for dealing with electronic consumer contracts. She analyses in detail the Brussels 1 Regulation, which modifies existing jurisdictional rules in consumer contract disputes, concluding that the Regulation is a coherent part of the European Community's stated objective to protect consumers as the 'weaker party' in consumer contracts. She also discusses, in the context of their proposed reform, the choice of law rules relating to consumer contracts as found in the Rome Convention on the Law Applicable to Contractual Obligations (1980).

Gillies then reviews the US position, outlining the jurisdiction and choice of law rules found in the case law and the *Restatement (Second): Conflict of Laws* (1971). She argues that a number of key issues identified in US cases 'illustrate the need for the adoption of specific legislative rules for electronic commerce activity and contracts'. The issues discussed include the distinction between active and passive websites, website activity as an economic activity in a forum state, website server location as a jurisdictional test, and the relevance of the place of receipt of goods and services.

Gillies' conclusion is that, while both the European and American developments are worthy and important regional initiatives that continue to influence the development of private international law rules, private international law 'should be harmonised globally in order to facilitate uniform application of jurisdiction and choice of law principles'. Such harmonisation does not, she suggests, require the creation of new rules for electronic contracts, but rather the adaptation of 'present offline rules for transactions that take place online'.

Axel Halfmeier's essay approaches the problem of internationalisation from a slightly different perspective than that of Gillies. He asks the question whether the growth of international electronic commerce, rather than, as widely assumed, greatly enhancing the importance of private international law rules, will in fact lead to the diminution and disappearance of private international law. His suggestion is that recent developments in European consumer protection law (whereby nation states are losing their regulatory powers) 'show that there are new mechanisms of European Union law that supplement or even replace traditional private international law doctrine'. Does this mean it is time to wave goodbye to private international law?

As Gillies does, Halfmeier discusses the impact on consumer contracts of both jurisdiction and choice of law instruments in European Union law. His main focus, however, is the decision of the European Court of Justice of 9 November 2000 in *Ingmar GB Ltd.* v. *Eaton Leonard Technologies Inc.* Although not a consumer law case, he argues that the decision expands the prospect of arguing successfully that the consumer law rules found in EC instruments are supermandatory rules. If so, 'a uniform minimum level of consumer protection would always exist before European courts regardless of conflict of laws rules'.

Halfmeier also examines non-contractual consumer protection law in the European Union, including the Treaty, the European Human Rights Convention and the E-Commerce Directive of 2000. These instruments highlight that EU law, while recognising that domestic laws of member states are theoretically applicable by virtue of private international law rules, requires scrutiny of those laws 'according to substantive European standards of rationality and necessity'. Halfmeier's conclusion is that while traditional private international law rules still exist, they 'are often blotted out by substantive EU rules'.

Conclusion

The essays by Gillies and Halfmeier indicate that the demands of a fair and effective consumer law in an age of electronic and global commerce will have far-reaching effects on the nature and content of private international law itself. The essays in the earlier sections of the book show that the same is true of consumer law's intersection with other branches of both private and public law. The essays not only provoke deeper consideration of the theme around which they were written, consumers' access to justice, but they also demonstrate that consumer law is fundamental to an understanding of the dimensions of a just, fair and efficient public and private justice system.

Part I
Perspectives on consumers' access to justice

2 Consumer redress and access to justice

IAIN RAMSAY

Introduction

The concept of access to justice has become an integral part of policy discourse in many countries. The attractiveness of its symbolism has made it a convenient wrapper for many proposed changes in court procedures and legal services. Access to justice is intimately connected with the rise of consumer protection and it is embedded in the United Nations Guidelines for Consumer Protection, which provide:[1]

> Governments should establish or maintain legal and/or administrative measures to enable consumers or, as appropriate, relevant organizations to obtain redress through formal or informal procedures that are expeditious, fair, inexpensive and accessible. Such procedures should take particular account of the needs of low-income consumers.

Governments should also 'encourage enterprises to resolve consumer disputes in a fair, expeditious and informal manner' and 'information on available redress and other dispute-resolving procedures should be made available to consumers'.[2]

In this essay I discuss two topics in relation to consumer redress and access to justice. My primary topic concerns the distributive impact of individualised complaint and redress procedures. I explore the question whether individualised redress procedures have a distributional tilt against lower-income and disadvantaged groups. I approach this question through an analysis of socio-legal research on three topics: consumer responses to problems with goods and services; the role of intermediaries in consumer disputes; and research on small claims courts. I then pose some questions raised by this research for thinking about reforms to the legal system and regulation of consumer markets. My second topic is the role of legal transplants in consumer law and the perils and promise of applied comparative law in this age of globalisation. Consumer law is a significant area of applied comparative law and consumer lawyers should therefore develop an understanding of the factors that will affect the success of consumer law transplants.

---

1 GA Res 248, 39 UN GAOR (106th plen. mtg), UN Doc A/Res/39/248 (1985).
2 *Ibid.*

These two topics are united by the theme that the study of consumer law and policy should be contextual and informed by an understanding of the role of law in society.

I enter at the outset some important caveats. Consumerism may be an international phenomenon but writing on law and legal institutions is likely often to reflect ethnocentric biases and indeed this is a peril of comparative law. I doubt that I am immune to these tendencies. In addition, the topic of consumers' access to justice is a large one and my approach is to provoke reflection based on a selection of studies rather than to attempt an exhaustive description. Finally, my focus is primarily on issues of economic loss sustained by consumers rather than physical injuries.

The development of the concept of access to justice

The contemporary concept of access to justice is associated with the large project on this topic under the direction of Mauro Cappelletti and Bryant Garth. They claimed in the late 1970s that they were describing a 'worldwide movement' to make rights effective in contemporary society. Using the metaphor of three waves they documented the development of legal aid (first wave) and reforms aimed at the representation of diffuse interests (second wave) within the legal system. The third wave represented a broader focus than legal representation and included the 'full panoply of institutions and devices, personnel and procedures, used to process, and even prevent, disputes in modern societies'.[3] Under this heading the authors included arbitration, mediation, small claims, neighbourhood justice centres, special tribunals for consumer complaints, rentalsmen, the use of paralegals, prepaid insurance plans, and legal simplification such as no-fault schemes. This last wave, coupled with a resurgence of interest in legal anthropology, drove the initial development of alternative dispute resolution as well as increasing research by sociolegal scholars into the various mechanisms in society through which individuals settled disputes.

The concept of access to justice exposed the gap between the liberal ideal of equality before the law and the reality of unequal access to justice for many in society, particularly those attempting to vindicate the new social rights that had developed in the twentieth century.[4] It was argued that modern societies of mass consumption generated diffuse problems where many individuals with small claims found themselves in dispute with large bureaucracies, and where 'mass injuries' were

---

3 M. Cappelletti and B. Garth (eds.), *Access to Justice: a World Survey* (Milan: A. Giuffrè, 1978), 49. For an interesting review of this work, see A. Sarat, 'Book Review: Access to Justice' (1980–1) 94 *Harv L Rev* 1911.
4 M. Cappelletti, 'Alternative Dispute Settlement Procedures within the Framework of the World-Wide Access-to-Justice Movement' (1993) 56 *Mod L Rev* 282.

a 'characteristic feature of our epoch'.[5] Consumer problems were often cited as the paradigm of the mass injury. They were individually small in monetary value, but large in aggregate, with individual 'one shot' consumers pitted against 'repeat player' organisations. The authors summarised their position:[6]

> There is a growing literature questioning the capacity of lawyers, courts, and court procedures to adapt themselves to the 'diffuse' and 'social' rights . . . such as rights of consumers, of environmentalists, of tenants, of poor people – which increasingly characterise modern societies.

At the outset there are four points that I would highlight about access to justice. First, access to justice and consumer protection shared common goals. They both had redistributive potential in their concerns for the protection of the poor, the unorganised, and the disadvantaged, and the idea of the right to dignity and self-respect in the face of corporate power.

Secondly, there has always been a tension between a narrow and a broad concept of access to justice.[7] The narrow dimension equates access to justice with access to legal institutions, whereas a broader approach is concerned with the general conditions of justice in society. A nagging question is whether the former conception has any substantial connection with achieving the latter objective. Thus, in this age of privatisation and the dominance of economic liberalism there is a suspicion that access to justice has been appropriated from being a serious critique of liberal systems of justice to being used to justify the political agenda of influential groups who may be more interested in cutting budgets than providing justice. A similar contrast exists in consumer protection where there is a distinction between mainstream ideas of consumer protection where the objective is that consumers should get more from the system and more radical concepts of consumerism where the goal is to change or transform the system. Thus Scott and Black note in relation to the privatisation of many services in the UK that although consumerisation may have appeared to increase accountability of service providers, consumers have had little opportunity to have an active voice in the development of these standards.[8]

Thirdly, there is sometimes the assumption in access to justice literature that society is a pressure-cooker filled with disputes.[9] Without the safety valve of access to legal institutions there will be the potential for an explosion, a breakdown of social order. At the least there may be problems in social relationships that cannot

---

5 M. Cappelletti, 'Vindicating the Public Interest through the Courts: a Comparativist's Contribution' in M. Cappelletti and B. Garth (eds.), *Access to Justice: Emerging Issues and Perspectives* (Milan: A. Giuffrè, 1978), 519.

6 Cappelletti and Garth, *Access to Justice: a World Survey*, 9.

7 See R. MacDonald, 'Access to Justice and Law Reform' (1990) 10 *Windsor Yearbook of Access to Justice* 287.

8 C. Scott and J. Black, *Cranston's Consumers and the Law* (3rd edn, London: Butterworths, 2000), 10.

9 See R. Kidder, 'The End of the Road? Problems in the Analysis of Disputes' (1981) 15 *Law & Soc'y Rev* 717, 719.

be solved and the continuance of exploitation and inequities in social relationships. Law itself will come into disrepute if it cannot respond to the problems of ordinary individuals. Laura Nader in her anthropological studies of consumer disputing in the USA expressed this sentiment when she argued that it was important for society to attend to the problem of 'little injustices'. She wrote:[10]

> Little injustices are the greater part of everyday living in a consumption society, and, of course, people's attitudes towards the law are formed by their encounters with the law or by the absence of encounters when the need arises. If there is no access for those things that matter, then the law becomes irrelevant to its citizens and, something else, alternatives to the law become all they have.

Finally, both consumer law and access to justice have often represented laboratories of applied comparative law. One thinks here of the class action, a common law device, which has made a successful bridgehead in Brazil;[11] of the cooling-off period which originated in England but is now ubiquitous;[12] of the spread of the Nordic idea of the ombudsman as a central mechanism of consumer redress in many countries.[13] The creation of ombudsmen in the 'private' sphere recognises the fact that large corporate bureaucracies may be no less likely than public bureaucracies to suffer from maladministration or abuses of discretionary power in their relations with individuals.[14]

What difference does a generation make?[15]

An important change is the resurgence of economic liberalism at the national and international level, which has had a significant influence on views of the role of the state in economy and society and which has driven a market

10 L. Nader (ed.), *No Access to Law: Alternatives to the American Judicial System* (New York: Academic Press, 1980), 4.
11 For an analysis of class actions in Brazil, see J. R. de Lima Lopes, 'Social Rights and the Courts' in T. Wilhelmsson and S. Hurri (eds.), *From Dissonance to Sense: Welfare State Expectations, Privatisation and Private Law* (Aldershot: Ashgate, 1999), 549.
12 For a history of the development of the cooling-off period, see B. Sher, 'The "Cooling-off" Period in Door-to-Door Sales' (1967–8) 15 *UCLA L Rev* 717.
13 See R. James, *Private Ombudsmen and Public Law* (Aldershot: Ashgate, 1997). See also R. James and P. Morris, chap. 8 herein.
14 See S. Deutsch, 'Are Consumer Rights Human Rights?' (1994) 32 *Osgoode Hall L J* 537, 552–3, arguing for the recognition of consumer rights as a form of human right: 'The big business organization should be considered less like an individual, who bargains on equal terms, and more like a government, which controls the private consumer . . . Consumer rights are intended to prevent abuse of power and, in this sense as well, are similar to other well-defined economic human rights which protect the individual against abuse of power by governments.'
15 The phrase is inspired by David Harvey: see 'The Difference a Generation Makes' in D. Harvey, *Spaces of Hope* (Edinburgh: Edinburgh University Press, 2000).

model of consumer protection as the facilitation of informed consumer choice.[16] At the same time, the concept of market failure, the lynchpin of economic analysis of consumer markets, has become increasingly amorphous. The rich literature that has arisen on the economics of information[17] has made it more difficult to identify sharp information failures in consumer markets.[18] It is possible to develop many hypotheses about the impact of information failures but there remains remarkably little empirical testing of these hypotheses. There is also the rise of behavioural economics. This has drawn attention to the extent to which consumers deviate from rational models of decision-making in existing neo-classical economic models. Not only has it drawn attention to many irrationalities in consumer information processing and decision-making, but also the extent to which producers exploit these irrationalities.[19] One consequence is that the sharp contrast between paternalism and consumer sovereignty in neo-classical approaches is undercut by this literature. Consumer sovereignty is both an economic concept and a political slogan that is frequently contrasted with the paternalism of a 'nanny state' that restricts or channels choices. But it is often very difficult to distinguish between situations where governments are responding to problems that prevent individuals from reaching a rational judgment and those where government is overruling individual preferences and substituting its own judgment. In addition, this literature suggests that simple assumptions

16 See, e.g., in relation to the EU, N. Reich, 'From Contract Law to Trade Practices Law: Protection of Consumers' Economic Interests by the EC' in T. Wilhelmsson (ed.), *Perspectives of Critical Contract Law* (Aldershot: Ashgate, 1993), 55. The famous *Cassis de Dijon* decision in the EU adopted implicitly a market failure approach to regulation, placing the burden on states to justify economic and social regulation in terms of market failure. In Australia, see E. Lanyon, 'Codes of Practice and Online Banking: an Australian Perspective' (2002) 8 *New Zealand Business Law Quarterly* 329, 330 where the comment is made that 'government emphasis on the role of codes reflects a change from a rights-based consumer protection model to a market-oriented model'. In the USA, the Federal Trade Commission adopted a market failure approach and the rational consumer test in its three-pronged test of unfairness, which holds a practice to be unfair '(a) if it causes a substantial injury to consumers; (b) if the injury is not outweighed by countervailing benefits to consumers or competition; and (c) if consumers could not reasonably have avoided the injury': Letter to Senators Ford and Danforth, Consumer Subcommittee on Commerce, Science, and Transportation, 17 December 1980. Greenfield comments that 'this three part test embodies reliance on the concept of a free market and is designed to permit intervention in the market only when there is some impediment to the operation of a free market': M. Greenfield, *Consumer Law: a Guide for Those Who Represent Sellers, Lenders, and Consumers* (New York: Little Brown, 1995), 92–3.
17 See, e.g., J. Stiglitz, 'The Contributions of the Economics of Information to Twentieth Century Economics' (2000) *Quarterly Journal of Economics* 1441.
18 This is the conclusion drawn by G. Hadfield, R. Howse and M. Trebilcock in 'Information-Based Principles for Rethinking Consumer Protection Policy' (1998) 21 *Journal of Consumer Policy* 131.
19 For a useful survey of behavioural economics and its applications to the legal system, see C. Sunstein (ed.), *Behavioral Law and Economics* (Cambridge: Cambridge University Press, 2000). For a consideration of the extent to which producers manipulate irrationalities in consumer information processing, see J. D. Hanson and D. A. Kysar, 'Taking Behavioralism Seriously: Some Evidence of Market Manipulation' (1999) 112 *Harv L Rev* 1420.

about consumer behaviour based on a rational weighing of costs and benefits may need to be modified. This has implications for several areas of consumer law[20] as well as for understanding consumer remedy-seeking behaviour.[21] These complexities and uncertainties in our 'scientific' understanding of market efficiency and consumer behaviour suggest that consumer policy-making cannot avoid difficult normative and distributional judgments against a background of empirical uncertainty.[22]

There is also a significant change in the nature of capitalism. We live in an era of shareholder-driven capitalism, where capital markets have a significant impact on corporate decision-making. This has two implications for consumer law and policy. While it is still possible to espouse the concept of consumer sovereignty as the organising principle of the market, a more accurate picture is one where the consumer is a means to ensure high short-term returns to satisfy the capital markets. This creates structural pressures on producers to cut corners where consumers are unlikely to detect problems and, where possible, to manipulate consumer choice to ensure high short-term profits.[23] Examples include the introduction of automobile leasing as a method of concealing automobile price rises,[24] the use of 'rebate coupons', which producers know are rarely used by consumers,[25] 'teaser rates' on credit card transfers where consumers are likely to underestimate the extent to which they will continue to carry a balance on their credit cards,[26] and 'interest free credit' offers where financiers know that many consumers will not repay the debt in the interest-free period. Some of the worst practices have been found in transitions to privatisation of utilities with widespread cases of fraudulent

---

20 Examples include advertising law and the regulation of marketing practices, information remedies such as cooling-off periods (does the existence of cognitive dissonance undercut the impact of this remedy?), designing information remedies that exploit the findings of behavioural economics in order to render them more effective, and the regulation of consumer credit.

21 See text accompanying n. 71 below.

22 See the interesting discussion of this issue in T. Rostain, 'Educating *Homo Economicus*: Cautionary Notes on the New Behavioural Law and Economics Movement' (2000) 34 *Law & Soc'y Rev* 973, 1002.

23 See D. A. Statt, *Understanding the Consumer: a Psychological Approach* (Hampshire: Macmillan, 1997), 295: 'Yet the economic hard times of the 1980s and 1990s have conclusively demonstrated how the corporate culture really views the consumer: as necessary profit-making fodder but a very distant second-best to the shareholder which invariably means the giant financial institutions that hold the largest blocks of company shares.'

24 See 'Leasing Fever', *Business Week* (7 February 1994), cover story, where the executive vice-president at Mitsubishi Motor Sales of America is quoted as stating that 'leasing provides a great camouflage for price increases'.

25 See Hanson and Kysar, 'Taking Behaviouralism Seriously', 1450, where they refer to W. Bulkeley, 'Rebates' Secret Appeal to Manufacturers: Few Consumers Actually Redeem Them', *Wall Street Journal* (10 February 1998), B1.

26 See L. Ausubel, 'The Failure of Competition in the Credit Card Market' (1991) 81 *American Economic Review* 50; L. Ausubel, 'Adverse Selection in the Credit Card Market' (Working Paper, Department of Economics, University of Maryland, June 1999).

door-to-door sales techniques in both Canada and the UK.[27] These practices are the result of intense competition so that consumer detriment is compatible with an apparently very competitive market. These developments do not mean that consumers are helpless victims of marketing practices, but these practices raise difficult regulatory questions since behavioural analysis suggests that individuals may continue to act irrationally, even if they are provided with accurate information. At a minimum, it suggests that greater attention should be paid to the most effective methods of communicating information to consumers. It is also useful to think about distributional issues here. Consumer detriment may benefit shareholders. This remains, I believe, in many countries, a regressive distributional effect. It is only major scandals such as those associated with pension mis-selling in the UK that might affect share prices, although there is little evidence that it has had a long-term effect on share prices of insurance companies.

Inequality has risen in many countries raising concerns about social exclusion, defined as the 'inability to participate effectively in economic, social, political and cultural life, and in some characterisations, alienation and distance from the mainstream society'.[28] I have described elsewhere the effects of these patterns of inequality in the growth of two-tier marketing and the 'alternative financial sector', which offers credit at very high prices to lower-income individuals, those with spotty credit records and those excluded from the mainstream financial system.[29] More generally, several writers have drawn attention to a sense of insecurity among many consumers, who, as individuals in a privatised world with reduced state redistributions, are increasingly required to plan their own futures against a volatile economic background.[30] A recent study of consumer bankruptcy in the United States,

---

27 In Ontario, Canada, there were many complaints about door-to-door selling during the privatisation of retail gas selling. In the UK, see, e.g., the response of National Association of Citizens Advice Bureaux to the White Paper, *Modern Markets Confident Consumers*, para 2.5, where it is stated that 'over the past two years, CABx throughout the country have advised clients who have experienced difficulties arising from the opening up of the gas and electricity markets to competition. CABx have been inundated with complaints about doorstep mis-selling. Consumers have also found it difficult to find transparent information about prices in order to make comparisons and make choices.'

28 K. Duffy, 'Social Exclusion in Europe: Policy Context and Analytical Framework' in G. Room (ed.), *Beyond the Threshold: the Measurement and Analysis of Social Exclusion* (Bristol: Policy Press, 1995), chap. 4.

29 See I. Ramsay, 'The Alternative Consumer Credit Market and Financial Sector' (2001) 35 *Canadian Business Law Journal* 325. See also H. M. Treasury, *Access to Financial Services*, Report of Policy Action Team 14 (1999); E. Kempson, C. Whyley, J. Caskey and S. Collard, Financial Service Authority, *In or Out? Financial Exclusion: a Literature and Research Review*, Consumer Research Report No. 3 (2000).

30 See, e.g., M. Castells, *End of Millennium* (Malden, Mass.: Blackwell Publishers, 1998), 358. The most cited author here is U. Beck, *Risk Society: towards a New Modernity* (London: Sage Publications, 1992). See also chap. 3, 'Beyond Status and Class'. For specific analyses, see, e.g., K. Rowlingson, P. Black, A. Harrington and W. Merrin, *A Balancing Act: Surviving the Risk Society* (London: NACAB, 1999).

entitled *The Fragile Middle Class*,[31] encapsulates this idea. This increased economic polarisation within countries of the North means that it is no longer possible to distinguish as sharply between consumer policy for 'developed' and 'developing' countries, and models developed in countries of the South, such as the Grameen Bank, are used as models for projects in countries of the North.[32]

The appropriate form of public regulation of consumer markets is a matter of much debate with interest in a variety of forms of 'self-regulation', 'co regulation', or programmes such as the EU regulation of unfair consumer terms, which envisages a significant role for private groups.[33] The reduction in the infrastructure of public regulation in many countries of the North suggests that they might learn from reform developments in newly emerging economies. In the latter countries there may be the problem of developing consumer protection without an existing infrastructure and also perhaps a distrust of government and government discretion in enforcement. In response to this perceived problem, writers have proposed models of 'self-enforcing' law[34] which would include the use of automatic sanctions with high penalties. There are already models of this form of law in consumer law and greater investigation might be made of their potential effectiveness.[35]

There has also been a movement from a grammar of politics which stressed redistribution, to one that focuses on identity, described by Nancy Fraser as a politics of recognition[36] and there has been the rise of the discourse of human rights. There is an ambivalent relationship between consumer protection and identity politics. On the one hand, it might be argued that the development of consumer law has been important symbolically in recognising the consumer as a rightsholder, and an important actor in civil society.[37] The development of consumer law involved a politics of recognition of the consumer as a citizen, and one writer has claimed that developments in consumer disputing over the past thirty years are 'enlarging the content of democratic citizenship by conferring new rights and protections for complaints which cannot easily or cheaply be pursued through the courts'.[38] The development

31 T. Sullivan, E. Warren and J. Westbrook, *The Fragile Middle Class: Americans in Debt* (New Haven: Yale University Press, 2000).
32 See, e.g., C. Lima Marques, 'Banking in the Information Society: a Brazilian Vision' in T. Wilhelmsson, S. Tuominen and H. Tuomola (eds.), *Consumer Law in the Information Society* (The Hague: Kluwer Law International, 2001), chap. 15.
33 See P. Rott, 'Injunctions for the Protection of Consumers' Interests after the Implementation of the EC Directive into English and German law' (2001) 24 *Journal of Consumer Policy* 401.
34 See B. Black and R. Kraakman, 'A Self-Enforcing Model of Corporate Law' (1995–6) 109 *Harv L Rev* 1911.
35 E.g., in a number of jurisdictions in North America a failure by an automobile repairer to provide consumers with the required documentation will result in the consumer receiving a free repair. See, e.g., s. 11 of the Motor Vehicle Repair Act, R.S.O. 1990, c. M.43.
36 See N. Fraser, 'From Redistribution to Recognition' in N. Fraser, *Justice Interruptus: Critical Reflections on the 'Postsocialist' Condition* (New York: Routledge, 1997).
37 See, e.g., Deutsch, 'Are Consumer Rights Human Rights'.
38 O. R. McGregor, *Social History and Law Reform* (London: Stevens, 1981), 7.

of consumer protection in countries of the South and newly emerging economies of Eastern Europe reflect this social transformation and recognition of consumer citizenship rights. On the other hand, there is the persistent critique of the concept of the consumer as citizen as an impoverished concept of passive citizenship where freedom is equated with 'freedom to buy what one wants'. Consumerism is equated with an individualisation of social problems and a decline of collective responsibility and political participation.[39] It is associated with an erosion of the social rights of citizenship.

The motor of many of these changes I have described is often viewed as the much-discussed concept of globalisation, a term that David Harvey claims first acquired prominence when American Express advertised the global reach of its credit card in the 1970s.[40] It is not possible within the confines of this paper to explore this slippery concept and its implications for consumer protection[41] but it is clear that globalisation has increased the international dimensions of access to justice and consumer protection as developments in communication technology facilitate the possibility of cross-border frauds. It has also spawned an increasing interest in comparative law and legal transplants, which has been reflected in consumer law scholarship.

Finally, there is the interest in a politics of the 'third way', advocated by writers such as Anthony Giddens.[42] Within this model, consumer policies might play a greater role within a model of 'positive welfare',[43] which would include a mix of educational, preventive and regulatory measures. This focuses on the role of consumer law as one part of a programme of welfare which might empower as well as redistribute. Consumer law is therefore a hybrid form of law that does not fit neatly into either private or public, private or social. In my view, it is neither obviously progressive nor regressive and addresses issues of social justice as well as being a market behaviour model of law. Understandings of consumer law are, however, a cultural phenomenon and I hesitate to generalise too broadly. Thus, in the USA, I believe that consumer law, particularly in the area of credit and debt, has often addressed issues of class and race inequality without necessarily naming them as such.[44] In countries without welfare states consumer protection may play a more significant role as a safety net to deal with the risks associated with consumption.

---

39 See generally G. Cross, *An All-Consuming Century: Why Commercialism Won in Modern America* (New York: Columbia University Press, 2000).

40 Harvey, *Spaces of Hope*, 13.

41 For a fuller exploration, see I. Ramsay, 'Consumer Protection in the Era of Informational Capitalism' in Wilhelmsson, Tuominen and Tuomola, *Consumer Law*, chap. 3.

42 See A. Giddens, *The Third Way and its Critics* (Malden, Mass.: Polity Press, 2000).

43 See A. Giddens, *Beyond Left and Right: the Future of Radical Politics* (Cambridge: Polity Press, 1994).

44 See I. Ramsay and T. Williams, 'Inequality, Market Discrimination, and Credit Markets' in I. Ramsay (ed.), *Consumer Law in the Global Economy: National and International Dimensions* (Aldershot: Ashgate, 1997), 233.

Socio-legal studies of consumer disputing

As a preliminary I wish to underline the importance of socio-legal re-search in consumer law. We still do not know much about the effectiveness of con-sumer laws, and policy-making is based often on assumptions about consumers and their motivations and decision-making. For example, there is little empirical data on whether central policies such as cooling-off periods actually have any im-pact on the market place. Hans Micklitz comments that although there have been nearly 10,000 court decisions under the German Unfair Contract Terms Act, 'no one knows whether and to what extent the situation of the individual has improved'.[45] Socio-legal research on consumer issues may be a powerful argument for change or for reorienting the focus of reform. There are many examples of such studies in consumer law, such as David Caplovitz's *The Poor Pay More*,[46] the exposure of racial and gender discrimination in competitive consumer markets,[47] or the description of what lawyers actually do when consumers approach them for advice.[48]

Access to justice literature drew on and stimulated 'gap' studies in law and so-ciety, which exposed the gap between the ideals of a liberal legal system and its realities where bargaining and power seemed to hold sway, and where 'repeat play-ers' had structural advantages over 'one-shotters' in the legal system.[49] Studies of the deformation of small claims courts into collection agencies, or the fact that the poor paid more, stimulated reform proposals directed to changes in legal rules and institutions.[50] It was assumed that changes in the law and legal procedures would bring the reality of civil justice closer to the ideal. However, a second wave of schol-arship expressed some scepticism about the efficacy of legal reforms and wondered whether reforms might do little to change the system in favour of the 'have nots' but might have an important legitimating effect in making the system seem just. Macaulay's study of the role of lawyers in delivering consumer rights concluded with the question whether consumer rights should be viewed as symbolism with-out any major substantive impact.[51]

45 H. W. Micklitz, 'Privatisation and Access to Justice and Soft Law – Lessons from the European Community' in Wilhelmsson and Hurri, *From Dissonance to Sense*, 565.
46 (New York: Free Press of Glencoe, 1963.)
47 See I. Ayres, 'Fair Driving: Gender and Racial Discrimination in Retail Car Negotiations' (1991) 104 *Harv L Rev* 817.
48 See S. Macaulay, 'Lawyers and Consumer Protection Laws' (1979) 14 *Law & Soc'y Rev* 114.
49 The description in this section of the development of socio-legal studies in consumer disput-ing draws on the excellent general outline of the development of law and society research con-tained in B. Garth and A. Sarat, 'Justice and Power in Law and Society Research: on the Contested Careers of Core Concepts' in B. Garth and A. Sarat (eds.), *Justice and Power in Sociolegal Studies* (Evanston, Ill.: Northwestern University Press, 1998), chap. 1.
50 See Garth and Sarat, *Justice and Power*, 4, citing as examples of this style of work: Caplovitz, *The Poor Pay More*; M. Galanter, 'Why the Haves Come out Ahead: Speculations on the Limits of Legal Change' (1974) 9 *Law & Soc'y Rev* 95; J. E. Carlin, J. Howard and S. L. Messinger, *Civil Justice and the Poor* (New York: Russell Sage Foundation, 1967).
51 Macaulay, 'Lawyers and Consumer Protection Laws', 161.

There was an emphasis in some research on how law was more of a disciplinary rather than emancipatory force. Abel questioned whether moves towards informal justice increased the power of state control over the disadvantaged and powerless, sacrificed the concept of rights, and served the political agenda of influential groups (such as judges or governments) interested in trimming budgets and dumping minor disputes out of the court system.[52] This perception led some researchers to alter the focus of their research so that within this new lens law itself was studied as an ideology, part of constituting social relations and individual subjectivity. Inspired also by the resurgence of interest in legal pluralism – the idea that individuals live in overlapping legal spaces and that a plurality of norms may operate in the same social space – some scholars have attempted to understand the role of law and legality in everyday life. Within this approach researchers are interested in how individuals construct ideas about law and legality and the extent to which law constrains and empowers individual action.

This turn to the study of law as ideology and its relation to ideology in general, what might be described as 'the invisible colour of daily life',[53] is of direct relevance to thinking about access to justice for consumers. It raises questions as to whether the categories of consumer law such as 'the rational consumer' may themselves be ideological concepts which elide class, gender and racial inequalities. Abstractions such as the reasonable consumer are taken to be unproblematic representations of the real world in which inequalities of social class, gender and race do not exist.

I would like to relate these developments in thinking about law and society to socio-legal research on three topics in consumers' access to justice: (1) consumer disputing; (2) the role of intermediaries; and (3) small claims courts. I do not propose a grand tour of existing research and I confess that my selections represent my own ethnocentric biases.

Consumer disputing and the problematic of law and everyday life

Studies of consumer disputing raise three concerns: (1) distributional issues in relation to individual dispute procedures; (2) issues of discrimination and the role of cultural capital; and (3) the adequacy of models of consumers as rational actors instrumentally weighing the costs and benefits of action.[54] Studies of individual problems in countries of the North indicate that consumer issues and money problems are often the most frequent problems encountered by

---

52 See R. Abel, 'The Contradictions of Informal Justice' in R. Abel (ed.), *The Politics of Informal Justice* (New York: Academic Press, 1982), 267.
53 See T. Eagleton (ed.), *Ideology* (London: Longman, 1994), 221.
54 The first concern is a leitmotif throughout much of consumer protection literature. Thomas Wilhelmsson has argued, for example, that two central forms of consumer policy, information remedies and individualised complaint procedures, are likely to reproduce social injustice: T. Wilhelmsson, 'Consumer Law and Social Justice' in I. Ramsay, *Consumer Law*, 217.

individuals.[55] There is a relatively high claiming rate in consumer problems compared with other potentially justiciable problems, and many consumers handle consumer problems without the intervention of a third party, so that much consumer disputing takes place at the level of two-party negotiations.[56] Genn *et al* in their 1999 English study claim that 'courts and ombudsmen play a minimal role in the resolution of consumer disputes'.[57] Complaint is thus a potentially important problem-solving mechanism for consumers. There is some evidence that consumer problems are experienced more frequently by women than men,[58] and several studies indicate that certain social groups may be more willing to complain and may be more successful when they do complain. An early study concluded that 'voiced complaints overrepresent problems . . . that are experienced by high socioeconomic status households . . . There is an underrepresentation of those in the lowest income groups, which seems to arise because socioeconomic position is associated with social attributes such as confidence.'[59] Genn *et al* found that consumers who had problems with faulty goods and services had higher incomes than the whole sample, but that those with money problems had slightly lower incomes. There is also a concern that lower-income consumers may have less success with complaining, although the evidence here is mixed.[60]

The central role of complaint is underlined by the fact that Genn *et al* found that in 40 per cent of cases consumers appeared to take no further action if the

---

55 See H. Genn *et al.*, *Paths to Justice: What People Do and Think about Going to Law* (Oxford: Hart, 1999), 24. The authors refer to recent studies in the USA and New Zealand which have similar findings: American Bar Association, *Legal Needs and Civil Justice: Major Findings of the Comprehensive Legal Needs Study* (1994); G. M. Maxwell, C. Smith, P. Shepherd and A. Morris, New Zealand Legal Services Board, *Meeting Legal Service Needs* (1999).

56 See Genn *et al.*, *Paths to Justice*, 106–7. In Canada, a study found that there was a relatively high claiming rate for consumer problems over $1000: N. Vidmar, 'Seeking Justice: an Empirical Map of Consumer Problems and Consumer Responses in Canada' (1988) 26 *Osgoode Hall LJ* 757.

57 Genn *et al.*, *Paths to Justice*, 156.

58 See P. Ewick and S. Silbey, *The Common Place of Law: Stories from Everyday Life* (Chicago, Ill.: University of Chicago Press, 1998), 236.

59 A. Best and A. Andreasen, 'Consumer Response to Unsatisfactory Purchases: a Survey of Perceiving Defects, Voicing Complaints, and Obtaining Redress' (1976) 11 *Law & Soc'y Rev* 701, 729. See also Office of Fair Trading, *Consumer Dissatisfaction: a Report on Surveys Undertaken for the Office of Fair Trading* (1986), 44: 'People in the AB social class are more likely to take action . . . the elderly (aged 65+) and the youngest age group (15–20) are much less likely to take action.' And see Ewick and Silbey, *The Common Place of Law*, 236, where the authors note that women reported significantly more consumer problems than men and that minorities experience more problems with insurance, utilities and creditors.

60 See L. Ross and N. Littlefield, 'Complaint as a Problem-Solving Mechanism' (1978) 12 *Law & Soc'y Rev* 199, 212: 'The factors producing generous responses to their complaints may be absent for economically disadvantaged groups.' Vidmar claims that lower-income consumers were as likely to have success with complaining as higher-income consumers: Vidmar, 'Seeking Justice'. See also K. McNeil *et al.*, 'Market Discrimination against the Poor and the Impact of Consumer Disclosure Law: the Used Car Industry' (1979) 13 *Law & Soc'y Rev* 695; Office of Fair Trading, *Consumer Dissatisfaction* (1991); Best and Andreasen, 'Consumer Response'.

complaint was not successful.[61] Some studies suggest that legal norms may not be
a significant factor in the success of a complaint and that success may be dependent partly on market norms and 'complaint competence', which may be related
to social class.[62] These findings suggest the importance of understanding the role
of the social norms of the market and the potential for reinforcing or regulating
such norms.[63] For example, I once suggested that the norm of 'satisfaction guaranteed or money refunded' might be introduced as a norm for the majority of consumer sales, since it provided a clear and straightforward remedy for a consumer.[64]
A model for the development of such a norm is the cooling-off period, which has become pervasive in consumer transactions such as door-to-door sales, distance selling, timeshares and consumer credit.[65] But cooling-off periods are rarely marketed
positively by producers in the same way as satisfaction guaranteed. There are also
different premises for the exercise of the right by a consumer. In a cooling-off period, one assumption is that a consumer has acted irrationally or been taken advantage of by high-pressure selling. This requires a consumer to see herself as either a
victim or an irrational person. The psychological concept of cognitive dissonance,
which suggests that individuals have difficulties in holding conflicting images of
themselves, means that one would predict that consumers, rather than admit that
they are not the smart individuals that they assumed themselves to be, will often ra-
tionalise their purchase as being of value, and consequently not exercise a cooling-
off right.[66] On the other hand, a 'satisfaction guaranteed' or 'trial period' promise

61 Fifty-six per cent of consumers reached an agreement after complaining but in 40 per cent of
   cases there was no resolution of the problem if two-party negotiations failed: Genn et al., Paths to
   Justice, 156–7.
62 See Ross and Littlefield, 'Complaint as a Problem-Solving Mechanism' 199, where the authors
   found that a department store serving middle-class consumers provided them with more generous remedies than those provided by the law and that this may have been related to market advantage in securing repeat purchases and the willingness and ability of the consumer
   to complain effectively. The authors wondered whether these factors would apply to disadvantaged groups. See also I. Ramsay, 'Consumer Redress Mechanisms for Defective and Poor Quality
   Products' (1981) 31 U Toronto LJ 117, where little evidence of legal rules having an impact on
   complaint handling was found. Rather, market norms, retailer discretion and consumer competence seemed to be key factors. For studies that indicate the insignificance of law at this level
   of disputing, see T. Ison, Credit Marketing and Consumer Protection (London: Croom Helm, 1979),
   251; R. Cranston, Regulating Business: Law and Consumer Agencies (London: Macmillan, 1979), 168.
63 There is now a growing literature in law and economics on the role of social norms. See, e.g., R.
   Ellickson, Order Without Law: How Neighbours Settle Disputes (Cambridge, Mass.: Harvard University
   Press, 1991); R. McAdams, 'The Origin, Development and Regulation of Norms' (1997) 96 Mich
   L Rev 338; E. Posner, Law and Social Norms (Cambridge, Mass.: Harvard University Press, 2000).
64 See Ramsay, 'Consumer Redress Mechanisms', 132.
65 See P. Rekaiti and R. Van Den Bergh, 'Cooling-Off Periods in the Consumer Laws of the EC
   Member States: a Comparative Law and Economics Approach' (2000) 23 Journal of Consumer Policy
   371.
66 Limited evidence suggests that cooling-off rights are rarely exercised. See Statt, Understanding the
   Consumer, 202–3: 'The theory of cognitive dissonance states that, because people have a powerful desire to be consistent, if they hold two psychologically inconsistent cognitions . . . they will
   need to find a way of reducing the resultant tension.' In relation to consumer decision-making,

does not require consumers to do more than change their mind about whether they really wanted the purchase. While cognitive dissonance may still be relevant, it may not be as strong in its impact. My hypothesis is therefore that cooling-off periods are currently relatively ineffective in practice in counteracting particular forms of mis-selling in markets such as door-to-door selling, distance selling and timeshares where the market incentive of the repeat purchase mechanism may be absent. They might be more effective, however, if framed as a requirement of 'satisfaction guaranteed' with a time limit for returning goods.

The above example suggests the importance of understanding the socioeconomic norms of market transactions, particularly if policy-makers wish to affect or reinforce these norms. We do not know a great deal about the relationships of legal norms to interactions at this level. There is the well-known metaphor of bargaining in the shadow of the law[67] but that evokes an image of an individual who knows her rights and the potential outcomes of a legal suit, and who rationally calculates its impact on her bargaining position. The most casual empiricism suggests that this is not an accurate picture of consumer market disputing.

One might hypothesise that where complaining is an individualised process there will be greater opportunities for variations in outcome related to the characteristic of the complainer and the ability of the complaint handler to discriminate among different complainers. Issues of discrimination have been highlighted in the consumer sales process and there is some evidence that discrimination might operate within the complaint handling process. Baker and McElrath, for example, suggest that in the wake of Hurricane Andrew, insurers took longer to investigate claims by Hispanics and Latino residents and also took longer to pay their insurance claims.[68]

The concept of 'cultural capital' may be helpful in understanding issues of discrimination in complaint handling. Cultural capital describes the phenomenon that those with higher occupational prestige will tend to have more influence and receive more deference from others based on greater poise and greater credibility.[69] A recent study of tax auditing in the USA found that cultural capital was correlated with the success of the taxpayers in an audit. This was reflected in such factors as the

it suggests that once a consumer has made a choice between two alternatives, then he or she will tend to downplay the negative aspects of the choice which has been made.

67 See R. Mnookin and L. Kornhauser, 'Bargaining in the Shadow of the Law: the Case of Divorce' (1979) 88 *Yale LJ* 950.

68 See T. Baker and K. McElrath, 'Insurance Claims Discrimination' in G. Squires (ed.), *Insurance Redlining: Disinvestment, Reinvestment, and the Evolving Role of Financial Institutions* (Washington, DC: Urban Institute Press, 1997). See also T. Chan, 'Service Quality and Unfair Racial Discrimination in Homeowners Insurance' (1999) 66 *Journal of Risk and Insurance* 83.

69 This has been described as the 'soft terrorism of middle class articulacy': P. Golding (ed.), *Excluding the Poor* (London: Child Poverty Action Group, 1986), x–xi. Birds and Graham in their empirical study of the insurance ombudsman found that 'people who get to Head Office are classic examples of "good complainants" or "squeaky wheels"': J. Birds and P. Graham, 'Complaints against Insurance Companies' (1993) 1 *Consumer LJ* 92, 101.

greater willingness of auditors to accept oral testimony from high-status taxpayers in relation to tax records. The issue here was not one of conscious bias but simply reflected the fact that the auditors 'automatically tend to grant more deference to people with high prestige than to others'.[70] In addition, the researchers found that higher-status individuals had higher expectations than lower-status individuals before the audit of being successful so that the results seemed to be a self-fulfilling prophecy. A further finding was that the introduction of a tax practitioner levelled the playing field, i.e., taxpayer prestige had no impact. This was explained partly by the fact that auditors who are dealing with repeat-player practitioners are less willing to bend the rules for fear of its impact on future cases. Researchers on court procedures have also suggested that status may affect the likelihood of an individual convincing a decision-maker of his or her credibility.[71] The concept of cultural capital is clearly of significance to any individualised procedure where decision-makers (corporate bureaucrats, lawyers, ombudsmen, judges, etc.) may be affected unconsciously by shared social beliefs that link status to attributions about personal abilities and social worth.

Many studies of consumer behaviour have collected primarily quantitative information on consumer responses to problems, correlating it with other variables such as demographic characteristics. Recent research by Ewick and Silbey[72] has combined quantitative analysis with in-depth qualitative interviews with individuals, which have explored how individuals think about and use the law in relation to everyday problems they encounter, such as consumer debt, problems with utilities, and defective automobiles. Their conclusions pose intriguing and difficult questions for policy-makers interested in the provision of effective consumer redress. The qualitative aspects of their research permitted the authors to probe the different understandings that individuals had of law as revealed in individuals' narratives. The authors expose a complex picture of law that challenges an instrumental model of law being wielded by rational actors. They argue that this instrumental model downplays the communicative role of law, which may be used to express one's relationship with others (for example, tolerating the noise of a neighbour to show that one is a good neighbour), one's own identity, or to assert values. Individuals would express statements in their narratives such as, 'there was enough to sue about but... really I'm not litigious'.[73] This speaker seems to assert an instrumental view of law in terms of costs and benefits but then in a reference to 'litigiousness' signifies both an individual characteristic (non-litigiousness) and a purpose for law that goes beyond self-interested calculation: law should not be used too often.

---

70 K. A. Kinsey, 'Which "Haves" Come out Ahead and Why? Cultural Capital and Legal Mobilization in Frontline Law Enforcement' (1999) 33 *Law & Soc'y Rev* 993, 1020.
71 See J. M. Conley and W. M. O'Barr, *Rules versus Relationships: the Ethnography of Legal Discourse* (Chicago, Ill.: University of Chicago Press, 1990).
72 Ewick and Silbey, *The Common Place of Law*.   73 *Ibid.*

The authors found that individuals seemed to hold three potentially contradictory views of law: (a) a universal set of norms separate from everyday life; (b) law as a game, where individuals may exploit the rules and where differential social and personal resources may be important; and (c) law as an arbitrary and capricious power. The conception of law as an arbitrary and capricious power included the idea that it was a power that seemed limited in its ability to affect everyday life. Thus interviewees talked about the futility of small claims judgments that could not be enforced, and the inability of the law to protect against the retaliation of others such as landlords. Individuals also developed methods of resistance and subterfuge to address the limits of the law and its arbitrariness. This approach to law seemed to be adopted most often by 'persons of colour, by women, or by unemployed and marginally employed working class men'.[74] Individuals in these situations seem to be often aware of the fact that the system is stacked against them and that the law is something that one bumps up against rather than an instrument of empowerment.

The findings of Ewick and Silbey are significant in emphasising the importance of social norms and the complex way in which ideas about legality and law are constructed and reproduced by individuals. It suggests that measures intended to affect social norms may be as important a strategy as reducing the financial costs of consumer action. One can observe in countries that have recently developed consumer protection regimes that it may take time for individual consumers to view themselves as rights holders and that this may be related to individuals' changing perceptions of the appropriateness of particular responses to consumer problems. At a more specific level, intermediaries may be a significant factor in affecting consumer behaviour and social norms about appropriate behaviour. For example, available consumer advice centres that are easily accessible may have a substantial impact on consumer behaviour and attitudes to defective problems and services.[75]

A final area of study of consumer problem-solving concerns marketing in lower-income areas. These studies have often shown the extent to which individuals may be locked in continuing (if not continual) relationships with retailers, lenders and others who service these markets. There are often 'fictive friendships', which are developed by the lenders so that economic relationships are embedded in personal and social relationships. Michael Hudson, in a recent exposé of the alternative financial sector in the USA, quotes the owner of a Rent-to-Own chain describing his top manager as a person who 'doesn't rent televisions. He doesn't rent

---

74 *Ibid.*, 235.
75 See Scott and Black, *Cranston's Consumers*, 104, where they cite D. Harris *et al.*, *Compensation and Support for Illness and Injury* (Oxford: Clarendon Press, 1984), and refer to the Oxford national study of accident victims, which found that a key factor in explaining the higher rates of claiming amongst road accident victims was the availability of information about legal rights immediately after the accident.

washers ... he doesn't sell anything. He develops relationships with people.'[76] Indeed, this finding seems confirmed by studies that suggest that consumers in the alternative credit sector are not necessarily price sensitive but appreciate being treated with dignity and respect, in contrast perhaps to their treatment by mainstream financial providers.[77] In a recent major complaint brought by the US Federal Trade Commission against Associates Finance, which is now part of Citigroup, for predatory lending in the subprime credit market,[78] the Commission argues that the Associates nurtured a relationship of trust in which consumers could rely on the Associates for sound advice about organising their finances. In fact, it is claimed that the company engaged in numerous deceptive practices to induce consumers to take out or refinance loans with high interest rates, costs and fees and to purchase high-cost credit insurance. These relationships may often represent situations where sellers attempt to dominate and control the consumer and where the costs to consumers of complaining about sellers may be high. In his study of the complaint-handling practices of the Walker-Thomas low-income retailer in Washington, DC, Greenberg noted that Walker-Thomas had many avenues of control over complaining consumers, which ranged from informing a consumer's social worker that her partner was working while receiving welfare, to ending access to credit or being flexible in repayments schemes. This example suggests the potentially dark side of relational contracting. It would also not be far-fetched to assume that consumers in this situation would often understand the law to be an arbitrary and capricious power, associated with social control rather than empowerment.[79]

The problems of consumers in lower-income markets are not new and are a continuing issue in consumer policy. The existing evidence suggests that complaint as a problem-solving mechanism is likely to be less effective in the markets described by Greenberg, than in the middle-class markets described by Ross and Littlefield. It suggests also that it is not a simple matter to affect these market relationships and it draws attention to the broader conception of access to justice. Legal rights and remedies are only one aspect of a public policy strategy that might reduce predatory

76 See M. Hudson (ed.), *Merchants of Misery: How Corporate America Profits from Poverty* (Monroe, Mo.: Common Courage Press, 1996), 152. See also R. D. Manning, *Credit Card Nation: the Consequences of America's Addiction to Credit* (New York: Basic Books, 2000), 200–2.
77 See Manning, *Credit Card Nation*, 202, where the author states that 'the industry's market research has shown that potential customers are more pride than price-sensitive, craving good treatment even more than low prices'. Some of the practices of the industry are said to include personalising greetings to customers, introducing high technology services, fostering long-term relationships with clients, and even sending inexpensive flower arrangements to funerals of local residents.
78 See Federal Trade Commission, *FTC Charges One of Nation's Largest Subprime Lenders with Abusive Lending Practices*, Press Release (6 March 2001). See http://www.ftc.gov/opa/2001/03/associates.htm.
79 See D. Greenberg, 'Easy Terms, Hard Times: Complaint Handling in the Ghetto' in L. Nader (ed.), *No Access to Law: Alternatives to the American Judicial System* (New York: Academy Press, 1980), 379.

lending and selling and high credit costs. Other initiatives must include the role of community development and the facilitation of credit unions in low-income areas. There is the need for what David Harvey terms the development of 'spaces of hope'.[80] The spatial metaphor illustrates the overlap of consumer issues with those of urban planning and the metaphor of 'the third way' suggests that consumer protection might be one part of a regime of positive welfare where a spectrum of facilitative and regulatory measures might be adopted. It is important to see the linkages between different policies. For example, strategies aimed at community redevelopment and the development of savings capacity among low-income consumers will be undermined by high-cost credit and predatory lending. Secondly, they underline the potentially regressive impact of individualised redress procedures, which require consumers to confront and negotiate with suppliers or third parties such as complaint managers and ombudsmen.

The role of intermediaries in the provision of access to justice

Intermediaries play an important role in the provision of access to justice for consumers. Intermediaries might include lawyers, social workers, debt counsellors or consumer advisors. They may influence the type of remedy that is obtained by a consumer, and they may also be important political actors in any proposed reforms of consumer rights. Intermediaries may 'mobilise' consumers, and heighten or dampen conflict. Stewart Macaulay showed that at the time of his study (the late 1970s) lawyers did not act as aggressive advocates on behalf of consumers.[81] Rather, they tended to mediate between businesses and consumers, sometimes 'cooling the client out' and acting as therapists. Macaulay argued that it was not only the economic realities of practice that deterred aggressive action by lawyers, but that lawyers' advice was affected by their values. They believed that there were legitimate and not so legitimate methods of solving consumer problems and at times distrusted consumers who complained, viewing them as 'flakes'. In addition, lawyers might fear losing work from local businesses if they were viewed as consumer advocates. These lawyers exercised a discretion in filtering away from the legal system disputes that in their view were not sufficiently important for the legal system. Legal action, represented by lawyers' practices, reflected and reproduced assumptions about appropriate consumer behaviour.

Bankruptcy is an important consumer remedy in the USA, and studies of the role of lawyers' advice to potential consumer bankrupts is a useful example of the influence of intermediaries over consumer choices. Studies indicate that a consumer's choice of a repayment programme or straight bankruptcy may depend on the

---

80 See Harvey, *Spaces of Hope*.   81 See Macaulay, *Lawyers and Consumer Protection Law*.

financial and ideological interests of the lawyers whom they consult.[82] Jean Braucher found in a study of US consumer bankruptcy lawyers that some viewed themselves as liberal crusaders protecting the economic underdog, where consumers were viewed as the victims of aggressive credit marketing; others emphasised individual responsibility for debts; while a final group viewed bankruptcy as the opportunity to educate clients into sound budgeting and financial management practices.[83] These ideologies represent a variety of conflicting social ideologies about debt and the morality of debt repayment, and they have a significant practical impact on outcomes for consumers.

We might hypothesise that *all* intermediaries are likely to bring with them a baggage of interests and values. Writers on debt counselling in Europe draw attention to the impact of the ideologies of these individuals on the approach to consumers and their handling of issues of overindebtedness.[84] These findings draw attention to the importance of the discretionary decisions of intermediaries and also the power dynamics between consumer and intermediary. A central question is whether intermediaries empower or control their clients. The evidence in relation to lawyers seems to be that in consumer protection lawyers tend to dominate their clients. One consequence of this finding is that the more complex a choice faced by a consumer, then the more likely this will confer power on a professional intermediary to channel a consumer in a particular direction. There is the need for greater understanding cross-culturally of the different roles of intermediaries such as lawyers, counsellors and advisors. Studies might investigate the different approaches of publicly and privately financed intermediaries and relate the findings on consumers to literature on welfare bureaucracies and their clients. It would be ironic if privatisation of services, which is often promoted in terms of consumer empowerment and choice, resulted in many cases in professional domination of consumer choice. There are also implications for the design of legal rules. 'Bright line' rules which reduce the need for intermediaries might be a desirable policy in certain areas. Finally, the power of intermediaries in shaping the law might also help to explain variations in the approach and substance of consumer protection.

---

82 See J. Braucher, 'Lawyers and Consumer Bankruptcy: One Code, Many Cultures' (1993) 67 *Am Bankr L J* 501; G. Neustadter, 'When Lawyer and Client Meet: Observations of Interviewing and Counseling Behaviour in the Consumer Bankruptcy Law Office' (1986) 35 *Buff L Rev* 177; T. Sullivan, E. Warren and J. Westbrook, 'The Persistence of Local Legal Culture: Twenty Years of Evidence from the Federal Bankruptcy Courts' (1994) 17 *Harv J L & Pub Pol'y* 801. I report some similar findings in relation to Canadian bankruptcy trustees in I. Ramsay, 'Market Imperatives, Professional Discretion and the Role of Intermediaries in Consumer Bankruptcy: a Comparative Study of the Canadian Trustee in Bankruptcy (2000) 74 *Am Bankr L J* 399.
83 Braucher, 'Lawyers and Consumer Bankruptcy'.
84 See N. Huls, 'Overindebtedness and Overlegalization: Consumer Bankruptcy as a Field for Alternative Dispute Resolution' (1997) 20 *Journal of Consumer Policy* 142, 157: 'Debt counseling is often provided by social workers with strong political and social beliefs which they readily impose on their clients and creditors.'

Small claims courts and consumers

Small claims courts have been an important instrument in common law jurisdictions for providing consumers with access to justice, and yet they have often seemed to fall short of meeting their promise.[85] This in turn has led to demands for reforms to make them even more accessible to litigants. I would like to introduce the conclusions from three socio-legal studies of small claims courts in England, Canada and the USA.

My first example is John Baldwin's study of the English small claims procedure,[86] where he explicitly assesses its success against the premise of access to justice. He concludes that:[87]

> the extent to which the small claims procedure has succeeded in facilitating access to justice has been at best limited. They continue to be used by very limited sectors of the population, particularly by professional people or those representing business interests. In so far as ordinary people are involved in small claims they are likely to appear as defendants, in other words those who are taken to court for non payment of debt.

Only about 20 per cent of contested claims were consumer disputes.[88] Nor did the small claims hearing bring closure to the dispute. Six months after the hearing, only half of all successful plaintiffs had received full payment. And any hope that the small claims context might provide an avenue through which the poor might find redress for their grievances 'seems to have no empirical support whatever'.[89] There is therefore a potentially significant class division in the users of the court with consumer debtors being generally in working-class occupations and consumer plaintiffs drawn from middle-class and professional groups.

My second example is McGuire and MacDonald's study of a small claims court in Montreal, Quebec.[90] This study is of particular interest because it focused on the role of the court within a multicultural community and, in addition, the court represents a very progressive model of small claims court. Lawyers are barred, corporations may not use the process, judges may play an activist role, and the court provides advice and assistance for the lay litigant. But the authors concluded that

---

85 I discuss these issues at greater length in I. Ramsay, 'Small Claims Courts: a Review' in Ontario Law Reform Commission, *Rethinking Civil Justice: Research Studies for the Civil Justice Review* (1996), vol. II, 489–544.

86 J. Baldwin, *Small Claims in the County Courts in England and Wales: the Bargain Basement of Civil Justice?* (Oxford: Clarendon Press, 1997).

87 *Ibid.*, 15.

88 A recent study in New Zealand found only 16 per cent of claims were consumer disputes: J. McDermott, 'Disputes Tribunals, Ombudsmen and Legal Aid in New Zealand' (1999) 7 *Consumer LJ* 465, 467.

89 Baldwin, *Small Claims*, 15.

90 S. C. McGuire and R. A. MacDonald, 'Small Claims Court Cant' (1996) 34 *Osgoode Hall LJ* 509.

in general the court continues to be used by well-educated, more affluent male professionals and business people running unincorporated businesses claiming for the price of unpaid goods and services, as opposed to consumers claiming in respect of defective products and services.

My final example is Conley and O'Barr's study of the experience of litigants in a small claims court in the United States.[91] The authors found that there was often a discord between what litigants wanted and what the legal system provided. Litigants were often seeking an intangible benefit such as wishing to tell their story, but this clashed with the court's need to process claims efficiently. In addition, individuals were often pursuing an agenda different from that of the court and often misperceived the power of the court to seek out and punish the other party, and were unclear as to the distinction between civil and criminal process. Thus, many expected the court to punish the defendant for exploiting the relationship. The authors conclude that the law often defines the problems of ordinary people in a manner that may have little meaning for them and that does not offer them the remedies they desire. But paradoxically the litigants did not blame the law but rather the particular actors involved, such as judges and administrators. Individuals learn that the law is a limited means of righting wrongs but that this limitation is attributable to the reality of the implementation of the law rather than the law itself. The authors conclude that 'it is hard to imagine a more effective mechanism for maintaining the status quo'.[92]

What should we conclude from these studies of small claims courts? I would not wish to draw overly broad conclusions about the overall success or failure of these courts from three studies,[93] but I think that they suggest some caution in viewing the facilitation of increased access to these courts as necessarily a progressive policy. It is possible that such a policy might not lead to a broadening of use but rather an increase in use by the same social groups as currently use the court. Perhaps there should be greater development of out-of-court alternatives such as ombudsmen. But there is some evidence that they are also colonised by the middle classes.[94] There is also the danger that the promise of increased access for individual claims may invite legislators to formulate legislation that relies on private remedies as a primary method for enforcing consumer statutes.

McGuire and MacDonald also ask the pertinent question in their study, why do women, the elderly and young, cultural minorities, immigrants, the less educated, the unemployed, and poorer consumers seem less inclined to invoke state

91 See Conley and O'Barr, *Rules versus Relationships*. 92 *Ibid.*, 165.
93 A more optimistic view of small claims courts is found in N. Vidmar, 'The Small Claims Court: a Reconceptualization of Disputes and an Empirical Investigation' (1984) 18 *Law & Soc'y Rev* 515. However, this study did not consider the demographic characteristics of court users.
94 See Birds and Graham, 'Complaints against Insurance Companies', 101: 'Respondents tended to be male, older and likely to be in social class AB.'

institutions in resolving their problems?[95] Is it because many of these groups do not perceive these institutions as relevant to solving their problems, and have they developed alternatives? To what extent does the view of law as an arbitrary and capricious power, something to be avoided or evaded, explain the reluctance of these groups to use the process? Finally, we might revise the 'pressure-cooker' model of society implicit in early access to justice literature, which imagines individuals striving to seek justice from the state but being barred by various costs. The picture drawn by Ewick and Silbey and other empirical studies suggests a more complex picture.

Summary

We might conclude that individualised redress procedures may have a distributional tilt against lower-income consumers and disadvantaged groups. A further conclusion might also be that an important goal for public policy may be to affect two-party complaint handling where the great majority of consumer problem-solving takes place. In relation to consumer problems, most consumers want to 'solve the problem' rather than assert legal rights. They want a refund, repair or replacement. Hirschman notes that voice is a costly mechanism and that it is 'conditioned on the influence and bargaining power'[96] of consumers. Policies might be addressed to upgrade the competence of consumers through the provision of information on complaint-handling practices of retailers. This might permit consumers to avoid firms with poor complaint records. A significant development of the past few decades has been the development by many firms of internal complaint mechanisms, often as part of a self-regulatory code of practice. In some cases, such as financial services, these are part of a broader ombudsman scheme. A cursory impression of their development is that they are initially developed grudgingly by firms and may be viewed partly as a method of containing criticism. Hirschman, in his classic work on voice and exit, argued that when organisations introduce channels for voice by consumers or clients, such as complaint mechanisms, there is a tendency over time to transform what should be a feedback mechanism into a method of institutionalising and domesticating dissent.[97] However, their development is often a continuing political process of adjustment to criticism so that over time standards may improve and the decisions of the complaint mechanism may even have some impact on general corporate practices, thus benefiting all consumers and not merely the 'squeaky wheels'. The development of the Financial Ombudsman service in the United Kingdom seems to fit this description.[98]

95 McGuire and MacDonald, 'Small Claims Court Cant', 550.
96 A. O. Hirschman, *Exit Voice and Loyalty* (Cambridge, Mass.: Harvard University Press, 1970), 405.
97 *Ibid.*, 124. See also L. Edelman and M. Suchman, 'When the "Haves" Hold Court: Speculations on the Organizational Internalization of Law' (1999) 33 *Law & Soc'y Rev* 941.
98 See R. James and P. Morris, chapter 8 herein.

The potentially regressive effects associated with individualised redress procedures might suggest that greater resources be invested in more public regulation of lower-income markets, recognising that lower-income consumers may suffer a relatively larger detriment than middle-class consumers when they experience losses arising from defective products or misrepresentations.[99] However, public enforcement is also reactive and its level is subject to social, economic and political influences. In the context of financial services in the USA, Caskey argues that larger resources are devoted to regulation of financial issues that affect middle-class consumers than are devoted to regulation of the 'alternative financial sector' that serves low-income consumers.[100] Class actions are a further alternative for addressing the limits of individualised redress procedures, although one study in the late 1980s suggested that they often piggybacked on public regulation[101] and could not be regarded as a substitute for public regulation. Class actions also raise the problem of monitoring the role of intermediaries, i.e., lawyers who conduct class actions.

A study of individualised redress procedures draws attention to two models of service delivery, described by Lawrence Friedman as routinisation and individualisation.[102] Routinisation simplifies access to justice by creating automatic entitlements based on bright line rules. It provides a uniform and universal approach to a problem and reduces the possibilities for the exercise of discretion. Individualisation, on the other hand, presupposes a custom-made solution based on the particular circumstances of an individual and the individual merits of the case. Routinisation reduces the extent to which individuals might be subject to the discretionary decisions of professionals and, it is argued, serves those 'who are inarticulate, unable or unwilling to press their particular claims'.[103] It might therefore have greater progressive effects. The importance of bright line rules in consumer protection was noted in the path-breaking work of the late Arthur Leff,[104] and this approach continues to be emphasised as the most appropriate method of protecting vulnerable consumers.[105] Routinisation underlines, therefore, the importance of 'self-enforcing' consumer laws, which in this era of cutbacks in public regulation

99 See Office of Fair Trading, *Vulnerable Consumers and Financial Services: the Report of the Director General's Inquiry* (1999), 10.
100 See J. P. Caskey, *Fringe Banking: Check-Cashing Outlets, Pawnshops, and the Poor* (New York: Russell Sage Foundation, 1994), 149–50.
101 See B. Garth, I. H. Nagel and S. J. Plager, 'The Institution of the Private Attorney General: Perspectives from an Empirical Study of Class Actions' (1988) 61 *S Cal L Rev* 353.
102 See L. Friedman, 'Access to Justice: Social and Historical Context' in M. Cappelletti and J. Weisner (eds.), *Access to Justice: Promising Institutions* (Milan: A. Giuffrè, 1978), 16–28.
103 See Sarat, 'Book Review', 1922.
104 See A. A. Leff, 'Unconscionability and the Crowd: Consumers and the Common Law Tradition' (1970) 31 *U Pitt L Rev* 349.
105 See J. Braucher, 'The Repo Code: a Study of Adjustment to Uncertainty in Commercial Law' (1997) 75 *Wash ULQ* 549.

merit further study. The potentially regressive distributional effects of *ex post* individual litigation also draw attention to the potential benefits of *ex ante* across-the-board protection such as exists within a licensing regime. The Crowther Committee on Consumer Credit supported the *ex ante* protection of licensing in consumer credit because of its advantage over individual actions in protecting those least able to protect themselves.[106]

The findings on intermediaries suggest that law reform might be most effective by affecting the incentives of intermediaries rather than consumers. If this is unlikely to be effective then it might be wise to reduce the role of intermediaries in the delivery of consumer protection and adopt the advantages of routinisation. However, this course of action is likely to be fraught with political difficulties since intermediaries may wield significant power in the political process.

Finally, there is the more general issue of instrumental, rational choice behaviour raised by Ewick and Silbey. They contrast a complex sociological view of individual action with that of the rational actor model where an individual views law as a commodity, the use of which depends on its price. This latter model is often influential in policy-making and has resulted in many changes designed to reduce costs of access to justice. But the failure of these policies in the area of small claims suggests the need for further reflection on the most appropriate mix of policy responses.

The comparative dimension: legal transplants and irritants

The discussion thus far has suggested some of the complexities for consumer policy-making posed by an interdisciplinary approach to understanding consumer behaviour and the role of law in consumer markets. These complexities are increased when the discussion takes a comparative and international turn and countries draw on foreign models for transplantation. Yet, consumer policy-making is often an exercise in applied comparative law. Policy-making exercises within the EU are generally preceded by comparative assessments of legal regimes within the EU as well as an assessment of US approaches.

The resurgence of interest in comparative law, which seems to be related to the interest in the 'transnational' or in 'globalisation', has stimulated reflection on the nature and methodology of comparative law.[107] This resurgence has revived

---

106 See Crowther Committee, *Report of the Committee on Consumer Credit*, Cmnd. 4596 (1971), para 6.1.19: 'The basic problem is that the law protects least those whom it is designed to serve most. The low income consumer is particularly open to oppression, yet he is usually unable – through ignorance, fear or sheer inability – to manage his affairs to avail himself of the protection which is offered to him by the process of litigation.'

107 For a general discussion of different approaches to comparative law, see A. Riles, 'Wigmore's Treasure Box: Comparative Law in the Era of Information' (1999) 40 *Harv Int'l L J* 221. The author notes that a LEXIS search reveals that from 1990 to 1996 the number of law review articles

debates on the role of law in development and the possibility of the success of legal transplants. It might be assumed that, given the global nature of consumerism and the potentially similar problems raised by the everyday consumption of goods and services, there would be significant possibilities for the convergence of legal regulation. For example, consumer problems with global credit card providers would not appear to differ significantly between countries. One extreme version of this argument is that as countries develop consumer societies and free market economies then there will be a convergence in the form of legal institutions for consumer protection. This argument, reminiscent of earlier theories of law and development,[108] does not seem to be sustained even within the EU where there have been significant moves towards harmonisation of consumer law. Wilhelmsson draws attention to the differing ideologies underlying consumer protection in Scandinavian countries and other countries of the EU,[109] as well as the significant differences that remain in national regulation, notwithstanding the existence of the harmonisation process. Even within countries such as the United States or Canada there remain many differences in state and provincial consumer laws, which partly reflect differing ideologies concerning consumer protection.[110] Globalisation seems to be compatible with significant diversity as well as uniformity, and capitalism takes a variety of forms in the contemporary world with little evidence of convergence. At the same time it would be interesting to assess the extent to which global corporations follow similar practices in different countries, notwithstanding differences in legal regimes. For example, all credit card companies in Canada have followed the practice of limiting a consumer's liability to $50 in the event of a card being lost or stolen. Yet, until recently, the companies were under no legal obligation to follow this practice in most Canadian jurisdictions. Their practice might be a consequence of market pressures in terms of good customer relations and the fact that in the USA there is a legal limit on consumer liability. However, Canadian credit card companies do not accept connected lender liability in relation to disputes with retailers, notwithstanding that this is a legal norm in many US states. An intriguing field for comparative research is understanding the factors that drive multinational

---

incorporating the term 'global' increased from 250 to 3,129 and that this was paralleled by an increase of articles using the term 'comparative law', which rose from 57 in 1990 to 224 in 1996.

108 See, e.g., J. Merryman, 'Comparative Law and Social Change: on the Origins, Style, Decline and Revival of the Law and Development Movement' (1977) 25 *Am J Comp L* 457.

109 See T. Wilhelmsson, *Is There a European Consumer Law and Should There Be One?* Centro di studi e ricerche di diritto comparativo e straniero Roma (2000), 19–20. The author notes that the European Court of Justice assumes an image of the consumer as a well-informed rational actor while Nordic consumer protection is based on the assumption of the consumer as a 'passive glancer' who does not read advertisements closely.

110 E.g., the Province of Quebec, Canada, has the most consumer-oriented legislation in Canada, which may partly reflect a period when Quebec was a more welfare-oriented society than the rest of Canada.

corporations to 'export' a particular legal standard throughout their global operations.[111]

If we should reject the idea of a convergence theory in the area of consumer protection, I think that the opposite extreme that legal transplants will fail because of the deep connection of law to culture is also not tenable in the area of consumer law. The cultural argument against transplants is overbroad and seems falsified by the extent to which there have been many legal transplants in the area of consumer law. A fruitful exploration of legal differences in consumer protection might focus on the interplay of organisational power, professional interests and legal culture in the development of the law. Carruthers and Halliday, in their comparison of the development of corporate bankruptcy in the USA and UK, show how the complex interplay between different groups and broader political ideologies resulted in different approaches to corporate bankruptcy in the USA and UK. They demonstrate that similar market economies did not adopt similar bankruptcy regimes, but rather that they were contingent on a complex interplay of professional interests, interest groups and ideologies.[112] This finding denied, therefore, a 'naïve functionalism' explanation which might assume a simple and direct connection between economic development and legal form.

A focus on the role of interest groups and the particular institutional structure associated with the area of law being studied was emphasised by Kahn-Freund, who stressed the relative political power of particular groups, such as lawyers, in affecting the success or failure of legal transplants.[113] More recently, Günther Teubner has argued that the success of legal transplants must be related to the existing institutional structures of industry/government relations and that the development of legal norms under directives such as the EU Unfair Contract Terms Directive will diverge because of the different nature of these institutional structures in the UK and Germany. He also proposes that we should use the term 'legal irritant' rather than legal transplant. The concept of an irritant is intended to describe the fact that importation of a legal concept may have unexpected, complex and long-term effects on the importing system.[114] Although Teubner seems to deny that these processes are about power and politics, it is difficult not to think of these developments without accounting for the power of interest groups as well as institutional traditions. It may be the case that self-regulation will be more effective within the corporatist tradition of Sweden or Austria where there has historically been greater co-operation

---

111 For an exploration of this issue, see D. Vogel, *Trading up: Consumer and Environmental Regulation in a Global Economy* (Cambridge, Mass.: Harvard University Press, 1995).

112 See B. G. Carruthers and T. C. Halliday, *Rescuing Business: the Making of Corporate Bankruptcy Law in England and the United States* (New York: Clarendon Press, 1998).

113 O. Kahn-Freund, 'On Uses and Misuses of Comparative Law' in O. Kahn-Freund, *Selected Writings* (London: Stevens, 1978).

114 G. Teubner, '"Legal Irritants": Good Faith in British Law or How Unifying Law Ends up in New Divergences' (1998) 61 *Mod L Rev* 11.

between business and government. However, I am sceptical that the dominant role of advertising self-regulation in the UK can be accounted for solely by institutional tradition rather than the historical power dynamics of industry/government relations in relation to advertising.[115] The 'irritant' of the EC Directive on Misleading Advertising does not yet seem to have significantly disturbed this structure. A detailed comparison of an apparently common development such as the consumer ombudsman might also reveal different stories concerning its functioning within Europe, Australia, New Zealand and Canada, and this may relate to the role of financial institutions within an economy, traditions of regulation within the financial industry, and the politics of regulation of this sector.

An interesting study of the potential impact of differing institutional structures of regulation is that of Geraint Howells and Thomas Wilhelmsson, who have drawn attention to different models of business/government relations within Northern Europe and North America, arguing that the USA represents in the consumer area a model of 'information and litigation' that compares to a Northern European model of 'regulation and administration'.[116] In addition, they argue that in the USA it is not seen as the proper role of federal agencies to shape the ethical basis of the market, in contrast to some European countries. In the light of their analysis they conclude that it may be dangerous to transplant institutions such as class actions to Europe where there is not the institutional structure of an entrepreneurial plaintiffs' bar and the incentives that exist in the US system. They might also have added that lawyers in the USA would have a significant political influence on any attempts to change the US system. There are also differing models of business/government relations within Europe. The resistance by the UK to the adoption of the German model of enforcement by private groups of unfair contract terms may reflect differing traditions of regulation within the two countries.[117]

These brief remarks suggest that an important role for consumer lawyers is to understand the potential complexities involved in consumer law transplants and that a political dimension should be a significant part of that analysis. We might hypothesise that if a rule is easily transplantable (such as a cooling-off period) then there is less likelihood that it will have a significant impact in changing practice. It may have symbolic impact, and that is itself a further dimension for analysis. The political dimensions of consumer law are also apparent in the competition to export

---

115 I provide a history of the development of the Advertising Standards Authority (ASA) in I. Ramsay, *Consumer Protection* (London: Weidenfeld and Nicolson, 1989), 388–96, describing the ASA as 'mandated self-regulation'. For a more recent account, see Scott and Black, *Cranston's Consumers*, 55–61.

116 See G. Howells and T. Wilhelmsson, 'EC and US Approaches to Consumer Protection. Should the Gap Be Bridged?' in *Yearbook of European Law* (Oxford: Clarendon Press, 1997), vol. XVII, 207.

117 See discussion in P. Rott, 'Injunctions for the Protection of Consumers' Interests after the Implementation of the EC Directive into English and German Law' (2001) 24 *Journal of Consumer Policy* 401.

models of consumer law to emerging economies where US and European models may provide alternative approaches to regulation. Dezalay and Garth have shown how the development of international commercial arbitration over the past twenty-five years has increasingly moved towards a US model.[118]

The area of over-indebtedness and consumer bankruptcy is a useful case study for comparative analysis. There has traditionally been a sharp distinction between the USA, with its open access to the 'fresh start' in bankruptcy for consumers, and continental European countries, where discharge of debts for individuals was unknown.[119] During the past decade, however, many countries in Europe have reformed their debt adjustment procedures and moved gingerly towards the idea of discharge. A superficial examination of these changes might suggest a convergence of legal regimes which are responding to the increasing problems of debt in a consumer credit society. Although the US model has provided some guidance to reforms, the landscape of debt adjustment procedures differs significantly in Europe,[120] so that the idea of convergence is only apparent on a superficial examination, and the USA and Canada continue to have much higher numbers of consumer bankrupts than European countries, including England.[121]

It would be interesting to compare, not the level of bankruptcy filings, but the level of over-indebtedness in North America and Europe. For example, commentators in England have recently expressed concerns about the high levels of consumer over-indebtedness.[122] These have not translated, however, into significant increases in bankruptcies, so an intriguing question relates to the differences in the response to over-indebtedness in England and North America. Perhaps it is simply reflecting a time lag, and these changes in over-indebtedness will be reflected ultimately in increased bankruptcies. A promising avenue of investigation might be the institutional structure for addressing problems of over-indebtedness. This would require an analysis not only of legal regimes but also the professional intermediaries

---

118 See Y. Dezalay and B. G. Garth, *Dealing in Virtue: International Commercial Arbitration and the Construction of a Transnational Legal Order* (Chicago, Ill.: University of Chicago Press, 1996).

119 See J. Niemi-Kiesilainen, 'Changing Directions in Consumer Bankruptcy Law and Practice in Europe and North America' (1997) 20 *Journal of Consumer Policy* 133.

120 See J. Niemi-Kiesilainen, 'Consumer Bankruptcy in Comparison: Do We Cure a Market Failure or a Social Problem?' (1999) 37 *Osgoode Hall LJ* 473.

121 See Sullivan, Warren and Westbrook, 'The Persistence of Local Legal Culture', 256–61. In 1997, the US bankruptcy rate was 5.1 per 1,000, Canada was 3 per 1,000, and England was 0.47 per 1,000.

122 The National Association of Citizens Advice Bureaux (NACAB), which is the primary provider of debt advice to consumers, indicated in 2000 that consumer debt problems brought to them had increased by 37 per cent over the past two years. In the year 1999/2000, Citizens Advice Bureaux in England and Wales handled nearly one million general debt enquiries. The chief executive of NACAB stated: 'Our CAB advisers are seeing more and more people who have been offered credit that they simply cannot afford to repay. This is a very worrying trend. Irresponsible lending exacerbates the problems of those trying to manage on low incomes or benefits. I urge consumers to think twice before taking on new consumer credit obligations': *Citizens Advice Bureaux Report a Rise in Consumer Debt*, Press Release (5 September 2000).

who deal with debt problems, their impact on consumer choices, and on the development of reforms. Such an investigation may require attention to the political power of these groups and the general configuration of interest groups in the development of the law. Layered onto this analysis would be the impact of the role of the state in protecting individuals against life's uncertainties, with more generous social security benefits in Europe and the absence of universal health care in the USA. A further explanation of these differences may lie in differing conceptions of the role of debt adjustment, differences that we might describe as cultural or ideological. Some authors have suggested that the 'fresh start' in US law represents values of the frontier and rebirth.[123]

The complexities involved in understanding the different approaches to consumer indebtedness in countries with not dissimilar economies suggests that there is an important role for comparative consumer law, which might develop through careful and detailed cross-national study of specific topics, informed by contextual and interdisciplinary analysis of the phenomena under investigation. Such an approach could have long-term importance in policy-making as well as in our understanding of the role of law in society.

---

123 See T. A. Sullivan, E. Warren and J. L. Westbrook, *As We Forgive our Debtors: Bankruptcy and Consumer Credit in America* (New York: Oxford University Press, 1989).

3   Consumer access to justice in common law
     countries: a survey of the issues from a law
     and economics perspective

ANTHONY J. DUGGAN

Introduction

Legal disputes are like contracts in reverse. A contract seals the outcome of the parties' negotiations. It avoids uncertainty and saves them the further transactions costs they would incur if the negotiations continued. A dispute keeps the outcome of the parties' engagement in suspense. It prolongs uncertainty and increases their transactions costs. Contracts lead to beneficial exchanges. Disputes lead to costly stand-offs. Dispute resolution benefits the parties in the same way a contract does. It seals the outcome between them, avoids uncertainty and saves further transactions costs. Settlement is a contractual form of dispute resolution. In default of settlement, adjudication may be necessary. Adjudication is a surrogate for the contractual solution.

The benefits of adjudication through the civil justice system are not limited to the parties themselves. There are social benefits as well. First, and most obviously, adjudication lowers the social cost of disputes by facilitating orderly dispute resolution. Rule is cheaper than misrule. A war of words in the courtroom is better than a shoot-out in the main street. This is the corrective justice function of the civil justice system. Secondly, and perhaps less obviously, the civil justice system avoids disputes. It does this by generating judge-made rules to guide future behaviour. When a court awards A (a consumer) a remedy against B (a firm), it internalises to B the cost to A of B's activity. B (and other like parties) will then take cost-effective preventive measures to avoid liability in future cases. This is the deterrence function of the civil justice system. The spill-over effects of the corrective justice function and the deterrence function help explain why governments subsidise the system. The aim is to encourage the optimal amount of litigation by transferring some of the costs from the litigant's pocket to the public purse.[1]

My thanks to Ted Tjaden and the staff of the Bora Laskin Law Library, University of Toronto, for research assistance, and to Michael Trebilcock, Catherine Walsh and Janet Mosher for helpful comments on an earlier draft. All errors are mine.
1 There are two questions: (1) Should the government be the sole provider of civil justice services? (the privatisation question); (2) Should the government subsidise the provision of civil justice services? (the subsidisation question). Privatisation and subsidisation are not mutually exclusive alternatives. See M. J. Trebilcock, 'An Economic Perspective on Access to Civil Justice in Ontario' in

What happens if people are overly discouraged from litigation? There are at least two likely consequences. First, there will be an under-supply of corrective justice. The implications are that some disputes that should have been resolved will not be resolved at all. Other disputes that should have been resolved by litigation will be resolved by less efficient methods, for example, costly self-help remedies or defensive measures. Secondly, there will be an under-supply of deterrence. The implication is that some avoidable disputes will not be avoided. A remedy award to A will cause B to modify its future behaviour if: (1) there are cost-effective measures open to B for avoiding future liability; and (2) litigation in future cases is certain. If litigation in future cases is uncertain, B no longer carries the full expected cost of its behaviour. B will spend less on preventive measures and this increases the risk of avoidable harm to A. In short, there will be too much consumer fraud, too many broken contracts, too many product defects and so on.

What happens if people are encouraged to litigate too much? Again, there are at least two likely consequences. First, there will be an over-supply of corrective justice. People will over-invest in dispute resolution at the expense of other activities, and they will over-invest in litigation at the expense of other methods of dispute resolution. Secondly, there will be an under-supply of B's product. Excessive litigation implies some unmeritorious lawsuits. This is because the lower the cost to A of suing B, the less influence the risk of losing the case will have on A's decision to proceed. B will either defend the case or settle. Both are costly options. If B decides to defend the case, it will avoid the cost of having to pay A (since A's claim is unmeritorious, B should win), but it will incur litigation costs. On the other hand, if B decides to settle, it will avoid litigation costs, but it will incur the cost of having to pay A. B's prices will rise to reflect the risk of unmeritorious law suits and this means that less of B's product will be bought and sold.

Are people encouraged to litigate too much? It is important to be clear at the outset about what the government's subsidy of the civil justice system amounts to. The government provides facilities (judges, administrative and support staff, court buildings and equipment, recording and reporting services). It recoups part of the cost of these expenditures through court fees and it pays the rest. Subject to the remedial measures discussed later in this paper, the costs of actually using the system (legal costs) are borne by litigants themselves. The legal costs burden encourages people not to litigate too much. Does it discourage them from litigating enough? The answer in most legal systems is probably, 'yes'. The problem is not just that legal costs are high. It is also that they have a substantial fixed component. Litigants must pay this fixed component regardless of the amount at stake in the dispute.

Ontario Law Reform Commission, *Study Paper on Prospects for Civil Justice with Commentaries* (Toronto: OLRC, 1995), 279, arguing for partial privatisation and subsidies targeted at deserving classes of case. Privatisation is a limited solution to the consumer access to justice problems discussed in this essay. Privatisation addresses the costs to the supplier of providing the service but it does not address the costs to the consumer of access to the service.

The consequence is to discourage all but relatively large claims.[2] The next section (pp. 48–50) develops this argument. The balance of the paper reviews some common solutions. The third section (pp. 50–58) looks at legal aid, contingent fees and class actions and public interest suits. These are all cost-spreading measures. The fourth section (pp. 58–63) looks at small claims tribunals, consumer affairs agencies and industry-specific dispute resolution schemes. These are all cost avoidance measures. The fifth section (pp. 64–65) looks at the role of substantive law in dispute resolution. The final section (pp. 65–67) makes some concluding observations.

The problem of legal costs

Litigation imposes direct and indirect costs on litigants. The main direct cost is lawyers' fees. Direct legal costs have a fixed component and a variable component. The fixed component is the minimum amount a party must spend to litigate a case. The variable component is any amount above the minimum a party chooses to spend having regard to the expected value of the judgment. The litigation costs of large claims are typically higher than the litigation costs of small claims. However, the difference lies in the variable component. The fixed component is probably about the same for both kinds of case.[3]

High fixed legal costs can make the litigation of small and even medium-sized claims uneconomical. Assume a case where the amount at stake is $1,000. A's and B's expected legal costs are $700. These are fixed costs. The small size of the stake makes it uneconomical for either party to spend more on the litigation. A estimates the probability of victory at 60 per cent. If the rule is that each party pays their own costs, A's expected benefit is $600 (60 per cent of $1,000) and her expected cost is $700. A is unlikely to go ahead with the suit. It is cheaper for her to forfeit the claim than incur the legal costs. If the rule is that costs follow the event, A's expected benefit is $600 (the same as before), and her expected cost is $560 (40 per cent of $700 + $700). This time the equation favours litigation, but only marginally. A's indirect costs are likely to tilt the balance back in favour of not proceeding.[4] Assume now that the amount at stake is $10,000 and all other figures are the same. A's expected benefit from the suit is $6,000. Her expected costs are the same as before: $700 if the rule is that each party pays their own costs and $560 if a costs follow the event rule applies. Under either rule, the equation heavily favours A going ahead with the

2 R. A. Posner, *Economic Analysis of Law* (5th edn, New York: Aspen Law and Business, 1998), § 21.9.
3 *Ibid.*, § 21.5.
4 Under a 'costs follow the event' rule, the winner recovers party to party costs (costs objectively assessed under itemised fee scales), not solicitor and client costs (the actual costs incurred). The winner must pay the difference. This factor alone may tilt the balance back in favour of not proceeding. Furthermore, the analysis in the text assumes A is risk neutral. If A is risk averse, the equation may not favour litigation after all.

suit.[5] The lesson is that conventional methods of pricing legal services discriminate systematically in favour of large claims and against small claims.

They also discriminate between A and B. A typically does not go to court often. For A, litigation with B is likely to be a one-off experience. A is a 'one-shotter'. B typically is a regular litigant. For B, litigation with A is more likely to be a routine matter. B is a 'repeat player'.[6] A and B face similar fixed legal costs. The difference is that a repeat player can achieve economies of scale in litigation more easily by spreading its costs over numerous cases. Economies of scale can make the litigation of small claims cost-effective for B. Since the litigation of a small claim is unlikely to be cost-effective for A, B has an advantage over A in the pre-trial bargaining process.

The indirect costs of litigation include information costs (for example, the cost of finding and instructing a lawyer), opportunity costs (for example, the cost of time off work) and emotional costs (for example, the costs that stress imposes on parties in dispute). Indirect costs also include insurance costs. Insurance costs are costs associated with the uncertain outcome of the dispute. A party may buy market insurance to cover the risk that the other party may eventually win. In that case, the insurance costs are the sum of the premiums. Alternatively, a party may create a reserve fund to cover the risk. In that case, the insurance costs are the costs to the party of not being able to use the reserve fund for other purposes (a kind of opportunity cost). Delay is an important contributing factor to the indirect costs of litigation. Pre-trial delay prolongs the uncertainty between the parties, increasing transactions costs, insurance costs and emotional costs.

A's indirect costs of litigation are likely to be higher than B's. As a repeat player, B will typically have the advantages routine brings. As a one-shotter, A will not. Routine lowers information costs (for example, B's lawyer may already be on hand), opportunity costs (for example, B may have staff whose job it is to run the case) and emotional costs (routine minimises the stress of conflict). If A is an individual and B is a firm, B will typically be wealthier than A. This means B's insurance costs will be lower. Insurance costs are determined by a party's attitude to risk. A risk averse party will spend more to cover a risk than a party who is risk neutral. The higher the amount at stake relative to the party's total wealth, the more risk averse the party is likely to be. If A is poorer than B, then, since the amount at stake is constant, A is likely to be more risk averse. A has a choice: (1) to incur the additional insurance costs; or (2) to carry the additional risk. Either way, her costs are higher than B's. A's higher indirect costs add further to B's bargaining advantage at the pre-trial stage. They increase the probability that A will drop the case altogether or settle with B at a discount (an amount less than the expected value of A's claim net of A's expected costs). Moreover, B has an incentive to delay the case. Pre-trial delays increase the

5 See J. Phillips and K. Hawkins, 'Some Economic Aspects of the Settlement Process: a Study of Personal Injury Claims' (1976) 39 *Mod L Rev* 497.
6 M. Galanter, 'Why the "Haves" Come Out Ahead: Speculations on the Limits of Legal Change' (1974) 9 *Law & Soc'y Rev* 95.

differential between A's and B's indirect costs and put even more pressure on A to drop the case or settle cheaply.

Repeat players sometimes have a greater stake in case outcomes than one-shotters. The outcome of A's claim may shape the outcome of other cases against B in future. This prospect gives B an incentive to settle with A at a premium (an amount higher than the net expected value of A's claim). A will agree to the settlement unless she: (1) is willing to fight the case on principle; and (2) values the principle more highly than the amount of the premium. Now consider the converse case. B brings a suit against A. A judgment in B's favour will create a precedent that disadvantages consumers. In that case, it may be in the collective consumer interest for A to settle the case with B at a premium. However, it is not in A's personal interest to pay B a premium unless she: (1) is willing to abandon the case on principle; and (2) values the principle more highly than the premium. B has a larger capacity to buy out A than A has to buy out B. This means that B is in a stronger position than A to determine the cases that go to judgment and shape the substantive law in its favour. A precedent in B's favour raises the odds against other As in later cases. B's 'position of advantage is one of the ways in which a legal system formally neutral as between "haves" and "have-nots" may perpetuate and augment the advantages of the former'.[7] The slow growth of judge-made product liability law, at least outside the United States, is perhaps an illustration of the point.

Cost-spreading solutions

High fixed legal costs disadvantage A in an absolute sense because they make the litigation of small claims uneconomical. They also disadvantage A in a relative sense because the problem is worse for A than it is for B. There are two main ways of addressing the problem. The first is to spread A's legal costs. The second is to avoid them. Cost-spreading solutions include legal aid, contingent fees and class actions. Cost-avoidance solutions include small claims tribunals, mediation by consumer agencies, and industry-specific dispute resolution schemes (tribunals, ombudsmen, compensation funds and the like). By and large, cost-spreading measures aim to give A at least some of B's advantages so that A can fight the case up at B's level. Cost-avoidance measures aim to give B at least some of A's disadvantages so that B must fight the case down at A's level.

Legal aid

There are two main legal aid models, the judicare system and the salaried lawyer system. The judicare system works for law like medicare works for medicine. It provides funding for the services of a private lawyer who acts for the applicant in more or less the same way as for a paying client. Under the salaried lawyer system the government establishes neighbourhood legal aid offices. Salaried lawyers employed by the government staff the offices. Whereas the judicare system is geared mainly to the provision of legal aid for litigation, the salaried lawyer system offers a range of other services as well, including legal advice, representation in dealings with other parties, and so on. Both systems are cost-spreading solutions to the access to justice problem. They transfer the costs of legal action from A to the taxpaying public.

The limitations of the judicare system are well known. Funding for legal aid is limited and it must be rationed. Means tests are one form of rationing. In bad times, a means test will exclude all applicants except the very poor. Even in good times, it will exclude all except the relatively poor. Consumer access to justice is not exclusively a poverty issue. The problem is a function of high direct and indirect legal costs relative to the expected value of A's claim. It is not a function of A's income level. Low-income consumers may face additional problems. For example, the indirect costs of litigation may be higher for them. However, that is a separate question and it requires special measures.

The other main form of rationing under a judicare system is to prefer some kinds of claim to others. Criminal matters usually get top priority. In bad times, criminal matters exhaust the funds and there is nothing left over for civil claims. In good times, some civil claims may be funded but typically not consumer claims. Agencies tend to favour family law and administrative law matters. Furthermore, judicare systems will nearly always have a 'reasonable grounds' requirement, or the like. To qualify for legal aid, applicants must demonstrate that they have reasonable grounds for taking, defending or being party to the proceedings. The reasonable grounds requirement means that: (1) the applicant must have a good probability of winning the case; and (2) there must be a substantial amount at stake. Unless both these conditions are met, it will be uneconomical for A to proceed with the case. *A fortiori*, it will be uneconomical for the agency to fund it. This means that so far as consumer access to justice is concerned, the judicare system fails where it is most needed. It perpetuates A's disadvantages. Even if there were enough money to fund consumer claims, the system would still not support test cases or small claims. The plaintiff in *Donoghue* v. *Stevenson*[8] would almost certainly have been denied legal aid on this basis.[9]

The judicare system focuses on the applicant's direct legal costs. It does nothing for indirect costs. This means that even if A did qualify for legal aid under the judicare system, there would still be a disincentive to go ahead with the case. The salaried lawyer system does better on this score because it addresses at least some of A's indirect costs. For example, it reduces information costs by locating legal

8 [1932] AC 562 (HL).
9 See R. Sackville, Australia, Commonwealth, Commission of Inquiry into Poverty, *Legal Aid in Australia* (Canberra: Government Publishing Service, 1975), para. 5.32.

offices in accessible places and it addresses emotional costs (client stress and apprehension) by encouraging office informality. In other respects, though, the salaried lawyer system has the same limitations as the judicare system. In bad times, there may be no assistance at all for consumer claims. In good times, there may be some assistance available for consumers in isolated cases. However, the consumer access to justice problem is a systematic one. Even in good times, legal aid does not have the capacity to address the problem systematically.[10]

Contingent fees

Under a contingent fee arrangement, A's lawyer accepts the case on a 'no-win, no-fee' basis. If A wins, the lawyer takes a percentage of the award. It is a form of credit contract. The lawyer lends A her services against a share of the claim.[11] Contingent fees are a cost-spreading solution to the access to justice problem. They transfer part of the expected legal costs from A to A's lawyer. A bears the expected cost of winning the case, and A's lawyer bears the expected cost of losing. A lawyer who specialises in contingent fee claims can pool multiple claims and diversify the risk.[12]

In the United States, where contingent fees are common, the rule is that litigants bear their own costs. In other common law countries, a 'costs follow the event' rule applies.[13] Contingent fees do not fit so easily with a 'costs follow the event' rule. There is no problem if A wins. In that case, there are two possible responses. One is to say that the contingent fee arrangement operates to exclude an award of costs. The other is to say that B pays A's party to party costs and the contingent fee covers the rest.[14] But what happens if A loses? In that case, A is not liable for her own costs at all, but she will have to pay B's costs. In other words, there is a residual risk that is not present in the United States system.[15] For example, assume a case where the amount at stake is $10,000. A conventional fee arrangement applies. A's and B's expected legal costs are each $5,000. A estimates the probability of winning at 60 per cent. In this case, A's expected benefit is $6,000 (60 per cent of $10,000) and

---

10 Civil law countries tend to be more generous in the provision of legal aid. Legal aid provision is typically on the judicare model. In Germany and some other countries legal aid for civil law matters is not limited to cases of poverty. Assistance is available to any party who in the light of 'personal economic circumstances' is wholly or partly unable to bear the costs of civil litigation. There is a merits test, but it is designed to screen out only hopeless or frivolous cases. Applicants do not have to show that they have reasonable grounds for taking, defending or being party to the proceedings: R. B. Schlesinger, H. W. Baade, P. E. Herzog and E. M. Wise, *Comparative Law: Cases Text Materials* (6th edn, Mineola, New York: Foundation Press, 1998), 393–401, 508.
11 See Posner, *Economic Analysis*, § 21.9.   12 *Ibid.*
13 The same is true in most civil law jurisdictions: Schlesinger *et al.*, *Comparative Law*, 403–5.
14 See R. C. A. White, 'Contingent Fees: a Supplement to Legal Aid?' (1978) 41 *Mod L Rev* 286, 295–6.
15 *Ibid.*

her expected cost is $4,000 (40 per cent of $5,000 + $5,000). Now assume there is a
contingent fee arrangement. The contingent fee is 30 per cent. This replaces A's
expected legal costs of $5,000. All other figures remain the same. In this case, A's
expected benefit is $4,200 (60 per cent of ($10,000 − $3,000)). A's expected cost is
$2,000 (40 per cent of $5,000). A is better off under the contingent fee arrangement
(a 4,200: 2,000 benefit-to-cost ratio is better than a 6,000:4,000 ratio), but the difference is less than it would be in the United States. In other words, contingent fees
are an improvement but not a panacea. One suggestion is to say that if A loses, B's
costs should be paid out of public funds.[16] That is a form of legal aid and it raises
the question, if A does not qualify directly for legal aid, why should she be allowed
to qualify indirectly? Insurance to cover A's risk of losing may be another option.[17]

Contingent fee arrangements have been banned until fairly recently in England
and the other Commonwealth jurisdictions.[18] The main concern has been that they
violate the laws against maintenance and champerty. Maintenance is the giving
of assistance to a litigant by a person who has no interest in the litigation and
no legally valid motive for interference. Champerty is a particular kind of maintenance, namely maintenance of an action in consideration of a promise to give the
maintainer a share of the proceeds. There is an agency costs problem with contingent fee arrangements. The problem arises because a contingent fee arrangement
in substance makes A and her lawyer joint owners of A's claim. A joint owner (A's
lawyer) may have an insufficient incentive to exploit the claim because she has to
share the reward for her efforts with the other co-owner (A).[19] This means that A's
lawyer may be tempted to settle the case quickly and cheaply in preference to in-
vesting more time and effort and running the risk of losing at trial.[20] The agency
costs problem is not a sufficient reason to ban contingent fees. There are other ways
of dealing with the problem. Posner suggests removing all restrictions on the outright sale of legal claims. A could then sell her claim to the lawyer and avoid joint
ownership.[21] A less provocative suggestion is to make out-of-court settlements subject to court approval if there is a contingent fee arrangement.[22] There may be other
issues that need to be addressed. Many Commonwealth jurisdictions now allow
contingent fees in one form or another.[23]

---

16 *Ibid.*   17 See text accompanying n. 25 below.
18 Civil law jurisdictions have also been traditionally hostile to contingent fees but some are now
    mellowing: Schlesinger *et al.*, *Comparative Law*, 391–2.
19 See Posner, *Economic Analysis*, § 21.9.
20 See White, 'Contingent Fees', 292. Posner, *Economic Analysis*, § 21.9, gives the following example:
    'Suppose the plaintiff's lawyer is offered a settlement of $100,000; if he goes to trial, there is a 90
    per cent chance that the plaintiff will win $150,000, but it will cost the lawyer $25,000 worth of
    his time to try the case; the parties are risk averse; and the contingent fee is 30 per cent. If the
    plaintiff agrees to the settlement, he will net $70,000 and the lawyer $30,000. If the case goes to
    trial, the net expected gain to the plaintiff rises to $94,500 [0.9 × ($150,000 − $45,000)] but the
    lawyer's net expected gain falls to $15,500 [$45,000 × 0.9 − $25,000].'
21 *Ibid.*   22 White, 'Contingent Fees', 293.
23 See S. Zindel, 'The Case for Contingency Fees' [1996] *New Zealand Law Journal* 295.

England has introduced a conditional fee scheme for certain kinds of litigation. The scheme allows A's lawyer to act on the basis that if A loses no fee is charged, but if A wins she pays an agreed multiple of the normal fee (a 'success fee'). Conditional fees are like contingent fees except that: (1) a contingent fee is an agreed percentage of A's winnings; and (2) under the English scheme, if A loses, she must still pay B's costs.[24] Because the 'costs follow the event' rule applies, there is still a substantial disincentive for A to litigate. In an attempt to mitigate the problem, the Law Society has devised an insurance scheme to cover A's risk of losing. However, the scheme applies only in certain kinds of case.[25] One of the main areas of concern about the new English scheme has been the potential for conflict of interest between lawyer and client. Because the conditional fee is a percentage uplift of the normal fee, the scheme gives A's lawyer an incentive either: (1) to settle the case quickly and cheaply; or (2) to drag the case out so that the costs and, therefore, the lawyer's success fee are increased.[26] These are variants of the agency costs problem that affect contingent fee arrangements.

Contingent fees are a partial solution to the consumer access to justice problem. The solution is only a partial one because at least in countries where a 'costs follow the event' rule applies, subject to the availability of insurance, A still bears a substantial portion of the expected legal costs. In any event, contingent fees are not a solution for small claims. The expected value of the claim must be at least high enough to cover the fee. The fixed cost component of legal fees means that A's lawyer's fee is not tied to the size of A's claim. Small claims do not necessarily mean low legal costs. Contingent fees address some indirect costs of litigation, but not others. For example, they reduce insurance costs because they shift at least part of the risk of losing to A's lawyer and this facilitates risk pooling. However, contingent fees do not address A's information costs, opportunity costs or emotional costs. Nor do they address the problem of delay.

Class actions and public interest suits

A class action is a proceeding that brings together for a single determination the claims of numerous persons against the same defendant that arise from a 'common nucleus of fact'. The action is brought by one or more members of the class on behalf of the class as a whole. Only the named representatives are party to the proceedings. This means, among other things, that they alone are liable for costs. However, judgment in a class action binds all members of the class. The class action is a cost-spreading solution to the consumer access to justice problem. The

---

24 See G. Woodroffe, 'Loser Pays and Conditional Fees – An English Solution?' (1998) 37 *Washburn LJ* 345.
25 *Ibid.*, 356.   26 *Ibid.*, 352.

aggregation of claims allows each party to achieve economies of scale. Notionally at any rate one set of legal costs is distributed among numerous claims. The result is to reduce A's disadvantage relative to B's.

This all assumes that class members share the legal costs. The default rule is that the class representative (A) alone is liable for costs, but class members may agree among themselves on a different arrangement. The trouble is that A may encounter hold-out problems in securing class members' agreement to contribute, particularly if the class is large. Each individual class member has an incentive not to contribute because if the other class members contribute, the action will go ahead and the individual will benefit anyway. If sufficient class members reason this way, the action will not go ahead. One alternative might be for A to apply for legal aid. This raises the issues about legal aid discussed earlier. Another alternative might be for A to make a contingent fee arrangement with her lawyer, assuming contingent fees are allowed. This raises the issues about contingent fees discussed earlier. In any event, the point is that the class action by itself is a limited solution to the consumer access to justice problem. It needs to be combined with other measures to ensure that A does not bear the whole cost herself.

The class action solution does not address A's indirect costs. On the contrary, it probably increases them. For example, given the complexity of a class action, A's information costs, opportunity costs and emotional costs may be higher than if A brought an ordinary claim. On the positive side, the class action minimises the other class members' indirect costs. The net result is to make A worse off but the class as a whole substantially better off. An obvious way to reduce A's burden is to name one or more other class members as co-plaintiffs. This will spread the indirect costs of the action among at least a sub-set of the class. This all assumes that class members other than the named representatives have no involvement in the litigation. If they do have an involvement, they will incur costs and the additional costs will reduce the net benefits of the procedure to the class. Class actions, like contingent fees, raise agency cost problems. The class members are joint owners of the claim, but the class representative (A) or, perhaps more accurately, A's lawyer, do all the work. It may be in the interests of A and A's lawyer to do less work even if this means compromising the claim. To guard against this risk, class members need to monitor the conduct of the case. Monitoring requires involvement, involvement increases costs, and additional costs reduce the net benefit of the procedure. The solution is to have the court act as monitor. The cost of monitoring by the court should be less than the aggregate cost of monitoring by individual class members. The larger the class, the greater the cost difference is likely to be. On the other hand, if judicial resources are already strained, the monitoring function may be a heavy additional burden for the courts to carry.

There may be other difficulties if the class is large and each class member's claim is very small. In that case, the cost of identifying each class member and processing her claim may exceed the amount of the judgment. Whether the class action should be allowed to proceed in this case depends on the importance of deterrence relative to compensation. From a compensation perspective, the concern is to make sure A gets paid. Who pays is a secondary consideration. From a deterrence perspective, the concern is to make sure B pays. Who gets the payment is a secondary consideration. From a deterrence perspective, the solution is to allow the class action to proceed but to make a *cy-près* distribution of the damages award. That means B is forced to pay, but the excessive costs of distributing the award among individual class members are avoided. The *cy-près* solution was used recently in Australia in connection with the enforcement of consumer credit laws. The credit laws impose civil penalties on a credit provider for contravention of truth in lending requirements. The penalty is payable to the debtor. In several cases, class actions for civil penalties were successfully brought on behalf of numerous debtors. In each case, the aggregate payment was very large but individual debtors' entitlements were very small. The credit provider was ordered to make the payment into a special trust which was established by statute to fund the provision of financial counselling and consumer information services.[27]

In common law jurisdictions outside the United States, class actions traditionally were restricted by civil procedure rules which said that class members must have the 'same interest' in the dispute. The courts held that the 'same interest' requirement precluded a class action for breach of contract where each class member had a separate contract with B. It made no difference that the contracts were identical.[28] The 'same interest' requirement also precluded class actions for a damages remedy because each class member's damages would have to be separately assessed, and so there was no sufficient common interest.[29] Many jurisdictions have taken steps in recent years to remove these traditional barriers and to facilitate class actions in other ways as well.

A public interest suit is a private action brought by A for an injunction to restrain B from engaging in unlawful conduct or for a declaration that B's conduct is unlawful. A sues in her own name, but her purpose is to benefit the public at large or a section of the public. The public interest suit is functionally like the class action. Both are mechanisms for achieving economies of scale in litigation. For example, assume B engages in a widespread misleading advertising campaign. A sues successfully for an injunction to stop the campaign. The consequence is to prevent loss to a large number of consumers. The loss to each individual consumer, if it had occurred, would have been small. The public interest suit provides an *ex ante* solution to this kind of problem. The class action provides an *ex post* solution.

---

27 A. J. Duggan and E. V. Lanyon, *Consumer Credit Law* (Sydney: Butterworths, 1999), para. 11.1.2.
28 See *Naken* v. *General Motors of Canada Ltd* (1983) 144 DLR (3rd) 385 (SCC) and the authorities discussed there.
29 *Ibid.*

In common law countries, restrictive standing requirements have traditionally limited public interest litigation. The basic rule, derived from nuisance law, was that the plaintiff must have a direct pecuniary or proprietary interest in the claim. In the misleading advertising example given above, A might not pass this test. The modern judicial trend is to relax the requirement, and in some countries there has been statutory intervention.[30] The Australian Trade Practices Act 1974 is an example. Part V of the Act prohibits false representations and other kinds of misleading and unfair conduct. Section 80 allows the Minister, the Australian Competition and Consumer Commission, or 'any other person' to sue for an injunction restraining B from engaging in conduct that is in contravention of the Act. The courts have interpreted the words 'any other person' to mean that there is no standing requirement at all. In the misleading advertising example given above, A would be free to sue.[31]

The main argument against relaxation of the standing requirement is that it would open the floodgates to litigation. In *Phelps* v. *Western Mining Corporation Ltd*, Deane J responded to this argument in the context of the Trade Practices Act 1974 (Cth), s. 80 as follows:[32]

> The argument that to give the words which Parliament has used their ordinary meaning would . . . 'open the floodgates of litigation' strikes me as irrelevant and somewhat unreal. Irrelevant, in that I can see neither warrant for concluding that the Parliament did not intend that floodgates be opened on practices which contravene the provisions of the Act nor reason for viewing that prospect, if it were a realistic one, with other than equanimity. Unreal, in that the argument not only assumes the existence of a shoal of officious busybodies agitatedly waiting, behind 'the floodgates', for the opportunity to institute costly litigation in which they have no legitimate interest but treats as novel and revolutionary an approach to the enforcement of laws which has long been established in the ordinary administration of the criminal law.

The action in *Phelps* was based on a claim made in advertising by the Uranium Producers' Forum which was alleged to be misleading in contravention of the Act. The court allowed the action to proceed even though Phelps had not been affected by the defendant's conduct to any greater extent than the public at large. In the end, Phelps dropped his action because of lack of funding. He had applied for legal aid. He was awarded only a quarter of his projected costs, on the ground that in a public interest suit the constituency should pay.[33] The explanation ignores the

---

30 See Kirby J's survey in *Truth About Motorways Pty Ltd* v. *Macquarie Infrastructure Investment Management Ltd* (1999) 169 ALR 616, 651–2 (HCA).

31 Section 80 of the Trade Practices Act 1974 (Cth) survived a constitutional challenge in *Truth About Motorways Pty Ltd* v. *Macquarie Infrastructure Investment Management Ltd* (1999) 169 ALR 616 (HCA).

32 (1978) 20 ALR 183, 189.

33 See M. Mobbs, 'Legal Aid in the Public Interest' (1978) 3 *Legal Services Bulletin* 231.

collective action problem. In this respect, public interest suits are no different from class actions. Like the class action, the public interest suit itself is a limited solution to the consumer access to justice problem. It needs to be combined with other measures to ensure that A's costs are spread among the group.

Cost-avoidance solutions

The previous section surveyed cost-spreading solutions to the consumer access to justice problem. These all involved facilitating A's access to the ordinary courts. This section looks at cost-avoidance solutions, namely small claims tribunals, mediation by consumer agencies and industry-specific dispute resolution schemes. These are all forms of alternative dispute resolution. They involve substitutes for the ordinary courts.

Small claims tribunals

There are two main kinds of small claims system: (1) court-based; and (2) tribunal-based. The court-based system uses the ordinary courts but it relaxes the rules of evidence and procedure and there are restrictions on costs. There may also be restrictions on legal representation and appeals. The court-based system is widely used in North America.[34] Tribunal-based systems are a more radical reform. The tribunal-based systems in a number of Australian states are a good example. The main features are as follows:

- The jurisdiction is limited to claims up to a specified amount arising out of a contract between a consumer and a trader.
- Consumers can sue traders, but traders cannot sue consumers in the tribunal.
- The consumer starts proceedings by filing a claim form and paying a nominal filing fee.
- Waiting time for hearings is a matter of weeks.
- The tribunal is constituted by a referee sitting alone. In some states (Victoria, for example) the referee must be a lawyer. In other states (New South Wales, for example) legal qualifications are not necessary.
- As a general rule, legal representation is prohibited.
- Evidence is given on oath, but otherwise the tribunals are not bound by the rules of evidence and procedure and they can inform themselves in any manner they see fit. Hearings are held in private.

34 See, e.g., I. Ramsay, 'Small Claims: a Review' in Ontario Law Reform Commission, *Study Paper,* 489.

- In some states (Victoria, for example) the tribunal must apply substantive law. In other states (New South Wales, for example) the tribunals are subject only to a 'fair and equitable' standard.
- There is no right of appeal.

Court-based small claims systems address the consumer access to justice problem primarily by reducing legal costs. This increases the cost-effectiveness of small claims litigation. Tribunal-based systems go much further. For example, they allow access only to consumers. The purpose is to prevent the monopolisation of scarce tribunal resources by traders' debt claims. Traders are repeat players. They can achieve economies of scale through the ordinary courts and hence they do not need tribunals.

The Australian tribunal-based systems prohibit legal representation. The purpose is to keep A's costs down. If legal representation were allowed, B would normally hire a lawyer. Then A would have to hire a lawyer too if she wanted to stay even. If A is forced to hire a lawyer, it may not be cost-effective for her to proceed with the claim. The prohibition of appeals is a related measure. The purpose is to avoid the risk that A's claim may end up in the ordinary courts after all. The risk may be high enough in some cases to make it not cost-effective for A to bring the claim in the first place. B may be tempted to inflate A's perception of the risk by threats of an appeal whether or not B really intends to follow through.

The absence of lawyers combined with exclusion of the rules of evidence and procedure and the prohibition of appeals increases the risk of wrong decisions. This is a cost of the system. However, the cost of not having the system must also be taken into account. A tribunal might decide a case wrongly in either A's or B's favour. The cost savings to A of the tribunal system probably exceed the higher risk of a wrong decision in B's favour. Imperfect justice for A is better than no justice for A at all. In any event, A has a choice. She can take tribunal proceedings or she can use the ordinary courts. The tribunals' lists are always full and this indicates a strong consumer demand for the low-cost alternative. The cost savings to B of the tribunal system may or may not exceed the higher risk of a wrong decision in A's favour. B might prefer the ordinary courts. Unlike A, B does not have a choice. B is bound by A's choice of forum. Why should A's preference trump B's? The answer is that if B could determine the choice, A's claim might not get off the ground at all. In other words, the cost savings to A of the tribunal system probably exceed the increased costs to B. Imperfect justice for B is better than no justice at all for A.

The prohibition on legal representation in the tribunals has an additional benefit. It reduces A's indirect costs. For example, it saves her the cost of finding and instructing a lawyer. Also, the absence of lawyers makes the proceedings more informal and this may reduce A's emotional costs. On the other hand, the absence of lawyers means that A has to prepare and present her own case and this will increase her indirect costs. The systems attempt to limit indirect costs by encouraging referees to take an interventionist role in proceedings. The idea is to help A along with whatever prompts, reassurances and the like may be necessary for her case. Tribunal registrars are also directed to help A prepare her claim and complete the claim form.

Small claims tribunals are used mainly by middle-income consumers. This seems to be a worldwide phenomenon.[35] Part of the reason is probably that the indirect costs of litigation are higher for low-income consumers. The special features of the tribunal-based systems are insufficient to offset these disadvantages.

It will be recalled that the main public benefits of the civil justice system are that it: (1) lowers the social cost of disputes by facilitating orderly dispute resolution; and (2) avoids disputes by generating judge-made rules to guide future behaviour.[36] Tribunal-based small claims systems involve a trade-off between these benefits. They maximise the first at the expense of the second. Tribunal-based systems are not geared to dispute avoidance because they do not generate rules. Tribunals do not deliver detailed reasoned judgments, their reasons are not published, and the prohibition of appeals prevents the leakage of small claims into courts where rules are fashioned. In short, tribunal-based systems do nothing to facilitate the growth of judge-made consumer laws.

Consumer agencies

Consumer agencies in many countries have authority to mediate disputes between consumers and traders. The costs and benefits of mediation relative to litigation in the ordinary courts are similar to the costs and benefits of small claims tribunals. One difference in theory is that parties to mediation have more control over the outcome of the case than they do in adjudication. A mediated solution depends on the parties' consent. Adjudicated solutions are imposed. An agreed outcome may make the parties jointly happier than an imposed outcome. In this sense mediation is a potentially superior alternative to small claims tribunals, particularly given the expected error costs of small claims tribunal proceedings. In practice, the quality of mediation outcomes turns on how good the mediator is. Consumer agencies may not always have enough funds to hire properly qualified mediators.

More fundamentally, many consumer agencies are in an ambiguous position. They are charged both with negotiating settlements on a consumer's behalf and mediating disputes between consumers and traders. The two functions are inconsistent. Negotiation requires the agency to take a partisan position on the consumer's behalf. Mediation requires impartiality. It may be difficult for an agency to switch from one function to another without losing credibility in the eyes of one or both parties.

35 *Ibid.*, 505–6.   36 See text accompanying n.1 and n.2 above.

There was a time when some consumer agencies in Australia had trouble deciding what to call themselves. In Victoria, for example, the agency was originally called the Consumer Protection Bureau. Its name was changed to Consumer Affairs.[37] The change implied a shift in the agency's mandate from partisanship to impartiality. It also implied an understanding that it is impossible for an agency to assume both stances at once. The Australian small claims tribunals are in a similarly ambiguous position. In Victoria, for example, the referee is directed by statute to attempt a settlement between the parties before proceeding to adjudication. There are similar provisions in the other States. The legislation is not clear on what this direction means. It probably means mediation. The trouble is that mediation and adjudication are incompatible processes. Mediation aims for agreed outcomes. Adjudication imposes outcomes. A party at the mediation stage may agree to a proposed outcome ('settlement') for fear that if she does not she will be punished later at the adjudication stage. Conversely, at the adjudication stage the losing party may conclude that she was punished for her lack of compliance at the mediation stage. Either way the integrity of the outcome is affected. The tribunals are aware of the tension. In Victoria, for example, the practice has been for the referee to suggest terms of settlement to the parties and then leave the room while they negotiate between themselves. The hands-off approach preserves the integrity of the adjudication process but at the cost of the mediation process. Unsupervised negotiation between the parties themselves is not mediation. The solution is to assign a mediator and a separate adjudicator to each case. However, this increases costs. Given budgetary constraints, the choice for the tribunals is either: (1) to put up with the procedural shortcomings and hear more cases; or (2) to cure the shortcomings and hear fewer cases. The consensus in Australia seems to favour the first alternative. The point of both these stories is that mediation occupies an ill-defined middle ground between negotiation and adjudication. The mediator can easily cross either boundary. In other words, there is a danger with mediation schemes that the product they deliver will turn out not to be mediation at all.

Industry-specific arrangements

Many industries are specially regulated. The cases vary from one country to another but familiar examples include motor vehicle dealers, travel agents and house-builders. Industry-specific regulation can take various forms. For example, it may be: (1) imposed by statute; (2) contained in a code of practice developed jointly by government and industry under a statutory scheme; or

---

37 The name has since been changed again. The agency is currently known as the Office of Fair Trading.

(3) contained in a set of rules developed by the industry itself with or without government authorisation. Most industry-specific regulation schemes include some kind of mechanism for resolving disputes between consumers and industry members, for example: (1) a specialist tribunal invested with powers of adjudication; (2) an ombudsman scheme; or (3) a compensation fund maintained by industry contributions.

Specialist tribunals and industry ombudsman schemes have many of the same costs and benefits as small claims tribunals. The main differences are as follows. First, specialisation tends to reduce hearing times. The decision-maker is already familiar with the industry and so there is less need for the parties to provide background information about the dispute. Shorter hearing times mean lower costs. Specialisation may also reduce error costs. Secondly, a specific industry focus facilitates communication between the decision-maker and industry members at large. It improves the signalling function of case outcomes. In this sense, industry-specific dispute resolution schemes do generate rules to guide future industry behaviour. They facilitate dispute avoidance within the industry in a way that non-specialist small claims tribunals do not. Thirdly, it is expensive to establish and maintain a dispute resolution scheme. Some costs are fixed, for example, office accommodation, staff salaries, equipment provision and so on. If there are n industry-specific dispute resolution schemes, then these costs will be incurred n times over. In this respect, industry-specific dispute resolution is a more costly alternative than small claims tribunals. These additional costs are the main trade-offs for the benefits already identified above. Fourthly, an industry-specific scheme depends for its effectiveness on its connection with the industry. This connection increases the risk of industry capture and the perception of bias in the industry's favour. Industry ombudsman schemes often address these problems by creating a buffer zone or Chinese wall between the industry and the ombudsman's office. For example, responsibility for the supervision of the office may be transferred from the industry itself to an independent committee or board of directors. The effectiveness of measures like this depends of course on how independent the committee or board is in fact and on the perception of the office's constituents. Fifthly, there is a risk that industry-specific schemes may be anti-competitive. For example, standards imposed on an industry via the de facto rule-making power described above may have the purpose or effect of increasing small firms' costs or discouraging innovation rather than improving industry efficiency. A partial response to this concern is government monitoring under regulatory impact assessment laws or competition statutes. This kind of monitoring is typically undertaken at the scheme's inception. To be fully effective it needs to be ongoing during the life of the scheme. Budgetary constraints may limit a government's capacity for ongoing monitoring.

Statutory compensation funds are common for some industries, for example motor vehicle dealers. The main features typically are as follows:

- Industry members must make periodic contributions to the fund in the form of statutory licence fees or otherwise.
- The fund is administered by an official or a committee designated by the statute.
- A consumer who suffers loss due to the default of an industry member can apply to be compensated out of the fund.

In theory, a scheme like this minimises A's costs. The procedure is administrative, not adjudicative. There is no dispute and so there is no hearing involved. The only direct cost to A is the cost of making the application. The main indirect costs are information costs. In practice, the fund is usually not big enough to meet all potential claims and this means it has to be rationed. Typical rationing measures include: (1) a cap on the amount of a claim; (2) a limit on the frequency of claims; and (3) a requirement that A must exhaust her legal remedies against B before making an application. In other words, compensation funds in practice are usually last resort alternatives for A. They do not avoid the need for A to sue B and they do not reduce A's legal costs. All they do is reduce the risk to A of B's insolvency. The risk of B's insolvency is a secondary consideration. It is irrelevant to cases where the expected value of A's claim makes it uneconomical for A to proceed with the case in any event.

Compensation funds are a form of insurance. Like all insurance, they create moral hazard problems. Assume a scheme limited by a requirement that A must exhaust her legal remedies against B before making an application. A knows that she is protected against the risk of B's insolvency. The risk of B's insolvency is a function of the amount B invests in management. The compensation fund gives B an incentive to cut its management costs and lower its prices. It gives A an incentive to take B's lower price in preference to the higher prices B's competitors continue to charge. B's competitors then have an incentive to respond in kind. If this happens, there will be a general decline in management standards across the industry. The insolvency risk will rise, increasing demand on the fund perhaps to the point where the fund is no longer viable. In this example, the compensation fund is insurance only against the risk to A of B's insolvency. If the fund covered other risks as well, for example, the risk of B's fraud or breach of contract, the moral hazard problem would be greater. A requirement that A must exhaust her legal remedies against B before making an application reduces the moral hazard problem by limiting the insurance coverage. Limiting the size of A's entitlement is another containment measure. In the context of conventional insurance arrangements, premium increases, no-claim bonuses and excess payment provisions perform a similar function. The aim is to achieve a trade-off between loss compensation (insurance) objectives and loss avoidance (deterrence) objectives. The need to address the moral hazard problem in one way or another means that compensation funds can never provide more than a limited solution to the problem of consumer access to justice.

Substantive law reform

Lawmakers have a choice in the making of substantive laws between rules and standards. Rules provide certainty in decision-making. Standards provide flexibility. Standards allow decision-makers to avoid injustice in hard cases. A statutory provision that prohibits particular contract terms is a rule. A provision that prohibits unconscionable contracts is a standard. Rules give content to a legal command *ex ante*, whereas a standard gives it content *ex post*. This means that rules are more costly for the legislature to draft, whereas standards are more costly for the courts to administer. There are clear trade-offs between the two alternatives.[38] The potential costs of a standards-based approach to substantive lawmaking can be summarised as follows:[39]

- Reliance on standards places an increased emphasis on fact finding and it allows greater scope for the mounting of arguable defences. The likely consequence is to increase both the complexity and the length of trials.
- A standards-based approach reduces the predictability of case outcomes, and this implies a decrease in the settlement rate. The further apart the parties' estimates are of the plaintiff's chances, the harder it will be for them to find common ground.
- The less precisely the law is stated, the higher the risk of judicial error. A standards-based approach implies a higher rate of appeals.
- A standards-based approach reduces the court's capacity for even-handedness and consistency. The consequence is to increase litigants' dissatisfaction with case outcomes and reduce public confidence in the system.
- A standards-based approach requires judges to act as '*ad hoc* legislators'.[40] It invests them with jurisdiction to determine policy questions. Some policy questions are better left to the legislature, whether for reasons of 'polycentricity' or otherwise.[41]

This catalogue implies that a shift from a standard to a rule may reduce legal costs by: (1) making trials simpler and shorter; (2) facilitating pre-trial settlements; and (3) lowering the incidence of appeals. In other words, substantive law reform may be a partial substitute for procedural reforms such as small claims tribunals and the like.[42]

---

38 See L. Kaplow, 'Rules Versus Standards: an Economic Analysis' (1992) 42 *Duke L J* 557; I. Erlich and R. A. Posner, 'An Economic Analysis of Legal Rulemaking' (1974) 3 *Journal of Legal Studies* 257.

39 See A. J. Duggan, 'Is Equity Efficient?' (1997) 113 *Law Quarterly Review* 601, 630–1.

40 Hon. A. M. Gleeson, 'Individualised Justice – the Holy Grail' (1995) 69 *Australian Law Journal* 421, 432.

41 See L. Fuller, 'The Form and Limits of Adjudication' (1978) 92 *Harv L Rev* 353.

42 Cf. R. A. MacDonald, 'Prospects for Civil Justice' in Ontario Law Reform Commission, *Study Paper*, 46–51, arguing that substantive law reform will not eliminate disputes. True enough, but

Section 15A of the Sale of Goods Act 1979 (UK), a 1994 initiative,[43] is an example of a substantive law reform measure that was drafted with the trade-offs between rules and standards in mind. Previous sale of goods law implied in a sale contract 'conditions' of correspondence with description, reasonable quality, fitness for purpose and so on. A 'condition' means a contract term, breach of which allows the buyer to reject the goods and terminate the contract. Until 1994, the Act drew no distinction between major and minor breaches. The consequence was to encourage opportunism on the buyer's part. The seller's breach could get the buyer out of an unprofitable contract regardless of whether the breach caused the buyer actual loss.[44] The courts could avoid this result only by saying that minor defects did not breach the implied condition, but if they did this the buyer would have no remedy at all, not even damages. The dilemma was caused by the rigid condition/warranty distinction the statute drew. Section 15A reforms the law by giving the court a discretion to disallow a buyer's rejection if 'the breach is so slight that it would not be reasonable for him to reject' the goods. In that case, 'the breach is not to be treated as a breach of condition, but may be treated as a breach of warranty'. The provision does not apply if the buyer is a consumer. Section 15A marks a shift from rule to standard. It reflects the legislature's judgment that for commercial transactions the benefits of a standard (preventing opportunistic behaviour by buyers) exceed the costs (increased uncertainty). Conversely, the exception reflects the legislature's judgment that for consumer transactions the costs of a standard exceed the benefits. The different treatment of consumer transactions can be explained on access to justice grounds. In the case of a consumer transaction, typically: (1) the buyer's claim is a small one; (2) the buyer is a one-shotter; and (3) the seller is a repeat player. Retention of the rule helps to make the buyer's claim viable by keeping down legal costs. Different considerations apply to commercial transactions where typically the buyer's claim is not a small one and both parties are repeat players.

Conclusion

Civil justice is a valuable commodity. It benefits the immediate parties to a dispute by avoiding uncertainty about entitlements. It benefits the public at large by: (1) avoiding the costs of social disorder; and (2) limiting the number of disputes. The economic objective is to achieve equilibrium in the market for consumer justice. Supply-side and demand-side market failures stand in the way. The supply-side market failure stems from the fixed-cost aspect of legal fees which makes the processing of small claims uneconomical. The demand-side failure stems from the

it may reduce them (i.e., it is *marginal* costs and benefits that matter, not total or average costs and benefits).

43 The provision was inserted in the principal Act by the Sale of Goods (Amendment) Act 1994 (UK).
44 See, e.g., *Cehave NV* v. *Bremer Handelsgesellschaft mbH* [1976] QB 44 (CA).

high indirect costs of consumer litigation. The solution is to spread or avoid A's costs. Cost-spreading measures include legal aid, contingent fee arrangements and class actions. Cost-avoidance measures include small claims tribunals, consumer agency mediation and industry-specific dispute resolution arrangements.

No single measure is a complete solution. Each has costs and benefits. Legal aid addresses the direct costs problem by spreading the costs among taxpayers. Legal aid on the salaried lawyer model, but not judicare, addresses some of the indirect costs problems as well. Funding restrictions make both kinds of legal aid a limited solution in practice. Contingent fee arrangements address the direct costs problem by sharing the costs between lawyer and client. They are only a partial solution because they do not facilitate small claims unless they are combined with other measures such as class actions. Contingent fee arrangements address A's insurance costs, but they do not impact on other indirect costs. Class actions address the direct costs problem by allowing the aggregation of claims to achieve economies of scale. The class action by itself is a limited solution. It needs to be combined with other measures, such as contingent fee arrangements, to make sure the costs of the action are spread among the class. Class actions address the indirect costs problem for all class members other than the named representative because it is the named representative and the named representative's lawyer who do all the work. The downside is a potential agency costs problem.

Small claims tribunals address the direct costs problem by providing a lower cost alternative to dispute resolution through the ordinary courts. They address the indirect costs problem by, for example: (1) limiting the use of lawyers; (2) speeding up hearings; and (3) minimising formalities. The trade-offs are higher error costs and a lowered commitment to dispute avoidance (deterrence). Consumer agency mediation in theory delivers similar benefits with lower error costs, but in practice it is limited by the variable quality of mediation facilities. Industry-specific dispute resolution arrangements in theory also deliver similar benefits to small claims tribunals, but with both lower error costs and a higher commitment to dispute avoidance. The trade-offs include: (1) higher establishment and maintenance costs; (2) a higher risk of industry capture; and (3) potential anti-competitive effects. Industry-resourced compensation funds are another form of cost-avoidance measure, but they are a limited solution because of moral hazard problems. Substantive law reform, in particular the substitution of rules for standards, is a surrogate for cost-avoidance procedural reform. Rules reduce uncertainty and this impacts on legal costs. The trade-off for increased certainty is reduced flexibility in decision-making which encourages opportunistic claims.

The normative implications of this assessment can be summarised as follows:

1. There should be a mix of cost-spreading and cost-avoidance measures to secure the benefits of both traditional litigation and alternative dispute resolution.

2. Contingent fee arrangements and class actions are both useful cost-spreading measures. Contingent fees separately or in combination with class actions facilitate the litigation of medium-sized to large claims, while class actions in combination with contingent fees facilitate the litigation of small claims in a mass disputes context.

3. Small claims tribunals are useful for cases where A's claim is too small to justify a contingent fee arrangement and there are insufficient claims to support a class action.

4. Mediation is useful for cases that fall outside the small claims tribunals' jurisdiction or where the parties have a valued ongoing relationship the adjudication process might damage.

5. Industry-specific arrangements may be appropriate for industries with a high volume of consumer complaints.

6. Legal aid, and particularly legal aid on the salaried lawyer model, should be sufficiently resourced and targeted to low-income consumers' needs.

7. Substantive law reform (the substitution of rules for standards) is another measure that might be targeted particularly to low-income consumers' needs. High indirect costs make dispute resolution disproportionately costly for low-income consumers. Rules reduce uncertainty. The more certain A's entitlement is, the less incentive B will have to contest it. A no-contest minimises A's costs. Rules in place of standards may be particularly appropriate for laws that affect low-income consumers more than others (debt collection laws, for example).

4   Rethinking consumer protection policy

MICHAEL J. TREBILCOCK

Introduction

While consumer protection policy has an ancient genesis, dating back at least to Roman times with the adoption in Roman law of various implied warranties against latent defects in the sale of goods, the current legislative and regulatory consumer protection framework in most industrialised countries largely finds its genesis in the consumer and more general policy activism of the 1960s and 1970s, during which period most of the major contemporary consumer protection statutes were first enacted or extensively elaborated.[1] As we enter the twenty-first century, pressures on these legal and regulatory regimes are mounting, spurred both by changes in the nature of modern industrial economies and by the evolution of economic theory. In terms of the former, the rapidity of technological change, globalisation and deregulation of formerly regulated monopolies have dramatically expanded the range of consumer products and services available in any given jurisdiction, making product and service-specific regulation increasingly problematic and intensifying the informational challenges faced by consumers. In terms of the latter, a veritable revolution in industrial organisation theory over the past two or three decades, particularly as it relates to market structure, bargaining power and information, has rendered simplistic structure–conduct–performance paradigms that keyed on a small number of variables (such as concentration levels) and that underpin many aspects of contemporary consumer protection policy also increasingly problematic. In particular, the burgeoning literature on strategic behaviour and game theory, transaction cost economics, contestability theory and information theory renders it much more difficult to characterise *a priori* the performance of given markets. I and my colleagues, Gillian Hadfield and Robert Howse, have reviewed some of these trends in previous writing.[2]

In our previous writing, we attempted to develop, consistently with the regulatory checklist approach recently developed by the Organization for Economic

---

1 See OECD Committee on Consumer Policy, *Consumer Policy during the Past Ten Years: Main Developments and Prospects* (Paris: OECD, 1983), chap. 1.
2 See G. K. Hadfield, R. Howse and M. J. Trebilcock, 'Information-Based Principles for Rethinking Consumer Protection Policy' (1998) 21 *Journal of Consumer Policy* 131.

Cooperation and Development (OECD) in its more general work on regulatory reform,[3] a series of questions or guidelines that are relevant specifically to the consumer protection field, and that, in our view, flow from an information-based approach to consumer protection policy, which we argue is the appropriate framework for analysing most consumer protection problems. In the following section, I briefly recapitulate our principal conclusions from our earlier analysis. In the third section (pp. 80–91), I then review a number of issues pertaining to the role of civil redress with respect to consumer protection problems. In the fourth section (pp. 91–97), I discuss the role of the courts in policing unfair contract terms. The fifth section (pp. 97–98) offers some concluding observations.

Principles for an information-based approach to consumer protection policy

Defining the problem

According to the OECD Regulatory Checklist, 'the problem to be solved should be precisely stated, giving clear evidence of its nature and magnitude, and explaining why it has arisen (that is, identifying the incentives of affected entities and their consequent behaviors)'.[4] A framework for consumer protection regulation should be able to provide policy-makers with certain relatively straightforward analytic tools for identifying whether a given situation is very likely, on the one hand, or very unlikely, on the other hand, to constitute a consumer protection problem of significance.

An essential first step in determining whether there is a consumer protection problem should be to characterise the market in question as either competitive, imperfectly competitive, or non-competitive (the case of monopoly). In very imperfectly competitive or non-competitive markets, problems of consumer protection may be in significant measure problems that have to be addressed through competition policy or economic regulation. The true focus of consumer protection policy, as distinct from competition policy or economic regulation, is, in our view, the quality and cost of consumer information. We begin, therefore, with a basic information-based model of a consumer transaction in which a consumer makes a decision about how many resources to expend on information about the transaction before proceeding. This then isolates two important characteristics of the market setting: (1) the value of information, by which we mean the benefit that

---

3 OECD, *The Design and Use of Regulatory Checklists in OECD Countries* (Paris: OECD, 1993).

4 OECD, *Recommendation of the Council of the OECD on Improving the Quality of Government Regulation (Including the OECD Reference Checklist for Regulatory Decision-Making and Background Note)* (Paris: OECD, 1995), 9.

information will probably bring to the consumer in terms of making a better choice about what goods or services to buy and on what terms; and (2) the cost of information. In general, we expect consumers to be better informed about the goods or services they buy and thus less likely to be in need of consumer protection where the cost of information is low relative to the value of information. Conversely, we expect consumer protection problems, in the sense of consumers not getting what they intended to buy, where information costs are relatively high or the value of information is perceived to be relatively low. We note in particular that the value of information is likely to be perceived to be low when consumers have reason to believe that most goods are what they expect and only the exceptional one is not.

We note here some tension in perspectives between competition policy and consumer protection policy. From a competition policy perspective, markets with low barriers to entry, low sunk costs, many rivals, and rapid rates of entry and exit will tend to conform with the textbook model of a fully competitive market. Yet from a consumer protection perspective, such markets (for example, used cars, home renovations) may present some of the most severe information problems that consumers confront. In addition, many service markets, even if (or especially if) structurally competitive, may present severe informational challenges to consumers, in part because services, by nature, are more 'experience' or 'credence' goods than 'search' goods that can be inspected before purchase. Yet much consumer protection policy assumes goods markets as its paradigm, despite the increasingly service-intensive character of modern economies.

In the case of a competitive market it is therefore necessary to ask whether, using this basic information model of a consumer transaction, there is some structural feature of this market that is likely to lead to anti-competitive behaviour with respect to information. Take, for instance, the market for cigarettes: manufacturers compete among themselves for market share but have a common incentive not to disclose information about the risks from smoking as long as these risks apply to all cigarettes. If there are no structural features of a market that suggest that anti-competitive behaviour, with respect to information, is occurring, then it is appropriate to narrow the focus somewhat and to ask whether forms of strategic behaviour (for example, fraud, deception or deliberate suppression of known material and low-cost information by individual sellers) are being engaged in by sellers that are unduly increasing the information costs to significant numbers of consumers, with large individual or aggregate physical or economic costs to them in terms of the gap between reasonable *ex ante* consumer expectations and the *ex post* costs and benefits of the transactions in question.

Given the high costs of investigating the safety of a given unfamiliar product prior to purchasing, it is not surprising that a general expectation that products on the market are acceptably safe is a crucial assumption of most consumer behaviour, influencing the value that consumers place on information. Not all cases where there are high safety risks are cases where these general expectations have been undermined or exploited by sellers who market products that do not meet the expectations. These expectations may not apply to activities such as bungee jumping, skateboarding or motorcycling, for instance, where the risks are fairly obvious. This leads to an important principle in identifying a consumer information problem related to safety risks: a consumer protection problem is much more likely to be present where there is no obvious reason for consumers to doubt their general expectation of safety, and so their expectation can easily be exploited. Even in the absence of exploitation by 'rogue' sellers, it may turn out that the expectation itself is based on a misperception of risk. For example, it turns out that most people systematically underestimate the risk of being killed in an automobile accident.[5] This suggests a likely consumer protection problem, since consumers are probably undervaluing information about the safety of automobiles.

But there is a related consideration that past government regulation as well as markets can create expectations of safety. For instance, it is quite likely that the legacy of deposit insurance has created expectations among many consumers that banks are safe institutions with which to place funds. With banks now in the business of selling many risky financial instruments, a gap may be arising between expectations and reality, signalling a genuine consumer protection problem.

An important implication of this focus on general consumer expectations is that the more obvious a consumer protection problem has become, the less of a problem it may come to be. Thus, once it becomes widely known or believed that, say, there are many scams in the timeshare industry, consumers will adjust their general expectations about these transactions, and (although some scams may continue to go on) there may no longer be a 'problem' that requires special attention from regulators. The same is likely to be true of dangerous drugs like thalidomide. This may lead to a dilemma for governments. Clearly, the greater the extent that consumers at large have misperceived the costs and benefits of a transaction based on their general expectations, the more likely it is that there is a problem that may require regulatory attention. At the same time, many pressures to regulate come *ex post*, once a problem is widely perceived, and therefore consumers at large have adjusted their expectations in light of it. This leads one to question, on an information-based approach, if there is a problem that any longer requires addressing. Hence, the special importance of devising early warning systems to alert policy-makers to potential problems in their incipiency so that pre-emptive action is facilitated. Timeliness is a prerequisite of effective government action. Markets are likely to solve most information problems, given time, although many consumers may be prejudiced in the meantime. A central issue is thus whether government can abridge these market lags.

---

5 See S. Breyer, *Breaking the Vicious Circle: toward Effective Risk Regulation* (Cambridge, Mass.: Harvard University Press, 1993), 34.

Deciding whether regulation is a necessary and feasible response

According to the OECD Regulatory Checklist, 'government intervention should be based on clear evidence that a problem exists and that government action is justified, given the values at stake and current government policies; the likely benefits and costs of action (based not on perfect government, but on a realistic assessment of government effectiveness); and alternative mechanisms for addressing the problem'.[6] The OECD goes on to state that 'a clear assessment of total costs and benefits – including those to businesses, private citizens, and administrations – likely to be realised in practice is crucial information for decision-makers'[7] and that regulators should routinely estimate the expected costs and benefits of each regulatory proposal and of feasible alternatives (quantitatively where possible, but at least qualitatively), and should make those estimates available in accessible format to administrative and political decision-makers.

The first principle here (albeit cast in negative terms) should be, in our view, that identification of a problem does not create a presumption that government should regulate. It is necessary to ask whether and why a market-based solution will not emerge in a reasonably timely and effective form, or why that solution may be socially sub-optimal. Of course, here a market-based solution means a solution that is influenced by background private law norms of tort, contract and property rights, which themselves bear the influence of government action. This question is easiest to answer where the market in question is not competitive or is very imperfectly competitive, or where the structure of the market itself suggests that anti-competitive behaviour with respect to information is likely to occur.

In the case of a competitive market, there are a number of characteristics that may lead to a hypothesis that a market-based solution is unlikely to emerge:

- Repeat transactions are rare, and consequently the performance incentives created by the possibility of repeat business from satisfied customers are blunted.
- Entry and exit costs in the industry are low, leading to the possibility of a large number of fly-by-night operators with few sunk costs and only modest investments in reputational capital.
- Many sellers or producers are extrajurisdictional, making redress through private law more difficult for consumers.
- Sellers characteristically have few assets against which a judgment may be enforced.
- The costs to consumers of a 'bad' transaction are delayed or potentially catastrophic, making *ex post* relief an inadequate or unsatisfactory solution.
- The small size of a typical transaction creates a significant disincentive to seeking *ex post* relief through the courts.

6 OECD, *Recommendation of the Council*, 9.   7 *Ibid.*, para. 29.

These criteria are not intended to be exhaustive, but rather simply to evoke the kinds of characteristics that suggest that a market may not work out the problem without government regulation. Once some features have been identified that point to the likely inadequacy of a market-based solution, then a second fundamental principle should come into play in determining whether there is a prima facie case that government should act: even where a significant market failure has been identified, government should act only where it is feasible and cost-effective to do so.

Here, an information-based approach suggests a fairly obvious analytical inquiry with respect to feasibility. Consumer protection regulation is only likely to make consumers better off if it either: (a) improves consumer estimates of the value of information; or (b) reduces the cost of information to consumers (or both). Regulation is most likely to improve consumers' estimates of the value of information where it is addressed to hidden risks or hazards that create a gap between consumers' general expectations and reality, or is addressed to certain demonstrable cognitive failures to appreciate the nature of particular kinds of risks. Regulators should be searching for gaps between expectations and reality, and asking themselves whether there is a real opportunity to address those gaps before consumer experience in the marketplace does so. This in turn suggests the vital importance of timely information and early warning mechanisms,[8] in assessing the likelihood of feasible and effective consumer protection regulation. It also suggests that there may be considerable benefit to inter-jurisdictional co-operation: one of the reasons governments may be in a position to identify gaps is access to information about problems that develop elsewhere but that have not yet reached local markets.

Knowing whether regulation is likely to improve consumers' estimates of the value of information means knowing something not only about the risks of a given product or activity, but also about the relevant groups of consumers. Some consumers' beliefs may be largely uninfluenced by regulation. Take, for example, various forms of non-traditional therapy or healing, such as health food remedies, meditation or massage. Expending public resources to police the healing claims being made for these products and services against objective, scientific standards may be pointless if the relevant group of consumers is already highly sceptical about the value of traditional medicine or mainstream science. Regulation of health food remedies on public safety grounds may nevertheless still be justified where these remedies may be used by third parties (such as children).

---

8 An example is the rapid alert system used by the European Commission with respect to food hazards, which has apparently worked well in a number of instances where significant hazards were identified prior to major contamination: D. Vogel, *Trading up: Consumer and Environmental Regulation in a Global Economy* (Cambridge, Mass.: Harvard University Press, 1995), 44–5.

With respect to the possibility of government reducing the cost of information, it is important to ask, what comparative advantage does government have in the information market? Why are governments going to be better than markets at generating low-cost information? Credit agencies, bond rating services, consumer publications, department store chains acting as screening agents for consumers, voluntary standards bodies and various other certification intermediaries, demonstrate that markets do generate mechanisms to provide information on the risk and value of transactions, although given the public goods nature of information, private information markets may still generate socially suboptimal quantities of information.

The following is an illustrative list of situations where governments may in fact have a comparative advantage over these mechanisms:

- Where the government itself is already engaged in the collection of information for another purpose (for example, in the regulation of financial institutions for macroeconomic stability reasons).
- Where it is difficult for a genuinely independent private market actor to obtain the necessary data (for reasons of consumer confidentiality, etc.).
- Where an independent private market information provider would have limited ability to deter inaccurate or fraudulent self-reporting by the sellers whom it is rating, thereby giving government an advantage because of its ability to use formal sanctions against such reporting.
- Where other jurisdictions are only willing or are more willing to import products where there is high-quality governmental consumer protection regulation, and so the government must regulate anyway for the sake of other jurisdictions' consumers.
- Where independent private market information providers or intermediaries simply create a second-order consumer protection problem because consumers face high costs in choosing such a provider, and assuring themselves about its independence, or the market for independent information is itself a monopoly or highly uncompetitive (the case in many jurisdictions with voluntary standard setting bodies).
- Where the most effective means of addressing information costs is by banning a product, i.e., some mandatory action that a private sector information provider would be legally unable to take (it may be much more costly to have to obtain specific up-to-date information to avoid purchasing a hazardous product than simply to arrive at the counter and find that it is unavailable).

This last kind of case takes us back to the first question, that of the accuracy of consumers' estimates of the value of information. In a world of many products and services and little time for search, consumers have no choice but to rely on fairly crude heuristic devices even to know when to seek information about a transaction.

Perhaps the most important and most durable of these devices, as discussed above, is the general expectation that products are reasonably safe, aside from risks that are obvious. From this perspective, health and safety regulation may be the most unambiguously valuable form of consumer protection regulation. The social value of such regulation may far exceed the number of lives saved by the particular precaution mandated (the conventional mode of economic evaluation), for in supporting general expectations of safety, such regulation reduces immensely the information and search costs that consumers face in all markets. In effect, it underwrites the heuristic device that is crucial to consumers' management of information cost problems generally.

Choosing a regulatory instrument

The implications of an information-based approach to policy-making for the choice of regulatory instrument are several. As a first principle, in a world of information overload, consumer protection instruments that actually generate information that is costly for consumers to interpret or access may be counterproductive. This principle may imply the re-evaluation of quite a wide range of consumer protection laws and regulations, especially those that mandate detailed disclosure of contents or ingredients, complex details of the price, terms and conditions of a transaction, or very specific caveats about the use of the product. Other instruments, such as licensing or permits for operating a business or engaging in a profession, may not reduce information costs at all, if they are not based upon relevant quality control standards (which is frequently the case). Indeed, such instruments may actually increase the gap between expectations and reality by giving the impression that a licence or permit indicates an actual level of safety or competence.

The corollary proposition is that cruder instruments, which often actually restrict consumer choice (such as bans of hazardous products), may in fact be more successful in lowering information costs. Thus, there may be a trade-off of some importance in instrument choice between reducing information costs effectively and maximising consumer choice. This suggests that particular attention should be paid to instruments that manage this kind of trade-off.

Simple warnings, unlike bans, actually retain consumer choice, but do not have the information cost problems associated with more sophisticated disclosure devices. For instance, prominent labelling of a substance as a poison is a low-cost way of providing important information to a consumer.[9] Depending on the value of the

---

9 Studies by Viscusi and others on hazard warnings suggest that this kind of information is likely to be reliably processed by consumers, while 'clutter' in labelling actually significantly alters recollections of the information being provided: W. K. Viscusi, W. A. Magat and J. Huber, 'Informational Regulation of Consumer Health Risks: an Empirical Evaluation of Hazard Warnings'

transaction, the consumer can choose: (1) to seek a substitute product without this classification if the information costs of finding out about the specific risks are high; (2) to investigate the details of the risks denoted by the expression 'poison'; or (3) to purchase the product and use it with care, based upon the kinds of precautions that most reasonable people would take in handling a substance labelled 'poison'.

Another instrument is mandatory use of information intermediaries, for example, in the case of medication, requiring that it be obtained from a pharmacist, or prescribed by a doctor, or both. Use of intermediaries may be an especially effective policy instrument for reducing information costs where the product has particularly severe risks for certain sub-groups and the intermediary has knowledge both of the risks and whether they are likely to affect the particular consumer in question. Generally a requirement that a product be obtained through a certain intermediary sends a crude but potentially effective signal to the consumer that there may be value in searching out more precise information and not relying on general expectations of safety.

Experience ratings may provide rather crude measures of quality or safety, but they nevertheless convey important information at low cost. For example, one could require that the number of times a professional has been the subject of complaints or investigation before a regulatory body be made publicly available. In some jurisdictions lists of restaurants that have been cited for health code violations are published in newspapers. Anecdotal evidence suggests that frequent flyers do pay attention to published information about the safety or on-time records of airlines. Unlike, for instance, product ratings such as 'AAA' or 'Canada Fancy' for food products, experience ratings do not require that consumers invest heavily in interpreting the information, or in assuring themselves of the bona fides of an official interpreter of the information (such as a rating agency). Experience ratings exploit one of the most important heuristic devices that individuals use to make decisions under uncertainty – the assumption that past behaviour is an indication of future performance. Governments could either provide this kind of information themselves or, in some cases, subsidise or otherwise facilitate the development of private for-profit or non-profit information intermediaries to perform this function. Similarly, governments could provide or otherwise underwrite the development of central data banks that record whether given suppliers of particular classes of goods or services maintain, for example, a guaranteed returns policy, product warranties (and basic terms), a complaints handling department (and how to access it), participation in an independent alternative dispute resolution regime (and how to access it), and records of violations of consumer protection and other laws. In important respects such a data bank would be the consumer analogue to credit-rating

(1986) 17 *Rand Journal of Economics* 351; W. K. Viscusi, W. A. Magat and J. Huber, *Learning About Risk: Consumer and Worker Response to Hazard Information* (Cambridge, Mass.: Harvard University Press, 1987).

bureaus utilised by merchants in dealing with consumers and, by strengthening reputational markets, would render a higher proportion of consumer transactions self-enforcing.

Standardised contract terms are an additional regulatory instrument. In many settings, consumers face a blizzard of contractual offerings that are often difficult to compare. This problem has become particularly acute in many service settings, in part as a result of deregulation – financial service charges, telecommunications charges, electricity charges – but also extends to other settings, such as insurance premiums and professional service charges. Here, standardising the format and content of contractual offerings while leaving a few key terms for tailored negotiation may facilitate the consumer search-and-selection process. On these key terms, government may have a useful role to play in sponsoring a centralised collection of data on competitive offerings that consumers can readily access before making purchase decisions.

In addition to, but not unrelated to, the trade-off between respecting consumer choice and lowering information costs, is a trade-off between restricting competition and trade and lowering information costs. Because an information-based approach suggests that often competitive markets are likely to solve many consumer protection problems on their own, consumer protection instruments that have an anti-competitive or trade-restricting effect may be counterproductive. Instruments such as licensing that directly restrict the number of competitors in the marketplace most obviously have an anti-competitive effect. A product safety instrument that specifies that the product must contain specific inputs, as opposed to meeting certain objective standards of safety (process rather than performance standards), may well exclude certain competing products from the marketplace, even if they are in fact safe. Similarly, requirements that a product be tested or certified by a particular certification entity before it is sold may have a trade-restricting or more generally competition-restricting effect, if the certification process has subjective or covert protectionist dimensions to it.

The trade-off for lower information costs is that less competitively restrictive standards may entail higher monitoring or enforcement costs. As a general principle, the choice of regulatory instrument has to be informed by the information costs of compliance or enforcement. The choice between product-specific regulation and general safety standards, for example, has to respond to the fact that it may be much less costly to verify that a product contains a particular design or device than to determine whether products of widely varying designs actually meet a given standard of safety performance. So too the choice between enforcement by a government agency as opposed to civil liability. One of the virtues of liability regimes such as tort and contract is that the responsibility for enforcement rests with the individual consumer who is best informed (at least cost) about the occurrence of a mismatch between intention and realisation in a consumer transaction. These information cost savings, however, come at the expense of a failure to share the costs of enforcement amongst all those who might benefit from enforcement, resulting in underenforcement: consumer protection laws which give a private right of action to harmed consumers are notoriously underutilised.

An emphasis on information costs in relation to enforcement also brings into focus the need to assess the efficacy of reputation and other market mechanisms to enforce standards. Regulation that harnesses these mechanisms may better achieve a number of consumer protection goals. Where industry standards are not generated by the market itself, the role for policy may be limited to organising the development of industry standards with respect, for example, to quality control: reputation and consumer responses may provide enforcement at low cost. In the biotechnology area, for example, some commentators have suggested that the role for government may be limited to requiring that food producers using biotechnology indicate this fact with a simple alert label; this could serve to create an incentive for producers efficiently to collect and communicate what consumers need to know (and, in response to the alert label, will demand to know before purchasing) about any risks posed by the novel food.[10]

Government may also have a role to play in helping to overcome collective action problems facing the development of voluntary industry codes with respect to acceptable business practices, complaints and dispute resolution mechanisms. Government may help define an appropriate set of standards, require participation in a regime, or certify regimes for compliance with industry-established standards. By paying close attention to information dynamics, policy designed in this way can be aimed at creative strategies for exploiting private compliance incentives and the lower costs of information to those on the ground, so to speak: producers and consumers themselves.

Attention to the costs of information also highlights important differences between regulatory regimes that focus on ongoing oversight for compliance with legislation, and those that focus on quick response mechanisms. The former pose much higher information costs than the latter in a world with accelerating product and service diversity. Against a background of generally effective incentives for product safety, generated by liability regimes, and of market incentives augmented by, for example, government-assisted reputation mechanisms such as those mentioned above, a regulatory regime that responds to identified product hazards with mandatory recall provisions and mandatory notification requirements for manufacturers that have become aware of product hazards rather than, for example, anticipating hazards, may achieve the best balance between the costs of accidents and the information costs of regulation. Here, as elsewhere, the cost of information, which lies at the heart of consumer protection problems in the first place, is a good guide to the development of creative and effective means of regulation.

---

10 See G. K. Hadfield and D. Thomson, 'An Information-Based Approach to Labelling Biotechnology Consumer Products' (1998) 21 *Journal of Consumer Policy* 193.

In summary, with respect to the choice of policy objectives for any proposed form of state involvement or intervention in a class of economic activities, it is of crucial importance that policy-makers identify the policy objectives to be served by state involvement or intervention with maximum clarity and precision. These provisions must have a sufficiently 'hard edge' to them so that it is possible to engage in a discriminating initial choice of policy instruments to serve those objectives and to re-evaluate, over time, how well the chosen instruments are serving the chosen objectives. Operational criteria for evaluating impacts on objectives need to be chosen so that it is possible to know whether the chosen instrument is making the problem better, worse, or having no impact at all; information systems need to be put in place from the outset to facilitate these evaluations; and commitments made to periodic programme evaluations that should be in the public domain, so that programme modifications are not primarily crisis-driven. In the past, too many consumer protection initiatives have been undertaken on faith and never been systematically evaluated or re-evaluated against rigorous empirical evidence on their actual effects.

With respect to each policy objective, a significant array of possible policy instruments are typically available and need to be evaluated (and periodically re-evaluated) comparatively, one against the other, in light of experience with their utilisation both in the jurisdiction in question in the past and other jurisdictions currently or historically. That is to say, historical, comparative, and empirical evidence will be critical to the choice and ongoing re-evaluation of policy instruments (or combinations of instruments). The efficacy of a given policy instrument (which I re-emphasise must be evaluated relative to available alternatives) can be assessed on two dimensions: (1) How completely does the instrument realise the chosen policy objective? (2) What public and private costs are likely to be entailed in the deployment of this instrument? In many contexts, there will be a trade-off between these two dimensions of instrument performance. That is to say, an instrument may realise a given policy objective fully, but at very high public and private costs. Another instrument may realise the policy objective, for example 80 per cent, but at much lower costs. Clearly in such cases choosing appropriate trade-offs between cost and effectiveness will be required. With respect to many policy objectives, dual sub-objectives will be relevant: (1) how to reduce the incidence of the offending conduct or activity; and (2) how to address the adverse consequences of residual forms of the conduct or activity in question, which in turn may implicate a combination of policy instruments. In addition, choices must be made as to whether to regulate or influence the supply-side or demand-side of the market and whether to regulate or influence inputs or outputs.

Even after these basic questions have been addressed, governments face important second-order choices between the direct administration of the instrument by a line department or agency of government; delegated administration by a statutory or administrative agency; delegated self-regulation by a professional or industry association; or private enforcement. A variety of factors may legitimately bear on these institutional choices, such as routinised mass decision-making entailing significant economies of scale (bureaucracies); the need for specialised expertise, large stakes and significant due-process concerns (an independent agency); cohesive professional and ethical norms (self-regulation, subject to appropriate checks and balances); and private enforcement to vindicate corrective justice or related rights (the courts). Moreover, in some cases, it may be appropriate to conceive of a combination of regulation (however administered) and private enforcement.

Once (1) the policy objectives have been defined with appropriate precision; (2) the case for some form of state intervention has been established; (3) the policy instruments to serve those objectives have been chosen; and (4) choices have been made as to the administrative or institutional forum in which responsibility for administering the chosen instruments will be vested, policy choices must then be made as to the nature of the decision-making process within the chosen forum. In particular, choices are required as to the relative emphasis on *ex ante* versus *ex post* decision-making and case-by-case adjudication versus generic determinations of classes of issues; the relative weight to be given to full oral hearings in case-by-case determinations versus more informal determinations, for example, on the basis of written records; and the relative emphasis on high-quality initial decisions and subsequent appeals/reviews of initial decisions, and the nature and locus of subsequent appeal/review processes.

In short, rigorous analysis of each of these categories of choices is required with respect to any perceived consumer problem. In making appropriate choices within each category, only limited progress is likely to be made through abstract analysis. Instead, what is required is serious attention to available empirical data ('taking the facts seriously') and historical and comparative experience. In many cases, ensuring that relevant data is systematically collected and analysed may be a necessary prelude to rational policy choices. Moreover, all choices (other than choice of policy objective) should be thought of as relative to available alternatives, thus requiring a comparative institutional framework of analysis. I now turn to the role of civil redress in an information-oriented consumer protection policy framework.

The role of civil redress in consumer protection policy

To what extent is civil justice a public good?

In considering issues that bear on the relationship between public and private provision (for example, private mediation, arbitration, etc.) of civil justice, we need to think clearly about what aspects of the provision of civil justice constitute a public good. It is traditionally argued by economists that services such as national defence and policing are public goods, in the sense that once they are provided beneficiaries of the services cannot be excluded from consuming them even if they do not pay for them. Similarly, if there are major positive externalities from the provision of civil justice, clearly it will be suboptimally supplied by private providers. Again, if there are very large economies of scale and scope in the provision of civil justice, one might view it as a kind of natural monopoly that if privately provided would have to be closely regulated or alternatively that should be publicly provided. Alternatively again, one could regard the provision of civil justice, even if not a natural monopoly, as necessarily entailing ultimately the deployment of the coercive powers of the state, which for good social and political reasons, we would not wish to see delegated to private agencies. My own tentative impressions are that unlike national defence or police services, most civil justice services can be priced and rationed. On the other hand, there may be major positive externalities from the provision of civil justice, such as providing an avenue for redressing grievances in a socially non-disruptive fashion (i.e., writs rather than rifles), and that a tightly co-ordinated and hierarchical system of civil justice provides some measure of consistency and predictability in decision-making by generating and interpreting legal rules which other parties can rely on as precedents in shaping their own conduct. Another example of an externality would be the incentive or deterrent effect on third parties of a decision to require one party to pay compensation to another in respect of some form of conduct (general rather than specific deterrence). On the other hand, I doubt that the inherent economies of scale or scope in the provision of civil justice require, for efficiency reasons, a single monopoly supplier (as evident from the growth of all kinds of alternative dispute resolution mechanisms, public and private). Yet, to the extent that even these systems depend for their ultimate efficacy on the state enforcing determinations or adjudications made by them, one probably needs to view private and public adjudication as complements, at least to some extent, rather than as substitutes, in that the public justice system may ultimately be called on to enforce awards, and is unlikely to do so without maintaining some degree of supervision over how these determinations have been reached. As one thinks about the channelling or screening process and the richness of the institutional options available for channelling different kinds of legal disputes, it strikes me as important to ask in each case whether there are public goods aspects to the class of dispute in question which require a public institutional presence (and what kind of presence).

From a law and economics perspective, in the present and other contexts, virtues are often seen in simply creating socially appropriate incentive structures and letting individuals make choices, in this case as to which institutional avenue of redress to pursue in the light of this incentive structure. In other words, pricing mechanisms are often preferred to command-and-control forms of regulation. In the present context, to the extent that we believe that the formal court system is both overburdened and overutilised from a social perspective, I would argue that the presumptive response should be to price the services provided by this system at fully allocated social cost so that all litigants utilising the system perceive not only their private costs but also the full social cost of the services provided. This is likely to have at least two effects: in many cases to induce settlement rather than litigation, and in other cases to utilise alternative forms of dispute resolution as a substitute for formal litigation. With respect to the second alternative, we need to ask, following my discussion of the public goods aspects of the provision of civil justice, whether inducing parties to rely on alternative forms of dispute resolution, including importantly private forms of dispute resolution, may compromise some of the public goods aspects of public provision. For normal two-party commercial and related litigation, it is not obvious to me that this is so. However, given that the determinations made by these alternative forms of dispute resolution must ultimately be enforced by the state, through the public courts, we need to think clearly about what forms of public supervision are required of these private alternative forms of dispute resolution. One could imagine *ex ante* certification by the legislature or some other public agency of these mechanisms, either with respect to the required qualifications of the arbitral personnel or the processes of decision-making that must be employed or both. Instead, or as well, one could imagine *ex post* judicial supervision, through rights of appeal or judicial review, although here, to the extent this *ex post* judicial oversight function more closely resembles a rehearing on the merits, to that extent these alternative dispute resolution mechanisms cease to be substitutes for, but are rather complements to, formal judicial adjudication and arguably contribute only modestly, if at all, to conserving judicial resources.

Supposing, as a presumptive matter, that all court services were priced at their fully allocated social cost; while this would *not* entail, obviously, any radical privatisation of the court system, it would promote a significant degree of *competition* amongst alternative providers of civil justice services. In addition, it would provide more resources to the public civil justice system, which could conceivably be deployed to increase the supply of services in that system or to targeted legal aid programmes. However, here we probably cannot avoid some *a priori* classification of classes of claims entailing major social or economic externalities where the parties to the dispute should not be required to bear the full social cost of resolving the dispute. I have in mind, first, that claims involving constitutional challenges to government legislation or regulations would fall into this category. Similarly, human rights claims are often likely to possess this characteristic. Again, major challenges to long-standing doctrinal rules or litigation over novel issues that have a test case character to them probably also present this dimension (applying something like the Supreme Court of Canada's 'public importance test' in reviewing leave applications). But surely these cases constitute a tiny percentage of the total workload of the formal court system. By publicly subsidising *all* civil litigation, we have substituted untargeted for targeted subsidies. On distributive justice grounds, targeted subsidies might, through, for example, the legal aid system, subsidise impecunious litigants with civil claims that potentially exhibit these significant externality characteristics, or entail significant impacts on their personal wellbeing (for example, family law cases), or in appropriate cases involving externalities the courts might waive the allocation of all or some of the fully allocated social costs of determining a dispute for other litigants. But, whatever the mechanism, surely we need to think hard about how to target the subsidies entailed in the public provision of civil justice much more finely, and outside the classes of disputes entailing targeted public subsidies foster competition between the public court system and alternative privately provided forms of dispute resolution.

One irony in this approach is that the case *against* maintaining a public monopoly in the provision of civil justice services seems strongest where only the litigants' interests are entailed, and the case *for* public provision seems strongest where there are major externalities associated with judicial decisions, thus increasingly focusing the resources of the formal court system precisely on those cases that many commentators have argued in the past are least appropriate for judicial adjudication, i.e., cases with major polycentric features or that involve major judicial balancing of competing values or entail, in effect, a major policy-making role.[11] We need to ponder whether we should be open to turning conventional wisdom about the appropriate role of judicial adjudication so sharply on its head.

A decision-tree framework for evaluating institutional options in the provision of civil justice

I find it useful, as a mental exercise, to trace through sequentially how one might respond to various classes of legally cognisable *interests* (not necessarily claims) from the moment at which the legislature or some other law-making body has determined that a particular class of citizens has a legally cognisable interest, taking that initial judgment for our purposes as a given. Here, it seems to me to be useful, at a middle level of reflection and abstraction, to consider the range of institutional options with respect to issues of cost, delay and access by reference to both supply-side and demand-side options at each juncture along this sequence. With respect to supply-side options, I have in mind options that would change the quantity or quality or nature of the supply of dispute resolution services. With respect to demand-side options, I have in mind various options that would change the configuration and level of demand for various kinds of dispute resolution services.

Public or private law enforcement

Assuming, for the sake of argument, that the legislature has decided that a particular group of citizens or constituency has a legally cognisable interest that the law should protect, perhaps the first issue that arises is whether this interest should be protected through public sanctions or private claims. In some cases, the

---

11 See, e.g., L. L. Fuller, 'The Forms and Limits of Adjudication' (1978) 92 *Harv L Rev* 353.

legislature could pre-empt subsequent disputes through criminal or regulatory prohibitions or requirements of one kind or another that are publicly enforced. Where the protected class is large and dispersed, and individual claims relatively small, public enforcement in many cases would seem to be more efficient than requiring individuals to prosecute their claims on an individual basis. Public enforcement authorities may be able to realise economies of scale, scope and specialisation in investigative and enforcement functions relative to private enforcers, and may have access to investigative powers that we would be reluctant to vest in private enforcers, and to penalties (fines and imprisonment) and other forms of deterrence (for example, licence revocation) not available in civil redress proceedings.[12] In some cases, it may be efficient to contemplate expanded utilisation of class action procedures in order to aggregate consumer claims and adjudicate them through the civil justice system but, nevertheless, a key threshold issue is whether to rely predominantly on public or private enforcement. In some cases, some combination of the two may be appropriate, in part as a check on the assiduousness of the public enforcement authorities.[13] Given fiscal constraints on government resources, there is likely to be a tendency to seek to provide relief to constituencies in an off-budget fashion, for example, through civil redress mechanisms, even though in principle it may be more efficient to deal with these concerns through publicly enforced sanctions or regulatory requirements. This may be largely a fiscal illusion in that while the government conserves on demands on its own expenditure budget, this may entail much more substantial aggregate costs of law enforcement, including costs privately borne, that are nevertheless real social costs. In general, a large volume of consumer civil claims should raise a presumption that other features of consumer protection policy are not working effectively, rather than being a source of policy satisfaction. In other words, consumer civil claims should be the residual, not primary, response to a consumer protection problem. A paucity of such claims is consistent both with the effective operation of policies (the best-case scenario) or the failure of such policies and denial of effective access to civil redress (the worst-case scenario). Some independent empirical referent is required to resolve this ambiguity.

Public legal education

Assuming that the state chooses not to rely exclusively on a public law response to these concerns, but instead, or in addition, assumes that there should be some significant role for private initiatives by citizens with legally cognisable interests in protecting these interests, a series of public policy initiatives, escalating in scale,

---

12 See K. Roach and M. Trebilcock, 'Private Enforcement of Competition Laws' (1996) 34 *Osgoode Hall LJ* 461.
13 *Ibid.*

might be contemplated. First, the state could largely confine itself to providing forms of public legal education either with a view to enabling citizens to avoid potential disputes in the first place by appropriately ordering their affairs or conduct, or educating them on how to prosecute complaints effectively on a self-help basis.[14] My own sense is that most citizens with legal grievances do not have in mind major constitutional challenges, applications for judicial review of administrative agency decisions, or human rights issues, but quite low-level or small-scale complaints against firms, landlords or bureaucracies, and indeed have a strong aversion to entanglement either with lawyers or courts, or anything that looks like lawyers or courts, not only because of the cost and delays but because of the stress and general unpleasantness associated with a structured adversarial process.

Informal dispute resolution

This leads me to another suggestion. Beyond providing public legal education in one form or another (which forms need to be carefully evaluated), the state might consider ways of either facilitating, or in some cases mandating, informal dispute resolution processes within firms, bureaucracies or other government agencies. My own casual impression is that for the average citizen, the principal frustration often experienced is getting an electronic voice on a telephone with a large firm or a government bureaucracy, or dealing with a low-level clerk with no authority to respond effectively to a complaint, or being shuffled endlessly from one person in the firm or agency to another. For example, requiring firms with retail sales over a certain size to provide a toll free 1–800 number and a designated person in charge of customer relations who is publicly identified in sales, other literature or receipts might respond to these frustrations. Indeed, a number of large retail chains or appliance or car manufacturers do this now. In addition, to proceed to another stage, one could imagine the state either facilitating, or in some cases mandating, the provision of some kind of internal or industry-wide informal arbitration system where citizens with a grievance that is not satisfactorily resolved in the customer-relations department can seek resolution through an informal adjudication process, perhaps principally based on letters and written material but entailing an independent adjudicator. As to whether the state should simply facilitate these mechanisms or mandate them is a difficult question. It could facilitate them by certifying personnel and processes and widely publicising the nature of these, allowing firms to opt into them as a way of signalling a commitment to quality of service, with the signal being rendered less ambiguous and more credible by virtue of the state having certified this informal arbitral regime. In other cases, the state may wish to mandate the creation

---

14 See, e.g., G. Kane and E. Myers, 'The Role of Self-Help in the Provision of Legal Services' in R. G. Evans and M. Trebilcock (eds.), *Lawyers and the Consumer Interest: Regulating the Market for Legal Services* (Toronto: Butterworths, 1982), chap. 15.

of such regimes on an industry-wide basis, if problems have been pervasive in an industry, rather along the lines of the New Home Warranty and Travel Insurance programmes in Ontario.[15]

There is also much to be said for greater utilisation of informal hotlines of the kind run by some government agencies such as the Consumer Protection Bureaux, Ombudsmen's Offices, the Employment Standards Branch or Better Business Bureaux. In order to give this kind of process teeth, apart from any public law enforcement sanctions that may be at the disposal of a public agency, I think greater use should be made of publicity, through periodic publication of the compilation of complaints by parties complained against and percentages of successful resolutions, thus enhancing the operation of reputational markets. To the extent that systematic data collection (itself an important early warning mechanism) from these more informal dispute resolution processes yields patterns of complaints that are better dealt with by pre-emptive legislation or regulation enforced through public sanctions, this in many cases is likely to be a preferable option to the prosecution of individual grievances.

In other cases, the state might consider making more widely available largely self-executing remedies, like the cooling-off period provided under consumer protection legislation for door-to-door sales, which provides an extremely low-cost remedy to consumers who may have been victims of overreaching tactics by door-to-door salesmen. Again, larger or more reputable firms already provide this assurance or signal of quality to their customers by providing a satisfaction-guaranteed or money-back assurance for all their sales.

Wholesale rather than retail civil justice

For other classes of disputes, other approaches may be more appropriate. For example, with respect to workplace injuries, Ontario, like most other jurisdictions, for most of the last century provided an administrative compensation system. Much more recently, Ontario has adopted a form of automobile no-fault insurance. New Zealand has adopted a much more comprehensive accident compensation scheme. In considering administrative agencies as alternatives to courts in the provision of civil justice services, one needs to think carefully about exactly what it is that these agencies can provide which courts cannot. One characteristic that they may possess is specialised expertise, even though they may continue to employ many of the same processes of inquiry and adjudication as courts. However, apart from specialised experience, they may also employ radically different processes for determining claims. With respect to workers' compensation, one can view processes of determining claims to be providing civil justice, in important respects, on a

15 See I. Ramsay, 'Small Claims Courts: a Review' in Ontario Law Reform Commission, *Rethinking Civil Justice: Research Studies for the Civil Justice Review, Volume 2* (1996), 489.

wholesale rather than *retail* basis, in that individualised determinations of fault on the part of employers are not required and compensation is largely provided according to a predetermined scale, so that individualised determinations of quantum are much less open-ended. With respect to other legal claims presently being processed through the formal court system and with respect to claims that presently, for the most part, do not find their way into any formal system of adjudication, we need to ask ourselves whether civil justice can be provided, in some range of these cases, on a wholesale rather than retail basis. Giving specialised administrative tribunals properly structured rule-making powers may sometimes facilitate this process.

Judicial oversight of non-judicial adjudicative systems

Assuming either in the case of many classes of small claims that we have gone the informal arbitral route, or in the case of other classes of larger claims we have chosen to assign them to an administrative agency to process to some extent on a wholesale rather than retail basis, we then need to think clearly about the relationship between these decision-making agencies and the formal court system with respect to rights of appeal or rights to judicial review. As noted earlier, this issue cannot be entirely escaped to the extent that determinations by these other agencies may ultimately have to be enforced through the coercive powers of the state, and courts quite properly are unlikely simply to enforce these awards mechanically without some assurance that justice has been done and some basic elements of due process respected. However, too expansive a role for a judicial oversight will clearly undermine a large part of the purpose for designing or fostering alternative dispute resolution mechanisms *as substitutes for* (not complements to) formal judicial adjudication. Informal arbitral mechanisms or wholesale rather than retail dispensation of civil justice are likely to raise difficulties for the courts, on the one hand, because the informal processes employed may seem sharply at variance with conventional judicial adjudication processes (and notions of due process) or, on the other hand, because civil justice dispensed wholesale will lack the individualised attention to the merits of claims on a case-by-case basis. Thus, some attention needs to be paid both to framing appropriate privative clauses in these regimes that strike an appropriate balance between the need for some judicial oversight and the need for considerable judicial deference, and also exploring more fully the notion of *ex ante* certification by the legislature of either the processes or personnel (or both) employed in these processes as a *quid pro quo* for substantial immunity from *ex post* judicial oversight.

Small claims courts

With respect to residual classes of small claims for which the above systemic responses are thought to be inappropriate or in any event have not been adopted,

I think we need to look harder at the current operation of small claims courts. Issues seem to me to arise here on both the supply and demand sides. On the supply side, it occurs to me that we should consider the idea of appointing part-time small claims court judges to sit either on a *pro bono* or nominal fee basis in evening or Saturday sessions, for example, lawyers with at least five years' experience. It may well be an attractive source of experience for practising lawyers with an interest in litigation (subject to conflict problems) to provide one evening or Saturday morning a month sitting on small claims court cases for a nominal fee. On the demand side, while I once thought that there was merit in the case for excluding lawyers from small claims courts, I now believe this view is probably ill-founded, in part because it is likely to lead to less focused and less well-prepared cases being presented by claimants and inefficient use of court resources being entailed in sorting through these claims. However, one could contemplate many of the legal services being provided by law students for nominal fees paid by litigants either to the students themselves or probably more commonly to the often publicly supported student legal aid clinics with which they are associated. More generally, I believe that we need to question the monopoly that lawyers have on the representational function in many contexts. While this monopoly has been eroded in some contexts (for example, the provision of legal services to citizens charged with traffic offences where former police officers in Canada now operate private legal services firms; non-lawyer representatives of injured workers with workers' compensation claims), there would seem much to be said for contemplating special training programmes for paralegals in community college programmes that are designed to provide a cadre of paralegals operating on their own account or in law firms who can provide low-cost representational services not only in small claims courts but in other dispute resolution fora (other than higher levels of formal judicial adjudication).[16]

In many of the above observations I have stressed the importance of providing effective means of resolving small-scale grievances, because I believe (correctly or incorrectly – we may want to ask how this impression can be verified) that for the great majority of citizens this is the kind of complaint that will be most commonly of concern to them and the frustrations they often currently experience in effectively prosecuting such a complaint are unlikely to be resolved by any formal process of adjudication.

Reforming the formal judicial adjudication process

At the end of this sequential analysis of policy responses to legally cognisable interests, we at last come to the role and functioning of the formal judicial adjudication

---

16 See, e.g., F. Zemans, 'The Non-Lawyer as a Means of Providing Legal Services' in Evans and Trebilcock (eds.), *Lawyers and the Consumer Interest*, chap. 9.

system.[17] I have already indicated that I favour investigating seriously the notion of presumptively pricing the services of the system at fully allocated social costs, with incentive implications that will feed back up the sequence of institutional options reviewed above. Beyond this suggestion, however, the complex trade-offs between costs, delay and access need to be addressed within the judicial adjudication system. One option that I do not think holds out much promise is simply to increase the number of judges and support staff in the traditional court system. Apart from the fact that the government may well feel it lacks the financial resources to fund a major expansion of the system, there are serious questions as to whether in the longer term this would have any significant effect on delay. This is an area where incentive issues have to be carefully analysed. For example, if doubling the number of judges in the system reduced the average delay in the general court system from filing a suit to resolving it from, for example, two years to two months, one could confidently predict the direction (if not the magnitude) of the likely effects. First, a number of cases that are presently settled, because of the costs and inconvenience of delay, will now be litigated, thus increasing the supply of litigated cases. In other words, the price of litigation relative to settlement has been reduced. Secondly, the reduced delay will draw cases into either the settlement or litigation stream that previously were not subject to formal suit at all. Thus, I would expect (as I believe past experience has tended to demonstrate in many jurisdictions) that increasing the capacity of the system has a short-run impact on delay, but this usually evaporates either largely or completely over time. However, this is not a reason for not utilising existing resources as productively as possible, even though this means speedier resolution of cases, which will also draw new cases into the court system, perhaps again increasing delay over the long term, but arguably improving access in the sense that more litigants actually have their day in court.

While it appears to be contrary to trends towards consolidating formal judicial adjudication into a general court system, it seems to me possible that some savings in costs (and possibly delay) could be achieved by greater specialisation in adjudicative functions (for example, a specialised commercial law court or a specialised family law court). This in turn is likely to lead to a more specialised Bar. Greater specialisation in turn is likely to lead to a higher rate of pre-trial settlement, simply because a higher level of specialised expertise on the part of advocates and judges is likely to reduce the degree of uncertainty about adjudicated outcomes.

By way of further encouraging settlement there needs to be some investigation of possible reforms to existing cost rules so that if, for example, a settlement offer is rejected and the result at trial is less favourable to the plaintiff than the settlement offer, the plaintiff bears all the defendant's legal costs from the time of the offer onwards. Conversely, if the result at trial is more favourable to the plaintiff than

17 See K. Roach, 'Fundamental Reforms to Civil Litigation' in Ontario Law Reforms Commission, *Rethinking Civil Justice*, 381.

any settlement offer from the defendant, the defendant should bear the full legal costs of the plaintiff from the time of the offer onwards.

I think that there is also a case for ensuring that the private parties and their agents (lawyers) more fully confront the social costs of delay that they engender in the system, for example, by seeking last-minute adjournments. Where these delays cause down-time in the utilisation of judicial and support staff, the cost of these delays should be imposed on the parties (including the lawyers) causing them.

More generally, it seems to me that a much wider range of matters could be determined on written rather than oral evidence, and that a severely reduced role should be provided for the discovery process. Most other institutions in our society, for example, families, firms, public sector agencies, private sector non-profit agencies, and indeed state cabinets, make far more important decisions than are often made by courts, without the dramatic ritual of 'the full-court press' that is typically entailed in formal adversarial proceedings.[18]

On the demand side, with respect to cases that would remain in the traditional court system, a variety of expedients for reducing legal costs might be contemplated. These costs can only be reduced by:

1. reducing the cost of inputs;
2. direct subsidies (for example, legal aid); or
3. spreading costs over individuals or through time.

With respect to (1), I have already noted the potential for an enlarged role for paralegal personnel in legal representation. With respect to (2), more experimentation with alternative delivery models for legal aid (community clinics, neighbourhood staff offices, duty counsel) may permit fuller realisation of economies of scale and specialisation relative to exclusive or predominant provision by the private Bar.[19]

With respect to (3), class action procedures may realise economies of scale in litigation where individual members of a class have similar claims, thus reducing the costs entailed in individual prosecution of each claim, and/or enhancing access where many of these individual claims might not otherwise have been brought (again, in important respects, a form of wholesale justice). Various forms of legal insurance may also permit some spreading and reduction of costs with respect to litigation. Here, my impression is that most existing prepaid legal service plans focus on legal services other than litigation.[20] This strikes me as perverse in many ways. Small-scale legal costs such as residential conveyancing or will preparation are relatively predictable and contained, and not typically the kind of costs that people

18 See M. Trebilcock and L. Austin, 'The Limits of the Full Court Press: of Blood and Merger' (1998) 48 *U Toronto LJ* 1.
19 See Report of the Ontario Legal Aid Review, *A Blueprint for Publicly Provided Legal Services* (Ontario Government, 1997), vol. I, chap. 7.
20 See, e.g., C. J. Wydrzynski, 'The Development of Prepaid Legal Services in Canada' in Evans and Trebilcock (eds.), *Lawyers and the Consumer Interest*, chap. 7.

find it rational to insure against. On the other hand, with litigation costs, which may be both substantial and unpredictable, individual insurance presents a problem, because of adverse selection and moral hazard problems, reflecting a possible predisposition for litigation on the part of an individual who would seek insurance or a greater propensity to litigate once insured, rendering private insurers circumspect about providing such insurance. Somewhat analogous to the disability insurance market, group insurance is likely to work best in this context, with a significant element of co-insurance. Group insurance also offers prospects of cost-reducing agreements being negotiated with legal service providers, who are offered some assured volume of work in return for volume discounts. In order to maximise the scope for this form of legal insurance, many traditional legal constraints, such as medieval rules on maintenance, champerty and barratry, and rules prohibiting restrictions on choice of lawyers may have to be re-evaluated. Along the same lines, a carefully crafted contingent fee regime may permit costs and risks of litigation to be shifted from plaintiffs to their lawyers, thus reducing the cost deterrent, and at the same time increasing access.[21] There may also be a useful deterrent role for punitive damages (as well as providing an inducement to assume the risk of suit) in some classes of consumer claims where successful claimants would have their damages multiplied by a factor (the reciprocal of the enforcement shortfall) that reflects the fact that not all victims with meritorious claims (particularly if they are small) will initiate actions.[22] However, where there is no enforcement shortfall, expected punitive damages are likely to be reflected in product or service prices, and consumers would probably prefer not to pay additional 'premiums' to cover amounts in excess of their actual losses.[23]

Judicial policing of unfair contract terms

In a consumer transaction context, a particularly important role is likely to fall to the courts in policing unfair contract terms. Obviously, as a matter of law, consumers are likely to have a legally effective array of remedies for outright misstatements by sellers of goods or services, either under misleading or deceptive practices legislation or at common law. However, beyond liability for misstatements, consumers may often wish to assert claims that contracts that they have entered into are excessively one-sided, relying on statutory or common law

21 See M. Trebilcock, 'The Case for Contingent Fees: the Ontario Legal Profession Rethinks its Position' (1989) 15 *Canadian Business Law Journal* 360.
22 See B. Chapman and M. Trebilcock, 'Punitive Damages: Divergence in Search of a Rationale' (1989) 40 *Ala L Rev* 741.
23 See A. Schwartz, 'The Myth that Promisees Prefer Supra-Compensatory Remedies: an Analysis of Contracting for Damages Measures' (1990) 100 *Yale L J* 369; M. Polinsky and S. Shavell, 'Punitive Damages: an Economic Analysis' (1998) 111 *Harv L Rev* 869.

doctrines of unconscionability. In addressing such claims, it is important that the courts do more than simply hold their fingers to the wind and strike down or modify contracts or contractual provisions by way of visceral reaction, rather than by applying a clearly articulated analytical framework. I have argued previously that serious pitfalls are likely to befall courts in this context in adopting unreflective 'smell' tests.[24] Many years ago, in a famous article on unconscionability,[25] Professor Arthur Allen Leff, in his characteristically iconoclastic way, concluded that:

> it is hard to give up an emotionally satisfying incantation, and the way to keep the glow without the trouble of the meaning is continually to increase the abstraction level of the drafting and explaining language . . . It is easy to say nothing with words. Even if those words make one feel all warm inside, the result of sedulously preventing thought about them is likely to lead to more trouble than the draftsmen's cozy glow is worth, as a matter not only of statutory elegance but of effect in the world being regulated.

Thus, courts, counsel and commentators seeking to justify reliance on a residual doctrine of unconscionability in consumer transactions must respond to Leff's challenge that it is 'easy to say nothing with words'.

In my view, the doctrine of unconscionability can be given a reasonably coherent and predictable structure, that is to say, move it closer to clear rules and away from amorphous standards through a focus on four key forms of contracting failure that singly or in combination may yield unfair (and inefficient) consumer contracts: (1) information asymmetries as to the terms of the contract or the financial risks entailed; (2) material non-disclosure; (3) various forms of cognitive incapacity that, even assuming the availability of relevant information, prevent a consumer from rationally processing that information; and (4) various forms of coercion.

Standard form contracts

Information asymmetries with respect to the terms of a consumer contract are likely often to arise with respect to standard form contracts. Standard form contracts have suffered a bad press from both judicial and academic members of the

---

24 See M. Trebilcock, 'The Doctrine of Inequality of Bargaining Power: Post-Benthamite Economics in the House of Lords' (1976) 26 *U Toronto LJ* 359; M. Trebilcock, 'An Economic Approach to Unconscionability' in B. Reiter and J. Swan (eds.), *Studies in Contract Law* (Toronto: Butterworths, 1980), chap. 11; P. Burrows, 'Contract Discipline: in Search of Principles in the Control of Contracting Power' (1995) 2 *European Journal of Law and Economics* 127.

25 A. A. Leff, 'Unconscionability and the Code – the Emperor's New Clause' (1967) 115 *U Pa L Rev* 485, 558, 559.

legal fraternity over many years.[26] At least in a consumer setting, the hostility to standard form contracts is predicated on two principal propositions. First, it is said that the use of standard form contracts is a manifestation of monopoly. Secondly, it is pointed out that the use of standard form contracts is typically characterised by imperfect information on the part of some of the parties to them. In both cases, the legal implications are much the same: courts should be extremely cautious about enforcing such contracts. These two arguments require evaluation.

The monopoly argument essentially rests on the take it or leave it character of most standard form contractual offerings. However, as I have argued elsewhere,[27] the principal justification for standard form contracts is the dramatic reduction in transaction costs that they permit in many contexts. That they may be offered on a take it or leave it basis is as consistent with the benign transaction cost conservation rationale for them as it is with a monopoly or collusion rationale. Simply observing the fact of standard form contracts yields no meaningful implications as to the underlying structure of the market. Indeed, we observe them being used in many settings where manifestly the structure of the market is highly competitive, for example, dry-cleaning stores, hotel registration forms, insurance contracts and so on. Indeed, even in the absence of standard form contracts, we observe many goods being offered on a take it or leave it basis in some of the most competitive retail markets in the economy. For example, corner variety stores (mom and pop stores) typically offer their goods on a take it or leave it basis, presumably to avoid the transaction costs entailed in haggling over price or product offerings.

The imperfect information argument against standard form contracts is clearly more substantial. Almost necessarily implicit in the transaction cost justification for standard form contracts is the assumption that parties will often not read them, or if they do, will not wish to spend significant amounts of time attempting to renegotiate the terms. Thus, to hold parties bound to standard form contracts which they had entered into and which they had not read or understood does not rest comfortably with a theory of contractual obligation premised on individual autonomy and consent. Clearly, in many, perhaps most, cases, meaningful consent is absent. Thus, to justify contractual enforcement of these kinds of standard form contracts requires us to move outside the purely internal, non-instrumental, basis for contractual obligation as deriving from the will of the parties, and appeal instead to external benchmarks of fairness. In this respect, I have argued first that problems of unfairness, resulting from imperfect information, are not as severe as they

26 See, e.g., F. Kessler, 'Contracts of Adhesion: Some Thoughts about Freedom of Contract' (1943) 43 *Colum L Rev* 629; T. D. Rakoff, 'Contracts of Adhesion: an Essay in Reconstruction' (1983) 96 *Harv L Rev* 1173; D. Slawson, 'Standard Form Contracts and Democratic Control of Law Making Power' (1971) 84 *Harv L Rev* 529.

27 See Trebilcock, 'The Doctrine of Inequality' and 'An Economic Approach'; D. Dewees and M. Trebilcock, 'Judicial Control of Standard Form Contracts' in P. Burrows and C. G. Veljanovski (eds.), *An Economic Approach to Law* (London: Butterworths, 1981), 93.

might seem at first sight. To the extent that there is a margin of informed, sophisticated and aggressive consumers in any given market, who understand the terms of the standard form contracts on offer and who either negotiate over those terms or switch their business readily to competing suppliers offering more favourable terms, this margin of competitive shoppers may effectively discipline the entire market, so that infra-marginal (less well-informed, sophisticated or mobile) consumers can effectively free-ride on the discipline brought to the market by the marginal consumers[28] (although there is a potential collective action problem if every consumer attempts to free-ride on the efforts of others in effective monitoring of contract terms).[29] However, where suppliers are able either to term or performance discriminate between marginal and infra-marginal consumers, this generalised discipline will be undermined, and there is a clear risk that the infra-marginal consumers will be exploited on account of their imperfect information as to the contract terms. Here, I have proposed that courts, in evaluating the fairness of standard form contracts in particular cases, should investigate the question of whether a particular consumer seeking relief from the contract or some particular provision in it has received a significantly inferior deal, either in terms of the explicit terms of the contract or in terms of the performance provided under it, to that realised by marginal consumers in the same market with the economic as opposed to personal characteristics of consumers in these two classes held constant.[30] In other words, where a supplier has deliberately exploited the ignorance by a consumer of terms generally available in the market for like goods or services to economically similarly situated consumers to exact terms substantially inferior to these generally prevailing terms, this should be viewed as unconscionable. In markets that are so badly disrupted by imperfect information that there is no identifiable margin of informed consumers from which appropriate benchmarks can be derived, then judicial sniping in case-by-case litigation seems less appropriate than legislative or regulatory intervention of the kind that has occurred in many jurisdictions, for example, with respect to various classes of door-to-door sales.[31]

Another form in which information asymmetries may manifest themselves is with respect to differential appreciation of the financial risks entailed in a particular transaction. This problem has arisen in an acute and recurrent form in

<hr/>

28 See also A. Schwartz and L. Wilde, 'Intervening in Markets on the Basis of Imperfect Information: a Legal and Economic Analysis' (1979) 127 *U Pa L Rev* 630.

29 See A. Katz, 'The Strategic Structure of Offer and Acceptance: Game Theory and the Law of Contract Formation' (1990) 89 *Mich L Rev* 215, 287.

30 Buckley suggests that in some such cases, courts may be more efficient 'screeners' of contract terms than some 'consumers': F. H. Buckley, 'Three Theories of Substantive Fairness' (1990) 19 *Hofstra L Rev* 33. However, Craswell is more sceptical of the ability of the courts to select superior terms to those selected by sellers: R. Craswell, 'Property Rules and Liability Rules in Unconscionability and Related Doctrines' (1993) 60 *U Chi L Rev* 1.

31 In other words, the problem is one of market failure, not transaction-specific contracting failure: A. A. Leff, 'Contract as a Thing' (1970) 19 *Am U L Rev* 131 (1970); A. Schwartz, 'Unconscionability and Imperfect Information: a Research Agenda' (1991) 19 *Canadian Business Law Journal* 437.

many recent cases involving family financial transactions, typically taking the form of a mortgage by husband and wife of the jointly owned matrimonial home to a bank or other financial institution to secure the financial indebtedness of a small business run by the husband which is in financial difficulties.[32] Here issues arise as to the scope of the duty of the bank not only to explain the legal terms of the mortgage to the wife in contexts where she typically delegates decision-making responsibility in family financial matters to her husband, but also to inform her of the nature of the financial risks involved, and perhaps go further by either recommending or insisting that she obtain independent legal advice. It may well be the case that duties of this kind should extend beyond the family context to other financial transactions such as franchising contracts, complex consumer credit arrangements or complex investment instruments.

Material non-disclosure

Contract law has traditionally taken an ambivalent position towards material non-disclosure of facts by one party that if disclosed would substantially impair the value of the bargain to the other party, often adopting a maxim of *caveat emptor*. From an economic perspective, the challenge is to design legal rules that create socially optimal incentives for information generation, on the one hand, and information dissemination, on the other, recognising that there will often be a tension or trade-off between these two objectives.[33] However, in general it is the case that a requirement of seller disclosure of material facts is more likely to promote efficient information dissemination, without seriously undermining incentives for information generation, than a requirement of buyer disclosure of material facts, which may undermine incentives to invest in information generation relating to privately and socially undervalued assets in the first place. Hence, in a consumer protection context, courts would often be warranted in treating seller non-disclosure of material facts as legally akin to material misrepresentation.

Cognitive incapacity

Under this category, I include cases where there has been no misrepresentation of information by one contracting party to the other and no non-disclosure of material facts, but rather where the two parties, while sharing equal access to the

---

32 See M. Trebilcock and S. Elliott, 'The Scope and Limits of Legal Paternalism: Altruism and Coercion in Family Financial Arrangements' in P. Benson (ed.), *The Theory of Contract Law* (Cambridge: Cambridge University Press, 2001), chap. 3.
33 See A. Duggan, M. Bryan and F. Hanks, *Contractual Non-Disclosure: an Applied Study in Modern Contract Theory* (Melbourne: Longman Professional, 1994); M. Trebilcock, *The Limits of Freedom of Contract* (Cambridge, Mass.: Harvard University Press, 1993), 106–18.

relevant body of information about the contract subject matter, have sharply differential capacities to evaluate the implications of that information for their respective welfare. Eisenberg[34] cites two sub-classes of case, both of which he argues should be addressed by a modern doctrine of unconscionability. The first sub-class of case he characterises as 'transactional incapacity'. The paradigm case he envisages is one where A knows or has reason to know of B's inability to deal with a given complex transaction, because of lack of aptitude, experience, or judgmental ability to make a deliberative and well-informed judgment concerning the desirability of entering into the transaction, and exploits that incapacity by inducing B to make a bargain that a person who had the capacity to deal with the transaction probably would not make. He cites as an example a very complex real estate proposal put by a commercial developer to an ageing testamentary beneficiary of a commercial building. He also cites the well-known judgment of Lord Denning of the English Court of Appeal in *Lloyds Bank Ltd* v. *Bundy*,[35] where an elderly farmer was induced by his son's bank to sign a guarantee of his son's indebtedness to the bank in circumstances where it was highly unlikely that the farmer was able to evaluate prudentially all the implications of the transaction. The other sub-class of case that Eisenberg identifies is what he calls 'unfair persuasion'. By this he means the use of bargaining methods that seriously impair the free and competent exercise of judgment and produce a state of acquiescence that the promisee knows or should know is likely to be highly transitory. Examples of such situations that he cites are a creditor obtaining a promise from a bereaved and distraught widow to pay debts of her husband's business shortly after his death, or a door-to-door salesman employing importuning and intrusive sales tactics.

I believe that both of Eisenberg's sub-classes of cognitive deficiencies fall comfortably within the concerns that in order for contractual promises to be binding, they should in general arise out of the autonomous consent of the parties and reflect base-line conditions of voluntariness and information. Thus, they seem entirely appropriate candidates for a doctrine of unconscionability.

Coercion/situational monopoly[36]

Situations sometimes arise where one party to a transaction takes advantage of a transitory situational monopoly vis-à-vis the other party of the transaction to extract extortionate terms (for example, in rescue-type situations), or alternatively more actively coerces the other party through physical, psychological or financial threats or intimidation into entering into a transaction that the latter would not voluntarily enter into (as in some of the family financial transaction

34 M. A. Eisenberg, 'The Bargain Principle and its Limits' (1982) 95 *Harv L Rev* 741.
35 [1975] 1 QB 326 (CA).   36 See Trebilcock, *The Limits of Freedom of Contract*, chap. 4.

cases referred to above). In some cases, all four forms of contracting failure may be present to a greater or lesser extent (again, as exemplified in some of the family financial transaction cases).

Conclusion

Consumer protection policy at the beginning of the new millennium is a much messier and more complex affair than those of us who were active in the policy-making process in this area in the 1960s and 1970s conceived it to be, in part because of the rapidity of technological change, deregulation of hitherto monopolised industries, and globalisation of markets, and in part because of increasing sophistication in economic theories that evaluate market structure, conduct and performance. These trends pose particular challenges for domestic and international competition policy and trade policy, in ensuring that consumers have available to them, at least potentially, a competitively effective array of product and service choices. They also pose formidable challenges for the distinctive domain of consumer protection policy, which should focus on informational impediments to the exercise by consumers of informed choices amongst the potentially available array of options open to them.[37]

In this essay, I have sketched how an information-based approach to consumer protection policy might orient thinking about policy choices in the contemporary consumer protection context. I then sought to situate the intractable problem of civil redress for typically small-scale consumer grievances within this broader panoply of public policy choices. For major health and safety concerns, it is difficult to conceive of policy choices that do not assign a central role to some form of direct government regulation, although striking the right balance between preemptive regulation that constrains consumer choices and regulation that attempts to ensure better informed choices is a difficult challenge. With respect to economic losses from transactions that entail a divergence between reasonable or well-settled consumer expectations and realisations, while again there is likely to be some (but probably a more limited) role for pre-emptive regulation that constrains consumer choices and also a role for information-oriented policies designed to improve the quality of consumer choices, civil redress mechanisms for resolving consumer grievances are likely to play a more significant role. In this respect, we face the daunting challenge of designing dispute settlement processes for what are commonly relatively small economic claims and for which the formal court system is often ill-adapted to respond effectively. However, for many citizens these are the only kinds of claims for which they are likely to seek redress from the legal system,

---

37 See N. W. Averitt and R. H. Lande, 'Consumer Sovereignty: a Unified Theory of Antitrust and Consumer Protection Law' (1997) 65 *Antitrust LJ* 713.

so that for the legal system to take the view, either wittingly or unwittingly, that because the claims are small they are trivial or unimportant, risks undermining the confidence of the general body of citizenry in the accessibility, even-handedness and responsiveness of the legal system. Thus, it is likely to be socially costly, in the long run, to leave this challenge unaddressed, even if addressing it requires imaginative consideration of unconventional options that may be unsettling to traditional habits of legal thought and practice. Finally, I have attempted to define a role for judicial policing of contractual unfairness in a consumer context by identifying four forms of contracting failure that either singly or in combination should inform the invocation and application of a residual doctrine of unconscionability.

Part II
Issues in contract and tort

5 Standard form contracts in Europe and North America: one hundred years of unfair terms?

LEONE NIGLIA

Gli astronomi di Perinzia si trovano di fronte ad una difficile scelta: o ammettere che tutti i loro calcoli sono sbagliati e le loro cifre non riescono a descrivere il cielo. O rivelare che l'ordine degli dei è proprio quello che si rispecchia nella città dei mostri.[1]

Introduction

For slightly more than a hundred years scholars have religiously held that standard form contracts contain terms that are unquestionably unfair as they shift upon customers as many as possible of the risks involved in the transactions, and have predicated that compulsory terms that internalise the risks on the drafter should be imposed.[2] This belief has proved contagious: legislators have enacted laws that ostracise unfair terms; judges and administrative agencies have successfully enforced such laws; comparative law scholars have considered the better law the one that prohibits such unfair terms, and have criticised legal systems where prohibitions of this kind have not existed. The purpose of this essay is to show that the traditional belief can no longer be accepted without question. A two-step argument suggests this. First, each decision on fairness *or* unfairness of a standardised term is a proxy for the decision-maker's choice of how to allocate the costs that society ought to bear in the face of the materialisation of the contractual risk at stake. Secondly, a law that ostracises certain terms for being unquestionably unfair will make society bear unnecessary costs at any time when a decision of fairness would minimise societal costs.

I am grateful to Roger Brownsword for helpful comments. Any errors remain, nevertheless, my own.

1 I. Calvino, *Le città invisibili* (Milan: Mondadori, 1983), 144, 145. My own reading of the passage is in the Conclusion on p. 127.
2 The first scholar who drew attention to the unfairness of standardised terms was the Frenchman R. Saleilles in passages of *Essai d'une théorie générale de l'obligation* (Paris: Librairie Cotillon, 1890); and *De la déclaration de volonté. Contribution à l'étude de l'acte juridique dans le code allemand (Art. 116 à 144)* (1st edn, Paris, 1901: 2nd edn, Paris, 1929).

Below are three main sections. The sections on the old paradigm (see pp. 103–121) consider a set of arguments that have been particularly influential in devising the essentials[3] of the established belief that certain standardised terms are unquestionably unfair.[4] The literature is large, but, at the risk of oversimplification, I suggest that one should consider two principal theories on standard form contracts, the first being dominant until the 1980s, whilst the second has developed since then. The first was held mainly by scholars interested in socio-legal analysis, the second by scholars trained in law and economics. The first holds that standard form contracts enable firms to exercise unjust power over customers. For this unjust power there are two explanations. One view suggests that the power results from the monopolistic position of firms in the market, whilst another suggests that it is purely institutional, that is, that the organisational power of firms leads them to adopt prejudicial standard form terms. The argument proceeds that it is this unjust power, be it monopolistic or organisational, that gives rise to standard form terms. Prejudicial terms are those that allocate risks to customers, often by altering their statutory rights. The rhetoric is one of subjection of customers to drafters' terms; standard form terms prejudicial to customers should be struck down so as to overcome such subjection. By contrast, law and economics theories maintain that firms are not necessarily exercising unjust power when they use standard form terms. To understand whether or not standard form terms are unfair, one must undertake an analysis based on the transaction costs involved in each bargain. The rhetoric is one of choice; standard form terms are prejudicial only if the reason they do not reflect the parties' preferences is high transaction costs. This view suggests, in line with the unfairness thesis cultivated by socio-legal thinking, that, because of high transaction costs, terms prejudicial to customers should be struck down, and that compulsory terms that internalise contractual risks on the drafter should be imposed. The section on the new paradigm (see pp. 121–127) considers that intellectual findings have been subservient to the unfairness belief, and for this reason have failed to show that a law conforming to that belief is unduly costly for society.

---

3 These sections are concerned with a limited aspect of the complex history of how the belief of unfairness began, as the sole purpose of this essay is selectively to identify some theoretical arguments that have been particularly influential in devising that belief, rather than to trace more generally further theoretical, dogmatic and historico-philosophical aspects, an issue that falls outside the reach of this essay.

4 By standardised terms I mean terms included in standard form documents formulated in advance by one party, typically the firm, accepted without modification by customers and shifting onto them as many as possible of the risks involved in the transaction. For this conventional definition, see K. Zweigert and H. Kötz (T. Weir trans.), *An Introduction to Comparative Law* (3rd edn, Oxford: Clarendon Press, 1998), 333; T. D. Rakoff, 'Contracts of Adhesion: an Essay in Reconstruction' (1983) 96 *Harv L Rev* 1174, 1177. In the essay standard form contracts (or terms), mass contracts (or terms) and contracts of adhesion are equivalent concepts, as are customer, adherent and client, and drafter and seller.

The old paradigm I. Sociology of law: standard form contracts and the power of the firm

The thrust of this section is to consider the findings of legal-sociological research on standard form contracting, which reveal the following central tenets: that standard form contracts are the product of the firm's questionable exercise of power; that standardised terms prejudicial to customers are unquestionably unfair; and that compulsory terms that place contractual risks on the drafter should be imposed.[5] Socio-legal thought has held to this in the context of sophisticated analyses that conceive of standard form contracts in relation to the enlargement of the firm under contemporary conditions of capitalist development. After pointing to the standardisation of contracts, scholars have explained how this led to the subjection of adherents, and finally have indicated how to overcome this subjection.

Origins of standardised contractual terms

Traditionally, contracts of adhesion are seen as the legal counterpart of the mass production and mass distribution characteristic of the free enterprise system. It is submitted that the latter 'made a new type of contract inevitable: the standardized mass contract',[6] for in this view 'the innate trend of competitive capitalism towards monopoly'[7] led to a form of authoritarian legislation as standard form contracts were 'effective instruments in the hands of powerful industrial and commercial overlords enabling them to impose a new feudal order of their own making upon a vast host of vassals'.[8]

---

5 The literature I refer to is essentially North American, but it illustrates the sorts of arguments fashionable in essays of European origin. The relationship between the two sets of developments is complex and as yet mysterious. F. Kessler's article of 1943 ('Contracts of Adhesion: Some Thoughts about Freedom of Contract' (1943) 43 *Colum L Rev* 629), a major North American essay, demonstrates how this authoritative writer was clearly indebted to his European legal–cultural background, as shown by his citation of the seminal 1936 work of Ludwig Raiser (*Das Recht der allgemeinen Geschäftsbedingungen* (Bad Homburg v.d.H.: Gentner, 1936 and 1961)), where the narrative of unfairness had been thoroughly conjured up. The belief of unfairness was indeed no less fashionable in Europe. For example, courts of various European countries were to state their belief in a relationship between monopoly power and the standardising of contract in the coming decades: this emerges in the wording of the *Reichsgericht* ('firms with a virtual monopoly of an essential trade exploit the general need for their services in order to gain for themselves advantageous terms incompatible with the law and in restraint of trade': RGZ 103, 82, 83 (quoted in Zweigert and Kötz, *Introduction to Comparative Law*, 336)). In England, see the famous statement by Lord Diplock in *A. Schroeder Music Publishing Co Ltd* v. *Macaulay* [1974] 1 WLR 1308, 1316, that standard form documents are the result of 'the concentration of particular kinds of business in relatively few hands'. Scholars of yesterday and of today show no less dedication: e.g., Saleilles, *Essai d'une théorie générale* and *De la déclaration de volonté*; Raiser, *Das Recht*; O. Kahn-Freund in the Introduction to K. Renner, *The Institutions of Private Law and their Social Functions* (London: Routledge, 1976), 38 ff.
6 Kessler, 'Contracts of Adhesion', 631.   7 *Ibid.*, 640.   8 *Ibid.*

Recently, standard form contracting has been conceived of more pragmatically as accommodating the institutional practices of modern business organisations,[9] as a legal manifestation of that history. The firm is seen as a complex organisation, whose functioning is embedded in the history of the development of free-market economic and social systems as large-scale markets are formed. In this view, contracts of adhesion are not the result of monopolistic power, but should be seen as intimately linked to the specific organisational form in which mass production and distribution most typically occur in our society.[10] Specifically, it is submitted that in the past century and a half, capitalist development has brought about a profound change in the structure of the firm. This change stemmed from the need to enlarge the enterprise and resulted in the growth of the large-scale enterprise.[11] The enlargement of the firm took place by the addition of new 'units' to the original ones. This was a process of backward and forward vertical integration.[12] Backward integration was a strategy meant to ensure that an adequate supply of necessary inputs would be available at a reasonable price; forward integration consisted of a strategy to ensure that mass production would indeed be transformed into mass sales.[13] Scholars have pondered on both the characteristics of the process of enlargement of the firm and its consequences upon contract theory and practice. Contract was looked at as a crucial part of this complex process, and two emergent needs of the enterprise have been identified:[14] first, the need to reduce serial transaction costs; and, secondly, the need to accommodate certain rigidities in internal organisation. The transaction costs to be avoided relate to: (1) information/negotiation on, and drafting of, contracts pertaining to each link in the chain of production and distribution; (2) uncertainties deriving from delays in, or interruptions of the chain of, production and distribution due to non-performances; (3) costs at the very end of the chain when customers buy the goods, including the information/negotiation/drafting costs of the contract between the firm and the customer; and, finally, (4) the costs of juridical risks avoidable if the firm transfers them to customers, by excluding liabilities and providing for short time limits for claims as well as using a range of well-known similar terms. The

---

9 See generally Rakoff, 'Contracts of Adhesion'.
10 Rakoff, 'Contracts of Adhesion', 1229.
11 *Ibid.*, 1220 ff. Prior to Rakoff's essay, Kessler, 'Contracts of Adhesion', 631, had already pointed to the structural changes of firms in relation to standard form contracts, and specifically to the growth of the large-scale enterprise. Kessler himself outlined the larger historical, social and economic context at the turn of the century in which the development of the enterprise took place: F. Kessler, *Freiheit unter Zwang im nordamerikanischen Vertragsrecht, in Festschrift für Martin Wolff* (Tübingen: Mohr/Siebeck, 1952), 68 ff.
12 A. D. Chandler, *Scale and Scope: the Dynamics of Industrial Capitalism* (Cambridge, Mass.: Belknap Press, 1990), 21 ff.
13 W. Lazonick, *Business Organisation and the Myth of the Market Economy* (Cambridge: Cambridge University Press, 1991), 193, commenting on Chandler's work.
14 I borrow this enumeration from Rakoff, 'Contracts of Adhesion', 1220 ff.

second set of enterprise needs includes the need to improve the efficiency of the firm by rendering its structure more operational, and solidifying the internal power structure. Efficiency is improved by easing co-ordination among departments, optimal use of managerial/legal talent and better internal control of salesmen.[15] An organisation's internal power structure needs to be solidified because discretion is power: the more discretion is given to subordinates, the more status and reward they acquire, so that, to maintain internal hierarchy, the routinisation of transactions through the use of standard forms is necessary since this reserves discretion to the positions further up the organisational hierarchy.[16]

Having argued thus, it is then submitted that the process of commercial enlargement and the consequent 'replacement of market transactions by managerial co-ordination'[17] involved the disappearance of the nineteenth-century practice of free contracting and the parallel creation of the standardised contract, the latter being the result of terms that accommodate the various needs described. These terms were then aggregated in different document forms depending on the relationships they were supposed to govern, i.e., between internal operative units, or between such units and the external market. As a consequence, standardised forms refer to terms governing firms' external relationship with the market (i.e., with customers). These terms serve the aim of rationalising the needs of firms in their external relationships. Since these terms are intrinsically unfavourable to the customer, there is an accumulation of forms which impose upon the adherent a large number of risks.[18] This process on the part of the modern firm resulted in terms both non-negotiable and detrimental to the adherents, because convenient to the drafters.[19] Last, but not least, scholars have argued that what makes standard terms harsher is that they are drafted by lawyers, whose professional ethos makes them eager to protect their clients.[20] This augments the firm's rigidity, and contributes considerably to the ongoing process of the standardisation of prejudicial contractual terms.

---

15 *Ibid.*, 1222–3.   16 *Ibid.*, 1223.   17 *Ibid.*, 1220.
18 It is a commonplace in the literature to explain unfair terms as those terms through which drafters shift contractual risks onto customers: e.g., D. Kennedy, 'Distributive and Paternalist Motives in Contract and Tort Law, with Special Reference to Compulsory Terms and Unequal Bargaining Power' (1982) 41 *Mod L Rev* 650; and the terms contained in the lists of the German Act on General Conditions of Business 1976, and in the EC Directive on unfair terms in consumer contracts April 1993: Council Directive 93/13/EEC of 5 April 1993, in OJ L95, 21 April 1993, p. 29. The distinction between economical and juridical risks is also commonplace: Kessler, 'Contracts of Adhesion', 631.
19 In the context of socio-legal analyses, non-negotiability arises from the complex institutional framework of relationships between units, and between units and customers, not simply from an analysis of transaction costs in terms of efficiency. For a note on this theoretical distinction, see Y. Ramstad, 'Transaction' in M. H. Hodgson, W. J. Samuels and M. R. Tool (eds.), *The Elgar Companion to Institutional and Evolutionary Economics* (Brookfield, Vt.: Edward Elgar, 1994), 334. The same argument applies to the finding of prejudicially onerous terms.
20 See Rakoff, 'Contracts of Adhesion', 1222.

Subjection

Scholars have then considered the way customers are affected by the practice of contracting *en masse*. Having considered the convenience to the firm of drafting standard form terms – mass contracting can shift specific risks on to customers, leading to their subjection to a web of onerous terms which they must confront once a specific risk concretises – the characterisation of the customer's situation in terms of subjection was a commonplace in this overall sociological perspective. Authoritative writers from diverse legal systems[21] emphasised this. Kessler, an authoritative German émigré, took the point as crucial. As he put it in his famous narrative:[22]

> The weaker party ... is frequently not in a position to shop around for better terms, either because the author of the standard contract has a monopoly ... or because all competitors use the same clauses. This causes a subjection more or less voluntary to terms dictated by the stronger party, terms whose consequences are only understood in a vague way, if at all.

In other words, contracting in this way excludes any bargaining process. Consistent with this view is the later claim that mass contracting is an impersonal phenomenon which sacrifices any bargaining process: contract becomes a thing.[23]

This overall explanation has remained in vogue for most of *Novecento*. Socio-legal scholarship of the early 1980s agreed on the subjection point, but criticised the monopolistic view and re-explained it in terms of institutional *qua* organisational domination. It has been submitted that the individual's failure to read or understand is simply the most visible symbol of a pervasive and complex institutional practice,[24] and that the customer is left only with the ability to choose the organisation by which he will be dominated.[25] On one crucial point, the old and the most recent views converge: whether standard form contracts are conceived of as a form of power of the firm in the market, according to the monopolistic view, or as a form

21 Notably, in France, Saleilles, *Essai d'une théorie générale* and *De la déclaration de volonté*; in Germany, Raiser, *Das Recht*, 248; in England, Kahn-Freund in the Introduction to Renner, *The Institutions of Private Law*.
22 Kessler, 'Contracts of Adhesion', 632. Raiser, *ibid.*, cited in Kessler's article of 1943, had already conjured up the idea of the economic and intellectual inferiority of the one party to the other, generally referred to as the 'strong bargaining power' of the firm as against the 'weakness' of customers/adherents.
23 See A. A. Leff, 'Contract as Thing' (1970) 19 *Am U L Rev* 131.
24 Rakoff, 'Contracts of Adhesion', 1228.
25 *Ibid.*, 1229. For studies that map institutional rigidities under competitive conditions, see, e.g., H. Beale, 'Legislative Control of Unfairness: the Directive on Unfair Terms in Consumer Contracts' in J. Beatson and D. Friedman (eds.), *Good Faith and Fault in Contract Law* (Oxford: Clarendon Press, 1995), 231; G. L. Priest, 'A Theory of the Consumer Product Warranty' (1981) 90 *Yale LJ* 1297. In the first half of the past century, K. N. Llewellyn, 'What Price Contract? An Essay in Perspective' (1931) 40 *Yale LJ* 704, 734, had already highlighted the accumulation of seller-protective clauses in highly competitive markets such as instalment sales, residential leases, investments and commercial banking.

of power of the firm due to institutional *qua* organisational factors, as argued by later socio-legal scholarship, they generate and allocate power in either case, and, in so far as they lead to subjection, they should concern us.[26]

Overcoming subjection: the case for compulsory terms

The most respected proposition of socio-legal scholars has been to suggest the imposition of compulsory terms: because customers are victimised, terms that are unfair on the customer should be replaced by terms that internalise risks on the drafter. A powerful legal–rhetorical tool to suggest this has been the argument that the customer's legitimate expectations ought to be protected: the subjection of customers is to be overcome by identifying and respecting their expectations. This requires an assessment on a case-by-case basis of the situations in which customers' expectations are endangered. In the words of one authoritative scholar:[27] 'In dealing with standardized contracts courts have to determine what the weaker contracting party could legitimately expect . . . and to what extent the stronger party disappointed reasonable expectations based on the typical life situation.'

This suggestion is aimed at reversing the abuse of power to which customers are seen to be subject. For standard form terms should be supported, given that they accommodate the modern conditions of transacting in the market, but such support should be limited by giving weight to customers' expectations; customers' expectations are to be respected by rules that both support the market and are socially acceptable. The bottom line of this 'rule of legitimate expectations' is to combat unfairness in typical life situations in which customers' expectations are endangered.[28] Much depends on what customers would have expected in each

---

26 Rakoff, 'Contracts of Adhesion'. From this vantage point, Rakoff's observation restates a viewpoint frequently found in socio-legal analysis: see K. Llewellyn, 'Book Review' (1939) 52 *Harv L Rev* 700, 701–2, commenting on O. Prausnitz, *The Standardization of Commercial Contracts in English and Continental Law* (London: Sweet & Maxwell, 1937).

27 Kessler, 'Contracts of Adhesion', 637.

28 There was a gradual development of the idea of legitimate or reasonable expectations in North American legal realist literature, an idea initially referred to by Llewellyn, 'Book Review', and attributed to moral grounds by F. Kessler and E. Fine, 'Culpa in Contrahendo, Bargaining in Good Faith, and Freedom of Contract: a Comparative Study' (1964) 77 *Harv L Rev* 401. It was then reconstructed as both a market policy and a customer protective instrument in the seminal work of S. Macaulay, 'Private Legislation and the Duty to Read Business Run by IBM Machine, The Law of Contracts and Credit Cards' (1966) 19 *Vand L Rev* 1051, which explains its parallel functions of supporting the market and of protecting customers. The concept was to become commonplace in North America: Leff, 'Contract as Thing'; Macaulay above; K. S. Abraham, 'Judge-Made Law and Judge-Made Insurance: Honoring the Reasonable Expectations of the Insured' (1981) 67 *Vand L Rev* 1151; Rakoff, 'Contracts of Adhesion'; Kennedy, 'Distributive and Paternalist Motives'; W. D. Slawson, 'The New Meaning of Contract: the Transformation of Contract Law by Standard Forms' (1984) 46 *U Pitt L Rev* 21; R. Craswell, 'Property Rules and Liability Rules in Unconscionability and Related Doctrines' (1993) 60 *U Chi L Rev* 1, 27 ff.; R. Craswell and A. Schwartz,

particular situation; they are protected by a legal intervention which modifies unfair contractual terms so as to satisfy those expectations.[29] More pragmatically, scholars consider a term to be prejudicial to customers whenever it alters statutory provisions,[30] for this may well amount to an unfair imposition of risks on customers, and as a result there should be a presumption that such standard form terms are unfair.[31] According to socio-legal scholars, unfair terms so identified shall represent the response of the law to the power relationships inherent in the development of the enterprise, challenging them by placing on firms more and more of the identified contractual risks, the attempted alteration of the prior legal rights of the customer being in itself sufficient evidence of the unfairness of the use of economic power.

The old paradigm II. Law and economics: standard form contracts and the market

Preliminary observations

This section addresses the approach to standardised terms adopted by those trained in law and economics.[32] It attempts to reconstruct the literature

Foundations of Contract Law (Oxford: Oxford University Press, 1994), 303 ff. (with an account of the literature), 337–8 (where it is said that categories of adhesion in contract and expectations overlap). In Europe, see, e.g., H.W. Micklitz, 'Ein einheitliches Kaufrecht für Verbraucher in der EG?' [1997] *EuZW* 229, 237; J. Steyn, 'Contract Law: Fulfilling the Reasonable Expectations of Honest Men' (1997) 113 *Law Quarterly Review* 433. Reference to legitimate/reasonable expectations can also be found in the context of law and economics studies on the law of contract in general: Craswell and Schwartz, *Foundations of Contract Law*, 304. I am particularly thankful to Duncan Kennedy for discussions on this point at Harvard Law School.

29 See Kessler, 'Contracts of Adhesion', 638.
30 Rakoff, 'Contracts of Adhesion', 1246.
31 *Ibid.*, 1246, 1258. In the narrative I simplify a more complex point. For, although Rakoff emphasises that one finds the principles for governing standard form terms in the 'background law', this stand is nonetheless flawed in the very context of the realist tradition which outlined the relative strength of any background law. This Rakoff himself recognises: 'in fashioning the applicable background rule, the court should of course consider what the applicant might reasonably expect; but just as relevant is the court's own sense of what is fair' (*ibid.*, 1269), and it is more evident in Rakoff's later work (T. Rakoff, 'Implied Terms: of "Default Rules" and "Situation Sense"' in J. Beatson and D. Friedmann (eds.), *Good Faith and Fault in Contract Law* (Oxford: Clarendon Press, 1995), 191 where he downplays the role of the background law. In light of this, Rakoff's reference to the background law is to be interpreted as an attempt to make the rule of expectations more certain. This also emerged from a private conversation with Todd Rakoff at Harvard Law School.
32 The literature is mainly of North American origin, but over the years use of economico-legal arguments in support of the belief of unfairness has become trite in European writings, as is shown by books and articles of the last decade: e.g., M. Adams, 'Ökonomische Begrundung des AGB-Gesetzes. Verträge bei asymmetrischer Information' in [1989] *Der Betriebs Berater* 781 ff.; J. Beimowski, *Zur ökonomischen Analyse allgemeiner Geschäftsbedingungen* (Munich: VVF, 1989);

in order to give a picture, first, of the various theories so far proposed, and, secondly, of the conventional criticisms made of them, singling out one of them for its efficiency-orientated credibility, the bulk of scholars having opted for the theory that compulsory terms ought to be imposed.[33] Because of high transaction costs, this prevailing view suggests – in line with the beliefs cultivated by socio-legal thinking – that it is not workable for the parties freely to agree on contractual terms, and that terms prejudicial to customers are therefore unquestionably unfair for not reflecting the parties' preferences and that compulsory terms favourable to customers should be imposed.

The underlying assumption of the economico-legal literature is that of the rational utility-maximising contractor, and its focus is on a form of legal analysis based on market competitiveness. The theorists with whom I will deal argue in terms of market competitiveness because of their normative commitments, it being their firm belief that rules should aim to fulfil the utilitarian goal of achieving the greatest net balance of satisfaction among individuals in a given society,[34] taking special account of the wealth-maximising agent/contractor. This leads such commentators to focus their analysis on the market and take the search for market competitiveness as their central analytical theme: the degree of *unfairness* of contractual terms depends upon the degree of competition within the market, and the latter in turn depends on the amount of information held by market actors during the making of the contract. In other words, the concern here is to ensure that market processes flow according to competitiveness, any distortion of which evidences a form of untenable market power which should be tamed.[35]

We are some distance from the exclusive concern to fight against the power of the firm which is characteristic of the socio-legal model. This shift in understanding sharply distinguishes law and economics analysis from the socio-legal model. The fundamental difference can be seen from the viewpoint of the firm or from that of the customer. The firm is now conceived of on the basis of the market, as an organisational structure that functions not according to institutional rigidities but in response to market processes, the decisions of the firm depending only on the degree

R. Pardolesi, 'Clausole abusive (nei contratti dei consumatori): una direttiva abusata?' (1994) 5 *Foro Italiano* 139; H.-B. Schäfer and C. Ott, *Lehrbuch der ökonomischen Analyse des Zivilrechts* (Berlin: Springer, 1995); H. Collins, 'Good Faith in European Contract Law' (1994) 14 *Oxford Journal of Legal Studies* 229; H. Kötz, 'The EC Directive on Unfair Terms in Consumer Contracts from an Economic and Comparative Perspective', Papers dedicated to Ole Lando (Copenhagen: Gadjura, 1997).

33 In 1981, P. Burrows and C. G. Veljanovski (eds.), *The Economic Approach to Law* (London: Butterworths, 1981), 93, noted that standard terms had suffered a bad press, but there has been much writing since then, as the account in the text demonstrates.

34 For a classical description of this philosophical assumption, see J. Rawls, *A Theory of Justice* (Oxford: Clarendon Press, 1972), 22 (and further references).

35 Here it is appropriate to refer to the category of market power as law and economics scholars commonly do, which shows how a conceptualisation that began life in the context of socio-legal analysis could become central to theoretical analysis of a different kind.

of transaction costs involved, and the manager operating inside or outside the firm depending on the costs implications of his or her options.[36] The second difference relates to the individual setting, by which I mean the contractual relationship between the adherent and the drafter. The role accorded to the individual contractual setting in the two models is quite distinct. The socio-legal model emphasises the situational fact of subjection and the challenge to contractual freedom within each individual setting, which constitute the preconditions for analysis and substantiate its thrust.[37] By contrast, the law and economics perspective abandons the vocabulary of subjection and assumes that the characteristic feature of the situation is lack of information on the part of the individual customer. A further difference ensues, for most economic theories even downplay the individual setting and focus on factors such as a number of marginal sophisticated customers rather than on the subjection of the customer in the context of the individual contractual relationship. They concentrate on the information supposedly available to the typical 'rational' customer rather than the more particular choices open to the concrete individual.[38] It is thought that focusing on the overall conditions of market competitiveness will result in the optimal combination of price and non-price terms and so make the parties within each individual contractual transaction better off.

One point deserves emphasis. Writers on law and economics agree in refusing to contemplate the lack of credibility of standard form contracting as such, admitting, at most, that the practice may be challenged by the imposition of compulsory terms. In the vocabulary of law and economics, this means that adhesion contracts cannot be inherently challenged as inefficient.[39] The following discussion of the efficiency of unfair terms must be seen in this light.

Protecting customers through compulsory terms

Efficiency-oriented theories

Efficiency-oriented theories start from the assumption that information/transaction costs play a decisive role in every putatively efficient regulation of standardised terms. Their effect is ascertained by considering what the scenario would be if no high information/transaction costs existed. Thus, law and economics writers project classical contract law into an ideal world characterised by perfect competition

---

36 See the seminal article by R. Coase, 'The Nature of the Firm' (1937) 4 *Economica* 386.

37 V. P. Goldberg (ed.), *Readings in the Economics of Contract Law* (Cambridge: Cambridge University Press, 1989), 167.

38 M. J. Trebilcock and D. N. Dewees, 'Judicial Control of Standard Form Contracts' in Burrows and Veljanovski, *The Economic Approach to Law*, 114–15.

39 See Craswell, 'Property Rules', 51 (and further references). This point is substantiated by scholars trained in law and sociology: e.g., Rakoff, 'Contracts of Adhesion', 1221 (indexing the advantages that stem from the use of standard form contracts).

and an absence of transaction costs.[40] The main idea is that in such a competitive and frictionless world both initial entitlements and any legal modification would be irrelevant – free bargaining amongst contractors would be sufficient to facilitate the optimal/superior allocation of resources.[41] Such a bargaining process would lead to reasonable clauses at the point where a more favourable obligation would make the buyers' gains exceed the seller's losses. Reasonableness is said to be achieved by comparing the gains and losses of buyer and seller on the basis of their willingness to pay.[42] On this view, any legislative reregulatory intervention is meaningless, and therefore undesirable.

Given this starting point, the real world of mass contracting becomes a problem for law and economics literature, since the fact that standard form terms commonly entail a fixed set of information costs raises the question of how parties deal with these costs. Writers have elaborated on the issue by considering the influence of the transaction costs involved in obtaining information and, as we shall see, the different theories on standardised terms turn on the various ways in which such an information requirement has been tackled. Here two main strands of thought, which tend to reconstruct the problem and offer solutions to it, may be identified: the deregulatory thesis, which furthers the idea of refraining from any attempt to reregulate such contracts; and a reregulatory position, which envisages different forms of reregulatory intervention. I begin with the former, in a section that aims to show the ultimate scholarly view: that the properly efficient solution is to impose compulsory terms in place of unfair contractual terms.

A deregulatory view

The deregulatory strategy is to decline to regulate standard form terms, though to call it deregulatory is perhaps to overstate it, since for those who propose this strategy it entails no more than abstention from any specific legislation/regulation on unfair terms. This is nonetheless a controversial position. A truly deregulatory policy is inconceivable in the realm of private law, whose complexity always leaves room for regulatory choices.[43] At the most, one has a choice between possible regulatory alternatives. I accordingly use the term 'deregulatory' to denote the minimal option of abstention from any specific legislative intervention on unfair terms that would aim to reregulate contractual practices by dictating a particular governing rule. This strategy focuses on information costs that customers can afford. It is therefore a bargaining solution, since it relies on the functioning of market

---

40 Leaving aside infancy and insanity, which undermine all contracts including standard form contracts.

41 See, e.g., L. Kaplow and S. Shavell, 'Do Liability Rules Facilitate Bargaining? A Reply to Ayres and Talley' (1995) 105 *Yale L J* 221; R. Coase, 'The Problem of Social Cost' (1960) 3 *J L & Econ* 1.

42 See Craswell, 'Property Rules', 21.

43 See D. Kennedy and F. Michelman, 'Are Property and Contract Efficient?' (1980) 8 *Hofstra L Rev* 711.

mechanisms, and is said to apply both when the market is competitive and when there is a monopoly. These are considered in turn.

Where there is no monopoly, it is argued that all customers will search for the most convenient offer whereby the expected marginal benefits of additional information equal the related marginal acquisition costs.[44] The supplier will adjust her/his offer to that point. Competitive equilibrium will thus always be achieved, with the customer obtaining the most convenient combination of price and terms. The claim is that the regime of competition ensures the efficiency of standard terms. Thus as Posner states:[45]

> If one seller offers unattractive terms, a competing seller . . . will offer more attractive terms. The process will continue until the terms are optimal . . . what is important is not whether there is haggling in every transaction; it is whether competition forces sellers to incorporate in their standard contract terms that protect the purchasers.

Only in the case of fine print or obscure terminology would excessive search costs be imposed on buyers. This, however, would be a case of fraud, and would not require specific regulation.[46]

A monopoly, according to some writers, differs from conditions of competition only as regards price, which is higher because the seller can compel the purchaser to buy at a price that would be lower under competitive conditions. The solution, so the argument runs, is to regulate the monopoly as such, rather than interfere with the printed terms themselves.[47] According to this view, standard form terms can never be questioned from an economic point of view, and all should be enforceable under the conditions outlined above. On this theory, the option of reregulating standard form terms is systematically excluded, whether there is competition or monopoly: any standard form term is fair because of its inevitable efficiency.

Reregulatory views

The reregulatory strategies agree that the competitiveness of the market guarantees the efficiency of mass contracting,[48] but differ from the theory just discussed in holding that the existence of imperfect information on the part of customers

---

44 The view is mentioned in R. A. Posner, *Economic Analysis of Law* (3rd edn, Boston: Little Brown, 1986), 85; and Goldberg, *Readings*, 169 (retracting his previous regulatory-oriented belief, 167).
45 See Posner, *Economic Analysis*, 102.
46 Fraud would, however, 'rarely (be) actionable': Posner, *Economic Analysis*, 103. Contrast the view of fraud as a powerful instrument for reregulating standard form contracts, preferable on distributive/paternalistic grounds even to the imposition of compulsory terms: Kennedy, 'Distributive and Paternalist Motives', 612.
47 See Posner, *Economic Analysis*, 102.
48 See M. J. Trebilcock, 'The Doctrine of Inequality of Bargaining Power: Post-Benthamite Economics in the House of Lords' (1976) 26 *U Toronto LJ* 359, 365; A. Schwartz and L. L. Wilde, 'Intervening in Markets on the Basis of Imperfect Information: a Legal and Economic Analysis' (1979) 127 *U Pa L Rev* 630.

constitutes a market failure which needs to be corrected through reregulation rather than left to the functioning of competitive mechanisms. There is a shift away from the market deregulatory solution towards a solution of market regulation, where the intervention may either support the choice of the contracting parties (the 'disclosure' solution) or make the decision for them (the 'compulsory' solution).

The two reregulatory strategies may be seen as consisting respectively of a property and a liability rule, to use a tool of analysis which extended to the field of contract formation,[49] a distinction made earlier in tort and property law,[50] and in the law of remedies.[51] The disclosure solution amounts to a property rule that X acquires an enforceable claim against Y whenever there has been a proper agreement[52] while the compulsory solution equates with a liability rule which obliges sellers to enforce those terms the court considers reasonable.

Reregulation through a property rule – disclosure

The disclosure view shares with the deregulatory theory the view that customers can afford information costs,[53] but imposes a policy of enforced disclosure in situations where there is no competitiveness as regards terms. According to the disclosure view, customers may well collect information until the point is reached at which the marginal cost of further search equals or is superior to the marginal gain, and if a sufficient number do so, they can influence the market process and thus obtain the preferred price/term combination. A detailed explanation of this position has been offered,[54] stating under what conditions the market may produce a monopoly as regards terms used by almost all firms. The basic assumption is that a search for price is less expensive than a search for other terms. The first hypothesis is that the market may be competitive as to the price if at least 35 per cent of buyers visit two or more stores before buying, and in such a case it can also be assumed that the market is competitive in relation to terms as well, unless they appear in fine print or arcane legal language. In case of fine print, the second hypothesis is that there would be a monopolistic market for non-price terms if, in a market competitive as to price, more than one-third of the 'comparison shoppers' are not term conscious.[55] In consequence, a duty of disclosure should be imposed both where

49 See Craswell, 'Property Rules'.
50 See G. Calabresi and A. D. Melamed, 'Property Rules, Liability Rules and Inalienability: One View of the Cathedral' (1972) 85 Harv L Rev 1089.
51 See A. T. Kronman, 'Specific Performance' (1978) 45 U Chi L Rev 351.
52 For this argument, see Craswell, 'Property Rules', 11–12.
53 See Schwartz and Wilde, 'Intervening in Markets', 643. This view of information is identical to that supported by theorists who uphold the deregulatory theory. The two strands of thought nevertheless diverge as regards customer ability to search, where, according to reregulatory views, but not according to deregulatory views, biases may exist.
54 Ibid.
55 Ibid., 653, 661. For further elaboration, see Trebilcock and Dewees, 'Judicial Control', 105 ff.

there is no price-competition, and where there is price-competition but an insufficient percentage of customers are aware of fine print terms. This involves a legal duty on the part of the public authorities *or* of the seller to make the customer read and understand the content of the contract.[56] Such a supply of information would decrease information costs and empower customers by affording them data otherwise unavailable to them for the reasons already described. The rationale assumes that where a certain percentage of customers become aware of this additional data, all customers are better off, because such a marginal group of customers forces the market to move towards the terms all customers would prefer.[57]

Various types of reregulatory devices are available to decision-makers, and there is extensive support for all of them. First, public authorities should either provide customers with a list of price-terms and of the firms charging them, or require firms to standardise and disclose their methods of quoting price-terms.[58] The latter instrument appears to be favoured.[59] It is thought that the legislator or the administration, rather than the judiciary, should carry out this disclosure policy, since litigation involves procedural expense and lacks appropriate remedies for moving the market towards competitive equilibrium.[60] There is also room for a wide range of solutions with regard to the duty of disclosure on the part of the drafting party. Apart from cases of fraud, there could be the requirement of presenting the terms of the contract in clear, bold print, and possibly of protecting the customer from information referred to but not contained in the contract form.[61] A stronger solution would be to impose a rule requiring that clauses diverging substantially from the reasonable expectations of the customer as reflected in the terms available to other customers at the margin of the market should be conspicuous, intelligible and perhaps specifically assented to.[62]

Reregulation through a liability rule – the option for compulsory terms

A different reregulatory theory is to impose a compulsory term that simulates the market outcomes which would have occurred had transaction costs been

---

56 For the first view, see Schwartz and Wilde, 'Intervening in Markets', 678 ff.; H. Beale, 'Unfair Contracts in Britain and Europe' (1990) 42 *Current Legal Probs* 197, 207 (but only in the context of a more elaborate approach). For the second view, see Trebilcock, 'Doctrine of Inequality', 373; A. Katz, 'Your Terms or Mine? The Duty to Read the Fine Print in Contracts' (1990) 21 *Rand J Econ* 518, 614. Contrast the 'old' North American doctrine of the 'duty to read' as summarised by Rakoff, 'Contracts of Adhesion', 1183 ff.

57 This shows that this strand of reregulatory policy is concerned less with the existence of information bias within the individual contractual setting, and more with the behaviour of a category of particularly active marginal customers.

58 See Schwartz and Wilde, 'Intervening in Markets', 673 ff. (with a detailed explanation of the problems raised).

59 *Ibid.*, 677.   60 *Ibid.*, 678.

61 See Trebilcock and Dewees, 'Judicial Control', 114–15.

62 *Ibid.*, 114.

non-existent.[63] This position takes seriously the bias due to information costs, and hinges on the idea that possible better terms are in fact hidden from customers, since they cannot be aware of them. Writers recognise the concrete difficulty customers experience in pursuing a market search in the hope of obtaining better terms,[64] and realise that they are not willing to take on the costs of acquiring and processing information with regard to terms that they do not see as relevant. Only if sellers make non-price terms a relevant bargaining point will customers start to shop around for better terms. Few customers, however, will behave in this manner, and even in this case producers can renegotiate the terms with such alert customers while leaving them intact for the majority of customers who are not ready to bargain. It is also argued that the few customers who are willing to fight for better terms are in fact irrelevant with regard to the overall market process, and that it is the producer who really influences market equilibrium: new producers are attracted into the market because of the amount of profits made possible by the writing of favourable terms, and it is this factor that drives the market towards a certain equilibrium. Whether this particular equilibrium will yield an optimal result for both producers and customers, however, is far from certain, especially in view of the so-called 'lemons equilibrium',[65] according to which an equilibrium of 'bad' contractual terms will result. This is so because sellers have no incentive to adopt better terms if poorly informed customers, not understanding the merits of better terms at a higher price, prefer to accept bad terms at a lower price.

For these reasons, and others to be exposed in what follows, writers aplenty have opted for the adoption of a 'compulsory term' solution, in effect a liability rule, since it would be for the court to determine if and to what extent a term imposed upon the customer was unreasonably prejudicial.[66] On this view, compulsory terms should be inserted in standard form contracts, terms that the customer would have preferred had no prohibitive costs existed. A variant of this opinion exists: it is argued that decision-making should aim to allocate the risk to the contractor able to prevent the materialisation of a given contractual risk at a lower cost than the other party, a matter to be ascertained by asking to whom the risk would have been allocated in a frictionless world. On this view, the decision-maker should look for what the parties would have agreed upon absent high transaction costs, and allocate

---

63 See Trebilcock, 'Doctrine of Inequality', 374.
64 The following reconstruction is borrowed from Goldberg, *Readings*, 170. See Llewellyn, 'What Price Contract?', 734 (who highlights the accumulation of seller-protective clauses in highly competitive markets such as instalment sales, residence leases, investments and commercial banking).
65 G. A. Akerlof, 'The Market for "Lemons": Quality Uncertainty and the Market Mechanism' (1970) 84 *Q J Econ* 488. Cf. Craswell, 'Property Rules', 49; V. P. Goldberg, 'Institutional Change and the Quasi-Invisible Hand' (1974) 17 *J L & Econ* 461, 486; Trebilcock and Dewees, 'Judicial Control'; Kennedy, 'Distributive and Paternalist Motives'.
66 Cf. Craswell, 'Property Rules', 12 (opting for liability rather than property rules, because of high transaction costs in the case of fine print terms); Katz, 'Your Terms or Mine?' (discussing the same point by a sophisticated economic model).

any unavoidable risk to the party who can take out insurance against it at the lowest cost.[67] This efficiency-oriented argument could constitute a criterion to test the credibility of any legislation or judicial decision, and some decisions have been justified or criticised on this basis:[68] the cheapest cost avoider would be, on this view, the drafter in any case.

Reregulation through default rules

A further reregulatory solution is based on default rules which liberate courts from having to decide which obligations are reasonable and which are not.[69] There are two versions of this idea – a majoritarian default rule, and a penalty default rule,[70] both of which should be considered. Under the majoritarian default rule, the law would provide for a set of protective requirements, e.g., a certain merchantable quality, which are to be observed unless any deviation from those requirements, such as a defect in the goods, is drawn to the buyer's attention. This would allow the drafter to escape liability for any such defect, and the parties would be encouraged to bargain and adjust the content of the contract according to their wishes. Under a penalty default rule, the law would provide for default terms so harsh for the drafter that he would consider it convenient to avoid them.

These solutions are only superficially different from, or composites of, those previously mentioned. First, as to the majoritarian version, the idea of a set of default rules avoidable by providing information, tenable in so far as it engages with information costs, is in this respect simply a variant of either the disclosure or the compulsory solution. Thus, where as a result of a default rule the drafter draws the buyer's attention to a term excluding a liability that would otherwise arise, he would simply be doing what is called for by the disclosure solution, and where the default rules apply, assuming that they are efficient in allocating the risk of the cheapest cost-avoider, the result is the same as under the compulsory solution. In either case, the economic bias of transaction costs remains.

The imposition of harsher terms under the penalty default rule simply favours the disclosure solution by deterring the seller from incurring the background rules, since he will find it more efficient to modify his terms rather than leave them intact. Nevertheless, the high transaction costs inevitably lead back to the previous reregulatory strategies so as to produce a sort of compulsory disclosure with all the difficulties of putting it into practice.[71]

67 See Kötz, 'The EC Directive', 210–11.   68 *Ibid.*, 212 ff.
69 See Craswell, 'Property Rules', 32 (criticising this view).
70 Here I draw on Craswell, 'Property Rules', 12–14, 32–4.
71 Cf. the treatment of this point in Craswell, 'Property Rules', 14 (drawing on I. Ayres and R. Gertner, 'Filling Gaps in Incomplete Contracts: an Economic Theory of Default Rules' (1989) 99 *Yale LJ* 87, 96; Calabresi and Melamed, 'Property Rules', 1106 ff.).

In failing to provide better solutions to the crucial issue of transaction costs, these default accounts, rather than offering a different type of regulatory solution, at best repeat the previous models.

Ultimate scholarly view in favour of compulsory terms

The analysis thus far has shown three alternative types of legal intervention. The deregulatory paradigm abstains from any reregulation, while the reregulatory paradigm may take the form of a disclosure policy (the imposition of a supply of information), or of a compulsory policy (the imposition of compulsory terms replacing those in the contract). In what follows, I call these the deregulatory, the disclosure and the compulsory theories. I now proceed to describe how the majority of scholars have heavily criticised the deregulatory and the disclosure views, whilst opting for the idea that compulsory terms ought to be imposed. This is a two-step critical analysis of the reasons underlying the three theories so far identified. First, I evaluate the claims to efficiency of both the deregulatory and disclosure theories, including the default accounts which overlap with the latter. Secondly, I refer to the arguments given by scholars for the compulsory solution over that of disclosure, the former solution being for them the solution truly justified on efficiency-oriented grounds.

On the illusory efficiency of the deregulatory, disclosure and default rules views

In this section, I outline the criticism that scholars have addressed to the efficiency of the disclosure policy. This amounts *a fortiori* to a criticism of the deregulatory policy, for if, as will be seen, transaction costs are a major barrier to customers' shopping around and bargaining, the deregulatory solution is shown to be equally inefficient. This applies also to the default account which overlaps with the disclosure solution.

Criticism of the disclosure policy must be accounted in two stages, since the policy itself has two aspects. It is deregulatory in abstaining from any regulation under conditions of price-competitiveness and where there are no fine print terms, and even in the latter case where a certain percentage of customers who can afford information costs exists, but it becomes reregulatory when it imposes a duty to disclose under conditions of non price-competitiveness, or where there is no minimum percentage of customers aware of fine print terms. The first criticism relates to the view that enough customers can afford the information cost of finding out what the best terms are so as to reach a percentage that influences the market and generates a new equilibrium in which the desiderated terms are offered.[72] The second

---

72 Another assumption of the reregulatory view is that customers are irrelevant to, and firms determinant of, the market equilibrium.

criticism relates to the sellers' side, and challenges the view that sellers can efficiently/conveniently provide for information so as to allow the market to achieve the optimal equilibrium.

Inefficiency of customers' acquiring information

Customers cannot be expected to search for better terms if their search costs would inevitably exceed any benefits so derived. Thus, no conscientious customer would pay any attention to subordinate terms. This has been argued on the basis of a series of arguments aimed at demonstrating that information costs always exceed the expected gains, since the various information costs normally confronting the customer are insuperable.

According to the literature under consideration, the information costs facing the customer fall into two categories.[73] First, there are those that range from having to read print, which may be tiny, to the greater difficulty of understanding the legalese in which it is couched. Secondly, there are transaction costs in altering the terms proposed or finding a seller who offers better terms. A further explanation of this point follows.

First, as to time spent in reading fine print and trying to understand legalese. A customer willing to take the effort of reading standard form contracts must use up an amount of time normally unavailable to him or her,[74] especially as the number of clauses normally included in any standard form contract is very large.[75] These difficulties are increased when, as often happens, fine print is used, which one writer has suggested may amount to fraud.[76] A further complication arises from the fact that adhesion contracts are drafted by experts who use legalese which a customer cannot understand unless he or she hires a lawyer. Since even lawyers often do not understand, or are incapable of explaining, the inevitable web of possible interpretations of each clause,[77] scholars conclude that the picture of a customer aware of the standard form contract is little more than a sham.

Secondly, as to time for bargaining and shopping around. This set of problems is more troublesome. A customer aware of the terms proposed and eager to improve the quality of the contract nonetheless faces costs in seeking to have them altered or finding a new seller who would provide better terms. Furthermore, customers are

---

73 The twofold set of information costs is signalled by Kennedy, 'Distributive and Paternalist Motives'.

74 Cf. M. I. Meyerson, 'The Efficient Consumer Form Contract: Law and Economics Meets the Real World' (1990) 24 *Ga L Rev* 583, 598.

75 *Ibid*.

76 See Posner, *Economic Analysis*, 85–6 (quoted also in Meyerson, 'The Efficient Consumer Form Contract').

77 See Meyerson, 'The Efficient Consumer Form Contract', 599, fn. 81 (and further references).

normally risk-averse,[78] and are reluctant to believe that a particular risk will occur. In sum, even customers aware of all the factors mentioned would still not face the acknowledged risks as they should,[79] and would in any case lack sufficient data for making a proper decision.[80]

Inefficiency of sellers' providing information

A second limb of criticism is designed to show that it is inefficient for sellers/ drafters to provide information.[81] First, customers do not need the information if they would continue buying even if it were not supplied, as is shown in the 'market for lemons' scenario.[82] Secondly, it is inefficient for sellers to insert better terms, for it is better for the firm to lose customers than to go to the effort of inserting better terms for clients who have asked for them.[83]

There are two further strategic grounds why sellers would see no advantage in proposing better terms. First, there is the scenario called 'freeloading'. Even if one assumes that customers are sufficiently informed and aware of any better terms, a non-compulsory solution Pareto-superior to the compulsory one would nonetheless fail, even on the supposition that the cost of educating customers, i.e. of informing them, is low enough to make it convenient for the seller to provide a better term for a higher price and thereby gain major benefits. What makes this strategy inconvenient is the fact that the first firm that initiates this strategy will see its competitors jump into the new business and gain those benefits at zero information cost. It is therefore better for the firm to 'sit tight and let someone else do it: no one undertakes the campaign'.[84] The disclosure idea is ineffective because it contains no incentive, but only an invitation for firms to disclose.

Another reason has been put forward for suggesting that this strategy is inconvenient. We have seen that just as it is not efficient for buyers to search for better terms and thereby contribute to the supposedly necessary percentage of shopping customers, so it is inefficient for sellers to provide information or introduce better terms. It is also possible to show that if customers were inefficiently to ask for better terms and firms were inefficiently/inconveniently ready to provide them, firms would nevertheless be likely to avoid doing so because it might act as a disincentive to customers and endanger the purchase.[85]

---

78 *Ibid.*
79 Cf. M. A. Eisenberg, 'The Limits of Cognition and the Limits of Contract' (1995) 47 *Stan L Rev* 211, 243.
80 See Meyerson, 'The Efficient Consumer Form Contract', 600 (and further references).
81 See, e.g., Craswell, 'Property Rules', 12. Some of the critical arguments that follow apply to the hypothetical case of a public authority providing information.
82 Akerlof, 'Market for "Lemons"'.
83 See Meyerson, 'The Efficient Consumer Form Contract', 600 (and further references).
84 Kennedy, 'Distributive and Paternalist Motives', 601.
85 See Meyerson, 'The Efficient Consumer Form Contract', 600 (citing Posner).

There is a further argument, which suggests that where the compulsory solution is juxtaposed with the disclosure solution, the former becomes more efficient. A mandatory disclosure policy would entail a set of costs that would make it more efficient to internalise the risks through a mandatory allocation of the latter to the drafter. This is so because any default mandatory replacement of contractual terms is efficient in so far as it allocates the risk of loss to the cheapest cost-avoider. This can be said to be true for any type of traditional background rule that allocates the risk in that manner. If one sees the non-compulsory solutions against this background one finds that there are two possible scenarios: either the term that the drafter intends to propose is more efficient than the default one, assuming that the latter is in a given case inefficient (for example, by providing for a negligence limitation), or it is less efficient. In the latter case, there is nothing to be said in favour of the drafter's strategy, given the inefficiency of the term proposed and the bias on seller choice which results from the transaction costs. In the first case, the greater efficiency of the term is to be set against the transaction cost of providing it, which can make the final choice of the drafter less efficient than the default alternative, since once again the drafter's choice is biased by the transaction costs.[86]

The efficiency of compulsory terms

The preceding account, which demonstrates how scholars overwhelmingly uphold the inefficiency of the disclosure solution, equally indicates that scholars consider the compulsory solution to be the truly efficient one. In the view of the majority of scholarly writings, the imposition of a compulsory term would save the customer the transaction costs of acquiring information and the seller those of disclosing information, without incurring the bias of either 'freeloading' or the 'market for lemons'. This last point is crucial, since it has been observed that even if customers were ready to pay for the costs involved in searching, these phenomena would render the compulsory term more efficient.[87] Moreover, scholars argue that the cheapest cost-avoider rationale, that the cost of the occurrence of a risk should be borne by the party in the best position to minimise it, leads to opting for the compulsory solution in its entirety. To conclude: the transaction costs on the side of both drafter and customer, together with the other biases described, have convinced the majority of scholars that solutions other than compulsory ones are untenable. Since transaction costs are too high to make the disclosure option available, they conclude that the compulsory solution is the only efficient one. To them, certain standardised terms are unquestionably harsh, as in the view of sociological literature,

---

86 *Ibid.*, 621, fn. 201. Moreover, this renders untenable a disclosure solution so framed that public authorities rather than drafters must provide the information. It is in fact inefficient to supply information, if this is more costly than the compulsory solution.
87 See Kennedy, 'Distributive and Paternalist Motives', 609 ff.

though not by reason of victimisation, but because of unfair surprise and lack of choice.[88]

The new paradigm: rethinking unfairness

Twenty years of law and economics writings have thus left unaffected the belief that certain standardised terms are unquestionably unfair. Scholars have only partly abandoned traditional thinking, as, once having discarded the tenet that customers are victimised, they tend invariably to regard the imposition of compulsory terms in lieu of unfair terms as the ideal economico-legal solution. This result is similar to that favoured by socio-legal scholars. Scholars share the consideration that prohibitive transaction costs make it unworkable for the parties to agree on the terms of their bargain, and they argue for compulsory terms on either of two grounds: compulsory terms would correspond to what customers would have preferred absent prohibitive transaction costs, or the drafter would be the best able to bear the risk contemplated in each unfair term.[89]

In this section, I suggest that an efficiency-oriented analysis must lead to the rejection of the view that certain standardised terms are unquestionably unfair. I argue that economico-legal and socio-legal findings have been too concerned with preserving the unfairness belief; and that for this reason they have failed to show that any legal system unquestionably conforming to that belief is unduly costly for society. I should add that my argument is not at all unknown to those scholars who at times advanced suggestions out of line with the unfairness belief. Some such suggestions were, however, rather vague: that flexible, rather than rigid, criteria for identifying unfairness are required.[90] Other suggestions were more pragmatic: that *ex casu* circumstances may lead to a decision not to declare unfair a term that alters the background statutory rules;[91] or that the relaxation of the test of unfairness should occur either when new goods or services are produced or new solutions are offered to legal problems;[92] or that distributive effects should be taken into account that may convince the decision-maker to relax the test of unfairness;[93] or that customers may shop around for the preferred term/price combination,[94] especially in

88 Beale, 'Legislative Control', 232 (criticising Kessler and referring to the writings of scholars such as Priest and Trebilcock in support of his view).
89 See text accompanying nn. 65–6 above.
90 See Beale, 'Legislative Control', 235; Trebilcock and Dewees, 'Judicial Control', 98 ff.
91 See Rakoff, 'Contracts of Adhesion', 1246 (stating that this is, however, exceptional and subsequently giving examples, 1266 ff.).
92 *Ibid.*, 1281–2. These are two instances that represent a partial return to Llewellyn's emphasis on the background role of commercial practices.
93 See Kennedy, 'Distributive and Paternalist Motives'; Rakoff, 'Contracts of Adhesion', 1231, fn. 201 (and approving a case in which distributive effects were taken into account, 1283).
94 See Rakoff, 'Contracts of Adhesion', 1225.

case of price-discrimination; or that due to changing market conditions customers may not be at a power disadvantage (for example, because they are able to protect themselves and/or because of effective competition) and as a result it is no longer always true that standard form terms are 'imposed' on customers by drafters with superior bargaining power,[95] and it is not always the draftsman who should internalise the risk in issue.

It is time to advance my chief argument, one that intentionally ignores the traditional belief, and for this reason sheds new light on each of the above scholars' suggestions. It is a two-step argument.[96] First, each decision on fairness *or* unfairness is a proxy for the decision-maker's choice on how to allocate costs that society ought to bear in the face of the materialisation of the contractual risk contemplated in the term under consideration. To consider unfair a term that limits the liability of the drafter for negligent performance is to make the drafter bear the costs implicated in bad performance; should that term stand, the customer will instead be the bearer of those costs. To give an example:[97] an English court struck down a standardised term limiting a farmer's liability to replace defective seeds; the farmer had to bear the costs of £61,000, the loss to the plaintiff, the latter having planted 30 lbs of seeds and discovered six months later that they were not cabbage seeds but loose leaves useless for human consumption. Significant collateral effects should also be considered: the decision may in turn force farmers to insure against this kind of risk and may raise the price of seeds on the market. Secondly, a decision-maker imposing compulsory terms in lieu of unfair ones in every contractual situation will allocate the relevant costs to the drafter, but this is not necessarily convenient for society. For efficiency requires that decision-makers minimise social costs by identifying the cheapest cost-avoider with respect to the contractual risks implicated in each bargain. On consideration of a particular bargain, the drafter may not be the best person able to prevent the materialisation of the contractual risk; in such a case, to impose a compulsory term results in the contractual risks being borne by those who cannot most efficiently bear them. A term prejudicial on its face may be, economically speaking, tenable, the customer being the cheapest cost-avoider, or untenable, the drafter being instead the cheapest cost-avoider: the decision-maker may thus consider the same term to be unfair in one case, but fair in another, depending upon which cost decision in each individual case best serves the purpose of minimising costs for society. Below is an illustration of my argument: compulsory

---

95 See P. S. Atiyah, *An Introduction to Law of Contract* (5th edn, Oxford: Clarendon Press, 1995), 336; O. E. Williamson, 'Comment' (1995) 151 *Journal of Institutional & Theoretical Economics* 49 (on theoretical grounds).

96 I do not think that the two are the sole arguments that should be of relevance for decision-makers. See Craswell, 'Property Rules', 65: 'There is much work still to be done in analyzing market failures and institutional competence for those cases where a liability rule would be most appropriate, and in developing criteria for evaluating the substantive reasonableness of contested obligations.'

97 *George Mitchell Ltd.* v. *Finney Lock Seeds Ltd* [1983] 2 AC 803, an example I borrow from Kötz, 'The EC Directive', 215.

terms are not to be imposed so as to replace supposedly unfair terms if hypothesis A suggests the contrary, for singling out terms as unquestionably unfair and invariably favouring the imposition of compulsory terms in such hypothesis is unduly costly for society. Hypotheses B and C show that to take costs seriously so as to minimise them may not consist of a straightforward search for the cheapest cost-avoider: the decision-maker may have to avoid decisions that, though not *too* costly, as costs would be efficiently allocated, are nevertheless *unduly* costly as costs would be wrongly allocated.

Hypothesis A: the case for avoiding compulsory terms too costly for society

Consideration of *ex casu* bargaining conditions of each party may entail that the cheapest cost-avoider, the one who can at least cost avoid the risk at stake in each contractual relationship, is the adherent. This is so when the adherent is superior to the drafter intellectually, by reason of his information or experience, or economically. A first illustration of intellectual superiority by reason of information is that of a standardised term being brought to the attention of the customer.[98] This may make the latter the cheapest cost-avoider, with society not incurring the higher costs to be faced by the drafter who would otherwise be obliged to incur liability. Consider *Barclays Bank Plc* v. *O'Brien*,[99] where a wife entered into an obligation to stand as surety for the debts of her husband. The fact that there was no shared economic interest between the guarantor and the debtor, as the wife had no pecuniary interest in securing the debts of the company in which her husband was involved, indicated that undue influence had occurred, and the security was held unenforceable.[100] However, the principle was stated that a guarantee is to be held valid and enforceable only where the creditor took reasonable steps to satisfy itself that the surety entered into the obligation freely and in knowledge of the true facts. This is so when the creditor warns the surety (in the absence of the principal debtor) of the amount of her potential liability and of the risks involved, and advises the surety to take independent legal advice. Another example is that of two or more offers at different prices with different 'risk' conditions. Writers acknowledge that[101] this model is optimal in that it is capable of promoting the welfare of the parties by enhancing their preferences, but warn that it needs testing, since prohibitive search costs may nevertheless be incurred in looking for the different price-offers that may

---

98 If this argument is correct, then the overwhelming scholarly belief that information costs are always too high for customers and/or drafters to afford them must be unsound.

99 [1994] 1 AC 180.   100 See Atiyah, *Introduction to Law of Contract*, 277.

101 See Atiyah, *Introduction to Law of Contract*, 311 (arguing that a wide range of choices may exist in today's markets); A. Schwartz, 'Legal Implications of Imperfect Information in Consumer Markets' (1995) 151 *Journal of Institutional & Theoretical Economics* 2, 31.

make an informed decision unachievable.[102] Subject to such qualifications, this solution seems well suited to the task of minimising costs: price discrimination is thus another instance in which the compulsory solution may be avoided. The adherent will be intellectually superior by reason of experience/expertise in the hypothetical situation of an adherent-lawyer specialising in insurance contracts but arguing that a standard term is unfair for lack of transparency.[103] Economic superiority of the adherent may exist, for example, should the adherent be a large, powerful firm capable of calculating interest rates and comparing those offered in the market. In order to minimise costs, it would be preferable that the firm makes this kind of comparison, rather than incurring the liability costs that the drafter ought to bear for unilateral imposition of unfair interest rates (unfair because they are calculated to the disadvantage of the client: for example, every three months rather than daily).[104]

The objective of minimising costs might convince the decision-maker to avoid compulsory terms on two further grounds: as recent socio-legal literature has suggested,[105] the test of unfairness could be disapplied, first, in the case of the invention of new legal solutions for complex problems, or, secondly, in the case of the making/marketing of a new, particularly sophisticated product. Here costs are saved that would arise from the persistence of legal problems *or* lack of the new products.

Hypothesis B: the case for avoiding compulsory terms unduly costly for society

Unlike non-economic analyses,[106] the economic literature places great emphasis upon the trade-off between price and non-price terms when unfairness is in issue.[107] This is a critical and contentious point, for consideration of the price

---

102 See the arguments of Schwartz, 'Legal Implications'.
103 In Europe, there are a number of studies where problem situations of this sort are referred to: e.g., H. Heinrichs, 'Die EG-Richtlinie über missbräuchliche Klauseln in Verbraucherverträgen' [1993] *Neue Juristische Wochenschrift* 1817, 1820; H. Heinrichs, 'Das Gesetz zur Änderung des AGB-Gesetzes' [1996] *Neue Juristische Wochenschrift* 2190, 2194.
104 Facts of this sort have been considered in Germany: see, e.g., J. Köndgen, 'Grund und Grenzen des Transparenzgebots im AGB-Recht. Bemerkungen zum Hypothekenzins und zum Wertstellungs-Urteil des BGH' [1989] *Neue Juristische Wochenschrift* 943, 952. Here, I assume that a plurality of offers of interest rates exists in the relevant market.
105 See n. 92 above.
106 Craswell, 'Property Rules', 30, notices this, criticising in particular the work of authors such as Rakoff and Slawson. The notorious exception is Leff, 'Contract as Thing', 155 (cited by Craswell). Contrast this with the European literature which is particularly sensitive to this issue: e.g., Beale, 'Unfair Contracts', 212; Atiyah, *Introduction to Law of Contract*, 311.
107 See Goldberg, *Readings*, 484; Craswell, 'Property Rules'; Kennedy, 'Distributive and Paternalist Motives'; Beale, 'Unfair Contracts'; Atiyah, *Introduction to Law of Contract*.

may lead one to reverse a preliminary conclusion that a term is unfair and that a compulsory term ought to be inserted that makes the drafter the bearer of the risk. It follows, too, that the imposition of compulsory terms entails distributive effects which decision-makers should take into account in deciding whether or not compulsory terms should be imposed. For, assuming that it is right to impose a compulsory term, in the light of the cheapest cost-avoider rationale, such imposition entails further costs on the firm and this may be reflected in a higher price. The decision-maker faced with a claim of unfairness must therefore re-evaluate the customers' willingness to buy in view of the altered combination of price and risks. In other words, the internalisation of risk by the cheapest cost-avoider is merely the first stage of the efficiency approach, which must then take into account the resulting price/better term combination.

This issue requires further discussion. Such price-oriented analysis differs depending on the structure of the market and the shape of the demand and offer curves in it, and thus homogeneous and heterogeneous markets must be analysed separately.[108] In the case of a homogeneous market, customers may sometimes be worse off because of a higher-price/gentle-term combination that they would not have agreed upon, or conversely, better off by a low-price/gentle-term combination where a compulsory term is imposed at no cost to them. More complicated is the case of a heterogeneous market, where customers have different preferences which need to be taken into account in the analysis.[109] There may be customers for whom the risk–price combination resulting from the imposition of the compulsory term is desirable, but there may also be some who are worse off since they would have preferred a lower-price–harsher-term combination. The seminal contribution by Ackerman,[110] as later adapted to mass contracting,[111] gives instances of conflict between decisions made respectively from efficiency-oriented and distributive motives.[112] Whether customers generally are better or worse off after the imposition of the compulsory term depends on whether the costs are passed on to them, which in turn depends on the shapes of the curves and structure of the market.[113] If a certain number of customers are going to be worse off,[114] the appropriateness of

---

108 I borrow this categorisation from Craswell, 'Property Rules'.
109 See Kennedy, 'Distributive and Paternalist Motives', 598; Craswell, 'Property Rules'; Beale, 'Unfair Contracts'.
110 B. Ackerman, 'Regulating Slum Housing Markets on Behalf of the Poor: of Housing Codes, Housing Subsidies and Income Redistribution Policy' (1971) 80 *Yale LJ* 1093. For Ackerman's reconstruction rephrased in classic law and economics vocabulary, see R. S. Markovitz, 'The Distributive Impact, Allocative Efficiency, and Overall Desirability of Ideal Housing Codes: Some Theoretical Clarifications' (1976) 89 *Harv L Rev* 1815.
111 See Kennedy, 'Distributive and Paternalist Motives'.
112 See R. Craswell, 'Passing on the Costs of Legal Rules: Efficiency and Distribution in Buyer–Seller Relationships' (1991) 43 *Stan L Rev* 361, 373.
113 See Kennedy, 'Distributive and Paternalist Motives', 605 ff.
114 See generally Kennedy, 'Distributive and Paternalist Motives'; A. T. Kronman, 'Paternalism and the Law of Contracts' (1983) 92 *Yale LJ* 763.

the measure will be in issue and the decision-maker will have to make a distributive choice whether to leave some customers better off and others worse off.[115]

Undoubtedly, to ascertain what is unduly costly for society may not be straightforward, but not to embark on this analysis at all might force customers to face situations where on closer inspection costs for society are unjustified. To test the above analysis, one can take the English case of A. *Schroeder Music Publishing Co Ltd v. Macaulay*.[116] The contract here required a songwriter to offer all his songs to the publisher for five years, extendable by the publisher for a further five years. This was excessively burdensome to the composer, for it deprived him of the profits of his subsequent success. The House of Lords upheld the songwriter's claim to avoid the contract. The decision was justified on the basis of inequality of bargaining power between the parties, yet it has been rightly criticised on the ground it would prevent many aspiring songwriters from getting their songs published. Contracts with beginners are in fact not very rewarding because of the many who want to be songwriters. Very few succeed.[117] In other words, consideration of conditions of highly competitive markets, such as the English music-publishing industry, should convince the decision-maker to relax the test of unfairness, a decision of unfairness being unduly costly for society in general.

Hypothesis C: avoiding compulsory terms unduly costly for institutional reasons

Institutional factors may militate against the imposition of a compulsory term. Indeed, in certain cases it may be better to retain a less efficient solution if the more efficient solution would be more costly to apply,[118] for it has been rightly noticed that 'all corrective policies involve some costs for administration and may impose some additional costs in the marketplace'.[119] Decision-makers must then ascertain whether or not imposing a compulsory term will lead to costs that outweigh the benefits of the intervention; and which institution is best able to identify the optimal solution without causing costs higher than those saved through its

---

115 At this point, the decision-maker will rely less on empirical data than on value judgments. This is agreed upon by writers, sometimes referring, rather contentiously, to paternalism: Kennedy, 'Distributive and Paternalist Motives', 624 ff.; Kronman, 'Paternalism', 764, 774; W. C. Whitford, 'Contract Law and the Control of Standardised Terms in Consumer Contracts: an American Report' (1995) 3 *European Review of Private Law* 193, 210 (referring to the desirability of favouring the interests of needy customers over the interests of those in better economic circumstances).

116 [1974] 1 WLR 1308. Here I borrow from Atiyah, *Introduction to Law of Contract*, 331.

117 See Atiyah, *Introduction to Law of Contract*.

118 See Craswell, 'Property Rules', 33 (considering the institutional costs entailed in any given decision).

119 See Trebilcock and Dewees, 'Judicial Control', 118.

intervention; and also whether courts or the parties are in the best position to choose the terms,[120] bearing in mind that distributive objectives may override any considerations based on grounds of efficiency.

Conclusion

Scholars have honoured the belief that certain standardised terms are intrinsically unfair, and they have sacrificed the objective of minimising social costs for the sake of that faith. This is shown by decoupling the efficiency argument from the legacy of traditional thinking, an operation that is also inevitable if intellectual analysis is to gain logical consistency. But what matters is more the social issue, and less the logical one of consistency. Having considered that legislation and judicial or administrative decisions that ostracise unfair terms and command instead the imposition of compulsory terms are too/unduly costly for society as a whole (as seen above in the discussion of the hypotheses A, B and C), should judges and administrative agencies continue striking down unfair terms whatever the costs might be for society? Similarly to what scientists have achieved in projecting the city of Perinzia[121] (meant to be a mirror of celestial harmony where nature and God's grace would shape the destiny of its inhabitants, but since its projection simply generating monstrous inhabitants), have scholars conceived of a belief meant to serve noble purposes to protect 'the weak' against abuse of private power but since its application merely generating unintended perverse effects? Do scholars face a dilemma similar to that of Perinzia's scientists either to admit they were technically wrong, in that their project has failed to reproduce on earth the celestial order; or to argue that they were right, as celestial harmony is in fact monstrous? Do scholars either admit that they were wrong, or argue that the law, as it is ('monstrous' because of its perverse cost effects), ought nevertheless to stand?

120 See, with specific regard to standard form contracts, Craswell, 'Property Rules', 38 ff. (arguing *inter alia* that 'the incentives and expertise governing' the parties' choice of terms should be balanced against 'the incentives and expertise governing the court's').
121 See Calvino, *Le città invisibili*, 144–5.

6   BSE, CJD, mass infections and the 3rd US Restatement

JANE STAPLETON

Introduction

In 1993 when I was writing *Product Liability*[1] I wanted an example of a risk that was almost unanimously regarded as negligible. I wanted to ask the question of whether a bizarrely remote suspected risk could deprive a defendant of the development risk defence in the 1985 European Directive on Product Liability.[2] My choice has turned out to be an even better illustration of the problems I was highlighting than I imagined. I wrote:[3]

> Should those now supplying meat be held liable if eventually it is shown that the factor responsible for bovine spongiform encephalopathy ('mad cow disease') *has* been passed via that meat to humans to cause Creutzfeldt–Jakob disease – a risk which as yet is given little credence in scientific circles, but a risk for which the technical means of *eventual* detection do exist?

This article is one step in looking at the challenge that bovine spongiform encephalopathy (BSE), Creutzfeldt–Jakob disease (CJD) and other mass infections[4] of product sectors throw out to the product liability regimes around the world. Certain characteristics make this challenge particularly severe. First, the dangerous

---

1 London: Butterworths, 1994. See also J. Stapleton, 'Products Liability in the United Kingdom: the Myths of Reform' (1999) 34 *Tex Int'l L J* 45; J. Stapleton, '*Restatement (Third) of Torts: Products Liability*, an Anglo-Australian Perspective' (2000) 39 *Washburn L J* 363; J. Stapleton, 'Comparing Australian Product Liability with EU and US' (2000) 28 *International Business Law* 195, reprinted in (2000) 10 *Australian Product Liability Reporter* 69.
2 Council Directive 85/374/EEC of 25 July 1985 on the Approximation of the Laws, Regulations and Administrative Provisions of the Member States Concerning Liability for Defective Products, 1985 OJ (L 210) (herein 'the Directive'). In response to the BSE/CJD crisis the Directive was amended by EC Directive 1999/34/EC to remove the potential for a Member State to bar claims concerning unprocessed primary products, on which exemption see Stapleton, *Product Liability*, 303–5.
3 Stapleton, *Product Liability*, 240–1. Note the comment of Lord Phillips *et al.*, *The BSE Inquiry* (London: HM Stationery Office, 26 October 2000): 'Right up to 1996 the [1989] Southwood Report was cited as if it demonstrated as a matter of scientific certainty, rather than provisional opinion, that any risk to humans from BSE was remote' (quoted by H. Pennington, 'The English Disease' in *The London Review of Books*, 14 December 2000, 3, 5).
4 On which see J. Cooke, *Cannibals, Cows and the CJD Catastrophe* (Milson's Point, NSW: Random House, 1998).

infection is not part of the condition of the product which the supplier 'intended' in the sense of 'desired'. Secondly, the dangerous infection is known or suspected to be 'generic', that is, potentially it has affected an entire product sector such as the beef industry or the blood product sector. Thirdly, this sector is an 'essential' product sector in that it does not have realistic substitutes. Fourthly, the dangerous infection in the product type is not present in each item of the product but testing each item for that infection is impossible or impractical. Fifthly, the dangerous infection was present before any 'manufacturing' or 'production' process occurred. And sixthly, the infection is not necessarily limited to one generation of products but can be transmitted to following generations.

In this paper I will concentrate on the situation under the US *Restatement (Third) of Torts: Products Liability* published in 1998. In a companion work, I have already considered how such cases may be handled under the European Directive which has served as the template for the special products laws adopted in the EU Member States, Japan[5] and Australia.[6]

General

Recently, the Reporters of the *Restatement (Third) of Torts: Products Liability*, Professor James Henderson, Jr. and Professor Aaron Twerski, argued that the sparse provisions of the European Directive are 'inadequate substantive standards in the form of overly simplistic rules of decision [that] will present judges and lawyers with conceptual difficulties in trying to respond to products liability claims rationally, consistently, and fairly'.[7] European complacency, the Reporters believe, is attributed to:[8]

> The idea that a vague, undifferentiating standard for defect is acceptable, and even preferable, because courts will 'work out the details' on a case-by-case basis . . . But the experience in the United States over the past forty years

---

5 See, e.g., T. Kitagawa and L. Nottage, 'Japan's First Judgment under its PL Law of 1994: Echoes of *Donoghue v. Stevenson*' (2000) 10 *Australian Product Liability Reporter* 121; L. Nottage, 'Global Harmony and Disharmony in Accident Compensation: Japan's New Product Liability Legislation Compared to the EC Directive and Part VA of the Australian Trade Practices Act' (1999) 66 *Hosei Kenkyu F1* (Journal of Law and Politics, Kyushu University).

6 See Trade Practices Act 1974, Part VA (Cth). See generally J. Kellam (ed.), *Product Liability in the Asia-Pacific* (2nd edn, Sydney: Prospect Media, 1999), chap. 1; J. Kellam, *A Practical Guide to Australian Product Liability* (Sydney: CCH, 1992); I. Malkin, 'Product Liability under the Trade Practices Act and at Common Law' (1998) 6 *Torts LJ* 204; I. Malkin and E. J. Wright, 'Product Liability under the Trade Practices Act – Adequately Compensating for Personal Injury?' (1993) 1 *Torts LJ* 63. The earlier study, passages of which are incorporated in this text, is J. Stapleton, 'Bugs in Anglo-American Products Liability' (2002) 53 *South Carolina L Rev* 1225.

7 See J. A. Henderson, Jr. and A. D. Twerski, 'What Europe, Japan, and Other Countries Can Learn from the New American Restatement of Products Liability' (1999) 34 *Tex Int'l LJ* 1, 2–3.

8 *Ibid.*, 14–15.

strongly suggests that courts – even fairly sophisticated courts that confront a
substantial and steady caseload of design defect cases – may require thirty or
forty years to 'get it right'. . . For the European Community . . . 'to leave it to
the courts' is to overlook the obvious gains to be had from drawing on the
American experience.

The Reporters even claim that 'a modern industrialised state's system of products
liability in tort [will be driven] to accept the organization of the defect concept reflected by recent developments in . . . [the United States]'[9] and manifested by the
Restatement (Third) of Torts: Products Liability.

In a recent article in the *Washburn Law Journal*[10] I put forward a number of reasons
why many non-Americans find this perspective less than compelling. Here I focus
on what seems to be the principal complaint of the Reporters. This is that laws such
as the 1985 Directive do not distinguish between types of defect. The reason the
Reporters complain about this is that it blocks products regimes that use the Directive or its clones from adopting the distinctive approach that the Reporters say
US courts found to be 'the only sensible standard for defect in classic *design* cases'.[11]
This standard, they argue, is the requirement that the plaintiff adduce convincing
proof of a reasonable alternative design (RAD) in most design cases but not in manufacturing cases. The Reporters argue that this requirement is mandatory in those
design cases – the vast majority – that fall outside certain 'special' classes of product
defect – a large residual class they call 'classic design cases'.

A heated debate took place in the USA over this RAD requirement which I discuss
elsewhere.[12] Here I will argue that a consideration of BSE, CJD and other mass infection cases casts doubt on both of the twin assumptions on which the Reporters built
the structure of the *Restatement (Third) of Torts: Products Liability*. The first of these is
the assumption that it makes sense, either theoretical or pragmatic sense, to carve
off for 'special' treatment classes of product claims according to certain proof shortcuts and according to product classes such as food. The second is the assumption
that for 'non-special' products, such as clothing, it makes sense to treat product
defect claims differently according to whether or not the product condition that
caused the injury is classed as a 'manufacturing defect', a condition that the Reporters define as departing from its intended design.[13] In short, my argument is
that had the Reporters addressed their minds to the BSE/CJD phenomenon that
was exploding in Europe at the time they formulated the *Restatement (Third) of Torts:*

9 *Ibid.*
10 Stapleton, '*Restatement (Third) of Torts: Products Liability*, an Anglo-Australian Perspective', 399.
11 See Henderson and Twerski, 'What Europe, Japan, and Other Countries Can Learn', 19 (emphasis added).
12 See Stapleton, '*Restatement (Third) of Torts: Products Liability*, an Anglo-Australian Perspective', 399.
An excellent example of the consumer perspective is J. J. Phillips, 'The Unreasonably Unsafe
Product and Strict Liability' (1996) 72 *Chi-Kent L Rev* 129.
13 See *Restatement (Third) of Torts: Products Liability* § 2(a). See text accompanying n. 39 below.

Products Liability in 1993 through 1998, they might well have realised the incoherence and inadequacy of both these fragmented arrangements of doctrine.

Structure of the *Restatement*: fragmentation according to certain proof shortcuts and according to product class

Structurally, the *Restatement (Third) of Torts: Products Liability* is an exceptionally elaborate affair. First, it gives special separate treatment to certain classes of products such as food and prescription drugs. The special classes are where there is a claim involving circumstantial evidence supporting inference of product defect (§ 3), a sort of generously reinterpreted *res ipsa loquitur* class; proof of noncompliance with product safety statutes or regulations (§ 4); manifestly unreasonable design, other terms for which are categorically defective design, generically defective design and egregiously dangerous product type (§ 2 cmt. e); components (§ 5); prescription drugs and medical devices (§ 6); food products (§ 7); and used products (§ 8).

While this separate treatment may reflect past case law fragmentation, it could be argued that the Reporters missed a critical opportunity for guiding US courts to a more coherent, less fragmented approach to product claims. For example, as we will see, the issues thrown up in the USA by 'naturally occurring' matter, such as bones in fish soup and viruses in oysters, are exactly some of those that constitute the core challenge that BSE/CJD-type infections present to our product regimes in whatever product type they occur. The BSE/CJD challenge is massively more serious because such risks can be generic to an entire class of 'essential' product such as beef, blood or vaccines.

It is similarly remarkable that human blood and human tissue, even when supplied commercially, are not subject to the *Restatement (Third) of Torts: Products Liability*. The Reporters briefly attempt to justify this omission on the basis that most States have 'blood shield' statutes limits:[14] 'The liability of sellers of human blood and human tissue to the failure to exercise reasonable care, often by providing that human blood and human tissue are not "products" or that their provision is a "service". Where legislation has not addressed the problem, courts have concluded that strict liability is inappropriate for harm caused by such product contamination.'

Again, it could be argued that the Reporters lost a crucial opportunity to address the underlying policy dilemmas that led to such artificial and anomalous[15] treatment of these infection cases. This is especially significant given that the issues

---

14 § 19, cmt. c. See also Reporters' Note on § 19, cmt. c.
15 That, prima facie, blood products fall well within the catchment of US product rules is illustrated by the (pre-blood shield statute) case of *Rostocki* v. *Southwest Florida Blood Bank, Inc.*, 276 So 2d 475 (Fla, 1973) which held that sale of blood constituted sale of a product and that the defendant blood bank was subject to common law strict liability for products commercially supplied.

involved in the US experience with hepatitis and HIV-infected blood products presented the very sort of policy issues of public interest (especially availability of the essential product type) versus private interest that the BSE/CJD phenomenon does.

In general it is surprising for a Restatement published in 1998 that there is no mention at all of CJD or of BSE,[16] while the sole mention of hepatitis and HIV occurs in the above obscure passage explaining the non-coverage of human blood and human tissue. Of course, the Reporters might defend this omission on the basis that there is little or no US products liability case law concerning such potentially 'generic' infections. But food chain contamination disasters, with the real prospect of inter-generational transmission, are not unknown in the USA. For example, in 1973 toxic chemicals were accidentally fed to dairy cattle in the State of Michigan with the result that virtually all of the 9 million in the State's human population became permanently contaminated by the hazardous chemical polybrominated biphenyl.[17] Other cases include the toxic waste dump at Love Canal[18] and the radiation leak from the Three Mile Island nuclear plant.[19] Foreign food chain disasters, such as the mercury contamination of food chains in and around Minamata Bay (Japan) in the 1950s which killed more than 1,000 and crippled thousands more, have also received prominent coverage in the USA.[20] Today American deer and elk carry a form of BSE and three American hunters have already died of CJD.[21] It is true that the most high profile of these cases were not formulated, and in many cases could not feasibly have been formulated, as products liability cases, but this merely goes to confirm the concern I share with other commentators that the

16 Or even of the Legionnaire's disease case law. See, e.g., *Brennen* v. *Mogul Corp.*, 557 A 2d 870, 872 (Vt, 1988) where a plumber sued the manufacturer of water treatment equipment when he allegedly contracted Legionnaire's disease while working on a cooling tower on the basis that the manufacturer's equipment and chemicals did not prevent growth of Legionella bacteria; *In re Horizon Cruises Litigation*, 101 F Supp 2d 204 (SDNY, 2000) passengers sued after a defective whirlpool filter caused them to contract Legionnaire's disease while aboard the defendant's cruise ship; *Humphry* v. *Riverside Methodist Hosp.*, 488 NE 2d 877 (Ohio, 1986) where the plaintiffs sued the hospital for negligence resulting from contraction of Legionnaire's disease; *Methodist Hospital* v. *Ray*, 551 NE 2d 463 (Ind Ct App, 1990) aff'd 558 NE 2d 829 (Ind, 1990) where the hospital negligently allowed its premises to become infected with Legionella bacteria; *Neill* v. *Western Inns, Inc.*, 595 NW 2d 121 (Iowa, 1999) where the plaintiff contracted Legionnaire's disease, allegedly while staying at a hotel operated by the defendant.

17 See J. Egginton, *Bitter Harvest* (London: Secker & Warburg, 1980), 14, 275, 281, 307: '[Scientists estimate] that only about 10% of the body burden of PBB [contamination] being carried by 9 million people would be excreted in their lifetimes.' For case law, see e.g., *Michigan Chemical Corporation* v. *American Home Assurance Company*, 728 F 2d 374 (6th Cir, 1984); *Oscoda Chapter of PBB Action Committee, Inc.* v. *Department of Natural Resources*, 268 NW 2d 240 (Mich, 1978).

18 Which occurred in 1978; see L. M. Gibbs, *Love Canal: the Story Continues* (Stony Creek, Ct.: New Society Publishers, 1998).

19 See J.V. Rees, *Hostages of Each Other: the Transformation of Nuclear Safety since Three Mile Island* (Chicago, Ill.: University of Chicago Press, 1994).

20 See A. Mishima (R. L. Cage and S. B. Murata, trans.), *Bitter Sea: the Human Cost of Minamata Disease* (Tokyo: Kosei Publishing Company, 1992); W. Eugene and A. M. Smith, *Minamata* (New York: Holt, Rinehart & Winston, 1975).

21 *Electronic Telegraph* (3 May 2001). See also *Wall St J* (24 May 2002) p. 1 and *Time* 12 Aug. 2002.

creation of special rules for injuries associated with commercially supplied products warps our law of obligation and blinkers us to important common themes that run through personal injury cases generally.[22]

Structure of the *Restatement*: fragmentation according to classification of dangerous condition

The second type of fragmentation under the *Restatement* arises where a product claim does not fall into one of the special product-type classes. In such circumstances the case will be dealt with under section 2 and thereunder according to whether the product condition is classed as a 'manufacturing defect', a design condition or a warning condition. Again, as we shall see, the Reporters of the *Restatement (Third) of Torts: Products Liability* lost the opportunity, squarely presented by the infection-in-food cases and HIV/CJD infection-in-blood cases, to examine the wisdom of the critical idea of a 'manufacturing' defect or, at the least, to forge an appropriate definition that would unambiguously classify such cases as within or outside the crucial notion of manufacturing defect.

In the fish soup case the deleterious element in the product, a residual stray bone, was present in the raw material well before any 'manufacturing' process began. In this case, as with the BSE/CJD cases, the production process was not the origin of the danger. In this sense such cases are not like the 'classic' form of manufacturing defect cited in the US products liability literature where the dangerous aspect is introduced into the product by the industrial process.

On the other hand, the Reporters' definition of 'manufacturing defect' is where the product departs from its 'intended' design. Certainly the soup producer would not have intended his or her soup to retain the dangerous bone in the sense of 'desiring' that it be present. This suggests the soup condition would fall inside the *Restatement* definition of 'manufacturing defect'. Moreover, the soup producer may well have been aware of the risk of its presence and have been unable to avoid that risk, at least by reasonable means. Emphasis on this aspect also brings the case close to another characteristic of the classic examples given in the literature of manufacturing defects, namely, where a producer of widgets suspects, fears or knows that one in 100,000 will contain a dangerous departure from the production line norm but rightly believes that it is impossible to avoid that risk, at least by reasonable means. This type of process-introduced but unavoidably dangerous condition was the very type that was targeted by the original reformers who, forty years ago, formulated the rule reflected in section 402A of the *Restatement (Second): Torts*. Today such conditions are unequivocally regarded as within the 'manufacturing defect' classification. That a plaintiff may be able to convince the court to accept this classification for his or her 'infected product' is critical because this classification brings

22 See Stapleton, *Product Liability*.

with it an automatic determination of defectiveness, quite independent of the sort of cost/benefit and reasonable alternative design considerations that might otherwise plague the plaintiff's argument for defectiveness.

How would a BSE/CJD case be dealt with under the *Restatement*?

We do not yet know how extensive the BSE/CJD infection has become. So far five and a half million animals have been slaughtered in Britain as a means of containing the BSE plague, and though only 113 humans are known to have died of the related wave of CJD, scientists have suggested that up to 135,000 people in Britain may have contracted CJD.[23] Imagine a raft of claims brought in the future by people infected with BSE/CJD from generic products such as meat,[24] dairy products,[25] blood[26] and blood products (e.g., vaccines and plasma),[27] human tissue,[28] leather[29] or woollen clothing and the water supply.[30]

23 See http://www.defra.gov.uk. In June 2001 it was reported that UK consumers might still be eating BSE-infected meat because of cross-contamination in abattoirs: J. Meikle, 'BSE Meat Risk from Abattoir Culls' *Guardian* (6 June 2001). So far the known human BSE/CJD death toll in the UK is at least 113 and scientists have suggested that up to 135,000 people in Britain have been infected: *The Telegraph* (15 January 2002); *The Times* (26 October 2001).

24 On 20 March 1996 the UK Government announced that BSE in cattle had been linked to CJD in people. Some months later the EU imposed a worldwide ban on British beef exports, which was lifted on 1 August 1999: D. Brown, 'France Had "No Excuse" for Failing to Lift Ban on British Beef' *Daily Telegraph* (20 June 2001). See also V. Elliott, 'Scientists to Test if Beef is the Cause of CJD' *The Times* (18 May 1999). The UK adopted a policy of slaughtering an estimated 5 million cattle aged more than 30 months in an effort to eradicate BSE. See generally Lord Phillips *et al.*, *The BSE Inquiry*.

25 See, e.g., D. Brown, 'Food Agency Urges Mass Screening of Sheep for BSE' *Daily Telegraph* (1 November 2000).

26 An early report of suspicions among a minority of scientists that CJD could be spread by blood donations: *The Independent* (8 October 1997). Plans made to ban plasma made from pooled donations of UK donors (in favour of imports) because of CJD risk: 27 February 1998. Ban put in place: *Guardian*, (14 May 1998). Report that 'Britain's blood supplies are almost certainly infected with the human form of mad cow disease, the Government has been told': *UK Mail* (20–6 July 1998). Superseded by UK scientists' upgraded warning that there is an 'appreciable risk' of people catching CJD through blood products. See *Guardian Weekly* (8–14 Aug. 2002).

27 The UK government concedes that blood products including vaccines may be at risk of contamination by CJD: *The Sunday Times* (22 February 1998). Thenceforward the Department of Health advised (a) that the CJD risk with current blood supplies was 'theoretical' but (b) that experts agree that there is no way of guaranteeing this. See United Kingdom, *Hansard*, House of Lords, 11th Volume of Session 1997–8, 5 June 1998, volume 590, column 680; 5th Volume of Session 1999–2000, 30 March 2000, volume 611, column 985; 7th Volume of Session 1999–2000, 7 March 2000, volume 345, column 124 WH.

28 An early report of suspicions of the possibility of CJD infection from donated implanted tissue: *UK Mail*, 8–14 December 1997.

29 In the largest study to date, researchers found a link between CJD and exposure to leather including wearing it: C. Hall, 'Research Fails to Find Link between Beef and CJD' *Daily Telegraph* (10 April 1998).

30 On suspicions that part of the UK water supply is contaminated with BSE/CJD see *The Independent* (30 August 1997), 8.

The history against which such claims will be seen is certain to be complex. In relation to each chain of infection to the end type of product there will have been a period where the firm weight of official scientific opinion was that such infection could not enter that particular type of product (for example, the 'cannot cross the species barrier into humans' phase of the BSE/CJD 'mad cow' disease story). Then there will have been a period of growing professional speculation that this might be possible. A third period is where the general population can foresee a real possibility that such infection of the product type might occur. For example, in relation to the entire meat, dairy and blood supplies in the UK many citizens now speculate that there is a risk that an individual product may be BSE/CJD-infected (even if only a tiny fraction of individual products in the class are infected); they are 'generically suspect'. That a similar suspicion exists abroad is illustrated by the banning in Australia, Canada and the United States of blood donations by people who had lived in the UK during the BSE/CJD outbreak.[31] Then a stage is reached when the chain of infection into the product type is confirmed. There may then be stages where a screening test becomes available but is of low reliability and finally a stage when a highly reliable test becomes available.

How would such cases be dealt with under the *Restatement (Third) of Torts: Products Liability*? First, one must look to see if they might fall into one of the special classes.

There seems no way BSE/CJD cases could be handled under section 3, which allows a plaintiff with circumstantial evidence supporting the inference of product defect to get to the jury even though he or she has failed to show the following: that the product departed from its intended design; or that a reasonable alternative design could have been adopted; or what type of product defect (for example manufacturing, design or warning) was present. This is because section 3 rests on an inference of defect,[32] and assumes a consensus about what defect means in relation to the relevant product. It follows that the clearest example of a case falling within section 3 is one where the product fails to perform its 'manifestly intended function' as where the brakes on a new car simply do not work and the driver is injured as a result. This falls squarely within section 3 because here, by definition, there is a consensus that this failure 'bespeaks' defect. But BSE/CJD-infected products will not usually fail in their intended function: infected clothing will still keep a person protected from the elements; infected vaccines may still protect from the targeted disease; infected food may still nourish; and infected blood may save a person from the threat of imminent death. It is not clear from section 3 what else besides a failure

---

31 *Guardian Weekly* (28 September–4 October 2000) (Australia); *Sunday Times* (18 July 1999) (Canada); *Wall Street Journal* (5 June 2001) (USA). The bans apply to those who spent more than six months in the UK between 1980 and 1996.

32 It is worth noting that because the US rule applies in the first instance to all suppliers up the chain of distribution it is immaterial to this provision that the facts do not implicate the behaviour of any particular party. Contrast the classic 'focused' *res ipsa loquitur* rule under which the facts must not only bespeak negligence but they must bespeak the negligence of the defendant.

to perform its manifestly intended function might bring a product within the ambit of the section, so we may assume the BSE/CJD cases will rarely if ever be clearly covered by section 3.

Let us now posit the hardest plaintiff's case: that at the time of trial none of the infected products can be shown to have failed to comply with product safety statutes or regulations, and so would not fall into section 4.

Next we must also recognise that it would be extremely unlikely for a US court to declare that any of such cases fall into the class of manifestly unreasonable design contemplated in section 2, Comment e. This highly controversial provision was reluctantly included by the Reporters to accommodate a few isolated decisions where a US court had, even in the absence of proof of a reasonable alternative design, declared the product design to be defective 'because the extremely high degree of danger posed by... [it] so substantially outweighs its negligible social utility that no rational, reasonable person, fully aware of the relevant facts, would choose to use... the product'.[33] The nature of BSE/CJD infection tends to apply to large market sectors where the risk seems low and the social utility is high in the context of available substitutes. UK citizens who eat beef[34] or accept blood transfusions from domestic donors[35] appreciate both sectors are generically BSE/CJD-suspect.

The end result, then, is that the treatment of the BSE/CJD cases under the *Restatement (Third) of Torts: Products Liability* would be highly fractured. BSE/CJD infection of vaccines will fall to be decided under section 6. BSE/CJD infection of meat and dairy products (and perhaps water) will fall to be decided under section 7, while BSE/CJD infection of human blood and human tissue will not be covered at all by virtue of section 19. BSE/CJD infection of leather or woollen clothing and so on will fall to be decided under the residual section, section 2, and therein will receive different treatment according to whether the product condition is classed as a manufacturing error (§ 2 (a)), a design condition (§ 2 (b)) or a warning condition (§ 2 (c)).

Despite the general claims of the Reporters for their *Restatement*, this fractured treatment that BSE/CJD cases would receive under the *Restatement* does not immediately seem to be the most effective way of addressing the 'conceptual difficulties in trying to respond to products liability claims rationally, consistently, and fairly'.[36] In this context the 'gains to be had from drawing on the American experience'[37] do not seem at all obvious. Perhaps the basic lesson from the USA here is that when a new legal rule emerges without a well-understood theoretical basis, which was certainly the birth conditions of section 402A of the *Restatement (Second): Torts*,[38] there is a temptation for courts to give the rule 'structure' by artificially

33 *Restatement (Third) of Torts: Products Liability* § 2, cmt. e.
34 See n. 23 above.   35 See n. 26 and n. 27 above.
36 Henderson and Twerski, 'What Europe, Japan and Others Can Learn'.
37 *Ibid.*   38 See generally Stapleton, *Product Liability*.

compartmentalising fact situations. Certainly it is easy in theory (if not forensically) to distinguish fact situations involving infection from eating meat from those involving infection from wearing infected clothing. The question is: Does the law have sound reasons to afford separate treatment?

Another feature of these sections (6, 7 and 2) that would be relevant to BSE/CJD cases is that their treatment of the issues depends on whether the product condition that caused the injury is classed as a 'manufacturing defect' defined as 'when the product departs from its intended design even though all possible care was exercised'.[39] Crudely, under all these sections reasonable care is no answer in manufacturing defect cases for which liability is, therefore, strict no matter which supplier in the chain is sued.[40] In contrast, in design or warning cases reasonable care is an answer. This means, for example, that a product with an unforeseeable *design* condition that causes harm cannot, by definition, be defective under the *Restatement (Third) of Torts: Products Liability*,[41] while a product with an unforeseeable *manufacturing error* that causes harm is, by definition, defective.

The problem here is that the US experience as set out in the *Restatement* gives little *conceptual* guidance as to how and why, in design conditions, the determination of unforeseeability exculpates from liability; but that in manufacturing error conditions the determination of unforeseeability does not exculpate from liability. Moreover, since treatment of unforeseeability is so dramatically different according to how we define 'manufacturing defect', the fact that this is so unclear that it is not possible to say how we should classify mass biological infections such as HIV and, no doubt, BSE/CJD is, as a practical matter, a considerable gap in US jurisprudence. Are such infected products to be classed as manufacturing errors because they depart from the intended, in the sense of desired, condition of the end product? Or is the rationale for the strict liability imposed in the case of manufacturing defects embedded in the idea that such errors are introduced into the product by the process of manufacture, in which case such BSE/CJD-infected products fall outside that classification and outside the strict liability imposed on 'manufacturing defects' because the infection was present in the raw materials of the product?

The treatment of infection cases by the *Restatement*: raw materials versus food

Though, as the Appendix shows, US courts have had considerable experience of cases involving infected products, the *Restatement (Third) of Torts: Products Liability*, that is the case law it tracks, seems confused when dealing with such cases.

39 *Restatement (Third) of Torts: Products Liability* § 2(a). See text accompanying n. 13.
40 Strict liability may be defined as liability in relation to which it is not an answer for the defendant to prove that its conduct was reasonable.
41 Stapleton, '*Restatement (Third) of Torts: Products Liability*, an Anglo-Australian Perspective', 388, fn. 89.

It baldly classifies certain infection contexts as being ones of manufacturing errors and subject to strict liability because they depart from the intended design:[42]

> When raw materials are contaminated or otherwise defective within the meaning of s. 2(a), the seller of the raw materials is subject to liability for harm caused by such defects . . . a basic raw material such as sand, gravel, or kerosene cannot be defectively designed . . . The same considerations apply to failure-to-warn claims against sellers of raw materials.
>
> [Concerning contamination of human blood and blood-related products by the hepatitis virus or the HIV virus.] Absent a special rule dealing with human blood and tissue, such contamination presumably would be subject to the rules of ss. 1 and 2(a). Those Sections impose strict liability when a product departs from its intended design even though all possible care was exercised in the preparation and marketing of the product.

On the other hand, the *Restatement (Third) of Torts: Products Liability* takes an exceptional attitude to food. Here the plaintiff cannot rely simply on the infection rendering the product a departure from its intended design and thus a manufacturing error. The plaintiff must also show the product fails the 'consumer expectations test'. Hence a harm-causing ingredient of the food product constitutes a defect only if a reasonable consumer would not expect the food to contain that ingredient.[43] Examples given include not only cases involving a failure to remove structural parts of the raw material such as a fish bone in fish chowder, a chicken bone in a chicken enchilada, and a pearl in an oyster, but also infection cases such as bacteria in clams and oysters.[44]

In fact, US case law on food infection cases is notoriously confused. It has failed to find a coherent line to distinguish 'adulteration' by infection, from infections that are 'an inherent aspect of the product'.[45] Moreover, this parallels the doctrinal confusion in the non-food infection contexts that have come to light. For example, to evade the difficult challenge to doctrine they present, certain (infected) live organisms such as parrots and gilts, have been judicially refused the classification of 'products' by US courts[46] in much the same artificial way some courts and statutes dealt with infected blood. In contrast, other courts have accepted the 'product' status of organic material but disagreed on the approach the law should take.

It is in this context of disarray that one should read the *Third Restatement*'s conclusion that, *in relation to food*, even infected substances are 'products' but that their defectiveness should be judged by 'consumer expectations.'[47]

---

42 *Restatement (Third) of Torts: Products Liability* § 5, cmt. c; § 19, cmt. c.
43 *Ibid.*, § 7.   44 *Ibid.*   45 *Ibid.*, § 2, cmt. h.
46 *Anderson* v. *Farmers Hybrid Cos.*, 408 NE 2d 1194 (Ill App Ct, 1980), infected gilts; *Latham* v. *Wal-Mart Stores, Inc.*, 818 SW 2d 673 (Mo App, 1991), psittacosis-infected parrot; *Malicki* v. *Koci*, 700 NE 2d 913 (Ohio Ct App, 1997), psittacosis-infected parrot.
47 *Restatement (Third) of Torts: Products Liability* § 7, cmt. b.

A consumer expectations test in this context relies upon culturally defined, widely shared standards that food products ought to meet. Although consumer expectations are not adequate to supply a standard for defect in other contexts, assessments of what consumers have a right to expect in various commercial food preparations are sufficiently well-formed that judges and triers of fact can sensibly resolve whether liability should be imposed using this standard.

The embrace of the consumer expectation test here is anomalous[48] and dangerous. Elsewhere I have argued that the consumer expectations test simply gives the fact-finder its head and is both normatively and empirically incoherent.[49] Even so, one might accept that it could be a *workable*, albeit theoretically unattractive, test where the fact-finder is the 'black-box' of a jury and where the issue involves a 'one-off' product condition such as an isolated incident of bacterial poisoning of shellfish.[50] But it is a wholly inadequate approach to the type of mass generic biological infection cases that are looming in Western Europe and perhaps elsewhere.[51] According to the *Restatement*, the USA seems to have had no case law experience of such generic infection cases formulated as products liability claims apart from the blood infection cases. And in the latter cases the consensus admission was that they were too hard to accommodate coherently within the US products rule, in other words, with an adequately convincing explication of the policy and moral issues at stake.

Contrasting gaps in case law experience

How was it that the anomaly in US products liability case law between the treatment of infection cases depending on whether they are food cases or not could develop? This was because of an accidental gap in the US experience, specifically the absence of generic infection cases formulated as cases of products liability. Such gaps occur in any system, even one with experience of 'forty years ... [with] fairly

---

48 Contrast the vigorous rejection of that test by the Reporters for design/warning cases (where they argue a cost–benefit approach is the only coherent one) and for manufacturing error cases (where they use the production line norm): *Restatement (Third) of Torts: Products Liability* § 2, cmt. g. And see Henderson and Twerski, 'What Europe, Japan and Other Countries Can Learn', 17–20.

49 Stapleton, '*Restatement (Third) of Torts: Products Liability*, an Anglo-Australian Perspective', 376–9.

50 On the other hand, the test's integrity, and hence its workability, will be immediately suspect in systems where the fact-finder is required to give empirical and/or analytical justifications for its determination. European and Australian judges will be acutely aware of what is expected of them and are therefore likely to reject consumer expectations as a controlling test of defect even in such one-off food cases.

51 BSE-infected animal feed and CJD-infected blood products have been exported by the UK: A. Osborn, 'EU Beefs about BSE' *Guardian* (16 February 2001).

sophisticated courts ... [confronting] a substantial and steady caseload'.[52] In the USA central gaps in the case law experience relate not only to these generic infection cases but also to development risks (unforeseeable dangers in the design) such as those at the centre of the thalidomide disaster in Europe which triggered products reform there.

In Europe the very low density across all jurisdictions of products liability cases, pre- and post-Directive, has also left a central but different gap in experience. There have yet to be many of the sort of claims that have put the main pressure on US products rules, namely those involving known or intended product conditions, that is advertent design choices, where the central issue is how much safety a consumer is entitled to. These so-called 'classic design cases' are ones that 'do not involve product malfunctions, violations of safety regulations, or egregiously dangerous products',[53] yet the 'plaintiffs nevertheless plausibly claim that the designs are unacceptably dangerous, and therefore, legally defective'.[54] My example of such a case is where the design of a chair is unable to withstand the weight of a person (weighing, say, 300 pounds).[55] The Reporters' example is of an axle failure where a car driven at thirty miles per hour hits an eight-inch pothole.[56] These are cases where the dangerous condition is part of the product line norm; it is known, it is intended and chosen by the producer, but there is not a consensus that this condition renders the product 'defective'. There is, in other words, no agreement that it is a *manifestly* unreasonable design (under § 2, cmt. e). In such cases as the chair and axle, people disagree on how much safety is enough.

The reason the *Restatement (Third) of Torts: Products Liability* attracted such controversy in the USA was the Reporters' concern to set out the tests they believed US courts had developed to control classic design cases. The Reporters assert that 'to find a defect on those facts, the court will require the jury to apply some sort of general normative standard regarding how much axle strength automobile designs should require'.[57] In other words, in these cases defectiveness would have to be determined by the cost–benefit (risk-utility) *reasonableness* principle to determine how much safety is enough.[58] According to the Reporters, classic design cases would also only succeed if the plaintiff could bring evidence of a reasonable alternative design (RAD). I have argued elsewhere, however, that in simple classic design cases

52 See Henderson and Twerski, 'What Europe, Japan and Other Countries Can Learn', 14.
53 *Ibid.*, 17.
54 See J. A. Henderson, Jr and A. D. Twerski, *Achieving Consensus on Defective Product Design* (1998) 83 *Cornell L Rev* 867, 876–7.
55 See Stapleton, '*Restatement (Third) of Torts: Products Liability*, an Anglo-Australian Perspective', 379, 390, 392, 395, 397.
56 See Henderson and Twerski, *Achieving Consensus*, 877.   57 *Ibid.*
58 See J. A. Henderson, Jr and A. D. Twerski, 'Arriving at Reasonable Alternative Design: the Reporters' Travelogue' (1997) 30 *U Mich J L Ref* 563, 588.

such as the chair and axle cases where the issue is simply how much strength and safety is enough, the issue of whether the plaintiff can show evidence of a RAD is a red herring because it is clear that the chair could be made stronger for more money or with loss of style values.[59]

In short, we seem to have a US regime that is incoherent in its approaches to infection cases. In particular, it would fail to provide any redress to BSE/CJD infections if they were contracted from human blood or human tissue. It might provide recovery in cases of BSE/CJD infections contracted from food only if a reasonable consumer would not expect the food to contain that ingredient. It might provide recovery in cases of BSE/CJD infections contracted from leather/woollen clothing without proof of defect, RAD or fault on the basis that these product conditions are to be classed, just as infected raw material cases are classed, as 'manufacturing defects' cases under section 2(a) (on the basis that the condition of such infected products departs from their intended design). Finally, the US regime might provide recovery only on the basis that the product condition was to be classed as a design case falling under section 2(b), namely defectiveness being determined by the cost/benefit reasonableness principle (and not the consumer expectations test) and RAD requirement.

The European Directive and its clones

Products case law experience on the Directive and its clones is still thin. Even now it has not exploded into the troublesome area of classic design cases and it is unclear whether the Directive will provide an acceptable structure within which to handle such cases as the chair and axle. However, the special experience of Europe in relation to thalidomide, a case of allegedly unforeseeable design condition, raises the question of whether it produced a products regime that will better be able to accommodate BSE/CJD mass infection cases than that set out in the *Third Restatement*. Certainly the Directive is not bedevilled by dubious classifications based on type of product or type of defect as the *Third Restatement* is.

Thalidomide ensured that unforeseeable product conditions received explicit treatment in the Directive, though ironically that treatment was pro-defendant: the highly controversial development risk defence. The critical 'defect' issue under Article 6 in unforeseeable product condition cases, as in all product cases under the Directive, is not what level of safety we *actually* expect,[60] for we do not expect,

---

59 See Stapleton, '*Restatement (Third) of Torts: Products Liability*, an Anglo-Australian Perspective', 379.
60 This cannot be the appropriate test for defectiveness under Article 6. Members of the public no doubt expect aspirin to be 100 per cent safe, but the fact that it is not 100 per cent safe does not, *per se*, render aspirin defective. See Stapleton, '*Restatement (Third) of Torts: Products Liability*, an

for example, that pregnancy drugs might deform our babies. The critical issue is what are we *'entitled* to expect', and *when* should we consider this in relation to the product: the time it was supplied or at the time of trial when we know its ghastly effects for certain.

Issues European courts will need to address include: whether the defect standard involves an evaluation of various incommensurable factors of costs and benefits or some other standard; *when* the apparent costs of the product should be evaluated (because it may well be that by the time of trial these are revealed to be much higher than expected at the time the product was commercially supplied, as was the case with thalidomide);[61] whether exculpatory motivations such as that behind the development risk defence (that there are some things even a reasonable producer can do nothing about and that, at least in some cases, that should provide exculpation) are also present in the definition of defect (for example, that the product may not be defective because it is essential, has no safer feasible substitutes, and the producer did all that the public interest could reasonably require); whether such infection cases are to be classed as 'manufacturing error' cases; and, if so, whether this excludes the development risk defence in Article 7(e).

So far the case law results under the Directive in relation to infected products have been mixed. The relatively unenlightening result in *Worsley* v. *Tambrands Ltd*,[62] which concerned an allegation arising from toxic shock syndrome associated with tampon use, was that there was no case to answer. Similarly in the case of *Lopez* v. *Star World Enterprises Pty.*,[63] a mass infected food case, brought under the Australian legislative clone of the Directive,[64] a judgment on the issues was precluded by the settlement of the action consequent on the bankruptcy of the defendant. *Ryan* v.

Anglo-Australian Perspective', 376–9. Another example is penicillin, which is one of the safest of antibiotics but has in rare cases been implicated in the death of users: A. L. Diamond, 'Product Liability and Pharmaceuticals in the United Kingdom' in G. F. Woodroffe (ed.), *Consumer Law in the EEC* (London: Sweet & Maxwell, 1984), 129.

61 In contrast, this critical hindsight/foresight distinction on which the development risk defence clearly rests and which gives it its force was not central to the thinking of the reformers behind section 402A of the *Second Restatement*. It was only after insightful academic work and the embarrassment of cases such as *Beshada* v. *Johns-Manville Prods. Corp.*, 447 A 2d 539 (NJ, 1982) (on which see Stapleton, *Product Liability*, 33) that it became widely appreciated in the USA that how its products regime treats unforeseeable defects is a litmus test for whether it imposes true strict liability; for strict liability is liability for which reasonable care is no answer and, as it is impossible to act carelessly in relation to a defect that is unforeseeable, imposition of liability for such a defect reveals that liability to be a strict one. US courts refuse to impose such liability for unforeseeable conditions classified as design conditions and warning conditions. This is why the *Third Restatement* correctly concedes that, despite the academic and judicial rhetoric of the 'strict liability' imposed on product manufacturers by the rule in section 402A, liability under that rule has always been based on unreasonableness in cases of conditions classified as design conditions and warning conditions.

62 [2000] PIQR 95 (Ebsworth J., QBD, 3 December 1999). See also [2000] C P Rep 43.

63 [1999] FCA 104 (28 January 1999).

64 Part VA of the Trade Practices Act 1974 (Cth). See Stapleton, 'Comparing Australian Product Liability with EU and US', 195–201.

Great Lakes Council,[65] a hepatitis-in-oysters case, was brought under the same legislation. The judge found the product defective and yet allowed the development risk defence. Both findings were upheld on appeal.[66] In *A* v. *OLVG Hospital Amsterdam*[67] a blood transfusion resulted in HIV infection and the court held that while the blood was defective it was protected by the development risk defence. In contrast, in *Re: Hepatitis C Litigation, A* v. *National Blood Authority*[68] over a hundred claimants sued the National Blood Authority over hepatitis C infection from blood. Mr. Justice Burton held that the blood was defective and that the development risk defence did not operate. Finally, *Henning Veedfald* v. *Arhus Amstkommune*,[69] the first product liability Reference for a Preliminary Ruling to be referred to the European Court of Justice concerning the Directive 85/374/EEC, concerned a tainted flushing fluid which ruined a kidney intended for transplantation. However, 'defectiveness' was not in issue and the questions for the court related only to general points not specific to infection cases, such as the meaning of the clause 'put into circulation' and whether the Directive imposed liability on non-profit suppliers.

More fundamentally, *Ryan's* case, like most infection cases,[70] highlights the artificiality of the product/service distinction in a law of obligations and the incoherence of the idea that products liability looks at the product and not the human behaviour surrounding its production and handling. In *Ryan's* case the hepatitis infection of the oysters could have been prevented by the reasonable care of the defendants,[71] so although the claim under the clone of the Directive failed, parallel claims in negligence succeeded. It shows how bizarre it is for there to be a liability regime that covers products alone. It is equally bizarre that we have a separate legal rule that covers BSE/CJD cases where the infection arose through contact with a tangible product such as food, which has been commercially supplied, but does

---

65 [1999] FCA 177 (5 March 1999).
66 On appeal as *Graham Barclay Oysters Pty. Ltd* v. *Ryan* [2000] FCA 1099 (9 August 2000) The case is now on final appeal to the High Court of Australia. An explanation of these findings is that the defectiveness of the product is assessed in the light of its costs as we know them at trial and in the light of the product's utility as judged at the time of circulation and the substitutes then available. Here the costs were considerable and the utility was low, because oysters as a food have many safe substitutes, hence defectiveness could be established. The defence was available, however, because there was no reliable way to screen for the defect in an individual oyster. The fairness of this result must be considered in the light of hypothetical fact situations such as if one imagines that the infection got into the oysters by means of the undetected unpredictable act of a terrorist.
67 District Court Amsterdam, 3 February 1999, *Nederlandse Jurisprudentie* 1999, 621. Also known as *Hartman* v. *Stichting Sanquin Bloedvoorziening* and *Scholten* v. *The Foundation Sanquin of Blood Supply*.
68 [2001] All ER (D) 293. See S. Pearl, 'Damaging Goods' (2001) 145 *Solic J* 424. The author acted as Consultant to the NBA.
69 ECJ, Case 203/99, judgment of 10 May 2001 (Danish Organ Transplant Solution) [2001] ECR1 – 3549. The DTI submitted comments to the ECJ.
70 See, e.g., the successful Australian Legionnaire's case argued solely in negligence: *Australian Current Law News*, 9 April 2001.
71 See Stapleton, '*Restatement (Third) of Torts: Products Liability*, an Anglo-Australian Perspective', 385.

not cover cases of BSE/CJD infection in a workplace such as a farm, dairy, abattoir or butcher's shop, by a service (for example, person-to-person infection in a commercial setting such as a doctor's or dentist's surgery), or by infection from environmental factors such as wind-carried pathogens. Why, for example, do we have a separate liability rule that covers only cases of foot and mouth infection by contact with infected products that have been commercially supplied, but not cases of infection by the wind from pyres burning slaughtered stock, or infection of those sent to do the slaughtering,[72] or other avenues of infection from not-yet supplied infected matter?

Conclusion

The Reporters of the *Third Restatement* are right to criticise foreign systems for their neglect of the important issues raised by classic design cases such as the strength-of-chair and strength-of-axle cases. But in relation to the challenge that mass infection cases pose to special product liability regimes, it would seem that the *Third Restatement* has little to offer in the way of coherent guidance. In contrast, it might have seemed that the Directive would provide a better model given that it does not require the classification of the defect, does not give separate treatment to claims based on certain evidentiary shortcuts, does not treat different product types such as food separately, and pays explicit attention to the exculpatory notion of the capacity of the defendant to respond to a risk. Yet the isolated case law concerning infected products that has so far emerged has not so far produced such a clear pattern.

Finally, it should be emphasised that, like classic design cases, mass infection cases would have, in any case, eventually arisen under pre-Directive legal rules such as the tort of negligence.[73] *Ryan's* case suggests that, despite all the energy thrown into the Directive and *Third Restatement*, the law of negligence may continue to provide citizens with a more flexible and coherent cause of action. Traditional general causes of action, such as negligence and warranty, also provide a clearer forum for courts to enunciate the complex moral and policy dilemmas that characterise generic mass infections of essential product sectors. The Canadian Supreme Court judgment in *Ter Neuzen* v. *Korn*[74] illustrates this. There, in a case involving HIV

72 See, e.g., 'Slaughterman Tested for Foot and Mouth' *Daily Telegraph* (23 April 2001); 'Foot and Mouth Man Not Told of Risk' *Daily Telegraph* (26 April 2001).
73 See, e.g., *The Creutzfeldt–Jakob Disease Litigation* QBD: 54 BMLR at 1 (7 April 1995); at 8 (19 July 1996); at 79 (19 December 1996); at 85 (18 November 1997); at 92 (18 December 1997); at 95 (23 March 1998); at 100 (27 April 1998); at 104 (22 May 1998); and at 111 (19 June 1998). Cases may also be taken under other statutory provisions, see, e.g., *Re: 'E'* v. *Australian Red Cross Society* (1991) 99 ALR 601; (1991) 105 ALR 53 (Full Federal Court) (an Australian case under Part V, Div 2 of the Trade Practices Act 1974 (Cth) involving HIV-infected blood products).
74 [1995] 3 SCR 674.

infection from an artificial insemination procedure, the Court was able to explain in detail its finding that 'it must be recognized that biological products such as blood and semen, unlike manufactured products, carry certain inherent risks. It would be inappropriate to imply a warranty of fitness and merchantability in the circumstances of this case. Moreover, any warranty would simply be to take reasonable care.' Of course, such traditional causes of action can still present formidable barriers of proof of causation and, in the case of the tort of negligence, proof of carelessness, particularly in latent infection cases. But there is still much that could be done to reorient evidentiary rules to be more claimant-friendly in cases brought against powerful commercial concerns.[75] An appreciation of how our liability rules cope with mass infections of major and/or important natural products will become even more critical as we cope with the recurrence of viruses such as foot and mouth disease[76] and we move into the era of genetically modified flora and fauna.

Appendix: A selection of US infection cases

Anderson v. Farmers Hybrid Co., 408 NE 2d 1194 (Ill App Ct, 1980) (diseased gilts).

Ayala v. Bartolome, 940 SW 2d 727 (Tex Ct App, 1997) (raw oysters contaminated by bacteria).

Bhagvandoss v. Beiersdorf, Inc., 723 SW 2d 392 (Mo, 1997) (bandages infected by microorganism *Rhizopus*).

Branch v. Willis-Knighton Medical Center 636 So 2d 211 (La, 1994) (hepatitis-infected blood).

Clime v. Dewey Beach Enterprises, 831 F Supp 341 (D Del, 1993) (applying Delaware law) (infected raw shellfish).

Kilpatrick v. Superior Ct., 11 Cal Rptr 2d 323 (Cal App, 1992) (infected raw oysters).

Johnesee v. Stop and Shop Co., 416 A 2d 956 (NJ Super Ct App Div, 1980) (hepatitis-infected canned soup).

Koster v. Scotch Associates, 640 A 2d 1225 (NJ Super Ct Law Div, 1993) (caesar salad contaminated with *Salmonella enteritidis* from raw eggs).

Latham v. Wal-Mart Stores, Inc., 818 SW 2d 673 (Mo Ct App, 1991) (psittacosis-infected parrot).

Malicki v. Koci 700 NE 2d 913 (Ohio Ct App, 1997) (psittacosis-infected parrot).

Savage v. Peterson Distributing Company Inc., 150 NW 2d 804 (Mich, 1967) (contaminated mink feed).

75 See e.g. *Fairchild v. Glenhaven Funeral Securities Ltd* [2002] 3 WLR 89 analysed in J. Stapleton, 'Lords a'leaping Evidentiary Gaps' (2002) 10 *Torts LJ* 276.

76 One estimate of the number of animals slaughtered in an attempt to control the Spring 2001 outbreak of foot and mouth in the UK is at least 6.5 million animals or more than 10 per cent of Britain's livestock: *Guardian Weekly* (10–16 October 2002). Compare the 5 million earlier slaughtered in an attempt to eradicate BSE in cattle; see n. 24 above.

Sease v. *Taylor's Pets Inc.*, 700 P 2d 1054 (Ore Ct App, 1985) (rabid skunk).

Simeon v. *Doe*, 618 So 2d 848 (La, 1993) (oysters infected with naturally occurring *Vibrio vulnificus*).

Snyder v. *American Ass'n of Blood Banks*, 659 A 2d 482 (NJ Super Ct App Div, 1995) (HIV-infected blood).

Thirsk v. *Ethicon, Inc.*, 687 P 2d 1315 (Colo Ct App, 1983) (surgery patient infected by a surgical bone wax contaminated with *Mycobacterium fortuitum*).

Worrell v. *Sachs*, 563 A 2d 1387 (Conn Super Ct, 1989) (infection from diseased parasite-carrying puppy).

Part III
Services and the consumer

7 Services of general interest and European private law

THOMAS WILHELMSSON

Privatisation and new tasks for private law

During the last decades of the twentieth century the state governments of most European countries have been the targets of reorganisational measures which have affected the relationship between the state and the market. Various methods of privatisation or marketisation have been used. Privatisation measures in the narrow sense have limited the extent of state ownership. In addition, public service functions have been contracted out to private bodies, or have been reduced, leaving the market to provide the service. Economic result-orientation and other market-oriented mechanisms have been introduced in the public sector. Once regulated branches of industry and commerce, as well as international trade and financial markets, have been deregulated.

Tracing the pressures related to such measures from the legal point of view, one should not conclude that they simply imply demands for deregulation of an excessive public sector and therefore mainly affect the field of public law. Various consequences for private law can also be envisaged. Some are rather self-evident: the shrinking of the tasks performed by public bodies and the market-orientation seem logically to imply an increase in the relative importance of private law within the legal order. More interesting than this assessment, however, are the possible consequences as to the content of private law. My essay will focus on some of these consequences.[1]

It is interesting to note, as a starting point, that one may assume that contradictory pressures on private law will follow from the privatisation/marketisation tendency. On the one hand, the ideology of deregulation and privatisation that is used to legitimate the cuts in public welfare may be used to justify 'deregulation' of private law as well. Indeed, there is evidence of such developments. For example, some features of English contract cases after Thatcherism have been explained with reference to the new ideological climate.[2] Such thinking would emphasise the view that

---

I thank Frey Nybergh for comments on this paper.

1 For a more general account, see the papers from a conference dealing with the issue of privatisation and private law collected in T. Wilhelmsson and S. Hurri (eds.), *From Dissonance to Sense: Welfare State Expectations, Privatisation and Private Law* (Aldershot: Ashgate, 1999).

2 See P. S. Atiyah, *Freedom of Contract and the New Right* (Stockholm: Juristförlaget, 1989).

the questions that may arise should, as far as possible, be left to be solved in the marketplace by the contracting parties, without interference from the state. Mandatory private law should be used very reluctantly.

On the other hand, one may refer to the fact that the withdrawal of the welfare state has not necessarily removed (although it may have altered) the welfare expectations of citizens. There is much empirical evidence of this fact available in Europe. Surveys made in several Western European countries have shown that the welfare state seems to enjoy relatively stable support among the majority of the population,[3] although the political élite often seems more sceptical. In Nordic countries in particular, the legitimacy of the welfare state is still strong; equality still functions as an important pressure for legitimacy in these countries.[4] The question therefore is how these expectations of citizens can be fulfilled in the new privatised environment. One way is to expect private law to move into the policy area which has been left vacant by the withdrawal of public law. If the citizens' welfare expectations are taken seriously, one may encounter stronger emphasis on private law regulation as a tool for channelling responsibilities and compelling the fulfilment of such expectations. When the provision of a service is moved to the marketplace, out of reach of internal public regulation, the regulatory need may be fulfilled by private law methods.

In other words, opportunities for developing new strategies in private law in the present social circumstances grow out of the contradiction between marketisation and welfarist expectations. This is a key starting point of my essay. What new private law means are to be envisaged when public services are, to an increasing extent, performed on the basis of a market rationality?

This essay does not analyse in detail the numerous ways in which private law in various countries has assumed this new type of responsibility. The actual situation is very different depending on the different legal and societal contexts, and it is strongly affected by traditions such as the much deeper cleavage between private and public law in the continental setting than in the common law. I will therefore analyse the new opportunities for private law against a limited societal and legal background, the European Union considered from a Nordic perspective that is, and in relation only to a subject that is delimited in several directions.

First, the development closely affects many so-called services of general interest which hitherto have been provided to citizens by the state or other public or semi-public bodies. The privatisation and/or marketisation of the providers of such services have placed new issues on the agenda, which may affect the legal

3 See the Summary by H. Ervasti, 'Kansalaiskritiikki ja hyvinvointivaltio' in P. Kosonen and M. Sakslin (eds.), *Sosiaalietujen muutokset: vastuunjaon ongelma* (Helsinki: Kansaneläkelaitos, 1998), 63, 65.
4 See P. Kosonen, 'Den nordiska välfärdsmodellen och dess framtid' in P. Letto-Vanamo (ed.), *Nordisk identitet. Nordisk rätt i europeisk gemenskap* (Helsingfors: Institut för internationell ekonomisk rätt vid Helsingfors universitet, 1998), 43, 50.

system in various ways. I limit myself here to discussing developments in respect of services of general interest, and the need for new private law rules in this context.

Secondly, even within the area of services of general interest, there is a multitude of new private law regulation models available. For example, I could discuss the expectations concerning various kinds of mandatory regulation of the contractual relationships between providers of such services and their clients (consumers).[5] Rather than describing the variety of these models, I will instead search for a more principled approach.

The move from public to private law implies a move from one set of principles to another. In an international legal discussion, it is especially important to focus on this switch of principles. This approach is also made interesting by the effect that developments in this area can have on general private law culture.

In this respect, the privatisation of some important public utilities opens up a very interesting new development in private law. If new private law principles develop to cover needs perceived to arise in privatised areas, it is then a relatively short step to extend them to cover such services of general interest which traditionally have been offered within the private sector as well, or even to extend them to cover consumer contracts in general. This is one of the reasons why it is important to discuss the issue on the level of private law *principles*, and not simply as a matter for concrete regulation related to each individual service. The new private law rules on privatised public utilities can become a Trojan horse (in a positive understanding of that metaphor) through which welfarist elements are allowed to be infused in private law, including consumer law, more generally. The development of private law in relation to services of general interest may 'infect' other areas of private law with more welfarist reasoning.

Public law principles through private law?

As long as a service is provided by a public entity, it is usually clear that a number of public law principles underlie its provision:[6]

---

5 In the Nordic countries, several studies concerning the problems connected with services of general interest have emphasised the need for improving the position of the consumers in the standard form contracts in use. See, e.g., TemaNord 1997:612, *Elavregleringens konsumenteffekter* (Copenhagen: Nordisk ministerråd, 1997), 65. For the view that mandatory rules in respect of these contractual relationships are required, see J. Heliskoski, M. Sunila, J. Tala and M. Varis, *Kuluttajien maksuvaikeudet ja välttämättömyyspalvelut* (Helsinki: National Research Institute of Legal Policy, 1996), 118. These expectations have been partially fulfilled: e.g., in Finland the amendment of the Act on the Electricity Market in 1999 (Act 466/1999), the new Chapter 6a (on electricity contracts), the Act on Water Services (Act 119/2001), Chapters 4–6, and the Act on Postal Services (Act 313/2001), Chapter 4.
6 See P. Arajärvi, 'Valtionhallinnon muutos ja yksilön asema' (1995) 24 *Oikeus* 383, 385.

- The principle of objectivity.
- The principle of equality.
- The principle that decisions are bound by purpose.
- The principle of proportionality.
- The principle of neutrality.
- The principle of compulsory provision of service.

Such principles have traditionally not been considered to be, as such or in similar form, directly applicable in a private law context. In addition, the principle of transparency (applied in the provision of public services in the Nordic countries, but not in all European countries) does not necessarily cover a privatised service, and the internal governmental methods of access to justice and of surveillance are often not applicable.[7] In addition, in bilingual and multilingual countries, like Finland, the requirement concerning provision of public services in minority languages is usually not extended to the private sector.

The question is whether private law, in spite of this traditional situation, can to some extent be used to fulfil the expectations of the public to be treated in accordance with such principles, even though the relevant service is privatised or marketised. Hence the title of this section: Public law principles through private law?

When speaking about services of general interest, from a welfarist point of view (with regard to the welfarist expectations of the citizenry), the question of *access to services* on reasonable terms seems especially acute. As long as a particular service is provided by the public sector, the above-mentioned public law principles of equality and of compulsory provision of that service apply. Every citizen has the right to receive the service on the same terms as other citizens. My first question is, therefore, to what extent and through what kind of principle can this right be upheld when the service is subject to private law rules only? I will discuss a private law principle of non-discrimination as a basis for access to service.

The discussion is taken a step further at the end of the essay. As the public sphere of government in the welfare state is expected to have a special responsibility towards the most disadvantaged citizens, as determined by the principle of compulsory provision of a service, there is a case for asking whether this expectation can also be upheld to some extent after privatisation. My theme here is a possible private law principle of *social force majeure* and protection against disconnection.

Services of general interest – the core area

Although the need for new ideas and rules in the field of services of general interest has been perceived to be strong, within both public law and private law,

---

7 *Ibid.*, 388 ff. However, public surveillance of privatised services is not necessarily completely removed by privatisation. With respect to the problems of legal ombudsmen in this context, see L. Lehtimaja, 'Privatisering ur laglighetsövervakningens synvinkel' (2000) 136 *Tidskrift, utgiven av Juridiska Föreningen i Finland* 587.

and the discussion concerning the regulation of such services has been intense in many countries, it is not possible to give any generally accepted definition of the concept.

The term 'services of general interest' is fairly vague and covers a wide group of varying situations. As a legal concept, it refers both to the concept 'services of general economic interest' used in the Treaty of Rome (now Art. 86), the precise meaning of which is purposely not spelled out in the Treaty but left to the member states to define,[8] and to various national doctrines such as the French doctrine of *Service Public*. These services are linked to tasks that are important for society and its economy as a whole.[9]

From the point of view of consumer policy, however, some of these services of general interest are more obviously in focus than others. Although consumers are interested in the reliable functioning of the infrastructure of society in general, consumer policy primarily looks at services offered directly to consumers. Of special interest, in the light of the privatisation and marketisation tendencies, are services that the consumer in the welfare state has grown to expect will, in some way or other, be offered or guaranteed by the public sector.

Such expectations have been connected especially to certain services that are considered to be necessary for the daily life of each citizen. These services are of primary interest in consumer law discourse. They are services that can be defined as necessary for 'a decent life' in modern society. They are services that are created to meet the basic needs of the people and are therefore viewed in Europe as social rights.[10] Although it is not possible to provide a strict legal definition of these necessary services, they generally have the following features:[11]

- The service fulfils a basic need of its users.
- There is often not any reasonable alternative to the service.
- There are few producers of the service.
- The service is based on a long-term relationship.

In discussions about such services, the focus has been on services that are significantly affected by privatisation. In this context, one usually encounters such services as the provision of electricity, gas and heating, water and telephone services, and perhaps also postal services. These are necessary services that a consumer in a modern society cannot reasonably be expected to do without. These services are usually termed *public utilities*.

---

8 It is common in this context to refer to the principle of member states' freedom to decide. See, e.g., the Communication from the Commission, COM(2000) 580 final 11.

9 C. Scott, 'Services of General Interest in EC Law: Matching Values to Regulatory Technique in the Public and Privatised Sectors' (2000) 6 *European LJ* 310, 313, distinguishes three types of service of general interest: the economic, the social and the strategic.

10 See the seminar memorandum of the EU conference on services of general interest in Helsinki 1999, arranged in connection with the Finnish presidency of the EU.

11 See Heliskoski *et al.*, *Kuluttajien maksuvaikeudet*, 15.

To this category, one could add transportation and health care. As the former is usually not based on any long-term relationship (although monthly and yearly tickets could perhaps be defined as such), and as the latter is tightly connected with general issues of social security, these services give rise to different questions from those which arise in connection with the services mentioned in the previous paragraph. Therefore, the former will not be specifically addressed in the following discussion.

The basic needs of the citizenry is a concept the content of which varies from time to time and which is largely socially and technologically determined. In society as presently constituted, certain *financial services* seem very important to the fulfilment of the needs of the citizen. The performance of day-to-day payments as well as the ability to receive payments is often dependent on access to a bank account, and in the mature 'credit card society' some form of access to credit cards is important. Although financial services are different from those services mentioned previously, in the sense that citizens have not traditionally expected the public sector to provide them, it is nonetheless important to include them in any current discussion of necessary services. In fact, the provision of means of payment (i.e., money) is undoubtedly considered a public task, and credit and bank cards are presently perhaps the most important means of payment. There has recently been much legal discussion of access to bank accounts and other financial services.[12]

In the context of the 'information society', it is also worthwhile to discuss the status of *information society services*. The Commission of the European Union, in its Green Paper on the information society generally, warns of potential 'inequalities between the information rich and the information poor'.[13] In the consumer marketplace, the benefits of increased choice, more convenient shopping and better information are certainly received to a greater extent by better-off consumers, while less fortunate consumers are usually not in a position to benefit to the same extent. A sound consumer policy should focus more on the needs of those consumers who do not have easy access to the new technology. It is important therefore to discuss the extent to which the developing rules and principles on the services dealt with in this chapter should apply to information society services as well.

Financial services and information society services are perhaps the best examples of services that run the 'risk' of becoming infected by the new principles developing in private law as a result of the privatisation of public utilities. Many financial services and information society services are now central to the infrastructure of

---

12 It is sufficient in this context to refer to F. Domont-Naert, 'The Right to Basic Financial Services: Opening the Discussion' (2000) 8 *ConsumerLJ* 63, as well as to the materials from the large conference on access to financial services arranged by the German Institut für Finanzdienstleistungen in Gothenburg in 2000.
13 COM(96) 389 final 2.

society, and the consumer cannot reasonably be expected to live without them. These aspects of those services can be treated as social rights in the same way that services provided by the 'traditional' public utilities are.

Some basic arguments

When discussing what may be achieved with the help of private law, one can point to some general legal arguments in order to provide a framework for discussion.

A principle of legitimate expectations

This is one of the emerging general principles of European consumer law.[14] The principle, elaborated for private law purposes by Hans-W. Micklitz for example,[15] may become a leading principle in European consumer law discourse.

Micklitz developed the principle of legitimate expectations on the basis of specific European Community legal materials such as the Products Liability Directive and the Products Safety Directive as well as documents such as the Green Paper on guarantees for consumer goods and after-sales services, which has recently also resulted in a directive.[16] In the European context, however, the principle can be defended from another point of view as well. It produces the necessary connection between private law principles and the more general principles of a constitutional and human rights character, and it builds a bridge between private law and other branches of European Community law. It may even be seen as a natural way of mitigating the obvious problems of legitimacy of European Community law, in that it connects the standards of behaviour to the expectations of those affected, instead of imposing purely abstract standards from above. The subjective element 'expectations' refers directly to the views prevailing among consumers, and the objective element 'legitimate' gives the courts the ability to screen these expectations by taking into account what enterprises can reasonably be expected to cope with.

As the legitimate expectations principle develops into a leading principle of European Community consumer law, it will confront established law that does not mirror the requirements of the principle. In such situations, the legitimate

---

14 See G. Howells and T. Wilhelmsson, *EC Consumer Law* (Aldershot: Dartmouth, 1997), 320–3.
15 H-W. Micklitz, 'Principles of Justice in Private Law within the European Union' in E. Paasivirta and K. Rissanen (eds.), *Principles of Justice and the Law of the European Union* (Brussels: European Commission, 1995), 259; H-W. Micklitz, 'Legitime Erwartungen als Gerechtigkeitsprinzip des Europäischen Privatrechts' in L. Krämer, H-W. Micklitz, and K. Tonner (eds.), *Law and Diffuse Interests in the European Legal Order* (Baden-Baden: Nomos, 1997), 245.
16 COM(93) 509 final.

expectations concept may be used as a tool for criticism, for pointing out inadequacies in the existing body of norms. This is one of the ways in which the legitimate expectations principle can be used in the context of services of general interest.

The concept of legitimate expectations combines an empirical and a normative approach in a fruitful way. The expectations of consumers are created on the basis of both the prevailing practices and the normative values that are deemed acceptable in a certain environment. This refers not only to market behaviour, but also to other aspects of life. The concept of legitimate expectations opens up legal discourse in various directions, as contractual expectations are tied to various other kinds of social expectations. As the expectations always arise in relation to a specific environment of practice and values, the content of the principle of legitimate expectations can differ depending on the setting. What is expected in one type of market might not be expected in another.

Thus, the principle of legitimate expectations may be applied differently in different countries, even within the European Union, because of variations in commercial and legal traditions. The Nordic economy, built to a large extent on relations of co-operation and trust between the actors in the marketplace, may give rise to a different interpretation of legitimate expectations from that which prevails in the commercial culture of Britain, which is founded more directly on the play of market forces.[17] The impact of the various legal traditions on the behaviour of the parties is relevant to the extent that the content of the law is internalised in a community (which might be a rather limited extent) as it then affects the expectations of the persons involved. A common European standard can therefore also reflect to some extent the various established patterns of consumer laws and consumer perceptions in the different countries concerned.

Described in this way, the principle of legitimate expectations cannot offer any definite answers for specific detailed problems of European law. It functions instead like a flexible background principle, allowing for national experiments and deviations while providing a direction in which the law should be developed. In this sense, it can offer useful guidelines for the development of the law in the area of services of general interest, keeping in mind the high welfarist expectations of the European citizenry.

First, one should recognise the expectation of the consumers that at least those services that have been publicly provided should remain subject to many of the *public law principles* mentioned earlier in this essay. For example, consumers have grown used to equal treatment in the provision of such services and they expect this state of affairs to continue. The principle of legitimate expectations may, in other words, function as a bearer of public law principles into private law.

17 Compare G. Teubner, ' "Legal Irritants": Good Faith in British Law or How Unifying Law Ends up in New Divergences' (1998) 61 *Mod L Rev* 11, on the differences between Germany and England.

Secondly, as the principle of legitimate expectations allows the differences between markets and lines of business to be taken into account, it is flexible enough to recognise the varying needs in different countries in relation to different services. The expectations concerning services of general interest may vary, for example, with respect to the conditions prevailing in different countries. For example, the loss of energy for heating is obviously more dramatic in the North than in the South of Europe.

Thirdly, the principle of legitimate expectations may imply that consumers can make claims of the kind that are discussed in this essay against private providers of services that have traditionally been run privately, or at least on the basis of market principles like most banks if they are generally expected to fulfil public functions. Because it may be difficult for consumers to perceive the difference between a bank offering them services that are regarded as necessities and a private 'public utility' enterprise, they may expect the same kind of principles to govern the performance of both kinds of enterprise. In other words, the principle of legitimate expectations may support the 'Trojan horse effect', enlarging the scope of the new principles of private law.

Arguments from corporate responsibility

A traditional private law relationship usually involves only two parties, whose interests, in the context of a dispute, are opposed. What one party wins, the other party loses. The fulfilment of one party's needs is necessarily effected at the other's expense. A person who demands a private law solution that respects his basic needs is therefore obliged to argue why and in what situations the other party should be obliged to contribute to such a solution. Therefore, a claim for a private law responsibility of providers of services can succeed only in cases in which this burden of reasoning can be fulfilled.

Some of the well-known arguments concerning *corporate responsibility* in private law doctrine can be used to defend a duty on (some) corporations to take into account the other party's needs. This is not the place to analyse these arguments in detail. A short enumeration of some basic arguments will suffice.

First, the bureaucratic image and economic power of large corporations imply an enhanced responsibility. People have a special trust in at least some such corporations. There should also be some connection between power and responsibility.

Secondly, a corporation may often, through the price mechanism, arrange for a given loss to be borne by a large number of consumers. The losses caused by the responsibility to take into account the special needs of some consumers can be borne by the consumer collective through (usually modest) price increases. From another perspective, one can describe this as a form of compulsory 'insurance' of the clients of the corporation.

Thirdly, enterprises should bear the responsibility for problems caused by them. For example, if the developing 'credit card society' causes problems for persons not able to function properly in that society, then the finance companies, which have made this development possible, should take some responsibility for solving the problems.

The enterprises and bodies that provide the types of services with which this essay is concerned are usually well suited to bearing certain social responsibilities. Because they are usually (at least partially) former public bodies, they still have a special standing with consumers, and consumers have legitimate expectations that they will carry a public responsibility. They are usually large and powerful corporations which have the ability both to carry the liability and to disperse their risks among a sufficiently broad collective of consumers. Even if they have not caused the relevant problems, they have usually come to the situation with an awareness of the expectations of the citizenry in respect of the services of general interest, and of the problems that will arise if those expectations are not met.

The basic rules of the marketplace

As a consequence of the privatisation or marketisation of service providers, the basic rules of the marketplace, in the context of which the enterprises operate, should apply to their behaviour. This can be defined as a minimum principle concerning the private law liability of privatised providers of services of general interest.

It should be self-evident that the providers of services of this kind, even though they have their historical roots in the public sector, should be subject to at least the same legal requirements as enterprises within other sectors. Normal rules on defective services should apply, as should rules on unfair contract terms. As self-evident as this seems, unfortunately the situation in practice is often rather different. Special public or semi-public regulations often put the consumer in a more disadvantageous position than, for example, the Directive on Unfair Terms in Consumer Contracts would allow, as several doctrinal analyses have shown.[18] In the era

---

18 See, e.g., P. Rott and B. Butters, 'Öffentliche Dienstleistungen und Vertragsgerechtigkeit im Lichte des Gemeinschaftsrechts (1999) *Verbraucher und Recht* 75–86, 107–17, on the situation in Germany. In Finland, the Consumer Ombudsman has been forced to intervene against providers of public utilities on the basis of the general fairness provisions on contract terms and marketing in the Consumer Protection Act. See, e.g., the yearly report of the Office of the Consumer Ombudsman, *Kuluttaja-asiamiehen ja kuluttajaviraston toiminta* (1999), 4 ff. To improve the situation, the Consumer Ombudsman has proposed that provisions on essential services should be incorporated into the Consumer Protection Act, in order to bring the consumer's position in this context into harmony with the principles of the Act: Consumer Protection 2/2000, English Summary, 6. The new special legislation on some services, n. 5 above, fulfils this wish only to an extent.

of privatisation and marketisation, this means that privatised enterprises and bodies can enjoy the fruits of functioning in a private law environment, without assuming the responsibilities involved. This is of course unacceptable.

This also means that there should be an interplay between the emerging new principles on services of general interest, and the legal principles within private law in general. The rules on services of general interest can be used not just to support the development of new principles of private law, as stressed earlier in this essay; there can and should be an influence in the other direction as well. I will show below how both the emerging principle of non-discrimination and the principle of *social force majeure* can be supported by materials from other areas of private law (i.e., consumer law) as well as being based on rules specific to services of general interest. The interplay means mutual support strengthening the status of the emerging principles.

Summary

To sum up this reasoning, one may conclude that the welfarist idea that enterprises have a social responsibility applies easily to providers of services of general interest. The legitimate expectations of consumers emphasise such a responsibility. The responsibility should be on at least the same level as the traditional responsibility of other actors in the marketplace. More is expected, however. The sector under scrutiny can and should be at the forefront in contributing to the development of new welfarist principles of private law. In the following part of this essay I will discuss some such principles.

The responsibility of enterprises providing services of general interest could be operationalised in various ways in various situations. One cannot and should not expect any consistent theory of private law 'after privatisation'.[19] In this essay, therefore, I can provide only a few illustrative examples of the social responsibility of enterprises in relation to services related to the consumer's basic needs.

The principle of non-discrimination and access to service

The privatisation of public functions, as well as the increased role of private actors with social functions such as banks and financial institutions, makes the question of access to certain services more important than before. It is expected that actors performing vital functions should have a responsibility to take into account the needs of all citizens. In the European Union this is acknowledged in several documents issued by the European Commission.

19 See G. Teubner, 'After Privatisation? The Many Autonomies of Private Law' in Wilhelmsson and Hurri, *From Dissonance to Sense*, 51.

With respect to services that are essential for living, such as electricity, water and telephone services, this expectation is recognised in the Communication from the Commission on services of general interest in Europe,[20] which covers the telecommunications, postal services, transport, electricity and broadcasting sectors. In the Commission report on the state of the liberalisation of the energy markets, the obligation of Member States to take measures to supply electricity to geographically isolated consumers and to sick and disabled consumers is expressly accepted.[21] The Commission extended this idea in its new Communication on services of general interest in Europe, where it noted that citizens in this context have concerns regarding both 'specific needs of certain categories of the population, such as the handicapped and those on low income' and 'complete territorial coverage of essential services in remote or inaccessible areas'.[22]

In addition, banks and financial institutions, for example, should be made responsible for providing relevant financial services and credit facilities within the whole European Union. The Commission has noted the problem of access to financial services for low-income people and expressed its support for action at the national level to solve the problem.[23] In later communications on financial services, however, this matter has been ignored.[24]

In general, there is said to be an agreement in the European Union that a universal service obligation should apply to services of general interest, although the understanding of what this concept should cover is variable. However, this obligation has been put into effect in only a piecemeal manner.[25] There is, in other words, still ample space and need for developing a private law principle of access to service.

In private law, such a principle can be reflected in, for example, various kinds of rules on compulsory contracting and protection against termination. These would, however, cover only part of the problem, and would not be sufficient in a situation where, for example, some service is not provided at all in some areas of the country. A more radical step would be to conceive of some kind of liability in damages for failing to provide necessary services, a question which is not further pursued in this context.

The generally accepted view among private lawyers is that rules concerning compulsory contracting constitute an exception, since they are contrary to the fundamental principle of freedom of contract. In a recent Nordic study concerning obligations to contract, which inure to the benefit of private persons, Frey Nybergh is critical of this view. On the basis of a review of legislation in the Nordic

---

20 COM(96) 443 final, item 8.   21 COM(1999) 198 final 10.
22 COM(2000) 580 final 7. Final version published also in OJ 2001/C 17/04.
23 COM(97) 309 final 7–8.
24 See COM(1999) 232 final. The latest status report in this area can be found in the Second Report from the Commission on Progress on Financial Services, COM(2000) 336 final.
25 See Commissioner M. Manfredi, Opening Speech, Conference on Consumer Protection and Services of General Interest (Helsinki, 9 September 1999).

countries concerning the provision of essential services such as electricity, gas, heating, water, telephone connection, health care, housing, transport, postal requirements, insurance and banking, Nybergh shows that the expressly regulated obligation to contract, as a restriction of the traditional concept of freedom of contract, assumes a more central position than that which one might expect upon a superficial review.[26] That conclusion leads Nybergh to argue in favour of adopting a more precise principle of an obligation to contract in Nordic law, which would extend at the very least to essential services, and according to which enterprises may not refuse to enter into contractual relations with a consumer without due cause.[27] At the same time, Nybergh manages to present a new perspective on the concept of freedom of contract: the positive freedom of contract, which meets expectations found in a consumer society, takes account of the consumer's freedom to consume (i.e., his or her freedom to enter into a contract for essential services), and therefore introduces into the notion of contractual freedom a certain measure of compulsion on enterprises to enter into contractual relations.[28] Nybergh's positive definition of contractual freedom, which includes an obligation to contract, is also meant to discourage economic discrimination. He seeks to establish that, where a consumer suffers from a social *force majeure* situation (for example, difficulties arising as a result of illness or unemployment), such disability can conceivably constitute a separate justification for not denying the consumer the right to enter into contractual relations referred to above.[29] I will return to the question of social *force majeure* in the next part of this essay.

As to the provision of electricity, similar ideas were earlier expressed by the Swedish researcher Ulf Stridbeck, who analysed the contractual relationship between the distributor of electricity and the consumer. He concluded his analysis with the claim that electricity is to be seen as a social right, which should influence the contractual relationship in various ways.[30]

As those who encounter problems in receiving proper services are usually less well-off citizens, rules of this kind are connected to the principle of equality. The weak consumers should receive services equally as easily as those who are better off. In other words, as a consequence of the privatisation measures, the public law principle of equality becomes more important within private law. In addition, equality of access has also been mentioned as one of the key issues when discussing consumer credit law and distributive justice.[31]

---

26 See F. Nybergh, *Avtalsfrihet – rätt till avtal* (Copenhagen: Nordisk Ministerråd 1997), 295. See also F. Nybergh, 'Dissonance in Freedom of Contract? How to Make Sense of it' in Wilhelmsson and Hurri, *From Dissonance to Sense*, 373.

27 *Ibid.*, 227 ff., 296 ff.   28 *Ibid.*, 77 ff.   29 *Ibid.*, 260 ff.

30 See U. Stridbeck, *Från kontrakt till social rättighet. En analys av förhållandet mellan eldistributör och abonnent* (Lund: Lund University Press, 1992).

31 See I. Ramsay, 'Consumer Credit Law, Distributive Justice and the Welfare State' (1995) 15 *Oxford Journal of Legal Studies* 177.

162   Services and the consumer

When one speaks of equality and the law, foremost in one's mind is the public law notion of equality, according to which the public sector should treat citizens equally. However, in the privatised and marketised society, where the dividing line between the public and private sectors is increasingly unclear, this reasoning, which is usually backed by constitutional provisions, must also carry greater weight in the private law area. If the starting point is the obligation to treat people equally in the public sector, it is difficult to ignore the idea of such an obligation in comparable private activities.

Therefore, a welfarist-inspired private law strategy related to services of general interest emphasises an equality principle that forbids discrimination of clients (a principle of non-discrimination). Such a principle should focus not just on racial and gender-related discrimination, although this is of course an important area,[32] but also on economic discrimination. The possibility of developing a private law principle of non-discrimination on the basis of European Community materials has already been discussed in general terms.[33]

The function of such a principle is closely connected with a demand for transparency: discrimination can be detected only if one knows on what conditions contracts are made with others. A private law response to the expectations of the citizenry should therefore include not just the principle of non-discrimination, but also the concomitant transparency requirements.

Thoughts on a principle of non-discrimination that run in a similar direction have been articulated by Dagmar Schiek,[34] who analysed the suitability of contract law for community tasks with reference to discrimination in contracting. Focusing on personal discrimination based on characteristics like race, ethnic origin, gender and disability, Schiek believes private law should provide protection against discrimination, as the market mechanism is incapable of guaranteeing the removal of discriminatory practices. She considers modern European contract law poorly equipped for this task, although European Community law contains several (inconsistent) prohibitions of personal discrimination, and a non-discrimination principle could in certain cases be tied to traditional contract law rules concerning compulsory contracting, immorality and implied promises. In the long run, therefore, one should work towards the development of a general non-discrimination principle in future common European contract law. In the short term, it would be more realistic, in the view of Schiek, to create specific non-discrimination legislation in certain sectors of contract law, concerning newly privatised public services

32 See I. Ramsay and T. Williams, 'Inequality, Market Discrimination, and Credit Markets' in I. Ramsay (ed.), *Consumer Law in the Global Economy* (Aldershot: Dartmouth, 1997), 233.
33 See T. Wilhelmsson, *Social Contract Law and European Integration* (Aldershot: Dartmouth, 1995), 203 ff.; and, with reference also to Nordic material, T. Wilhelmsson, 'Contract and Equality' (2000) 40 *Scandinavian Studies in Law* 145.
34 D. Schiek, 'Contract Law, Discrimination and European Integration' in Wilhelmsson and Hurri, *From Dissonance to Sense*, 405; D. Schiek, *Differenzierte Gerechtigkeit* (Baden-Baden: Nomos, 2000).

for example. One encounters again the idea that regulation of public services can function as a forerunner for a more general private law principle.

In the Nordic setting, it seems possible to base the development of a general principle of non-discrimination in contract law on certain existing legal materials. Such materials can be found not just in specific areas like labour law,[35] but within the general part of contract law as well.

In one respect, the relevance of a principle of non-discrimination has been explicitly acknowledged, in theory at any rate, in Swedish and Finnish law. This is found in the application of the general fairness clause in s. 36 of the Contracts Act, which gives the courts power to adjust contracts that are found to be unfair. The preparatory work with respect to the Swedish general clause expressly states that discrimination should constitute a ground for adjusting contractual terms. In this context, particular reference is made to cases of discrimination on the basis of race, skin colour, origin or faith, since these have been criminalised in the Swedish Penal Code.[36] A similar view is to be found in the preparatory works to the Finnish general clause: a contractual term that is used for systematic discrimination on the basis of gender, age, race, nationality, religion, membership of organisations, etc., should be subject to adjustment.[37] However, these provisions are not always helpful when faced with the important 'poor pay more'[38] problem of economic discrimination, since different treatment based only on variations in risks or costs seems to be accepted. The preparatory work to the Swedish general clause specifically emphasises that differences that emanate from economic circumstances, for example, differences in costs between different customers, cannot usually be regarded as discrimination.[39]

In spite of these express references, discussion on contract and discrimination continues to have a low profile. In the Nordic context, therefore, it is especially interesting to discuss private law remedies which are related to access to services of general interest. This focus can place the general issue of a private law principle of non-discrimination higher on the agenda.[40] The new rules on

---

35 As we know, equality between the sexes in the workplace has been the subject of particular attention from legislatures both internationally and nationally. Equality legislation is today heavily influenced by European Community law. Finnish labour law, alongside the specific legislation on gender equality, contains a rule prohibiting discrimination on other grounds in the Employment Contracts Act, s. 17.3 (by Act 611/1986): 'The employer shall treat employees without prejudice so that no person, without due cause, is treated differently to another on the basis of birth, religion, age, political or trade union activities or any other comparable circumstance.'

36 See the law drafting report, SOU 1974:83, 148.

37 Finnish Government Bill 247/1981, 16.

38 The well-known phrase stems from D. Caplovitz, *The Poor Pay More: Consumer Practices of Low-Income Families* (New York: Free Press 1963).

39 SOU 1974:83, 147.

40 In a decision of the Finnish Market Court, economically motivated discrimination was held to be contrary to law (Finnish Market Court 1982:21). The facts of the case were somewhat peculiar, however, since one could also rely, at least in part, upon specific legislation. According to

compulsory contracting, concerning some of the services of general interest, strengthen the general tendency towards an acceptance of a general principle of non-discrimination in contract law.

In summary, the discussion concerning private law in the era of privatisation reflects a perceived need for new thinking concerning the content and tools of this area of law. Services of general interest are a good testing ground for such discussions. When public supervision and control become more lenient, enterprises offering such services should be required, with the help of private law, to adhere to certain fundamental principles, namely, general access to the service, equal treatment of the consumers, and transparency in relation to the consumers.

The principle of provision of services and the disadvantaged citizens

The principle of non-discrimination of the weak and vulnerable may even lead to a principle whereby these consumers are in some situations given more favourable treatment than others. Financial institutions, as well as other actors performing services of general interest to the consumers, may, to some extent, be made responsible for the economic welfare of their clients.

The most effective and comprehensive regulations of this kind are the consumer bankruptcy schemes that exist or have been drafted in various countries. Such a scheme could be described as a kind of (partial) private responsibility of the creditor(s) for the social security of the debtor. Bankruptcy schemes are mentioned here to show that the notion of a special responsibility of private enterprises for the wellbeing of weak consumers is not as strange as it may at first seem.

A growing number of social problems result from the ever more common cases of over-indebted consumers. It is well known that the causes of such situations of over-indebtedness are not necessarily attributable to mismanagement by the consumer. Empirical research from many countries demonstrates quite clearly that the most common causes of over-indebtedness are to be found elsewhere. In most cases, the economic problems of consumers seem to be caused by more or less unexpected changes in their life situation. Often their difficulties in paying their debts

---

s. 12 of the then Electricity Act, the Electricity Authority was obliged to observe terms and conditions for the supply of electricity approved by the Ministry of Trade and Industry. According to the terms and conditions fixed by the Ministry, one was entitled to require security for payment of electricity supplies to private households only where compelling reasons existed, which were required to be examined in advance. The mere fact that the consumer lived in rental accommodation could not, according to the Market Court, constitute such a compelling reason. A contractual term and condition pursuant to which a consumer who lived in rental accommodation was required to provide security for payment of debts based upon the supply of electricity was considered to be unfair.

are a consequence of unemployment, illness, divorce and other marital problems, increased costs for accommodation, and the like.[41]

In various countries, the recognition of this reality has resulted in (somewhat limited) discussion concerning the need for, and the possibilities of, developing new private law principles that would strengthen the position of (consumer) debtors. In some countries, there are also examples of existing legislation that pays explicit attention to such circumstances. A development in this direction can be discerned in Nordic law, especially in Finland, but also in Sweden and Norway. New elements in legislation and legal practice have prompted discussion of a possible new principle of 'social force majeure'.[42] Elsewhere, this principle has been characterised as an expression of a solidary contract law.[43]

I discuss this principle in other places.[44] I will here simply note that the principle of social *force majeure*, as I have defined it, should be applied when (i) the consumer is affected by some special occurrence such as an unfavourable change in his health (physical or mental illness, personal injury), work (unemployment, reduced work, strike and lockout), housing (termination of lease), or family situation (divorce, death or injury of family member); (ii) there is a causal connection between this occurrence and the consumer's difficulties in paying; (iii) the consumer did not foresee the special occurrence when he or she concluded the contract; and (iv) the occurrence was not the fault of the consumer.

Various legal consequences may be attached to social *force majeure*. The responsibility of the enterprise is normally a 'negative' responsibility; the enterprise loses certain rights against consumers who have run into economic difficulties because of social *force majeure*. Interest on delayed payments as well as other similar remedies can be mitigated in cases where the debtor's difficulties are due to illness, unemployment or similar causes.

In cases where termination of a contract would cause loss to the consumer, social *force majeure* should prevent the enterprise from terminating the contract, at least for a period. This is especially important in the case of long-term contracts concerning services of general interest. Consumers affected by social *force majeure* should not have their situation worsened by being prematurely cut off from services like electricity, water, heating and telephone.

In the European Union, national limitations on the possibility of electricity companies disconnecting consumers because of debt are permitted.[45] An example of

---

41 For references to this research, see T. Wilhelmsson, *Critical Studies in Private Law. A Treatise on Need-Rationality in Modern Law* (Dordrecht: Kluwer Academic Publishers, 1992), 181 ff. Many later studies in various countries confirm these well-known results.

42 *Ibid.*, 180 ff.

43 See B. Lurger, *Vertragliche Solidarität* (Baden-Baden: Nomos, 1998), 133.

44 See T. Wilhelmsson, 'Social Force Majeure – a New Concept in Nordic Consumer Law' (1990) 13 *Journal of Consumer Policy* 1.

45 COM(1999) 198 final 10.

such a limitation, where the provisions are expressly focused on the situation of so-cial *force majeure*, is the new Finnish legislation on electricity contracts.[46] According to this law, the time during which the consumer cannot be disconnected is extended to two months if the consumer's difficulties in paying his or her bills are due to severe illness, unemployment, or some other specific reason that was not the fault of the consumer. A similar rule is adopted in the new Finnish Act on Water Services. In the case of social *force majeure* the disconnection of water supply and of soil water ser-vice cannot take place until ten weeks after the time when the customer was given notice of disconnection.[47] The law on services of general interest again appears as an area that can contribute to the development of general private law in a more wel-farist direction by strengthening the emerging doctrine of social *force majeure*.

A society that claims to be welfarist even though services are privatised or mar-ketised cannot withdraw from its responsibility to ensure that more unfortunate members also have ongoing access to the services that the fulfilment of our basic needs require. If public law measures do not achieve this, the private law principle of social *force majeure* can, in certain circumstances and for some cases, prove to be useful.[48]

---

46 Act 466/1999, Chapter 6a, Section 27h.   47 Act 119/2001, Section 26.

48 It has to be remembered that private law rules may have a wider impact through various kinds of collective actions of organisations or public authorities concerning the fairness of standard form conditions (based on, e.g., Art. 7 of the Unfair Contract Terms Directive). The Finnish Consumer Ombudsman has in some cases reacted against standard contract terms on remedies in which no exception for social *force majeure* was mentioned, and the Finnish Market Court has even found unfair a clause that prescribed a (relatively small) extra payment in case the consumer wanted to have the due date of a telephone bill postponed because of over-indebtedness because the clause did not recognise the situation of social *force majeure*: Market Court 1999:18.

8   The new Financial Ombudsman Service in the United Kingdom: has the second generation got it right?

RHODA JAMES AND PHILIP MORRIS

Introduction

While the new Financial Ombudsman Service ('the FOS') in the United Kingdom owes much to its predecessors, its size and scope mean that we are witnessing the birth of a new form of the ombudsman remedy. The FOS brings together eight existing complaints schemes[1] and will be organised according to product, rather than provider, as has been the case with the existing ombudsman schemes. The stated rationale behind the political decision to establish a single 'one-stop' organisation, taken evidently at ministerial level, is to reduce confusion (though the empirical evidence to support this is conspicuous by its absence) and possible duplication as far as consumers are concerned, while responding to the blurring of traditional distinctions between the industry sectors, as firms are restructured and products packaged together.[2] The move to a statutory ombudsman with overarching responsibilities, to replace the existing fragmented patchwork quilt of mostly voluntary schemes, was almost inevitable once the discredited, largely self-regulatory regime in the financial services sector was replaced by a single statutory regulator in the shape of the Financial Services Authority ('the FSA').[3] There were other dynamics at work here, too, and we need to trace, briefly, the history of the ombudsman remedy in the United Kingdom and also to locate the present developments in the context of the Blair Government's Modernising

The authors are Associate Members of the British and Irish Ombudsman Association, which is the professional self-regulatory body for Ombudsman schemes in the British Isles. We are grateful to Walter Merricks, Chief Ombudsman, for agreeing to a personal interview as part of this research project and commenting on an earlier draft of this essay. Needless to say, all views expressed, unless otherwise indicated, should be attributed to the authors alone.

1 Banking Ombudsman, Building Societies Ombudsman, Investment Ombudsman, Insurance Ombudsman, Personal Insurance Arbitration Service, Personal Investment Authority Ombudsman, Securities and Futures Authority Complaints Bureau and Arbitration Scheme, Financial Services Authority Direct Regulation Unit and Independent Investigator.

2 See FOS, *Laying the Foundations First Annual Report: 26 February 1999–31 March 2000* (Chair: Andreas Whittam-Smith), 2.

3 The transition from the Financial Services Act 1986 (UK) to the Financial Services and Markets Act 2000 (UK). For an interesting concise account, see I. MacNeil, 'The Future for Financial Regulation: the Financial Services and Markets Bill' (1999) 62 *Mod L Rev* 725.

Justice project. This project is now well advanced following implementation of the Access to Justice Act 1998 (UK), the introduction of new rules on civil procedure, and the introduction of a funding code by the new Legal Services Commission which will govern decisions on financial assistance for legal action. We are where we are today because of developments in the early 1980s, when private power responded to pressure, albeit usually covert pressure, to provide some sort of consumer-friendly redress mechanism and also because of the drive towards providing 'proportionate' remedies which lies at the heart of the Government's civil justice reforms.

The fact that we are now examining an 'ombudsman' remedy instead of, say, an arbitration scheme or some other form of alternative dispute resolution ('ADR'), is because the 'ombudsman' became the remedy of choice for the private sector during the 1980s and early 1990s. The reasons for this development have been well documented[4] and will not be rehearsed here. It suffices to say that ombudsmen form part of a wider movement towards ADR.[5] The voluntary adoption of this type of remedy resulted from a complex set of imperatives, not founded solely on defensive responses to the threat of statutory intervention or on the need to present a consumer-responsive image to counter public concerns about the consumer-unfriendly practices common in many of the sectors. Indeed, consumer organisations were pivotal in the setting up of some of the early schemes.

The claim has always been that the ombudsman provides a cheap and easy solution for the consumer with a complaint against the company and that, on the whole, ombudsmen have provided a valuable consumer redress mechanism in the UK. In reality, given the type of claim at stake, ombudsmen are usually the *only viable* means of redress, not so much an *alternative* to the courts.[6] They offer a free service to the individual complainant, they conduct their investigations in private using inquisitorial and informal processes, and their processes are based on the assumption that the complainant will not need legal assistance to make use of them.

---

4 See, e.g., J. Birds and C. Graham, 'Complaints Mechanisms in the Financial Services Industry' [1988] *Civil Justice Q* 313; R. James, *Private Ombudsmen and Public Law* (Aldershot: Dartmouth, 1997); P. E. Morris, 'The Banking Ombudsman I and II' [1987] *J Bus L* 131, 199; P. E. Morris and J. A. Hamilton, 'The Insurance Ombudsman and PIA Ombudsman: a Critical Comparison' (1996) 47 *Northern Ireland Legal Quarterly* 119; P. E. Morris and G. Little, 'The Ombudsmen and Consumer Protection' in P. Cartwright (ed.), *Consumer Protection in Financial Services* (London: Kluwer Law International, 1999), chap. 2; P. Rawlings and C. Willett, 'Ombudsman Schemes in the United Kingdom's Financial Sector: the Insurance Ombudsman, the Banking Ombudsman, and the Building Societies Ombudsman' (1994) 17 *Journal of Consumer Policy* 307.
5 For a fascinating study, see M. Palmer and S. Roberts, *Dispute Processes: ADR and Primary Forms of Decision Making* (London: Butterworths, 1998).
6 See Rawlings and Willett, 'Ombudsman Schemes'.

Ombudsmen in the financial services sector

Ombudsmen had been well established in the public sector,[7] and the introduction of the 'voluntary' ombudsman in the private sector in turn fuelled a further and diverse development of the model. It may be that the undisputed independence of the public sector ombudsmen, and the consequent legitimacy attached to the title, attracted corporate bodies to adopt that type of remedy, even while they were adapting it to suit their particular circumstances. The idea certainly took root in the 1980s, and, where corporate power itself failed to embrace the ombudsman solution, government in certain cases imposed one by statute, largely following the template of the voluntary schemes. We were left with a tapestry of differently constituted ombudsmen, public, private and hybrid, covering a wide area of services from financial and legal services, to estate agency and other areas such as funeral directors. But most have, however, been concentrated in the financial services sector and it is interesting that financial services have provided the focus for a number of informal consumer remedies within the European Union ('EU'). The first EU 'out of court' complaints network has recently been introduced to cover financial services, bringing together thirty-five different national schemes.[8]

As to existing schemes in the UK financial services sector, three in particular are worthy of mention in illustrating the different forms of ombudsman that are to be subsumed within the new FOS. Comparison of their salient features enables a tentative assessment to be made of the possible impact of the new arrangements. These schemes are the Insurance Ombudsman Bureau ('the IOB'), the Building Societies Ombudsman Scheme ('the BSOS') and the Personal Investment Authority Ombudsman Bureau ('the PIAOB'). The IOB was the first such scheme in the UK, having been introduced in 1981, and it is the archetypal voluntary self-regulatory scheme, deriving its power from a contractual relationship between the Insurance Ombudsman Bureau and its member insurance companies.[9] The BSOS was set up in 1987 under the provisions of the Building Societies Act 1986 (UK) which required[10] all societies to belong to an ombudsman scheme, the building society movement having failed to take the hint and follow the banking sector in introducing a voluntary scheme. The PIAOB was introduced in controversial circumstances

---

7 Since the introduction of the Parliamentary Ombudsman under the Parliamentary Commissioner Act 1967 (UK).

8 FIN-NET, IP/01/152 (Brussels, 1 February 2001).

9 This was the main rationale behind the court's decision in R v. *Insurance Ombudsman Bureau, ex parte Aegon Life Insurance Ltd* (*The Times*, 7 January 1994), which is fully discussed in James, *Private Ombudsmen*, 4–12, 30–2, and in P. E. Morris, 'The Insurance Ombudsman Bureau and Judicial Review' [1994] *Lloyd's Maritime and Commercial Law Quarterly* 358. The ruling and reasoning in *Aegon* has recently been approved in R v. *Personal Investment Authority Ombudsman Bureau, ex parte Mooyer* (unreported, Administrative Court, 5 April 2001).

10 On pain of criminal penalty.

in 1994 under the recognition requirements of the Financial Services Act 1986 (UK), set up and funded by a self-regulatory body but authorised and operating under legislation. The underlying reasons for its introduction to handle insurance business complaints with an investment element owed much to the insurance industry's concern about the perceived pro-consumer bias of the then Insurance Ombudsman.[11]

Many of the salient features of the IOB derived from advice given by the National Consumer Council ('the NCC') which was canvassed for support by the founder insurance companies who decided to set up the scheme. The NCC stipulated minimum conditions that would have to apply if the scheme were to receive its blessing. These were, briefly, that there should be an institutional structure which would provide an intermediate and independent body, with a lay majority, to oversee the ombudsman scheme and to separate the industry from the ombudsman. The NCC also specified that the ombudsman should be given the power to make substantial awards and that, although the consumer should be free to take advantage of the ombudsman remedy, its existence should not prejudice the consumer's right to take his or her case to court if unhappy with the ombudsman's decision. In other words, the complainant should not be bound by the ombudsman's decision. These stipulations influenced the ombudsman template that was then devised, although the extent to which the industry devolved power to the intermediate body was to vary from scheme to scheme. The IOB is in legal terms a limited company, with a membership open to insurance companies and supervised by a Board of up to twelve members. But responsibility for running the ombudsman scheme is vested in a separate Council which has a majority of lay members, and an independent Chair, together with industry representation. The ombudsman is responsible to the Council which is entrusted with the power of appointment and reappointment; but the Board retains important powers, notably in approving the ombudsman's terms of reference and therefore determining jurisdiction.

The BSOS, although set up under statutory requirements, largely followed the IOB model. Again, an Ombudsman Council was created to act as a buffer between the ombudsman and the industry. Here the Council appoints the ombudsman, subject to approval by the Board, and the Board has the ultimate power to remove the ombudsman from office. Although, because of its statutory origins, the Board does not have the same type of power to alter jurisdiction, in instances where jurisdiction was unclear, the Board has proved reluctant to agree to extensions to jurisdiction. This issue arose quite early in the scheme's life over the question of negligent surveys and valuations.

11 See the discussion in Morris and Hamilton, 'The Insurance Ombudsman'; and J. Farrand, 'An Academic Ombudsman' (Centenary Lecture Series, Department of Law, University of Sheffield, 16 November 2000).

The Personal Investment Authority ('the PIA') again constituted an Ombudsman Council to appoint the ombudsman and oversee the PIAOB scheme, but the
Council has close links with the PIA. The PIAOB is a company limited by guarantee,
the PIA Board is also the Board of the PIAOB, and three PIA Ombudsman Bureau
Board members are also members of the Bureau's Council. It is the PIAOB Board
that has responsibility for setting the budget and case fees and for overseeing the
administration of the Bureau, and the PIAOB General Manager is accountable to
the PIA Board, though the General Manager has no role in complaint handling.
Interestingly, in this scheme it is for the ombudsman to decide whether or not a
complaint falls within his or her terms of reference. This has been a contentious
matter in other schemes where the industry has been unwilling to cede power on
this issue.

Civil justice reforms

While the incoming New Labour Government had reform of financial
services regulation as one of its early agenda items, it also had plans to reform
the civil justice system. The ombudsman remedy has a place in these reforms. In
its *Modernising Justice* White Paper,[12] the Government argued that access to justice should mean the provision of effective solutions proportionate to the issues at
stake. This would not necessarily entail court proceedings. The shift towards ADR
and a civil justice system where courts are a forum of last resort is evident from
two further discussion papers published by the Lord Chancellor's Department as
part of the Modernising Justice project. In one, on alternative dispute resolution,[13]
ombudsmen feature as exemplars of decision-making bodies providing 'alternative
adjudication'. The second paper, *Civil Justice 2000. A Vision of the Civil Justice System in
the Information Age*,[14] highlights the policy, cultural and technical challenges that lie
ahead in providing an integrated justice system where there will be 'a much wider
focus for the civil justice system and much more variety in the services provided and
in the means of delivery'.[15]

Ombudsmen are to be part of this increased variety. Guidance on the funding
code brought into force by the new Legal Services Commission in April 2000 has, as
one of its objectives, the wider use of ombudsman schemes by allowing legal help
to be offered to enable a client to pursue a complaint. If that avenue achieves the
desired outcome, then further funding for the purpose of representation in civil

12 Lord Chancellor's Department, *Modernising Justice* (White Paper) (London: HM Stationery Office,
    1998).
13 Lord Chancellor's Department, *Alternative Dispute Resolution* (Discussion Paper) (London: HM
    Stationery Office, 1999).
14 Lord Chancellor's Department (Consultation Paper) (London: HM Stationery Office, 2000).
15 *Ibid.*, para. 3.6.

proceedings will not be available. If the relevant ombudsman finds that the complaint has no merit then this may be taken into account in assessing the client's chance of success in other actions for which funding is sought. The failure to pursue a complaint is a factor that might count against an applicant for legal representation, particularly in certain housing cases and clinical negligence cases. As one commentator has said, these proposals, 'far from relegating ombudsman schemes to the margins, create newly formalised responsibilities, which effectively grant certain ombudsmen what amounts to the final and authoritative say'[16] in their respective spheres of work.

The Financial Ombudsman Service

The FOS has existed in 'shadow' form since early 2000, staff have been in post, most handling complaints under the jurisdiction of the existing eight complaints schemes, and the FOS occupies extensive offices in London's Docklands area. It is expected finally to assume its powers under the Financial Services and Markets Act 2000 (UK) in November 2001. The FOS will be the largest ombudsman scheme in the world, with an annual budget of around £27 million, and a staff of 450–500.[17] The FOS is organised into five divisions: customer contact, banking and loans, investment, insurance and a management support and services division. The intention is that it will retain the benefits of existing expertise from the prior sectoral schemes while providing a single point of entry for the consumer. It is also argued that it provides the opportunity for greater consistency in decision-making by adopting an organisational matrix based on product rather than provider lines. Thus, complaints about mortgages, for example, will now be decided by one ombudsman, rather than by a banking ombudsman or a building society ombudsman depending upon the type of institution that had provided the financial product. The customer contact division will have an important role to play in what the Chief Ombudsman has characterised as a 'front to back' system, with the emphasis on providing skilled and informed help to complainants when they first approach the service, with the objective of facilitating the early resolution of complaints.

While the FOS is obviously a new scheme, it inevitably owes much to the existing schemes it replaces, the Chief Ombudsman acknowledging that in devising the rules and operational detail for the new service it has proved necessary to adopt a 'brownfield' rather than 'greenfield' philosophy. The transitional arrangements

---

16 N. O'Brien, 'Ombudsmen: Flyswatters or Lion-Hunters?' (2000) 14 *The Ombudsman* 11.
17 See W. Merricks, 'Lessons from Merging the Financial Ombudsman Schemes' (paper presented at the British and Irish Ombudsman Association Annual Conference, University of Warwick, 25 May 2001).

have yet to be finalised at the time of writing, and it may be several years before the FOS's new jurisdictions are completely on stream. In the words of the Chief Ombudsman, 'there is still a large quantity of brownfield mud there'.[18]

The FOS will have both a compulsory and a voluntary jurisdiction, and it is anticipated that about 10,000 firms will be covered by the scheme. The process has been designed to deal with 300,000 inquiries a year, and 12,000 telephone calls a day, with about 38,000 decisions expected to be made a year.[19] The comparatively small number of estimated decisions a year reflects the emphasis on early resolution. The very magnitude of the service, however, presents an unprecedented challenge if the traditional virtues associated with ombudsmen are to be retained. It probably also represents a shift from the ombudsman perceived as an identifiable decision-maker to an ombudsman service operating as an acknowledged bureaucracy where a number of subsidiary ombudsmen seek to make consistent decisions within a highly formalised managerial structure, and where the Chief Ombudsman fulfils a function more akin to that of a corporate style Chief Executive than a quasi-judicial decision-maker.

Constitution and structure of the FOS

The first point to make is that, unlike the three comparator sectoral schemes mentioned earlier, here the industry is firmly at arm's length from the ombudsman. Funding comes from the industry, but the scheme operates on a statutory basis with close links to the regulator, the FSA, rather than to a company. Both the FOS and the FSA have rule-making responsibilities under the Financial Services and Markets Act 2000 (UK).

The FSA has been given responsibility for a raft of crucial matters. Thus, the FSA will, *inter alia*, approve the FOS annual budget, determine the scope of the voluntary jurisdiction, define which complainants should have access to the compulsory jurisdiction, decide the overall monetary limit on awards and the types of loss amenable to compensation in the compulsory jurisdiction, and grant its approval to any scheme rules put forward by the Ombudsman Company (the Financial Ombudsman Service Limited). Therefore, while the FOS enjoys virtually unfettered operational autonomy in grievance resolution and a considerable degree of room for manoeuvre on policy matters, the FSA retains significant 'ownership' of crucial aspects of the scheme with the result that the FOS cannot claim to be wholly independent of the FSA. Nor should it be forgotten that the FOS will be enforcing FSA regulatory standards and is expected itself to perform a quasi-regulatory role by acting as an 'early warning' mechanism for the FSA.

18 Personal interview with the authors (24 October 2000) [hereinafter 'Personal interview'].
19 See Merricks, 'Lessons'.

The aim of the proposals is principally to provide individual consumers with an informal, quick and user-friendly alternative to the courts, but there will also be a relationship between the FOS and the FSA as regulator where a complaint reveals the need for supervisory or disciplinary action of some form. This represents an improvement on some of the existing schemes where, in the case of the banking and building society schemes, for example, there is no explicit provision for feedback from the ombudsman to the regulator. In the case of the building societies there seems to be minimal contact between the ombudsman and the Building Societies Commission, which has responsibility for monitoring the prudential side of regulation. Similarly, there seems to be minimal contact between the Bank of England[20] and the Banking Ombudsman. Rather, the schemes were seen as freestanding grievance-resolution mechanisms having an entirely separate existence from any regulatory agency.

While the two interests are functionally distinct, that of complaint handler and regulator, there will inevitably be communication between the two. At the same time, however, too intimate a relationship with the regulator can raise questions about the genuine independence of the ombudsman. There is a delicate balance to be struck here, and to an extent this has been recognised by a formal Memorandum of Understanding on the exchange of information agreed by the FSA and FOS.[21]

Turning to the detailed institutional arrangements, under the provisions of the 2000 Act, the FSA created a company, the Financial Ombudsman Service Limited, to administer the scheme. The Chair and Board of the Ombudsman Company were appointed by the FSA, the Chair's appointment approved by HM Treasury. The Act[22] specifies that the terms of appointment of the Board and the Chair, and in particular the terms governing removal from office, must be such as to secure their independence from the FSA in the operation of the scheme. The Board has been appointed and is composed of twelve 'public interest' members, including consumer affairs representatives and Michael Barnes, an eminent figure in the UK ombudsman world, as a former Legal Services Ombudsman and former Chair of the British and Irish Ombudsman Association ('the BIOA'), and Richard Thomas, now Director of Public Policy at solicitors Clifford Chance, but previously Director of Consumer Affairs at the Office of Fair Trading, and Head of Public Affairs at the National Consumer Council. In that latter post, Thomas was instrumental in the creation of the Insurance, Banking and Building Societies Ombudsmen schemes. The Chair of the Ombudsman Company Board is Andreas Whittam-Smith, currently President of the British Board of Film Classification and founding editor of *The Independent* newspaper.[23]

20 The FSA is to take over the relevant regulatory functions of both the Building Societies Commission and the Bank of England.
21 See Merricks, 'Lessons'.   22 Sch. 17, para. 3(3).   23 FSA Press Release (22 February 1999).

The Board appointed Walter Merricks, the then Insurance Ombudsman, as the Chief Ombudsman, and appointments were swiftly made to posts of individual product ombudsmen and their panel ombudsmen. Once again the Act[24] requires that their terms of appointment must be consistent with the independence of the persons appointed. The terms of the new appointments and arrangements as to security of tenure are not in the public domain, but the FOS has been accepted into full membership of the BIOA, which indicates that the FOS meets that body's rigorous criteria regarding independence and accountability.

Clear lines of accountability are built into the scheme by virtue of the fact that the FOS and the Chief Ombudsman are required to submit annual reports on the discharge of their statutory functions to the FSA.[25] Copies of the reports will be made available to the Treasury and to Parliament. Moreover, the Chairman of the Ombudsman Company Board may be required to present evidence to an appropriate Parliamentary Select Committee. As to legal accountability, the FOS will almost certainly be subject to judicial review, something that the Chief Ombudsman is sanguine about, provided that it 'is confined to its proper function, that is to say checking whether the decision-maker has acted lawfully rather than substituting the court's opinion for that of the decision-maker who has been entrusted with that responsibility by Parliament'.[26]

Funding will still flow from the industry. The FOS, in relation to the compulsory jurisdiction, will be funded by means of a standing charge (calibrated by reference to the scale of activities entered into by firms based on a number of indicia) and case fees based on usage.[27] The Act[28] confers on the FSA a broad enabling power to promulgate rules that give detailed effect to this principle. Funding for complaints falling under the voluntary jurisdiction will be specified in FOS standard terms which will be contractually binding on those firms subscribing to the voluntary jurisdiction.

Adequate funding will obviously be crucial, and this was a matter that concerned the Joint Parliamentary Committee in its consideration of the ombudsman provisions during the passage of the Bill through Parliament. One of that Committee's recommendations was that the ombudsman scheme should be required to report annually to Parliament on the adequacy of its budget. The Committee expressed the hope that the Parliamentary Select Committee that takes evidence on the FSA's report would, as part of its examination, consider whether the ombudsman scheme was adequately funded.[29] While broadly accepting the point about adequate

---

24 Sch. 17, para. 4(2)(a).   25 Sch. 17, para. 7.   26 Personal interview, n. 18 above.
27 For discussion of the policy issues and detailed draft Rules, see generally FSA and FOS, *Funding the Financial Ombudsman Service. A Joint Consultation Paper* (Consultation Paper 74) (November 2000).
28 Section 234.
29 See Joint Parliamentary Committee, *First Report on the Financial Services and Markets Bill* (29 April 1999), para. 291.

funding, the Government response did not provide a strong endorsement of the Committee's recommendation, preferring to refer to the provisions in the Bill that gave the FSA responsibility for approving the budget in line with its responsibility to maintain an effective complaints handling system. The response stated that the scheme operator's annual report on the discharge of its functions could include material about resources and the use to which they had been put: 'The Government would regard it as helpful for Parliament to take an interest in these reports in connection with its broader scrutiny of the regulatory system.'[30]

Accessibility

The existing schemes have been comparatively accessible and have collectively attracted a large number of complaints. The creation of the FOS has been portrayed as a 'populist measure', the result of a political decision that something needed to be done to make reform of financial services regulation more attractive to the population at large and that this could be achieved by ending the incoherence of an 'alphabet soup' system of ombudsmen with different powers and procedures.[31] That said, the introduction of a 'one-stop shop' for consumers with a grievance against a financial services provider will surely improve matters for those consumers who have been confused by the plethora of schemes from which to choose.

The FOS will be open to a wider constituency than simply consumers. Complaints may be brought to the FOS by private individuals but also by certain types of small businesses and charities, i.e., those with a turnover or income of less than £1 million, and also by trustees where the trust has a net asset value of less than £1 million.[32] Ease of use and accessibility for consumers is one of the claims made in favour of ombudsmen, and most of the existing schemes have had a good record in endeavouring to ensure that complainants find their processes relatively easy to use. The FOS will continue this tradition. Evidently the Chief Ombudsman is concerned to ensure that the 'virtues of smallness' characteristic of the existing schemes should be continued and the aim is that consumers should be able to choose their preferred mode of communication as far as possible, whether it be by telephone, letter or e-mail, with matters only formalised when necessary to avoid confusion or to have a finally recorded decision.[33]

Knowledge of ombudsman schemes in general is increasing and the FOS has already received considerable editorial coverage in the press through its issues of news bulletins and press releases. The Chief Ombudsman is chary of particular

30 HM Treasury, *Response to the Joint Committee's First Report on the Financial Services and Markets Bill* (17 June 1999), VIIB.
31 Personal interview, n. 18 above.   32 DISP 2.4.3R.   33 See FOS, *Laying the Foundations*.

emphasis being placed on general profile raising lest there be accusations of 'touting for business' which could impair the FOS's relationship with the industry. What is more important, in his view, is that consumers with a grievance know that they have ultimate recourse to the ombudsman.[34]

Internal procedures as a gateway for complainants

Again, as has been customary with other ombudsmen, there is a gateway, operated by the firms themselves, which governs access to the ombudsman, since complainants have to exhaust the internal complaints procedures within firms before having recourse to the ombudsman. The operation of these internal procedures has not always proved helpful in the existing schemes with the suspicion that member companies were able to manipulate their systems to deter or at least delay complainants taking the matter further. This 'conspiracy theory' may be extreme; there may simply have been a failure in administrative systems. Research published in the early 1990s found that some financial institutions were prepared to admit that the good intentions of head office were not always translated into appropriate action at branch level.[35] In any event, a number of studies[36] have shown that consumers often experience frustrating delays at the internal complaints stage before they can take their complaint to an ombudsman. Crucially, in the existing schemes, the ombudsmen have weak powers in relation to supervision of these complaint procedures.

So this 'gateway' is vital and this is one aspect where the role of the regulator in relation to complaints should prove beneficial. Firms subject to the compulsory jurisdiction are required by FSA Rules[37] to have specified complaint-handling procedures.[38] They are also applied in most cases to voluntary jurisdiction firms by contract. The Rules prescribe minimum standards for complaint handling. Complaints must be in writing and must be designed to deal with 'any *expression of dissatisfaction* whether oral or written and whether justified or not'[39] relating to that firm's provision of, or failure to provide, a financial service activity. The

---

34 Personal interview, n. 18 above. For a full articulation of this view, see S. Edell, 'Access and Visibility: a Private-Sector View' in R. Gregory *et al.* (eds.), *Practice and Prospects of the Ombudsmen in the United Kingdom* (Lampeter: The Edwin Mellin Press, 1995), 67–72.

35 See R. James, M. Seneviratne and C. Graham, 'Building Societies, Customer Complaints, and the Ombudsman' (1994) 23 *Anglo-Am L Rev* 214.

36 See National Consumer Council, *Ombudsman Services: Consumers' Views of the Office of the Building Societies Ombudsman and the Insurance Ombudsman Bureau* (London, 1993); J. Birds and C. Graham, 'Complaints against Insurance Companies' [1993] *Consumer LJ* 92; R. James and M. Seneviratne, *Offering Views in Both Directions: a Survey of Member Agencies and Complainants on their Views of the Ombudsman for Corporate Estate Agents Scheme* (Sheffield, 1996).

37 DISP 1 FSA Handbook Rules and Guidance, reproduced in FSA and FOS, *Complaints Handling Arrangements Response on CP49, a Joint Policy Statement* (December 2000), Annex A.

38 Made under s. 138 and para. 13 of Sch. 17, Financial Services and Markets Act 2000 (UK).

39 DISP 1.2.1R (emphasis added).

complainant must allege that he or she has suffered or may suffer financial loss, material distress or material inconvenience.[40] Financial loss here includes consequential or prospective loss, in addition to actual loss. Hence, this covers loss that has not yet crystallised because of the type of product involved, for example, pensions or endowment mortgages.[41] The Rules advise that complaints procedures should fit the size and type of organisation of the firm concerned, that regard should be had to the BS standard on complaints systems,[42] and that firms may use a third party administrator for handling complaints.

The availability of the complaints system must be notified to customers at or immediately after the point of sale, a copy of the procedures must automatically be provided on receipt of a complaint, and every branch or sales office must advertise the coverage of the FOS.[43] That these are mandatory requirements is a welcome improvement on the previous situation, where these were often matters covered only by codes of practice.

Furthermore, firms must take reasonable steps to ensure that their employees are aware of, and implement, the internal procedures, and that they have appropriate monitoring procedures to check compliance with the complaint handling rules both in relation to individual complaints and to any systemic problems identified. Certainly, research in the early 1990s revealed a gap between the professed commitment to complaints procedures (and ombudsman schemes) by senior management, and that of those who were working in branch offices, face to face with the customer.[44] The rules specify time limits at various stages of the complaint handling process: a written acknowledgement must be sent within five days of receipt of the complaint, within four weeks firms must send the complainant either a final response or a holding response that indicates when the firm will make further contact, and that contact itself must be within eight weeks of the original receipt of the complaint.[45] The final response letter must indicate clearly the complainant's right to take the case to the FOS if dissatisfied and must also explain that there is a six-month deadline for taking a complaint to the ombudsman.

These provisions have been covered in detail as they represent a significant advance on the previous schemes where the only sanctions that could be applied were weak ones, in that the ombudsmen could simply make *recommendations* as to procedures and time limits and could in some instances penalise tardy complaint handling by awards of compensation for inconvenience. Here, the regulator is able to

40 DISP 1.3.1 (1)(c)R.   41 DISP 1.3.2 (G).
42 British Standard's Institution *Complaints Management Systems Guide to Design and Implementation* (London: BSI, 1999; BS8600).
43 DISP 1.2.8 (1)(2)(3)R.
44 See C. Graham, M. Seneviratne and R. James, 'Publicising the Bank and Building Societies Ombudsman Schemes' [1993] *Consumer Pol'y Rev* 85; James, Seneviratne and Graham, 'Building Societies'.
45 DISP 1.4.1R, 1.4.4R, 1.4.5R.

impose standards through rules. The rules relating to internal complaints procedures will be monitored by the FSA through its roving inspection teams. These provisions should do much to improve accessibility, and represent one benefit of having a regulator with statutory duties in relation to complaint handling and the ombudsman scheme. It will also provide a more effective system for rectifying systemic problems.

There are interesting reporting requirements, too, which go far beyond any existing provisions.[46] Firms must keep records of complaints for up to three years from receipt of the complaint, and must report to the FSA, twice yearly, on the total number of complaints received by the firm, broken down according to categories and generic product types, also indicating the number of complaints closed within four and eight weeks and the total number of complaints outstanding at the end of the reporting period. Whether this might ultimately lead to the publication of 'league tables' remains to be seen. The FOS evidently perceives there to be mixed signals emanating from the Government and the FSA regarding this possible transplant of 'Charterism' into the private sector.[47] Some of the existing sectoral schemes, notably the Banking Ombudsman, did collect statistics on numbers and types of complaint per bank, but did not publicise them. Interpretation of such statistics in the consumer interest is not clear-cut, and there is some fear that publication might make individual firms more adversarial and legalistic in their dealings with the ombudsman, which would hinder the FOS in its conciliation and adjudication functions. It might also lead to firms seeking to 'buy off' complainants, with the possibility that systemic problems would thereby remain concealed.

A firm is required by the Rules to co-operate fully with the ombudsman in the handling of complaints against it[48] and this includes, but is not limited to, producing requested documents, adhering to any specified time limits, attending hearings, and complying promptly with any settlements and awards.[49]

FOS procedure

In terms of procedure, the ombudsmen will pursue a paper-based inquisitorial approach, and the Chief Ombudsman is concerned to ensure that their procedures are easy to use and meet the complainant's preferences.

The broad thrust of the FOS complaint handling procedures are set out in published Rules, and those on eligibility of complainant and time limits obviously match those already discussed in relation to the firms' own procedures. There is generally a back-stop time limit of six years after the event complained of, or, if later, no more than three years from the date on which the complainant became

---

46 DISP 1.5R.   47 Personal interview, n. 18 above.   48 DISP 1.6.1R.   49 DISP 1.6.2G.

aware, or ought reasonably to have become aware, that he or she had cause for complaint.[50]

The Rules are heavily influenced by due process requirements. On receipt of the complaint, if the ombudsman considers that the complaint is ineligible under the jurisdiction Rules, or that it is one that should be dismissed without consideration of its merits, he or she must give the complainant an opportunity to make representations before making a decision. If the ombudsman then decides that the complaint must be dismissed, he or she must give the complainant reasons for the decision and inform the firm of the decision.[51] Again, if the ombudsman decides that an investigation is necessary, he or she must give both parties an opportunity to make representations during the investigation stage, and send the provisional assessment to both parties giving them a time limit within which to respond. If either party indicates disagreement with the provisional assessment within the time limit prescribed, the matter then proceeds to determination.[52] It is at this point that the provisions of Article 6 of the European Convention on Human Rights ('the ECHR'), the so-called fair trial guarantee, may come into play.

The ombudsman is required to endeavour to resolve complaints at the earliest possible stage, and if there is a reasonable prospect of resolving the complaint by mediation he or she may attempt to negotiate a settlement between the parties.[53]

In handling complaints, the ombudsman has considerable autonomy as to the evidence required and may give directions as to the issues on which evidence is required, whether or not that should be oral or written evidence, and the way in which the evidence should be presented.[54] The ombudsman may exclude evidence that would be admissible in court, or include evidence that would be inadmissible. The ombudsman may accept information in confidence so that only a summary or edited version is submitted to the other party. He or she may take account of the failure of either party to provide information and make a decision on that basis. The ombudsman may also dismiss a complaint if a complainant fails to supply required information.[55]

In exercising these powers, the ombudsman may designate members of staff to whom the powers may be delegated,[56] and we understand that these powers will be delegated to the panel ombudsmen who work in product divisions headed by principal ombudsmen.

Possible impact of the Article 6 provisions of the European Convention on Human Rights

Under the Human Rights Act 1998 (UK), the FOS as a public body has to observe the provisions of the ECHR. The fair trial provisions in Article 6 have caused

---

50 DISP 2.3.1R (1)(c).   51 DISP 3.2.4R; 3.2.7R.   52 DISP 3.2.10R.   53 DISP 3.2.8R.
54 DISP 3.5.1R.   55 DISP 3.5.2R.   56 DISP 3.7.1R.

some concern in the ombudsman community, and the BIOA lobbied unsuccessfully for an exemption in regard to affected ombudsman schemes to be incorporated into the 1998 Act. Article 6(1) states that:

> in the determination of his civil rights and obligations or of any criminal charge against him, everyone is entitled to a fair and public hearing within a reasonable time by an independent and impartial tribunal established by law. Judgment shall be pronounced publicly.

Since the FOS in its decision-making may be determining the civil rights of both the complainant and the firm against which a complaint is made, it has to be open to the parties to request a public oral hearing.

The decision of the European Court of Human Rights, and the reasoning adopted, in *Scarth v. United Kingdom*,[57] where the private nature of the small claims arbitration proceedings in the UK county courts was held to be in breach of Article 6, made it clear that there was likely to be little flexibility if the matter came to court in relation to an ombudsman. Counsel's opinion was that the FOS and other similarly constituted ombudsmen must make provision within their procedures for the fair trial guarantee.

The recent House of Lords decision in *Alconbury*,[58] however, albeit in an entirely different context, suggests that the UK judiciary will not necessarily be prepared to interpret Article 6 requirements in a way that would undermine established practices. *Alconbury* concerned the constitutional boundaries between the executive and the judiciary, and their Lordships reiterated their reluctance to interfere in the freedom of the elected executive to define and implement policy. The House of Lords held that the availability of judicial review provided adequate jurisdictional control to meet the Article 6 requirements, particularly given the power of the court to intervene on grounds of proportionality and material errors of fact.[59]

It is unclear at this stage whether the *Alconbury* ruling will alter the FOS's view as to the need to provide for oral hearings where requested, given that as a statutory body it will be subject to judicial review. If the FOS were to take the line that such hearings are not required, it would be interesting to see how the courts would view a challenge if either party to a dispute sought to bring an action under Article 6. It may well be that adopting a similar approach to *Alconbury* would lead the courts to maintain the integrity of an alternative dispute resolution mechanism where judicial review is available, and would resist attempts to impose a trial-type appeal system. But it may be that *Alconbury* represents one extreme of judicial restraint because of the particular constitutional context of the case, and in the different context of ombudsmen the courts may take an entirely different view where

---

57 ECHR, judgment of 22 July 1999, [1999] ECHR 33745/96.
58 R. *(on the application of Alconbury Developments Ltd)* v. *Secretary of State for the Environment, Transport and Regions* [2002] 2 WLR 1389.
59 On this latter point, see R v. *Criminal Injuries Compensation Board, ex parte A* [1999] 2 AC 330.

a 'rival' adjudicator is concerned; their apparent antipathy to ombudsmen has been documented and this might lead them to support calls from either party for an 'Article 6 hearing'.[60]

What can be said at this juncture is that there are clearly dangers if the oral hearing were to become a regular feature of FOS processes. Hearings could impair the user-friendly and speedy nature of the remedy and there would be considerable cost implications. The FSA originally made it clear that provision would be made within the ombudsman procedures to comply with the Article 6 provisions, but that the emphasis would remain on protecting the underlying policy of the 2000 Act that the FOS exists to resolve complaints quickly and with minimum formality. The Chief Ombudsman has indicated that while details remained to be decided, the emphasis in the hearings would be on maintaining an inquisitorial approach without the legalistic trappings of a court.[61] He concedes that a number of unresolved issues remain as to the extent to which legal representation will be allowed, and as to how to manage a situation where one party wants an oral hearing but the other does not.[62]

Jurisdiction

In demarcating the range of coverage of the FOS, a dual policy has been pursued: to ensure that the new scheme covers the same activities as the previous sectoral schemes, and to incorporate a necessary measure of flexibility which permits the scope of the scheme to be subsequently broadened in the light of operational experience and changes within the industry. The mechanisms used to attain these objectives are the compulsory jurisdiction ('the CJ') and the voluntary jurisdiction ('the VJ'). The former is determined by the FSA, whereas the latter is specified by the FOS subject to the approval of the FSA.[63] Despite the different institutional architects of the rules, close collaboration between the FSA and FOS has taken place with the aim of ensuring, to the maximum extent possible, that from the consumer's perspective the treatment of a complaint should be the same irrespective of whether it is lodged under the CJ or the VJ.[64]

Broadly speaking, the CJ embraces all regulated activities as delineated in the Regulated Activities Order 2001,[65] plus mortgage lending and unsecured lending

---

60 See, e.g., R. Nobles, 'Keeping Ombudsmen in their Place. The Courts and the Pensions Ombudsman' [2001] *Public Law* 308.

61 FOS, *Annual Review and Reports and Financial Statements, 1 April 2000, 31 March 2001*, 14, where the Chief Ombudsman remarks that 'the "right" to a fair hearing may turn out to be more limited than at first believed, and less of a challenge to the informality of our dispute resolution process'.

62 Personal interview, n. 18 above.

63 Sch. 17, Parts III and IV, Financial Services and Markets Act 2000 (UK).

64 FSA and FOS, *Consumer Complaints and the New Single Ombudsman Scheme. A Joint Consultation Paper* (Consultation Paper 33) (November 1999), 15.

65 The Financial Services and Markets Act 2000 (Regulated Activities) Order 2001.

taking the form of overdrafts, loan accounts and cards where such activities are provided by authorised firms and the provision of general insurance services by banks and building societies. Moreover, all ancillary activities are caught, including advice in connection with those activities. Aspects of the activities that may form the subject of a complaint include not only their provision or non-provision, but also the manner of their administration.[66] In a nutshell, the CJ mirrors the aggregate coverage of the eight sectoral schemes replaced by the FOS, guaranteeing that there are no cracks into which consumers' complaints may fall. The ambit of the CJ is not, however, set in concrete; its future expansion to cover all authorised firms' financial services activities, whether regulated or not, is regarded as a longer-term objective by the FSA.[67]

The VJ jurisdiction is essentially a contractual arrangement, governed by standard terms, between the FOS and VJ participants. While the scope of the VJ is 'potentially very wide', since it can cover the financial services activities of authorised and unauthorised financial services firms,[68] the FOS is determined, principally for logistical reasons, to open it up in a controlled way. In short, it will be expanded at a rate and to activities consistent with the FOS's ability to handle the anticipated volume of complaints.[69] The intention is to make the VJ available to unauthorised mortgage lenders (e.g., direct mortgage lenders not conducting any authorisable activities and thus not caught by the CJ) in order to create a level playing field with their authorised rivals and authorised firms whose activities are currently covered by membership of an existing scheme.[70] The FOS's longer-term strategy is to expand the VJ to cover all authorised firms' financial services activities not brought within the VJ, the activities of mortgage intermediaries, and the conduct of general insurance intermediaries currently subject to the self-regulatory regime administered by the General Insurance Standards Council.[71]

We thus have in place arrangements that in terms of substantive coverage can be loosely characterised as 'existing coverage plus'. Consumers will encounter no gaps in coverage, when compared with the *status quo ante*, and there is an in-built provision for controlled expansion in FOS jurisdiction, albeit on a voluntary basis, which takes into account the FOS's complaints handling capacity and the dynamics of the financial services industry.

A final point on the FOS jurisdiction is that a series of qualifications and inroads into it have been borrowed from the sectoral schemes. Thus, a firm's in-house complaints procedure must have been used and exhausted before recourse is made to the FOS; complaints about general interest rate policies or lending decisions or the application of standards, tables and principles to the calculation of bonuses,

---

66 The full list and technical details can be found at DISP 2.6.1–2.6.5G.
67 See FSA and FOS, *Consumer Complaints*, 23.
68 FOS and FSA, *Complaints Handling Arrangements; Feedback Statements on CP 33 and Draft Rules* (Consultation Paper 49) (May 2000), 17.
69 See FSA and FOS, *Consumer Complaints*, 24.
70 See FOS and FSA, *Complaints Handling Arrangements*, 17.   71 *Ibid.*, 17–18.

surrender values, etc., cannot be made.[72] The first exclusion means that local settlement of consumers' financial services grievances will continue to be the norm, and the latter three provisos underline the accepted wisdom that it is no part of an ombudsman's role to intrude upon the legitimate commercial autonomy of financial services firms.

Unlike the PIAOB and the Banking Ombudsman schemes, however, there is no 'test case' provision whereby the FOS could refer difficult or complex cases raising issues of legal principle to the courts for a definitive resolution. The Chief Ombudsman regards such a power as unnecessary, given the power of early termination of complaints which are more appropriately resolved in the court system.[73] While it is true that the PIAOB and Banking Ombudsman schemes indicate that use of this power is very rare, there may be some merit in revisiting this issue in the future. A power of prompt termination in no way guarantees that the dispute will actually go to court. Moreover, an institutionalised link[74] between the FOS and the courts would establish a potentially fruitful vehicle for the development of a new corpus of financial services law spawned by the Act and the rapidly burgeoning FSA regulations and guidance.

Operating standards

One of the key advantages of the ombudsman technique as a consumer redress mechanism is the capacity to transcend strict legal rules and draw upon a range of extra-legal standards in a manner that usually operates to the benefit of the consumer. This power is vital in the financial services industry where there is characteristically acute inequality of bargaining power between the product or service provider and the purchaser, coupled with, perhaps most notoriously in the insurance sector, a body of legal doctrine heavily weighted against the consumer. It is, moreover, a crucial tool for private sector ombudsmen in developing to the fullest extent their quality control activities, that is to say using individual complaints as a vehicle for stimulating higher standards of business conduct within the industry.

So far as the FOS is concerned, the overriding criterion to be used by the ombudsman in dispute resolution is to do 'what is, in his opinion, fair and reasonable in all the circumstances of the case'.[75] In assessing the precise requirements of

72 The full list of provisos to the FOS's jurisdiction can be found at DISP 3.31. (1)–(17)R.
73 Personal interview, n. 18 above.
74 As proposed by Lord Woolf, *Access to Justice* (London: HMSO, June 1995), 140, who saw considerable benefits in cases being transferred between ombudsmen and the courts as appropriate.
75 Financial Services and Markets Act 2000 (UK), s. 228(2); DISP 3.8.1R. In terms of the transition from the sectoral schemes to the FOS, the Treasury is proposing that complaints made before but not resolved by 1 December 2001 ought to be resolved by reference to the rules of the old schemes even if these do not incorporate a fair and reasonable standard, but complaints lodged

fairness and reasonableness in particular cases, the ombudsman is directed to take into account 'the relevant law, regulations, regulators' rules, guidance and standards, relevant codes of practice and, where appropriate, what he considers to have been good industry practice at the relevant time'.[76]

The power to use a subjective fair and reasonable standard has in the past proved controversial in connection with ombudsmen, but it now seems to be accepted as an essential element in an ombudsman's armoury. Both the IOB and BSOS included this in their remit. In contrast, the PIA opted to follow the advice of Lord Ackner that such a standard exposed the industry to being 'the hostage to fortune of uncertain and therefore unpredictable liability which may result from the Ombudsman acting as the embodiment of the conscience of the industry, a wholly subjective perception subject to no appellate process', and was therefore unacceptable.[77] Accordingly, it confined the ombudsman to recourse to extra-legal standards enshrined in codes and guidance issued by the PIA itself. This prompted charges that the PIAOB offered a distinctly inferior mode of redress in comparison with the IOB,[78] charges that the first Ombudsman was keen to rebut by contending that the level of consumer protection furnished by codes and regulatory guidance rendered a fair and reasonable criterion otiose.[79] Certainly the experience of the IOB and BSO schemes indicate that the availability of this admittedly subjective power is essential to do justice in individual cases where the law, codes and regulatory guidance are deficient in some respect. Furthermore, exercise of the power does not necessarily involve 'palm tree' justice dispensed by an ombudsman. This is a discretionary power which can be structured by reliance on a series of broad equitable principles and the gradual emergence of a corpus of informal, persuasive precedent used to guide decision-making in the future.[80]

At first glance it is somewhat surprising that Parliament has granted the FOS this broad licence given the 'tensions'[81] and 'strife'[82] that its creative use by the second Insurance Ombudsman, Julian Farrand, generated during the early to mid-1990s.

after 1 December 2001 but relating to an act or omission prior to 1 December 2001 ought to be determined by FOS rules including the fair and reasonable standard: HM Treasury, *The Transition to the New Ombudsman Scheme and the Investigation of Complaints against the Financial Services Authority. A Consultation Document* (March 2001), paras. 2.2–2.5, 3.3.

76 DISP 3.8.1(2) R.

77 Lord Ackner, *Report on a Unified Complaints Procedure* (London: PIA, July 1993), para. 93.

78 See Morris and Hamilton, 'The Insurance Ombudsman', 146.

79 Stephen Edell, *Annual Report of the Personal Investment Authority Bureau 1994–95*, 21.

80 See, in particular, the discussion by Julian Farrand in Insurance Ombudsman Bureau, *Annual Report 1989*, paras. 1.1–1.59. See also the comments by Farrand's successor, Laurie Slade, that the demands of fairness and reasonableness should not be an 'esoteric secret' and required the identification of some basic principles as guidance: Insurance Ombudsman Bureau, *Annual Report 1995*, paras. 2.3.3, 2.4.1–2.4.6.

81 *Annual Report 1995, ibid.* (Chair: Barbara Saunders), 11.

82 Insurance Ombudsman Bureau, *Continuing Growth and Evolution: Annual Report 1999* (Ombudsman: Laurie Slade), 7.

These strained relationships existed apparently not merely between the IOB and the industry, but also within the IOB constitutional structure itself.[83] There is an emerging consensus in the UK ombudsman community that the fair and reasonable standard is defensible in voluntary schemes where sponsor firms can choose freely to submit to its application and enjoy the freedom to withdraw at any point in time. Conversely, the standard is far less easy to support in compulsory schemes,[84] unless there are special provisions that take account of this, such as the power of building societies in the BSOS to defy what would otherwise be a binding award by invoking the so-called 'publicity option'.[85] Incorporation of the power and its paramount status, which clearly permit its use to override legal or established extra-legal standards (such as FSA rules or sectoral codes),[86] underlines the point that the FOS has scope for creativity, dynamism and self-renewal in dispute resolution; and, therefore, that one of the best features from a consumer protection perspective of the sectoral schemes has been retained.[87] As a necessary counterbalance to this power, though, the FOS is firm in its commitment to a key theme of consistency in decision-making, that is to say, the development of consistent policies articulating how the FOS will approach commonly encountered problems. This will provide firms with a predictive tool in relation to complaints referred to the FOS, and assist in ironing out different approaches employed by the sectoral schemes to resolve the same problem.[88] For the FOS, therefore, the fair and reasonable standard will be tempered by the values of predictability and consistency, which are of critical importance from an industry perspective. Clearly the FOS is sensitive to the need not to alienate the industry by a cavalier use of the fair and reasonable standard. It is aiming to develop a principled and transparent approach to use of the standard, mindful that the capacity to traverse the parameters of legality and issue determinations which bind firms but not consumers 'should make us act with care and responsibility'.[89]

Turning to sectoral codes and regulatory guidance, these will frequently serve to mitigate the impact of financial services law on consumers. In sharp contrast with the PIAOB, BSOS and IOB schemes, however, FOS rules do not explicitly provide that if the law requires consumers to be treated less favourably than do codes and regulatory guidance, then the latter is to prevail. It is hard to see how this principle

---

83 Morris and Hamilton, 'The Insurance Ombudsman', 124–5.
84 A proposition that even the arch exponent of the fair and reasonable criterion in private sector ombudsmen schemes is inclined to support: Farrand, 'An Academic Ombudsman', 14.
85 See the provision in the scheme's terms of reference to the effect that if a building society chose to defy the Ombudsman's award, the Ombudsman could publicise that fact in such manner as the Ombudsman decided: Office of the Building Societies Ombudsman, *Building Societies Ombudsman Scheme* (August 1998), para. 33(A) and (B).
86 Personal interview, n. 18 above.
87 See the concerns expressed regarding the FOS on this in Insurance Ombudsman Bureau, *Continuing Growth and Evolution*, 21.
88 See further on this FOS, *Laying the Foundations*, 8.   89 *Ibid.*

can now be abandoned in view of the oft-stated policy that the FOS will maintain the same levels of consumer protection furnished by the sectoral schemes. The assumption must be that it will be implicitly read into FOS rules. FSA guidance is proliferating at a rapid pace and in practice will provide the level of detail, clarity and precision to resolve many complaints reaching the FOS without the need to refer to sectoral codes or the fair and reasonable standard. Indeed, there are likely to be entire categories of complaints where the basis for dispute resolution is to be found in specific regulatory guidance. The classic example of this is the PIA–FSA joint guidance[90] on the quantification of loss and compensation in complaints alleging the mis-selling of endowment mortgage policies. What then is the precise interrelationship between the fair and reasonable standard and these extra-legal sources? The fair and reasonable standard is clearly the ultimate source of authority within the scheme and thus will override a code or regulatory standard if an ombudsman deems that appropriate in a particular complaint. But, in addition, at least judging from the experience of the sectoral schemes, it is likely also to perform a developmental function: a provision in a code or regulatory edict may be regarded by an ombudsman as the 'bare minimum'[91] open to embellishment by the requirements of fairness and reasonableness. Thus, the consumer interest may be asserted not just during the formulation and regular revision of codes and guidance, but also, in cases where the ombudsman discovers deficiencies or lacunae during the continuous process of conciliation and adjudication within the FOS itself.

So far as good industry practice is concerned, this is a standard criterion utilised by private sector ombudsmen. There has, however, been a long-running debate as to its precise meaning, with two schools of thought emerging. According to what may be loosely termed the 'codification school', the role of an ombudsman is to identify and apply in the process of resolving disputes *industry-determined* precepts of good practice. In contrast, the 'reform school' holds that an ombudsman's function is to *establish* standards of good practice which may, where a balanced analysis of consumer interests requires it, be more exacting than those currently accepted as good practice throughout the industry. This debate first reared its head as far back as 1989 in the Jack Report on *Banking Services Law*,[92] which started from the premise that the industry itself cannot enjoy the sole prerogative in determining standards

---

90 PIA and FSA, *Endowment Mortgage Complaints* (Consultation Paper 75) (November 2000). See also FSA, *Endowment Mortgage Complaints Feedback on CP75 and 'Final' Text* (Policy Statement) (May 2001). While this guidance is directed primarily at the handling of endowment mortgage complaints by regulated firms themselves, it will be relevant to the FOS in dealing with such complaints post-N2.

91 See, e.g., Office of the Building Societies Ombudsman, *Building Societies Ombudsman: Annual Report 1996–97*, 32.

92 *Banking Services: Law and Practice Report by the Review Committee*, Cm. 622 (Chair: R. B. Jack), paras.15.11–15.13, chap. 16.

of good practice without conferring on the ombudsman a mission to develop independently standards of good banking practice.

In the insurance sector, the PIAOB and IOB adopted diametrically opposed postures, the former tending to confine itself to a codification role, whereas the latter was much more openly reformist in its philosophy and practice.[93] While the proliferation of sectoral codes of good practice and FSA guidance (not to mention the presence of the fair and reasonable criterion) will probably render the issue less important in the FOS scheme, there will inevitably be some complaints that involve an assessment of the adequacy of an industry practice. The clearly subjective wording of FOS rules on this point indicates the incorporation into the scheme of power in an ombudsman to reshape good practice (which was in any event a power explicitly or implicitly assumed by most of the sectoral ombudsmen). Hence, the wording and underlying spirit of the FOS strongly suggest a licence to reappraise and revamp even established practices in the various sectors covered by the scheme where the fair treatment of consumers warrants it.

Finally, although neither the scheme rules nor the Act make any reference to maladministration, it is almost certainly the case that the FOS will utilise it as an operating standard. Maladministration requires essentially a subjective, flexible standard of good administration which can be drawn upon, and in light of which a diverse range of administrative mistakes can be condemned, but which typically precludes scrutiny of the substantive merits of a decision unless it is thoroughly bad.[94] While the concept owes its origins and subsequent evolution to the Parliamentary Ombudsman, it has been embraced by the private sector schemes,[95] usually by implicitly reading it into their terms of reference. In the context of the FOS, however, it may well be the case that there will be less need to have recourse to maladministration given the precise standards of business conduct articulated in FSA regulations and the various sectoral codes. Even where an administrative error is not covered by these provisions, the fair and reasonable standard provides an adequate basis for resolving the grievance, with the result that maladministration, in explicit terms at least, will probably be relegated to the role of a residual operating standard.

Remedies

The provision of effective remedies by the FOS is vital not only if it is to be viewed as a credible consumer redress mechanism, but also if it is to fulfil its

---

93 See the discussion in Morris and Hamilton, 'The Insurance Ombudsman'.
94 For a full account of its genesis and subsequent development by the UK Parliamentary Commissioner for Administration, see A. W. Bradley, 'The Role of the Ombudsman in Relation to the Protection of Citizens' Rights' [1980] *Cambridge LJ* 304; A. J. Callaghan, 'Maladministration' [1988] *Ombudsman Journal* 1; House of Commons, *Maladministration and Redress* (First Report of the Select Committee on the PCA) (1994–5), 112; and C. Harlow and R. Rawlings, *Law and Administration* (2nd edn, London: Butterworths, 1997), 425–7.
95 James, *Private Ombudsmen*, 221.

potential as an agent for stimulating higher standards of business practices within the financial services industry. The initial signs on this are very promising: the FOS retains the best features of our three comparator sectoral schemes and goes beyond them by furnishing, albeit as a last resort option, 'judicial teeth' for the enforcement of an ombudsman's award.

Essentially, the FOS has dual compensatory and injunctive remedial powers, which may be combined or used in the alternative. First, if a complaint is decided in favour of the complainant, a determination can include a money award which the ombudsman considers compensation for financial loss or other loss such as pain and suffering, damage to reputation, or distress and inconvenience. Compensation for non-pecuniary loss may be awarded irrespective of whether a court of law could do so.[96] There is a £100,000 overall ceiling on awards which is enshrined in the Act[97] itself and reflects the position in our three comparator sectoral schemes. Interestingly, and in line with powers conferred on the IOB and BSOS but not the PIAOB, where such awards are limited to £1,500,[98] there is no limit, within the overall £100,000 ceiling, on the non-pecuniary element within the ombudsman's awards. While this permits the FOS considerable latitude to ensure that awards reflect the full range of complainant losses, the evolution of internal guidelines to structure the discretion of individual ombudsmen is imperative in view of the cogent evidence that quantification of compensation for such matters as distress and inconvenience is an inherently subjective exercise on which reasonable ombudsmen presented with the same set of facts may reach very different solutions.[99] This point is of critical importance in the context of the FOS, where decision-making power is dispersed amongst a large panel of ombudsmen working in distinct divisions endowed with considerable operational autonomy. Secondly, the ombudsmen enjoy a power to issue a direction akin to that of an injunction, namely the ability to order a firm to 'take such steps in relation to the complainant as [he] considers just and appropriate' regardless of whether a court could order those steps.[100] This will doubtless prove particularly valuable where proper redress for the consumer requires, instead of or in addition to compensation, the provision of a formal apology or a change of decision or the reappraisal of a decision or administrative action.

Once an ombudsman's award has been made or a settlement reached, the firm is required to comply promptly with any monetary award or direction issued, or any settlement that it agrees to at an earlier stage of the procedure.[101] Replicating

---

96 DISP 3.9.1.G, 3.9.2R, 4.2.8R.
97 Financial Services and Markets Act 2000 (UK), s. 229, which is limited to the CJ but is effectively extended to the VJ by FOS standard terms for VJ participants. The ombudsmen may recommend a figure in excess of the ceiling, but this is not binding on a firm: s. 229(5), DISP 3.9.5G.
98 FOS, *Annual Report of the Personal Investment Authority Ombudsman 1999–2000*, Appendix 1, Ombudsman's Terms of Reference, para. 5.5.
99 See the account of a role-play exercise highlighting this in Insurance Ombudsman Bureau, *Annual Report 1994*, para. 2.15.
100 DISP 3.9.1.G, 4.2.8.R.   101 DISP 3.9.13.R, 4.2.10.R.

the practice in sectoral schemes, the complainant at any point prior to formal acceptance of an ombudsman's award is free to reject it and pursue his or her legal rights in court.[102] On paper, therefore, the FOS redress machinery can be regarded as biased in favour of consumers, though the point may be more theoretical than real given that a complainant whose case has been rejected by the FOS is unlikely to obtain redress in a court restricted to the application of legal standards. Perhaps the most distinctive feature of the entire FOS architecture, compared with the three sectoral schemes, is that ombudsmen's monetary awards may be enforced in the county court (or in Scotland in the Sheriff Court) as though such award were a normal court order, and the ombudsman's directions may be enforced, at the behest of the complainant, in the same manner as an injunction.[103] In order to facilitate judicial enforcement, the FOS is required to maintain a register of each money award and directions issued.[104] In practice, recourse to this judicial enforcement machinery is likely to be extremely rare: failure to comply with FOS awards will in the vast majority of cases be due to the financial services firm having gone into insolvent liquidation, with the result that the complainant will have no option other than to turn to the new unified Financial Services Compensation Scheme for redress.[105]

This stands in stark contrast to the IOB and PIAOB, which were empowered to issue binding awards against member firms, but where the power was not underpinned by possible judicial enforcement, and the BSOS, whose awards were generally binding subject to the 'publicity option' granted to building societies to defy an ombudsman's award on pain of that fact being publicised in a manner directed by the ombudsman. Provision for binding (and judicially underwritten) ombudsman awards and directions, in the context of a statutory and compulsory scheme, represents a sharp departure from orthodox theory in the ombudsman community which has long reasoned that this is acceptable in voluntary schemes which firms are free to join and leave, but not in compulsory schemes on the basis this would infringe the 'constitutional principle', which holds that the courts should ideally be the ultimate arbiters of an individual's legal rights. Such a principle if indeed it exists is only implicit in our (largely) unwritten constitution. It now appears to have been overridden by the political imperative for a modernised financial services regime with, as a central feature, stronger consumer redress machinery. Once again, however, it may be that this issue is more symbolic than real: it is difficult

---

102 DISP 3.8.2.(2)–(4).
103 Financial Services and Markets Act 2000 (UK), Sch. 17, Part III, para. 16, and s. 229(9)(a) and (b) respectively.
104 DISP 3.9.14R, 3.9.15G, 3.9.16 G.
105 Details of which can be found in Financial Services and Markets Act 2000 (UK), Part XV and Sch. 10; FSA, *Financial Services Compensation: Scheme Draft Rules* (Consultation Paper 58), (July 2000). Ombudsman schemes and compensation funds are conceptually distinct consumer protection mechanisms. Ombudsmen provide redress in relation to live firms by the firm whereas compensation schemes are designed to provide compensation cover as a back-stop: FSA, *Consumer Compensation* (Consultation Paper 5) (December 1997), 17.

to envisage many firms opting to defy an ombudsman's award or direction with the advance knowledge that a consumer could rectify this by invoking the enforcement apparatus of the courts.

If a complainant rejects an ombudsman's determination there is no further right of appeal or review within the FOS institutional structure. The only option is to pursue the matter via an action on the substantive merits in the court system. This contrasts with formal practice in the IOB and the BSOB, where the Chair of Council performed an attenuated review function at the request of the disappointed complainant. In the IOB, this involved a check by the Chair that the IOB's procedures had been followed (with an apology to the complainant if they had not),[106] and in the BSOS, the Chair restricted himself or herself to checking that the ombudsman had discharged his or her duties with impartiality to both sides.[107] A complainant claiming a fundamental procedural defect in the FOS or a substantively perverse determination by an ombudsman can probably turn to the remedy of judicial review. It is almost certain that the FOS meets the criteria for judicial review of private sector ombudsman schemes as articulated in *Aegon*.[108] Exposure of the FOS to the discipline of judicial review grafts a necessary measure of legal accountability onto the scheme. There are, however, real fears that judicial review could slip its leash of scrutinising the legality (in terms of the *vires*) of FOS procedures and determinations, and in practice result in courts substituting their opinions on the substantive merits of complaints in place of those of the ombudsmen.[109] If this were to occur on a regular basis, the spectre looms of a more legalistic *modus operandi* and substantive decision-making ethos within the FOS, which would undermine its entire *raison d'être* as a speedy, informal and effective consumer redress mechanism.

Quality control activity

All ombudsmen are confronted with a tension between the redress of individual grievance, a court substitute role, and performance of a quality control function whereby the individual complaint may be used as a vehicle for raising standards of administrative and business practice, a quasi-regulatory mission, in the constituency subject to the ombudsman's jurisdiction.[110] While the ombudsman technique is intrinsically better suited than the courts to engage in quality control

106 Insurance Ombudsman Bureau, *Annual Review 1996*, 3; Insurance Ombudsman Bureau, *Annual Report, March 1999*, 3.
107 Office of the Building Societies Ombudsmen, *Building Societies Ombudsman Scheme: Annual Report 1993–4*, 4.
108 R v. *Insurance Ombudsman Bureau, ex parte Aegon Life Assurance Ltd* (*The Times*, 7 January 1994).
109 Personal interview, n. 18 above. See also Farrand, 'An Academic Ombudsman', 16.
110 See N. Lewis and P. Birkinshaw, *When Citizens Complain: Reforming Justice and Administration* (Philadelphia: Open University Press, 1993), 123.

activity,[111] the extent to which a particular ombudsman scheme actually performs a quality control role turns on a number of factors, not least the presence of a direct regulator operating in close proximity to the ombudsman and the personal predilections of the ombudsman as to what his or her primary role should be.

Certainly those sectoral ombudsmen having close links with regulatory agencies, such as the PIAOB and the IMRO Investment Ombudsman, have tended to take a more restricted view of their role, seeing it as principally a quasi-judicial redress of individual complaints function, which ought not to intrude upon the territory of a regulator.[112] Judging the FOS posture on this is very difficult in view of the infancy of the scheme, but the Chief Ombudsman has expressed a definite preference for the primary focus being redress of individual grievances while acknowledging that some quality control activity is inevitable given the lacunae and uncertainty in sectoral codes and FSA regulatory standards that concrete complaints-handling experience will reveal.[113] The fair and reasonable standard will obviously be an indispensable tool in performing this task. For the Chief Ombudsman, the dividing line between the FOS's quasi-judicial function and the FSA's role as regulator is clear, but these functions are complementary, with the FOS having a role to play in facilitating the FSA's regulatory activities.[114]

The FSA itself at an early stage in the gestation of the FOS acknowledged the value of this link between complaints-handling and regulatory processes, observing that:[115] 'complaints are an important source of regulatory information. They can provide valuable early warnings of problems in particular firms or sectors, with particular products or with particular regulatory requirements. They may indicate the existence of a more widespread, systemic problem which requires the FSA's attention.' This aspiration has been translated into regulatory reality by conferring on the FOS an open-textured power to pass information on to the FSA, which is necessary for the latter to discharge its regulatory functions.[116] Clearly there are limits to this linkage. In particular, the FOS retains the unfettered discretion as to when to invoke it and what information is provided,[117] and the Chief Ombudsman is aware of the possible threat to the perceived independence of the FOS flowing from too intimate a relationship with the FSA.[118] But both bodies regard it as constituting the FOS as an 'important part of the new regulatory system with a crucial role to play in enabling the FSA to fulfil its consumer protection objective'.[119] This can be regarded as a form of *indirect* quality control activity in contrast with the

111 *Ibid.*
112 See Morris and Hamilton, 'The Insurance Ombudsman', 142; P. E. Morris, 'The Investment Ombudsman. A Critical Review' [1996] *J Bus L* 1.
113 Personal interview, n. 18 above.   114 *Ibid.*
115 FSA, *Consumer Complaints* (Consultation Paper 4) (December 1997), 24.
116 DISP 3.10.(3)R.
117 See FSA and FOS, *Consumer Complaints*, 57.   118 Personal interview, n. 18 above.
119 *Ibid.*, which is expressly articulated as a regulatory objective for the FSA in s. 2(2)(C) of the Financial Services and Markets Act 2000 (UK).

direct impact on business practices stemming from the identification and rectification of systemic deficiencies in firms' practices exposed by the FOS's case-work activity, which will be disseminated to (and hopefully absorbed by) the industry in the FOS's Annual Reports and a monthly newsletter which the FOS has already started to publish. A potentially powerful engine for quality control activity is the power of the FOS to issue guidance[120] articulating its posture on categories of specific complaints. Such guidance may well act as a potent incentive for firms to reappraise their business practices and help to stimulate prompt local settlement of consumer grievances. Even at this early stage in the life of the FOS, it has exhibited real zeal in utilising this power, issuing guidance on its approach to complaints about variable interest rate TESSAs (tax exempt special savings accounts), reductions in interest rates on savings and deposit accounts to (allegedly) unfair levels, and endowment mortgages.[121] This power will have to be used with care and sensitivity if the FOS is to avoid industry charges of arrogating to itself a quasi-regulatory mission.[122]

The above refers to quality control at the tip of the 'complaints iceberg'.[123] Accounts of ombudsman schemes in both the public and private sectors have an unfortunate tendency to lapse into myopia by ignoring the extent to which service providers may themselves use complaints as 'jewels in the crown'; as an informed basis for continuous improvements in service standards.[124] Given the expectation that the vast majority of consumers' financial services complaints will continue to be resolved in-house, coupled with FSA monitoring of internal complaints procedures and the requirement to maintain and regularly file with the FSA complaints statistics, firms themselves will have both the means and incentive to engage in complaints analysis as a means of improving business practices. This will not only serve to minimise the risk of FSA disciplinary action and/or regulatory intervention, but also possibly enhance a firm's competitive position in the market. Quality control activity triggered by patterns of complaints should not be seen as a threat or as the sole prerogative of the FOS and FSA. A responsive and forward-looking firm should instead view complaints statistics as a valuable measure of consumer satisfaction which represents an opportunity to improve the quality of service provided.

---

120 Sch. 17, para. 8, which is expressed in open-ended terms.
121 Full details of which can be gleaned from the FOS website: www.financial-ombudsman.org.uk.
122 Allegations that the FOS would strenuously deny, depicting its briefing notes as merely providing external users with an indication to how complaints falling within a particular category are likely to be considered: FOS, *Annual Review*, 16.
123 Which formal consumer complaints clearly are. A large-scale empirical study of access to advice and justice reports that less than 1 per cent of consumers who took formal action to resolve their grievance ended up obtaining an ombudsman's adjudication: H. Genn, *Paths to Justice: What People Do and Think about Going to Law* (Oxford: Hart Publishing, 1999), 156–7.
124 For a full discussion of this process, albeit in the context of public-sector complaints handling and redress, see Harlow and Rawlings, *Law and Administration*, 405–6.

Conclusions

Our preliminary study of the FOS is necessarily tentative given the lack of a track record in complaints-handling under its own jurisdiction. Confident statements on whether the FOS represents an improvement on the previous 'patchwork quilt' of sectoral schemes requires an empirical study over several years which examines the internal functioning of the FOS, its relationship with the FSA, and, perhaps most crucial of all, complainants' experiences of the service it provides[125] and its effect on internal complaints handling by financial services firms.[126] A major deficiency in ombudsman research, in sharp contrast with studies of the judiciary, is the failure to analyse and highlight the different nuances in philosophy and detailed decision-making that different individuals may bring to the same ombudsman office.[127] While, historically at least, there has been a major barrier to this type of research in the form of a lack of case digests published by ombudsmen, the FOS represents fertile ground for just such a project in several years' time given its publication of divisional case digests and accessibility to academic researchers.

There are, however, some provisional observations that can be made. While the FOS has claimed that the scheme is evolutionary rather than revolutionary, in that it covers the same ground as the sectoral schemes and retains their best features,[128] this is to some extent disingenuous. In terms of its sheer size, range of coverage of the industry, statutory underpinning and close links with the lead regulator, the FOS will arguably be a different type of species from the previous ombudsman schemes in the financial services industry. The effective nationalisation of a private sector industry, which the creation of the FOS entails, in particular the provision of a single point of entry for complaints and the emergence of a logical internal divisional structure, will almost certainly reduce consumer confusion while permitting the retention of specialist subject and dispute-resolution expertise accumulated in the sectoral schemes. On the other hand, there must be real fears that the birth of such a massive organisation will result in some loss of the high levels of personal service and informality offered to complainants by the sectoral schemes. A related concern is that the individualised justice regarded as inherent in 'ombudsmanry' may be dissipated as sectoral codes and regulatory standards become ever more detailed and pervasive. The Chief Ombudsman and his team of panel ombudsmen will need to be vigilant to prevent this by preserving their statutory discretion to resolve

---

125 Along the lines of the National Consumer Council commissioned study of complainants' experiences of two sectoral schemes: *Ombudsman Services*.

126 For an example of this type of research, see Birds and Graham, 'Complaints against Insurance Companies'.

127 See S. Lee, 'Ombudsman over All Our Shoulders' (UK Ombudsman Association, Conference Report, 17–18 October 1991), 18.

128 See FOS, *Laying the Foundations*, 2.

complaints by reference to the fair and reasonable criterion, even if this cuts across legal and extra-legal standards.

Specific strengths of the FOS can be identified even at this early juncture. The provision of judicial enforcement for ombudsmen's awards and directions is a significant advance on the position in the sectoral schemes. While it will probably be rare for a complainant to have to utilise this machinery, its effect in bolstering an ombudsman's bargaining power in negotiating with obstreperous firms should not be underestimated. That said, within the FOS there is a powerful organisational ethos favouring early and informal resolution of complaints, with formal adjudication regarded, at least in crude quantitative terms, as very much the exception to the rule.[129] Accordingly, it may well transpire that judicial machinery for the enforcement of FOS awards proves to be of symbolic rather than practical importance.

Links between the FOS and the FSA create rich potential for quality control activity that, over time, may lead to improved standards of business practice which benefit all consumers of financial services, not merely those with sufficient knowledge and determination to lodge a formal complaint with the FOS. Perhaps most important of all, the requirement for firms to establish and publicise in-house complaints procedures, the stringent time limits for internal resolution of complaints, and continuous FSA monitoring of internal complaints procedures, lay the foundations for the gradual evolution of a bifurcated complaints structure involving the vast majority of disputes being resolved locally and informally, with only the most intractable complaints raising difficult or complex factual or legal issues reaching the FOS.

129 For confirmation of this, see the statement by the Chief Ombudsman in FOS, *Annual Review*, 15.

9 Economic appraisals of rulemaking in the new society: why, how, and what does it mean? The challenge for the consumer

JENNY HAMILTON AND MIK WISNIEWSKI

Introduction

By the mid-1980s there was already a fully fledged, and very significant, market in financial services in the UK. This sector (loosely encompassing banking, insurance and securities) was regulated through a mix of some limited statutory regulation (for example, brokers) but primarily through an informal 'gentlemen's club' model of self-regulation. In 1986 the Thatcher Government replaced this by a formal bureaucratic regulatory structure consisting of formally recognised self-regulatory organisations operating under a statutory umbrella body known as the Securities and Investment Board ('the SIB').[1]

The reasons for this reform were primarily market related: the internationalisation of the financial services sector, particularly the entry of foreign businesses into the UK after the removal of certain anti-competitive structures, and the government's desire to widen the share ownership base. Foreign businesses could not necessarily be relied upon to adopt the norms of the British 'gentlemen's club'. Equally, UK private citizens could not be expected to go where they had never gone before into stocks and shares unless they were convinced the market was 'safe', particularly after the financial scandals that occurred in the late 1970s and early 1980s. A new structure was needed to ensure that new players in particular adopted certain standards, and to reassure the private investor that the market was clean and safe. The financial services sector was too important to the UK economy to risk having its reputation tarnished. New regulation was required not in order to interfere with or undermine the operation of the market but in order to support its growth.[2]

In 1997 Tony Blair's Labour Government took office. One of its first acts was to announce that the existing regulatory structures for the UK financial services would be reformed and replaced by a single statutory regulator. Although the reform had been foreshadowed in Labour's election Business Manifesto, the radicalism of the

---

1 This new structure governed all 'investment' business, typically securities and long-term insurance products. General banking and general insurance business remained outside this structure. See further J. Black, *Rules and Regulators* (Oxford: Clarendon Press, 1997), 46–77.
2 For a fuller explanation, see L. C. B. Gower, *A Review of Investor Protection: a Discussion Document* (London: HMSO, 1982).

reform ultimately took many by surprise.[3] The new regulatory structure introduced in the Financial Services and Markets Act 2000 combines the regulation of securities, insurance and banking under one regulator (replacing nine existing regulators), and arguably makes the new regulator, the Financial Services Authority ('the FSA'), one of the most powerful financial sector regulators in the world.[4] It replaces the previous regulatory structure with one that is entirely statutory.

The public reason most often given by the Government to justify this reform was one of 'protecting the consumer'. There was a perception that the regulators had been 'captured' by the industry they were supposed to regulate.[5] Consumer protection was therefore thought to be at the heart of the new regulatory regime. This reason was consistent with the strong communitarian values traditionally associated with Labour ideology.

But what is perhaps most radical about this new structure, given the Labour Government's concern to ensure adequate consumer protection, is the extent of the rule-making and enforcement powers given to the 'super-regulator' and the level of apparent independence of the regulator from government.[6] How could consumer protection be guaranteed in such circumstances? If consumer protection was to be at the heart of the new, but very independent, regime then mechanisms had to be put in place to curtail the exercise of regulatory discretion for purposes other than consumer protection. One obvious method is the introduction of specific statutory objectives. Unlike the previous legislation, the new legislation contains a number of explicit statutory objectives. In addition, it contains seven statutory 'principles' that are to guide the regulator in discharging its functions. These objectives and regulatory principles are intended to impose discipline on the use of regulatory discretion and provide a measure of regulatory accountability. Given the public rhetoric accompanying the reforms, we would have expected consumer interests to be at the heart of these objectives and principles.

Significantly, however, only one of the four objectives contains a reference to consumer protection, namely 'securing the appropriate degree of protection for

3 See M. Blair, L. Minghella, M. Taylor, M. Threipland and G. Walker, *Blackstone's Guide to the Financial Services and Markets Act 2000* (London: Blackstone Press, 2000).
4 See further J. Hamilton, 'Financial Services Regulation' in L. MacGregor, P. Prosser and C. Villiers (eds.), *Regulation and Markets beyond 2000* (Aldershot: Ashgate, 2000), 243; Blair *et al.*, *Blackstone's Guide*, 17–36.
5 There were also other less public reasons. The Government had to find a new home for banking regulation after granting the Bank of England independence; international co-operation and coordination required a rationalisation of the multiple regulator structure, as did the fight against financial crime. See further Blair *et al.*, *Blackstone's Guide*, 12–16; Hamilton, 'Financial Services Regulation', 249–50.
6 The new regulator is a private company limited by guarantee. Although this is an unusual regulatory structure, it is modelled on its predecessor, the SIB. There were pragmatic reasons why the Government chose not to change this model; a change in structure would have required legislation, which in turn would have created delay in implementation of the new regime. See further Blair *et al.*, *Blackstone's Guide*, 19–20.

consumers', while the other three are for 'maintaining market confidence', 'promoting public understanding of the financial system' and 'reduction of financial crime'.[7] Furthermore, the seven guiding principles make no reference to consumer protection. Instead, their emphasis is upon the importance of competition in the market, and the need for cost-effective regulation.

What we would have expected from a Labour Government was a much stronger commitment to 'public interest' regulation and less emphasis on economic efficiency as a general regulatory theme. What we got was an affirmation of an economic approach to regulation that is not as far removed from the neo-liberal values of the Conservatives as might have been expected. At the heart of this regime is a strong affirmation of market efficiency, individual responsibility and the need for regulatory efficiency. Included is a statutory requirement for the regulator to conduct a cost–benefit analysis ('CBA') of any proposed new regulation. This was not a requirement of the previous regime introduced by the Thatcher Government in 1986, although in practice some regulators did carry out a CBA of proposals. Regulation in the interests of consumers, it seems, is to be pursued only in so far as it does not impose too great a cost on the industry.

The reasons for the introduction of CBA into the process of lawmaking

One explanation for the introduction of CBA is pragmatic. In the financial sector where capital is extremely mobile, it is possible that the Labour Government believed it had little choice but to accept the broad neo-liberal economic principles as pursued under Thatcher. Too much regulation brought with it the risk that financial sector businesses would take flight and relocate. A strong commitment to the market and to an economic rather than a distributive or 'public interest' rationale for regulation was required to reassure the market that its operations would not be unduly constrained, and that it would not be burdened with excessive and costly regulation. Requiring a CBA to be conducted on all proposed new regulation was a means of reassurance.[8] While publicly Labour could speak of the need for strong measures to protect consumers, the reality was that this was constrained by practical economic considerations. At the same time, few would disagree that regulation inevitably costs – the end user – the consumer. It is important that regulators consider the economic impact of imposing regulation, including the impact on consumers. While a CBA does not provide for particular

7 Financial Services and Markets Act 2000, s. 2(2).
8 The need to reduce the burdens of regulation on industry is a theme pursued by the Conservative Governments since the 1980s but has continued to be a strong theme under Labour, pursued primarily through the Better Regulation Unit of the Cabinet Office.

regulatory outcomes,[9] it nevertheless operates as an important and appropriate discipline on the use of regulatory discretion.

However, it is also possible that there is another explanation for the introduction of CBA, an explanation arising out of the new Labour ideology and its particular view about the role of government and individuals in society. The current Labour ideology (the 'Third Way') is much more positive about markets than earlier social democratic governments. Markets are not just seen as engines of wealth creation, they provide individuals with a variety of opportunities for action.[10] This ideology has been located somewhere between liberalism, conservatism and socialism. It encompasses the socio-economic practices associated with liberalism, including a belief in the rule of the law, the consumer and the managerial efficiencies that flow from a mixed economy and from competition, together with an emphasis on human wellbeing pursued in part by the welfare state (especially in areas such as health and education) and in part by the exercise of personal responsibility.[11]

Influential in the development of the ideology of the 'Third Way' is work by sociologists such as Anthony Giddens and, through him, Ulrich Beck. To provide a crude summary, both believe that we have entered into a new phase of modernity, one that is primarily concerned with the risks generated by human progress. For Beck the nature of society has changed.[12] We now recognise that scientific knowledge and rationality cannot provide us with the means to control the social and natural worlds. Rather, precisely because of the knowledge we have accumulated through the period of enlightenment and industrialisation, we recognise that there is no certainty in the scientific and natural worlds. For every scientific 'breakthrough' there are new uncertainties and new risks to be faced. As a result, we now live in a 'risk society', a society he describes as 'designat[ing] a stage of modernity in which the threats produced so far on the path of the industrial society begin to predominate'.[13] The primary concerns of the 'industrial society' or the 'class society' – the elimination of scarcity – have been replaced, he believes, with the quest for safety (in the financial sector witness the explosion in the development and use of risk-management products such as derivatives since the 1970s).[14] Further, we are engaged in a period of 'individualisation' or liberation in which the individual is freed from status-based classes and traditions, which provided collective sources of meaning in industrial society, but simultaneously thrown into the

---

9 Section 155 of the Financial Services and Markets Act 2000 simply requires a CBA to be carried out, and to be published together with the draft rules as a part of the consultation process. In addition, the regulatory principles only require the FSA to 'have regard to' the need for cost-effective regulation.

10 R. Mullender, 'Theorizing the Third Way: Qualified Consequentialism, the Proportionality Principle, and the New Social Democracy' (2000) 27 *Journal of Law and Society* 413.

11 See M. Freeden, 'The Ideology of New Labour' (1999) 70 *Political Q* 42.

12 U. Beck, *Risk Society* (London: Sage, 1992).   13 *Ibid.*, 6.

14 For a discussion of the role of risk in the development of financial products, see P. Bernstein, *Against the Gods. The Remarkable Story of Risk* (New York: John Wiley & Sons, 1996).

turbulence of the global risk society in which '[we] are being expected to live with a broad variety of different, mutually contradictory, global and personal risks'.[15] To deal with the uncertainty of the risk society requires the development of the 'differential politics' of what Beck terms 'reflexive modernity',[16] namely democratic participatory networks which transcend the system boundaries of the modern state. These networks would challenge the orthodoxy of experts and provide a forum for consensus-building co-operation between industry, science, politics and the populace.[17]

Anthony Giddens, advisor to Tony Blair and one of the prime influences on 'Third Way' ideology, has further developed the concept of 'reflexive modernity'.[18] Like Beck, Giddens accepts that we live in a risk society, a society in which we know that most risk is not externally imposed upon us but is generated by humans as part of techno-economic development.[19] We are dominated by science and technology, which no one completely understands, but which can also generate a diversity of possible futures. We no longer trust governments or experts to make the best decisions or to provide the right answers. They also live in the risk society and face the same uncertainties as we do.

For Giddens, however, risk represents opportunity and an expansion of choice. Every new development, while it may bring new and uncertain risks, also brings new opportunities and new choices. We, as individuals, cannot bury our heads in the sand, or expect others to make the right choices for us. We do not really trust them enough to do that anyway. What we need instead is the ability to be able to engage with 'experts' in order that we can better understand the choices and risks. As individuals we are thus empowered to make our own choices about how we wish to lead our lives. Creating in individuals the capacities effectively to use those opportunities is a key role for government.[20] At the same time Giddens also emphasises that with choice comes personal responsibility for the negotiation of risk.[21] As such, the role of government is no longer about automatically providing a collective

---

15 Beck, *Risk Society*, 7.
16 Reflexive modernisation has been defined as 'self-confrontation with the effects of risk society that cannot be dealt with and assimilated in the system of industrial society': U. Beck, A. Giddens and S. Lash, *Reflexive Modernisation* (Cambridge: Polity Press, 1994), 6.
17 Beck, Giddens and Lash, *Reflexive Modernisation*, 29–30. The authors acknowledge that such networks would not necessarily guarantee consensus, but they would provide a forum for identifying risks and uncertainties and 'winners and losers', so improving the preconditions for political action.
18 Giddens describes reflexive modernity as 'coming to terms with the limits and contradictions of the modern order': A. Giddens, 'Risk and Responsibility' (1999) 62 *Modern L Rev* 1, 6.
19 See Giddens, 'Risk and Responsibility', 1.
20 See also R. Mullender, 'Theorizing the Third Way: Qualified Consequentialism, the Proportionality Principle, and the New Social Democracy' (2000) 27 *Journal of Law and Society* 493.
21 Acceptance of personal responsibility is a key theme for Giddens. See A. Giddens, *The Third Way. The Renewal of Social Policy* (Cambridge: Polity Press, 1998), 65–6. For a discussion of the differences and similarities between Gidden's and Beck's concept of reflexive modernity, see S. Lash, 'Reflexivity and its Doubles' in Beck, Giddens and Lash, *Reflexive Modernisation*, 110.

safety net for bad decision-making but about providing the mechanisms to enable individuals to manage risk.[22] We are returning, it seems, to a more privatised model of governance in which there is more individualised risk, and less sense of collective responsibility.[23]

Whether or not we agree with Beck or Giddens about the nature of modern society, removing decision-making in 'technical' areas such as financial services from the purely political arena and entrusting it to experts with a strong commitment to open and consultative decision-making can be understood in the context of 'reflexive modernity' as part of a process of creating the opportunity for engagement and dialogue.[24] Requiring the use of economic appraisal measures such as CBA ensures the inclusion of economic expertise into the decision-making process. Beck would describe this as the process of the 'de-differentiation' of various sub-systems.[25] Requiring its publication as part of a general consultative process is intended to ensure that consumers are empowered by it, in the sense that it will inform their dialogue with others in that process, and also to inform their decision-making.[26]

These various strands of Labour ideology referred to above all run through the new financial services regime. The communitarian objective of 'well-being' is reflected in the general objective of 'consumer protection' while personal responsibility is underscored by the proviso to the consumer protection objective that consumers must accept responsibility for decision-making.[27] Empowering consumers is reflected in the 'promoting public awareness of the markets' objective. The potential of the market as an instrument of wealth generation is reflected in the objective of 'market confidence', underpinned by the emphasis on competition and cost-effective regulation in the underlying regulatory principles. The decision-making

---

22 See Giddens, 'Risk and Responsibility', 7.
23 Risk discourse is most prominent in relation to the natural environment. For a discussion of the influence of risk discourse on other areas of the modern social environment, see, e.g., J. Braithwaite, 'The New Regulatory State and the Transformation of Criminology' in D. Garland and R. Sparks (eds.), *Criminology and Social Theory* (Oxford: Oxford University Press, 2000), 47; L. Ruhl, 'Liberal Governance and Prenatal Care: Risk and Regulation in Pregnancy' (1999) 28 *Economics and Society* 95. As Ruhl notes, the individualisation of responsibility for risk is dependent on the willingness of individuals to assume responsibility to 'self-regulate'. Self-regulation has been identified as a key element of advanced liberal rule.
24 Although, as one staff member of the FSA has commented, removing financial services regulation from the political arena was also self-serving. Financial services regulation is a 'bad risk' for the government as inevitably there will be crisis or scandal. Publicly, it wants to be seen to keep its distance while at the private level it is still keeping at least one finger in the pie.
25 See B. Lange, 'Economic Appraisal of Law-Making and Changing Forms of Governance' (2000) 63 *Mod L Rev* 294.
26 For a critique of Giddens' view of reflexive modernity, see, e.g., Z. Bauman, *Postmodern Ethics* (Oxford: Blackwell, 1993), 203: 'The type of reflexivity in which the public is trained by risk-assessments offered for popular knowledge to use, fends off and deflects the blows which otherwise would, perhaps stand a better chance of aiming at the true causes of present dangers: all in all it helps the technology inspired strategies of efficiency maximisation . . . to survive their unprepossessing consequences and so to emerge . . . intact.'
27 Section 5(2)(d) of the Financial Services and Markets Act 2000.

process itself reflects the process of 'de-differentiation' with its requirement for consultation with industry (through the FSA's own Practitioner Panel), consumer representatives (through the FSA's Consumer Panel), 'experts' (through the use of CBA, for example) and the public (through the general consultative process which must precede any new regulation).

The place of CBA in the lawmaking process

Under the Financial Services and Markets Act 2000, the regulator (the FSA) has three main functions:

1. To authorise those who want to carry on a 'regulated activity' in the UK.[28]
2. To make rules. In addition to the power to make rules for certain specific purposes specified in the Act, the regulator has extensive general powers under Part X to make rules 'protecting the interests of consumers'. The regulator can specify that those rules are to apply in different ways to different persons, activities or investments,[29] and it has power to waive the rules for individual firms.[30] In other words, not only does the regulator make the rules; it can apply them flexibly as it thinks fit and the rules need not be applied consistently across firms or across the industry.[31]
3. To enforce the rules. The regulator has responsibility for enforcing its rules and the power to impose penalties for breach (including unlimited fines), and for prosecuting certain criminal offences under the Act.

In discharging its duties and functions, however, the FSA must so far as possible act in a way that is compatible with the four statutory objectives:[32]

---

28 The Act sets out threshold conditions for authorisation, although the regulator has discretion over how certain conditions are interpreted in individual cases, e.g., the FSA must be satisfied the applicant has 'adequate resources'.

29 Section 156.   30 Section 148.

31 These rules are not subject to any prior parliamentary approval, and the Government has no power directly to intervene in rulemaking. However, as under the previous legislation, and in line with the pro-competition ideology underlying this regime, the Act requires the Director General of Fair Trading (DGFT) (head of the non-ministerial government department, the Office of Fair Trading, which has responsibility for consumer and competition affairs) to keep the rules and practices of the FSA under review. Any significant anti-competitive effect is to be reported to the UK Competition Commission and if the Commission finds that effect is unjustified, the Treasury must order the FSA to take appropriate action (e.g., to change the rule). Similar powers were enjoyed under the 1986 regime and were used fairly extensively by the DGFT to challenge rules made by regulators in the retail sector. The disagreement between the regulator and the DGFT was not over the purpose of consumer protection but over the extent to which consumers conformed to the economic model of the 'rational, well informed consumer'. See further Black, *Rules and Regulators*, 147–84.

32 Financial Services and Markets Act 2000, s. 2(2).

1. Maintaining confidence in the financial system ('market confidence').
2. Promoting public understanding of the financial system ('public awareness').
3. Securing the appropriate degree of protection for consumers ('consumer protection').[33]
4. The reduction of financial crime.

While general rules therefore cannot be made to further objectives other than consumer protection, neither, it seems, should such rules be incompatible with these other objectives. However, the 'consumer protection' objective is qualified by (amongst others) the requirement that the FSA must have regard to 'the general principle that consumers should take responsibility for their decisions', and 'the need consumers may have for advice and accurate information'.[34] This objective seems more oriented towards issues of 'information asymmetry' ensuring that consumers are provided with sufficient information to enable them to make a rational and informed decision about the risks and benefits of particular products.[35]

Section 155(2)(a) imposes the requirement that a CBA accompany the draft of any new regulation and that the draft and accompanying CBA be published as part of the general consultation process that should precede the introduction of any new rule.[36] However, the outcomes of the CBA do not impose any particular obligations on the regulator in terms of the specific regulatory proposal. The legislation simply requires the regulator to have regard to the need for cost-effective regulation in pursuing its statutory objectives. Other than the discipline imposed through conducting and publishing the CBA, the regulator's discretion is not circumscribed by the outcome of the CBA.

Nevertheless, the view expressed by the Chairman of the FSA is that regulation is 'only justified in the presence of substantial market imperfection, and only where

---

33 'Consumer' has a particular meaning under the Act. Section 138 defines a consumer as any person who uses or contemplates using any services provided by, or whose interests may be affected by, those regulated by the Act. A consumer need not be a private person. Thus, the definition is wider than that generally used in other UK consumer legislation.
34 Section 5.
35 And consistent with the Labour Government's general concern for information asymmetry. See Department of Trade and Industry, *Modern Markets: Confident Consumers* (White Paper, 1999), www.dti.gov.uk/consumer/whitepaper. Despite the Labour Government's general concern to provide for social inclusion, particularly in financial matters such as banking, there is no explicit encouragement for the regulator to take non-economic factors such as distributive goals into account when exercising regulatory functions, nor to regulate for social goals such as universal access to financial services, although the Government is currently encouraging the industry to provide for universal access at least to basic banking and credit facilities. In this respect, credit unions have recently complained that proposed FSA prudential rules might in fact prohibit them from providing such universal service.
36 Unless such consultation would cause delay, prejudicial to the interests of consumers: s. 155(7).

the cure is not worse than the disease'.[37] He identifies two particular strands of market imperfection which he believes justify intervention on behalf of the consumer: systemic risk (i.e., the risk that a failure of one institution will lead to a 'run' on other institutions), and information asymmetries where the consumer is unable to make a rational decision maximising his or her own welfare because of inadequate information. Otherwise, the best protection for the consumer is acquired through the operation of competitive markets. (Of course, this approach still leaves considerable discretion in terms of identifying when and where information asymmetries arise.)

But even in these two situations of market failure regulation should only be imposed, he believes, where it satisfies CBA. For the regulator, CBA (and also risk analysis which is the initial 'trigger' for possible regulatory intervention[38]) appears to be at the forefront of regulatory activity. This in turn suggests an approach to regulatory decision-making that will be guided very much by quantitative rather than qualitative factors.

Cost–benefit analysis – what is it?

What is CBA?

CBA is a technique grounded in microeconomic theory for assessing the net social value of a project, policy or measure.[39] According to the US National Center for Environmental Decision-making Research:[40]

> A properly constructed cost benefit analysis will attempt to measure the change in economic welfare associated with all costs and all benefits uniquely generated by a project.

The New York Governor's Office of Regulatory Reform similarly defines CBA as:[41]

---

37 H. Davies, 'Why Regulate?' (speech of 4 November 1998), www.fsa.gov.uk/pubs/speeches/sp19.html.
38 See FSA, M. Foot, 'Our New Approach to Risk-Based Regulation. What Will Be Different for Firms?' (2000), fsa.gov.uk/pubs/speeches/sp69.html.
39 See A. K. Dasgupta and D. Pearce, *Cost Benefit Analysis: Theory and Practice* (London: Macmillan, 1972); E. J. Mishan, *Cost–Benefit Analysis* (2nd edn, London: George Allen & Unwin, 1977); P. G. Sassone and W. A. Schaffer, *Cost–Benefit Analysis: a Handbook* (New York: Academic Press, 1978); M. Thompson, *Benefit–Cost Analysis for Program Evaluation* (New York: Sage, 1980); R. Sugden and A. Williams, *The Principles of Practical Cost–Benefit Analysis* (Oxford: Oxford University Press, 1978).
40 US National Center for Environmental Decision-Making Research Tools, *Cost–Benefit Analysis*, www.ncedr.org/tools/othertools/costbenefit/module5.htm.
41 New York Governor's Office of Regulatory Reform, *Cost–Benefit Handbook*, www.gorr.state.ny.us/gorr/cba-glossary.html.

A conceptual framework which is designed to compare a policy's incremental and total costs to its incremental and total benefits. C/B analysis considers all gains (benefits) and losses (costs) regardless of to whom they accrue.

CBA is undertaken from the perspective of the economy as a whole and considers all benefits and costs, financial or otherwise, arising from a project. A benefit is defined as any gain in human wellbeing, often referred to as welfare or utility in economics, and a cost is defined as any loss in wellbeing. So, for example, a regulatory initiative to reduce industrial air pollution would incur and impose various costs: on industry the costs of complying with the additional regulations, and on the regulator the costs of introducing and monitoring compliance. However, there may well be other, indirect, costs incurred. For example, some industry may relocate to avoid the new regulations with a subsequent cost to the economy in terms of reduced employment and income. Benefits would include improved air quality for residents, consequent health improvements, and perhaps economic benefits for those firms supplying the equipment that industry now requires to meet the new regulations. In this way CBA contrasts markedly with traditional financial appraisal or evaluation which is undertaken from solely the viewpoint of a particular firm or agency.

A monetary value is then placed on each of the costs and benefits identified and the net benefit determined.[42] Thus, CBA attempts to identify the most economically efficient way of meeting a stated public policy objective. The projects being evaluated may be construction based, such as the building of an airport, dams or roads. They could also be policy-based initiatives, in education, health care or social inclusion, for example, or they could be regulatory interventions, in financial services or in environmental control, for example. The theoretical foundation of CBA is well established, although a number of key practical difficulties remain which are discussed briefly later. It is important to note, however, that the term CBA is often used in a much more informal way, implying simply that the costs and benefits associated with some decision(s) have been identified and evaluated although not necessarily in quantitative terms, and not necessarily in monetary value terms. To add to the confusion, a number of terms have come to be used almost interchangeably, such as cost–benefit appraisal, impact analysis and cost-effectiveness analysis.

How did CBA develop?

CBA has a relatively long history with its origins traceable to Dupuit, a French engineer and economist who established the foundation of what economists would refer to as marginal analysis that an investment decision should

---

42 'C/B analysis has attempted to quantify and put monetary values on the costs and benefits to arrive at a net-benefit figure, which could be positive or negative': *ibid.*

meet the criterion of its benefits outweighing its costs. The theoretical underpinnings of marginal analysis were developed in the nineteenth century, with major contributions from the British economist Alfred Marshall. However, the practical development of CBA came primarily as a result of the US Federal Navigation Act of 1936. This required that the US Corps of Engineers carry out projects for the improvement of the waterway system 'if the benefits to whosoever they accrue are in excess of the estimated costs'.[43] This implied that systematic methods for measuring such benefits and costs would be required. Formal guidance on cost–benefit appraisal of water investment projects began to appear, notably in the so-called Green Book from the sub-committee of the US Federal Interagency River Basin Committee in 1950 and Circular A-47 of the US Bureau of Budget.

However, it was not until the 1950s that economists began to provide a more rigorous, theoretical and consistent measurement and analysis framework based primarily on the welfare economics literature that had emerged over the previous two decades, most noticeably that of Kaldor and Hicks. The Kaldor–Hicks criterion (also known as Potential Pareto Superiority) established that projects with net benefits were justified in spite of the fact that there would be those suffering a loss in welfare as a result of the project. The justification put forward was that because the project showed a net benefit then, in principle at least, those benefiting from the project could fully compensate the losers and still retain some benefit from the project.[44]

Undertaking a CBA

In principle, undertaking a CBA follows a straightforward methodology:[45]

> Identify the policy options available; for each policy option assess the impacts the policy is likely to have; identify the costs and benefits associated with these impacts; determine a valuation of these costs and benefits over the lifetime of the policy option; compare the net benefit from each policy option.

In practice, of course, there are considerable theoretical and practical difficulties involved.[46] As Fraiberg and Trebilcock comment: 'Cost–benefit analysis . . . is subject to serious uncertainties.'[47] These include the following:

---

43 See D. Pearce, 'Cost–Benefit Analysis and Public Policy' (1998) 14 *Oxford Review of Economic Policy* 84, 85.

44 Pearce, 'Cost–Benefit Analysis'.

45 J. L. Moore, *Cost–Benefit Analysis: Issues in its Use in Regulation*, Congressional Research Issue Brief 95–760 ENR (Washington, DC: National Council for Science and the Environment, 1995), www.cnie.org/nle/rsk-4.html.

46 See A. Boardman, D. Greenberg, A. Vining and D. Weimar, *Cost–Benefit Analysis: Concepts and Practice* (New Jersey: Prentice Hall, 1996).

47 See J. D. Fraiberg and M. J. Trebilcock, 'Risk Regulation: Technocratic and Democratic Tools for Regulatory Reform' (1998) 43 *McGill LJ* 835, 846.

Difficulty in predicting policy impacts

The detailed impact of a policy option may be difficult to predict because 'lack of information about the consequences of actions . . . often confounds the analysis'.[48] In the case of air pollution, for example, predicting the reaction of industry in terms of potential relocation because of the extra costs incurred is clearly problematic.

Identification of costs and benefits

The difficulty of predicting policy impacts also makes the identification of all subsequent costs and benefits difficult to predict.

Valuation of costs and benefits

The valuation of costs and benefits is a particularly complex task. As Fraiberg and Trebilcock comment: 'The entire method is contingent on the ability to value accurately both costs and benefits.'[49] Some of the difficulties related to this include calculating a monetary value for a particular cost or benefit,[50] estimating the value placed on particular costs and benefits in a non-market environment, and establishing the time period over which the analysis is to be conducted.

Indirect estimating methods are frequently necessary in CBA because many of the benefits and some of the costs will typically have no private sector equivalent and consequently no market prices exist that can be used to place a monetary value on these benefits and costs. For example, legislation to regulate industrial air pollution may improve the quality of air for local residents. However, there is no direct way of placing a monetary value on this since clean air is not an economically traded good. Similarly, 'consumer confidence' in the financial sector is not a good that can be measured in monetary terms. Cost–benefit analysts frequently approximate the value of benefits and costs using a number of estimating and survey methods. In the clean air example, property prices may be used as a proxy value measure with the logic that comparing property prices in an area with high air pollution and one with low air pollution will give an indication as to the monetary value the consumer places on the difference in air pollution. Alternatively, a structured survey may be used to ascertain the monetary value local residents might attach to such a benefit. Needless to say, such indirect valuation methods generate considerable debate.[51]

---

48 US National Center for Environmental Decision-Making Research Tools, *Cost–Benefit Analysis*.
49 Fraiberg and Trebilcock, 'Risk Regulation', 858.
50 'Inevitably, some costs and benefits resist the assignment of dollar values': R. Clarke, 'Computer Matching by Government Agencies: the Failure of Cost/Benefit Analysis as a Control Mechanism' (1995) 4 *Information Infrastructure & Policy* 29.
51 See, e.g., H. Pildes and C. Sunstein, 'Reinventing the Regulatory State' (1995) 62 *U Chi L Rev* 1; J. Adams, *Risk* (London: UCL Press, 1995).

Often the issue of time is also critical in CBA.[52] The evaluation of costs and benefits needs to take into account the time value of money, given that costs will be incurred and benefits accrued over some period and at different times during that period. This requires that 'future costs and future benefits should be discounted to their present values'.[53] The principle is simple: a cost incurred now, say of $10 million, is not equal to a benefit of $10 million accrued in three years' time. The common method of taking time value into account is to discount future monetary returns back to the base year in which costs/benefits first started to accrue. However, this requires the use of an appropriate discount rate, the choice of which may critically alter the net benefit value, and also requires assumptions about the time-life of the policy option.

Attitudes to risk

CBA assumes a risk-neutral decision-maker, someone who is indifferent to the possibilities of significantly better or worse outcomes. In principle, the use of additional approaches involving decision theory and the calculation of expected value together with sensitivity analysis could go some way to minimising this criticism of CBA. As Pearce points out, however, 'sensitivity analysis . . . is not a feature of most modern CBAs and should be'.[54]

Decision analysis is an approach intended to allow decision-makers to incorporate risk into the decision-making process. The approach assumes that any decision is likely to have several possible outcomes that are largely outside the control of the decision-maker. Each of these outcomes will have different consequences (a net cost benefit) and each of these outcomes will have a different likelihood (risk) of occurring. The approach then calculates the weighted average consequence (cost–benefit) of that decision by summing the probability of each outcome multiplied by the likelihood of that outcome occurring. This weighted average, known as the expected value of that decision, thus takes into account all possible outcomes from some decision and their respective likelihoods (risks). The expected values from different possible decisions can then be compared, and the one with the highest expected value would normally be preferred. Sensitivity analysis can also be undertaken to assess under what circumstances the preferred decision would change. For example, the likelihood of outcomes from some decision could be re-evaluated (assuming a more pessimistic or a more optimistic outlook), the expected value using these new likelihoods calculated, and the preferred decision reassessed.

---

52 'Cost benefit analysis is a technique for . . . assessing . . . costs and benefits . . . over a relevant time period': Moore, *Cost–Benefit Analysis*.
53 New York Governor's Office of Regulatory Reform, *Cost–Benefit Handbook*.
54 Pearce, 'Cost–Benefit Analysis', 94.

Value judgments

Given the uncertainties and assumptions involved in CBA, value judgments are frequently made by analysts although not always in a transparent way, leading Lave to comment: 'The same economist might do quite different cost–benefit analyses of the same issue, depending on who the client is.'[55] In the USA, where CBA has been required of executive agencies proposing regulations since at least 1981,[56] a congressional committee stated that 'the most significant factor in evaluating a cost–benefit study is the name of the sponsor'.[57]

Distributive justice

The issue of distributive justice is often raised in criticisms of CBA. By its very nature, CBA is concerned only with the net benefit of a proposed action, aggregated over the whole economy, or at least those parts judged to be affected. CBA is not primarily concerned with the distribution of the benefits and costs over different parts of the economy. In principle, a policy showing an overall net benefit may impose large costs on a few sections of the economy and small benefits over a large section. In the earlier example of air pollution, a few sections of industry may have to incur large additional costs as a result of the proposed regulation whilst the benefits are felt by a large number of individuals, albeit any one individual receives only a small benefit. In the financial sector, where compliance costs are inevitably passed on, some consumers may as a result be excluded from the market (smaller investors paying proportionately higher sums for products).

Cost-effectiveness

Whilst there are methods of minimising these difficulties in particular CBA studies, they add to the complexity and assumptions that underpin the analysis. This in turn adds to the actual cost of undertaking a CBA. As Moore comments, 'formal cost benefit analysis ... demands costly ... expertise and data'.[58] This leads to what has been referred to as 'excessive proceduralism', where the actual cost of conducting the CBA outweighs the benefits from conducting the CBA.[59]

55 L. B. Lave (ed.), *Quantitative Risk Assessment in Regulation* (Washington, DC: Brookings Institute, 1982), 23.
56 Although its genesis lay in the National Environmental Policy Act 1969: R. Baldwin, *Rules and Government* (Oxford: Clarendon Press, 1995); Pildes and Sunstein, 'Reinventing the Regulatory State'.
57 Baldwin, *Rules and Government*, 194.   58 Moore, *Cost–Benefit Analysis*.
59 See Fraiberg and Trebilcock, 'Risk Regulation', 870.

CBA in the FSA

In October 1999, the FSA published a CBA of statutory regulation of mortgage advice. Mortgage lending and advice were not originally intended to be a regulated activity under the new regime. However, consumer groups (and some members of Parliament) lobbied for its inclusion so that it would be subject to FSA regulation. In July 1999, the Government launched a consultation on the matter and also commissioned the FSA to undertake the CBA.[60]

The use of CBA by UK governments is not new. It has been used internally by certain government departments since the 1970s, although few were published. In addition, from the mid-1980s the Conservative Government required all government departments to undertake compliance cost assessments ('CCAs') of all regulatory proposals to be introduced by secondary legislation. The purpose of a CCA was to inform ministers of the costs to industry in complying with the regulation. CCAs had to be submitted to the Enterprise and Deregulation Unit ('the EDU') within the Department of Employment. However, it has been suggested that the EDU was not created to represent the public interest but rather to act as the proxy voice of business and that it considered departmental proposals purely from the viewpoint of business.[61]

In 1997, the new Labour Government replaced the CCA with a regulatory impact assessment which requires a CBA to be undertaken wherever a government department or agency proposes new legislation or proposes to exercise rule-making powers.[62] The requirement to conduct a CBA has been extended by the Government to non-agency regulators such as the FSA. This is consistent with the Government's strategy of 'ensuring that regulations are necessary, properly costed, practical to enforce and straightforward to comply with'.[63]

The FSA has proposed 'a six-stage process based on a six-part impact analysis' with the six stages of the process set out as:[64]

1.   Decide upon the scope and depth of the analysis including the number of options to be assessed.
2.   Use the six-part impact analysis model to assess the likely effects of each option.
3.   Qualitatively compare the effects of the options.
4.   Reject those options that are inferior.
5.   Estimate the costs and assess the benefits of the remaining options.

---

60 This was the first high-profile CBA conducted by the new regulator.
61 See Baldwin, *Rules and Government*.
62 See Cabinet Office, *Good Policy Making: a Guide to Regulatory Impact Assessment*, www.cabinet-office.gov.uk/regulation/2000/riaguide.
63 Better Regulation Unit, *Access Business* (1995), www.open.gov.uk/co/bru/access.htm.
64 A. Alfon and P. Andrews, *Cost–Benefit Analysis in Financial Regulation* (London: FSA, 1999), 14.

6. Provide an output that illustrates the relative advantages, disadvantages and net benefits of the options under consideration.

The six-part impact analysis model is intended to provide a stimulus to thinking widely about the costs and benefits of the proposals. The six impacts to be considered as part of a CBA are set out as:

1. Direct costs of designing, monitoring and enforcing regulations.
2. Compliance costs incurred in order to comply with the proposals.
3. Changes in the quantity of the goods sold, influenced by the extent to which the product price would be affected by the proposals.
4. Changes in the quality of the goods offered, for example through mandatory minimum standards.
5. Changes in the variety of the products offered which may lead to better consumer choice.
6. Changes in the efficiency of competition which itself may bring further consumer benefits.

In terms of introducing additional regulations, costs could arise in any of the six impact categories whilst benefits could arise only in categories (3)–(6). From the proposed framework it appears that the FSA has attempted to take a number of the practical difficulties of applying CBA into account in order to develop a pragmatic approach that will be sufficiently robust to assist FSA policy-makers.

Difficulty in predicting policy impacts

The six-stage impact analysis set out by the FSA is clearly an attempt to introduce a consistent and standardised approach to detailing the likely impact of some policy option, reinforcing the view that 'a fundamental requirement of sound policy development is to ensure that no significant impact of the proposal is overlooked'.[65] Similarly, the last stage of the proposed process, providing an output, also appears to be an attempt to ensure that the CBA is transparent in terms of the assumptions and limitations of its impact analysis.[66]

Identification of costs and benefits

The FSA provides further guidance in an attempt to ensure a robust approach to the identification of likely costs although little practical detail is included. Three

---

65 Quality of Regulation Team, New Zealand Ministry of Commerce (1999). As Moore comments, when reviewing the developments still needed for effective CBA, 'needs may include . . . guidelines to ensure consistency': Moore, *Cost–Benefit Analysis*.
66 'To enable the public and policymakers to assess the quality of an agency's cost–benefit analysis and the conclusions the agency reached, the agency should fully disclose important assumptions and major points of uncertainty': New York Governor's Office of Regulatory Reform, *Cost–Benefit Handbook*.

broad categories of likely costs are detailed: direct costs (as in the impact analysis earlier), compliance costs (which are defined as the incremental costs of compliance caused by regulation) and indirect costs.[67] As for benefits, the guidance comments optimistically that 'reference to the list of impact categories . . . should usually help to identify the benefits of any given measure'.[68]

Valuation of costs and benefits

The FSA's methodology appears implicitly to recognise the difficulties of assigning monetary values to some impacts with the output stage of the approach allowing for the reporting of 'any other advantages or disadvantages that have been identified', regardless of whether these have been quantified.[69]

Interestingly, however, the obligation on the FSA to conduct a CBA does not actually require the quantitative valuation of associated benefits.[70] This actually implies that the CBA requirement on the FSA is more of a cost-effectiveness analysis requirement.[71] Thus, whilst costs will be quantified, benefits will be assessed qualitatively.[72]

The third aspect of valuation that typically proves problematic, that of discounting future costs/benefits to present-day values, appears to be largely irrelevant to the FSA. Although there is some discussion in the FSA's documentation

---

67 See Alfon and Andrews, *Cost–Benefit Analysis in Financial Regulation.*
68 The FSA guidelines suggest that an assessment of the impact of an increase in the compliance costs on business volume of sales should be done by estimating the price consumers would be prepared to pay for the increase in quality. This is done by an analysis of consumer 'willingness to pay'. For a critique of the 'willingness to pay' as opposed to the 'willingness to accept' model, see Adams, *Risk*, 98. As Adams points out, willingness to pay assumes a permissive law (i.e., it assumes the consumer has no right to quality unless he or she is prepared to pay), whereas willingness to accept assumes a restrictive law (i.e., the provider has no right to supply poor quality products unless he or she is willing to compensate the consumer).
69 See C. Goodhart, P. Hartmann, D. Llewellyn, L. Rojas-Suarez and S. Weisbrod, *Financial Regulation: Why, How, and Where Now?* (London: Routledge, 1988), 65: 'Cost–benefit analysis . . . is notoriously difficult to complete successfully, not least in the financial sector. This is true primarily because it is difficult to quantify the benefits of regulation and supervision.'
70 'An important feature of the . . . statutory requirement for CBA is that it requires estimation of costs but not of benefits. Benefits may be assessed in qualitative terms. . . . Full quantitative evaluation of costs and benefits is difficult to achieve . . . It is usually possible to identify the most *cost-effective* of the available options by using a combination of qualitative and quantitative information': Alfon and Andrews, *Cost–Benefit Analysis*, 8 (emphasis added). See also Moore, *Cost–Benefit Analysis*: 'Costs . . . are typically easier to estimate than benefits.'
71 'Cost effectiveness analysis . . . [is] typically used in situations where it is either difficult, impractical or inexpedient to monetize the benefits of alternative programs or regulations . . . [However,] costs are measured in monetary terms. The approach [is] often employed when comparing alternative programs or regulations for achieving a particular goal': New York Governor's Office for Regulatory Reform, *Cost–Benefit Handbook.*
72 Other regulatory agencies clearly take a different view on the need for CBA as opposed to cost-effectiveness analysis: 'accepting the quantitative difficulties, a full CBA is desirable wherever a major regulation is proposed': Quality of Regulation Team, New Zealand Ministry of Commerce.

of discounting approaches and issues, it appears almost as an afterthought and is relegated to a short footnote:[73] '*Sometimes* costs and benefits would arise in different time periods. It is then necessary to discount the costs and benefits (to the present) to compare them.'

It is difficult to think of a regulatory change that would *not* have an impact over more than the first year and yet the discounting of costs (benefits not being quantified) appears to be seen as irrelevant.[74]

Attitudes to risk

Although the FSA guidance frequently comments on the difficulties caused by uncertainty in a CBA context, there is little explicit discussion of risk *per se* or of possible methods of incorporating risk into the CBA process.

Value judgments

As commented earlier, the CBA process proposed by the FSA requires an output stage which allows for reporting on some of the wider issues and assumptions made in the CBA. Only time will tell whether these assumptions are made explicit.

Distributive justice

The FSA makes it clear that the focus of a CBA is on the overall economic efficiency of a proposed initiative, that is, whether there is an overall net benefit regardless of who the recipients of the benefit are:[75] 'A regulator who does not use CBA ... runs the risk of delivering a stream of outputs that may reflect the given objectives but lead to unintended (economic) inefficiency.'

At the same time, however, the door is left open to consider the distributive justice issue: 'In some cases, evaluation of a policy might be facilitated by applying distributional weights to the costs and benefits'.[76] The CBA team within the FSA states that distributive justice concerns are not typically identified in the CBA process, that being left to other parts of the consultation process.

Cost-effectiveness

Throughout the FSA guidance, the emphasis is on ensuring a cost-effective approach to CBA rather than a comprehensive, rigorous and quantified

---

73 Alfon and Andrews, *Cost–Benefit Analysis*, 13 (emphasis added).
74 Again, the FSA's view contrasts with those of other agencies: 'the result of a CBA will generally be expressed in dollar terms as a net present value (NPV)': Quality of Regulation Team, New Zealand Ministry of Commerce. See also Moore, *Cost–Benefit Analysis*: 'In comparing benefits and costs that occur at different points in time, it is necessary to translate future dollar values into present values so that comparison is done from a common point of reference.'
75 Alfon and Andrews, *Cost–Benefit Analysis*, 10.   76 *Ibid.*, 12.

analysis.[77] Whether the focus on pragmatism rather than rigour will deliver useful results remains to be seen. The FSA's CBA on mortgages may provide an indication.

An analysis of the CBA accompanying the proposal to regulate mortgage advice

The FSA published its report on the CBA of statutory regulation of mortgage advice in October 1999 (FSA 1999). As the FSA commented, 'This CBA is intended to be an objective assessment of the impacts of regulating mortgage business under the legislation that will result from the Financial Services and Markets Bill'.[78]

The background to the analysis

For a variety of reasons, competition in the domestic property mortgages market in the UK had increased markedly during the 1990s resulting in greater choice, and arguably improved value, for consumers but also resulting in increased complexity with product proliferation and increasing attempts by suppliers at product differentiation. The FSA concluded that there appeared to be a case for statutory regulation of mortgage advice given by lenders and intermediaries to consumers. The conclusion was based on the likelihood of consumer detriment arising from a partial lack of competitiveness and from unsuitable sales of both mortgage and mortgage repayment products. However, the industry itself, in the guise of the Council of Mortgage Lenders ('the CML'), had already developed proposals for voluntary regulation of mortgage advice to be in place by 2002 (the CML code). The context of the CBA, therefore, was one of whether additional statutory regulation would prove beneficial.

Approach

The overall approach taken by the FSA followed that set out earlier in this paper. To begin with, broad policy options were identified. These were as follows:

- The Standard Case ('SC'). This option was, in broad terms, to give the proposed voluntary regulation (the CML code) a formal statutory basis.

77 *Ibid.*, 10: 'Regulatory options are compared only to the extent necessary to determine which of them is most likely to yield the greatest excess of benefits over costs.'
78 FSA (1999), 30.

- The Enhanced Coverage Case ('ECC'). This option would extend the SC to cover all loans secured on residential property.
- The Minimal Coverage Case ('MCC'). This option was much narrower in terms of the type of lending it would cover, restricting itself to equity release, foreign currency and mortgages covered by the Consumer Credit Act. The CML code would apply to the other areas of lending.
- The Lighter Regulation Case ('LRC'). This would have the same coverage as ECC but some of the proposed ECC regulatory requirements would not apply (mainly relating to advice on staff training qualifications).

The FSA then went on to examine the impacts of each of the four options using the six-impact model described earlier.

Direct costs

These were estimated by the FSA itself at around £12 million per year regardless of the policy option. The FSA used a model developed to estimate the cost of regulating professional firms that was felt to be transferable. The FSA also makes clear that there is considerable uncertainty around this figure relating primarily to the reaction to regulation of some 8,000 mortgage advisors currently exempt from regulation.

Compliance costs

The estimation of compliance costs for each of the policy options was conducted on the FSA's behalf by a consultancy firm. Samples of lenders and intermediaries were asked to estimate the one-off and annual recurring costs of new systems and processes required to comply with the different options for statutory regulation. The estimates were then scaled upwards using the existing distribution of firm size in the industry to give total industry compliance costs. For SC, these were estimated at £36 million as a one-off cost and £32 million per annum as a recurring cost. For ECC the one-off cost was estimated as £40 million and recurring costs at £32 million. The MCC was not regarded as a viable option by interviewees, with a number of lenders and intermediaries indicating that they would withdraw from providing advice on the forms of mortgage subject to regulation under the MCC. As a result, this option was neither costed nor evaluated in any further detail. For the LRC option, accurate estimates of the compliance costs could not be obtained. The main reason for this was that the sample firms were not actually asked to estimate the cost for this option but rather to subtract certain training costs from the SC option. Firms indicated their uncertainty and reluctance to cost this difference. However, it was estimated that these might be in the order of 50 per cent with the effect of reducing the one-off costs to £24 million and recurring costs to £17 million. These costs are summarised:

Cost (£ million)	SC	ECC	MCC	LRC
Direct	12	12	12	12
Compliance:				
One-off	36	40	–	24
Recurring	32	32	–	17

The FSA then reviewed the potential impact under the remaining four areas. Given that these were seen largely as benefits, and following the FSA approach not to quantify benefits, they were evaluated qualitatively.

Quality

Under this impact the FSA looked at the main areas of consumer detriment associated with unsuitable mortgages (i.e., unsuitable repayment vehicles, redemption charges, tied products, possession, general unsuitability) and attempted to evaluate the impact that statutory advice regulation might have from the consumer perspective. Their conclusion was that the benefits from the SC and ECC options were likely to be higher for the LRC option, given the latter has fewer requirements for staff training and competence, and that the benefits for ECC would extend to more loans. However, they also concluded that: 'the benefits ... might not be enormous'.[79]

Quantity and variety

The FSA concluded that 'the[se] remaining two categories ... are not very important in the context of this CBA' with the view that neither quantity of products sold nor the variety of products sold were affected in any marked way by statutory regulation.[80]

Competition

Under this heading the FSA assessed the impacts on disclosure, CAT (charges, access and terms) standards, regulation of advice and enhancing competition. The general conclusion was that benefits from regulation were possible but difficult to predict with any certainty because of the complexity of the situation. However, the FSA did conclude that[81] 'none of the differences between the Standard Case, Enhanced

79 *Ibid.*   80 *Ibid.*   81 FSA (1999), 27.

Coverage Case and Lighter Regulation Case are considered particularly relevant... Similar benefits could be anticipated from each of them.'

Overall, the FSA concluded that: 'the costs of statutory regulation... will be small... statutory regulation could in principle produce significant benefits'.[82] The FSA further concluded that the ECC option was likely to be more cost-effective than the SC option, and that both the ECC option and LRC option were likely to bring the benefit of enhanced competition. The former, however, would also enhance suitability whilst the latter would be cheaper.

Critique

Clearly, the FSA has applied its version of CBA to a difficult and complex area and to an area where there is little, if any, experience from other regulatory bodies. To some extent this CBA can be seen as an initial attempt to integrate CBA into the policy process in the FSA. So how did the FSA do?

Source of policy options

The options that the FSA considered were sufficiently distinct, although they apparently lacked detail, which caused problems later in their detailed costings. It is, however, far from clear why the FSA considered these options, or whether there were others under consideration at any time. The FSA reports that the options were drawn up in consultation with the Treasury. One wonders, then, why one of the options (MCC) was later judged not to be a viable option by the industry itself. Arguably, some discussion at the option identification stage with the industry itself, those incurring the costs, and with consumers, those likely to benefit, would have been productive in terms of helping to scope the CBA.[83]

Impact analysis

The FSA followed its own impact analysis process in conducting the CBA. On the costings side, there are a number of issues to consider. First, although the

---

82 *Ibid.*
83 The Financial Services Consumer Panel's Annual Report 2000 indicates that it provided some advice to the FSA on this CBA. See *Consumer Panel Annual Report 2000*, Appendix 3, www.fs-cp.org.uk/public/pdf/000312.annualreportwebsite.pdf. It is clear from the submission to HM Treasury by the Consumer Panel that it was critical of two of the options for regulation considered in the CBA: Consumer Panel, *Mortgage Regulation: Financial Services Consumer Panel Response to HM Treasury Discussion Paper on Mortgage Regulation* (November 1999), www.fs-cp.org.uk/public/pdf/000312.annualreportwebsite.pdf.

FSA reports its own direct costs at around £12 million, these appear very much in a black-box manner with little explanation or justification, and do little for transparency. The estimation of compliance costs was a complex and difficult task. However, whilst the consultancy company undertaking this work developed a robust methodology to try to ensure firms sampled were costing impacts consistently and rigorously, the sample size itself was quite small.

For lenders, an initial sample of sixteen firms was chosen (out of a total of 120) although it is not clear exactly how these were selected. Four of these did not take part because of staff time commitments. The resulting sample of 12 included 5 of the largest 8 lenders, 3 of the 22 middle-sized lenders and 4 of the 103 small lenders, although the sample was estimated to cover about 55 per cent of the advisors employed by lenders.

For intermediaries, the initial sample was twenty-seven (out of an estimated almost 14,000). The final sample size was 16, including 4 from the 28 largest companies, 8 from the approximately 400 medium-sized companies and 4 from the approximately 13,000 smaller intermediaries, and covered only an estimated 7 per cent of the advisors employed by intermediaries. As the consultancy company itself commented:[84] 'The combined effect of the relatively small sample size and the hypothetical nature of the questions asked of the interviewees is that the estimates (of cost) are subject to considerable margins of error.'

There was some attempt made to consider the distributional effects of these costs, splitting them between lenders and intermediaries. For the SC option, for example, the one-off compliance cost of £36 million was split at £13.7 million for lenders and £22.4 million for intermediaries, whilst the recurring costs were put at £14.1 million and £18.3 million respectively. The implications of this distributive effect, however, was not discussed. Similarly, the impact analysis in terms of cost focused only on the costs borne by the industry directly. The FSA reported that, in the case of intermediaries, a substantial part of training costs would be borne by individuals undertaking the training in their own time. This 'could add another £40million to total compliance costs' but was not considered further.[85]

The evaluation of benefits as part of the CBA is qualitative rather than quantitative, although the logic of both the evaluation and the limitations are clearly set out in the analysis document. However, the evaluation of benefits is to some extent dominated by the caveat that it is, arguably, difficult to get any real sense of the possible scale of the benefits. Interestingly, there is no record of any attempt to identify the benefits or the general 'worth' to the consumer, either with consumers directly or with consumer groups.[86]

84 Europe Economics (London, 1999), 28, although no attempt is made to quantify these.
85 FSA (1999), 20.
86 For the Consumer Panel's criticism of the attempts to identify and measure benefits in this CBA, see the *Consumer Panel Annual Report 2000*, para 5.3.

Comparison of costs with benefits

The FSA conclude that the incremental costs of regulation under any of the three options are 'small' and that regulation 'could' produce significant benefits. Arguably, this leaves the reader with the impression that, on balance, there is a net benefit from regulation. However, it is difficult from the reported analysis to see the real evidence for this conclusion. Ingeniously, the FSA reports that, even if the full cost of statutory regulation was passed on to consumers, this 'would increase the cost of a mortgage of £60,000 by 15 pence per month'.[87] However, a different perspective can be developed using the FSA's own cost results. The FSA itself assumes that firms would write off costs over a five-year period. The costs involved in statutory regulation can then be presented as:

Costs (£ million over five years)	SC	ECC	LRC
Total Direct	60	60	60
Compliance:			
One off	36	40	24
Total recurring	160	160	85
Total	256	260	169

Presented this way, the analysis raises some interesting questions. Would the benefits felt from regulation (primarily by consumers) be worth at least £250 million in the SC option? Would the total benefits from the ECC option be at least £90 million more than the benefits from the LRC option? Put another way, is the benefit derived from the 'enhanced suitability' of products arising from the ECC option worth the extra cost of £90 million, given that the FSA's perceived key difference between these two options was that the ECC would enhance suitability whilst LRC would not. The FSA's consultancy company also reported that the total of direct and compliance costs, if passed to consumers, might add £20 to a mortgage. Would the consumer (i.e., the borrower) feel this extra cost was worthwhile in terms of regulation of mortgage advice? Unfortunately, in spite of its own call for 'lateral thinking', the FSA did not consider its own results in this way.

As has already been commented, the FSA's approach to CBA pays scant attention to the time value issue of costs and benefits. Applying discounted cash flow analysis to the data in the above table (using an assumed discount rate of 8 per cent and ignoring inflation and tax implications), the net present value figure for the ECC option is £230 million whilst that for the LRC option is £150 million. Would this have helped identify a preferred policy option?

87 FSA (1999), 27.

Final outcome

After submission of its CBA to the Government, and after consideration of the results of its own consultation exercise, the Government decided that while the FSA should regulate mortgage advertising and regulate for product disclosure by lenders, it should not regulate mortgage advice.

We are confident in surmising that this outcome was privately welcomed by the FSA. The FSA already has the considerable task of taking over the functions of nine regulators and welding them together into one coherent scheme, without having to take on a new and additional area of responsibility. In addition, the regulation of advice in the investment sector had proved problematic for the FSA's predecessor, the SIB.[88] Regulating for advertising and product disclosure, on the other hand, fits very well with the regulatory ethos of the FSA providing information to the consumer to enable consumers to make their own informed decisions. On the other hand, the Consumer Panel of the FSA, which has responsibility for monitoring and promoting consumer issues, expressed regret at the Government's decision, believing inadequate or inappropriate advice to be at the heart of consumer detriment.[89]

Did CBA add value?

As discussed earlier, the FSA's CBA approach was designed deliberately to be 'cost-effective'. Clearly, the CBA that was undertaken was not without cost (both to the FSA and to the sample of firms who committed time and effort to providing cost data). In spite of this there is no discussion as to the value added by the CBA itself to the policy process, nor whether the analysis actually influenced policy. As the FSA comments elsewhere:[90] 'The central problem of CBA is to identify extremely complex (and to an extent unknowable) interactions within an economy and reduce them to a set of propositions that are simple enough to be readily understood and yet realistic enough to be useful.'

The potential impact of CBA in the future for consumers of financial services

One of the commonly stated advantages of CBA is that it minimises excessive regulation, the costs of which are inevitably and ultimately borne by the

88 See Black, *Rules and Regulators*, chap. 4.
89 Financial Services Consumer Panel, Press Release (19 December 2000), www.fs-cp.org.uk/public/mn.pr977237752.
90 Alfon and Andrews, *Cost–Benefit Analysis*, 25.

consumer. Thus, CBA is presented as a valuable but neutral tool in the process of decision-making. In imposing a discipline on the regulator it also prevents that regulator from acting in its own interests to further its importance and power (and individual careers) by identifying more 'risk' and introducing more regulation.

However, one acknowledged difficulty with the use of CBA is the problem of identifying which costs and which benefits should count. This inevitably involves value judgments. For example, product information disclosure has been a significant element of the regulatory regime for long-term insurance products such as endowment mortgages. Providers are required to disclose anticipated rates of returns to investors to enable investors to make comparisons between different product providers and between this type of product and other investment products (for example, the personal equity plans or its recent replacement the 'individual savings accounts'). Consumers should therefore be able actively to shop around and bring competitive pressure to bear. However, comparative growth rates do not take into account other costs to consumers. The UK Consumers' Association has estimated that only around 30 per cent of endowments are held till maturity. The surrender values for such products are notoriously low in the first few years and consumers cashing in such policies would lose not only the anticipated rate of return, but also the hefty charges associated with early surrender. They could in fact get back far less than they had put into the fund. If the consumer were to cash in a similar equity product such as a Personal Equity Plan or Individual Savings Account, all he or she would lose would be the anticipated rate of return. A significant number of consumers would have been better off putting money into a fund with a lower projected rate of return than into an endowment mortgage.[91] A meaningful CBA would need to identify and take into account these behavioural issues in order to present a truer reflection of costs and benefits. Yet the Consumers' Association notes that in the past regulators in the financial sector have been reluctant to engage in this sort of exercise. More complex behavioural issues which can affect regulatory output do not appear to have been acknowledged and incorporated into the policy process in this instance.

The FSA relies heavily upon the industry for estimates of compliance costs and in this respect the industry becomes 'privileged' in the regulatory process. It has the ear of the regulator and is in a potential position at least to influence outcomes through its submission of costings. Industry might view cost estimating as an opportunity to engage in bargaining with the regulator, something that seems to be implicitly recognised by the FSA's consultancy experts in this case. The industry is of course a large and diffuse body and this must work to some extent against the possibility of 'regulatory capture'. The only apparent counterweight to the possibility of regulatory 'bargaining' is the experience of the

91 Consumers' Association (2001), www.which.net/campaigns/with_profits/problems2.html.

regulatory staff, together with the expertise on the Financial Services Consumer Panel.[92]

There is also another danger with the use of CBA, in that it could be used to mask policy decisions by 'obscuring central issues in a web of economic technicalities and arcane language'.[93] To quote another author, 'cost-benefit analysis is almost always used not to make decisions, but to justify decisions that have already been made'.[94] It has already been noted that in the case of the CBA for mortgage advice there was no indication of how the four regulatory alternatives were decided, and whether they were the only possible regulatory alternatives. Although the outcome of the CBA was transparent, the process itself was not.

Further, is there a risk that the introduction of economic analysis might lead the regulator to favour modes of regulation that minimise the need for elaborate CBA calculations? CBA itself costs, and this cost takes resources away from the job of regulating. Again, regulating for information disclosure is probably easier to quantify, in terms of costs at least, than more interventionist regulatory strategies such as product regulation and regulation of advice.

Unlike the Better Regulation Unit guidelines, the FSA CBA does not set out to identify distributional issues such as who would in fact incur the benefits/costs if the regulation were to be imposed. The FSA apparently believes that distributional issues are more properly identified as part of the general consultation process, but we would argue that identifying them at the end of the CBA process is arguably too late; the preferred option(s) has (have) already been determined.

How consumers might try to ensure their voices are better heard in the process

Systems theorists might suggest that the introduction of economic appraisal represents an attempt to integrate other sub-systems, such as economics, into lawmaking. They have questioned the ability of economic appraisal techniques such as CBA to impact upon the 'traditional' lawmaking process because of the limited ability of one sub-system (for example, economics) to impact on the dynamics of other sub-systems (for example, lawmaking). Regulation, in so far as it hands lawmaking to specialist agency bodies such as the FSA, represents an attempt to integrate these other sub-systems into the lawmaking process, but without controlling substantive outcomes. In other words, it changes procedural processes without attempting to direct substantive outcomes.[95]

---

92 The Consumer Panel has the right to commission its own research. However, that ability is constrained by its limited financial resources.
93 Baldwin, *Rules and Government*, 202.   94 Adams, *Risk*, 107.
95 See further Lange, 'Economic Appraisal'.

But a central debate in government policy-making is the rationality for adopting economic language based on monetary representations of value in the first place. Money is used as the representation of value because it is the value of the marketplace. Even some economists and accountants have conceded that not everything relevant to decision-making through CBA can be translated directly into money. One of the key difficulties with CBA, as already noted, is to identify which costs and benefits count and what values to attach to them. On what basis are such decisions to be made?

There is now a considerable body of research that suggests that cultural filters influence both the selection of information and the ways in which we approach decision-making. Cultural theorists have applied cultural principles to analyse the different premises from which decisions are made. One mode of cultural analysis that has dominated the discussion is the 'grid-group' analysis first developed by Mary Douglas[96] but extended by subsequent cultural theorists such as Schwarz and Thompson[97] and Thompson, Ellis and Wildavsky.[98] Cultural theory primarily grew out of a desire to understand the nature of risk and of risk-taking behaviour. Theorists[99] discerned the presence of order and pattern in risk-taking behaviour and in the beliefs and biases that underpinned it, and have identified the existence of shared interpretational frameworks that exist and that enable communities to make sense of their (social and natural) environment.[100] Thus, cultural theorists proposed that all people approach decision-making from one of four 'ways of life':[101] hierarchists, egalitarians, individualists and fatalists.[102] While these typologies are not immutable (we can move between them given the right circumstances), cultural theorists would suggest that we are all predisposed to one of these typologies. As a result, we have a recognised view of reality and a set of value systems that influences how we approach decision-making.

Typically, members of 'big business', 'big government' or 'big bureaucracy' would be members of the 'hierarchist' typology. At the risk of gross oversimplification, hierarchists are biased towards the belief that nature (or possibly markets) will be good to them if properly managed. They are respecters of both scientific and administrative authority and they believe in research to establish 'the facts'. They also take a 'top-down' approach to decision-making. They are not 'individualists' who

---

96 *Cultural Bias* (Occasional Paper 35, London, Royal Anthropological Institute, 1978).
97 M. Schwarz and M. Thompson, *Divided We Stand: Re-Defining Politics, Technology and Social Choice* (Hemel Hempstead: Harvester Wheatsheaf, 1990).
98 M. Thompson, R. Ellis and A. Wildavsky, *Cultural Theory* (Boulder, Col.: Westview Press, 1990).
99 For discussion of the theoretical roots and development of cultural theory, see J. Tansey and T. O'Riordan, 'Cultural Theory and Risk: a Review' (1999) 1 *Health, Risk and Society* 70.
100 It is this focus on preference formation that is said to distinguish cultural theory from public choice theories, which focus on preference realisation: Thompson, Ellis and Wildavsky, *Cultural Theory*.
101 Subsequently refined by Adams as 'typologies of bias': *Risk*, 36.
102 In fact, subsequently extended by Thompson, Ellis and Wildavsky to five so as to include the 'hermit': *Cultural Theory*, 100.

believe in market forces and are hostile to regulators, nor 'egalitarians' who view nature as fragile and precarious and who will always favour the 'precautionary' principle, nor are they 'fatalists' who do nothing because we are all doomed anyway. Cultural theorists would suggest that the dominant (hierarchist) approach, which places primary value on scientific knowledge and which often dismisses alternative or non-expert perspectives as irrational, fails to recognise and acknowledge the values and beliefs that underlie scientific and technical knowledge.[103] In the context of the use of CBA as a regulatory tool, one such belief is the belief in the rationality of decisions based upon a mathematical calculation of the monetary values attached to the various costs and benefits identified as appropriate.[104]

Cultural theorists suggest that these typologies can help to explain why individuals, groups and societies can appear to approach an issue such as risk from quite different perspectives, as well as explaining how they engage in decision-making. Furthermore, they would argue that any decision-making, including decision-making at state level, must include representatives from these four typologies if it is to be effective and to engage society. Others may not agree that the world can be reduced to four 'ways of life'.[105] Nevertheless, it is suggested that decision-makers need to be aware of subtle differences of perception in order to recognise and engage more complex patterns of social difference.[106]

Adopting the insights of cultural theorists, what should the process of conducting a CBA look like? We would suggest that it would not involve a 'top-down' approach to CBA. A top-down approach places particular emphasis on the importance of 'experts' in establishing the appropriate policy parameters. Once done, the policy-makers then set out to engage in dialogue with consumers, armed with their expert knowledge. Typically this dialogue will take place in the context of an expert/lay divide (so beloved of hierarchists). Rather it should begin with a broad consultation exercise endeavouring to include a broad range of perspectives (acknowledging the existence of cultural filters for decision-making), and focused on inclusiveness and consensus building. This consultation would then form the basis for the development of policy objectives defining and clarifying options already identified and/or defining additional options which in turn could be subjected to CBA according to agreed criteria by which to identify and assess costs and benefits.

103 Schwarz and Thompson, *Divided we Stand*, chap. 1.
104 See further Adams, *Risk*, 93.
105 For critiques of cultural theory, see Tansey and O'Riordan, 'Cultural Theory and Risk'. See also C. Lockhart and R. Coughlin, 'Building Better Comparative Social Theory through Alternative Conceptions of Reality' (1992) 45 *Western Political Quarterly* 793, who argue that cultural theory devotes insufficient attention to the origins and evolution of social institutions and fails to explain how biases are constructed and activated and why people act on one bias in one social sphere (e.g., work), but on another bias in another sphere (e.g., family).
106 A. Stirling and S. Mayer, *Rethinking Risk: a Pilot Multi-Criteria Mapping of a Genetically Modified Crop in Agricultural Systems in the UK* (Sussex: SPRU, University of Sussex), have developed multi-criteria mapping as a means of opening up regulatory processes to a wider range of constituencies and perspectives. For a description of multi-criteria methodology, see chap. 2.2.

Thus, the process would begin with consultation rather than end with consultation. It would represent an acknowledgement that expert perceptions of risks and expert perceptions of which values should count in the CBA process are themselves culturally constructed, and that other perceptions are possible and no less valid. One of the most important keys to the process of decision-making is the recognition of the assumptions on which proposals are made. Such a consultative exercise might reveal, for example, that consumers are more concerned with issues of social inclusion or risk identification than regulating advice.

While the FSA clearly recognises the importance of consultation and openness in decision-making, it appears in this case to have been predominantly an 'end of process' openness. Once the policy parameters have been set, once the CBA has been done, then the consultative process becomes genuinely open. We can speculate that the policy parameters were set by an 'expert committee'. As far as we are aware, government and some industry representatives (who would likely share the same typology of bias in the view of cultural theorists) were consulted in the process, but it is not at all clear to what extent others such as consumers were included.[107]

The particular value of the cultural theorising is not, we believe, in the 'truth' of typologies of bias. The value is in the potential new insight it gives into the decision-making (including lawmaking) process. It provides another perspective by which to analyse processes and identify avenues for change. In the political process perhaps the call of the consumer should be for greater transparency and involvement in the process of setting policy parameters and identifying values. If the assumption of individual responsibility is a defining feature of modern society in which there are few certain outcomes, then by the same token individuals should have greater input into the decision-making process. That input should not be confined to the level of commenting on, approving, or choosing between options identified by experts. It should extend to the level of identifying the values and the options representing those values that are put on the table for consideration in the first place. Empowering, in the sense used by Beck, involves not only making choices and accepting responsibility at the individual level, it also includes involvement in the decision-making process at the 'state' level. A system that emphasises responsibility but denies citizens the opportunity to know or to influence the 'rules of the game' is unlikely to be empowering. Once the science has been 'done' and presented to the consumer a particular cultural view about what is important and what is valuable already dominates. It is too late for other voices to be heard.

Conclusion (well, so what?)

It is possible to interpret the imposition of the requirement for a CBA in a number of ways: as an exercise of political expediency; as an attempt to integrate

107 FSA (1999), 20. A brief reference list in the *Consumer Panel Annual Report 2000* indicates that it was consulted but it is also clear that the Panel did not agree with two of the policy options.

sub-systems into lawmaking; or as creating the opportunity for public engagement and dialogue in a world increasingly preoccupied with risk and risk management, and in which individuals are required to accept greater responsibility for outcomes. Irrespective of what might have been the political motives behind the introduction of CBA into the regulatory process, it is nevertheless to be welcomed as a worthwhile attempt to acknowledge and incorporate an assessment of cost–benefit impact into the regulatory process. Despite the flaws identified above, the FSA set out a clear process and framework to be followed in conducting the CBA.

While the process and framework might have been clear, it was nevertheless flawed and as such its value in terms of enhancing the dialogue between regulator, the regulated community and the consumer was limited. Its value could be enhanced by incorporating greater consumer involvement in setting the parameters of the CBA and greater consumer focus and improved transparency.

The motivation behind the consideration of mortgage advice regulation was consumer protection. Despite being the potential beneficiary of any new regulation, the consumer appears to have been conceived of as external to the process of identifying the possible alternative regulatory responses, and external to the process of planning the CBA. Consumers might well have had particular insights into the process of the CBA, including the identification of alternative policy options and who to involve in the process. At the same time, the process needs to focus more on the benefits and their perceived value to consumers, rather than the general paternalistic view that 'this will be of considerable benefit to customers'. Again, consumers might have valuable input into discussions of what benefits are involved in regulation, and what value to place on those benefits. While consumers might not be able to comment upon the technical output of a CBA, they will nevertheless have a view on how the process itself should be conducted. Finally, the process requires more transparency during its key stages, particularly in deciding what policy options will be evaluated in the CBA and in making clear the key assumptions used in quantifying costs and qualitatively assessing benefits.

Any assumptions about the likely outcomes of a particular regulation necessarily involve a risk analysis as part of the process of decision-making. In other words, the assumption that the imposition of regulation X will, with certainty, result in outcome Y in turn relies upon certain assumptions about how the industry will behave in response to that regulation. However, there is always a risk that the industry will find ways to sidestep the regulation, or indeed that consumers will respond in a way not anticipated by the regulators. While regulatory processes are within the control of the regulators, regulatory outcomes are not. There appears to be a presumption in this CBA that there is only one possible outcome per regulatory option whereas, in fact, there may be a number of possible outcomes. The incorporation of decision analysis and sensitivity analysis into the CBA process, enlightened by the insights of cultural theory, which recognises the validity of different articulations and assessments of risk, might allow the regulators to identify multiple potential outcomes and to assess their relative risk of occurrence. The ultimate result may be that at the end of the day a different policy option is preferred to the 'expert' preferred choice.

This is an area in which we believe the CBA process could benefit from further research. Whatever might have been the political motivations behind the introduction of economic analysis tools into the regulatory process, the value of such tools in terms of producing desired regulatory outcomes would benefit from research into how the insights of cultural theorists, for example, might impact upon the process of CBA and affect ultimate regulatory policy and outcomes.

Part IV
Consumer bankruptcy law

10 Access to the discharge in Canadian bankruptcy law and the new role of surplus income: a historical perspective

THOMAS G. W. TELFER

Introduction

While Canadian debtors have never had an unconditional entitlement to a discharge in bankruptcy, Canadian courts have long recognised the important function that the discharge plays in the rehabilitation of the debtor. The Canadian discharge, originally based upon the English model, has differed from the American concept of fresh start in that Canada has traditionally relied on judicial discretion to impose conditions or limitations on the order of discharge in appropriate circumstances.[1] Although the courts in Canada have had the ability to impose conditional discharges upon bankrupts, including requirements to pay money from future income, conditional discharges under the traditional regime are only one option and courts have had the discretion to grant an unconditional discharge where it has been merited. The often cited rationale for the release of debts is that it permits the debtor's 'rehabilitation as a citizen, unfettered by past debts'.[2] The discharge, it is argued, allows the debtor to once again become a productive member of the open market economy.

More recently, however, there has been a reconceptualisation of the role of the discharge in bankruptcy law and perhaps more broadly a new view of debtor rehabilitation has emerged.[3] The rising number of consumer bankruptcies over the last decade led many to claim that something must be done to stem the rising tide. The assumption was that many debtors could really afford to pay more to their creditors and that the bankruptcy regime was too easy on debtors. In response to this perceived crisis over consumer bankruptcies Parliament amended the Bankruptcy and Insolvency Act in 1997. In reforming the law, Parliament transformed the concept of debtor rehabilitation.

I would like to thank the New Zealand law firm of Chapman Tripp for their sponsorship of the Research Scholarship Programme which provided research assistance for this project.
1 See J. Ziegel, 'The Philosophy and Design of Contemporary Consumer Bankruptcy Systems: a Canada–United States Comparison' (1999) 37 *Osgoode Hall LJ* 203, 209, noting that the unconditional entitlement to a fresh start has never been a part of Canadian law.
2 See, e.g., *Industrial Acceptance Corp.* v. *Lalonde* [1952] 2 SCR 109.
3 Iain Ramsay suggests that there has been a 'reconceptualization of the debtor as a deviant': I. Ramsay, 'Models of Consumer Bankruptcy: Implications for Research and Policy' (1997) 20 *Journal of Consumer Policy* 269, 271.

232 Consumer bankruptcy law

The amendments curtailed the ability of a debtor to obtain access to an unconditional discharge. The new statutory regime encourages debtors to file a proposal and discourages debtors from taking advantage of the straight bankruptcy regime. Where a debtor does file for bankruptcy the legislation requires debtors to make mandatory payments of surplus income to the trustee. In assessing whether a bankrupt is entitled to an unconditional discharge the trustee must assess whether the bankrupt could have made a viable proposal and whether the bankrupt has co-operated by making surplus income payments. The focus of the current regime presumes that many debtors have the ability to make repayments to their creditors from surplus income and sets out new mandatory repayment levels. Whereas traditional bankruptcy discharge policy referred to the rehabilitation of the debtor, Parliament now asks debtors to rehabilitate their debts by making payments out of surplus income.

The new amendments have not escaped criticism. Canadian academics pointed out that there was little empirical evidence to suggest that many debtors had surplus income.[4] Recent empirical studies have supported the initial criticisms and have found that few debtors have surplus income to justify a regime mandating payments from future income.[5] Beyond pointing out the faulty empirical basis of the reforms, critics have also asked what consequences follow from adopting a more restrictive bankruptcy discharge regime. What impact will a regime have that encourages or directs debtors to enter into a repayment regime whereby they commit a portion of their future income to creditors?

Those who have favoured the more traditional view of rehabilitation have speculated that restricting access to the discharge and mandating consumer proposals may have perverse effects. Debtors may lose the incentive to work knowing that they are committing the fruits of their labour to the repayment of debt during the life of a plan. Empirical work on the success of the repayment plans may shed light on this issue. However, as bankruptcy scholars debate the merits of moving to a more restrictive bankruptcy regime, one should not lose sight of the fact that the debate is not new. The 1997 reforms are not the first time that Canada has restricted access to the discharge.

The characterisation of the debtor as a deviant[6] and the claim that bankruptcy law interferes with an obligation to repay debts has arisen in the past. Indeed in Canada it lay at the heart of the debate over bankruptcy in the late nineteenth and early twentieth centuries. Canada briefly experimented with bankruptcy

---

4 See J. Ziegel, V. Black, E. Edinger, R. Cuming, and I. Ramsay, 'Consumer Bankruptcies and Bill C-5: Five Academics Claim the Bill Turns the Problems on their Head' (1996) 13 *National Insolvency Review* 81.
5 See I. Ramsay, 'Individual Bankruptcy: Preliminary Findings of a Socio-Legal Analysis' (1999) 37 *Osgoode Hall LJ* 15; S. Schwartz, 'The Empirical Dimensions of Consumer Bankruptcy: Results from a Survey of Canadian Bankrupts' (1999) 37 *Osgoode Hall LJ* 83.
6 See Ramsay, 'Models of Consumer Bankruptcy', 271.

legislation shortly after Confederation and enacted the Insolvent Act 1869 and the Insolvent Act 1875. The Canadian experience illustrates the progression of increasing restrictions on the discharge between 1869 and 1877 followed by a complete denial of the discharge by the repeal of federal bankruptcy law in 1880. Canadian debtors were denied access to a bankruptcy discharge for a period of nearly forty years until the enactment of the Bankruptcy Act 1919. Perhaps what is of interest to a contemporary audience is the impact of a non-bankruptcy or strict bankruptcy regime on debtors, creditors and society generally.

While repeal in 1880 satisfied those who claimed that the discharge interfered with the higher obligation to repay debts, the absence of a discharge had a profound effect upon credit relations. The near forty-year absence of the discharge provides numerous examples of complaints of debtors engaging in deceptive or fraudulent conduct under defective provincial legislation. Evidence also suggests that debtors left Canada for the United States to avoid creditors.

In the nineteenth century, the discharge proved to be one of the most contentious issues and in many respects became the focal point for those who sought repeal. However, by 1919 it was argued that bankruptcy legislation was a necessity. What had been deemed an evil in 1880 became an essential form of business regulation after the First World War. By 1919 creditors recognised the discharge as part of the larger bankruptcy scheme that enhanced collection goals. Creditors demanded and sought the return of a national uniform bankruptcy law in 1919. The Bankruptcy Act 1919 included provisions for the release of debts.

Debate over bankruptcy law in the nineteenth century involved very different considerations than the current reforms.[7] Consumer bankrupts as we know them today did not exist in nineteenth-century Canada. Only those who engaged in buying and selling were eligible under the rudimentary nineteenth-century statutes. Further, there were independent ideological, institutional and interest group factors[8] that explain the pattern of legislation in the nineteenth and early twentieth centuries, and that are no longer applicable in the present setting.

Giving historical perspective to a contemporary issue is not to suggest that particular patterns of legislation will be repeated or are predetermined.[9] However, the current debates might be better informed by a consideration of the origins of the law.[10] An understanding that similar fundamental issues have been debated in

7   See Ziegel, 'Philosophy and Design', 207, noting that the current controversy differs from the historical experience because of the development of consumer bankruptcies.
8   See T. Telfer, 'Reconstructing Bankruptcy in Canada: 1867–1919, from an Evil to a Commercial Necessity' (SJD Thesis, University of Toronto, 1999). On the relevance of institutional factors see generally D. Ernst, 'Law and American Political Development 1877–1938' (1998) 26 *Reviews in American History* 205.
9   See B. Trujillo, 'The Wisconsin Exemption Clause Debate of 1846: an Historical Perspective on the Regulation of Debt' [1998] *Wis L Rev* 747.
10 See J. Honsberger, 'Philosophy and Design of Modern Fresh Start Policies: the Evolution of Canada's Legislative Policy' (1999) 37 *Osgoode Hall LJ* 171, 172, maintaining that any attempt

the past (i.e., 'we have indeed been there before'[11]) may illustrate the historic rationale for the development of the discharge. Further, the historical perspective may
raise issues that require further study in the contemporary setting.

As a recent critical review article in the *Journal of Policy History* illustrates, one
should not too easily dismiss the historical experience when developing modern
policy alternatives.[12] Further, the historical experience may illustrate, as Michael
Katz's study does for poverty, that certain 'shop worn ideas' or assumptions about
debtor behaviour have persisted over time. These assumptions about debtors continue to hamper reform in the modern context as they did in the nineteenth
century.[13]

The following section of this essay begins by briefly examining the 1997 amendments and the official government rationale for the more restrictive regime. The
new focus on surplus income suggests that bankruptcy rehabilitation is now concerned with the repayment of debts rather than the more traditional notion of rehabilitation, which focused upon returning the debtor to the credit economy freed
from past obligations. The question raised by contemporary critics, which is yet to
be answered, is whether the current restrictions on the discharge and the encouragement of debtor repayment plans will have any impact on debtor behaviour. The
essay suggests that the current debates can be better informed by an examination
of the historical record, and reminds readers of the historic role that the discharge
played in bankruptcy policy. The concluding part of this essay considers the impact
of a restrictive or non-bankruptcy regime from an historical perspective and illustrates how debtors responded when faced with a difficult or non-existent path to a
discharge.

The 1997 amendments: the new debtor responsibility Act?

The demand for reform

The number of consumer bankruptcies increased more than fourfold
from 19,572 in 1985 to a record high in 1997 of 85,297.[14] The dramatic increase
sparked a debate about whether it was 'too easy for a consumer debtor to file for

to design a modern fresh start policy must start from where we are, how we got here and from
where. See also J. Honsberger, 'Bankruptcy Administration in Canada and the United States'
(1975) 63 *Cal L Rev* 1515; J. Honsberger, 'Bankruptcy: a Comparison of the Systems of the United
States and Canada' (1971) 45 *Am Bankr LJ* 129.

11 C. J. Tabb, 'A Century of Regress or Progress? A Political History of Bankruptcy Legislation in
1898 and 1998' (1999) 15 *Bankr Dev J* 343.

12 J. Zeliser, 'Clio's Lost Tribe: Public Policy History since 1978' (2000) 12 *Journal of Policy History*
369. I am indebted to Daniel Ernst for his discussions on this point.

13 M. Katz, *The Undeserving Poor: from Poverty to the War on Welfare* (New York: Pantheon Books, 1989).

14 Office of the Superintendent of Bankruptcy, *Bankruptcy Statistics*, www.strategis.ic.gc.ca/SSG/
br01011e.html.

bankruptcy relief and obtain a quick discharge of debts'.[15] The statistics 'set off alarm bells among creditors and federal bankruptcy officials'. It was feared that an easy bankruptcy declaration would threaten the 'integrity of Canada's credit system'.[16] Critics claimed it was an abuse of the Bankruptcy and Insolvency Act to allow debtors to use bankruptcy law as a means to evade payment of 'just obligations'.[17]

In many ways critics were responding to the perceived failure of the earlier 1992 reforms. While retaining the basic framework of discretion-based conditional discharges, Parliament in 1992 streamlined the discharge process providing that a bankrupt could obtain a discharge within a period of nine months. In addition, Parliament introduced new consumer proposal provisions with the hope that consumers would not opt for straight bankruptcy but would rather utilise the new Division III, Part 2 provisions.[18] The 1992 consumer proposal regime had the aim of 'reducing the number of consumer bankruptcies by allowing individuals in financial difficulty an opportunity to present debt repayment plans over a longer period of time, and an opportunity to negotiate with creditors settlements of amounts owing'.[19] However, the aim of diverting people away from straight bankruptcy into repayment plans did not succeed.[20] For the first four years of the new regime, consumer proposals remained largely static at about 3 per cent of total filings.[21] The 1992 amendments did not, according to one author, provide enough incentives 'to offset the attraction of consumers being able to obtain an unconditional discharge from their debts nine months after bankruptcy'.[22] The increasing number of bankruptcies even after the 1992 amendments led many to believe that further action was required.

In addition to the claim that bankruptcy law was too easy on debtors, critics claimed that many bankrupts had surplus income and could have made a viable proposal. There was a widespread assumption that many debtors could have paid

15 J. Ziegel, 'Canada's Phased in Bankruptcy Law Reform' (1996) 70 *Am Bankr LJ* 383; Ramsay, 'Individual Bankruptcy', 17, noting the growing newspaper coverage since he began his consumer bankruptcy research project.
16 J. Ziegel, 'Canadian Perspectives on the Challenges of Consumer Bankruptcies' (1997) 20 *Journal of Consumer Policy* 199.
17 Honsberger, 'Bankruptcy Administration', 186, summarising arguments of critics of bankruptcy.
18 See J. Ziegel, 'Canadian Bankruptcy Reform, Bill C-109 and Troubling Asymmetries' (1996) 27 *Canadian Business Law Journal* 108, 111.
19 G. Marantz, R. Chartrand, B. Goldberg and S. Golick, '*The Bankruptcy and Insolvency Act.* The New Look after 40 Years' (1992–3) 8 *Banking and Finance Law Review* 195, 213.
20 See Ziegel, 'Canadian Perspectives', 210.
21 'Consumer Proposals as a Proportion of Total Personal Filings' (2000) 20(2) *Insolvency Bulletin* 36.
22 J. Ziegel, 'Introduction to the Symposium on Consumer Bankruptcies' (1999) 37 *Osgoode Hall LJ* 1, 8; I. Ramsay, 'Market Imperatives, Professional Discretion and the Role of Intermediaries in Consumer Bankruptcy: a Comparative Study of the Canadian Trustee in Bankruptcy' (2000) 74 *Am Bankr LJ* 399, 433–4.

off their debts over time.[23] It was argued that the 1992 amendments might have encouraged individuals who had an ability to pay 'to avoid doing so'.[24] If consumer bankruptcies were rising out of control, a new mechanism had to be found to reduce the numbers of bankruptcies.[25]

Bill C-5 and the new surplus income regime

In order to encourage more debtors into the proposal regime Parliament further amended the Bankruptcy and Insolvency Act. The legislation was approved by Parliament on 25 April 1997 and came into force on 30 April 1998.[26] In introducing the Bill into the House of Commons, the Parliamentary Secretary to the Minister of Industry claimed that 'Canadians want to be assured that no one is slipping away from financial obligations by using bankruptcy as an easy way out. Canadians want assurances that the piper will be paid.'[27] While the legislation amended the principal Bankruptcy and Insolvency Act, it might as well have been called the Insolvent Debtor Responsibility Act.[28] The Office of the Superintendent of Bankruptcy described the new provisions:[29]

> Insolvent debtors will be expected to consider submitting a viable proposal to creditors as a preferred option and responsible alternative for discharging their debt.

23 See Ziegel, 'Philosophy and Design', 232.
24 R. Marantz and R. Chartrand, 'Bankruptcy and Insolvency Law Reform Continues: the 1996–1997 Amendments' (1997–8) 13 *Banking and Finance Law Review* 107, 127. See also Ziegel, Black, Edinger, Cuming and Ramsay, 'Consumer Bankruptcies', 81, summarising their submission to the Industry Committee of the House of Commons.
25 In testimony before the House of Commons Standing Committee on Banking, Trade and Commerce, Robert Klotz, Chair of the National Bankruptcy and Insolvency Section, Canadian Bar Association, referred to the problem of the rising number of bankruptcies and stated that he agreed 'with the government's efforts to promote the use of consumer proposals to avoid and reduce the number of personal bankruptcies'. See House of Commons, Standing Committee on Industry, *Evidence of Proceedings* (17 September 1996), 1600.
26 *An Act to Amend the Bankruptcy and Insolvency Act, the Companies Creditors' Arrangement Act and the Income Tax Act*: S.C. 1997, c. 12.
27 *House of Commons Debates* (27 May 1996), 3030–3031 (M. Bodnar, Parliamentary Secretary to Ministry of Industry).
28 During the hearings of the House of Commons Standing Committee on Industry, government officials presented an overview of the Bill and discussed the policy rationale behind the reforms. David Tobin from the Department of Industry segregated the reforms in Bill C-5 into different categories. The category dealing with consumer bankruptcies was classified as 'Encouraging Responsibility'. Under this heading Mr. Tobin outlined the surplus payment requirements in the Bill: House of Commons, Standing Committee on Industry, *Evidence of Proceedings* (11 June 1996), 1640 (D. Tobin, Director General, Corporate Governance Branch, Department of Industry).
29 Office of the Superintendent of Bankruptcy ('OSB'), 'Final Phase of New Bankruptcy Legislation Comes into Force' (1 May 1998), www.strategis.ic.gc.ca/SSG/br0106le.html. In an earlier press release the OSB stated that 'the amendments seek to assert the need for responsible action by insolvent debtors': 'Bill C-5 Receives Royal Assent' (25 April 1997), www.strategis.ic.gc.ca/SSG/br01011e.html.

In cases where, as a last resort, bankruptcy is filed, debtors with surplus income will be obligated to contribute their fair share to the creditors in the bankruptcy process, as a condition of their discharge from bankruptcy ... These amendments promote debtor responsibility in this area.

The amendments 'attempt to encourage more consumer proposals as an alternative to bankruptcy and greater financial contribution by the bankrupt to creditors'.[30] Several mechanisms have been utilised to achieve this goal. Bankrupts face new mandatory income payment requirements. Under the revised s. 68, the Superintendent has established a Directive which sets out standards 'for determining the portion of the total income of an individual bankrupt that exceeds that which is necessary to enable the bankrupt to maintain a reasonable standard of living'.[31] The trustee is required to consider the standards in the Surplus Income Directive,[32] and the debtor's available monthly income (after deducting allowable expenses), and then must determine whether or not the debtor has an available surplus income.

For example, in 2002 the Surplus Income Directive allowed a single person a monthly income of $1602 whereas a family of four is allowed $3015.[33] Calculations of surplus income are based upon a comparison of the allowable standards with the debtor's available monthly income. A debtor must pay over 50 per cent of his or her surplus income where the surplus monthly income is equal to or greater than $100 and less than $1,000. Where the surplus monthly income is $1,000 or more the debtor is required to pay at least 50 per cent and may be required to pay up to 75 per cent of the surplus income.[34]

Once the surplus income amount is fixed, the trustee is required to 'take reasonable measures to ensure that the bankrupt complies with the requirement to pay.'[35] Surplus income payments are to be made during the nine-month period between the declaration of bankruptcy and the discharge.[36] The provision 'implements a policy which requires bankrupts who have surplus income to pay the same into the estate for distribution among creditors'.[37] However, as Iain Ramsay points out, the surplus income rules are 'crude bright-line standards which make no distinction between different regions and provide little scope for tailoring budgets to the individual circumstances of debtors'.[38]

---

30 Marantz and Chartrand, 'Bankruptcy and Insolvency Law', 125.
31 Bankruptcy and Insolvency Act RSC 1985, c B-3 as amended, s. 68(1) ('BIA'). See *Re O'Reilly* (2001) 28 CBR 4th 68 (BCSC): 'The rationale behind these standards is to leave the bankrupt with sufficient funds to pay for the necessaries of life and to ensure all individuals in bankruptcy are treated in the same manner insofar as the payment of surplus income is concerned.'
32 Office of the Superintendent of Bankruptcy, *Directive 11R Surplus Income* (3 October 2000), www.strategis.ic.gc.ca/SSG/br01055e.html ('Directive 11R').
33 Directive 11R, Appendix A.   34 Directive 11R, s. 7.   35 BIA s. 68(3)(c).
36 Directive 11R, s. 13. See also Ramsay, 'Market Imperatives', 404.
37 *Re Aubin* (2000) 20 CBR (4th) 181, 182 per Registrar Ferron (Ont. SCJ). The provision does not operate as a garnishment order that can be served upon employers.
38 Ramsay, 'Market Imperatives', 431.

Some measures in the 1997 regime are designed to protect the debtor. The bankrupt is able to ask for mediation if he or she disagrees with the trustee's assessment. Where mediation fails or the bankrupt refuses to comply with the requirement to pay, the trustee may make an application under s. 68(10) and ultimately the court is charged with fixing the amount that the debtor is required to pay.[39] However, as Jacob Ziegel notes, it is unrealistic to place the onus on an unsophisticated and asset-poor debtor to challenge the trustee's decision where the trustee is bound to follow a statutory scale.[40] Few cases have been found where a trustee's assessment of surplus income has been challenged in the courts. However, in one case a debtor who had started to make payments under a proposal that ultimately failed was unable to claim the partial payments as credit towards the s. 68 payment obligation.[41]

As noted by the Manitoba Court of Appeal, s. 68 of the Act, 'as re-enacted in 1997, provides a quite different regime for the attachment of the post-assignment income of a bankrupt'. The trustee fixes the amount the bankrupt must pay to the bankrupt estate without having to make an initial application to the court.[42] Under the former s. 68, in order to reach a bankrupt's post-bankruptcy income, a trustee was required to make an application to the court for an order 'directing the payment to the trustee of such part of the money as the court may determine, having regard to the family responsibilities and personal situation of the bankrupt'.[43] However, given the percentage of bankrupts who are unemployed and the poverty median levels of consumer bankrupts in general, Ziegel notes that under the former regime applications under s. 68 were 'more of an aspiration than a reality'. Ziegel concludes that under the former provisions, trustees disliked making formal applications as the results did not often warrant the effort.[44] Trustees now have a much broader power to capture post-bankruptcy income and available statistics indicate

---

39 BIA s. 68(10). For a discussion of the procedure under s. 68, see Re Landry (2000) 192 DLR (4th) 728, 739 (Ont. CA). See also Re Laybolt (2001) 27 CBR (4th) 97 (NSSC). The statute has also been amended to make it a bankruptcy offence, punishable by fine or imprisonment or both, to refuse to pay the surplus income requirement when ordered by a court: BIA s. 198(2). A Quicklaw search did not reveal any such prosecutions to date.

40 Ziegel, 'Canadian Bankruptcy Reform', 120. Also relevant is whether the courts under s. 68(10) have the discretion to vary the Standards. Houlden and Morawetz suggest that the courts still have a discretion: L. W. Houlden and C. H. Morawetz, Bankruptcy and Insolvency Law of Canada (3rd edn, Toronto: Carswell, 1990), 6–77. Re Deymen (1998) 4 CBR (4th) 67 (Sask. QB) notes that the Superintendent's Standards have been given statutory force. Re Missal (1999) 14 CBR (4th) 123, para 8 (Alta QB) concludes that 'under special circumstances the court may relieve a bankrupt from making all of the guideline payments. Similarly the court can as a condition of discharge require the bankrupt to make payments over and above the superintendent guidelines.' See also Re Croft (2001) 196 NSR (2d) 164 (NSSC), Re Weatherbee (2001) 25 CBR (4th) 133 (NSSC).

41 Re Missal (1999) 14 CBR (4th) 123 (Alta QB).

42 Re Berthelette (1999) 174 DLR (4th) 577, 582 (Man. CA). Where the debtor refuses to pay, the trustee may bring an application to the court pursuant to s. 68(10).

43 RSC 1985, c. B-3 am. 1992, c. 27, s. 34; rep and sub. 1997, c. 12, s. 60(1). For a discussion of a difference between the two versions of s. 68, see Re Landry (2000) 192 DLR (4th) 728 (Ont. CA).

44 Ziegel, 'Canadian Perspectives', 211.

that about 16 per cent of debtors are currently required to make surplus income payments.[45]

Beyond the repayment requirement, straight bankruptcy is made less attractive by the new provisions governing the discharge. Under the Bankruptcy and Insolvency Act, a first time bankrupt will be automatically discharged nine months after the bankruptcy unless the discharge is opposed.[46] However, the recent amendments have restricted access to an unconditional discharge. The trustee is required to recommend whether or not a bankrupt should be discharged subject to conditions, 'having regard to the bankrupt's conduct and ability to make payments'.[47] Under the new provisions the trustee is specifically to consider the following matters in making a recommendation:

(a) whether the bankrupt has complied with a requirement imposed on the bankrupt under s. 68;
(b) the total amount paid to the estate by the bankrupt, having regard to the bankrupt's indebtedness and financial resources; and
(c) whether the bankrupt, if the bankrupt could have made a viable proposal, chose to proceed to bankruptcy rather than to make a proposal as the means to resolve the indebtedness.[48]

Directive 12 further specifies the following standards to be applied by trustees in recommending conditions of discharge. Under the terms of Directive 12, a trustee shall recommend a conditional discharge where the trustee is of the opinion that:

(a) the bankrupt refuses to comply with the requirement to make surplus income payments to the estate;
(b) the total amount paid to the estate by the bankrupt is disproportionate to the bankrupt's indebtedness and financial resources; or
(c) at the time of assessment, the bankrupt could have filed a viable proposal but chose instead to file an assignment in bankruptcy.[49]

Payments required under conditional discharges are to be determined in accordance with the Directive on Surplus Income.[50] Again, the bankrupt is able to

45 See Ramsay, 'Market Imperatives', 404–5, citing Office of the Superintendent of Bankruptcy Statistics for period 1 August to 31 December 1999.
46 BIA s. 168.1(1)(f).
47 BIA s. 170.1(1). Notwithstanding a trustee's conclusion that the bankrupt could not have made a viable proposal, a creditor may still oppose the discharge on the basis of s. 173(1)(n). See, e.g., Re Fauser (2000) 19 CBR (4th) 189 (Alta. QB). See ss. 168.1(1)(c) and 170(7).
48 BIA s. 170.1.
49 Office of the Superintendent of Bankruptcy, Terms of Discharge, Directive 12, s. 4, www.strategis. ic.gc.ca/SSG/br01056e.html.
50 Office of the Superintendent of Bankruptcy, Terms of Discharge, Directive 12, s. 5(3), www.strategis. ic.gc.ca/SSG/br01056e.html. Under Directive 12, conditional discharges are to be up to twelve months in duration. Thus a bankrupt may face a requirement to pay income for a period of twenty-one months when taking into account the original nine-month bankruptcy period. See Directive 12, s. 5. See also Ramsay, 'Market Imperatives', 431.

challenge the trustee's recommendation by mediation and then ultimately in the courts.

In reviewing an application for a discharge, the court is now required to consider two new statutory factors which will preclude the granting of an unconditional discharge. Under s. 172(2) a court shall refuse the discharge, suspend the discharge or impose conditions if any of the facts listed in s. 173 are proven. Now included in the list are:

> (m) the bankrupt has failed to comply with a requirement to pay imposed under s. 68;
> (n) the bankrupt, if the bankrupt could have made a viable proposal, chose bankruptcy rather than a proposal as the means to resolve the indebtedness.

Thus debtors who opt for a straight bankruptcy without considering making a proposal may not achieve their goal of obtaining a clean break from past obligations. Under the new provisions courts are precluded from making an unconditional discharge where the debtor ignored the possibility of making a proposal to creditors.

A review of reported and unreported cases to date illustrates that at least in those instances where the matter has worked its way up to the courts, the provisions are being used to preclude unconditional discharges.[51] In addition, the courts have seized upon the viable proposal obligation to send a message that one should consider repayment of debts before looking to bankruptcy. In Re Imbeault the court concluded that the bankrupts had decided to:[52]

> take the easy way out. They have an income. They did not offer a viable proposal to their creditors . . . Unfortunately, there is a tendency for bankrupts to ignore a hard look at their spending habits, eliminate unnecessary expenses and make viable proposals to their creditors. Instead they take the easy way out, no doubt encouraged by the volume of advertising by trustees.

---

51 In Re Ollivier (1999) 11 CBR (4th) 87 (Alta QB), the court concluded that the bankrupt had substantial excess income and that a viable proposal could have been made. The court imposed a conditional order of discharge for one year requiring the bankrupt to pay $200 per month. In Re Kanovsky (2000) 21 CBR (4th) 273 (Man. QB), the court refused an absolute discharge on the basis of the trustee's recommendation that the bankrupt had substantial surplus income. The court ordered that the bankrupt contribute $20,000 to the estate within five years. See also Caisse Populaire de Shippagan Ltee v. Ward (2000) 21 CBR (4th) 211 (NB QB) (conditional discharge upon payment of $15,000 over three years); Re Neudorf [1999] OJ No. 3101 (QL) (SCJ) (conditional discharge upon payment of $5,234.33 at the rate of $300 per month); Re Khosla (2000) 19 CBR (4th) 240 (Alta QB) (discharge refused on a number of grounds including the bankrupt's refusal to pay surplus income requirements); Re Nosal [2001] SJ No. 559 (QL) (QB) (failure to pay surplus income to trustee, discharge conditional upon bankrupt paying $5,000 in monthly instalments of $200). However, compare Re Hynes (2000) 20 CBR (4th) 98, 104, para. 24 (NSSC) (discharge granted where debtor's income did not meet minimum guidelines: 'The Bankrupt is entitled to retain a reasonable amount of her income to sustain herself and her family').
52 [2000] AJ No. 1430 (QL) para. 7–8 (QB).

Similarly, in *Re Illes* the court in referring to the obligation to consider a viable proposal noted that 'bankruptcy should be a last resort. A debtor should first try to compromise their debts directly with their creditors or with the assistance of a trustee, be encouraged to consider other options before taking an assignment.'[53]

It has been argued that the effect of these new provisions 'may encourage many debtors to consider a proposal first, rather than a bankruptcy, as a solution to their financial problems'.[54] That is putting it rather mildly. The new regime is specifically 'designed to make straight bankruptcies a less attractive route and to steer consumers more energetically towards consumer proposals'.[55] Indeed the Senate Standing Committee on Banking Trade and Commerce explicitly recognised this in its report on the Bill:[56]

> Bill C-5 contains a number of provisions designed to reduce the attractiveness of consumer bankruptcies and to encourage more insolvent debtors to opt for a consumer proposal under Part III Division 2 of the BIA.

The aspirations of Parliament appear to have been initially met. The number of Division 2 proposals has increased from 1,791 in 1993 to 12,392 in 2000 whereas since 1997 bankruptcy filings have decreased.[57] In a recent report, the Office of the Superintendent of Bankruptcy noted that over the period 1995 to 1999 'there has been a noticeable change in the mix of insolvency filings' with an increase in the total proportion of filings that are proposals.[58]

Rehabilitation reconsidered

The theme of the legislation is clearly debtor responsibility. A review of the Parliamentary Debates and Committee Hearings reveals not only a strong commitment to this theme but also suggests that Parliament has redefined debtor rehabilitation. During the introduction of the Bill the Parliamentary Secretary to the

53 (2000) 20 CBR (4th) 239, 241 per Registrar Laycock (Alta QB).
54 Marantz and Chartrand, 'Bankruptcy and Insolvency Law Reform Continues', 128.
55 Ziegel, 'Canadian Bankruptcy Reform', 111–12.
56 Senate, Standing Committee on Banking, Trade and Commerce, 12th Report (4 February 1997).
57 Statistics available for 2001 indicate that to the end of October, 11,096 Division 2 proposals were filed. Since 1997, the number of consumer bankruptcies has fallen from a high of 85,297 in 1997 to 75,137 in 2000. To the end of October 2001, there were 66,669 consumer bankruptcies. See Office of Superintendent of Bankruptcy, *Bankruptcy Statistics*, www.strategis.ic.gc.ca/SSG/br01011e.html.
58 Office of Superintendent of Bankruptcy, *The National Insolvency Forum National Report* (March 2000), 13. Ramsay notes that proposals are now 13.6 per cent of consumer bankruptcy filings nationally: Ramsay, 'Market Imperatives', 434.

Ministry of Industry indicated that in drafting the Bill the government had been guided by three principles:[59]

> First, Canadian bankruptcy law will continue to provide a framework in which it is preferable for consumers or businesses to reorganize their affairs rather than declare bankruptcy. Second, the legislation emphasizes the importance of measures to promote consumer rehabilitation. We want to create an environment in which consumers can act as responsible citizens. Third, the legislation is aimed at promoting fairness to both creditors and debtors.

The aim of rehabilitation is not new. Modern bankruptcy legislation has traditionally raised debtor rehabilitation as a goal of bankruptcy law. However, Parliament's recent focus on the rehabilitation of debts and the requirement to make payments from future income contrasts with more traditional notions of debtor rehabilitation that focused on the freedom from the burdens of debt.

While the Canadian form of the discharge since 1919 has always recognised the ability of the courts to impose conditions, including the requirement for debtors to pay a fixed amount over time from future income,[60] nevertheless Canadian courts have consistently recognised the importance of debtor rehabilitation through the granting of a discharge. Rehabilitation of the debtor has been the focus of a number of statements by the judiciary. What is important to recognise is that there is a 'nexus between the extinguishment of debts and rehabilitation'. When using the latter term, many courts suggest that they mean 'restoration of the debtor to a former state of solvency; and that is synonymous with discharge itself'.[61] For example, the Ontario Court of Appeal in the recent case of *Simone* v. *Daley* stated:[62]

> An important purpose of bankruptcy legislation is to encourage the rehabilitation of an honest but unfortunate debtor, and to permit his or her

59 *House of Commons Debates* (27 May 1996), 3033 (M. Bodnar, Parliamentary Secretary to Minister of Industry).
60 See, e.g., *Marshall* v. *Bank of Nova Scotia* (1986) 62 CBR (NS) 118, para. 29 per Hutcheon JA (BCCA). In *Marshall*, the British Columbia Court of Appeal stated that the judge must balance 'the rehabilitation of the bankrupt, and that rehabilitation being supported by sufficient income to provide the requirements of living in an appropriate manner, against the rights of the creditors, who may on that balance be entitled to receive an additional sum'. The focus in Canada has been on the rehabilitation of honest but unfortunate debtors. Canadian courts have also recognised the need to impose conditions where there has been misconduct on the part of the debtor. See, e.g., *Bank of Montreal* v. *Giannotti* (2000) 197 DLR (4th) 266 (Ont. CA). Numerous courts have expressed the need to balance the rights of the debtor to be rehabilitated with the interests of the creditor and the broader public. See e.g., *McAfee* v. *Westmore* (1988) 49 DLR (4th) 401 (BCCA).
61 J. Ferron, ' "Rehabilitation" and "Fresh Start": Concepts that Never Were' (1996) 13 *National Insolvency Review* 39. See also Canada, *Bankruptcy and Insolvency: Report of the Study Committee on Bankruptcy and Insolvency Legislation* (Ottawa: Information Canada, 1997), 87, where the Committee stated: 'We believe that, in respect of the individual debtor, the principal objective of the bankruptcy system should be to rehabilitate him and give him an opportunity to make a fresh economic start in life.'
62 (1999) 170 DLR (4th) 215, 226–7 per Blair J (Ont. CA).

reintegration into society – subject to reasonable conditions – by obtaining a discharge from the continued burden of crushing financial obligations which cannot be met.

The Supreme Court of Canada in *Industrial Acceptance Corp.* v. *Lalonde*[63] also linked the concept of debtor rehabilitation to the discharge. Justice Estey stated that 'the purpose and object of the *Bankruptcy Act* is to equitably distribute the assets of the debtor and to permit his rehabilitation as a citizen, unfettered by past debts'.[64] Similarly, the British Columbia Court of Appeal in *Re Irwin* stated that one of the purposes of bankruptcy law is to enable an 'honest debtor, who has been unfortunate in business, to secure a discharge which will give him a fresh start and enable him to resume the place in business life for which he is equipped by training and experience'.[65] The purpose of bankruptcy law is 'to make possible the rehabilitation of a bankrupt as a citizen free of the burden of past debts'.[66]

In contrast, the recent reforms have cast rehabilitation in a newer light. Rehabilitation will now be achieved by a greater commitment on the part of the debtor to the repayment of debts. Debtor responsibility will ensure that debts are rehabilitated on behalf of the creditors.[67] On the third reading, the Parliamentary Secretary to

---

63 [1952] 2 SCR 109.

64 *Ibid.*, 120, per Estey J. The Supreme Court of Canada later recognised that rehabilitation did not solely result from the discharge. In *Vachon* v. *Canada (Employment & Immigration Commission)* [1985] 2 SCR 417, 430, the Court noted that rehabilitation begins when the debtor is put into bankruptcy with measures that are designed to give him the minimum needed for assistance. More recently, the Supreme Court recognised that while the first purpose of bankruptcy law was to distribute the debtor's assets, the second 'was to provide for the financial rehabilitation of insolvent persons': *Royal Bank of Canada* v. *North American Life Assurance Co.* [1996] 1 SCR 325, 337, per Gonthier J.

65 (1994) 112 DLR (4th) 164, 180, per Rowles JA (BCCA). See also *Re Newsome* [1927] 3 DLR 828 (Ont. SC [Bktcy]); *Re Blahut* (1970) 14 CBR (NS) 82, 83, per Houlden J (Ont. SC); *Re Beaumont* (1976) 22 CBR (NS) 287 (BCSC).

66 *Re Gaklis* (1984) 49 CBR (NS) 303 (NSSC). See also *Cleve's Sporting Goods Ltd* v. *Jones* (1986) 58 CBR (NS) 304 (NSCA); *Re Munro* (1986) 62 CBR (NS) 269, 274 (Sask. QB), varied (1987) 70 CBR (NS) 260 (Sask CA) ('The purpose of the Bankruptcy Act with respect to individual debtors is to permit their rehabilitation as citizens free from an overwhelming burden of debts.'); *Re Green* (1925) 5 CBR 580 (NBSC) ('the Legislature has always recognised the interest that the State has in a debtor being released from the overwhelming pressure of his debts, and that it is undesirable that a citizen should be so weighted down by his debts as to be incapable of performing the ordinary duties of citizenship'); *Re Wensley* (1985) 59 CBR (NS) 95 (Alta QB); *Zemlak* v. *Zemlak* (1987) 42 DLR (4th) 395, 405 (Sask. CA) ('We accept that it is a basic purpose of bankruptcy laws to give debtors a fresh start in life free from creditor harassment and from the worries and pressures of too much debt').

67 Robert Klotz, Chair of the National Bankruptcy and Insolvency Section, Canadian Bar Association, in testimony before the House of Commons Standing Committee on Industry claimed that the 'responsible alternative' to bankruptcy was a consumer proposal. He claimed that the consensus in the credit community was that it is better to 'encourage debtors to take the responsible step of addressing their creditors on a consensual basis through a proposal': House of Commons, Standing Committee on Industry, Evidence of Proceedings (17 September 1996), 1600.

the Minister of Industry summed up the leading principles behind the consumer bankruptcy reforms:[68]

> Bill C-5 also addresses consumer bankruptcy. It provides an opportunity for debtor consumers to be rehabilitated and to act responsibly. I believe the vast majority of consumers who run into major financial difficulties want to fulfil their obligations. I am sure that we all know of stories where someone has run up their debts and regards bankruptcy as an easy way to discharge their responsibility, easier that is than taking the rough measure necessary to pay back creditors over time.
>
> The legislation before us puts more pressure on debtors to rehabilitate. It encourages consumers to act more responsibly by repaying at least a portion of their debts when they can.

Similarly, the Parliamentary Secretary for the Minister of International Trade claimed that the government 'wanted to see if there was some way debts could be rehabilitated and put over a longer period of time. In this way Canadians could maintain their dignity. It is not a dignified thing for many Canadians to be forced into personal bankruptcy.'[69]

No longer will the discharge be the prime means of debtor rehabilitation. The route to rehabilitation now lies through repayment plans. When the debate moved to the Senate, Senator Kirby concluded that bankruptcy laws 'affect the moral and ethical tone of the marketplace in which we count on people to be responsible citizens and responsible debtors'. According to Senator Kirby, rehabilitation still lay at the core of bankruptcy law. However, rehabilitation was no longer linked to the discharge:[70]

> One of the basic intentions of the amendments in Bill C-5 is to provide an opportunity for debtor consumers to be rehabilitated quickly and to act responsibly. One of the major thrusts of these amendments is to encourage debtors to rehabilitate rather than declare bankruptcy. The bill also encourages consumer debtors to act more responsibly by repaying, where they can, at least a portion of their income.

Not only did Parliament recast debtor rehabilitation, but there was also an explicit acknowledgement that that regime recast the balance in favour of creditors:[71]

> Indeed, honourable Senators, the current rules do not encourage responsible debtor behaviour. The new rules contained in the amendments which form Bill C-5 take steps to make the bankruptcy process more fair and reasonable

68 *House of Commons Debates* (22 October 1996), 5532 (M. Bodnar, Parliamentary Secretary to Minister of Industry).
69 *House of Commons Debates* (22 October 1996), 5543 (R. MacDonald, Parliamentary Secretary to Minister for International Trade).
70 *Debates of the Senate* (28 October 1996), 2110 (M. Kirby).   71 *Ibid.*

to creditors. They, in effect, shift the balance which is substantially more fair and reasonable to creditors.

Academics have subsequently criticised the shift in the balance. The reforms have been characterised as 'coercive' and meeting 'the creditors' fondest expectations'.[72] However, it is important to note that there has been more than a shift simply in favour of creditors. As evident from the comments in Parliament and the structure of the legislation itself, there has been a shift away from viewing the discharge as a means of rehabilitation towards a notion that debt repayment plans offer a more responsible way to rehabilitation. Several Canadian and American scholars have noted this broader trend. Iain Ramsay, for example, notes that the oldest paradigm of bankruptcy law was a response to deviant behaviour. He argues it evolved from its criminal law origins into a routinised administrative procedure to allow an individual re-entry into the world of credit. However, more recently Ramsay suggests, there has been a reconceptualisation of the 'debtor as a deviant'.[73] He argues that this 'reconceptualization views the debtor as a person in need of treatment for a failure to manage their finances adequately'.[74] He points to a broader continuing belief that 'a relaxation of insolvency standards will affect commercial morality and reduce consumers' sense of responsibility to repay debts'.[75]

A similar debate has been raging in the United States where a number of authors have noted the shift in attitudes. William Whitford in a recent paper illustrates what he calls the 'lessened public commitment to the core values that have historically justified a fresh start in consumer bankruptcy'.[76] Perhaps emblematic of that change is the recent Congressional effort to enact legislation that would impose a means test as a mechanism to keep debtors out of Chapter 7 when they are deemed to have an ability to pay creditors, and force debtors into a Chapter 13 repayment plan.[77] The new emphasis on debt repayment from future income suggests that there has been a 'paradigm shift' in the 'collective public assumptions concerning the opportunity to discharge individual debts in bankruptcy'.[78] Thomas Jackson noticed this general trend in a 1985 article on the discharge:[79]

72 Ziegel, 'Canadian Bankruptcy Reform', 120. See also Ziegel, 'Philosophy and Design', 232.
73 Ramsay, 'Models of Consumer Bankruptcy', 271.   74 Ibid.
75 Ibid., 272. See, e.g., the comments by Master Funduk in Re O'Keefe [2001] AJ No. 521, para. 7 (QL) (Alta QB): 'Debtors who overuse credit are not unfortunate. They are financially irresponsible, some might even say stupid.'
76 W. Whitford, 'Changing Definitions of Fresh Start in US Bankruptcy Law' (1997) 20 Journal of Consumer Policy 179, 191.
77 See H. R. 333, Bankruptcy Abuse Prevention and Consumer Protection Act of 2001; S. 420 Bankruptcy Reform Act 2001. 'Bill on Bankruptcy to Make it Harder to Wipe out Debts', New York Times (13 March 2001). For an interest group explanation of why the debate has changed, see E. Warren, 'The Changing Politics of American Bankruptcy Reform' (1999) 37 Osgoode Hall LJ 189.
78 R. Coulson, 'Consumer Abuse of Bankruptcy: an Evolving Philosophy of Debtor Qualification for Bankruptcy Discharge' (1998) 62 Alb L Rev 467.
79 T. Jackson, 'The Fresh Start Policy in Bankruptcy Law' (1985) 98 Harv L Rev 1393, 1431–2.

Bankruptcy legislation has been moving in the direction of permitting and legislators have even been contemplating requiring an individual debtor to satisfy some or all of his existing liabilities out of his future income stream. Thus bankruptcy law appears to be relaxing its protection of human capital and enhancing its protection of existing tangible assets.

Critics of efforts to steer debtors into repayment plans raise two objections. First, they challenge the assumption that vast numbers of debtors have escaped through bankruptcy with surplus income. In Canada, two separate empirical studies have called into question the view that large numbers of debtors have surplus income.[80] Iain Ramsay concludes that 'there is little evidence from the data that there are substantial numbers of individuals who can pay their debts, but are successfully using the system as a method of "washing out" their debts'.[81]

A second challenge, however, is to query the impact of the more restrictive regime upon debtor behaviour. The merits of mandatory repayment plans have been debated for some time in the United States and some have raised the issue of whether it would provoke consumer resistance and lessen incentives to work.[82] The United States Bankruptcy Commission Report in 1973 suggested that imposition of a mandatory repayment plan 'would be almost bound to encourage the debtor to change employment and, if necessary to move to another area'. Petitioning debtors turned away by the court 'would be motivated to change jobs and locations to get away from creditors'.[83] Margaret Howard argues that requiring debtors to complete a repayment plan conflicts with the value of economic rehabilitation and does nothing to return a debtor to economic productivity. The debtor, she argues, is held in 'economic limbo while tied to past obligations'.[84] Repayment plans, it is argued, discourage enterprise[85] and economic productivity.[86] Restrictions on the availability of the discharge will have an impact on the debtor's willingness to act entrepreneurally.[87]

Thomas Jackson notes that the preservation of human capital and exempting future income from creditors is one of the justifications for the discharge. Of the various forms of wealth, human capital is the least diversifiable but also has the

80 See Ramsay, 'Individual Bankruptcy'; Schwartz, 'Empirical Dimensions'.
81 Ramsay, 'Individual Bankruptcy', 78.
82 See Ziegel, 'Philosophy and Design', 245, summarising traditional arguments against a mandatory repayment plan.
83 *Report of the Commission on Bankruptcy Laws of the United States* (1973), 159.
84 M. Howard, 'A Theory of Discharge in Consumer Bankruptcy' (1987) 48 *Ohio St LJ* 1047, 1062, 1085.
85 See Coulson, 'Consumer Abuse of Bankruptcy', 523, arguing that mandatory repayment plans may have the result of 'discouragement of enterprise by those debtors who see themselves three to five years as working for their creditors rather than themselves or family'.
86 See Whitford, 'Changing Definitions', 191.
87 See J. Czarnetzky, 'The Individual and Failure: A Theory of the Bankruptcy Discharge' (2000) 32 *Ariz St LJ* 393, 463. It is not clear whether the author's entrepreneurial hypothesis has application to all individual debtors, particularly consumer debtors.

most direct bearing on the future wellbeing of the debtor and those who depend upon him or her.[88] He argues that if the discharge did not protect human capital many individuals would 'substitute leisure' for work to avoid having to pay creditors.[89]

In the Canadian context, it has been suggested that the new regime may in fact deter people from using bankruptcy altogether. Under the new legislation, it is argued, debtors may lose their incentive to work and the regime itself may encourage deviancy on the part of debtors to avoid debts.[90] The 1970 Study Committee on Bankruptcy also recognised this theme. The report concluded that 'whenever the right to bankruptcy as an "escape door" is restricted, or when it is too difficult to become a bankrupt, there is a great danger that debtors will resort to crime and desert their families they can no longer support and their responsibilities they can no longer face'.[91]

The Canadian reforms, which have been in effect since 30 April 1998, may provide a source of empirical study to test the above claims. Further, the traditional absence of a discharge in many European countries might provide comparative evidence on the impact on debtors in a restrictive or non-discharge regime. Iain Ramsay suggests that if there were detailed empirical studies from Europe that illustrated the reduced motivations in debtors to continue working 'it would be a powerful argument against reducing the availability of the discharge in North America'.[92]

While it is conceded that these studies may provide ammunition for those who oppose the new restrictions, it should be noted that it is not the first time in Canadian history that limitations have been placed upon the discharge. Canada briefly experimented with bankruptcy legislation in 1869 and again in 1875. In reaction to the claim that bankruptcy law made it too easy to escape obligations, Parliament throughout the 1870s sought to make it more difficult to obtain a

88 T. Jackson, *Logic and Limits of Bankruptcy Law* (Cambridge, Mass.: Harvard University Press, 1986), 256. Jackson, however, suggests that there is merit to allowing debtors to choose whether to protect human capital at the expense of other assets by electing for a liquidation plan or by choosing to protect current assets at the expense of human capital by opting for a repayment plan. He suggests that individuals are unlikely to make errors in judgment in choosing whether to protect human capital or current assets. This assumes, however, that debtors are fully informed and understand the consequences of the decision.

89 *Ibid.*, 256–7.

90 I. Ramsay, Professor of Law, Osgoode Hall Law School, House of Commons, Standing Committee on Industry, *Evidence of Proceedings* (25 September 1996), 1600. In reaction to the recent Congressional bankruptcy reform efforts, Lawrence King stated in a *New York Times* interview: 'I fear this will end up creating an underground economy . . . people will go off the books. They'll ask to be paid in cash. They'll get a false Social Security number. They'll move.': 'Bill on Bankruptcy to Make it Harder to Wipe out Debts', *New York Times* (14 March 2001).

91 Canada, *Report of the Study Committee on Bankruptcy and Insolvency Legislation* (1970), 87.

92 Ramsay, 'Models of Consumer Bankruptcy', 283. For an overview of European reforms, see J. Niemi-Kiesiläinen, 'Consumer Bankruptcy in Comparison: Do We Cure a Market Failure or a Social Problem?' (1999) 37 *Osgoode Hall LJ* 473.

discharge before finally ending a debtor's right to obtain a release from the burdens of debt by repealing the bankruptcy statute in 1880. It was not until 1919 that Canada again adopted a national bankruptcy regime.

While independent historical factors explain the pattern of legislation in the late nineteenth and early twentieth centuries, what might be of interest to the contemporary debate is how creditors and debtors responded to a restrictive or non-bankruptcy regime. The historical record does indeed reveal evidence of debtor deviance and efforts to flee the jurisdiction for the United States. Contrary to the assumption that the notion of a fresh start is a twentieth-century concept, the history of Canadian bankruptcy law illustrates that there was recognition that the discharge had an important role to play in returning the debtor to the productive economy. Creditors also recognised this and after experiencing nearly forty years without a national law ensured that the new Bankruptcy Act of 1919 contained a discharge.

The discharge in Canadian bankruptcy law: a historical perspective[93]

The Pre-Confederation era

Prior to Confederation, there was little consensus on the need for bankruptcy statutes in the various colonies and provinces that would ultimately make up Canada. Many regions never enacted any bankruptcy statutes prior to entering Confederation. The only major statutes enacted prior to 1867 were the Lower Canadian Bankruptcy Act of 1839 and the Province of Canada Acts of 1843 and 1864.[94] One of the first recorded comments on the merits of the discharge can be found in a pamphlet authored in 1831 by a leading proponent for bankruptcy reform in Nova Scotia:[95]

> In cases of insolvency it also appears conformable to the immutable principles of justice that the effects of the debtor should be divided among all his creditors in proportions according to the amount of their claims. Nothing can be more simple than an arrangement of this kind, and it at once would restore the honest man to the power of pursuing his occupations without the perpetual annoyance of duns, the embarrassment and wretchedness of an undecided situation, and the tortures of dependence which to the honourable mind are worse than death.

93 For a detailed account, see Telfer, 'Reconstructing Bankruptcy'; T. Telfer, 'The Canadian Bankruptcy Act of 1919: Public Legislation or Private Interest?' (1994–5) 24 *Canadian Business Law Journal* 357.
94 Canada, House of Commons, Select Committee, *Third Report of the Select Committee on Bankruptcy and Insolvency* (17 April 1868), 8. Also reported in (1868) *Lower Canada Law Journal* 46, 52.
95 B. Murdoch, *An Essay on the Mischievous Tendency of Imprisoning for Debt and in Other Civil Cases* (2nd edn, Halifax: Cunnabell, 1831), 18.

A similar view was expressed in *Upper Canada Law Journal* editorials. Written during the period when no bankruptcy law governed the provinces of Canada, the authors expressed concern over the lack of a discharge. In the absence of a discharge, a debtor would continue to have 'the millstone of debt about his neck'.[96] Debtors burdened with debt were of little use to society. 'The man may be useful if free; he is worse than useless if he is not.'[97] In the absence of a discharge, debtors took extreme measures. Individuals, 'driven in self defence' to remove themselves from the reach of creditors, left for the United States as they found Canadian laws 'void of mercy'. The 'expatriation' of traders was a loss to Canada.[98]

John Abbott, Solicitor General of the Province of Canada and Dean of Law at McGill, drafted the Insolvent Act of 1864, which was the most significant piece of bankruptcy legislation in the pre-Confederation period. In the introduction to his text on the Act, Abbott outlined the need for reform:[99]

> There has been for some years past an urgent demand in Canada, for a law creating a summary mode of realizing and distributing the estates of Insolvents, and of affording relief from liability, to debtors making full disclosure and delivery of their estates to their Creditors. The absence of such a law left the failing debtor no chance of success in any future enterprise, unless he could succeed in the almost hopeless task of procuring a discharge from every one of his creditors. Thus many such were tempted to secure their remaining assets by dishonest devices, rather than leave themselves destitute by resigning themselves to their Creditors.

The Act of 1864 would influence the later post-Confederation statutes passed in 1869 and 1875. In many respects it was a more liberal regime than its later counterparts as Parliament would subsequently restrict the legislation in response to demands for a tougher regime. The Act of 1864 permitted both voluntary and involuntary proceedings. However, like the later Acts of 1869 and 1875, Abbott retained the historic trader rule to limit the scope of the legislation.[100] Bankruptcy law in England had been traditionally limited only to traders. Only those engaged in the business of buying and selling were brought within the purview of the legislation. In England, the trader rule can be traced to 1571 and was abolished in 1861.[101] Debtors not engaged in business were not eligible for the discharge.

---

96 'A Bankruptcy Law Required' (1863) 9 *UCLJ* 141.
97 'Bankruptcy and Insolvency' (1861) 7 *UCLJ* 10, 11.
98 'Shall We Have a Bankrupt Law?' (1858) 4 *UCLJ* 2, 3–4.
99 J. Abbott, *The Insolvent Act of 1864* (Quebec: Rollo and Adam, 1864), preface.
100 The trader rule only applied in Canada East while in Canada West any person unable to meet his engagements was able to make an assignment in bankruptcy: Insolvent Act of 1864, s. 2. In Canada West, the trader rule applied to involuntary proceedings. Thus, only traders could be forced into bankruptcy. See s. 3(2) of the Act.
101 See L. Friedman and T. Niemira, 'The Concept of the "Trader" in Early Bankruptcy Law' (1958) 5 *St Louis U LJ* 223.

The discharge was tightly controlled by the creditors. Debtors were required to obtain the consent of a majority in number of creditors representing three-quarters in value of the liabilities. If the creditors agreed in the requisite numbers an application could be made to the court for confirmation of the discharge.[102] At confirmation, any creditor could object to the discharge on the grounds of, among others, 'fraud or evil practice in procuring the consent of the creditors to the discharge'.[103] The court could either confirm the discharge absolutely or conditionally, or make an order for suspension. Debtors who were unable to obtain the consent of creditors could apply to the court for a discharge after one year.[104]

The Act of 1864 did not escape criticism. In 1867, a Resolution of the County of Huron asked for the repeal of the Insolvent Act of 1864. The council viewed 'with great apprehension, the action taken by so many parties, in taking advantage of the Provisions of the Insolvent Act of 1864'. 'It is notorious that numbers, daily increasing, resort to the Act to shirk their just debts, which they might exert themselves to pay, had they not so facile a method to relieve themselves from their debts.'[105]

Arguments along these lines would continue to be raised throughout the nineteenth century.

The Insolvent Act 1869

Following Confederation, the Dominion Parliament enacted the Insolvent Act of 1869 which created a uniform bankruptcy regime for the new country. The legislation, like its 1864 predecessor permitted both voluntary and involuntary proceedings and was limited to traders. One author suggested that the inclusion of voluntary proceedings was in accordance with the spirit of modern bankruptcy law.[106] However, this was an overly optimistic view. By adopting a voluntary procedure in 1869, Parliament may have moved beyond what was acceptable to society. Voluntary proceedings proved contentious after 1869. Parliament abolished this right in 1875.[107]

The discharge provisions of the Insolvent Act of 1869 illustrated society's deep mistrust of debtors. Parliament took steps to tighten further access to the discharge. Like the Act of 1864, debtors required creditor consent and subsequent court approval in order to obtain a discharge.[108] The court retained the discretion to suspend the discharge for up to five years. Creditor consent was not always possible, and the Act provided a separate route to the discharge. After one year, debtors could

102 Abbott, *Insolvent Act of 1864*, 63.   103 Insolvent Act of 1864, s. 9(6).
104 Insolvent Act of 1864, s. 9(11).
105 Resolution of Corporation of the County of Huron, at June Session 1867.
106 J. Edgar, *The Insolvent Act of 1869* (Toronto: Copp Clark, 1869), 38.
107 Insolvent Act of 1875.
108 Insolvent Act of 1869, ss. 94, 98, 101. See *Austin v. Gordon* (1872) 32 UCQB 621.

apply for a judicial discharge.[109] However, creditors could effectively block this alternative route. A majority of the creditors representing three-fourths of the claims could apply to the court requesting suspension, or classification or both. The court did not have any independent discretion on this issue and had to follow the direction of the creditors.[110]

In a further innovation the legislation permitted the court to issue a second-class discharge. Both a first- and second-class discharge released a bankrupt from his debts. However, the classification of discharges represented an official statement as to the moral trustworthiness of a debtor. First-class discharges were awarded in most cases where the bankruptcy had arisen from unavoidable loss or misfortune.[111] The court granted second-class discharges when:[112]

> The Insolvent has been guilty of misconduct in the management of his business, by extravagance in his expenses, recklessness in endorsing or becoming surety for others, continuing his trade unduly after he believed himself to be insolvent, incurring debts without reasonable expectation of paying them ... or negligence in keeping his books and accounts.

England introduced the classification of discharges in 1849 and abandoned the regime in 1861.[113] John Abbott followed this lead when he drafted the Insolvent Act of 1864 and excluded a class system.[114] However, the Insolvent Act of 1869 reintroduced official moral judgment into bankruptcy proceedings. John Popham, author of a text on the 1869 Act, offered a rationale for the class system:[115]

> It would seem but just there should be a distinction between the discharge given to an insolvent whose losses were unavoidable, and whose dealings were honourable; and that to another whose conduct bordered on recklessness or fraud, though insufficiently so to warrant a refusal of his discharge.

The Insolvent Act of 1875 and repeal

There was a consensus that the Act of 1869 had not gone far enough. Creditors required further means of discovering and punishing fraud.[116] The new Liberal government responded with a more creditor-friendly regime. The Insolvent Act of

109 See Abbott, Insolvent Act of 1864, 70. See also Insolvent Act of 1864, s. 9(10); Insolvent Act of 1869, s. 105.
110 Insolvent Act of 1869, s. 107.
111 See J. Popham, The Insolvent Act of 1869 (Montreal: Dawson Bros, 1869), 138.
112 Insolvent Act of 1869, s. 103.   113 Popham, Insolvent Act of 1869, 138.
114 Edgar, Insolvent Act of 1869, 120.   115 Popham, Insolvent Act of 1869, 138.
116 C. Beausoleil, La loi de faillite (Montreal: S.N., 1877), 2.

1875 came into force on 1 September 1875.[117] The '"poor creditor" proposes now to take his innings, the "poor debtor" having had ... a good time of it for many years past'.[118] Although the 1869 legislation had contained many provisions favourable to creditors, the 'object of the [1875] bill was to give the creditors greater control of the estate'.[119]

Like the 1869 Act, the Insolvent Act of 1875 also applied only to traders.[120] However, the most significant policy change was the decision to abolish voluntary assignments.[121] The Insolvent Act of 1875 only allowed creditors to initiate proceedings.[122] If bankruptcy law sought to balance the interests of creditors and debtors, the abolition of voluntary proceedings represented a sharp turn in favour of creditors.[123] Voluntary assignments were no longer acceptable in the public eye.[124]

The discharge provisions further restricted the eligibility of debtors to obtain a release of their debts.[125] Like the Act of 1869, debtors required both creditor consent and the approval of a court in order to obtain a discharge.[126] Debtors could also apply for a judicial discharge after a one-year wait.[127] The court had the discretion to suspend or grant a second-class discharge if the debtor engaged in some form of misconduct. The court, according to one author, had a duty to ensure that 'the insolvency law is not used as a mere white-washing machine'.[128]

The Insolvent Act of 1875 also introduced another new hurdle for debtors. Under s. 58, a judge had the discretion to suspend or refuse the discharge altogether if it appeared that the dividend from the estate would not pay 33 cents in the dollar. One Member of Parliament explained the rationale for the new limitation:[129] 'Anyone whose estate could not pay 33 cents in the dollar, who had not been overtaken by some unexpected calamity, had no right to be whitewashed or to receive credit again.'

117 Insolvent Act of 1875, s. 148. See S. Clarke, *The Insolvent Act of 1875* (Toronto: Copp Clark, 1877), 2. The Insolvent Act of 1875 repealed the Insolvent Act of 1869 and amending Acts.
118 'Review of MacMahon, *Insolvent Act of 1875*' (1875) 9 *Can LJ (NS)* 259.
119 *House of Commons Debates* (19 February 1875), 239; *House of Commons Debates* (20 March 1875); *House of Commons Debates* (25 March 1875). See also I. Wotherspoon, *The Insolvent Act of 1875* (Montreal: Dawson Bros, 1875), 38.
120 'The list of "trades, callings or employments" which is given is copied from the English Act': 'The Act Respecting Insolvency', *Monetary Times* (26 March 1875), 1006.
121 'The abrogation of the power of voluntary assignments ... is the greatest change effected by the present Act': Wotherspoon, *The Insolvent Act of 1875*, vi.
122 Insolvent Act of 1875, ss. 3, 4, 9.
123 See Wotherspoon, *The Insolvent Act of 1875*, 38; L. J. De la Durantaye, *Traité de la faillite* (Montreal: Chez L'Auteur, 1935), 25.
124 De la Durantaye, *Traité de la faillite*, 25.   125 Wotherspoon, *The Insolvent Act of 1875*, vii.
126 The Act of 1875 also required creditors to consent to a discharge. Debtors had to obtain the agreement of a majority of creditors representing three-quarters of the value of liabilities.
127 The discharge provisions in the Insolvent Act of 1875 are found in ss. 49–66. See Clarke, *The Insolvent Act of 1875*, 161–2.
128 Wotherspoon, *The Insolvent Act of 1875*, 175.
129 *House of Commons Debates* (25 March 1875), 912.

However, the 33 cents in the dollar restriction was ineffective as courts refused to exercise their discretion and deny a discharge even when dividends did not meet the minimum level. Critics pointed to the discretionary power of the judge being exercised in a 'compassionate spirit'.[130] When a creditor forced a debtor into bankruptcy, the dividend rarely reached the 33 cents level.[131] In 1877, Parliament amended the Act and imposed a requirement of a dividend level of 50 cents in the dollar before a debtor could obtain a discharge.[132]

In 1878[133] and 1879 the Government faced several private member Bills calling for the repeal of all insolvency legislation.[134] No longer committed to retaining the federal law, and uncertain how to proceed, the Government established a committee to study the matter.[135] The committee's bill was a compromise that purported to appeal to the 'repealers ... and [to] the champions of insolvency law and insolvency principles'.[136] Its purpose was described as follows:[137] 'They had stripped the old Act of its evil as thoroughly as if they had repealed it, and had furnished the commercial community with what they did desire, a law by which the creditors might possess themselves of an insolvent's estate and fairly divide among themselves its proceeds.'

Bill No. 85, if enacted, would have become the Insolvent Act of 1879.[138] The committee listed several evils associated with the bankruptcy regime. It had given rise to recklessness and extravagance in trade. Rather than inducing men to extricate themselves from financial difficulties through hard work, the Insolvent Act of 1875 was available as an 'easy process of starting anew in life, free from the load of debt'. The committee specifically intended to 'diminish the facilities now possessed by a debtor for obtaining a discharge'. In addition, it sought to increase the grounds of opposition to the discharge and to extend and increase the 'precautions for ascertaining the conduct of the insolvent'.[139] It 'struck the axe at the root of that evil' by requiring a debtor to obtain the consent of creditors representing 4/5 in

130 *House of Commons Debates* (26 February 1877), 292.
131 Ibid., 293. See 'Some Provisions of the New Insolvent Act', *Monetary Times* (3 September 1875), 265.
132 40 Vict., c. 41., (1877), ss. 14, 15.
133 In 1878, another repeal Bill was introduced but did not pass: *House of Commons Debates* (18 February 1878), 349. It was agreed on 27 March 1878 to delay the Bill six months: *House of Commons Debates* (27 March 1878), 1453. For criticism of the ease in which discharges were granted, see 'Proposed Repeal of the Insolvency Laws', *Monetary Times* (19 April 1872), 826.
134 See Bills presented on 19, 20 February, and 3, 4 March 1879: *House of Commons Debates* (19, 20 February, 3, 4 March 1879), 41, 48, 107, 126.
135 See *House of Commons Debates* (7 March 1879), 189. See also J. Bicknell, 'The Advisability of Establishing a Bankruptcy Court in Canada' (1913) 33 *Canadian Law Times* 35, 43.
136 *House of Commons Debates* (29 April 1879), 1605 (Girouard).   137 Ibid., 1599.
138 Bill 85, *An Act to Repeal the Insolvent Act of 1875, and the Acts Amending it, and to Make Provision for the Liquidation of the Estates of Insolvent Debtors*, 1st Sess., 4th Parl., 1879, s. 135.
139 The *Journal of Commerce* reproduced a memorandum attached to the report of the Parliamentary Committee: 'The Insolvent Law' (1879) *J of Commerce* 274.

number and 4/5 in value.[140] 'They had made it impossible for [a debtor] to obtain his discharge as a matter of right, under any circumstances whatever, from the obligations he had voluntarily assumed.'[141]

The House of Commons debated Bill 85 at length. However, in the end it unexpectedly abandoned the comprehensive reform bill to consider Bill 15, which simply proposed to repeal the Insolvent Act of 1875.[142] The House of Commons voted to repeal the Insolvent Act of 1875 on 5 May 1879.[143] The repeal bill failed to gain support in the Senate.[144] However, the following year a repeal bill quickly gained approval in both chambers.[145] The bill to repeal the Insolvent Act of 1875 received assent on 1 April 1880.[146]

The impact of repeal

By repeal, Parliament had responded to the claims that bankruptcy law impaired a sense of responsibility and rewarded debtors.[147] It was claimed that bankruptcy law caused commercial failure.[148] If the Act caused failure, repeal would prevent commercial ruin.[149] The link between bankruptcy law and commercial immorality was derived from the fundamental principle that 'he who owed should pay'.[150] Bankruptcy law provided a temptation to ignore one's higher duty. In a pamphlet entitled *Fallacy of Insolvency Laws and their Baneful Effects*, Thomas Ritchie, an importer from Belleville, Ontario, explored this theory:[151]

> Statutory law should be so framed as to lead men to observe the laws of
> nature, to have regard to the responsibilities of their position and observe the

140 *House of Commons Debates* (29 April 1879), 1597 (Colby). Bill 85, s. 44.
141 *House of Commons Debates* (29 April 1879), 1596.
142 The House divided 99–77 in favour of delaying consideration of the reform Bill: *House of Commons Debates* (29 April 1879), 1621. The House immediately thereafter resumed debate on Bill 15. Bill 15, *An Act to Repeal the Acts Respecting Insolvency Now in Force in the Dominion*, 1st Sess., 4th Parl., 1879. See Bicknell, 'Advisability of Establishing a Bankruptcy Court', 44.
143 *House of Commons Debates* (5 May 1879), 1783–4. See 'Editorial' (1879) 15 *Can LJ (NS)* 119; 'Editorial' (1879) 15 *Can LJ (NS)* 146.
144 *Debates of the Senate* (9 May 1879), 537.
145 Bill C-2, *An Act to Repeal the Acts Respecting Insolvency Now in Force in Canada*, 2nd Sess., 4th Parl., 1880. See *House of Commons Debates* (19 February 1880), 103–11.
146 See *Debates of the Senate* (12 March 1880), 152; (1 April 1880), 219. The Senate voted 47–17 in favour of repeal. See *An Act to Repeal the Acts Respecting Insolvency Now in Force in Canada* SC 43 Vict, c. 1, 1880.
147 See *Debates of the Senate* (23 May 1872), 788. See also *Debates of the Senate* (23 May 1872), 746, 747; *House of Commons Debates* (23 April 1872), 120, 121, 140. See also R. M. F., 'Legislation upon Insolvency' (1873) 2 *Canada Monthly* 419–22.
148 See *Debates of the Senate* (28 May 1872), 789.
149 The debate over the Insolvent Act of 1875 and its subsequent amendments and repeal took place in the midst of a serious depression that lasted from 1874 until 1878.
150 *House of Commons Debates* (7 March 1879), 206 (Houde).
151 T. Ritchie, *The Fallacy of Insolvency Laws and their Baneful Effects* (Belleville, 1885), 18.

obligations they are naturally under to their fellow men. And conversely, the state has no right whatever to enact any law that will tempt men to break those, or even extend increased opportunity or facility to disregard the duties and responsibilities of their condition in life, and this all insolvency laws practically do.

While the repeal movement succeeded, it is important to note that during the 1870s many members of Parliament continued to advance the notion that some debtors were deserving of a discharge. Prime Minister Sir John A. Macdonald claimed that 'when a man made a clean breast of his affairs, and gave his estate honestly for the benefit of his creditors, he ought to have relief'.[152] In a direct challenge to the idea that debtors failed through moral weakness, Members of Parliament argued that honest but unfortunate debtors deserved a discharge.[153]

Members also recognised the broader implications for the Canadian economy and society if there was to be no discharge. The debtor was of no use to his community in a state of perpetual debt.[154] The right of discharge did not belong, therefore, to the 'poor debtor', but rather it was in the 'public interest'.[155] The lack of discharge had an economic impact. Debtors who wished to remain in Canada would be forever dependent upon the will of creditors.[156]

There was another option. Debtors burdened with debts, it was claimed, would leave the country. One Member claimed that if a debtor could not obtain his discharge in Canada, 'he would follow his 500,000 fellow Canadians to the United States'.[157] Another referred to the lack of bankruptcy law in Ontario prior to Confederation, noting that 'many useful members of society . . . were obliged to leave the country, for judgments piled up one after another'.[158] Canadian debtors built up American industry, while the Canadian economy suffered.[159] Given the negative connotations of financial failure and the possibility of receiving the official stigma of a second-class discharge, it is not surprising that debtors continued to leave Canada.[160] The Minister of Justice, Edward Blake, acknowledged in 1877 that debtors continued to abscond to the United States.[161]

---

152 *House of Commons Debates* (11 May 1869), 258.
153 *House of Commons Debates* (26 February 1877), 305.
154 *House of Commons Debates* (21 April 1869), 36.
155 *House of Commons Debates* (3 April 1877), 1111.
156 *House of Commons Debates* (3 April 1877), 1104.
157 *House of Commons Debates* (24 March 1875), 880.
158 *House of Commons Debates* (26 February 1877), 286.
159 *House of Commons Debates* (7 March 1879), 211 (Ross). See also 'The Law Regarding Insolvency' (1878) *J of Commerce* 431, where it was argued that the abolition of a discharge would lead debtors to abscond.
160 Burley's study of Brantford indicates that those who failed often could not face the public shame. Many fled and some even committed suicide rather than confront creditors, friends and families with their financial failure: D. Burley, *A Particular Condition in Life: Self Employment and Social Mobility in Mid-Victorian Brantford* (Montreal: McGill–Queen's University Press, 1994), 176–7.
161 *House of Commons Debates* (19 April 1877), 296.

Following repeal, Parliament debated twenty bankruptcy bills between 1880 and 1903. All failed and the provinces sought to fill the gap by enacting legislation dealing with the distribution of debtors' assets and the prohibition of preferential payments. However, under the Constitution provincial jurisdiction did not extend to the granting of discharges, and debtors and creditors had to struggle on with a no-discharge regime.[162]

Opponents of bankruptcy law sought to prevent its return and argued that 'the country has profited by the repeal of the Act'. Members of Parliament claimed that debtors and creditors conducted business on a more responsible basis after repeal.[163] As no discharge was available under provincial law, debtors were, according to the *Monetary Times*, encouraged to deal fairly with their creditors because if they did not 'they cannot free themselves from liability for their debts'.[164] Repeal of the Insolvent Act of 1875, it was argued, had eliminated reckless credit.[165] In an 1882 letter to John A. Macdonald, one merchant celebrated the demise of the Insolvent Act. Its abrogation, according to the author, had done more for the prosperity of the country than Macdonald's National Policy.[166] Throughout the 1880s and 1890s Members of Parliament continued to make the argument that debtors had a responsibility to repay debts.

Support for the discharge continued to be based upon notions of forgiveness, and the importance of freeing a debtor from the burdens of debt. However, increasingly one finds evidence of how debtors responded to a non-discharge regime. A letter to Prime Minister Laurier lamented the fate of helpless debtors who were obliged to remain idle while others less skilled succeeded. Families 'who have seen better days are obliged to accept humble positions and a good useful Father is helpless or brokenhearted'.[167] Without a legislative discharge, debtors had to rely on the good will of creditors. According to one author this resulted in a 'civil lynch law' whereby creditors refused the discharge and took all means short of violence to persecute the debtor in order to recover the amount owed.[168] A debtor who had fled to the United States to avoid his creditors wrote to Laurier with a personal plea for insolvency reform:[169]

162 The provincial efforts and constitutional position is discussed in Telfer, 'Reconstructing Bankruptcy'.
163 *Debates of the Senate* (17 April 1894), 240.
164 Creditors, on the other hand, who advanced credit unwisely 'will have themselves to blame if their debtors do not ultimately have to pay or go out of business': 'Without a Bankrupt Law', *Monetary Times* (16 July 1880), 67.
165 *Debates of the Senate* (17 April 1894), 240.
166 Letter of E. Giles to John A. Macdonald (15 May 1882), *Macdonald Papers*, PAC MG 26A, Vol. 384, pt. 1, Reel c-1756, No. 180377–180378.
167 Letter of Christie & Co to Laurier (17 February 1906), *Laurier Papers*, PAC MG 26, Vol. 403, Reel c-850, No. 107234.
168 Letter of J. L. F. to the Editor, *Monetary Times* (20 April 1883), 1181. See also *House of Commons Debates* (6 March 1883), 120.
169 Letter of Debtor to Laurier (18 December 1909), *Laurier Papers*, PAC MG 26, Vol. 603, Reel c-884, No. 163911.

Is it humane or Christian, that men who have lost their all by fire, by endorsing for a friend who abused their confidence, by unforseen land slides in business and otherwise, should have the gates of mercy closed to them forever?

Many debtors had little choice but to flee to the United States. Absconding debtors had been a problem prior to Confederation and the issue had been raised briefly during the debates of the 1870s. The repeal of federal bankruptcy legislation in 1880 put further pressure on debtors.[170] Members of Parliament pointed to the increasing problem of fleeing debtors. Creditors who insisted upon their 'pound of flesh' had the effect of 'driving many a man out of the country to do business in the United States'.[171] Without a discharge the debtor had no option but to 'go to a new country where he can make a fresh start without having around his neck the millstone of debt which he cannot throw off in Canada'.[172] One such Canadian debtor, who moved to Erie, Pennsylvania, wrote to Laurier demanding that an insolvency law be enacted. He referred to the:[173]

multitude of men banished from Canada for the reason that they can never be free so long as you neglect to give them protection [from] the merciless visits of the Sheriffs and the Bailiffs . . . My own case represents many thousands of men obliged to live in another country, rather than return to be pounced on and harassed by some Loan Co., Bank, or . . . lawyer, for debts and Judgments beyond hope of ability to pay.

However, sympathy for exiled debtors was not the sole reason to support a bankruptcy law discharge. The problem of absconding debtors had a detrimental impact on Canadian business. Fleeing debtors meant the loss of 'our good but unfortunate trading population'.[174] Driving 'men out of the country' was a loss and not a gain to the community.[175] One company, concerned with the extent of migration to the United States, wrote to Laurier and claimed that 'an Insolvent Act would reclaim so much good active brain power, and that it would be equal almost, if not quite as good as one year's Immigration to Canada'.[176] Debtors fled to the United

170 Bliss notes that, between 1880 and 1896, several hundred thousand Canadians migrated to the United States: M Bliss, *Northern Enterprise: Five Centuries of Canadian Business* (Toronto: McClelland & Stewart, 1987), 249. This shift in population must be re-evaluated in light of the repeal of federal bankruptcy legislation.
171 *House of Commons Debates* (29 March 1882), 608 (Gault); *House of Commons Debates* (18 May 1903), 3250.
172 *House of Commons Debates* (5 May 1887), 283 (Edgar).
173 Letter of Debtor to Laurier (18 December 1909), *Laurier Papers*, PAC MG 26, Vol. 603, Reel c-884, No. 163911.
174 *House of Commons Debates* (5 May 1887), 283 (Edgar).
175 Letter of J. L. F. to Editor, *Monetary Times* (9 February 1883), 885. See also *House of Commons Debates* (18 May 1898), 3254.
176 Letter of Christie & Co to Laurier (17 February 1906), *Laurier Papers*, PAC MG 26, Vol. 403, Reel c-850, No. 107234. See also letter of Soclean Chemical Company to Laurier (9 August 1907), *Laurier Papers*, PAC MG 26, Vol. 470, Reel c-850, No. 127611, referring to the fact that many people were compelled to leave Canada following the bursting of the Toronto boom.

States to obtain 'a new lease on life'. The lack of a discharge deprived Canada of 'active and enterprising individuals'. If there had been a proper bankruptcy law they would have 'remained at home and would now be taking part in the development of Canada'.[177]

While support for a discharge was often framed in terms of the underlying value of forgiveness and sympathy for an unfortunate debtor, the credit community had a particular interest in seeking bankruptcy legislation that contained a discharge. For example, the inability of debtors to obtain a release of their old debts meant fewer customers for creditors wishing to sell goods on credit.[178] Individuals heavily burdened with debt were of no use to creditors as new customers as it was 'no advantage to creditors to have a debtor die poor'.[179] A wholesaler who conducted business in Ontario and the four Western provinces wrote to the Department of Justice and complained of the lack of individuals who were able to enter into business:[180]

> In the West, with large numbers of young men who have joined the forces, it is necessary for the proper carrying on of business here that a number of the older men should go back into business, but as a result of unwise Real Estate speculation, many of these are tied up with old judgments and debts that they cannot under any circumstance ever pay.

Further, the lack of discharge drove debtors to 'means flavouring of trickery and deception' in order to re-establish their livelihood.[181] Without a discharge, debtors had an incentive to engage in 'crookedness and deception'.[182] Debtors sequestered assets,[183] and arranged their affairs so as to become judgment proof.[184] To avoid creditors, debtors traded in the name of their wife or behind the name of a

177 *Saturday Night* (10 January 1914), 1, where it is claimed that exiled Canadian debtors were to be found in 'every leading city of the American Union'. This point was also made at a Liberal Party convention in Winnipeg. See letter of Henry Detchon to the Minister of Justice (17 September 1917), *Department of Justice Papers*, PAC RG13 A2, Vol. 213, File 1081. See also letter of Soclean Chemical Company to Sir Wilfred Laurier (9 August 1907), *Laurier Papers*, PAC MG26, Vol. 470, Reel c-850, No. 127611. See also *House of Commons Debates* (18 May 1903), 3249.
178 'The lack of any legal discharge for an old debt may prove an injustice towards new creditors': Letter of J. L. F. to Editor, *Monetary Times* (9 February 1883), 885.
179 Christie and Co. Wholesale Dealers in Lumber [etc.] (17 February 1906), *Laurier Papers*, PAC MG26, Vol. 403, Reel c-850, No. 107231.
180 Letter of R. J. White and Co Ltd Wholesale Dry Goods to Department of Justice (17 April 1918), *Department of Justice Papers*, PAC RG13 A2, Vol. 221, File 735.
181 'Insolvency Legislation' (1902) 35 *Can LJ* 179, 180.
182 A. McMaster, 'The Bankruptcy Act' (1912–13) 2 *Canadian Chartered Accountant* 236, 241.
183 *Saturday Night* (10 January 1914), 1.
184 This included transferring property to a wife to evade legitimate debts. In Ontario the enactment of the Married Women's Property Act 1884 abolished the role of the husband as trustee over the woman's property. Under the Act, women were entitled to hold and convey property. This created opportunities for spousal transfers to avoid debts. Chambers found over 130 cases of attempted fraud in unreported court documents: L. Chambers, *Married Women and Property Law in Victorian Ontario* (Toronto: University of Toronto Press, 1997), 155.

company or took the dramatic step of leaving the country.[185] Debtor misbehaviour led to a growing acceptance on the part of creditors that some legislative reform was required.[186]

The intensity of competition between creditors increased dramatically without a bankruptcy law. Without a discharge, 'it is in the power of one vindictive creditor to hinder the debtor from making further restitution to his other creditors. Is this wise or right?'[187] Other creditors 'not attempting to blackmail but are acting honestly, obtain a reduced amount and they are injured... thus the preferential creditors who are paid some special amounts get something more while the other creditors get less than they should receive'.[188] Thus while a discharge could be sold as assisting poor unfortunate debtors, creditors who had experienced the brief absence of discharges found that the provision could operate in their favour.

The renewed debate and the Bankruptcy Act of 1919

After 1903 bankruptcy law reform disappeared from the Parliamentary agenda until the issue was revived, largely by a creditor interest group, during the economic downturn which began in 1913. Creditors came to accept the necessity of the discharge as a means of improving the standard of debtor conduct and a way to enhance their collection efforts. The Canadian Credit Men's Trust Association ('the CCMTA'), an organisation that represented various authorised trustees operating under the provincial assignment statutes, was well placed to recognise the needs of creditors, and the draft bill of 1919 reflected their influence.[189] Several defects in the provincial assignment Acts led the CCMTA to demand new legislation.[190] The CCMTA identified at one of its meetings 'four defects or omissions' in the provincial legislation:[191]

> *Firstly*, the lack of uniformity relating to insolvency laws in Canada; *secondly*, the absence of machinery for compelling an insolvent debtor under certain circumstances to turn over to a trustee for creditors his property for pro rata

185 See McMaster, 'The Bankruptcy Act', 237. One author summarised options available to debtors under the provincial regime. Debtors had the option of leaving the country, carrying on business in the name of their wife, forming companies, awaiting the Statute of Limitations, or obtaining releases from those creditors who were willing to grant them. See Bicknell, 'Advisability of Establishing a Bankruptcy Court', 44.
186 The specific problem of creditors being defrauded by transfers between spouses is discussed in Chambers, *Married Women*, 148–65.
187 Letter of J. L. F. to Editor, *Monetary Times* (9 February 1883), 885.
188 *House of Commons Debates* (5 May 1887), 284.
189 The role of the CCMTA is discussed in Telfer, 'The Canadian Bankruptcy Act'.
190 The CCMTA originally demanded uniformity in provincial legislation, but later sought federal legislation. Their four stated defects could not have been remedied by provincial amendments.
191 'Proposed Bankruptcy Act', *Monetary Times* (1 September 1917), 14. See also McMaster, 'The Bankruptcy Act', 238.

distribution among creditors (involuntary bankruptcy); *thirdly*, the ratification by the court of composition and extension agreements when approved by a certain majority of creditors (say 75 per cent) thereby binding the minority, and *fourthly*, the right of an honest but unfortunate debtor to obtain his discharge.

The English Bankruptcy Act of 1883 provided the ideal solution. The CCMTA retained a solicitor to draft a bill and he closely followed the English model. In 1919, after a near forty-year absence, Parliament reasserted its jurisdiction over bankruptcy and insolvency law and passed what many came to realise to be an essential form of business regulation. The Bankruptcy Act of 1919, in the words of one author, was 'a very radical change in the relationship of debtors and creditors'.[192] The Act of 1919, which was largely based upon the CCMTA bill, would remain in force for the next thirty years and set the framework for much of twentieth-century Canadian bankruptcy law.[193]

The discharge was no longer perceived as an evil, as in the nineteenth century, but it was proclaimed as a necessary form of business regulation. The new acceptability of the discharge reflected the underlying interests of creditors who demanded reform. Canada opted for a discharge because it met the legal needs of the credit community.

The new federal legislation allowed debtors to apply for a discharge and obtain a release of their debts. However, in a significant change from nineteenth-century statutes, debtors were no longer required to obtain prescribed levels of creditor consent to obtain a discharge. The ultimate discretion for the granting of the discharge lay with the courts and not creditors. The courts would therefore assume a function that creditors had been unable to carry out. The private remedy of individual creditor release encouraged dishonest competition among creditors. The private release did not operate as a check on debtor misconduct, as creditors sought their immediate best deal and did not concern themselves with the larger public goal of improving commercial morality:[194]

> Under the bill it is recognised that the Court, seized of all the circumstances, would be in a better position to decide as to whether the debtor should be given his discharge, than creditors whose interest in the Estate is in many cases too immediate and personal to permit unbiased judgment.

Creditors were willing to give up this role of monitoring debtor behaviour in favour of a judicial system that provided better control over debtors. The court, on hearing

---

192 F. Lucas, 'The New "Bankruptcy Act"' (1920) 40 *Can LT* 668.
193 The next major revision of bankruptcy law occurred in 1949. Ziegel notes that although the 1919 Act has been amended many times, 'the 1919 Canadian Bankruptcy Act still provides the conceptual framework for the current Bankruptcy and Insolvency Act': Ziegel, 'Canada's Phased in Bankruptcy Law Reform', 383.
194 S. Jacobs, 'The Proposed Bankruptcy Act' (1918) 3 *Proceedings of the Canadian Bar Association* 164.

the debtor's application, could grant or refuse an absolute order of discharge or suspend the operation of the order for a specified period. Alternatively, the court could
make an order conditional upon payment of a portion of the debtor's after-acquired
earnings.[195] This basic model provided the conceptual framework for Canadian
bankruptcy law for most of the twentieth century.

By 1919 creditors recognised the discharge as part of the larger bankruptcy
scheme that enhanced collection goals. After the First World War the discharge
was an accepted feature of the bankruptcy statute. Statements in the House of
Commons that emphasised the fundamental importance of the discharge were
not challenged. The near forty-year absence of the discharge provided numerous
examples of debtors engaging in deceptive or fraudulent conduct under defective
provincial legislation. Whereas the discharge had been feared as an evil in the
nineteenth century, by 1919 it had become a commercial necessity.

Conclusion

The 1997 reforms and the existing law of consumer bankruptcies and
proposals are currently being examined by a Personal Insolvency Task Force established by the Office of the Superintendent of Bankruptcy. The Task Force was
prompted by the legislative five-year review of the Bankruptcy and Insolvency Act
due in 2002.[196] The Task Force itself recognises 'accessibility' as one of the key criteria that will serve as a measure against which final recommendations must be
gauged:[197]

> *Accessibility*: going bankrupt in Canada must be seen as a right, not a privilege.
> Accordingly access to the system must be simple, inexpensive and readily
> available throughout the country.

As this essay has illustrated, the 1997 reforms have reshaped the notion of debtor
rehabilitation and significantly affected a debtor's access to the straight bankruptcy
remedy by encouraging more debtors into the proposal regime. Rehabilitation has
always played an important role in modern bankruptcy law; however, it has traditionally been linked to the release of debts.

195 The Bankruptcy Act of 1919, ss. 58, 59. See also N. Martin, 'A New Bankruptcy Act' (1918–19) 8
   Canadian Chartered Accountant 24, 29. No provision existed for an automatic discharge as exists in
   modern Canadian legislation. If a debtor did not make an application, he remained a bankrupt
   indefinitely. The automatic procedure was not added until 1949. See E. Martel, 'The Debtor's
   Discharge from Bankruptcy' (1971) 17 *McGill LJ* 718, 724.
196 Office of the Superintendent of Bankruptcy, *Personal Insolvency Task Force Terms of Reference* (August
   2000), 1. In addition, the Task Force terms of reference note that beyond the mandated review,
   'the single most important event giving rise to this task force is the rapid escalation in the number of personal bankruptcies over the years'. At the time of this essay going to print, the report
   of the personal Insolving Task Force had not been published.
197 *Ibid.*, 5.

The reforms in part can be explained by the concern that something had to be done about the alarming number of bankruptcies. Bankruptcy, however, is a term defined by Parliament, which it may choose to alter. It remains to be seen whether shifting people out of straight bankruptcy and into repayment plans will solve underlying problems of rising levels of consumer indebtedness. Indeed, one is reminded of the nineteenth-century claim that bankruptcy law caused commercial failure.[198] After all, if the legislation was the root of financial failure, repeal would prevent commercial ruin.

As we struggle with the merits of the current reforms, we should not lose sight of the historical perspective or the possible implications of placing restrictions on the discharge. Throughout the history of bankruptcy law, governments have experimented with various forms of bankruptcy legislation. Indeed, the entire history of bankruptcy law from its origins in England to its transplant to the United States and Canada, has been one of reforms shifting between debtor and creditor interests.[199] One author characterised the continuous reforms in nineteenth-century England as a 'legislative pendulum' that 'oscillated from one theory to another, as the imperfections of each were experienced in succession'.[200] Another author characterised nineteenth-century English efforts at bankruptcy reform as follows:[201]

> The process of bankruptcy reform was slow and tortuous, often beset by conflicting interests, and by the contradictions between traditional morality and economic necessity. In theory nothing should have been simpler than to construct a set of just and rational bankruptcy laws... The tortured history of bankruptcy legislation, however, demonstrates the problems of translating moral and legal theories into practice. Often conflicting interests were involved: justice for the creditor vs mercy for the debtor; moral outrage over bankruptcy vs recognition of economic realities; idealism vs pragmatism.

Indeed, the current reforms may be part of the legislative pendulum that has moved away from the traditional sense of debtor rehabilitation (i.e., returning the debtor

---

198 See text above at notes 133–46.
199 On the shifting balance between debtor and creditor interests in the history of US bankruptcy law, see, e.g., C. J. Tabb, 'The Historical Evolution of the Bankruptcy Discharge' (1991) 65 *Am Bankr LJ* 325; C. Warren, *Bankruptcy in United States History* (Cambridge, Mass.: Harvard University Press, 1935); P. Coleman, *Debtors and Creditors in America: Insolvency, Imprisonment for Debt and Bankruptcy, 1607–1900* (Madison: State Historical Society of Wisconsin, 1974).
200 B. Bowen, 'Progress in the Administration of Justice during the Victorian Period' in *Select Essays in Anglo American Legal History* (New York: Lawbook Exchange, 1992), 516, 548. For a discussion of the struggle between official and creditor control over bankruptcy proceedings, see V. Lester, *Victorian Insolvency: Bankruptcy, Imprisonment for Debt and Company Winding up in Nineteenth Century England* (Oxford: Oxford University Press, 1995).
201 B. Weiss, *The Hell of the English: Bankruptcy Law and the Victorian Novel* (Lewisburg, Pennsylvania: Bucknell University Press, 1986), 40. Dunlop also traces this contradictory response of Victorian society: C. Dunlop, 'Debtors and Creditors in Dickens' Fiction' (1990) 19 *Dickens Studies Annual* 25, 26.

to the productive economy) back to a renewed sense of debtor responsibility for the repayment of debts. As this essay has illustrated, the recent Canadian reforms are not the first time that Canada has restricted access to the discharge. Nineteenth-century bankruptcy legislation made it progressively more difficult for debtors to obtain a discharge and Parliament ultimately eliminated the legislation in 1880. In response to the initial restrictive legislation and the subsequent repeal in 1880, debtors took steps to avoid their creditors. The absence of a discharge was a policy failure and, by 1919, bankruptcy law became a commercial necessity.

While the history of bankruptcy law is replete with episodes of various governments tightening or removing access to the discharge, Edward Balleisen's study of bankruptcy law in antebellum America illustrates how the US Bankruptcy Act of 1841 and the discharge contributed to the dynamism of the American economy. The 'ability of bankrupts to gain legal absolution from old debts unleashed a range of economic energies'. The opportunity for bankrupts to return to the economy encouraged risk taking and allowed debtors to pursue new ventures after their encounter with bankruptcy law.[202] In Canada, after the repeal of the federal legislation in 1880, there could be no releasing of economic energies. In the absence of a discharge between 1880 and 1919 debtors opted out of the Canadian economy altogether.

202 See E. Balleisen, *Navigating Failure: Bankruptcy and Commercial Society in Antebellum America* (Chapel Hill: University of North Carolina Press, 2001), 18, 167–8, 198. A similar conclusion could be drawn with respect to the impact of the Bankruptcy Act of 1898. On efforts to establish a national Act in 1898, see B. Hansen, 'Commercial Associations and the Creation of a National Economy: The Demand for Federal Bankruptcy Legislation' (1998) 72 *Business History Review* 86; R. Sauer, 'Bankruptcy Law and the Maturing of American Capitalism' (1994) 55 *Ohio St LJ* 291; Tabb, 'A Century of Regress or Progess?'.

11   The death of consumer bankruptcy in the United States

CHARLES JORDAN TABB

Introduction

Consumer bankruptcy in the United States as it has existed for over a century[1] narrowly escaped death in the year 2000. But that venerable institution is on death row; only the execution date remains to be set. The 106th Congress passed a major bankruptcy 'reform' bill in December 2000.[2] The fundamental purpose of the Reform Bill is to deny many consumer debtors an immediate discharge of their debts in a Chapter 7 liquidation bankruptcy,[3] leaving only the Hobson's choice of forgoing bankruptcy relief altogether or attempting to 'repay their creditors the maximum that they can afford'[4] in a Chapter 13[5] repayment plan. Only a pocket veto[6] of the Reform Bill by then-President William Clinton on 19 December 2000 granted a temporary reprieve.

The salvation of consumer bankruptcy may be short-lived. If possible, the fate of traditional consumer bankruptcy has been hanging by an even more precarious thread in the 107th Congress than ever before. In March 2001, both chambers overwhelmingly passed slightly different versions of a bankruptcy reform bill.[7]

Also published in (2002) 18 *Bankr Dev J* 1.

1 The historical development of the discharge policy in the United States is traced in C. J. Tabb, 'The Historical Evolution of the Bankruptcy Discharge' (1991) 65 *Am Bankr LJ* 325.
2 H.R. 2415 passed the House of Representatives by voice vote on 12 October 2000, see 146 Cong. Rec. D1072–01 (daily ed. 12 October 2000), and passed the Senate 70–28 on 7 December 2000. See 146 Cong. Rec. S11729–02 (daily ed. 7 December 2000). H.R. 2415 is referred to as the 'Reform Bill', or 'RB'. The bills passed in the 107th Congress (H.R. 333 (referred to as 'House Bill' or 'HB') and S. 420 (referred to as 'Senate Bill' or SB')), see n. 7 below, are included in the reference to the 'Reform Bill' in the many instances in which the three bills are the same. In those few instances in which the bills in the 107th Congress differ from H.R. 2415, they are separately cited.
3 11 U.S.C. §§ 701 *et. seq.* (Chapter 7). Title 11 of the United States Code is commonly known and will hereafter be referred to as the 'Bankruptcy Code' or 'Code'.
4 147 Cong. Rec. H133–01 (daily ed. 31 January 2001) (remarks of Rep. Gekas). Representative George Gekas has been the primary sponsor of the bankruptcy bill in the House of Representatives.
5 11 U.S.C. §§ 1301 *et. seq.* (Chapter 13).
6 The President can block enactment of a bill that has been passed by both houses of Congress simply by not signing the bill (thus 'pocketing' the bill), if the bill is presented to the President within ten days of the adjournment of Congress: US Const. Art. I, § 7, cl. 2.
7 The House of Representatives passed H.R. 333, Bankruptcy Abuse Prevention and Consumer Protection Act of 2001, 107th Cong., by a vote of 306–118 on 1 March 2001, 147 Cong. Rec. H600–01

President George W. Bush has made it known that he supports the bankruptcy legislation and, unlike his predecessor, will sign a bankruptcy bill.[8] All that apparently remained was for the House and the Senate to appoint conferees, reach a compromise in conference regarding the handful of differences in the two chambers' passed bills, and present the conference version to the willing President for signature.

Why, then, has a bill not been enacted, as of June 2001? Only the remarkable fortuity of a 50–50 split in the Senate, which led to a political impasse between Democrats and Republicans over the number of conferees each party was entitled to appoint, held up the process.[9] Due to that impasse, a conference has not yet been convened. The problem had nothing at all to do with the merits of the bankruptcy bill. That particular logjam has now been removed, though, with the defection of a Republican senator (James Jeffords of Vermont) to the ranks of independents, giving the Democrats control of the Senate as of 6 June 2001.[10] Democrats now are entitled to appoint more Senate conferees, clearing the way for a possible conference with the House. The new Democratic Senate Majority Leader has announced that he wants a conference with the House.[11] It is possible, though, that the controlling Senate Democrats led by new Judiciary Committee Chair Patrick Leahy[12] might favour a slightly less harsh (to debtors) version of the bankruptcy bill than would the controlling House Republicans, making the exact outcome of a conference hard to predict.[13] Furthermore, even getting to a conference will require proponents of the

(daily ed. 1 March 2001); the Senate passed S. 420, Consumer Bankruptcy Reform Act, 107th Cong., by a vote of 83–15 on 15 March. See 147 Cong. Rec. S2379 (daily ed. 15 March 2001).

8 See 'House Passed Bankruptcy Bill 306–108, Bush Supports Legislation', *American Bankruptcy Institute* (2 March 2001), www.abiworld.org/headlines/today.html. President George W. Bush's narrow victory in the 2000 election over Vice-President Albert Gore probably sealed the fate of the traditional conception of consumer bankruptcy in the United States. Gore, a liberal Democrat, probably would have followed in the footsteps of his predecessor, President Clinton, and used the threat of a veto to ameliorate to some degree the harshness of bankruptcy reform against consumer debtors. Bush, a conservative Republican, can be expected to embrace the full rigour and vigour of the consumer credit industry's decades-long efforts to make the bankruptcy laws tougher on individual debtors.

9 The Senate Democrats insisted that they should be entitled to appoint the same number of conferees as the Republicans. The Republicans urged with equal fervour that they should be entitled to appoint one more conferee than the Democrats, on the ground that they still had ultimate control of the Senate, since the tie-breaking vote would be cast by Vice-President Cheney, a Republican. See 'Still No Deal for Conference Committee', *American Bankruptcy Institute* (10 May 2001), www.abiworld.org/headlines/today.html.

10 See 'Jeffords Party Switch Shifts Balance of Power in Senate, Future of Bankruptcy Legislation Unclear', *American Bankruptcy Institute* (25 May 2001), www.abiworld.org/headlines/today.html.

11 See 'Daschle Wants Conference on Bankruptcy Reform Bill', *American Bankruptcy Institute* (11 June 2001), www.abiworld.org/headlines/today.html.

12 See 'Grassley Pessimistic about Chances for Bankruptcy Legislation', *American Bankruptcy Institute* (13 June 2001), www.abiworld.org/headlines/today.html.

13 See 'Biden's Choice to Chair Foreign Relations Panel Could Affect Bankruptcy Bill', *American Bankruptcy Institute* (30 May 2001), www.abiworld.org/headlines/today.html. Knowledgeable observers on the Hill believe that a key indicator of whether the Senate leadership wants the bill is

legislation to overcome nettlesome delaying tactics (such as a filibuster) by the Bill's opponents.[14]

The overwhelming support for bankruptcy reform in both chambers,[15] coupled with the fact that the two bills passed in 2001 are remarkably similar on most (albeit not all) crucial points,[16] suggests that a compromise bill could still be forged. The Senate bill's $125,000 limitation on the homestead exemption[17] which certain factions in the House strongly oppose[18] is perhaps the biggest stumbling block to consensus. And, even if by happenstance no bill is enacted in 2001/2, the credit industry's determined and well-funded push for reform, which has been heeded in the halls of Congress, is quite likely to bear fruit in the very near future.

Assuming that it does become law, the Reform Bill would radically reshape the contours of the United States consumer bankruptcy laws in favour of financial institutions and to the detriment of needy individual debtors. For many debtors the promise of a financial 'fresh start' in life that the United States bankruptcy law has long offered[19] would become a cruel and ephemeral illusion. Bankruptcy reform in its current form is draconian for those financially vulnerable 'fragile middle class' debtors who have been the most in need of bankruptcy relief.[20] Perversely, however, the bill still offers substantial succour to wealthier debtors who own multi-million dollar mansions,[21] drive expensive cars and send their young scions to private schools. The reformers' mantra of 'stopping abuse' thus rings hollow in light of what the bankruptcy Reform Bill actually would do.

whether Senator Joseph Biden, a strong proponent of the credit card industry's pet provisions, is named as a conferee; if not, that would send a signal that the Senate does not want reform this year.

14 See 'Wellstone Intends to Filibuster Bankruptcy Conference', *American Bankruptcy Institute* (19 June 2001), www.abiworld.org/headlines/today.html.

15 See n. 7 above.

16 For a comparison of the two bills' consumer bankruptcy provisions, see 'Major Effects of the Consumer Bankruptcy Provisions of the 2001 Bankruptcy Legislation (H.R. 333 and S. 420)', *American Bankruptcy Institute*, www.abiworld.org/mainpoints.pdf.

17 SB § 308(2).

18 'House Republicans Raise New "Tax" Issue on Bankruptcy Bill', *American Bankruptcy Institute* (14 June 2001), www.abiworld.org/headlines/today.html.

19 See *Local Loan Co. v. Hunt*, 292 U.S. 234, 244 (1934). The justifications for the discharge policy are explained in C. J. Tabb, 'The Scope of the Fresh Start in Bankruptcy: Collateral Conversions and the Dischargeability Debate' (1990) 59 *Geo Wash L Rev* 56, 89–103. See also C. J. Tabb, *The Law of Bankruptcy* (Westbury, N.Y.: Foundation Press, 1997), § 10.3, 699–701.

20 See generally T. Sullivan, E. Warren and J. Westbrook, *The Fragile Middle Class: Americans in Debt* (New Haven: Yale University Press, 2000).

21 One of the most important differences in the House and Senate bills concerns this point, *viz.*, whether to limit the dollar amount of a homestead that a debtor may exempt. The House bill has no dollar limit. The Senate adopted an amendment offered by Senator Kohl that caps a debtor's homestead exemption at $125,000. See 147 Cong. Rec. S2336 (daily ed. 15 March 2001), SB § 308(2). The Administration favours the House version. See 'Senate Approves Bankruptcy Bill 83–15, Conference Faces Hurdles', *American Bankruptcy Institute* (16 March 2001), www.abiworld.org/headlines/today.html.

This essay explores the phenomenon of consumer bankruptcy reform in the United States at the dawn of the third millennium. After opening with a brief explanation of the parameters of traditional consumer bankruptcy in the United States, I will examine what the Reform Bill does to consumer bankruptcy: how it undermines the 'fresh start' for needy debtors, while leaving major loopholes available for the wealthy and well advised.

Prologue: traditional consumer bankruptcy in the United States (and the push for reform)

Traditional consumer bankruptcy in the United States

Consumer bankruptcy in the United States since 1898 has enjoyed a strong and unmistakably debtor-friendly posture.[22] The central tenet of the consumer bankruptcy system in America has been to offer all 'honest' individual debtors a freely available, immediate, unconditional debt discharge in exchange for the surrender of current non-exempt assets, if any. Since distributions are made to creditors in only about 5 per cent of all liquidation bankruptcies, this trade is a good one indeed for most debtors. The reality is that in most cases debtors give up nothing and yet are released from their debts. Debtors then may enjoy their future earnings free from the claims of their creditors. The vehicle for the realisation of this debtor's dream is Chapter 7 of the Bankruptcy Code.[23]

Notably, since 1898 the consumer bankruptcy law in the United States has not required any of the following as a requisite of discharge:

- consent of creditors;[24]
- payment of a minimum percentage dividend or minimum amount of debt, either in the initial bankruptcy distribution or over time out of future earnings;[25]
- proof of financial need (for example, insolvency, either on a balance sheet or ability to pay[26] basis);

22 See Tabb, 'Historical Evolution', 370. For an excellent overview of the American consumer bankruptcy system, see J. Braucher, 'Options in Consumer Bankruptcy: an American Perspective' (1999) 37 *Osgoode Hall LJ* 155.

23 11 U.S.C. §§ 701 *et. seq.*

24 The 1898 Act was the first United States bankruptcy law that did not either require creditor consent or permit creditor dissent to discharge. See Tabb, 'Historical Evolution', 364. Earlier United States laws, in effect from 1800–3, 1841–3, and 1867–78, contained such limitations: Tabb, 'Historical Evolution', 346 (1800 law), 351–2 (1841 law), 356–7 (1867 law).

25 As with the creditor consent restriction, all American bankruptcy acts until 1898 imposed some minimum dividend limitation on the discharge: *ibid.*, 346–7 (1800), 352 (1841), 356–7 (1867). The 1898 Act abandoned use of the minimum dividend: *ibid.*, 364.

26 The notable exception to this is the 'substantial abuse' barrier to Chapter 7 relief, enacted as part of the 1984 Amendments. See § 707(b). While Congress eschewed any rigid 'ability to pay'

- proof that the bankruptcy was caused by unavoidable misfortune rather than the debtor's fault or improvidence; or
- suspension of the discharge for a period of time.[27]

Instead, the only limitations on the availability and scope of a debtor's discharge have been of three types. First, some debtors are denied a discharge upon proof of a statutory ground in § 727(a) evidencing the debtor's failure to co-operate in connection with the bankruptcy case itself.[28] For example, a debtor who hides assets and fails to report them and turn them over to the trustee would be denied a discharge.[29] Few debtors run afoul of the discharge bar, however. Secondly, under § 523(a) some types of debts are exempted from a general discharge.[30] These debts may arise out of the debtor's misconduct, such as debts for fraud,[31] or from wilful and malicious injury,[32] or may favour worthy creditors, such as for alimony and child support.[33] Thirdly, a debtor is permitted to agree to 'reaffirm' an otherwise dischargeable debt,[34] effectively waiving the discharge as to the reaffirmed debt.[35]

An individual consumer debtor has another option.[36] She may file under Chapter 13 and retain all of her assets, exempt or not, in exchange for paying creditors under a court-approved payment plan for three years. Under the plan the debtor must pay creditors at least as much as they would have received in a Chapter 7 liquidation case,[37] and must devote all of her 'disposable income' to the plan for three years.[38] The granting of the discharge is deferred until the completion of this payment plan.[39] Resort to Chapter 13 is entirely voluntary with the debtor, however; creditors may not force a debtor into a Chapter 13 payment plan.[40]

A debtor thus is free to play to her strengths in choosing the appropriate chapter under which to file. If she has significant future earning capacity but few existing non-exempt assets, she would choose Chapter 7, but if she has substantial non-exempt property that she hopes to retain, she might instead select Chapter 13.[41] For most debtors, though, the preferred choice is Chapter 7: about 95 per cent

guidelines as indicative of *per se* abuse, courts have gleaned a congressional intent that payment ability at least be a factor in assessing abuse. The reforms pushed by the consumer credit industry would impose a firm 'means test' assessing a debtor's ability to pay part of her debts as a predicate to being permitted to proceed with Chapter 7 relief. See pp. 276–88.

27 English law has given the court discretion to condition or suspend a debtor's discharge since 1883: D. G. Boshkoff, 'Limited, Conditional, and Suspended Discharges in Anglo-American Bankruptcy Proceedings' (1982) 131 *U Pa L Rev* 69.

28 Tabb, *The Law of Bankruptcy*, § 10.1, 692–3.   29 11 U.S.C. § 727(a)(2), (4).

30 Tabb, *The Law of Bankruptcy*, § 10.1, 693.   31 11 U.S.C. § 523(a)(2).   32 11 U.S.C. § 523(a)(6).

33 11 U.S.C. § 523(a)(5).   34 11 U.S.C. § 524(c).   35 Tabb, *The Law of Bankruptcy*, § 10.33, 748–9.

36 Technically, an individual consumer debtor is also permitted to file under Chapter 11. See *Toibb* v. *Radloff*, 501 U.S. 157 (1991). However, for many reasons, particularly Chapter 11's greater complexity, most individuals would prefer to file under Chapter 13. In some circumstances, though, Chapter 11 is a better choice for the debtor. See Tabb, *The Law of Bankruptcy*, § 12.3, 901–3.

37 11 U.S.C. § 1325(a)(4).   38 11 U.S.C. § 1325(b).   39 11 U.S.C. § 1328(a).

40 11 U.S.C. § 303(a).   41 See Tabb, *The Law of Bankruptcy*, § 12.3, 900–1.

of all Chapter 7 cases are 'no asset' cases that result in no payment to unsecured creditors out of current non-exempt assets. The most valuable 'asset' most consumer debtors possess is their earning capacity, the future fruits of which are protected by the Chapter 7 discharge.[42]

Origins of the means test: the consumer credit industry's push for reform

Creditors typically have exactly the opposite interest from the debtor, and, assuming the debtor is going to file for bankruptcy,[43] would vastly prefer a scheme in which a debtor could be forced to make payments on her debts over time out of her future earnings, in effect, an involuntary Chapter 13 regime. Those desires have fuelled the consumer credit industry's reform efforts for nearly forty years, and underlie the current push for 'means testing'. The consumer credit industry has been waging an almost ceaseless and relentless battle to reshape consumer bankruptcy since the mid-1960s. Indeed, the first roots of the 'can pay' campaign were planted in the early 1930s, with hearings held in 1932 on a bill to establish wage earner plans.[44] In 1938 Chapter 13 was enacted to permit such payment plans, but on a purely voluntary basis.[45] In the 1960s Congress considered several bills that would screen out of Chapter 7 those debtors with the ability to pay substantial amounts of their debts.[46] At every turn, though, Congress definitively rejected this approach as unwise, unsound, unworkable and possibly unconstitutional.[47]

The first congressional bankruptcy review commission, reporting in 1973, concluded 'that forced participation by a debtor in a plan requiring contributions out of future income has so little prospect for success that it should not be adopted'.[48] Following this lead, in the 1978 massive revision of the nation's bankruptcy laws[49] Congress flatly rejected the suggestion of forcing supposed 'can pay' debtors into involuntary payment plans.[50] Yet, in the face of this history of rejection, a recent Congress had the temerity to state that the proposed legislation propounding

42 *Ibid.*, §1.24 80.
43 The first preference for most creditors is that the debtor not file for any sort of bankruptcy at all. Much of the pending reform legislation is designed to make filing for bankruptcy more difficult, thus limiting access. If, however, a debtor is going to file, the creditors normally would prefer that the debtor attempt to repay debts under Chapter 13.
44 S. 3866, 72nd Cong. (1932).   45 Chandler Act, Ch. 575, 52 Stat. 840, § 621 (1938).
46 H.R. 12784, 88th Cong. (1964); H.R. 292, 89th Cong. (1965); S. 613, 89th Cong. (1965); H.R. 1057, 90th Cong. (1967); H.R. 5771, 90th Cong. (1967).
47 See discussion of this history in H.R. Rep. No. 95–595, 95th Cong., 1st Sess. 120–1 (1977).
48 Report of the Commission on the Bankruptcy Laws of the United States, Part I at 159, H.R. Doc. No. 93–137, 93rd Cong., 1st Sess. (1973).
49 See Pub. L. No. 95–598, 92 Stat. 2549 (1978).
50 See S. Rep. 95–989, 95th Cong., 2nd Sess. 32 (1978); H.R. Rep. No. 95–595, 95th Cong., 1st Sess. 120–1, 322 (1977).

means testing 'is merely an extension of this longstanding effort to ensure that bankruptcy is reserved for those truly in need of debt forgiveness'.[51]

The ink on the 1978 law was barely dry before the consumer credit industry renewed its assault. Central to their efforts was the publication in 1982 of a study funded by the industry itself that asserted that many debtors could repay significant amounts of their debts without difficulty.[52] Using this study as fodder, bills were introduced in the 97th and 98th Congresses, which included ability-to-pay screening tests for Chapter 7.[53]

In 1984 Congress finally gave creditors part of what they sought by denying access to Chapter 7 for an individual consumer debtor if granting relief to the debtor under that chapter would constitute a 'substantial abuse'.[54] The apparent intention was that such a debtor would then have to file 'voluntarily' under Chapter 13 if she wanted bankruptcy relief at all. Congress hedged, though, and declined to state explicitly that it would be a 'substantial abuse' for a debtor to proceed under Chapter 7 if the debtor had the ability to pay a substantial portion of her debts out of future earnings. Still, courts have interpreted § 707(b) as permitting consideration of ability to pay as one factor in weighing substantial abuse.[55]

Discontented with what it perceived to be the ineffectiveness of the substantial abuse test in kicking debtors out of Chapter 7, in the early 1990s the consumer credit industry renewed its efforts for a firm and unequivocal 'means test' that would bar supposed 'can pay' debtors from Chapter 7.[56] One chamber or the other passed differing versions of this legislation over the ensuing years. A new industry-funded study again concluded that some debtors could repay some of their debts.[57] The industry thought it had the perfect vehicle to push its cause when Congress in 1994 established a second blue-ribbon bankruptcy study commission.[58] Alas, the Review Commission, under the thoughtful supervision of its Reporter, Professor

---

51 S. Rep. No. 106–49, 106th Cong., 1st Sess. 4 (1999).
52 See Credit Research Center, Krannert Graduate School of Management, Purdue University, Ind., USA, Monographs No. 23–4, *Consumer Bankruptcy Study* (1982). The study concluded that at least one-third of consumer debtors could repay a significant portion of their debts. However, critics have pointed out a number of significant flaws in the study. See, e.g., T. A. Sullivan, *et al.*, 'Rejoinder: Limiting Access to Bankruptcy Discharge' (1984) *Wis L Rev* 1087; T. A. Sullivan, *et al.*, 'Limiting Access to Bankruptcy Discharge: An Analysis of the Creditors' Data' (1983) *Wis L Rev* 1091.
53 Senator Dole introduced S. 2000 in 1982. Congressman Evans introduced H.R. 4786 the same year. These measures were reintroduced in the 98th Congress as H.R. 1169 and S. 445. See 146 Cong. Rec. S11683–02 (daily ed. 7 December 2000).
54 11 U.S.C. § 707(b).   55 See, e.g., *Green v. Staples (In re Green)*, 934 F 2d 568 (4th Cir. 1991).
56 These efforts (through the 105th Congress) are detailed in C. J. Tabb, 'A Century of Regress or Progress? A Political History of Bankruptcy Legislation in 1898 and 1998' (1999) 15 *Bankr Dev J* 343, 344–53.
57 See Ernst and Young Economics, Consulting and Quantitative Analysis, T. Neubig, *et al.*, 'Chapter 7 Bankruptcy Petitioners' Repayment Ability under H.R. 833: the National Perspective' (1999) 7 *American Bankruptcy Institute Law Review* 79, 81.
58 Bankruptcy Reform Act of 1994, Pub. L. No. 103–394, 108 Stat. 4106.

Elizabeth Warren of Harvard, and its Chairman, Brady Williamson, thoroughly reviewed but then categorically rejected the notion of means testing when it issued its report in the fall of 1997.[59] Only two of the nine commissioners expressed support for means testing[60] notwithstanding the credit industry's fevered promotion of that scheme.

Congress now apparently agrees with the dissenters[61] that the vagueness of the substantial abuse test and procedural restrictions[62] have weakened the effectiveness of § 707(b) as a means of screening out 'can pay' debtors and channelling them into Chapter 13. A 1999 Senate Report, commenting on a prior reform bill, observed: 'In sum, from its inception, section 707(b) was designed with serious defects which have rendered the section unusable.'[63]

The current Reform Bill would eliminate any indirection and enact explicitly the essence of what the consumer credit industry has long sought. As Representative George Gekas, the primary champion of bankruptcy reform in the House, explained when introducing the new version of the Reform Bill (H. R. 333) in 2001 in the 107th Congress:[64]

> An important feature of the new bill, will be that certain provisions will be put into place which will make certain that those people who have an ability to repay some of their debts *will be compelled to do so*, so that instead of a Chapter 7 filing which will give that automatic almost-fresh start, we will be able *to shepherd some of those debtors into Chapter 13* and propose a plan and adopt a plan by which they could over a period of time repay some of the debt out of their then-current earnings.

Consumer bankruptcy after the fall

The means test

The heart of the reform effort[65] is to impose means testing as a gatekeeping device that would close the Chapter 7 door to those debtors who are judged to have some ability to repay their creditors out of future income. The idea is to

---

59 National Bankruptcy Review Commission Final Report, *Bankruptcy: the Next Twenty Years* (20 October 1997), 89–91.
60 *Ibid.*, Commissioners Edith Jones and James Shephard, *Additional Dissent to Recommendations for Reform of Consumer Bankruptcy Law*, 10–25.
61 See S. Rep. No. 106–49, 106th Cong., 1st Sess. 6 (1999).
62 Creditors and the trustee are prohibited from requesting or even 'suggesting' dismissal for substantial abuse, leaving it up to either the bankruptcy judge to act *sua sponte*, which he rarely does, or to the United States trustee to make a substantial abuse motion.
63 See S. Rep. No. 106–49, 106th Cong., 1st Sess. 6 (1999).
64 147 Cong. Rec. H133 (daily ed. 31 January 2001) (remarks of Rep. Gekas) (emphasis added).
65 See H.R. Rep. No. 105–540, 105th Cong., 2nd Sess. 55 (1998).

'requir[e] bankrupts to repay their debts when they have the ability to do so'.[66] Imposition of a means test has been the Holy Grail sought by the consumer credit industry for over a third of a century.

The means test checks for projected surplus income. Debtors whose income exceeds allowed expenses by a certain minimum amount are deemed to have the 'means' to repay their creditors. A debtor who fails the means test would be dismissed from Chapter 7, thus leaving a Chapter 13 repayment plan as the debtor's only remaining bankruptcy alternative. As Senator Chuck Grassley stated: 'The bill . . . sets up a flexible formula . . . to channel those with repayment capacity to Chapter 13.'[67]

Means testing expands dramatically on the concept of 'substantial abuse' dismissal under § 707(b). According to the reformers, a debtor with even a modest amount of projected surplus income should *not* be permitted to obtain an immediate bankruptcy discharge simply by relinquishing her non-exempt assets in a liquidation bankruptcy under Chapter 7. If the debtor wants a discharge, she should have to pay for the privilege by giving her creditors the income surplus. As Senator Grassley has argued, 'it's not fair to permit people who can repay to skip out on their debts'.[68]

Superficially, means testing has some appeal. Accepting Grassley's premise, it is hard to argue that 'it *is* fair to permit people who can repay to skip out on their debts'. The spectre of the proverbial rich doctor filing for bankruptcy, stiffing his creditors and then enjoying a life of luxury unfettered by his just debts, understandably draws our ire. That is the picture the consumer credit industry paints.

But is it an accurate picture? The pitch for means testing rests on several critical and often unstated assumptions. If any of these assumptions do not hold, the seemingly 'obvious' case for means testing starts to disintegrate. Means testing may be a simple answer to the wrong questions. Professor Jean Braucher has cogently referred to means testing as a 'distraction'.[69]

The question we need to ask is whether the game is worth the candle. Is there even a problem that needs to be fixed? Is there a 'game' that is worth being played? If there is a possible problem, then we need to ask two follow-up questions. First, to play the game, is it worth burning the means-testing 'candle'? That is, will the costs associated with means testing be worth any benefits that might be gained? Secondly, is means testing the *right* candle to burn? Does the solution lie in stepping

66 S. Rep. No. 106–49, 106th Cong., 1st Sess. 4 (1999).
67 Press Release, Sen. Chuck Grassley (31 January 2001), www.senate.gov/~grassley/releases/2001/p01r-31.html.
68 146 Cong. Rec. S5383 (daily ed. 20 June 2000) (remarks of Sen. Grassley).
69 J. Braucher, 'Increasing Uniformity in Consumer Bankruptcy: Means Testing as a Distraction and the National Bankruptcy Review Commission's Proposals as a Starting Point' (1998) 6 *Am Bankr Inst L Rev* 1.

up the policing of consumer debtors or in asking creditors to be a bit more diligent in handing out credit?

What is the 'game'? Reformers say the name of the game is 'fixing the bankruptcy crisis'.[70] They assert that a crisis exists because of (1) the substantial rise in the *number* of consumer bankruptcy filings in the United States in recent years, and because of (2) the substantial losses allegedly 'caused' by those filings. Reform advocates then take the leap of faith that *debtors* are causing the crisis, that debtors are abusing the law by taking out too much credit, living the high life, and sliding down the easy path of discharge when they could repay a significant portion of their debts.

This portrait is grossly exaggerated and factually unsupported. There is no doubt that the number of consumer bankruptcy filings has increased substantially. Total bankruptcy filings went from 331,264 in 1980 to 1,253,444 in 2000, and consumer bankruptcies went from 287,570 in 1980 to 1,217,972 in 2000 both approximately a fourfold increase.[71] Of those consumer cases, 838,576, or almost 70 per cent, were filed under Chapter 7.[72] No one in the United States is happy about those numbers (except perhaps debtors' attorneys). But ascertaining the *cause* of this rise is not so easy.

Studies show that the vast majority of Chapter 7 bankruptcies are caused by medical problems, divorce, or job lay-offs.[73] Furthermore, the financial circumstances of debtors filing for bankruptcy today are as desperate as they ever have been.[74] Indeed, the *real* incomes of the bottom 60 per cent of American families have actually declined since 1980. Thus, the 'abuse' mantra is a canard.[75]

Furthermore, other studies show that the increase in the number of consumer bankruptcies is closely correlated with the increase in the amount of outstanding consumer credit,[76] and with the rate of credit card defaults.[77] The level of personal debt has never been higher.[78] Credit issuers in the United States have made credit readily available to debtors, flooding debtors with endless solicitations to take on

---

70 See S. Rep. No. 106–49, 106th Cong., 1st Sess. 2 (1999).

71 See 'U.S. Bankruptcy Filings 1980–2000 (Business, Non-Business, Total)', American Bankruptcy Institute, www.abiworld.org/stats/1980annual.html.

72 See 'Non-Business Bankruptcy Filings by Chapter 1990–2000, per quarter', American Bankruptcy Institute, www.abiworld.org/stats/1990nonbuschapter.html.

73 See 'A Bad Bankruptcy Bill', *San Francisco Chronicle* (15 March 2001).

74 See National Bankruptcy Review Commission Final Report, *Bankruptcy*, 83–4; E. Warren, 'The Bankruptcy Crisis' (1998) 73 *Ind LJ* 1081, 1094–1100.

75 See E. Warren, 'A Principled Approach to Consumer Bankruptcy' (1997) 71 *Am Bankr L J* 483, 493.

76 See, e.g., R. M. Lawless, 'The Relationship between Nonbusiness Bankruptcy Filings and Various Basic Measures of Consumer Debt' (1 October 2000), www.law.missouri.edu/lawless/bus.bkr/filings.htm; National Bankruptcy Review Commission Final Report, *Bankruptcy*.

77 See L. M. Ausubel, 'Credit Card Defaults, Credit Card Profits, and Bankruptcy' (1997) 71 *Am Bankr L J* 249, 250.

78 Americans are spending one-seventh of their take-home pay on debts: 'Debt Pinches Consumers', *CNN Financial News*, cnnfn.cnn.com/2001/06/20/news/wires/consumers.debt.wg/.

more and ever more credit. In the last several years, approximately *three billion* solicitations for credit cards were mailed every year,[79] an average of nearly twenty offers for every single American between the ages of eighteen and sixty-four. Another study found that one-third of all college students had four or more credit cards![80] Credit card issuers do all of this for the very simple reason that they make a very large amount of money. Industry profits surged 44 per cent from 1998 to 2000.[81] Yet, while inundating debtors with credit offers, credit issuers express consternation when some debtors are unable to pay the crushing debt load. While debtors may not all be blameless, neither are the creditors.

Nor is it fair to assume that most debtors can repay a significant portion of their debts. An empirical study by Professors Culhane and White, which was funded by the non-partisan American Bankruptcy Institute, concluded that only 3.6 per cent of Chapter 7 debtors in their study were possible 'can pay' debtors.[82] A study by Bermant and Flynn for the Executive Office of United States Trustees concluded: 'Only a small percentage of current Chapter 7 debtors have income sufficient to repay any portion of their unsecured debts.'[83]

The 'candle' (that reformers want to burn) is means testing. The game is worth the candle, reformers urge, on the assumptions that (1) means testing would recoup a significant portion of the illicit bankruptcy losses, and (2) step one could be effected at an acceptable cost. Neither assumption is warranted. First, the reformers' assertion that means testing would result in the collection of an additional $3 billion a year from debtors[84] is very dubious. Respected non-partisan studies would generously put the figure at less than $1 billion. The Culhane and White study determined that 'a more realistic estimate would be $450 million', and that 'even under the overly optimistic assumptions' of the credit industry studies, creditors would 'collect at most an additional $930 million from can pay debtors'.[85] The Bermant and Flynn study concluded, 'we believe that the final return to

---

79 See 'Credit Card Issuers Aggressively Expand Marketing and Lines of Credit on Eve of New Bankruptcy Restrictions', *Consumer Federation of America* (27 February 2001), www.abiworld.org/travpr.pdf; D. J. Saunders, 'Of Puppies, Kittens, and Huge Credit-Card Debts', *San Francisco Chronicle* (22 May 2001), citing report by credit-card research firm BAI Global Inc.
80 See Saunders 'Of Puppies'.   81 See 'Credit Card Issuers'.
82 See M. B. Culhane and M. M. White, 'Taking the New Consumer Bankruptcy Model for a Test Drive: Means-Testing Real Chapter 7 Debtors' (1999) 7 *Am Bankr Inst L Rev* 27, 31. The Culhane and White study was based on an earlier bill, H.R. 3150, 105th Cong., which differed from the pending Reform Bill in several particulars. For example, that earlier bill did not have a safe harbour provision. These differences would suggest that the number of 'can pay' debtors under the Reform Bill would be even *lower* than the 3.6 per cent estimated by Culhane and White, perhaps even as low as 1 per cent or 2 per cent.
83 See Executive Office of United States Trustees, G. Bermant and E. Flynn, *Incomes, Debts, and Repayment Capacities of Recently Discharged Chapter 7 Debtors* (January 1999), www.abiworld.org/legis/reform/eoust-99jan.html.
84 See S. Rep. No. 106–49, 106th Cong., 1st Sess. 2 (1999).
85 Culhane and White, 'Taking the New Consumer Bankruptcy Model for a Test Drive', 31.

unsecured creditors under means testing as proposed would be less than $1 billion annually'.[86]

Secondly, means testing would create a huge new bureaucratic burden for courts, trustees, debtors and debtors' attorneys – for everybody in the bankruptcy game, that is, *except* creditors. The Congressional Budget Office estimated that an earlier version of the Reform Bill (H.R. 3150) would cost $214 million in the first five years, plus $8–16 million more to pay the new judges that would be needed to apply means testing.[87] As Professor Warren has pointed out, 'someone would have to pay for means testing'.[88]

In light of these facts, Professors Culhane and White concluded that 'the net gains to unsecured creditors, in sum, appear small relative to the costs likely to be imposed on the great majority of Chapter 7 debtors, as well as trustees, judges, and taxpayers'.[89]

Professor Warren, the Reporter for the National Bankruptcy Review Commission, laments:[90]

> With a means test in place, either the system would have to commit vastly more resources to reviewing the circumstances of each failing debtor in Chapter 13 or it would make bankruptcy relief unavailable for people who could not repay their creditors … In the latter case, the safety valve that keeps consumer debt burdens in check would be lost. The consumer bankruptcy system would not be strengthened; it would be destroyed.

The candle that reformers do *not* want to burn is to require the consumer credit industry to monitor their own behaviour. They could do this, first, by being more responsible and diligent in selecting those to whom they extend credit. In recent years many large credit issuers have become very active in marketing credit to debtors, often without worrying much about the debtor's creditworthiness. The credit issuers engage in this policy for the simple reason that they like to make money. As noted earlier, credit card industry profits went up by 44 per cent from 1998 to 2000. Credit card issuers can make a lot of money by charging extremely high interest rates to their legions of debtors. That a certain percentage of those debtors will default is *already* factored in to the high interest rates charged. Should it be any surprise that many of those debtors will default and then seek refuge in bankruptcy? And when they do, are the creditors really blameless? Yet, the pending reforms would give consumer lenders the go-ahead to proceed merrily along the careless path they have chosen.

86 Bermant and Flynn, *Incomes*.
87 See Culhane and White, 'Taking the New Consumer Bankruptcy Model for a Test Drive', 32 n. 21.
88 Warren, 'A Principled Approach', 504.
89 Culhane and White, 'Taking the New Consumer Bankruptcy Model for a Test Drive', 61.
90 Warren, 'A Principled Approach', 506.

Indeed, with means testing in place, credit issuers can be expected to become even *more* aggressive in soliciting and extending credit, because the credit issuer would have less reason to fear a bankruptcy discharge.[91] If past evidence is any guide, this expansion of credit in turn would cause more debtor defaults. But, with means testing in place, those economically burdened debtors would have no place to turn.

A second way that the consumer credit industry could be policed is to require credit issuers to *disclose* more information to their debtors. With this information, debtors might be able to make more prudent choices. Scholars have long pointed out that one of the primary justifications for the bankruptcy discharge is the fact that debtors are not able to make accurate forecasts about the likelihood of future defaults.[92] Debtors systematically underestimate future risks and overestimate their future prospects. One suggestion that has been made is to require credit card lenders to disclose in a conspicuous manner how long it will take a debtor to pay off the balance if he or she makes only the minimum payments required. Even this modest idea has been resisted by the credit industry. Ironically, reform proponents claim that the Reform Bill *would* enhance disclosures.[93] But this 'disclosure' would only require a notice on a credit-card bill of a toll-free number that a debtor could call if she wanted to find out how long it would take to pay off the debt.

Means testing under the Reform Bill

Let us turn now to a more detailed examination of the particulars of means testing, as provided for in the act that passed both houses of Congress in December 2000 (H.R. 2415). That Reform Bill served as the template for reform in the 107th Congress; the separate bills passed in the two houses in March 2001 (H.R. 333, S. 420) are virtually identical to H.R. 2415 with respect to means testing.[94]

As the following discussion will explain, there are numerous problems with the means test, not only in its basic conception but also in its specific application. A glaring flaw is that *all* individual debtors would be required to file a means test calculation with their schedules,[95] even though studies estimate that less than a quarter of those debtors would actually be subjected to means testing. The heart of the means test is the 'presumption of abuse', which compares the debtor's projected future income with expenses to ascertain whether that debtor supposedly could repay a

---

91 See Braucher, 'Increasing Uniformity', 8.
92 See T. H. Jackson, 'The Fresh-Start Policy in Bankruptcy' (1985) 98 *Harv L Rev* 1393.
93 Press Release, Sen. Chuck Grassley (31 January 2001), www.senate.gov/~grassley/releases/2001/p01r1-31.html.
94 In a handful of instances the Senate Bill (SB) differs from the House version and the Reform Bill, and is separately noted.
95 Reform Bill § 102(a)(2)(C).

certain amount or percentage of her debts, in which event the debtor is deemed to be a presumptive abuser. Both the income and the expense components are quite problematic, as will be seen below.

The presumption of abuse

Section 102 of the Reform Bill contains the principal provision for means testing. The vehicle used is a dramatic expansion of the current provision in § 707(b) for dismissal of an individual consumer debtor's case for 'substantial abuse'. Under the Reform Bill, the statutory reference is changed simply to 'abuse'.[96] More important than the jargon used is the substantive change that the new statute would create a *presumption* of abuse if the debtor has a certain level of projected income in excess of allowable expenses.[97] The theory driving the reform is that the debtor could and should devote this excess net income to the payment of creditors in a Chapter 13 plan. If the presumption is triggered and is not rebutted, the court *must* dismiss the case, unless the debtor avails himself or herself of the 'option' to convert to Chapter 13.[98]

Under § 102(a)(2)(C) of the Reform Bill, the threshold level of excess income that will trigger the presumption of abuse is determined according to the following calculation:

- Net monthly income (i.e., income less deductible expenses) multiplied by sixty months (i.e., five years) is not less than the lesser of
- 25 per cent of the debtor's non-priority unsecured claims, or $6,000, whichever is greater, OR
- $10,000

Note first that the required repayment period is pegged at *five* years (sixty months), an expansion of 67 per cent over the current presumptive *three*-year length of a Chapter 13 plan.[99] No explanation is given for this rather dramatic increase. Given that today two-thirds of Chapter 13 debtors fail to complete performance of a three-year plan, the statutory presumption that debtors should be judged against a projected five-year pay-out from income is unsupportable.

Secondly, the test assumes that nothing will change regarding the debtor's income and expenses for five years! If the notion of change is considered at all, even implicitly, then the formula works only if both income and expenses happen to change by exactly the same amount. The premise of no change (or identical change) is handy, to be sure, but also preposterous.

Thirdly, any debtor who can repay $10,000 over that five-year period is presumptively an abuser, no matter how small a *percentage* of his or her debt that represents.

---

96 Reform Bill § 102(a)(2)(B)(i)(III).   97 Reform Bill § 102(a)(2)(C).
98 Reform Bill § 102(a)(2)(B)(i)(II).   99 11 U.S.C. § 1322(c).

In short, any debtor with net income of $166.67 a month is presumptively barred from Chapter 7 relief. Furthermore, a debtor with debts of $24,000 or less is deemed an abuser if he or she can pay $100 a month to creditors.

Some examples will illustrate the application of the test. Consider first a debtor with debts of only $20,000, income of $2,500 per month, and allowed expenses of $2,400 per month. This debtor would be a presumptive abuser as she has $100 in net income theoretically available, and thus over sixty months could pay $6,000. Or, as a second example, consider an unusual single debtor with $800,000 in debt, income of $2,970 per month and allowed expenses of $2,800 per month. This second debtor also would be a presumptive abuser as she supposedly could pay $170 per month, for sixty months, for a total of $10,200, thus satisfying prong two of the test. That debtor would thus be denied bankruptcy relief under Chapter 7 even though she could pay her creditors just a shade more than 1 per cent of the debt owed.

The new 'abuse' test demonstrates the truth of the adage that 'the devil is in the details'. Looking at the details shows how complicated and cumbersome, as well as how unfair and subject to manipulation, the proposed means test would be. I first will examine the income side of the ledger, and then the expense deductions. Both are flawed.

Income

The means test requires ascertainment of income and expenses. Let us begin with income. Income, called 'current monthly income', is defined as the average monthly income that the debtor (or the debtor and the debtor's spouse in a joint case) received from *all* sources, without regard to whether it is taxable income, for the six months prior to bankruptcy, *plus* any amount contributed by someone else on a regular basis to the debtor's household expenses. [100] The only income excluded is that from social security benefits and war crimes reparations.

Thus, believing apparently that 'what is past is prologue', the Reform Bill takes the debtor's historical earnings record and presumes that the debtor will *continue* earning that same income for the next five years. If the debtor believes this income projection to be unwarranted (for example, because the debtor has been laid off), the debtor bears the burden of raising that argument as 'special circumstances' to rebut the presumption of abuse.[101] Thus, for the purposes of triggering the presumption of abuse, the means test would count income from a job the debtor no longer has!

Conversely, because of its purely retrospective focus, the income component of the Reform Bill's means test will *not* capture a debtor whose income prospects are about to improve dramatically. The bright young law school graduate who has accepted a job with a big city firm for $100,000 could blithely file for bankruptcy under Chapter 7 without having to worry about the means test.

100 Reform Bill § 102(b).   101 Reform Bill § 102(a)(2)(C).

So, too, could a clever debtor carefully manipulate his income by keeping it un-usually low in the six months before filing bankruptcy to ensure that he keeps his net income just below the threshold amount that would trigger a presumption of abuse. For example, a debtor who has regularly worked overtime in the past might be well advised to eschew overtime work for the six-month pre-bankruptcy income-calculation period so that the debtor could escape means test scrutiny and qualify for Chapter 7 relief. The wisdom of a congressional test that creates an incentive for bankrupt debtors to work less and earn less is suspect.

Expense deductions

If income is problematic, the expense (or deduction) side is even worse. Obviously it is imperative to provide for expense deductions to arrive at a net income figure, because debtors cannot devote *all* of their income to the payment of creditors. Everyone has necessary expenses such as food, clothing, shelter and utilities. But how to decide what deductions to allow?

Current Chapter 13 offers a possible model, using an open-ended standard in which the bankruptcy judge exercises discretion. A debtor must devote all of her 'disposable income' to payments under the Chapter 13 plan.[102] 'Disposable in-come' is defined simply as income received by the debtor that is not reasonably nec-essary for the maintenance or support of the debtor or the debtor's dependents.[103] Bankruptcy judges make case-by-case decisions on a regular basis about what types and amounts of expenses in a debtor's proposed budget are 'reasonably necessary' for a debtor's 'maintenance or support'.

Yet, making such individualised determinations is time consuming and labour intensive, and inevitably leads to differential treatment of debtors in like situations. One judge's necessity may be another judge's luxury. The current reformers worry that bankruptcy judges might be too soft on debtors and not require debtors to 'tighten their belts' enough. Another problem with using a 'chancellor's foot' type of approach to gauge deductions, when means testing is employed as an up-front screening device, is that many debtors cannot know *in advance* with any certainty whether they will pass the means test.

Accordingly, a central aspect of the Reform Bill supposedly is to take most of the discretion away from the bankruptcy judges in assessing allowable expense deductions.[104] The amounts and categories of permitted expense deductions are largely set in stone pursuant to congressional edict. Furthermore, these allowances are relatively parsimonious, excepting only a few areas that the reformers sought to favour.

The end result is a system where many honest debtors are treated no better than taxpayer cheats, while a few shrewd debtors would be able to arrange their

102 11 U.S.C. § 1325(b)(1).　103 11 U.S.C. § 1325(b)(2)(A).
104 See J. F. Williams, 'Distrust: the Rhetoric and Reality of Means-Testing' (1999) 7 *American Bankruptcy Institute Law Review* 105, 128.

affairs to live luxuriously and yet pass the means test into the hallowed halls of Chapter 7.[105] Furthermore, it is doubtful whether the Reform Bill even achieves its goals of predictability, consistency and ease of administration.

The categories of deductions from income allowed by the Reform Bill may be divided into four main groups: (1) living expenses; (2) secured debts; (3) priority claims; and (4) miscellaneous favoured expenses.

Living expenses: IRS Collection Standards

A significant policy decision that the reformers made was to gauge allowable living expenses by reference to the Collection Standards of the Internal Revenue Service.[106] The IRS uses those Standards to determine how much a delinquent tax-payer should be permitted to keep for herself; the rest is supposed to be remitted to the government. In principle, then, the underlying premise of the bankruptcy Re-form Bill is that consumer bankruptcy debtors deserve to be treated like delinquent taxpayers. A corollary concept is that private creditors are entitled to the same rights and benefits the government has in collecting taxes. Both notions are revolutionary, extraordinary and unsupported. It is little wonder that the consumer credit indus-try is so anxious to obtain the passage of the Reform Bill; never in American law has a private creditor been able to attain such a privileged status. Yet Congress has stead-fastly deflected all efforts to jettison use of the IRS Standards. The only concession made to those upset about use of the IRS Standards is that a debtor may be allowed to add 5 per cent to the allowance for food and clothing if the debtor demonstrates that the increase is 'reasonable and necessary'.

Nor is use of the IRS Collection Standards even limited to Chapter 7. Under the Reform Bill, the expenses allowed to a Chapter 13 debtor under § 1325(b) for pur-poses of calculating whether the debtor is devoting all 'disposable income' to plan payments would be based on the IRS Standards, not the debtor's actual expenses as under current law, if the debtor's income exceeds the state median for a family of like size.[107]

Aside from the policy issue implicated, use of the IRS Standards to determine liv-ing expenses would present many difficulties. One concern with the Standards in a bankruptcy context is the arbitrariness (and seeming unfairness) of some of the distinctions that would be drawn. Furthermore, these distinctions could reward ingenious planning. For example, the IRS Allowance for Housing and Utilities is based on the county of the debtor's residence. To use my home State of Illinois as an illustration, a debtor with a family of four who lives in Cook County (Chicago)

---

105 Some of the loopholes in the Reform Bill that permit wealthy debtors to shield assets from cred-itors are discussed in at pp. 294–6.

106 Reform Bill § 102(a)(2)(C). The Collection Standards are set out in volume II, Internal Revenue Manual, at § 5323, and exhibits 5300–45 to –51.

107 Reform Bill § 102(h).

would be allotted $1,355 per month for housing. If that same debtor were to move across the county line (to DuPage or to Lake County), that debtor would be allotted an extra $336 per month for housing[108] or $20,000 more for the sixty months of the means test. Thus, making that move might well be the difference that would enable the debtor to pass the means test. As another example, consider the IRS Allowance for Food, Clothing, and Other Items, which differentiates on the basis of income. A debtor with a family of four and an annual income of $70,000 would be allotted almost $5,000 per year more (and thus $25,000 for the sixty months of the means test calculation) for food and clothing than would a debtor with a $50,000 income.[109] Do wealthier people have to eat more?

Consider another problem that would arise. The IRS Standards fail to differentiate between *owners* and *renters* (or *lessees*) in both the housing allowance and the transportation allowance. That is good and well for the IRS, perhaps. But in the context of a bankruptcy means test, it does not work. Why not? It does not work because the means test provides a *separate* deduction for payments on *secured* debts, as will be explained below. Therefore, a debtor with *actual* secured debt payments for housing or for a car that are *greater* than the IRS allocation would be entitled to deduct that larger amount. This result provides a perverse incentive for debtors to take on substantial secured debt prior to bankruptcy; by increasing allowable expense deductions, a debtor may be able to pass the means test.

Nor should one forget the problem of timing. The expenses allowed to the debtor under the IRS Standards are only good for *today*. Yet the debtor will be incurring expenses for the next five years (the period covered by the means test). And it is hardly a revelation to suggest that expenses are likely to *increase* over that five-year period. It is true that under the means test, a debtor's income (like expenses) also is projected forward from the present into the five-year future, without any adjustment for projected changes. In that sense, the comparison made is between apples and apples. But they are rotten apples. Whether a debtor passes or fails the means test depends on the difference between income and expenses. The *only* way the Reform Bill's means test will give an accurate picture of that total difference, even assuming that the present calculations and allowances are correct, is if both the income and expense components either do not change one penny *or* change by exactly the same amount, for five full years. Neither prospect is likely, to say the least. Nor is this a picking over nits. When a debtor can be denied access to Chapter 7 bankruptcy relief if the means test calculation reveals an excess of income over expenses of as little as $100 per month, even the slightest adjustment could make all the difference.

Finally, the Reform Bill's use of the IRS Collection Standards will not even provide the certainty and ease of computation so earnestly sought. Bankruptcy judges

---

108 See www.irs.ustreas.gov/prod/ind.info/coll.stds/cfs-il.html.
109 See www.irs.ustreas.gov/prod/ind.info/coll.stds/cfs-other.html.

still will have to make subjective judgment calls on an individualised, case-by-case basis. Nor should this be surprising; it is inescapable. People (even including bankruptcy debtors) face different issues and problems and have different needs in their lives. One debtor may have a child with a serious and costly illness; another debtor may need to commute an unusually long way to work to earn a decent wage. The possible variations are as endless as the number of debtors who file for bankruptcy. A serious attempt to provide nearly absolute advance certainty would run afoul of the principle of individual justice. Debtors thus will still not be able to know for sure in advance whether they will pass means test scrutiny, and like debtors may be treated differently.

How is certainty lost? First, the IRS Standards include a category for 'Other Necessary Expenses', which is a catch-all designed to capture everything that a debtor needs that is not reflected in the distinct Standards for housing, transportation and food and clothing. This residual classification offers some modicum of needed flexibility for the IRS to account for differences between debtors. In the Reform Bill, a deduction is permitted for a debtor's *actual* monthly expenses that fall within this 'other' category.[110] But that then means that a bankruptcy judge will have to pass on the reasonableness and necessity of each debtor's actual 'other' expenses.

The second way certainty is lost is through the possibility that a debtor may try to *rebut* a presumption of abuse by showing 'special circumstances' warranting an adjustment of income or expenses, as explained below.[111]

In sum, use of the IRS Standards is not only dubious as a matter of principle, but the very certitude supposedly promised by invocation of those Standards would be ephemeral. In practice, the Standards may prove both unworkable and unfair.

Secured debts

The Reform Bill allows a debtor to deduct her average monthly payments on account of secured debts.[112] These payments include (1) any payments contractually due to secured creditors for the sixty months following the bankruptcy petition date and (2) additional payments to secured creditors necessary for the debtor to retain her primary residence, motor vehicle, and any other property necessary for support of the debtor and her dependents. Category (2) payments typically would be used for the purpose of curing arrears.

The deduction for secured debts in calculating the means test is understandable, since the bankruptcy law allows secured creditors to insist on full payment out of their collateral, even in Chapter 13.[113] If the premise of means test scrutiny is to steer supposed 'can pay' debtors into Chapter 13, then the test must take the realities of a putative Chapter 13 into account. It would be patently unfair to rule a

---

110 Reform Bill § 102(a)(2)(C).   111 *Ibid.*   112 *Ibid.*   113 11 U.S.C. § 1325(a)(5).

debtor ineligible for Chapter 7 under the means test by denying a full secured debt deduction, when that debtor would have to pay the same secured debt in full in a Chapter 13 plan. Indeed, in such a world a debtor easily could be unable to proceed *either* in Chapter 7 or in Chapter 13.

Having said that, the problem that arises is one of moral hazard and perverse incentives. In effect, for purposes of the means test a debtor is *rewarded* for having large amounts of secured debt. For the housing and transportation expenses, a debtor with actual secured debt expenses greater than the IRS Standards would be entitled to deduct those larger actual debt expenses. In applying the means test the bankruptcy judge is not asked to examine the circumstances under which the debtor *incurred* the secured debt. Such an inquiry could only be raised in a general good faith assessment. The only question under the means test is whether such secured debt payments are actually due after the bankruptcy filing. Thus, a debtor who plans carefully can manipulate her net income prior to filing bankruptcy so that she will be able to pass the means test. All that the debtor need do is take on additional secured debt. Alternatively, in the months preceding bankruptcy a debtor could choose to pay down her *un*secured debts, at the expense of her *secured* debts, and thus would have a higher amount of secured debt when the means test is computed.

As an example of the first tactic, assume a hypothetical debtor with monthly net surplus income of $800 (a means test failure for sure)[114] who is driving a paid-off ten-year-old vehicle. That debtor then might decide to buy a new Mercedes a month before filing Chapter 7, incurring a monthly payment of $750 on the new car. With net income now reduced to a mere $50 a month, the debtor could easily pass means test scrutiny.[115] Is this really a wise system?

Priority claims

Priority claims present problems for means testing under the Reform Bill that are similar to the problems raised by secured debts. Under bankruptcy law, priority claims are paid first amongst unsecured claims, after satisfaction of secured claims.[116] A Chapter 13 plan can only be confirmed if it provides for full payment of priority claims.[117] As was true with secured debts, then, a means test that is designed to channel debtors into Chapter 13 must of necessity take into account what debts those debtors will be required to pay as a matter of law in the event they do end up in Chapter 13.

---

114 The debtor would be able to pay $48,000 over sixty months, well above the $10,000 figure that would always constitute a means test failure: Reform Bill § 102(a)(2)(C).
115 The debtor now would be able to pay only $3,000 over sixty months, substantially below the $6,000 floor that is the smallest possible repayment amount that would be expected under the means test: *ibid.*
116 Tabb, *The Law of Bankruptcy*, § 7.7, 494.   117 11 U.S.C. § 1322(a)(2).

Accordingly, the Reform Bill grants debtors an expense deduction for all priority claims.[118] The Bill also includes a deduction for actual administrative expenses that would be incurred by the debtor in a Chapter 13 case, up to a maximum of 10 per cent of plan payments.

Granting a deduction for priority claims is inevitable but, like the deduction for secured debts, raises moral hazard problems and creates perverse incentives that reward pre-bankruptcy planning that undermines congressional aims. A debtor who is considering filing Chapter 7 and whose net income is close to the margin for triggering the presumption of abuse might choose *not* to pay priority claims in the months preceding bankruptcy. Instead the debtor could use any available dollars to pay non-priority unsecured debts. For example, a debtor with a substantial priority alimony debt might postpone paying that debt prior to bankruptcy. Then the full amount of the alimony debt will count as a direct deduction from income, perhaps enabling the debtor to pass the means test. The wisdom of a test that rewards a debtor for *not* paying the very debts that Congress has declared to be most important (and thus entitled to priority) seems open to question.

Miscellaneous favoured expenses

Finally, in the Reform Bill Congress has singled out a few favoured types of expenses as ones that a debtor may deduct from income *in addition* to her other deductions for IRS-blessed living expenses, secured debts and priority claims. These excluded expenses are: (1) amounts incurred that are reasonably necessary to maintain the safety of the debtor and the debtor's family from family violence; (2) the continuation of actual and reasonably necessary expenses for the care and support of an elderly, chronically ill or disabled member of the debtor's household or immediate family (excluding dependents of the debtor); and (3) actual expenses up to $1,500 per minor child per year, for the debtor's minor children to attend private school, if the debtor documents the expenses and gives a detailed explanation as to why they are reasonable and necessary.[119]

How can the reformers justify the discriminations made? Why should a debtor who wants to send her children to a private school be allowed to do so and credit that amount against any means test calculation, while debtors who send their children to the public schools are not given any correlative privilege? And why should a debtor who is *already* caring for a disabled relative be allowed a deduction while a debtor who needs to *start* doing so after filing for bankruptcy is not?

These expenses are likely to further undermine the predictability of the means test and embroil the bankruptcy judge in discretion-driven litigation. When is it 'reasonable and necessary' to send your child to a private school? To care for a disabled relative? To expend money to protect one's family?

118 Reform Bill § 102(a)(2)(C).   119 *Ibid.*

Nor should the current exclusion for charitable contributions be forgotten. Under § 707(b), in considering the question of abuse the court is precluded from considering the debtor's 'charitable contributions'. A debtor thus is allowed to make substantial contributions to charity, rather than paying her creditors, without being considered an 'abuser'. The Reform Bill does not touch this loophole.

Finally, debtors again are invited to try to manipulate the system. A debtor who spends $1,500 a year on private school can eat up $7,500 (per minor child!) over the sixty-month means test period of otherwise available net income. Sending Junior to First Baptist Academy rather than P.S. 100 could be the difference in whether the debtor is entitled to obtain an immediate discharge in a Chapter 7 or not.

Rebuttal of the presumption of abuse

One of the key ideas driving the reform is to limit the discretion of the bankruptcy judges in screening debtors for ability to pay.[120] This ideal was sought in order to put some teeth into the means test, unlike the substantial abuse test, which the credit industry views as a dead letter. Thus, if the presumption of abuse is triggered, the debtor can *rebut* the presumption only by proving 'special circumstances' such that either the income or expense side must be adjusted sufficiently to drop the debtor's sixty-month net income below the presumptive abuse amounts. The debtor must demonstrate that she has 'no reasonable alternative' to making the adjustment. Furthermore, the debtor must itemise and explain each asserted adjustment *and* provide documentation of the same.[121] Plainly, Congress intended to make it very hard for debtors to escape the rigours of the means test on an individualised basis. As explained below, the *in terrorem* availability of sanctions against debtor's counsel when a Chapter 7 case is dismissed under the means test is likely to chill most attempts to invoke the 'special circumstances' exception.

Safe harbour

Partially in response to the concerns expressed about the administrative burden that would be created by imposition of a means test, the reformers have created a 'safe harbour' that will exempt from its operation debtors whose family incomes fall below specified income medians. This screening would be done on the front end, excusing below-median debtors from the means test. The idea is that the 'truly poor' will not be subjected to means test scrutiny, leaving vulnerable only those with above-median incomes. Independent studies based on earlier versions of the Reform Bill estimate that somewhere between 18 per cent[122] and 24 per cent[123] of all Chapter 7 filers have incomes above the applicable safe harbour median income

---

120 See Williams, 'Distrust', 128–9.   121 *Ibid.*   122 See Bermant and Flynn, *Incomes*, 4.
123 See Culhane and White, 'Taking the New Consumer Bankruptcy Model for a Test Drive', 33.

and thus would be subjected to means testing. Splitting the difference and applying a 21 per cent figure to the 838,000 Chapter 7 filers of 2000 would mean that approximately 175,000 debtors would have to be screened under the means test. While this approach is preferable to means testing *all* debtors, 175,000 cases is still a very large number.

Furthermore, *all* debtors would be required to file a means test calculation with their schedules, no matter how low their income might be.[124]

The safe harbour uses *State median incomes* (for families of like size to the debtor's family) as the barometer. If the combined current income of the debtor and the debtor's spouse is less than or equal to the median income in the debtor's state for families of like size, then a means test motion may not be brought.

What are those median income levels? For all families in the United States, the median income in 1999 was $40,816.[125] Currently, the Bureau of the Census only publishes information on *State* median incomes for a family of four, so exact information is not available for other family sizes.[126] Still, some sense of the range of probable medians can be gleaned from existing information. For 1999, the most recent year for which the Census Bureau has published State median incomes, the United States median for a family of four was just under $60,000. The various State medians for four-person families ranged about $15,000 above and below the $60,000 mark, from a low of $44,947 (New Mexico) to a high of $75,505 (Connecticut). National median income information, which is available for families with less than four people, indicates that the median drops about $8,000 per person from the four-person level for families of three ($51,190) or two ($43,342) people. For single debtors, the single 'earner' figure is used for the safe harbour; in 1999, that number was $31,948.[127]

Sanctions

The Reform Bill also provides for *sanctions* to be imposed against a debtor's *counsel* if the case is dismissed as an abuse under § 707(b) and the court finds that the attorney violated rule 9011 (bankruptcy's equivalent to civil Rule 11).[128] The Reform Bill defines the content of the necessary rule 11 certification by the attorney so that virtually any dismissal could trigger sanctions. How does the Bill accomplish this neat trick? The Bill provides that the attorney's signature 'constitute[s] a certification that the attorney has ... determined that the petition ... does not constitute an abuse'.[129] Nor is there a 'good faith' exception. Thus, any dismissal for abuse

---

124 Reform Bill § 102(a)(2)(C).
125 See US Census Bureau, *Money Income in the United States: 1999*, 11, www.census.gov/prod/2000pubs/p60–209.pdf.
126 In passing the Reform Bill in December 2000, Congress announced in the Section by Section Explanation that 'it is expected that the Bureau of the Census will promptly make available state median income information by family size': 146 Cong. Rec. S11702 (7 December 2000).
127 See US Census Bureau, *Money Income*, 26.   128 Reform Bill § 102(a)(2)(C).   129 *Ibid.*

by definition will contradict and belie the accuracy of the attorney's certification, and expose that attorney to the risk of sanctions. In effect, the debtor's attorney is compelled to become a guarantor of the petition. That is, the debtor's attorney effectively faces *strict liability* with regard to the permissibility of her client's Chapter 7 filing.

The sanctions authorised are, first, payment to the trustee for all reasonable costs in bringing the dismissal motion, including reasonable attorney's fees. As if that were not enough, the court also is supposed to order payment of a civil penalty.[130]

The probable effects of this sanctions rule are: first, to increase the costs to debtors of filing a Chapter 7 case; secondly, to deter such filings, even when a plausible argument might be made that the filing is not an abuse; thirdly, to increase the number of *pro se* Chapter 7 filings; and, fourthly, to drive competent and ethical attorneys out of the consumer bankruptcy debtor field.[131] Any rational debtor's attorney would file a Chapter 7 case (if at all) only after doing considerable independent investigation of the debtor's finances. That investigation will not be free for debtors. Many attorneys will not even bother to try, and instead will refuse to file Chapter 7 cases except in the clearest qualifying cases (probably those in which the debtor's income is below the safe harbour median). Chapter 13 filings (which would be likely to rise) are much more expensive for debtors.

Furthermore, attorneys will not be willing to risk sanctions in close Chapter 7 cases. Thus, one would expect it to be quite rare for a debtor to file a Chapter 7 case with the income–expense calculation showing abuse, in the hope of persuading the court that she faces 'special circumstances'. That supposed safety valve is likely to become a dead letter. With qualified, ethical debtors' attorneys either unwilling to file Chapter 7, or willing to do so only for an exorbitant fee, debtors will be left to the clutches of disreputable attorneys or to their own devices in filing *pro se*. The sanctions rule in short order probably will curtail Chapter 7 filings, make bankruptcy more expensive for debtors, and decrease the quality of legal advice those debtors will receive.[132]

---

130 *Ibid.*
131 Many of the same concerns are echoed in J. L. Dam, 'Bankruptcy Law Puts Lawyers out of Work', *Lawyers Weekly USA* (16 March 2001), www.lawyersweekly.com/alert/usa/finalbankruptcy.htm, quoting H. Sommer, one of the leading consumer bankruptcy attorneys in the country: 'Attorneys will be serving fewer people and charging them more.'
132 As the American Bar Association's General Practice, Solo and Small Firm Section, lamented in a May 2001 letter to Congress vehemently opposing this provision and asking that it be deleted: 'Bankruptcy proceedings function more efficiently and with less loss of rights when all parties are represented by competent counsel ... The rule changes the attorney from an advocate for and representative of the client to his policeman. The legislation creates an unwaivable conflict of interest because the attorney must, in effect, inform against his client ... Further, the attorney must verify independently the representations of his client. The cost of verification will make competent bankruptcy attorneys shy away from representing debtors, and will require attorneys to become furniture appraisers rather than counsellors ... Attorneys will find it difficult if not impossible to settle cases with the trustee ... This proposed section creates a

Notwithstanding the apparent statutory threat to debtors' counsel, it is of course possible that in practice some bankruptcy judges will shy away from reading the statute in the way described above because of its harshness, and instead will sanction attorneys only on more traditional grounds. Even so, though, many of the negative effects of the statute described above are still likely to occur because the new sanctions rules would be on the books and attorneys would be understandably hesitant to incur even the risk of sanctions. Why should they?

Creating entry barriers

The sanctions rule just discussed is likely to erect a significant artificial entry barrier to Chapter 7 filings in addition to the general screening done via the means test. The Reform Bill contains additional provisions that also will create entry barriers. Harvard professor Elizabeth Warren has analogised the effect of the Reform Bill to inflicting a thousand paper cuts on consumer debtors, noting that one can die from that many small cuts. University of Chicago professor Douglas Baird, vice chair of the National Bankruptcy Conference, states that 'the big change is the paperwork' and opines that consumers and their lawyers 'will be drowning in paper'.[133]

What are some of these new requirements? For starters, the Reform Bill might be styled the 'full employment for credit counselling agencies' bill. Why? First, *every* individual debtor must complete a briefing with an approved credit counselling agency in the 180 days prior to bankruptcy as a *condition of eligibility* for bankruptcy relief.[134] Complying with the counselling requirement will be both a hassle and an expense for debtors. While exceptions are permitted upon proof of exigent circumstances, this device will make filing for bankruptcy more difficult. Note too that this eligibility test is *not* limited to debtors whose incomes are above the relevant median income level; even the poorest debtor will have to either go through credit counselling or convince the bankruptcy court to grant an exception.

As if it were not enough to force debtors to go through credit counselling as a condition of even being permitted to file for bankruptcy, the Reform Bill also introduces an 'educational' requirement as a *condition of discharge*. An individual debtor

substantial burden to finding counsel to represent debtors in most consumer cases. Knowledgeable counsel will stay away because they will not seek to become their client's insurer. Counsel will either charge substantial sums of money (which most debtors will be unable to afford) or will not take cases. This effectively denies clients timely and important representation at the time that they need it most. This, then, will deny access to the bankruptcy court system by many debtors, since they will not be able to obtain or afford competent legal advice': L. Feinstein, Chair of ABA General Practice Section, posted to bankrlaw@polecat.law.indiana.edu by M. S. Stern at marc@hutzbah.com (25 May 2001).
133 Dam, 'Bankruptcy Law'.   134 Reform Bill § 106(a).

must complete an instructional course on personal financial management or be denied a discharge. This limitation is imposed in both Chapter 7 and Chapter 13.[135] The educational requirement will again add a burden for debtors in terms of cost and time. Nor is there even an exception for exigent circumstances.

Another significant new set of requirements is that debtors must file a lot more paperwork. And, the sanction is harsh if *all* of the paperwork requirements are not complied with by day forty-five of the case: dismissal is *automatic*.[136] More paper, more paper cuts. Preparing these documents will take time and cost money, more barriers to entry. One example is that a debtor must file her most recent tax return, and provide a copy to the trustee before the first creditors' meeting, *and* send a copy of her tax return to any *creditor* who requests it.[137] New income statements, and projections of future income, must be filed. The debtor must file wage statements from her employer.[138]

Aside from the substantial cost to debtors that all of these new requirements will impose, one should not forget about the massive costs to the bankruptcy system as a whole. Administering the means test and all of these attendant new rules will be extremely expensive and burdensome. It is as if Congress is trying to impose the worst of the welfare and tax systems on the bankruptcy bureaucracy. Given the absence of compelling evidence of abuse, the imposition of these massive costs and burdens is hard to justify.

Deteriorating discharge

The Reform Bill systematically weakens the discharge available to consumer debtors. How? First, it *extends the time* between discharges. Under current law, debtors must wait six years after receiving a discharge in a case before they can obtain a discharge in a Chapter 7 case.[139] The Reform Bill would extend the time bar to *eight* years.[140]

Secondly, under current law there is no time bar between discharges if the debtor's *second* case is a Chapter 13 case, rather than a Chapter 7. This different rule makes sense, because a debtor must earn a discharge in Chapter 13 by making payments over the life of the plan.[141] Also, Congress wanted to encourage debtors to choose Chapter 13. No more. Now, the Reform Bill would impose a *five-year* bar

135 Reform Bill § 106(b) (Chapter 7), § 106(c) (Chapter 13). This instructional course can be offered by a for-profit enterprise, and by telephonic or online means: Reform Bill § 106(e). A veritable 'cottage industry' of internet-based financial management providers thus could well come into being. Quality control is likely to be a significant problem.
136 Reform Bill § 316.   137 Reform Bill § 315(b)(2).   138 Reform Bill § 315(b)(1).
139 11 U.S.C. § 727(a)(8). The exact measuring points for calculating the time bar are when the two cases are commenced, rather than the dates the discharges are granted.
140 Reform Bill § 312(1).   141 11 U.S.C. § 1328(a).

on receiving bankruptcy discharges when the second case is under Chapter 13.[142] This prohibition apparently would apply even if the debtor were to complete performance under the plan, and would apply no matter how high a percentage of debt the debtor were to pay under the plan.

The Senate Bill is slightly less onerous, erecting a *three*-year Chapter 13 ban rather than a five-year ban, if the first case was under Chapter 7, 11 or 12 and a two-year ban if the first case was under Chapter 13; the Senate Bill also includes an 'extreme hardship' exception.[143] The House Bill, though, retains the full five-year across-the-board bar.[144]

Thirdly, the 'loading up' presumption of fraud under § 523(a)(2)(C) is greatly expanded. Under current law a presumption of fraud arises if the debtor obtained 'luxury goods or services' of more than $1,075 within the sixty days prior to bankruptcy, or if the debtor received cash advances of more than $1,075 within that sixty-day period. Such eve-of-bankruptcy 'load ups' on cash or luxury goods are presumptively fraudulent. Under the Reform Bill, the luxury goods presumption would be dramatically expanded to all luxury goods totalling only $250 or more, and reaching back a full ninety days.[145] While the House Bill continues this minuscule $250 figure,[146] the Senate Bill adopts a $750 luxury goods floor.[147] All the bills expand the reach of the cash advance presumption, with the dollar amount needed to trigger the presumption dropping to $750, and the reach-back period extending back seventy days.[148]

This provision is a tricky back-door way of making a lot of credit card debt non-dischargeable. Consider a debtor who takes out cash advances of just $75.01 per week to buy groceries for her family, for the ten weeks prior to bankruptcy. That debtor presumptively is a 'fraud' and would have the burden of rebutting the presumption in order to discharge the credit card debt. Adding to the perversity and to the overall impact of the Bill as a trap for the unwary is the fact that the debtor *could* discharge the credit card debt if she charged the groceries *directly* to her credit card. It is the taking out of the cash advance even to use for general necessary living expenses that triggers the fraud presumption.

Another significant problem with the expanded presumption is that it will provide cover for credit card companies to bring more dischargeability complaints alleging fraud, without having to worry about their own potential liability. One of the biggest congressional concerns prior to the enactment of the 1978 Bankruptcy Code was the prevalent creditor practice of bringing 'strike' suits alleging fraud, confident that many debtors would not have the financial means or the savvy to fight. Instead, many debtors would just settle the litigation by agreeing to reaffirm part

142 Reform Bill § 312(2). The time is measured from the times the first and second cases are commenced.
143 Senate Bill § 312(2).   144 House Bill § 312(2).   145 Reform Bill § 310.
146 House Bill § 310.   147 Senate Bill § 310.   148 Reform Bill § 310.

of the debt.[149] In 1978 Congress enacted § 523(d), which in its current form gives the debtor a weapon to contest this abusive creditor practice by enabling the debtor to recover costs and attorneys' fees from a creditor who brings a fraud complaint that is 'not substantially justified'. However, it would be almost impossible for a debtor to bring a successful action against the creditor under § 523(d) with regard to debts covered by the expanded presumption of fraud proposed by the Reform Bill.

Fourthly, *all* student loans are made non-dischargeable (subject to the 'undue hardship' exception), even if they are not made or guaranteed by a governmental unit. The 1997 Commission Report recommended *repealing* the student loan exception to discharge.[150] Instead, this expansion of the exception is the congressional response.

Fifthly, the Chapter 13 'superdischarge' would be further weakened. In the original 1978 Code, Congress created the concept of a 'superdischarge' in Chapter 13, under which a debtor who completed performance under her plan would be able to discharge almost all types of debts, even many of those debts that would be excluded from discharge in Chapter 7. Under the Reform Bill, however, most types of § 523(a) debts now would be made non-dischargeable in Chapter 13 as well.[151] Among others, this expansion would include the credit card 'fraud' debts just discussed.

Sixthly, as explained above, the debtor must complete a personal financial management course during the case or be denied a discharge.[152]

One of the primary concerns expressed by many critics about the Reform Bill is that the expansion in the number (and type) of creditors whose claims would not be discharged would hurt not only debtors, but also weaker creditors whose claims are *already* excepted from discharge, by expanding the field of creditor-contestants who would be free to pursue collection from a debtor after bankruptcy. In particular, concerns have been expressed about the harm that would befall women and children trying to collect alimony and child support from 'deadbeat dads'.[153] Those debts are already non-dischargeable, meaning that the alimony and support claimants may try to collect from the dad post bankruptcy.[154] Now, though, those women and children might face post-bankruptcy competition from Visa, Master-Card and the like, whose debts would be more likely to escape discharge under the Reform Bill,[155] as explained above.

---

149 H.R. Rep. No. 95–595, 95th Cong., 1st Sess. 131 (1977).
150 National Bankruptcy Review Commission Final Report, *Bankruptcy*, Recommendation 1.4.5.
151 Reform Bill § 314(b).   152 Reform Bill § 106(b).
153 See, e.g., Letter from 82 Law Professors (7 September 1999), www.abiworld.org/legis/ profcrit.html; D. E. Rovella, 'Bad for Debtors, Worse for Mothers', *National Law Journal* (9 April 2001); E. Warren, 'The New Women's Issue; Bankruptcy Law', *Christian Science Monitor* (10 September 1999), www.csmonitor.com/durable/1999/09/10/fp11s1-csm.shtml.
154 11 U.S.C. § 523(a)(5), (15).
155 See Statement of Senator Edward M. Kennedy on the Bankruptcy Reform Act of 2001 (5 March 2001), (2001 WL 5420389).

Secured creditor windfalls

The Reform Bill's beneficence for non-debtor parties is not limited to *un*secured creditors. Secured creditors join in the bounty as well. Several provisions provide significant benefits to secured creditors.

First, the Reform Bill would come close to eliminating 'strip down' of secured debts. What is 'strip down'? Simply stated, it is the reduction of a secured claim to the value of the collateral itself.[156] Assume, for example, that a debtor buys an automobile on credit. Two years later, when the debtor files Chapter 13, the debtor owes a total debt of $10,000, but the automobile securing the debt is worth only $7,000. Under current law, the debtor would be allowed to 'strip down' the secured debt to the $7,000 collateral value; the debtor would accomplish this by confirming a Chapter 13 plan that would pay the secured creditor $7,000 (plus interest) on the secured claim.[157] The remaining unsecured balance of $3,000 would be paid *pro rata* with all other unsecured claims. In so providing, Chapter 13's plan confirmation rules are merely implementing the general rule in § 506(a) that defines the extent of a secured claim (*viz.*, to the value of the collateral, but no more). Note that if the debtor were to return the vehicle to the creditor, the creditor would not get any more money than under the strip down plan, assuming that the creditor would only be able to sell the vehicle for its value.

The Reform Bill would take even this modest benefit away from debtors. In a section piously titled 'Restoring the Foundation of Secured Credit', the Bill prohibits using the § 506 principle in a Chapter 13 plan in order to strip down a secured debt on a motor vehicle if: the debt is purchase money (which it almost always is); the vehicle was acquired for the debtor's personal use; and the debt was incurred within *five years* (three years under the Senate Bill) of bankruptcy.[158] Effectively, this rule would end most strip downs on automobiles. The new anti-strip down provision was lobbied for vigorously by the major auto companies,[159] and by current White House Chief of Staff Andrew Card in his prior position with the Automobile Manufacturers' Association. In addition, under the Reform Bill, strip down is prohibited on *any* type of property ('any other thing of value') if the debt was incurred within one year prior to bankruptcy.[160]

The effect of this rule will be to make it much more difficult for debtors to confirm (and, if they somehow confirm, to complete performance under) a Chapter 13 plan. The reason is that they will have to pay more to their secured creditors. In the example given above, the debtor would have to pay $10,000 plus interest, rather than just $7,000 plus interest. Ironically (for the unsecured creditor lobby), the rule would divert money from the pockets of unsecured creditors to the pockets of secured

---

156 See Tabb, *The Law of Bankruptcy*, § 7.29, 555–62.   157 11 U.S.C. § 1325(a)(5)(A).
158 Reform Bill § 306(b); SB § 306(b).
159 See T. Hamburger, 'Auto Firms See Profit in Bankruptcy-Reform Bill Provision', *Wall Street Journal* (13 March 2001).
160 Reform Bill § 306(b).

creditors. Were the consumer credit industry lobbyists paying attention? Mostly though, the anti-strip down provision will make Chapter 13 even more problematic for debtors. This outcome is ironic (or even perverse), given that Congress in the very same bill is trying to force debtors into Chapter 13 via the means test.

The enhanced difficulty for debtors to confirm and complete a Chapter 13 plan under the Reform Bill is starkly demonstrated by the findings of a 1999 study by the National Association for Chapter 13 Trustees 'NACTT'.[161] The NACTT Study analysed the impact of an earlier reform bill (S. 625) that contained very similar anti-strip down rules to those in the current Reform Bill. According to the NACTT Study, 20.79 per cent of existing Chapter 13 cases could not be confirmed. That would mean that over 70,000 fewer Chapter 13 cases every year could be confirmed. The harm to unsecured creditors is dramatic: 44.78 per cent of existing Chapter 13 cases that would be confirmed would propose substantially reduced distributions to unsecured creditors. Nearly a quarter of a million Chapter 13 cases that currently are confirmed every year would provide smaller or no distributions to unsecureds. Nationally, proposed distributions to unsecured creditors in those cases that would still be feasible would be reduced by $100 million.[162]

A second and related provision further feathers the secured creditor nest. A recurring issue in valuing collateral (for the purpose of ascertaining the amount of the secured claim under § 506, as explained above) is deciding what *standard* of valuation should be used.[163] That is, should the focus be on the *retail* or replacement cost (what it would cost the *debtor* to replace the item on the retail market), or should the focus be on *wholesale* or foreclosure cost (what the *creditor* could realise on the collateral at foreclosure)? Most of the time creditors want their collateral to be valued higher. Under current law, though, the answer depends on the projected use or disposition of the collateral.[164] If the debtor is retaining the collateral, then replacement value (to the debtor) might be appropriate.[165] But if the concern is adequate protection to the creditor, due to the imposition of the stay, then perhaps foreclosure value (to the creditor) should be used, since that is all the creditor is losing.

Here again the Reform Bill says 'creditors always win'. For individual debtors in Chapter 7 or 13, personal property collateral is to be valued at 'replacement' value, which the Bill defines as retail value.[166] Since creditors could not get this much for the collateral if the debtor were simply to turn the collateral back to the creditors, this provision gives a windfall to secured creditors.

161 National Association of Chapter 13 Trustees, *Results of Informal Survey on Impact of Section 306(b) of S. 625* (25 May 1999) (copy on file with author). The bill that governed the study, S. 625, was quite similar to the current Reform Bill with regard to strip down, prohibiting strip down (1) if the debt was incurred within five years of filing and the collateral was a motor vehicle and (2) if the debt was incurred within six months of filing for any other type of collateral. The study was conducted by thirteen trustees in twelve districts, who analysed every tenth Chapter 13 filing made in their district in January 1999.

162 *Ibid.*   163 Tabb, *The Law of Bankruptcy*, § 7.27, 549–52.   164 11 U.S.C. § 506(a).

165 See *Associates Commercial Corp.* v. *Rash*, 520 U.S. 953 (1997).

166 Reform Bill § 327(2); Senate Bill § 326(2).

There is more. One of the major issues in consumer bankruptcy law today is what a debtor must do in order to retain collateral if she is current on her payments at the time of bankruptcy.[167] The problem lies in § 521(2), which requires a debtor to state her intention with respect to personal property collateral that is consumer goods. The issue is whether the debtor may simply continue making required payments and retain the collateral (known as 'ride through'), or whether instead she must either *redeem* the property under § 722 (which would require an immediate cash-out of the collateral value) or *reaffirm* the entire debt under § 524(c), in order to keep the collateral. The circuit courts are about evenly divided.[168] The Reform Bill again concludes, 'creditor wins'. Under the Bill, the debtor in this situation must either redeem or reaffirm, or the automatic stay is lifted and the secured creditor can foreclose.[169]

Exemption bonanza and other privileges for the rich

The reader by this point might assume that the Reform Bill adopts an unabashed anti-debtor policy. Close, but not quite; if a debtor is *really* rich, and has the benefit of excellent legal counsel, then the debtor might be able to dodge the harsh consequences of the Bill and continue to live a life of luxury, unencumbered by his creditors. What loopholes does the Bill leave for wealthy, well-informed debtors?

To begin with, harking back to the discussion of the means test, a debtor who plans well might be able to pass the means test by the simple expedient of increasing certain expenses that the means test permits to be deducted from income in making the calculation. For example, a debtor who owes secured debt is entitled to deduct all of the upcoming payments on that secured debt irrespective of how or when the secured debt was incurred.[170] The smart move for a debtor is to buy a Mercedes on credit shortly before filing. The debtor can then keep the Mercedes, make payments to the Mercedes secured creditor and deduct all Mercedes payments from income in computing the means test. The Mercedes-debtor thus might well be able to obtain access to Chapter 7 and to the discharge available thereunder, whereas the Chevrolet-debtor would not.

Nor must the well-informed debtor limit himself to buying fancy cars. He also can spend $1,500 per child per year on private schools.[171] The debtor can make charitable contributions of up to 15 per cent of gross income.[172]

---

167 See Tabb, *The Law of Bankruptcy*, § 7.26, 547–8.
168 Compare *Capital Communications Federal Credit Union* v. *Boodrow* (*In re Boodrow*), 126 F. 3d 43, 53 (2nd Cir. 1997) (debtor may retain property without redeeming or reaffirming), with *Taylor* v. *AGE Federal Credit Union* (*In re Taylor*), 3 F. 3d 1512, 1517 (11th Cir. 1993) (debtor may retain property only if she redeems or reaffirms).
169 Reform Bill § 304(1)(c).   170 Reform Bill § 102(a)(2)(C).
171 *Ibid.*   172 11 U.S.C. §§ 707(b), 548(d)(3).

But all of these other loopholes pale in comparison to the 800-pound gorilla of loopholes, the homestead exemption. Under the Bankruptcy Code, a debtor may select the exemptions offered by State law.[173] All States allow debtors to exempt their homestead, which is an important and understandable debtor protection. But in five States (Texas, Florida, Iowa, Kansas and South Dakota) the homestead exemption is *unlimited*. A debtor who plans well enough to pour his assets into purchasing an enormously valuable homestead is entitled to keep the entire homestead for himself, free from his creditors.

Debtors, as one might imagine, have not failed to notice this benefit. Some of the more notable debtors who have taken advantage of the homestead privilege include actor Burt Reynolds, who kept a $2.5 million home in Florida while discharging debts of $10 million; former baseball commissioner Bowie Kuhn, who, just before his New York law firm filed for bankruptcy, moved to Florida and bought a million dollar home in exclusive Ponte Vedra Beach; and former Texas governor John Connally, who kept a 200-acre ranch, large home and swimming pool despite his bankruptcy.[174] Then there is Paul Bilzerian, who was one of the legendary corporate raiders on Wall Street in the heady days of the 1980s but who fell from grace when sentenced to prison for rampant securities fraud. Bilzerian has filed for bankruptcy and kept a mansion in Florida, not once but twice. Six months after his first bankruptcy case was closed (which paid $400,000 to creditors owed $300 million), Bilzerian filed again, listing debts of $140 million and assets of just over $15,000. Those assets do not include, of course, his 37,000 square foot Florida abode worth $5 million, which he is free to keep under Florida's unlimited homestead exemption.[175]

The 1997 Commission recommended capping the amount of the homestead exemption available to a debtor.[176] The specific dollar amount of the cap was less important than imposing some limit, be it $100,000 or even a more generous $250,000. But under any plausible cap, Bilzerian, Reynolds, Connally and Kuhn would lose their homes.

Until 2001, both houses of Congress steadfastly rejected the cap notion. Neither the Reform Bill passed in 2000 nor the 2001 House Bill contains a cap. The only small limitations the Reform Bill and the House Bill would impose are that the debtor must have had the home and must have resided in the generous homestead state for two years before bankruptcy,[177] thus emphasising the importance of good planning. Also, the debtor must not have fraudulently converted non-exempt assets to purchase the homestead shortly before bankruptcy.[178] If the debtor fails the two-year test, then a $100,000 cap is imposed.

173 11 U.S.C. § 522(b)(1).
174 See 'Should Debtors Be Able to Keep Homes?', *USA Today* (26 June 2000).
175 See American Bankruptcy Institute (8 January 2001), www.abiworld.org/headlines/todayshead.html.
176 National Bankruptcy Review Commission Final Report, *Bankruptcy*, Recommendation 1.2.2.
177 Reform Bill §§ 307, 322(a).   178 Reform Bill § 308(2).

Why has Congress not stopped this obvious and flagrant abuse? States' rights, pure and simple. Senators and congressmen from unlimited homestead exemption states vociferously defend their State's right to offer whatever homestead exemption they wish to debtors. Some of those legislators have a lot of clout on the Hill on the Reform Bill. One of the principal attractions for these States is to draw wealthy debtors to their States.[179]

In the most significant break from prior reform bills, the Senate in 2001 for the first time adopted a homestead exemption cap (of $125,000).[180] In so doing, the Senate sought to eliminate the most embarrassing and most obvious entitlement for the wealthy, a provision that had helped expose the whole process to scathing ridicule. As a *Washington Post* editorial observed:[181]

> The reform in Congress probably will increase hardship: It toughens the rules for ordinary debtors, most of whom declare bankruptcy not out of irresponsibility but because of catastrophic medical bills, unemployment or divorce. At the same time the reform does too little to clamp down on an egregious loophole known as the homestead exemption, which is used by wealthy debtors.

But at the same time, the Senate's imposition of a dollar limitation on the homestead exemption created a stumbling block to reaching agreement on a compromise bill with the House, which remains adamantly opposed to a homestead cap. Indeed, the Senate's homestead provision effectively dissuaded the House from simply taking up and passing the Senate Bill as a means to avoid a formal conference. If and when a conference is convened, the homestead exemption will have to be resolved. The House has the advantage of support from President Bush, who hails from a prominent unlimited homestead State (Texas). If the reform process hangs up over the issue of how generous a homestead to allow rich debtors in a handful of States, while the main thrust of the Bill is to make bankruptcy tougher for lower- and middle-income debtors, that would be ironic indeed (some might say poetic justice).

Conclusion

How did we come to this pass? An article in *Time* magazine asked, 'What is the real reason Congress is doing this?'[182] Their answer: 'Because the legislation is just what banks, credit-card companies, debt consolidators and other

179 See E. A. Posner, 'The Political Economy of the Bankruptcy Reform Act of 1978' (1997) 96 *Mich L Rev* 47.
180 Senate Bill § 308(2).   181 'The Rich Win', *Washington Post* (9 June 2000).
182 D. L. Barlett and J. B. Steele, 'Soaked by Congress', *Time* (15 May 2000).

financial-services businesses ordered.'[183] Ordered how? Two ways: huge campaign contributions to key congressmen by the consumer credit industry and intensive lobbying efforts by very influential lobbyists. The *New York Times* agrees, opining that 'heavy lobbying and huge campaign contributions guaranteed big victories in both houses'.[184]

The industry has carefully nurtured both sides of the party aisle, both in terms of which lobbyists have been used and which congressmen have been targeted for contributions. How would you handicap the chances of a bill that has been pushed by lobbyists the likes of Haley Barbour (former chairman of the Republican National Committee); Lloyd Bentsen (former Senator, Treasury Secretary and Democratic Vice-Presidential nominee); and Andrew Card Jr (then president of the American Automobile Manufacturers' Association and now President Bush's Chief of Staff)?[185] Would you be surprised to discover that controversial Senator Robert Torricelli of New Jersey (then head of the Democratic Senatorial Campaign Committee), who has been one of the leading Democrat sponsors of the bankruptcy bills, accepted a contribution of $150,000 from credit card giant MBNA?[186] Or that Republican Congressman Bill McCollum, who introduced the first means testing bill in 1997, has received $225,000 from the consumer credit industry? Taking no chances, MBNA was the single largest corporate contributor to President Bush's 2000 presidential campaign.[187]

Since 1997, the finance industry has spent an estimated $5 million on lobbying for the bankruptcy bill and over $20 million in political contributions, with $2.2 million in contributions just to members of the House and Senate Judiciary Committees (which have responsibility for bankruptcy legislation).[188] The paltry $1.3 million spent on lobbying by groups opposed to the reforms (such as the National Consumer Law Center) pales in comparison.

Yet, there is widespread public opposition to a bankruptcy reform bill that bears any resemblance to the bills that have passed the congressional chambers. In May 2001, the Consumer Federation of America released a poll that found that *only 28 per cent* of those interviewed thought President Bush should sign the bankruptcy legislation.[189] Rarely in American history has there been such a dissonance between

---

183 *Ibid.*
184 'An Unfair Bankruptcy Bill', *New York Times* (13 December 2000); 'Hard Lobbying on Debtor Bill Pays Dividend', *New York Times* (13 March 2001).
185 See 'Bill on Bankruptcy Makes it Harder to Wipe out Debts', *New York Times* (14 March 2001).
186 See Barlett and Steele, 'Soaked'.
187 See 'Hard Lobbying on Debtor Bill Pays Dividend', *New York Times* (13 March 2001); G. Miller, 'Bill Making Bankruptcy Filings Harder for Individuals Nears OK', *Los Angeles Times* (15 March 2001).
188 See 'An Unfair Bankruptcy Bill', *New York Times* (13 December 2000); 'The Rich Win', *Washington Post* (9 June 2000), estimating $20 million in political contributions and $5 million in lobbying expenses.
189 *National Opinion Poll on Bankruptcy Legislation*, Opinion Research Corporation International, www.abiworld.org/research/cfapoll.html.

the attitudes of most Americans and the position taken by a substantial majority of Congress.

The May 2001 poll confirms results from another independent poll taken in June 2000, which revealed that 'most Americans oppose making it more difficult for low- and moderate-income families to declare bankruptcy'.[190] Almost 60 per cent of those surveyed in the 2000 poll did not believe that bankruptcy should be made more difficult for low- and moderate-income families. The only major reforms that those surveyed did favour were adding provisions that would (i) discourage credit card companies from making risky loans (64 per cent), and (ii) limit the ability of wealthy individuals to keep expensive homes (84 per cent). Ironically, those two reforms have *not* been included in the Reform Bill (except for the Senate's homestead provision).

As noted above, numerous major newspapers and magazines have expressed strong opposition to the bankruptcy bills. Leading the way is a prominent *Time* article, 'Soaked by Congress'.[191] The *Washington Post* is quite hostile to the bill, publishing editorials such as 'Bad Ideas on Bankruptcy'[192] and 'The Rich Win'.[193]

The *New York Times* has been equally adamant in its opposition to the bankruptcy bills. One editorial, addressing the bill that passed Congress in December 2000, was entitled 'An Unfair Bankruptcy Bill',[194] and decried the 'distorted bankruptcy bill' that 'amounts to a handout to the credit card industry'. An earlier *Times* editorial referred to the pending legislation as 'A Gift for the Credit Card Industry', and described the bills as 'stuffed with gifts to the credit card industry'.[195] The overall assessment: 'the overwhelming impact would be to hurt unsophisticated debtors and go easy on the well-healed'. On the eve of the Senate's passage of the bill in March 2001, the *Times* lamented that 'for many debtors, the idea that bankruptcy offers a true, fresh start would disappear', while at the same time 'financial analysts say enactment of the bill would mean billions of dollars in extra profits for credit-card issuers'.[196]

A *Boston Globe* editorial called the bill that passed Congress in December 2000 a 'Punitive Measure'.[197] This echoed the *Globe*'s statement in a prior editorial that this was a 'bad bankruptcy bill',[198] which 'includes punitive provisions that only a banker could love . . . or congressmen at the receiving end of the $6 million that banks, credit-card companies, and other financial institutions donated during the first half of this year alone'.

In a May 2001 article, nationally syndicated columnist Debra Saunders issued a scathing indictment of the push for bankruptcy legislation:[199]

190 Press Release, Consumer Federation of America (13 June 2000), www.abiworld.org/research/cfapoll.pdf. The poll was conducted by Opinion Research Corporation International.
191 Barlett and Steele, 'Soaked'.   192 18 February 2000.   193 9 June 2000.
194 See 'An Unfair Bankruptcy Bill', *New York Times* (13 December 2000).
195 *New York Times* (30 May 2000).
196 'Bill on Bankruptcy Makes it Harder to Wipe Out Debts', *New York Times* (14 March 2001).
197 *Boston Globe* (18 December 2000).   198 *Boston Globe* (17 October 2000).
199 See Saunders, 'Of Puppies'.

Financial institutions can profit handsomely from cardholders' runaway debt... Meanwhile, expect the same banks to bellyache to Congress about carefree deadbeats who rack up debt. Their lobbyists have been pushing for a tough new bankruptcy bill to protect them from their own rapacious business practices... It is astonishing how united Washington can be when it comes to passing laws to protect banks from themselves... The President... (wrongly) endorses bankruptcy regulation to protect banks from the free-market consequences of their risky lending choices.

The vast majority of America's bankruptcy law professors have repeatedly expressed their vehement opposition to the bankruptcy reform bills. About 100 professors have written to Congress on four separate occasions imploring Congress not to pass such a bill.[200] Only *two* law professors have urged passage.[201] The professors opposed to the Reform Bill have expressed particular concern about the negative impact on women and children, and the unfairness of the homestead exemption loophole. But the consumer bankruptcy reform train keeps on running. It is a shame that innocent consumers will be the ones who will get run over.

---

200 See Letter from 82 Professors of Bankruptcy Law to Senators Orrin Hatch and Patrick Leahy (7 September 1999), www.abiworld.org/legis/profcrit.html; Letter from 69 Professors of Bankruptcy Law to Senators Orrin Hatch and Patrick Leahy (2 November 1999), www.abiworld.org/legis/bills/106anal/99nov2proflett2.html. See also B. A. Markell, Letter from 57 Law Professors (24 March 1998) (copy on file with author); Letter from 93 Professors (30 October 2000) (copy on file with author).

201 See Letter from T. J. Zywicki, Assistant Professor of Law www.abiworld.org/legis/bills/106anal/gmulaw.html.

Part V
Procedure and process issues

12 Privatisation and power: dispute resolution for the Internet

ELIZABETH G. THORNBURG

Introduction

Despite clichés about 'Internet speed', disputes that arise on and about the Internet can be time-consuming to resolve, factually complex and legally murky. In response, Internet players with market power are opting out; mandatory arbitration is replacing both substantive law and court procedure, and technological 'remedies' are providing self-help without any 'dispute resolution' at all. These alternative procedures tend to move faster than courts and cost their corporate creators less than lawsuits. They are also structured to maximise the success of the powerful. But faster is not always better. Cheap is not always fair or accurate. Market power is not always used to achieve the public good. And the power to make the rules is often the power to win the game. The Internet is a largely privatised world, and private actors are creating structures under which governments and their courts are increasingly irrelevant. Some enthusiasts, in fact, look forward to the day when computer code makes courts unnecessary. Bill Frezza, in *Internet Week*, envisioned complete automation of Internet dispute resolution and enforcement: 'What if there were a way ... that does not rely on judicial intervention to interpret rights or the police power of the state to enforce them? A way in which laws, *along with their enforcement*, could be designed into the products or transactions themselves?'[1]

Ironically, this freedom from government control is supported by the government. In 1997, the Clinton Administration released a document setting out a blueprint for the promotion of electronic commerce.[2] The *Framework for Global Electronic Commerce* (more commonly called the 'Magaziner Report') is organised around a set of principles encouraging privatisation. While the Magaziner Report notes that government action may be necessary to protect consumers, its general rule is that parties should be able to do business with each other on the Internet under whatever terms and conditions they agree upon. As Professor Michael

---

A lengthier discussion of these issues can be found in E. G. Thornburg, 'Going Private: Technology, Due Process, and Internet Dispute Resolution' (2000) 34 *U C Davis L Rev* 151.

1 B. Frezza, 'How the Internet Will Change the Rule of Law', *Internet Week* (22 September 1997) (emphasis added).

2 *A Framework for Global Electronic Commerce* (1997), www.ecommerce.gov/framewrk/htm.

Froomkin has pointed out, the Magaziner Report portrays 'the private sector . . . in its heroic mode, needing only to have moribund rules removed to allow its un-leashed animal spirits to carry the day. In effect, the private sector rules, or should rule.'[3] The role of the government is to provide a legal environment that allows pri-vate parties to rely on and enforce the deals they have made and to take full advan-tage of what technology makes possible.

This combination of private forces, government co-operation, and technologi-cal feasibility is creating a disturbing trend. The courts are being marginalised and squeezed out of dispute resolution. When the technology of the Internet is capable of providing a remedy attractive to those with the power to design it, there is incen-tive to use it. When the 'law', procedural as well as substantive, is unappealing, a combination of contract and technology minimise its impact.[4] Further, the bene-fits of this privatisation are not evenly distributed but result in some clear winners (for example, trademark owners, copyright holders, corporate repeat players) and some clear losers (for example, consumers, small businesses). The use of contract is already moving much of this dispute resolution out of the courtroom. We are not far from a time when technology makes it possible to move it out of the realm of the human. Lawmakers on state, national and international levels need to focus on this phenomenon and impose some minimal standards of due process and public policy before the underlying Internet architecture is too well entrenched to control.

This essay will discuss three contexts in which Internet disputes have become privatised in ways that provide substantial advantages to the already powerful: (1) the domain name dispute policy of the Internet Corporation for Assigned Names and Numbers ('ICANN'), a form of mandatory online arbitration for the benefit of trademark owners; (2) the use of 'digital rights management technology' to pro-vide computer-activated self-help to those seeking to impose and automatically enforce contract terms, even terms at variance with real world substantive law; and (3) contractual 'shrinkwrap' or 'clickwrap' clauses creating their own 'law' by man-dating binding arbitration in consumer transactions.[5]

These scenarios and their probable technological extensions, if left unchecked, will have several consequences for the power of courts as institutions and for due process to litigants. First, they result in privatised justice. These processes take place independently, with little or no participation or sanction from government

---

3 A. M. Froomkin, 'Of Governments and Governance' (1999) 14 *Berkeley Tech L J* 617, 620.
4 See M. A. Lemley, 'The Law and Economics of Internet Norms' (1998) 73 *Chi-Kent L Rev* 1257, 1259: 'The common goal of these quasi-private ordering advocates is to decentralise governance and return control to the people – at least, the people who write the contracts.'
5 This essay addresses only arbitration clauses that are imposed *ex ante* in transactions between a business and a consumer, especially those included in standard form contracts of adhesion. It does not question the potential benefits of arbitration clauses genuinely negotiated between par-ties with equal bargaining power, voluntary mediation programmes, or even arbitration options meaningfully presented to a consumer after a dispute has arisen when there is no attached ex-haustion requirement.

actors. Secondly, the processes shift procedural advantage to certain powerful players. Thirdly, the mechanisms do not protect certain traditional components of due process in dispute resolution. Aspects of litigation such as affordable access to justice, notice, discovery, collective action, live hearings, confrontation of witnesses, a neutral decision-maker and a transparent process may be absent from these privatised processes. Fourthly, by eliminating the courts as the arbiters of disputes, these processes decrease the power of government to shape and enforce substantive law. The 'law' becomes what is specified in the contract or programmed into the software, and courts lose the ability to enforce mandatory rules and to subject contractual 'law' to the needs of public policy. Public interests that balance private property rights under real world governments (including free speech, an intellectual commons and consumer protection) need not be included in privatised systems.

Governments can either allow this to happen, or they can choose to intervene. Rather than repeat platitudes about the 'unique qualities of the Internet' we must choose the shape of dispute resolution for the future. Models based on private contract or law-free private international arbitration will not adequately protect the needs of consumers or society.

Three worlds of privatised dispute resolution

Domain name disputes

The problem

On the Internet, a system called 'domain names' is used to locate people and organisations. Domain names translate the long strings of numbers that computers use to send data from one computer to another into words that are easier for humans to use. For example, the domain name 'www.amazon.com' locates an Internet site for Amazon.com, Inc. at Internet address 208.216.182.15 and a particular host server named 'www'. The 'com' part of the domain name reflects the purpose of the organisation (in this example, 'commercial') and is called the top-level domain name. The 'amazon' part of the domain name defines the organisation or entity, and together with the '.com' is called the second-level domain name. These second-level domain names must be unique on the Internet; there can be no more than one amazon.com. That was no problem in the early days of a small number of largely academic and governmental users. It poses a huge problem now, with businesses all over the world scrambling to acquire the second-level domain name that the public associates with their business and to wrest those domain names from people who first registered them. Many were registered by individuals or small businesses who intended to use the name. In addition, a new type of entrepreneur, called a 'cybersquatter', made a business out of registering well-known domain names for the purpose of selling them back to the trademark owner at inflated prices. The price reflected both the trademark owner's strong desire to use its name as a domain name and the probable cost of litigation to acquire the domain name.

The system

The Internet's domain name system has since 1998 been administered by ICANN, a private non-profit corporation, under the authority of a series of understandings with the US Department of Commerce.[6] One of its first charges was to create a dispute resolution policy to allow cheap, fast resolution of conflicts regarding rights to domain names. ICANN approved its Uniform Domain Name Dispute Resolution Policy[7] and Rules for Uniform Domain Name Dispute Resolution Policy[8] on 24 October 1999, and they went into effect on 1 December 1999. ICANN imposes this policy on all approved Registrars, and through them onto all who acquire domain names.

The ICANN policy allows a trademark holder who alleges that a domain name infringes on its mark to submit a complaint to any dispute resolution provider ('DRP') approved by ICANN.[9] The complainant must allege and convince the arbitrator that:

1. the domain name is identical or confusingly similar to the complainant's trademark or service mark; and
2. the domain name holder has no rights or legitimate interests in the domain name; and
3. the domain name has been registered and is being used in bad faith.

The policy also provides a non-exhaustive list of circumstances that are 'evidence' of bad faith:

1. the domain name holder registered or acquired the domain name primarily for the purpose of selling it to the owner of the trademark or service mark or to a competitor of that complainant, for valuable consideration in excess of documented out-of-pocket costs; or
2. the domain name was registered in order to prevent the owner of the trademark or service mark from using its mark in a domain name, provided that the domain name holder has engaged in a pattern of such conduct; or

6 See ICANN, *Approved Agreements among ICANN, the US Department of Commerce, and Network Solutions, Inc.* (10 November 1999), www.icann.org/nsi/nsi-agreements.htm.
7 ICANN, *Uniform Domain Name Dispute Resolution Policy* (26 August 1999) [hereinafter *ICANN Policy*], www.icann.org/udrp/udrp-policy-24oct99.htm.
8 ICANN, *Rules for Uniform Domain Name Dispute Resolution Policy* (26 August 1999) [hereinafter *ICANN Rules*], www.icann.org/udrp/udrp-rules-24oct99.htm.
9 At the time this essay was written, the approved DRPs were: (1) World Intellectual Property Organisation (WIPO); (2) The National Arbitration Forum (NAF); (3) eResolution (eRes); (4) CPR Institute for Dispute Resolution (CPR). See ICANN, *Approved Providers for Uniform Domain Name Dispute Resolution Policy* (17 October 2000), www.icann.org/udrp/approved-providers.htm.

3. the domain name was registered primarily for the purpose of disrupting the business of a competitor; or
4. by using the domain name, the owner has intentionally attempted to attract, for commercial gain, Internet users to its Website, by creating a likelihood of confusion as to the source, sponsorship, affiliation or endorsement of its Website or of a product or service on its Website.

The domain name holder (the 'respondent' under the ICANN policy) has three possible affirmative defences (note, however, that their elements overlap considerably with the complainant's burden of proof):

1. before any notice of the dispute, the domain name holder used, or made demonstrable preparations to use, the domain name or a name corresponding to the domain name in connection with a *bona fide* offer of goods or services; or
2. the domain name holder has been commonly known by the domain name (even absent a trademark or service mark); or
3. the domain name holder is making a legitimate non-commercial or fair use of the domain name, without intent for commercial gain to misleadingly divert consumers or to tarnish the trademark or service mark at issue.

These standards involve the resolution of fact-intensive issues such as confusing similarity, bad faith, the intent behind registration, fair use and whether conduct would tarnish a trademark or service mark. You might expect the resolution of such disputes to involve procedural devices such as discovery or live hearings or cross-examination. You would be wrong. Rather, the main point of this policy is that it is fast and cheap. The complaint is filed[10] in writing, and it must describe the manner in which the domain name is similar to the trademark, why the domain name holder has no rights in it, and why the domain name should be considered as having been registered and used in bad faith. The complaining trademark owner must also attach documentary or other evidence, including the trademark or service mark registration. The complainant pays the filing fee.

The domain name holder/respondent must be sent notice within three calendar days and has twenty days from the commencement of the proceeding to submit a response. That response must address specifically the statements in the complaint as well as any applicable affirmative defences. If the respondent fails to respond,

---

10 Just as a plaintiff in litigation can choose the forum (within limits), the complainant here can choose any of the approved dispute resolution providers: *ICANN Rules*, § 4(d). While it is still too early to draw conclusions, it appears that the different providers have statistically stronger and weaker tendencies to rule in favour of the trademark owner. As of late summer 2000, WIPO had ruled for the trademark holder more than 80 per cent of the time, while eResolution did so about 55 per cent of the time. The complainants seem to have noticed. While WIPO got 29 per cent of the complaints filed in January 2000, it got 61 per cent of the complaints filed in July 2000. See M. Geist, 'WIPO Wipes out Domain Name Rights', *The Globe and Mail* (24 August 2000).

the case will be decided on the basis of the complaint. The ICANN rules provide that there 'shall be no in-person hearings (including hearings by teleconference, videoconference, and Web conference)' unless the arbitrator 'determines, in its sole discretion and as an exceptional matter, that such a hearing is necessary for deciding the complaint'.[11] The arbitrator is given fourteen days in which to decide the case. The decision is supposed to be in writing and provide the reasons on which it is based. If the arbitrator rules for the complainant, ICANN will require the cancellation of the domain name or its transfer to the complainant. The only way for the domain name holder to prevent the cancellation or transfer is to file a lawsuit against the trademark owner and provide a file-stamped copy of the complaint to ICANN within ten business days. Thus, the whole process should be resolved in less than two months.

The original purpose for the ICANN dispute resolution process was to create a remedy for a narrowly defined group of particularly egregious cases. During the initial drafting process, the procedure was said to be available 'only in respect of deliberate, bad faith, abusive, domain name registrations or "cybersquatting"'.[12] ICANN's staff repeated this promise after receiving public comments on the proposed policy. They assured concerned commentators that 'the policy . . . calls for administrative resolution for only a small, special class of disputes', namely those 'involving "abusive registrations" made with bad faith intent to profit commercially from others' trademarks'.[13]

Nevertheless, the dispute resolution procedure has been used in all sorts of trademark/domain name disputes and even disputes involving un-trademarked famous names. Between 1 December 1999 and 31 July 2000, 1,330 new complaints were filed, involving 2,252 domain names.[14] Of the 1,193 domain names disposed of by decision, only about 19 per cent were decided in favour of the domain name holder. The rest resulted in transferring the domain name to the trademark owner (900), cancelling the domain name (14), both cancelling and transferring challenged names (4), or in a split decision (44).

The ICANN process is mandatory in the sense that once a complaint is filed it will be processed by the dispute resolution provider unless the complaint is settled or withdrawn. If the domain name holder does not respond, it will almost certainly lose, and ICANN will order its domain name transferred or cancelled. It is

---

11 ICANN Rules, § 13.
12 WIPO, Final Report of the WIPO Internet Domain Name Process (30 April 1999), § 135(i), wipo2.wipo.int/process1/report/finalreport.html.
13 Anonymous, 'Does the UDRP Provide for Constructive Notice of Trademarks?' (2000) 1 Internet L & Bus 584, 586 (quoting ICANN, Second Staff Report on Implementation Documents for the Uniform Dispute Resolution Policy (25 October 1999), § 4.1(c)), www.icann.org/udrp/udrp-second-staff-report-24oct99.htm.
14 See ICANN, Statistical Summary of Proceedings under Uniform Domain Name Dispute Resolution Policy, providing daily updated summary of the status of proceedings, www.icann.org/udrp/proceedings-stat.htm.

not mandatory in the sense that the ICANN rules do not preclude the filing of a lawsuit, either during the proceeding or after its conclusion. A trademark owner who believes that, given its particular circumstances, a lawsuit would be more advantageous is free to pursue that option instead of, or in addition to, the ICANN procedure.

As technology develops, this process may become automated, rendering even faster and less expensive dispute resolution. Trademark owners could develop software to search out domain names that they deem confusingly similar to their trademark. The software could then automatically generate a cease-and-desist letter. If the domain name is not transferred or cancelled within a short period of time, the computer could generate an automated complaint, which it will file with ICANN, which will use an algorithm to 'resolve' the dispute. No human arbitrators are required. The ICANN computer will notify both parties of the result by e-mail. If the trademark owner prevails and the ICANN computer does not receive notice that the domain name owner has filed a lawsuit within ten days, ICANN's computer will automatically order the relevant Registrar to cancel or transfer the domain name to the complainant.

Fanciful? Maybe. It would require a complex and sophisticated programme. A human might at least be required to examine the supporting documentation to see if it is consistent with the parties' allegations.[15] Greater automation and speed, however, are sufficiently prized for there to be an incentive to design such a programme, and generous rewards for its designer.

Trusted systems and digital rights management technology

The purpose of copyright law is to give authors an incentive to create and distribute new works. Without such protection, it is feared, authors would not be adequately compensated and would not, therefore, create. The point, though, is to achieve the broader public purpose of providing public access to a larger body of material. Copyright law thus involves a balancing of interests between the needs of authors and the needs of the public. Because of these public interests, the rights of copyright holders are not absolute. For example, the doctrine of 'fair use' gives individuals power to use limited portions of a copyrighted work to further education or debate on the topic.[16] Also, the buyer of copyrighted works (at least in traditional

---

15 The current rules require both complainant and respondent to include a statement that 'the information contained . . . is to the best of [the filer's] knowledge complete and accurate, that [the pleading] is not being presented for any improper purpose, such as to harass, and that the assertions . . . are warranted under these Rules and under applicable law, as it now exists or as it may be extended by a good-faith and reasonable argument': *ICANN Rules*, §§ 3(b)(xiv), 5(b)(viii), 15(d). These provisions appear to be modelled on Rule 11 of the Federal Rules of Civil Procedure. There is, however, no sanction available against a party who falsely makes these statements.
16 17 U.S.C. § 107 (2000).

media) acquires 'first sale' rights, allowing her to dispose of the purchased copy as she sees fit; she can keep it, lend it out or give it away.[17]

Improvements in technology have often been seen as a threat to copyright owners. The Internet concerns copyright owners for at least two reasons. First, digital technology has both reduced the cost and increased the quality of copies of copyrighted material. An infinite number of almost perfect copies can be made for almost no cost. More importantly, the Internet allows multidirectional communication, so people with digital copies of copyrighted works can share their copies with a huge number of other users. Instead of worrying about one record purchaser making one audiotape copy of music for a friend, copyright holders are worried about websites making free, unauthorised copies of copyrighted material available to literally millions of Internet users.

Litigation about copyright disputes can be protracted and expensive (and often futile), and the interim losses great, if a person insists on litigating her competing rights to the relevant intellectual property. Companies are therefore integrating protective software into copyrighted material such as digital copies of books, music, video and computer programmes distributed over the Internet. Such 'trusted systems' (also called 'digital rights management systems' or 'DRMs') turn the threat of digital technology into an opportunity for copyright owners not only to protect rights under existing law but also quietly to attain a number of new ones.

Trusted systems are attached to the digital copies of the work, and they ensure that copyright holders can track every use made of the digital copies, trace where every copy resides on a network, and determine what is being done with the work at any given time. Trusted systems also 'have the ability to secretly report back to the copyright owner via the network on what the user was doing with the work, and the ability to search the consumer's hard disk and report back on what else was there'.[18] If an unlicensed use is detected, the system can disable the product from working at all.[19]

Trusted systems, then, 'delegate enforcement and control to computers'.[20] Consumers have no way to disregard the digital contract: the software simply will not make an unauthorised copy, or perform any other act not allowed by the trusted system software. Whatever terms are in the contract are automatically enforced.

Trusted system enthusiasts note that they provide for greater control than copyright law; the DRM, rather than copyright law, controls the use of the product. For example, the creators of trusted systems anticipate that fair use of copyrighted material must be purchased with a licence. So would first sale rights: the right to read,

---

17 17 U.S.C. § 109 (West. 1996).
18 P. Samuelson, 'Intellectual Property and the Digital Economy: Why the Anti-Circumvention Regulations Need to Be Revised' (1999) 14 *Berkeley Tech LJ* 519, 543 n. 134.
19 *Ibid.*, 543 n. 136.
20 M. Stefik, 'The Bit and the Pendulum: Balancing the Interests of Stakeholders in Digital Publishing' (1999) 16 *Computer Law* 1, 4.

watch or listen to a work would be licensed separately from the right to read it again, copy it, print it or do whatever. So would the right to make a backup copy. Each use would be licensed, and charged an associated fee.

For procedural purposes, the point is that trusted systems constitute automated self-help.[21] They are not a dispute resolution system in the traditional sense. Rather, this technology pre-empts the court system by building into the product itself the mechanism for asserting claimed property rights. The copyright holder needs no recourse to the courts to enforce its copyright because the copyright is self-enforcing. There will be no 'efficient breach' of a copyright licence, because there can be no breach at all. Because there will be no way to use breach to test purported agreements, courts will not be examining the legality of the bargain. This is a very efficient method of dispute resolution from the standpoint of the copyright holder. At a minimum, the trusted system flips the parties' procedural posture. Instead of the copyright holder suing to enjoin a breach and to collect damages, the user who believes his rights were restricted by the trusted system must bring a lawsuit to sue for damages for being denied what he believes to be a legitimate use of the product. Since any individual user's money damages may be fairly minimal, these lawsuits may never materialise.

One might think that just as fast as engineers can design trusted systems, other engineers can figure out how to disable them. The US government, however, has once again come to the rescue of the copyright owners. The Digital Millennium Copyright Act[22] prohibits the circumvention of technological protection measures, and bans devices whose primary purpose is to enable circumvention of technical protection systems. There are serious criminal penalties for wilfully violating the anti-circumvention rules,[23] and it is not a defence that no act of underlying infringement (for example, illegal copying of a protected work) ever took place.[24]

Mandatory binding arbitration of consumer disputes

In a perfect world, businesses would always sell products that conformed to their descriptions and were free from defects. Further, consumers would pay for those products promptly and reliably. Since neither the Internet nor the physical world reaches such perfection, disputes arise between merchants and consumers. The processing of those disputes can be disruptive to businesses, distressing to the consumer, and expensive for both. In the case of modestly priced consumer goods,

---

21 See J. E. Cohen, 'Copyright and the Jurisprudence of Self-Help' (1998) 13 *Berkeley Tech LJ* 1089, 1093.
22 17 U.S.C. § 1201 (2000).
23 17 U.S.C. § 1204(a)(1) (mandating up to five years in jail and fine of up to $500,000 for first offence).
24 See Samuelson, 'Intellectual Property', 556.

the cost of resolving a dispute can easily exceed the cost of the items themselves. It is therefore natural that businesses have sought alternatives to conventional litigation for such matters.

Merchants have a strong incentive to preselect a privatised decision-maker to enforce the 'law' as specified in the contract.[25] To this end, they can include an arbitration clause specifying the arbitral body, the location of the arbitration, the substantive and procedural law to be applied (or creating its own 'law') and the grounds, if any, for appeal. Two developments have made mandatory arbitration clauses increasingly feasible: (1) American courts' increasing willingness to enforce arbitration agreements, even those contained in consumer contracts of adhesion;[26] and (2) a creeping acceptance of 'buy now, terms later' contracts in which terms such as arbitration clauses are added after the consumer's initial purchase.[27]

Under the Federal Arbitration Act,[28] where parties have entered into a contract that calls for mandatory binding arbitration, that agreement will be enforced.[29] That means that if a consumer attempts to ignore an arbitration clause and file suit in court instead, that suit will be dismissed. It also means that courts will enforce the arbitral award. The federal courts have interpreted the Act broadly. For example, an ambiguous contract will be interpreted in favour of arbitration rather than litigation.[30] When a party seeks to avoid an arbitration agreement on grounds of coercion, fraud or duress, those defences are to be construed narrowly.[31] Relying on the preference for arbitration, courts have severely limited the grounds for appealing an arbitral award.[32]

25 For multinational sellers, arbitration has an added advantage. While judgments rendered in one country may be difficult to enforce in another, international arbitral awards are widely enforced under the New York Convention on Recognition and Enforcement of Arbitral Awards. In the United States, federal courts are given a broad grant of jurisdiction to enforce these awards: 9 U.S.C. § 201 (2000).
26 See generally M. E. Budnitz, 'Arbitration of Disputes between Consumers and Financial Institutions: a Serious Threat to Consumer Protection' (1995) 10 *Ohio St J on Disp Resol* 267, discussing types of arbitration clauses and governing federal and state statutes; B. G. Garth, 'Privatisation and the New Market for Disputes: a Framework for Analysis and a Preliminary Assessment' in S. S. Silbey and A. Sarat (eds.) (1992) 12 *Studies in Law, Politics, and Society* 367, comparing private justice and public justice and the trend towards their combination; J. R. Sternlight, 'Panacea or Corporate Tool?: Debunking the Supreme Court's Preference for Binding Arbitration' (1996) 74 *Wash U L Q* 637, criticising courts' increasing deferral to mandatory binding arbitration clauses.
27 See, e.g., *Hill v. Gateway 2000, Inc.*, 105 F 3d 1147 (7th Cir. 1997), cert. denied, 522 US 808 (1997). See also *Carnival Cruise Lines, Inc. v. Shute*, 499 US 585 (1991) (enforcing choice of forum clause printed on consumer cruise ticket received after payment).
28 9 U.S.C. §§ 1–16 (2000).   29 *Ibid.*, § 2.
30 See *Moses H. Cone Mem'l Hosp. v. Mercury Constr. Corp.*, 460 US 1, 24–5 (1983).
31 See *David L. Threlkeld & Co. v. Metallgesellschaft Ltd*, 923 F 2d 245, 248 (2nd Cir. 1991) (holding party to arbitration clause absent showing of special circumstances), cert. dismissed, 501 US 1267 (1991); *Cohen v. Wedbush, Noble, Cooke, Inc.*, 841 F 2d 282, 285 (9th Cir. 1988) (rejecting unconscionability defence in light of policy favouring arbitration).
32 See I. R. Macneil, R. E. Speidel and T. J. Stipanowich, *Federal Arbitration Law: Agreements, Awards and Remedies under the Federal Arbitration Act* (Waltham, Mass.: Little Brown & Co., 1996) Section

The online seller may also be attracted by the availability of online arbitration. This allows both the original transaction and the resolution of any related disputes to take place without the physical presence of the parties. There are currently more than half a dozen online dispute resolution providers, as well as conventional providers offering online options. Some provide online mediation, some have algorithms that settle cases based on offers from opposing parties, and some actually resolve the disputes based on an e-mailed complaint and response. These providers tend to be for-profit entities, and the drafter of the contract (the seller) gets to choose the provider. Sellers can thus choose a system of online arbitration with an acceptable cost structure and an attractive set of procedural rules.

The trend towards privatisation through mandatory arbitration has helped the repeat player achieve its goal of more favourable substantive law, more favourable procedural law and a potentially more favourable decision-maker. Assuming that this type of arbitration is cheaper and faster than conventional litigation, it has achieved both efficiency and preferred outcomes. The consumer, on the other hand, has potentially been deprived of her home State's consumer protection law, forced to litigate or arbitrate in an inconvenient forum and been given procedural systems that may limit her ability to prove a meritorious case.[33]

Consequences of privatised dispute resolution

The technology of the Internet, together with its surrounding political and legal environment, provide new contexts for old problems: the effects of differing resources on procedural systems, the advantages of repeat players, the cost of justly resolving economically small disputes, the allocation of the burden of legal uncertainty, the disharmony of potentially applicable law. When it comes to the Internet, the government's awe of the booming 'new economy', the rapid speed of technological change and the market power of the major players tends to lead towards private solutions to these public problems. This section of the essay will

nos. 40.1.4: 'Over the years, the courts have taken a fairly uniform approach to awards: Awards should be confirmed and enforced as is unless there is clear evidence of a gross impropriety.'

33 If the consumer has paid for the transaction using a credit card, US law passed in the 1970s may provide a better remedy than the arbitration clause. Among its other requirements, Regulation Z requires the issuer to provide certain dispute and error resolution services: 12 CFR § 226.13 (2000). This will provide incentive for online sellers to help perfect the technology required for other kinds of electronic payment systems that would not be burdened by Reg Z's consumer protections. See J. K. Winn, 'Clash of the Titans: Regulating the Competition between Established and Emerging Electronic Payment Systems' (1999) 14 *Berkeley Tech L J* 675, 686–8. See also 'Alternative Dispute Resolution for Consumer Transactions in the Borderless Online Marketplace', *Comments to the Federal Trade Commission from the National Consumers League, the Electronic Privacy Center, and Consumer Federation of America* (23 June 2000), www.ftc.gov/bcp/altdisresolution/comments/ncl.htm.

314 Procedure and process issues

discuss some of the consequences of this choice: (1) shift of procedural advantage to the already powerful; (2) due process gaps; and (3) privatised substantive law in favour of trademark holders, copyright owners and sellers. Just as in the physical world differential resources and repeat player status provide advantages, so too with the Internet. These processes shift the cost of making a claim and the burden of uncertainty onto the less powerful disputant.

Shift of procedural advantage

Each of the three processes works to shift certain procedural advantages from the civil litigation norm. For example, the domain name process and trusted system technology both operate to give one disputant the equivalent of a preliminary injunction without requiring the usual quantum of proof or applying the normally applicable law. Courts generally approach preliminary injunctions with caution, because they operate under several disadvantages. The issue must be determined before full discovery; there has been little time to research the applicable law; there has been no determination that the plaintiff will ultimately be entitled to an injunction; and granting an interim injunction may do significant harm to the defendant or to third persons, sometimes harm that is difficult to compensate retroactively.

Because of these circumstances, courts generally use a balancing test in deciding whether to issue a preliminary injunction. They consider the plaintiff's probability of success on the merits and the harm to the plaintiff if the preliminary injunction is not granted. It must be a type of harm that cannot be adequately redressed by awarding an injunction and/or damages at the conclusion of the lawsuit. Against this courts balance the probable harm to the defendant if the injunction is wrongfully granted, and also consider the impact of a preliminary injunction on the public interest. If the plaintiff successfully convinces the court that the balance of justice favours the preliminary injunction, it will generally be required to post a bond to help compensate the defendant for the damage that may be caused by an injunction that is later reversed.

From a procedural standpoint, the party seeking the injunction must hire a lawyer to draft a complaint, gather information both informally and through discovery and request a hearing in which it presents to the judge the evidence that it believes justifies the preliminary relief. Such hearings can be elaborate and expensive since the court must consider the strength of the plaintiff's case on the merits, and the damages to both parties that could flow from issuing or not issuing the injunction. The more fact-intensive the issues, the more evidence-intensive the hearing is apt to be; live testimony, cross-examination of witnesses, introduction of documents and other tangible evidence, and oral argument from the attorneys would all be typical of a preliminary injunction hearing.

ICANN *domain name disputes*

In the case of domain name disputes, the trademark holder is in the position of a plaintiff. Absent the informal ICANN process, the trademark holder has to file a lawsuit against the domain name owner, alleging trademark infringement and violation of the newly passed Anti-Cybersquatting Consumers Protection Act ('ACPA').[34] The lawsuit will seek cancellation or transfer of the domain name and, possibly, statutory or actual damages. The plaintiff will have to locate and serve the domain name owner. To secure a preliminary injunction hearing, it will need to assemble (and put into admissible form) the information needed to prove that it will ultimately prevail on the merits, and that it will be irreparably injured if it has to wait until the conclusion of the litigation for relief. Its lawyer will need to write a brief arguing to the court why it satisfies the requirements for preliminary relief.

What about the domain name holder? It will need to file an answer, which, in federal court, will require a paragraph-by-paragraph response to the complaint. It will also be allowed to assemble evidence for the preliminary injunction hearing, including evidence showing that its use of the domain name is legitimate and that it has acted in good faith. At the hearing, it will be allowed to call its own witnesses and cross-examine the witnesses called by the trademark owner. It, too, will write a brief addressing its defences on the merits and its probable harm should an injunction be granted.

Compare this to the ICANN process, which grants the equivalent of a preliminary or even permanent injunction to a trademark holder with much lower procedural hurdles. The trademark owner files a complaint amounting to a fact pleading, and attaches evidence of the trademark. If the domain name owner has done anything in writing that suggests bad faith (such as offering to sell the domain name at an inflated price), the writing can also be attached. The trademark owner pays a filing fee. The domain name holder prepares and files a written response, and can also attach any documents that might be in its possession showing good faith. There is no discovery. There is no hearing to prepare for. There is no brief to write, except to the extent that arguments are included in the complaint or response. The substantive standards to be applied are unique to ICANN, and require somewhat less of the trademark owner than the corresponding US law. The case is quickly assigned to an arbitrator, and a decision reached within fourteen days. If the arbitrator rules for the trademark owner, the ruling results in cancellation or transfer of the domain name, which is the final relief the trademark owner seeks. In the absence of a lawsuit, then, the ICANN process operates not as a preliminary injunction but as a final and permanent one. Even if the domain name owner has the will and resources to challenge the ICANN result, the procedural advantage has shifted: it is

34 15 U.S.C.A. § 1125(d) (2000) (amending s. 43 of Lanham Act).

the domain name holder, not the trademark owner, who must file a lawsuit, and it is cancellation or transfer that becomes the default result.

Trusted systems

It is difficult to compare an automated process, which most closely resembles self-help, to the process for acquiring a preliminary injunction. There are, however, some parallels. Consider the relationship of the copyright owner to its licensee absent the DRMs. If the owner believes the licensee is breaching the licence agreement by engaging in unlicensed uses, it must file a lawsuit. In that lawsuit it can seek damages for past breaches, and it may seek injunctive relief, although damages are the norm in breach of contract cases. It might request a preliminary injunction ordering that the challenged practice cease for the duration of the lawsuit. To secure such an injunction, it would have to meet the requirements discussed above.

The DRMs eliminate the need for an injunction and completely reverse the parties' procedural posture. One type of DRM prevents the licensee from engaging in an unauthorised use (or charges fees for expanded use, as if it were an award of damages measured by a licence fee). This is the equivalent of an injunction against the expanded use. Another type of DRM disables the software when it detects an unauthorised use. This constitutes an injunction against the expanded use and a penalty against the user, termination of her licence. Whether the best analogy is a preliminary rather than a permanent injunction depends on the reaction of the licensee. If she does nothing, the DRM has in effect granted a permanent injunction. If the licensee has sufficient motivation and resources to contest the DRM's action, she can file a lawsuit charging breach of the licence agreement and seeking damages. During the pendency of that lawsuit, however, the licensee has still lost use of the product. In this sense, the action of the DRM functions as a preliminary injunction.

The DRMs arguably provide the starkest shift of procedural advantage. The licensor does not even have to file a complaint, much less prove an entitlement to an injunction. The enforcement procedure was pre-programmed into the software. The licensee receives no notice of the action, no opportunity to argue that it had not breached the licence, and has no third-party decision-maker considering the law and the facts. And it is, once again, the party on the 'losing' end of the Internet process that must fight inertia and file a lawsuit.

Due process gaps and repeat player advantages

When a lawsuit is filed and processed in a court in the United States, certain procedural steps are available as of right to the parties. Some of these are required by constitutional due process. Others have come to be assumed as part of a fair system for learning about and resolving complex factual disputes, and for applying the law to those facts. Privatised processes can be designed to forgo those procedures that their designers deem too expensive or too disadvantageous. The processes discussed in this essay tend to eliminate or minimise many important procedural rights implicit in a court proceeding: affordable access to the courts, discovery, collective action, oral hearings, cross-examination of witnesses, the use of unbiased decision-makers, process transparency and written, reasoned opinions. Changes to these procedural devices are not mere matters of institutional quirk or economic efficiency. It is not surprising that the repeat players who have created (or lobbied in favour of) the privatised processes have created processes that work to their benefit.[35]

Access to justice

The dispute resolution processes created for the Internet sometimes shift the burden of initiating suit. If the domain name holder who has lost the ICANN proceeding cannot afford to hire an attorney to draft a complaint and to pay the filing and service fees for a lawsuit, the domain name is gone. If the consumer whose software has been disabled by a DRM cannot afford to pay the filing and service fees for a lawsuit, the software is gone. The mere fact of shifting the benefit of inertia has changed the likelihood that a party can seek outside adjudication of its claims.[36]

In addition, some of the private processes charge higher initial filing fees than would a corresponding court process. This is particularly true of mandatory arbitration clauses, although the cost will vary from provider to provider, and the impact will vary from consumer to consumer and with the cost of the disputed item. If the costs are too high for the consumer to afford, the claim will not be filed. If the costs are excessive in relation to the value of the disputed product, the claim will not be filed. Best practices within the dispute resolution community indicate that arbitration services in consumer cases should be available at a 'reasonable cost to consumers based on the circumstances of the dispute, including among other things, the size and nature of the claim, the nature of goods or services provided,

---

35 See Garth, 'Privatisation', 368; C. Menkel-Meadow, 'Do the "Haves" Come out Ahead in Alternative Judicial Systems? Repeat Players in ADR' (1999) 15 *Ohio St J on Disp Resol* 19.
36 Even non-binding but mandatory arbitration can decrease access by increasing costs. If, for example, a consumer were required to first exhaust any internal dispute procedure used by the merchant, then to use a third-party arbitration procedure that is not binding on either party, and only *then* file a lawsuit, the process has increased the consumer's cost in time and money of seeking relief. This explains why the dispute resolution proposal of the e-commerce giants requires such exhaustion and why consumer groups object to it. See B. Krebs, 'Groups Embrace E-Commerce Dispute-Resolution Plan', *Newsbytes* (7 June 2000), describing industry-led proposal regarding dispute resolution methods for e-commerce consumers; Electronic Commerce and Consumer Protection Group, *Guidelines*, § XIV [hereinafter *Guidelines*], explaining dispute resolution guidelines for e-commerce merchants), www.ecommercegroup.org/guidelines.htm.

and the ability of the consumer to pay'.[37] In a private system, however, the drafter of the arbitration provision need not follow best practices.

The problem of excessive fees is not an imaginary one. In *Hill* v. *Gateway 2000, Inc.*,[38] Gateway's arbitration clause called for a dispute resolution provider, the International Chamber of Commerce, whose filing fee was $US4,000. This far exceeded the cost of the computer that was the subject of the dispute. Even modest sounding fees can be excessive under certain circumstances. The National Arbitration Forum has a relatively modest $US49 fee for filing consumer claims.[39] However, there are additional fees for hearings. And, if the consumer loses, NAF has a cost-shifting system that means that the consumer could be required to pay the merchant's fees. Even a $US49 fee is a sufficient deterrent when filing a claim for damages from a defective $US50 programme or $US75 dress ordered off the Internet.[40] Some courts will refuse to enforce arbitration clauses if they find the fees to be excessive. Other courts enforce them without seriously discussing the problem of costs. When this happens, the fees restrict access to justice.[41]

Adequate discovery

Discovery exists as a litigation tool in order to provide all parties with access to all relevant information. Once the parties are aware of that information, they can present a fuller account to the trier of fact. This, in turn, leads to fairer and more accurate trial outcomes. Discovery is essential where at the outset of the lawsuit the stronger party is most likely to have the bulk of relevant information, while the weaker party is apt to lack such information. When a private dispute resolution system limits discovery, it limits a device that otherwise serves to equalise the parties' relative positions within the lawsuit: 'to the extent that the private system's inquiry is less thorough, the private system permits the underlying power of the stronger party to persist undeflected'.[42]

---

37 American Arbitration Association, *Consumer Due Process Protocol: Statement of Principles of the National Consumer Disputes Advisory Committee*, Principle 6(1) (1998) [hereinafter *AAA Statement of Principles*], www.adr.org/education/education/consumer.protocol.html.
38 105 F 3d 1147 (7th Cir. 1997), cert. denied, 522 US 808 (1997).
39 The American Arbitration Association's filing fee for consumers is $US125: American Arbitration Association, *Arbitration Rules for the Resolution of Consumer-Related Disputes* (1 April 2000). Responding parties also pay a $US125 fee for the arbitrator plus a $US500 administration fee. See www.adr.org.
40 This problem of the cost of disputing small ticket items is also a problem in real world transactions. Consumers in such situations are probably better served by effective return/refund policies than by an inexpensive dispute resolution process.
41 Fees are not the only barriers to access. Another common device is the forum selection clause. The adhesion contracts may not only specify arbitration but also choose a forum that is convenient to the seller but extremely inconvenient for the consumer. Unfortunately, this problem is not confined to Internet transactions but also exists in litigation generally. For that reason, ICANN is to be commended for generally making the domain name holder's domicile a proper forum for a lawsuit challenging the arbitral findings: *ICANN Rules*, § 1.
42 Garth, 'Privatisation', 382.

None of the systems under review permits as much discovery as a civil lawsuit, and many provide none at all. Arbitrators under the ICANN dispute resolution system base their decisions on a complaint from the trademark owner and, in the absence of default, a response from the domain name registrant. Each side gets only one chance to submit its position and attach documents to which it already has access. Although theoretically the arbitrator can request further statements or documents, the arbitrator can only request documents that she knows about, and such action seems highly unlikely when the decision must be rendered in fourteen days. That process leaves the complainant with no method of learning more about the respondent's intent or use of the domain name; it leaves the respondent with no method of learning more about the trademark owner's right to the mark. This lack of discovery might be relatively insignificant in the egregious cases of cybersquatting for which the process was designed. It will be more problematic in genuinely contested cases and cases in which the complainant is relying on a common law right rather than a registered trademark. It is certainly not a good model for the resolution of Internet disputes generally.

Arbitration of consumer disputes may or may not involve discovery. Since the arbitration system is created by a contract drafted by the seller, it is unlikely to include discovery if the seller believes that discovery would be either harmful or too expensive. Neither the American Arbitration Association's *Statement of Principles* for consumer arbitration nor the *Guidelines* recently promulgated by the Electronic Commerce Consumer Protection Group mentions a right to discovery.[43] It is apparently not considered to be an industry 'best practice'.

The online consumer knows that the product she purchased is defective. She knows the way(s) in which she believes the product has failed to meet her needs, or to live up to its description. She does not, however, have access to records concerning the product's design or manufacture, complaints from others that might show the existence of a defect or the seller's knowledge of the problem, or internal communications concerning the product. Neither does the consumer have access to the people who made the relevant decisions. An arbitration system that allows a dispute to be decided when only the defendant has access to this relevant and potentially incriminating information will lead to inaccurate and one-sided results.

The cost of undertaking thorough discovery for very small claims is a problem for both real space and cyberspace. It may not be rational to spend $US10,000 resolving a dispute over a single $US50 product. Decisions about how to allocate cost are political decisions about policy, not simple economic calculations. Should the cost be borne by the consumer, the manufacturer or the taxpayer? If discovery is required for a fair and accurate resolution, a process that is conducted without

43 *AAA Statement of Principles*. Nor do the AAA consumer arbitration rules contain any mention of discovery: *Guidelines*. Contrary to what one might expect from its name, the Electronic Commerce Consumer Protection Group is not composed of consumer advocates but of America Online, AT&T, Dell Computer Corporation, IBM, Microsoft, Network Solutions, Time Warner Inc. and Visa USA Inc.

discovery is no more than a sham. The apparent existence of an inexpensive mechanism for resolving disputes may convince the buyer *ex ante* that it is safe to make a purchase. But it will not serve the unhappy consumer of a complex and defective product.

Collective action

One of the ways to change the ratio of product cost to dispute-related transaction costs is through collective action. In other words, if one purchaser of a $US50 defective widget is unhappy, it seems irrational to spend $US10,000 resolving her claim. However, if 100,000 purchasers of that widget are unhappy, the $US10,000 seems more reasonable. The problem of the potential defendant who does a small amount of harm to a large number of people is one reason that courts allow class actions.

The potential for class actions is also exactly the reason some businesses require arbitration rather than litigation of consumer disputes. Consider this advice given to businesses developing commercial websites: 'Companies should consider including dispute resolution clauses requiring arbitration, which may, in some instances, serve as a defense to the certification of a class action against the site owner.'[44] Shrinkwrap with an arbitration clause will often protect the seller from a consumer class action. While some courts have allowed class arbitration,[45] many have found that the existence of the arbitration clause precludes a class action.[46]

Without the ability to bring a class claim, consumers are deprived of a mechanism that helps undo the repeat player advantage. A single consumer may easily decide that the costs of arbitration are too high given her personal stake in the outcome. Consumers are also deprived of a dispute structure that permits adequate discovery.

44 R. N. Dreben and J. L. Werbach, 'Top 10 Things to Consider in Developing an Electronic Commerce Website' (1999) 16 *Computer Lawyer* 17, 19. See also Budnitz, 'Arbitration of Disputes', 268: 'Arbitration programs [imposed by financial institutions] were initially intended to avoid class action lender liability suits demanding punitive damages.'
45 See *Blue Cross of Ca.* v. *Superior Court*, 78 Cal Rptr 2d 779 (Ct. App. 1998) (allowing class action because arbitration agreement did not prohibit it); *Navarro-Rice* v. *First USA Bank*, No. 97009–06901 (Or. Ct. App. 1998) (noting that bank added arbitration clause after class action was filed), (cited in M. E. Budnitz, 'Recent Developments in Consumer Arbitration Case Law: 1997–1999' in Practicing Law Inst., *Corporate Law and Practice Course Handbook Series* 744 (April–May 1999), Westlaw 1113 PLI/Corp 725). See also J. R. Sternlight, 'As Mandatory Binding Arbitration Meets the Class Action, Will the Class Action Survive?' (2000) 42 *Wm & Mary L Rev* 1.
46 See *Champ* v. *Siegel Trading Co.*, 55 F 3d 269, 275–7 (7th Cir. 1995) (denying class certification in arbitration proceeding because no provision for such certification in arbitration agreement); *Lieschke* v. *Realnetworks, Inc.*, Lexis No. 99 C 7274, 99 C 7380 (N.D. Ill. 2000), 2000 WL 198424 (dismissing as unnecessary and premature plaintiffs' motion regarding future court proceedings); *Randolph* v. *Green Tree Fin. Corp.*, 991 F Supp. 1410 (M.D. Ala. 1997) (denying class certification because agreement between parties did not provide for class certification for arbitration purposes); *Med Center Cars Inc.* v. *Smith*, 727 So 2d 9 (Ala. 1998) (holding plaintiffs not entitled to class-wide arbitration).

Where discovery is allowed at all in arbitration, it is apt to be discovery that is 'reasonable' in relation to the amount in controversy and the resources of the parties. Discovery that would be denied for the single claim might be permitted for a class claim. Limiting arbitration to a single transaction by a single buyer provides a double advantage to the seller; fewer claims will be filed, and those that are filed are less likely to succeed.

Meaningful hearings

Conventional litigation includes, as a matter of fairness, a right to present evidence to the fact finder and to respond to evidence offered by one's opponent. In an adversarial system, the reliability of evidence is tested through the combination of physical presence, oath, cross-examination and observation of demeanour by the trier of fact. Trusted systems allow no presentation at all, and hence no use of hearings to test evidence. The ICANN process and consumer arbitration purport to include adversarial fact-finding, but the fact finder acts either without a live hearing or with a sharply curtailed one. When the operative facts are essentially uncontested, a decision based on written statements should be sufficient. When facts are disputed, however, the lack of a hearing can distort the fact-finding process.

Under the ICANN dispute resolution procedure, any kind of hearing would be extremely unusual. The ICANN rules virtually prohibit video conferences, telephone conferences and Web conferences. Instead of hearing witnesses, the arbitrator makes her decision based on written submissions and accompanying documents. The pleadings are not even made under oath, but rather under an assertion of good faith.

Arbitration, as always, depends on the rules agreed to by the parties. While traditional commercial arbitration may include an elaborate hearing that is hardly different from a non-jury trial to the court, consumer arbitration clauses are apt to prohibit or limit hearings.[47] Even when a hearing is provided, it is more likely to be an opportunity to present one's claim orally, and to listen to the other side present its claim, than a chance to cross-examine witnesses.[48] The procedure provided may be called a hearing but is actually a 'document hearing', a euphemism for

47 The consumer arbitration service provided by the Better Business Bureau, however, generally uses oral hearings and allows the party to present witnesses and to question the witnesses presented by the other party: Better Business Bureau, *Rules of Arbitration [Binding]* (1998), § 20 [hereinafter *BBB Rules*], www.bbb.org/complaints/bindarb.asp.
48 See, e.g., Electronic Commerce and Consumer Protection Group, *Guidelines, Commentary to Guidelines*, stating that the 'procedure allows parties to present their arguments and facts to the forum and to hear the arguments and facts of the other party'. Under the AAA's own rules for consumer arbitration, the default 'desk hearing' (covered by the $US125 fee) involves only the arbitrator reviewing the documents. For an extra $US100, either party can secure a telephone hearing. The only way to get an in-person hearing is to switch to the gigantically more expensive Commercial Arbitration Rules.

the arbitrator sitting down and reading the relevant papers. A hearing may also be an 'online hearing', in which the parties participate through e-mail.[49] Another way arbitration rules limit the scope and content of the hearing is through time limits. Arbitration providers may severely limit the number of minutes available to both sides to present their cases in small consumer disputes.[50] None of these processes is well suited to resolve contested facts.

How might this lack of evidentiary hearing impact on consumers? Procedures that make it harder to present a sufficient quantum of credible information will systemically hurt the party with the burden of proof. If the consumer's complaint was drafted by the consumer herself, without legal assistance, it may seem less 'credible' compared to the seller's response, where legal involvement is more likely. The writing may be less clear or less sophisticated; it may include facts that are not legally relevant, or it may omit facts that would have been both relevant and helpful. Even clearly drafted consumer statements are less helpful than live testimony and a chance to challenge defence witnesses. As the consumer has the burden of proof, any weakness, or even any 'tie' in terms of the weight of the written evidence will go to the seller. Further, if the arbitrator has any pro-defendant bias, the lack of live evidence may make it less likely that the consumer's presentation can counteract that bias.

The industry trend seems to be towards more rather than less automation of arbitration processes. There is already substantial use of 'on the papers' hearings in place of oral hearings. Use of an online process to resolve online disputes is also mentioned often, purportedly as a way to solve the problem of consumer inconvenience or overcome personal jurisdiction limits.[51] When technology will allow computers to actually resolve the dispute itself, that will be the next step. The consumer would still instigate the arbitration procedure, probably paying the filing fee with some form of electronic cash. Then each party could be directed to answer a series of questions, the answers to which are deemed relevant to the outcome. Then the programme would take that information and determine the outcome. The seller, as the party who writes the contract and thus chooses the arbitration rules, would get to write the programme.

---

49 Under NAF rules, for example, hearings for claims less than $US1 million will be conducted online unless all parties agree otherwise: National Arbitration Forum, *Code of Procedure*, Rule 26 [*NAF Code of Procedure*], www.arb-forum.com/arbitration/NAF/code-060101.pdf. Online hearings are conducted using e-mail or other electronic means: Rule 2(P).
50 NAF limits consumer hearings (for which one must pay extra) to a maximum of one hour if the claim is for less than $5,000: *ibid.*, Rule 34.
51 See, e.g., L. J. Gibbons, 'Rusticum Judicium? Private "Courts" Enforcing Private Law and Private Rights: Regulating Virtual Arbitration in Cyberspace' (1998) 24 *Ohio N U L Rev* 769, 785, noting that consumers can participate from home; Krebs, 'Groups': 'Maybe the answer would be to have a new Cyber court to handle these disputes' (quoting Nancy Ellis of Webdispute.com); B. Mitchener, 'Cybercourts Emerge As Way to Resolve Internet Disputes', *Wall Street Journal* (21 March 2000), B9.

Unbiased decision-makers

Due process also requires a neutral decision-maker. Among other things, this requires that the tribunal not have a personal interest in the outcome. It also requires an unbiased decision-maker. Sometimes bias is direct, as when the arbitrator has a prior financial relationship with one of the parties or a financial stake in the dispute. Other times it is indirect, growing out of cultural or professional biases.

Contract-based arbitration of consumer disputes may involve a more subtle kind of direct bias. Responsible providers of arbitral services have codes of ethics requiring arbitrators to disclose any direct conflicts of interest such as prior representation of a party, a financial stake in the outcome, or family relationship to a party. The kind of direct bias that may exist in contractual arbitration clauses stems instead from the volume of business that a repeat player can bestow.[52] Sellers write the contracts with the arbitration clauses and thus get to choose the arbitration provider: 'In this era of entrepreneurial ADR, the arbitrator often does have a subtle but substantial economic interest in the outcome of the case in that his or her ability to get future cases depends, at least in part, on party satisfaction.'[53] It is not the one-shot consumer that the arbitrator needs to satisfy for business development; it is the repeat player seller who is capable of bringing numerous cases to the arbitrator.[54]

Indirect bias is harder to pin down. Arbitrators, unlike conventional judges, are often valued for their substantive expertise in the subject area. The expertise is considered to be a positive factor, but it comes with a flip side: expertise can bring about bias. Is indirect bias likely to be a problem in any of the privatised systems? It would be interesting to study the identity and backgrounds of the arbitrators participating in the ICANN cases (and it may vary by provider). Are they trademark lawyers? If so, do they tend to represent parties taking a particular position in trademark litigation? Are they former judges or academics? Is there any statistically significant correlation between the arbitrators' backgrounds and their decisions in contested cases? Similarly, a study of arbitrators in consumer disputes would be interesting. Are they tilted toward corporate defence lawyers?

Arbitration can also be an area in which repeat players have an informational advantage. In the ICANN process, it is the trademark owner who gets to choose the dispute resolution provider.[55] The trademark holder has the expertise to access and

52 See Garth, 'Privatisation', 382: 'If decision-makers depend on a certain clientele for their business, and that clientele has a particular perspective or long-standing practice, we should not be surprised if that perspective or practice is not challenged.'
53 R. C. Reuben, 'Constitutional Gravity: a Unitary Theory of Alternative Dispute Resolution and Public Civil Justice' (2000) 47 UCLA L Rev 949, 1063.
54 Trial Lawyers for Public Justice, for example, alleges that the National Arbitration Forum markets its arbitration services as providing a defence for financial services companies against lawsuits from their consumers, and that MCI has a very close financial relationship with its mandatory arbitration service provider: Trial Lawyers for Public Justice, *Letter to Federal Trade Commission* (22 March 2000), 8–9, www.ftc.gov/bcp/altdisresoution/comments/blandjr.pdf.
55 *ICANN Policy*, § 4(d).

analyse the outcome of prior ICANN proceedings and take advantage of any perceived patterns. For example, if statistics would show that WIPO arbitrators were more likely to rule for trademark holders than eResolution arbitrators, trademark holders would file with WIPO.[56] In consumer dispute arbitration, the seller has already chosen the provider. Once that is done, individual arbitrators may be assigned, subject to challenge. Alternatively, parties may be permitted to choose from a list. The consumer is unlikely to have any information about the prior rulings or background of the suggested arbitrators. The seller, however, may have a record or other source of information on arbitrator-by-arbitrator decisions.[57] This superior knowledge about the general attitudes and tendencies of the arbitrator gives a further advantage to the repeat player.

Process transparency

In addition to the litigants' interest in disputes, the public has an interest in the fairness of the process, the subjects under dispute and the outcome of those disputes. When disputes are litigated in a court, the public generally has access to this information. Privatised processes, in contrast, allow the parties to keep the matter secret. This may result in the public, or even the government, lacking information about important issues of public health or safety or product reliability. It may allow companies who have committed wrongs that are hard to discover to hide the problem from a greater number of people. It allows material to be removed from public access without public knowledge. It also allows questionable processes to persist free of public scrutiny.[58] This section assesses the comparative transparency of the Internet processes, considering the amount of information available to the public and the content of that information.

ICANN is to be commended for its policy of making most decisions freely available on the Internet at its website. In addition, the ICANN decisions tend to set out the allegations of the parties and describe the supporting documents, and they explain the arbitrator's reasons for her decision. This process, then, is largely transparent.

The other two processes, however, proceed in secrecy. The trusted system automatically 'resolves' the dispute through its ability to control the software; it happens automatically in the licensee's home or office. One would have to read the

56 See K. McCarthy, 'Who the Hell Does WIPO Think it Is?' *The Register* (16 September 2000): 'One rule of domain name argument is that the complainant can decide which body to take its dispute to. Is it any surprise then that big, powerful companies choose WIPO when it has a crystal-clear policy of favouring Goliath over David?'
57 E.g., filings with the FCC allege that MCI's dispute resolution provider gave MCI quarterly reports on the dispute outcomes, and specially trained arbitrators who would hear MCI cases. It also received financial benefits if it asserted jurisdiction over cases brought to it by MCI: Reuben, 'Constitutional Gravity', 1059, n. 531.
58 Opaque processes are also a problem for the parties. It is difficult to know whether one has been treated fairly, and difficult to know the reason one won or lost.

code to understand the process. This is about as opaque as a system can get. Arbitration providers advertise privacy as one of their major advantages.[59] In truly consensual arbitration proceedings, secrecy may be desired by both parties. In the kind of consumer arbitration discussed here, it is the seller/contract drafter who has chosen the secret process. If 1,000 lawsuits were filed against a manufacturer, the public would certainly find out. If 1,000 claims in arbitration were filed against the same company, it is much more easily hidden. Further, the arbitration processes themselves tend to be relatively opaque. Each party presents its position, but there is no record made of the proceeding, and generally the arbitrator need not explain her decision. Where the arbitrator has drawn on her own expertise, in addition to material submitted by the parties, there is no information about what, if anything, the arbitrator considered.

There is a growing trend towards encouraging arbitrators in consumer cases to at least briefly explain their decisions.[60] For example, the AAA *Statement of Principles* states that at 'the timely request of either party, the arbitrator should provide a brief written explanation of the basis for the award'.[61] Similarly, the CPR Institute for Dispute Resolution rules require that the arbitrator 'shall state the reasoning on which the award rests unless the parties agree otherwise'.[62] From a democratic standpoint, a written opinion helps demonstrate that the private process was legitimate, rational and fair. It can help both parties guide their future conduct. Public availability of opinions might also narrow the knowledge gap between the parties when choosing arbitrators.[63] Currently there is no requirement that opinions be explained, and contract drafting parties can even prohibit the publication of opinions.[64] The result is 'maximum freedom and minimal public scrutiny for the institutions with the economic power to take full advantage of what private dispute resolution has to offer'.[65]

---

59 See, e.g., the NAF chart on 'arbitration vs. litigation' in National Arbitration Forum, *About the Forum: Choose the Forum*, www.arb-forum.com/about/index.asp.

60 The consumer arbitration rules of the Better Business Bureau do require that the arbitrator render a written decision that explains the reasons for the award: *BBB Rules*, § 28.

61 *AAA Statement of Principles*, Principle 15. This is an interesting development, as AAA rules for consumer disputes do not require the arbitrator to explain her decision. Indeed, the former tendency was *not* to explain so as to make it harder to show, on appeal, that the arbitrator did not follow the law. Statutorily, neither the Federal Arbitration Act nor the State laws under the Uniform Arbitration Act require arbitrators to make findings of fact or conclusions of law or otherwise to reveal the reasoning behind their awards: Reuben, 'Constitutional Gravity', 1083.

62 *Ibid.*, 1084.

63 Granted, trial-level decisions in courts are not always informative. A general jury verdict merely finds for one of the parties. However, it will be based on a (theoretically) complete explanation of the law to be applied. A trial court decision in a non-jury trial generally includes some mechanism for requiring the judge to make findings of fact and conclusions of law. See, e.g, Fed R. Civ. P. 52; Tex. R. Civ. P. 296.

64 In addition, drafting parties can also charge extra for an opinion and thus discourage the consumer from requesting an explanation.

65 Garth, 'Privatisation', 386.

Loss of government control over law

The privatisation of dispute resolution transfers control over the process from the courts to the party who creates the procedural rules. Perhaps less obviously, it also transfers control over the substantive rules applied within those processes. Part of the appeal of the private systems is their ability to circumvent the law that would otherwise apply. The result is a depreciation of public order. 'The disputants, through contract, create private law and private courts to adjudicate their dispute, and, so long as their own private laws are applied, they have contracted for and achieved private justice adjudicated by a ... decision-maker of their choice.'[66] A court would apply the law created by the government, whether through legislation, regulation or common law. Even when considering the parties' contractual agreement, courts will sometimes refuse to enforce it because mandatory law overrides it. However, mandatory law is jeopardised when private processes and private decision-makers are involved. The private system allows the more powerful party to avoid the impact of what would have been mandatory law.

In all of the processes considered by this essay, privately chosen rules are being substituted for public law. ICANN's policy and rules were developed by a private body.[67] Many groups had input into these rules, but they were not primarily looking out for the interests of the public at large. Now the arbitrators privately accredited by ICANN, and privately chosen by trademark owners, are creating their own body of ICANN common law. With a body of hundreds of decided cases, ICANN arbitrators have begun to cite other ICANN arbitrators.[68] Although they also may cite national law, it is clear that 'the law of ICANN' is developing as a body of law about domain names, separate and apart from the law of any country or from any international treaty.[69]

---

66 Gibbons, 'Rusticum Judicium', 772. Note the dream of one technology believer, Frezza, 'How the Internet will Change the Rule of Law': 'Think about the impact on commerce of laws that ... are algorithmically defined and enforced with certainty, anywhere and everywhere. Imagine laws in which mobs of uninvolved third parties have no say, have no power and have to mind their own business.'

67 Not surprisingly, at least one ICANN complainant has already responded to a domain holder's claim of a first amendment right to expression by arguing that as a private body, ICANN cannot violate the first amendment: *Wal-Mart Stores, Inc.* v. *Walsucks*, Case No. D2000–0477 (WIPO, 20 July 2000), www.arbiter.wipo.int/domains/decisions/html/d2000-0477.html.

68 See M. Geist, 'Domain Name Wars Heat up', *The Globe and Mail* (4 May 2000), remarking that early cases are forming the basis for new global cyberlaw, with standards and legal tests divorced from traditional intellectual property law. See, e.g., *3636275 Canada* v. *eResolution.com*, Case No. D2000–0110 (WIPO, 10 April 2000), (finding in favour of complainant, doing business as 'eResolution', and stating that 'although entitled to consider principles of law deemed applicable, the Panel finds it unnecessary to do so in any depth. The jurisprudence which is being rapidly developed by a wide variety of Panelists world-wide under the ICANN Policy provides a fruitful source of precedent.'), www.arbiter.wipo.int/domains/decisions/html/d2000-0110.html.

69 This could create a strange situation where a party actually files a lawsuit to avoid the result of the ICANN decision. That lawsuit will be decided under the laws of some actual country, which

In the area of copyright, the planned operation of trusted systems allows contract to triumph over copyright. No access to copyrighted works is granted without permission. The parties' agreement is said to trump the content of copyright law, as if there were no national component to it and no interests involved other than those of the contracting parties.[70]

Even within the realm of contract law, the loss of court supervision is a serious matter.[71] From the standpoint of the legal system, as well as for individual transactions, private systems eliminate the ability of courts to apply mandatory contract and consumer protection law. A court might hold that certain contract terms are unenforceable, or that certain warranties cannot be disclaimed, or that certain remedies cannot be waived. It might require certain indications of true consent or adequate notice before other terms are enforced. When these values are incorporated into published opinions, they help not only the individual consumer in the case before the court but also consumers as a group. When a private arbitrator rules, it binds no one other than the parties before her. Even if she were to rule for the consumer, it would create no precedent. Further, the arbitrator, applying the private law contained in the terms and conditions page, or trusted systems software applying its program, need not apply laws benefiting consumers.

Some arbitration providers represent that the arbitrators will apply the applicable law, although this would include the provisions of the contract. Under the AAA rules of consumer arbitration, for example, the arbitrator is to apply 'any identified, pertinent contract terms, statutes, and legal precedents'.[72] The National Arbitration Forum also advertises that its arbitrators are supposed to apply applicable law.[73] The former online service, Cybertribunal (perhaps because it was administered by a law faculty), said that it would apply the law agreed to by the parties or, absent agreement, the 'national law with which the conflict has the closest links'.[74]

Arbitrators, in fact, need not apply the law at all. The consumer arbitration service offered by the Better Business Bureau provides in its rules that 'arbitrators are not bound to apply legal principles in reaching what the arbitrator considers to be

may differ from the domain name policy. The WIPO global standards may work only as long as they are not challenged.

70 For an argument that federal copyright law pre-empts certain kinds of contract terms that would be allowed under UCITA, see G. L. Founds, 'Shrinkwrap and Clickwrap Agreements: 2B or Not 2B?' (1999) 52 *Fed Comm LJ* 99.

71 From a systemic perspective, it decreases the supply of case precedent that guides commercial actors in planning their conduct and informs consumers of their rights: C. A. Carr and M. R. Jencks, 'The Privatisation of Business and Commercial Dispute Resolution: a Misguided Policy Decision' (1999–2000) 88 *Ky LJ* 183, 188.

72 American Arbitration Association, *Arbitration Rules for the Resolution of Consumer-Related Disputes* § 13(c), www.adr.org/rules/commercial/000411ab.htm.

73 National Arbitration Forum, *An Overview of the Forum*, www.arb-forum.com/about/index.asp.

74 M. S. Donahey, 'Current Developments in Online Dispute Resolution' (1999) 16 *J Int'l Arb* 115, 125, noting that Cybertribunal has been succeeded by eResolution.

a fair resolution of the dispute'.[75] Online services may also be law free. The original online dispute resolution service, the Virtual Magistrate, said that it would apply a standard of 'reasonableness in light of all available information'.[76]

When governments lose control over disputes, they lose a large amount of control over the law. This is particularly true in a country like the United States in which much of the implementation and enforcement of legal norms is left to private litigation. The trend in Internet dispute resolution to move disputes out of the courts and into private processes is changing not only the litigants' own process rights but also the substantive law.

Conclusion

Privatisation is indeed all the rage, but some of its manifestations need to go the way of the pet rock. The privatisation currently reigning on the Internet is not the kind of libertarian nirvana envisioned by its architects. The old-style libertarians are busy designing open source code, creating programs that provide free access to music even more untraceably than Napster, and acting as vigilantes in the war against spam. The new privatisation is instead the anti-regulation sentiment of corporate actors seeking to maximise their profits.

This is not an area where we can expect industry self-regulation to provide adequate limits to overreaching.[77] Evidence of market choices is already emerging. Trademark owners strive to stretch local marks to global control through the dot-com domain name. Copyright owners are preparing to license every conceivable use of copyrighted material and to use self-help to avoid outside supervision. And merchants are using standardised contracts to impose both substantive and procedural terms that dilute the rights of the consumer. Companies purporting to adopt consumer-friendly 'best practices' are agreeing to little more than the bare minimum required by the most lenient jurisdiction's law. Consumer transactions in particular often take place under conditions of pervasive and persistent market failures that prevent an economically rational outcome from being reached through pure market forces.

Both code and contract can be controlled. Governments can provide minimum acceptable standards even for private systems of resolving disputes, and can where appropriate prohibit the parties from using technological devices to administer

---

75 *BBB Rules*, § 28.
76 A. Almaguer and R. W. Baggott III, 'Shaping New Legal Frontiers: Dispute Resolution for the Internet' (1998) 13 *Ohio St J on Disp Resol* 711, 726.
77 Given the trend towards privatisation, a developing body of case law will also not be available to create a useful set of legal limits. Many disputes will not reach courts, especially courts that issue published decisions. Further, courts are by their nature limited to deciding the cases before them on the facts before them and are thus less able to implement rules that have a broader effect.

self-help remedies. Although technology-specific regulation would be quickly out-dated, certain actions can be required or prohibited. Further, governments can identify substantive law that may not be varied by contract.

Left unchecked, market forces and their legislative allies are ignoring important public interests. The e-commerce boom comes with associated costs, and absent government regulation the companies involved will externalise those costs onto consumers and the public at large. Governments need to impose certain standards, or technological choices will make it increasingly difficult to embed important values in the dispute resolution process. Reasonable minds can disagree about the exact dimensions of government intervention that would protect procedural due process guarantees and require the enforcement of substantive norms. It is clear, however, that regulation is required. The US Government has bent over backwards in its effort to please the major players on the Internet. It is now time to lean the other way.

13 Armageddon through aggregation? The use and abuse of class actions in international dispute resolution

RICHARD O. FAULK

Introduction

A troubling and dangerous phenomenon has emerged onto the international litigation landscape. The system of justice understood and appreciated by citizens in most democratic states, one that guarantees individual plaintiffs and defendants their 'day in court', is increasingly being sidestepped by procedural rules that allow entrepreneurial lawyers to aggregate claims into massive controversies that, for all practical purposes, cannot be tried. Although these massive cases arise in varying formats, they share a single intimidating characteristic: the designed imposition of enormous and intolerable risks which defendants cannot prudently accept by insisting on their 'day in court' in a jury trial.

Although some courts have refused to accept this type of 'judicial blackmail', the practice has not been disapproved uniformly. Indeed, the mere threat of international class actions, especially those regarding human rights violations occurring in other countries, has produced gigantic settlements in the United States. The recently concluded slave labour and Holocaust victims' class actions against German companies and the Swiss banks are illustrative. In those controversies, sovereign states and major international institutions paid billions of US dollars to resolve claims by many persons residing outside the United States arising from activities occurring wholly outside the United States. Moreover, the settlements occurred not only in the absence of any adverse rulings on the merits of the case, but also, at least in so far as the Germans were concerned, despite favourable rulings holding that the matters were not justiciable in United States courts. Most importantly, the settlements occurred *before* classes were certified, thereby demonstrating the coercive effects of class allegations.

The use of these techniques by entrepreneurial lawyers is understandable in view of their predictable effects, namely, enormous and relatively prompt settlements and extraordinary fee recoveries for the lawyers themselves. With few exceptions, the public record conclusively demonstrates that once a controversy is aggregated

Also published in (2001) 10 *MSU-DCL J Int'l L* 205.
Armageddon is the biblical site of the final climactic battle between the forces of good and evil: Revelation 16:16.
The opinions stated herein are solely those of the author.

to the point where the 'blackmail' threat arises, settlement is inevitable unless the threat is eliminated by interlocutory appellate review or bankruptcy. As a result, major controversies that involve large numbers of claims, and that have a significant impact on the public interest and private coffers, are involuntarily decided outside of the judicial process, thereby bypassing all of the procedural safeguards, protections and guarantees the litigation process provides to participants in all other types of case.

Unfortunately, the unfairness of this phenomenon has an impact on individual plaintiffs as well as defendants. Settlements achieved in mass tort cases are fraught with potential conflicts of interest between individual plaintiffs and their counsel. Moreover, the potential for collusive settlements that end the controversy, compensate plaintiffs' counsel highly and undercompensate individual plaintiffs cannot be disregarded. Unless the system permits sufficient attention to individual claims and adequate representation of individual interests, there are genuine risks that individual plaintiffs' rights may be trampled on in the stampede to settlement.

The use of American or, for that matter, any other nation's collective liability devices to resolve claims of non-resident foreign litigants represents a major intrusion into the internal social policies and cultures of other sovereign states. Although 'globalism' may be useful as a commercial cliché, its intrusion into jurisprudence is disturbing, especially when procedural devices that are not yet recognised internationally are used to resolve claims arising from conduct that occurs beyond the forum state's borders. Accordingly, it is prudent that proposals seeking to expand the use of the class device internationally, or that would allow the international enforcement of class action judgments by treaty, should be evaluated cautiously. To the extent that such proposals are considered, they should not focus solely upon enhancing claimants' access to justice. They must also guarantee that defendants are not oppressively denied their opportunities to be heard.

There are three serious obstacles to compromise on this issue. First, the necessity of class actions is questionable in systems outside the United States. Secondly, longstanding civil law principles militate against the creation and implementation of class action practices that depend upon equitable principles and discretionary certification and administration. Finally, the selective adoption of American-style class action rules by individual nations, such as those in the European Community, threatens a barrage of 'forum shopping' by litigants and counsel who seek to create 'transnational' class actions. Although each of these issues will be discussed below, this essay does not purport to solve these problems. Instead, it questions whether there is a need to create them in the first place. Any attempts to introduce class action practice into the international arena should be approached with the utmost caution, with full awareness of the cultural limitations of the forum's system of jurisprudence, the serious potential for abuse inherent in the process, and the consequences of enabling extraterritorial class actions within the forum's national courts.

Are international class actions necessary?

Are class actions necessary to motivate responsible behaviour?

The debate over the scope and utility of class actions is a controversy over fundamentals, namely, the role of private litigation in governance. Differing cultures have widely contrasting views on that subject. In the United States, there is a strong tradition, especially in civil rights litigation, that supports the utility of class actions to have an impact on social policy and to modify behaviour. Outside the United States, virtually no nations have such a tradition. Instead, other countries commonly rely upon governmental regulation and public enforcement proceedings to protect the public interest. The concept of the 'private attorney general', a citizen or advocate who 'represents' the public interest and who uses the judicial system, as opposed to parliamentary action, to advance social aims or redress public wrongs is not commonly accepted outside the United States. This fundamental disagreement over the role of private litigants and the judiciary underlies many of the obstacles to expanding class action procedures into Europe and other regions.

There are serious questions regarding the necessity of class actions involving claims beyond those for arithmetically calculable damages.[1] Given the extensive reliance on governmental regulation and enforcement in the European Union and elsewhere, as well as the pervasive social welfare systems already in place, there is little 'incentive' to use class actions seeking tort damages as tools of social engineering.[2] To date, no studies have been published establishing that, in liberal social democracies, there is a need for tort litigation to regulate corporate behaviour. There is no empirical evidence that threats of litigation are necessary to coerce responsible behaviour and regulatory compliance, nor is there evidence that current regulations and compensation programmes are inadequate to protect personal and public interests. It would require a 'revolutionary change in European

1 For reasons of space, and not necessarily of philosophy, this essay addresses the issues of class action abuse solely in the 'mass tort' context, where individual amounts in question are typically insufficient to motivate claimants to file individual actions, and where damages are intangible and not susceptible to arithmetical calculation. Nothing in this essay should be construed as suggesting that serious obstacles do not exist to unrestricted recognition of class actions for commercial claims.

2 This essay recognises a distinction between US-style 'class actions' and 'group actions', as that term is used in certain European and Latin-American countries. A 'class action' is a proceeding where a representative plaintiff seeks to obtain relief on behalf of a group of similarly situated persons, and where the judgment in the action is binding on those persons, irrespective of whether they are actually joined as parties to the case. Generally, a 'group action' does not bind absent persons, but instead permits groups of plaintiffs to consolidate their claims in a single proceeding. See generally R. Faulk, 'The International Class Action: a Commentary on the Geneva Group Action Debates' (BNA 2000) 1 *Class Action Litig Rep* 325, 326–7. There is an unfortunate tendency to confuse these two terms under the general category of 'class actions' when they are actually different proceedings.

policy' if these nations' pervasive regulatory mechanisms were declared ineffective in favour of a need for 'supplemental regulation through compensation'.[3]

Indeed, it appears that the cultures of most democracies, other than the United States, have already determined that tort litigation is not an effective or efficient method to achieve social or personal justice.[4] In those nations, social security systems are the major methods of providing compensation and care for persons who have sustained an injury.[5] Moreover, in most of those systems, the compensation levels are relatively high and the victims are not required to show 'causation' by a particular responsible person or product.[6] By contrast, the American tort system does not concentrate upon predictable and complete compensation, but rather depends upon the subjective judgment of juries to determine liability, causation and damages. Although damages may, in some cases, be extraordinarily high, recoveries are not necessarily so, nor are they assured.

Such inconsistency and subjectivity not only increase risks for the litigants, but also imperil the 'harmonisation' necessary for international co-operation and business development. In the European Union, 'harmonisation' of commercial laws and activity is a fundamental goal. Allowing isolated courts to create and enforce their own variable standards, standards that may or may not be consistent with the considered policies of EU statutes and regulations, undermines the very purpose underlying international economic alliances and political organisations.

Even now, such problems are appearing under treaties where the United States is a party, such as the North American Free Trade Agreement ('NAFTA'). In some US jurisdictions, litigation pressure on certain products, such as gasoline additives, has prompted States to restrict or ban the use of those products within their borders.[7]

---

3 C. J. S. Hodges, 'Multi-Party Actions: a European Approach' in 'Lessons from the Land of Litigation Fever: Should the Class Action Be Exported or Quarantined?' (2000) *International Bar Association Proceedings* 19. See generally C. J. S. Hodges, *Multi-Party Actions* (Oxford: Oxford University Press, 2001).

4 See Hodges, 'Multi-Party Actions: a European Approach', 20: 'Europe neither needs nor wants US-style class action litigation'; Hodges, *Multi-Party Actions*, Foreword by Steyn LJ, discussing problems with the use of US-style class actions in Europe, and concluding that 'the introduction of United States style class actions cannot but contribute to such unwelcome developments in our legal system'. See generally Faulk, 'The International Class Action', 326. Significantly, the European Commission, after studying the necessity of class actions for improving 'access to justice', concluded that such devices were not appropriate in EU products liability cases: Report from the Commission, *On the Application of Directive 85/374 on Liability for Defective Products*, COM (2000) 893 final (European Commission, 31 January 2001), 27: 'At this stage, there is no indication that action concerning access to justice specifically with regard to product liability cases would be appropriate'. See www.europa.eu.int/comm/internal.market/en/goods/liability/liability2.htm.

5 See Hodges, *Multi-Party Actions*, 16–17.   6 *Ibid.*

7 See R. Faulk and J. S. Gray, 'MTBE: Can the Controversy Be Contained?' (BNA 2000) 14 *Toxics L Rep* 603, 607, updated as R. Faulk and J. S. Gray, 'Crisis? What Crisis? Containing the MTBE Controversy' in R. Faulk, *Stopping the Speeding Locomotive: Perspectives on Toxic Tort and Environmental Litigation* (Houston: Gardere, 2000), 14; further updated as R. Faulk and J. S. Gray, 'Salem Revisited: Updating the MTBE Controversy' (BNA 2000) 2 *Class Action Litig Rep* 125, examining the national and international controversy regarding groundwater contamination allegedly caused by methyl tertiary butyl ether.

Foreign companies that manufacture and distribute the restricted or banned products have made claims for compensation under NAFTA because the States' actions violate the Treaty's free trade guarantees.[8] The jurisdiction of the World Trade Organisation is also implicated in such a controversy, removing the dispute to the global arena. This example illustrates the perils created by attempts to harmonise commercial relations between unpredictably litigious societies and more stable regulatory democracies. Even policies set through international agreements may be challenged when litigation influences participating states or their subdivisions to take contrary political action. Such disputes are inevitable where the policies of one participating nation, such as the United States, are highly influenced by private litigation, as opposed to uniform regulatory standards.

Incompatibility of contingent fee principles

The 'entrepreneurship' of contingent fees, a hallmark of American class action litigation that promotes risk-taking by the plaintiffs' bar,[9] seems flatly incompatible with the 'fee shifting' tradition of most other nations, which discourages litigants and their counsel from taking similar risks. Indeed, as stated above, outside of the United States, it appears that the international community *distrusts* litigation as a means for social reform, preferring instead to focus on individual claims and requiring the litigants to take responsibility for asking society's institutions to resolve their personal disputes. This is shown by the prevailing 'costs follow the event' requirement in non-American jurisdictions. This rule typically requires unsuccessful litigants to bear major portions of their opponent's legal expenses. The 'costs follow the event' principle facilitates judicial administration by discouraging the filing of weak cases and by encouraging early settlements before costs escalate.

Although contingent fees have been accepted in a few common law and civil code nations, they are disallowed elsewhere.[10] Contingent fees, like legal aid programmes, supposedly enhance consumers' access to justice by enabling poorer litigants to pursue claims without the intimidation of an attorney's fees.

---

8 See Faulk and Gray, 'MTBE: Can the Controversy Be Contained?', 607; Faulk and Gray, 'Salem Revisited: Updating the MTBE Controversy', 127.

9 See R. B. Cappalli and C. Consolo, 'Class Actions for Continental Europe? A Preliminary Inquiry' (1992) 6 *Temp Int'l & Comp LJ* 217, 290, 292 n. 257: 'The primary actor in the American class action is the class lawyer pursuing significant fees'; J. Coffee, 'Understanding the Plaintiffs' Attorney: the Implications of Economic Theory for Private Enforcement of Law through Class and Derivative Actions' (1986) 86 *Colum L Rev* 669, 678: 'Our legal system has long accepted, if somewhat uneasily, the concept of the plaintiff's attorney as an entrepreneur who performs the socially useful function of deterring undesirable conduct.'

10 See generally W. J. Lynk, 'The Courts and the Market: an Economic Analysis of Contingent Fees in Class Action Litigation' (1990) 19 *J Legal Stud* 247.

Unfortunately, this altruistic principle has not proven uniformly effective when applied in progressive social welfare states. In the United Kingdom, for example, the 'costs follow the event' rule was originally suspended in cases where the plaintiff participated in a legal aid programme. Although litigation proliferated, so did the number of questionable claims and the costs associated with handling them.[11] Ultimately, the number of persons actually helped by the system declined dramatically.[12]

More importantly, as in US class actions, a practice arose known as 'legal aid blackmail', where defendants, who could expect reimbursement in other types of cases, were forced to settle weaker claims that might not have been filed previously, or that would have been tried to judgment under the 'costs follow the event' rule.[13] To correct this injustice, the UK has now restored the 'costs follow the event' rule and now generally applies the rule to contingent fee cases. Parties may, if they choose, purchase private insurance to cover the risk, but they remain primarily liable for their opponents' costs if their case fails.

The UK's experience with contingent fees illustrates the problem of permitting class action litigation in social welfare societies. Private litigants, especially tort litigants, can seldom finance class actions without the financial support of their counsel. In most nations, contingent fee agreements are either impermissible or, if permitted, fail to shield the claimant from the burden of paying the opponent's expenses. Hence, society's policy of discouraging frivolous claims and facilitating early settlement, both admirable goals, also discourages aggregating claims to the point where the danger of 'blackmail' arises. In combination with advanced social welfare programmes, the 'costs follow the event' rule ensures that injured parties are predictably and consistently compensated by non-judicial means, and that defendants' behaviour is controlled by regulations issued and enforced by legislative institutions, which are typically more politically responsive and accountable than courts.

Are class actions compatible with civil law jurisprudence?

Long-standing civil law principles militate against the creation and implementation of class action practices. Unlike common law nations,[14] civil law systems[15] generally eschew judicial discretion. Common law legal principles reflect

11 See generally Hodges, *Multi-Party Actions*, 9.   12 *Ibid.*   13 *Ibid.*, 12.
14 Common law systems exist in the United States, Great Britain, Ireland, Canada, Australia and New Zealand, and have 'substantial influence on the law of many nations in Asia and Africa': J. H. Merryman, *The Civil Law Traditions: an Introduction to the Legal Systems of Western Europe and Latin America* (2nd edn, Stanford, Ca.: Stanford University Press, 1985), 4. The traditional date marking the beginning of the common law is 1066, the year of the Norman Conquest: *ibid.*, 3.
15 The civil law tradition is the dominant legal structure in most of Western Europe, all of Central and South America, substantial portions of Asia and Africa, and 'a few enclaves in the common

a 'preference for pluralism' and the 'predominance of reasonableness', qualities that are largely foreign to civil law jurisprudence.[16] Unlike the civil law, the common law does not always insist on the 'right answer'; instead, only a 'reasonable' approach is required, defined as an approach that accepts that a problem has 'many reasonable answers'.[17] Civil law systems, on the other hand, primarily depend upon specific statutes, regulations and rules adopted in the parliamentary process and strictly enforced by a relatively inflexible judiciary.[18]

In the United States, these differences are exacerbated by the fundamental political variances between parliamentary democracies (even in sister common law nations) and the American constitutional structure. In America, unlike in a parliamentary democracy, lawmaking is not wholly entrusted to any single branch of government. Neither the executive nor the legislative branches completely control the process and, as a result, laws are almost invariably the result of many compromises. Therefore, American courts, rather than being charged with finding precise solutions to specific problems, are charged with effectuating compromises, a responsibility that naturally entails acceptance of one 'reasonable' approach over others rejected or accommodated in the legislative process.[19] This hallmark of the American system promotes even greater discretion than the equitable flexibility encountered in other common law jurisdictions. As Professor Christie has noted, 'this is an important philosophical difference which the proponents of the globalisation of law cannot afford to ignore'.[20]

Rule 23 of the Federal Rules of Civil Procedure, the American rule governing class actions arising from mass torts, is laced with deference to judicial discretion.[21] This is not surprising because the rationale for class actions originated in courts of equity.[22] American class action jurisprudence originated with a noble vision,

---

law world (Louisiana, Quebec, and Puerto Rico)': Merryman, *The Civil Law Traditions*, 3–4. It dates back at least to 450 BC, the approximate date when the XII Tables of Roman Law were published: Merryman, *The Civil Law Traditions*, 2.

16 See G. P. Fletcher, 'Comparative Law as a Subversive Discipline' (1998) 46 *Am J Comp L* 683, 699.

17 *Ibid.* See also G. C. Christie, 'Some Key Jurisprudential Issues of the Twenty-First Century' (2000) 8 *Tul J Int'l & Comp L* 217, 230.

18 See Merryman, *The Civil Law Traditions*, 23–4, 47, noting that, consistently with Roman and French legal traditions, written constitutions, specific statutes and decrees, criminal, civil and commercial codes, as well as international treaties, generally constitute the exclusive sources of law in civil law nations, as opposed to judicial precedents.

19 Christie, 'Some Key Jurisprudential Issues', 230.   20 *Ibid.*, 223.

21 According to Professors Cappalli and Consolo, the broad discretionary powers conferred by Rule 23 effectively transform the American class action judge into 'the manager of a small welfare-type bureaucracy whose purpose is to determine and distribute entitlements to a beneficiary group': 'Class Actions' 292 n. 261.

22 Courts of equity were originally created in England to vary the strict operation of the law in the interests of justice. Eventually the courts of law and the courts of equity were merged into a single common law tradition that consists of the original common law 'and the tempering influence of equity'. Comparative law scholars have remarked that the modern civil law is 'what the common law would look like if there had never been a court of chancery in England': Merryman, *The Civil Law Traditions*, 50–1.

namely, to resolve *equitably* large controversies involving large numbers of persons who have common claims against common defendants. In early experience, the 'common claims' were typically held by persons with small claims, which could not be efficiently litigated. Class actions gave small claimants an opportunity to recover damages from defendants who, in the absence of a class remedy, would be unjustly enriched by retaining an aggregated ill-gotten gain.[23] Even the most recent cases have underscored the importance of this equitable goal.[24]

Essentially, therefore, class actions were first designed, in the interests of equity, to promote the filing of litigation that would otherwise never be prosecuted. They were allowed because, as a matter of policy, wrongdoers should not be allowed to reap unscrupulous gains from multitudes of victims who, without the class device, would probably forgo claims for relief in court because their losses were relatively small. While individual amounts in controversy remained relatively small, this jurisprudence clearly served the purpose of precluding 'unjust enrichment'. Unfortunately, these relatively altruistic concepts carry within them seeds of abuse: the potential to proliferate litigation and the tendency to exaggerate the significance and merits of claims.[25] In such cases, courts face a 'fundamental dilemma' which requires them to 'balance the harm caused by court-sanctioned solicitation of claims' against the 'benefits of increased law enforcement through realistic compensation of private attorneys and economic leverage for small claims'.[26]

---

23 See *Deposit Guaranty Nat'l Bank* v. *Roper*, 445 US 326, 338–9 (1980) per Burger CJ.: 'The aggregation of individual claims in the context of a class wide suit is an evolutionary response to the existence of injuries unremedied by the regulatory action of government. Where it is not economically feasible to obtain relief within the traditional framework of a multiplicity of small individual suits for damages, aggrieved persons may be without any effective redress unless they may employ the class-action device.'

24 See *Amchem Products, Inc.* v. *Windsor*, 521 US 591, 617 (1997) per Ginsburg J.: 'The very core of the class action mechanism is to overcome the problem that small recoveries do not provide the incentive for any individual to bring a solo action prosecuting his or her rights. A class action solves this problem by aggregating the relatively paltry potential recoveries into something worth someone's (usually an attorney's) labour.'

25 See generally *Southwestern Refining Co., Inc.* v. *Bernal*, 22 SW 3d 425, 438 (Tex 2000) per Gonzales J.: 'Aggregating claims can dramatically alter substantive tort jurisprudence. Under the traditional tort model, recovery is conditioned on defendant responsibility. The plaintiff must prove, and the defendant must be given the opportunity to contest, every element of a claim. By removing individual considerations from the adversarial process, the tort system is shorn of a valuable method for screening out marginal and unfounded claims. In this way, "class certification magnifies and strengthens the number of unmeritorious claims"' (citing *Castano* v. *American Tobacco Company*, 84 F 3d 739, 746 (5th Cir. 1996)). See also J. A. Siliciano, 'Mass Torts and the Rhetoric of Crisis' (1995) 80 *Cornell L Rev* 990, 1010–11; F. E. McGovern, 'Looking to the Future of Mass Torts: a Comment on Schuck and Siliciano' (1995) 80 *Cornell L Rev* 1022, 1023–4, each observing that mass tort cases have a tendency to attract many unmeritorious claims. In short, 'if claims are not subject to some level of individual attention, defendants are more likely to be held liable to claimants to whom they caused no harm': *Southwestern Refining Co.* v. *Bernall, ibid.*, 438 per Gonzales J.

26 J. W. Moore, *Moore's Federal Practice* (2nd edn, Albany, NY: M. Bender, 1996) § 232.02[1], 23–37.

From this underlying equitable rationale, American class action jurisprudence arose that broadly supported early and easy class certification, and which placed defendants under significant pressures to settle.[27] In order to promote the policies against 'unjust enrichment', procedural rules were promulgated in the United States that granted broad discretion to trial judges. Both trial and appellate courts construed the class action rule liberally. Even on appeal, class certifications were typically reviewed under a liberal 'abuse of discretion' standard. Under this standard, certification must be affirmed even if the evidence adduced at the hearing is severely conflicting.[28] A trial court abuses its discretion only when it acts arbitrarily or unreasonably, or without reference to any guiding principles.[29]

Given the equitable origins of class actions, it is understandable that Rule 23 does not specifically address many of the problems that contribute to class action abuse. Arguably, some problems are broadly encompassed in their wording, but the effectiveness of these factors, standing alone, can only be judged by experience, and experience demonstrates that the rule is not sufficiently specific, predictably to preclude the abuses described in this essay.[30] As class action jurisprudence developed in the United States, and as mass tort controversies proliferated, most notably asbestos litigation, the courts became less sensitive to the equitable underpinnings of

27 Relying on this jurisprudence, which was developed to 'empower' litigants with small claims, many courts in the United States made overreaching decisions that were supposedly 'consistent' with traditional class action principles. Examples from a single jurisdiction, Texas, illustrate the situation that occurred nationally. See, e.g., *St Louis Southwestern Railway Co.* v. *Voluntary Purchasing Groups, Inc.*, 929 SW 2d 25 (Tex App Texarkana 1996, no writ) (class certification should be resolved 'as soon as practicable' after the action is filed and the determination may be made solely on the basis of the pleadings); *Microsoft Corp.* v. *Manning*, 914 SW 2d 602 (Tex App El Paso 1993, no writ) (when considering class certification at such an early stage, before supporting facts are fully developed, the court should favour maintaining the suit as a class action because the court may always modify or decertify the class later); *Life Ins. Co. of the Southwest* v. *Brister*, 722 SW 2d 764 (Tex App Fort Worth 1986, writ dism'd w.o.j.) (plaintiffs are not required to prove a prima facie case of liability to secure class certification and the probability of their success on the merits is not relevant to the class certification issue); *Microsoft Corp.* v. *Manning, ibid.*, 615 (to the extent the court hears evidence at the class certification hearing, the rules of evidence do not apply. In particular, the court may base its conclusions on evidence that may be inadmissible at trial, even if the supporting proof fails to satisfy admissibility standards for scientific evidence); *Microsoft Corp.* v. *Manning, ibid.*, 613 (the identity of a class may, under appropriate circumstances, be 'national' in scope, and variations in State law across the nation do not necessarily preclude certification of 'national' classes, especially if the party opposing the class fails to establish that the variations will render the case unmanageable). Under the laws of some States, unnamed class members are not considered parties for the purpose of discovery after a class is certified: e.g., Tex R Civ P 42(f).

28 See, e.g., *Microsoft Corp.* v. *Manning, ibid.*, 607; *Vinson* v. *Texas Commerce Bank*, 880 SW 2d 820, 823 (Tex App Dallas 1994, no writ).

29 See, e.g., *Downer* v. *Aquamarine Operators, Inc.*, 701 SW 2d 238, 242 (Tex 1985), cert denied, 476 US 1159 (1986).

30 See generally R. Faulk and K. L. Colbert, 'Reforming an Abusive System: Curtailing Class Certification in Toxic Tort and Environmental Litigation' (1997) 11 *Toxics L Rep* 241, reprinted in Faulk, *Stopping the Speeding Locomotive*, examining the historical progression of class action abuse in the United States and proposing reforms to preclude 'blackmail' situations in mass tort cases.

class actions as a safeguard against 'unjust enrichment' and developed another rationale: the 'judicial economy' served by aggregating thousands of claims into a single proceeding.[31] According to these courts, there was simply no alternative to class certification to manage these massive controversies efficiently and effectively.[32] Once 'judicial economy' became the overriding consideration, Rule 23's lack of specificity exacerbated the problem by permitting trial courts to exercise broad discretion to certify cases merely on the *allegation* of a mass tort crisis, instead of requiring proof that such a controversy actually existed or that the claims had any demonstrable merit.[33] This practice resulted in uninformed certifications that created gigantic controversies – controversies that placed defendants under such intolerable settlement pressures that they were termed 'judicial blackmail'.[34] This pattern of abuse not only promoted the creation of artificial controversies, but also motivated the resolution of those controversies on economic grounds, rather than on their merits.

The movement to correct these abuses in the United States has taken many approaches, but the actual and proposed reforms generally have a single common objective, namely, the restriction of trial court discretion. From the judicial

31 See Faulk and Colbert, 'Reforming an Abusive System', 247–8. The individual claims involved in mass tort actions are rarely impractical to litigate economically. In an alleged class seeking lifetime 'medical monitoring' costs or property value diminutions, the individual amounts in controversy may easily exceed $US100,000. If personal injury and death causes of action are added, the individual claims may exceed $US1,000,000. Given these amounts of alleged damages, it seems clear that any injured party has a strong incentive to litigate. The original underpinnings of the class device, namely avoidance of unjust enrichment, are vitiated in this situation. It is unnecessary to 'promote' or 'foster' litigation through a class action in these circumstances: *ibid.*, 242.

32 This evolution was not swift, but rather occurred after a long series of decisions that rejected many other creative methods of dealing with the asbestos controversy. See generally Faulk and Colbert, 'Reforming an Abusive System', 247. Indeed, the first federal appellate court to permit an asbestos mass tort class action explicitly did so only out of 'necessity': *ibid*. Thereafter, however, the use of class actions in mass tort cases expanded throughout the United States until the very same court emphasised the importance of a showing of necessity and predictability as a prerequisite to class certification of such controversies: *Castano* v. *American Tobacco Company*, 84 F 3d 734 (5th Cir. 1996) (discussed in *ibid.*, 248).

33 *Ibid.*, 249–50.

34 See, e.g., *Castano* v. *American Tobacco Company*, 84 F 3d 734, 746 (5th Cir. 1996) per Smith J.: 'In the context of mass tort actions, certification dramatically affects the stakes for defendants. Class certification magnifies and strengthens the number of unmeritorious claims. Aggregation of claims also makes it more likely that a defendant will be found liable and results in significantly higher damage awards. In addition to skewing trial outcomes, class certification creates insurmountable pressure on defendants to settle, whereas individual trials would not. The risk of facing an all-or-nothing verdict presents too high a risk, even when the probability of an adverse judgment is low. These settlements have been referred to as judicial blackmail.' See also *In Re Rhone-Poulenc Rorer, Inc.*, 51 F 3d 1293, 1300 (7th Cir. 1995) per Grady J., cert. denied, 116 S. Ct. 184 (1995): 'With the aggregate stakes in the tens or hundreds of millions of dollars, or even in the billions, it is not a waste of judicial resources to conduct more than one trial, before more than six jurors', to determine whether a major segment of the industry 'is to follow the asbestos manufacturers into Chapter 11 [bankruptcy proceedings].'

perspective, the trend of the reforms, either through judicial action or rulemaking, is to limit the exercise of discretion by setting more specific certification standards that require a 'rigorous analysis' and that limit the discretion formerly held by the trial courts to 'certify first and ask questions later'.[35] From a rule-making perspective, proposals were made to incorporate the judicial reforms into Rule 23 as specific guidelines for certification proceedings.[36] Even so, however, the restricting case law and the proposed reforms stress the importance of experience gained through trials and appeals of individual claims to determine whether a mass tort is sufficiently 'mature' to have the 'predictable vitality' necessary for class certification.[37] As a result, they still call for the exercise of broad discretion, restricted only by a requirement that the discretionary decision be informed by real historical experience, rather than based upon speculation.[38] They do not purport to divest the courts of discretionary power in the class certification process, but rather confine the exercise of discretion to circumstances where there is adequate information to determine whether a proposed class action will truly satisfy the Rule 23 requirements.

35 See, e.g., *Amchem Products, Inc.* v. *Windsor*, 521 US 591 (1997). In *Amchem*, the US Supreme Court emphasised the importance of carefully scrutinising the standards to ensure that the proposed class is 'sufficiently cohesive to warrant adjudication by representation' (623). As a result of these decisions and principles, the current trend in the federal and state judiciary requires courts to perform a 'rigorous analysis' before ruling on class certification to determine whether all prerequisites to certification have been met. See *General Tel. Co. of the Southwest* v. *Falcon*, 457 US 147, 161 (1982); *In re American Medical Sys., Inc.*, 75 F 3d 1069, 1078–9 (6th Cir. 1996). A cautious approach to class certification is now essential in many jurisdictions. See, e.g., *Southwestern Refining Co., Inc.* v. *Bernal*, 22 SW 3d 425 (Tex 2000). As the Supreme Court stressed in *Amchem, ibid.*, 620: 'Courts must be mindful that the rule as now composed sets the requirements they are bound to enforce . . . The text of a rule . . . limits judicial inventiveness.' See also *General Motors Corp.* v. *Bloyed*, 916 SW 2d 949, 954 (Tex 1996) per Cornyn J., emphasising 'the importance of the trial court's obligation to determine that the protective requirements of [the class action rules] are met'.
36 See, e.g., Faulk and Colbert, 'Reforming an Abusive System', 249–50, setting out specific proposals to amend Rule 23 to provide more specific guidance for trial court discretion. The amendments proposed in that article are set out in the Appendix to this essay. See also D. M. Franklin, 'The Mass Tort Defendants Strike Back: Are Settlement Class Actions a Collusive Threat or Just a Phantom Menace?' (2000) 53 *Stanford L Rev* 163, 182–9, describing the official proposed amendments to Rule 23.
37 Professor Francis E. McGovern first proposed the concept of 'maturity' as a prerequisite to certifying American mass tort class actions in 'Resolving Mature Mass Tort Litigation' (1989) 69 B U L Rev 659. See also R. Faulk, R. E. Meadows and K. L. Colbert, 'Building a Better Mousetrap? A New Approach to Trying Mass Tort Cases' (1998) 29 *Texas Tech L Rev* 779, 786–8. Generally, it permits class certification of a mass tort controversy only when there has been a sufficient history of trials and appeals to justify a conclusion that a real judicial crisis involving meritorious cases exists. The concept has been embraced in a number of federal decisions. See, e.g., *Castano* v. *The American Tobacco Company*, 84 F 3d 734 (5th Cir. 1996). The principle is also enshrined in primary reference materials for United States judges: *Manual for Complex Litigation*, § 33.26.
38 Rule 23 remains a 'flexible' rule, but its criteria must be more carefully applied. See, e.g., *General Tel. Co. of the Southwest* v. *Falcon*, 457 US 147, 160 (1982) per Stevens J.: The 'flexibility' of Rule 23 'enhances the usefulness of the class-action device, [but] actual, not presumed, conformance with [the Rule] remains . . . indispensable'.

Even this 'restricted' discretion, however, goes far beyond the authority of most civil law judges. In civil law nations, judicial service is a bureaucratic career, and the judge's function is narrow, mechanical and relatively uncreative.[39] As Professor Merryman, a leading American comparative law scholar, once explained:[40]

> [The civil law judge] is a kind of expert clerk. He is presented with a fact situation to which a ready legislative response will be readily found in all except the extraordinary case. His function is merely to find the right legislative provision, couple it with the fact situation, and bless the solution that is more or less automatically produced from the union. The whole process of judicial decision is made to fit the formal syllogism of scholastic logic. The major premise is in the statute, the facts of the case furnish the minor premise, and the conclusion inevitably follows.

This *deductive* reasoning approach is the antithesis of the United States common law tradition, which uses *inductive* reasoning to resolve legal issues, inferring general principles of law from specific principles found in the federal and state constitutions, statutes and prior judicial decisions.[41] The difference between these approaches 'cuts at the very heart of the dichotomy' between the two traditions.[42] As the great American jurist Oliver Wendell Holmes wrote, 'the life of the [common] law has not been logic: it has been experience'.[43] Consistent with the American tolerance for compromise and degrees of indeterminacy, Justice Holmes recognised that, under the common law, 'the felt necessities of the time, the prevalent moral and political theories, intuitions of public policy, avowed or unconscious, even the prejudices which judges share with their fellow-men, have a good deal more to do than the syllogism in determining the rules by which men should

---

39 See Cappalli and Consolo, 'Class Actions', 291: the Euro-Continental judge 'is profoundly different both in his role in the legal system as a type of state bureaucrat and in his relatively passive role in the legal process, notwithstanding the frequent references to his "inquisitorial" powers in preparing a case on the facts'. See also Merryman, *The Civil Law Traditions*, 38: 'Judicial service in the civil law countries is a bureaucratic career; the judge is a functionary, a civil servant; the judicial function is narrow, mechanical, and uncreative'; C. R. Giesze, 'Helms-Burton in Light of the Common Law and Civil Law Legal Traditions: Is Legal Analysis Alone Sufficient to Settle Controversies Arising under International Law on the Eve of the Second Summit of the Americas?' (1998) 32 *Int'l Law* 51, 62: 'In contrast to the rigorous analysis that characterises the application of US law before an American court, civil law analysis usually consists in the mere mechanical application of the law.'

40 Merryman, *The Civil Law Traditions*, 36. See also Giesze, 'Helms-Burton', 61: 'Given the traditional lack of equitable interpretive powers in the civil law system, contemporary civil law judges and lawyers are trained during their formative years to become strict constructionists of the law in accordance with a scientific approach to jurisprudence. They must literally interpret and strictly apply legal principles in accordance with deductive reasoning techniques, doctrinal writings, and legal dogma. Reliance on simple common sense, derived from daily human experiences, generally does not form part of the civil law analytical framework.'

41 See J. F. Smith, 'Confronting Differences in the United States and Mexican Legal Systems in the Era of NAFTA' (1993) 1 *US–Mexico LJ* 85, 87–8.

42 *Ibid.*   43 O. W. Holmes, *The Common Law* (Boston, Ma.: Little Brown & Co., 1881), 1.

be governed'.[44] US courts are highly flexible and rely largely upon common sense, based on the 'reasonableness' derived from the compromises inherent in the American political structure, as the linchpin of their analysis.[45] This flexibility is derived from the broad discretionary and equitable powers traditionally granted to common law judges to resolve controversies.[46]

In civil law nations, however, the syllogism rules. Once the question is cast in syllogistic form, the result follows with 'inescapable necessity' because 'there is no room for discretion when logic is compelling'.[47] Civil law judges may not make decisions based upon 'social values' or 'comparative costs or benefits' unless such an approach is specifically authorised by statute.[48] This limitation is critical to the structure of civil law societies, where legislative bodies, rather than judges, are entrusted with the responsibility of resolving large economic and political issues affecting social welfare.[49]

Limits on judicial discretion have deep roots in the civil law tradition, where revolutionary societies distrusted independent judiciaries, preferring instead to concentrate law-making power in parliamentary bodies that were viewed as more responsive and accountable to popular opinions.[50] Given these limitations on discretionary authority, the modern civil law judge 'would be absolutely unable to execute, in credible fashion, the same functions as an American judge' in presiding over a proposed class action.[51] If civil law judges lack sufficient discretion to apply certification standards fairly, and if they lack the administrative authority to supervise a certified class action effectively, they certainly lack the discretion necessary to implement the protections necessary to avoid class action abuse.

Indeed, transplanting class action practice into such a rigid system may even *increase* the risk of abuse, however well intentioned the civil law judiciary might be.

44 *Ibid.*   45 See Merryman, *The Civil Law Traditions*, 37–8, 50–1.
46 *Ibid.*, 51: 'As to judicial discretion, common law judges traditionally have inherent equitable power: they can mold the result in the case to the requirement of the facts, bend the rule where necessary to achieve substantial justice, and interpret and reinterpret in order to make the law respond to social change . . . Hence the common law judge is less compelled by prevailing attitudes to cram the dispute into a box built by the legislature than is his civil law counterpart. Even when the case involves the application of a statute, the common law judge has some measure of power to adjust the rule to the facts.' See also Giesze, 'Helms-Burton', 92 n. 78: 'Unlike her civil law counterpart, a US common law judge would not be hamstrung by the absence of statutory law, because she possesses inherent equitable powers to interpret statutes.'
47 A. N. Yiannopoulos, *Louisiana Civil Law System* (2nd edn, USA: Claitor's Pub. Div. Coursebook, 1977), 89–90. See also Smith, 'Confronting Differences', 87–8: 'To paraphrase Holmes by inversion, the life of the civil law has not been experience but logic.'
48 See Cappalli and Consolo, 'Class Actions'.   49 *Ibid.*
50 The drafters of the Napoleonic Code of 1804 believed that judicial corruption was one of the principal causes of the French Revolution and, to avoid past abuses, they drafted the Code to curtail judicial discretion: Merryman, *The Civil Law Traditions*, 14–18, 29–30, 36. The fundamental distrust of unrestrained judicial discretion underlies the structure of most civil law judicial systems: Giesze, 'Helms-Burton', 92 n. 62; Smith, 'Confronting Differences'.
51 See Cappalli and Consolo, 'Class Actions', 291.

Although stricter guidance for judges can certainly protect against abuses, unyielding allegiance to inflexible standards may create even greater dangers. In the more flexible atmosphere of the common law, experience has shown that class certification has a major impact on substantive law by magnifying personal principles into general societal concerns.[52] Aggregation in civil law systems may have similar effects, as Professor Edward Cooper has observed:[53]

> Class action devices will change the real-world effect of some existing substantive laws, and it may be difficult to predict which laws will be the most affected. Some substantive laws have little meaning because little enforced. Providing an efficient procedural tool that leads to widespread enforcement changes [sic] may transform the social, political, and economic reality. Not everyone will be pleased.

Moreover, even without juries, many are concerned that aggregating tort claims enhances their significance and value beyond the range normally allowed in foreign systems. There are concerns that the size of awards will necessarily increase with the perceived magnitude of their impact on large numbers of plaintiffs.[54] Other voices raise concerns that the difficulty of apportioning and allocating compensatory damages between mass tort plaintiffs will lead to de facto awards of punitive damages, which are typically not allowed outside the United States, especially in civil code jurisdictions. As Judge Dag Bugge Norden of Norway remarked at a recent conference, 'it is sometimes easier to figure out what the culprit is supposed to pay than to calculate how the injured should be compensated'.[55]

It is, of course, impossible to foresee precisely what principles and policies may be magnified (or restricted) by class certification in civil law cultures. Civil jurists strictly adhering to traditional methods certainly have greater potential to create such results than do common law judges who may exercise precautionary discretion to avoid them. Inflexible aggregate enforcement may transform laws into major weapons of social policy in ways that their drafters never envisioned. Civil law countries with no culture of using litigation as a tool for public policy may find themselves swamped by 'progressive' litigants who resort to the courts to achieve social change instead of using the traditional parliamentary process. This concern deserves close attention in civil law societies, where 'unlucky drafting is not easily cured by judicial creativity and mistaken choices are not readily cured by amendment'.[56]

Even if civil courts had the discretionary power to certify and manage class actions, they lack the institutional safeguard of *stare decisis* essential to the common

52 See authorities cited in nn. 25, 34 above.
53 E. H. Cooper, 'Class Action Advice in the Form of Questions' (2001) 11 *Duke J Comp & Int'l L* 215, 219.
54 See Faulk, 'The International Class Action', 326.   55 *Ibid.*, 326–7.
56 Cooper, 'Class Action Advice', 11.

law tradition.[57] As a result, they are not structured to implement the lessons learned as mass controversies mature through individual trials and appeals.[58] The bias against *stare decisis* is inherent in the political structure of civil law nations,[59] and is a basic axiom in legal education of their lawyers and judges.[60] Even if civil law jurists were somehow empowered with sufficient equitable discretion to certify and manage class actions, the absence of *stare decisis* guarantees that protections against abuse fashioned by courts with experience in prior class actions will not be applied consistently. As a result, the jurisprudential memory necessary for handling aggregate controversies will never arise. Litigants will have no assurance that the 'fairness' of one civil law tribunal will not be entirely rejected by another even if the courts are confronted by similar facts.

Of course, it is entirely possible that adjustments may be made that ultimately resolve the difficult dichotomies between the common law and civil law traditions. At this point, however, reliance on discretion will be difficult in procedural systems that rely on detailed and controlling rules.[61] Although the specific solutions may not be apparent at this time, it seems clear that the US class action practice is ill-suited to wholesale export to civil law nations. To the extent those nations develop devices that permit aggregate resolution of legal controversies, those solutions must emerge from their own unique traditions and not from transplanting the US model to foreign soil.

In that regard, civil law systems do not lack tools for dealing with mass controversies. In certain situations, a private civil proceeding may be annexed to a criminal or administrative case and, upon conviction or resolution of the public matter, a civil court may quantify damages and render a private judgment for the annexed claimants.[62] When numerous private claims are involved, civil courts may

---

57 See Merryman, *The Civil Law Traditions*, 47: Judicial decisions 'are not a source of law' in the civil law tradition, 'it would violate the rules against judicial lawmaking if decisions of courts were to be binding on subsequent courts'.

58 From an historical perspective, it is not surprising that *stare decisis*, which has its origins in *equitable* considerations, is foreign to civil law jurisprudence, which does not recognise equitable considerations in judicial analysis. See *Marbury v. Madison*, 5 US (Cranch) 137 (1803) (partially deriving American rule of *stare decisis* from the Court's 'equitable powers').

59 In some nations, such as Chile, *stare decisis* is even forbidden by constitutional mandate: Giesze, 'Helms-Burton', 92 n. 71. Under the civil law, the absence of *stare decisis* is seen as necessary 'to ensure that questionable judicial decisions grounded on literal statutory construction do not disrupt the delicate balance of power in the civil law tradition': *ibid.*, 62. Of the civil law nations, Mexico is a notable exception because it permits *stare decisis* ('jurisprudential obligata') when the Mexican Supreme Court renders five consecutive and consistent decisions involving the same legal issue.

60 See, e.g., J. M. Perillo, 'The Legal Professions of Italy' (1966) 18 J *Legal Educ* 274, 278: 'Legal education gives [the student] a strong orientation towards scholarly doctrine as opposed to judicial precedent and towards the orthodox dogmatic approach of the academic establishment.'

61 See Cooper, 'Class Action Advice', 14.

62 See generally Hodges, *Multi-Party Actions*, 3. Given the civil law tradition's emphasis on regulation and public enforcement as an alternative to private litigation, this paradigm is an excellent compromise because it enables co-ordinated private claims when a defendant is found publicly

appropriately consolidate the claims and select one or more claims as a 'model' claim for individual attention. The court may then use the 'model' claim to guide its inquiries and decisions on the remaining cases similarly to a non-binding 'bellwether' trial under US practice.[63]

Many nations now permit 'group actions', which allow multiple claimants to aggregate their causes of action and which enable them to pursue those claims in a single forum.[64] Generally, these suits are designed to vindicate 'diffuse public interests' such as consumer protection, unfair competition and false advertising, instead of individual rights.[65]

These 'group' actions are not truly 'class actions' within the American understanding of the term. In 'group actions', the plaintiffs must affirmatively join the case and agree to be bound by the result. Joinder can be accomplished in varying ways, such as being a member of an association, which is then named as the plaintiff, or by transferring the individual claimants' rights to a named representative. Typically, these cases do not allow a party to be impressed into the case *involuntarily*, as in American class actions, subject only, in some instances, to a right to 'opt out'. This distinguishing characteristic of the American 'class' device is generally unavailable under 'group action' procedure. Moreover, many states restrict the utility of the 'group action' to injunctive proceedings, as opposed to suits for money damages.[66] As a compromise aggregation device, the 'group action' offers many of the advantages of aggregation, while avoiding many of its oppressive pitfalls. It remains to be seen, however, whether civil law jurists can handle such complex controversies effectively, especially if the cases are expanded into the mass tort arena.

International class actions and global liabilities

International class actions in United States courts

Although recent judicial decisions have taken giant steps towards returning American class action litigation to the noble aspirations of its origins, much more work is required before the fallacy of 'judicial economy' is completely banished from certification deliberations. Efforts to amend the rules of procedure

responsible. Contrary to the US class actions paradigm, it permits aggregation only upon a prior finding that the defendant's conduct violated legitimate public interests.

63 See Faulk and Meadows, 'Building a Better Mousetrap?' collecting and reviewing authorities regarding the use of 'bellwether' trials of selected plaintiff groups in American mass tort cases.

64 See Hodges, *Multi-Party Actions*, 22–4; Fernandez, 'Class Actions in Spain?' in 'Lessons from the Land of Litigation Fever', 5–6.

65 See Cappalli and Consolo, 'Class Actions', 292 n. 270, discussing distinction between 'diffuse' and 'differentiated' interests.

66 See J. M. van Dunne, 'Class Actions: a Continental View of the American Cathedral' in 'Lessons from the Land of Litigation Fever', 3.

to incorporate these judicial reforms have generally failed with the single exception of allowing a discretionary interlocutory appeal from class certification in the federal courts.[67] Moreover, the State courts' attitudes towards class certification vary considerably, from those that abide by the traditional 'judicial economy' approach, to those that apply the narrower perspectives of some federal circuits.[68] As a result, class action litigation in the United States is now characterised by 'forum shopping', where plaintiffs' counsel carefully select those jurisdictions where courts have the broadest discretion in class certification and management.[69] Hence, the controversy rages on and the problems of abuse remain unresolved. For defendants stranded in jurisdictions where discretion reigns supreme, 'judicial blackmail' remains a real possibility.

The 'blackmail' threat of American class action litigation, as American courts use that term, has already been felt outside of the United States. The most obvious examples, cases seeking class recoveries by Holocaust survivors and workers impressed into slave labour by the Third Reich, have already had their desired effects. For example, even though the slave labour class claims have, to date, proved unsuccessful in US courts,[70] the German Government recently orchestrated and implemented a comprehensive settlement of the controversy and, in the process, provided for billions of German marks to be paid to labourers and millions of American dollars to be paid to American class action lawyers. Germany created a special foundation that will pay up to $US5 billion in compensation from a fund comprised of contributions from government and industry. The agreement was delayed by 'haggling over how much of the foundation's money should be paid to the American lawyers, who were hoping to secure large contingency fees, as is customary in class-action suits'.[71] Attorney payments were ultimately capped at $US50 million, with two arbiters selected 'to make sure that any legal fees would not be exorbitant'.[72] Unfortunately, the victims themselves will only recover between $US2,500 and $US7,500 each.[73]

It would be naïve to presume that the threat of American class actions was not a major factor in the German Government's decision. These claims have

---

67 See Fed. R. Civ. P. 23(f).
68 See generally *Southwestern Refining Co.* v. *Bernal*, 22 SW 3d 425 (Tex 2000) (examining competing lines of authority in various jurisdictions). See also R. Faulk, 'The Florida Tobacco Class Action Verdict: Can it Happen in Texas?', posted at www.gardere.com, comparing Florida and Texas class action procedures.
69 See Faulk, 'The Florida Tobacco Class Action Verdict', noting that the procedure that permitted the $US145 billion class action verdict against the tobacco industry in Florida is not available in Texas.
70 See, e.g., *Iwanowa* v. *Ford Motor Company*, 67 F Supp 2d 424 (DNJ 1999) (slave labour claims raise non-justiciable 'political questions' that were entrusted to other branches of government responsible for the political settlement of wars and the payment of reparations).
71 W. Drozdiak, 'Germany Sets Funds for Slaves of Nazis: $5 Billion Will Go to Aging Survivors', *Washington Post* (18 July 2000).
72 *Ibid.*   73 *Ibid.*

jeopardised German business activities even outside the context of the litigation, such as the merger between US investment bank Bankers Trust and Deutsche Bank AG. Similar class action claims are currently pending against numerous Austrian companies.[74] Recently, the Austrian Parliament approved a compensation fund exceeding $US400 million to partially resolve the American class action claims.[75] Apparently, neither the German nor Austrian Governments nor their various defendant industries have any intention of seriously defending the American class actions in court, irrespective of their apparent lack of legal merit, in view of the social, political and moral pressures engendered by the lawsuits' allegations. Even more recently, IBM, a global enterprise headquartered in America, was sued in a New York federal court for its alleged involvement in supplying data management tools that allegedly facilitated the Holocaust.[76]

Although the Nazi-era claims raise particularly heinous allegations, it is not difficult to foresee how other allegations, such as those arising from mass torts, might produce similar results. In a real sense, these cases have transformed the American class action into an 'international' proceeding, thereby allowing American private litigation to have an impact on business and personal activities far beyond the borders of the United States, even though the impacted cultures might never empower their own courts to exert similar influences.

Presently, the power of these 'international' class actions is primarily exerted through moral, political and diplomatic pressure. Although it is questionable whether American class action judgments are actually *enforceable* against defendants' assets located outside the United States, the adoption of American-style class action rules by other nations, however, may render such judgments enforceable, at least in part. If such rules are adopted, foreign defendants may no longer be able to resist enforcement by arguing that the American class action is fatally dissimilar and fundamentally contrary to their homeland's judicial procedures[77] and public policies.[78] Indeed, even without formal adoption of class action principles in other

74 See K. Richter, 'Settlement of Nazi-Era Claims in Austria Remains Elusive', *Wall Street Journal, Europe* (28 July 2000); C. Rhoads, 'Breuer Seeks Resolution of War Claims', *Wall Street Journal, Europe* (8 February 1999).
75 See Richter, 'Settlement of Nazi-Era Claims'. The fund will not completely resolve the suits because the US class action lawyers will only drop the claims 'if the slave labour agreement includes a firm commitment to set up a similarly extensive solution for restitution of Jewish property'.
76 See J. O'Sullivan, 'IBM's Hands Are Clean', *Chicago Sun-Times* (13 February 2001).
77 EU courts have refused to enforce foreign judgments that are contrary to their own procedural rules. See, e.g., Judgment of 17 May 1978, 1979 Cour de cassation, *Journal du droit international* 1979, 380; Judgment of 18 January 1980, Cours d'appel de Paris (le ch), *Revue critique* 1981, 113; Judgment of 9 October 1991, 1992 Cour de cassation, *Revue critique* 1992, 516 (refusing to enforce foreign judgments that are not accompanied by written reasons). See generally P. F. Schlosser, 'Lectures on Civil Law Litigation Systems and American Cooperation with those Systems' (1996) 45 *Kan L Rev* 9, 47 n. 136.
78 See, e.g., Judgment of 4 June 1992, 118 BGHZ 312 (313) (FRG) (refusing to enforce portion of American judgment that awarded punitive damages). This German decision was criticised for 'going too far' because although it disallowed the punitive award, the court enforced a $200,000

nations, American class action awards soon may be rendered enforceable by treaty. For example, enforcement might ultimately be permitted by the Hague Convention on Jurisdiction and Foreign Judgments in Civil and Commercial Matters, a critical agreement that has, to date, not been approved.

If American class action judgments become enforceable against non-US assets, can there be any doubt that entrepreneurial American lawyers will attempt to transform the United States into the 'Courthouse for the World'? Under such a scenario, the 'long arm' of American justice may reach out to have an impact on business practices on a global basis, thereby depleting the coffers (and regulating the conduct) of any entity 'doing business' in the United States irrespective of where the entity's coffers are located. The global consequences of this strategy should not be underestimated. If sovereign states, such as Germany, are currently bowing to US class action pressures even without existing enforcement mechanisms, the threat of collectible judgments may prove overwhelming.

The political impact of enhancing the power of American jurisprudence in this manner is nothing less than imperialistic. Accordingly, any reforms that permit the proliferation of the class device, either procedurally or though enforcement of United States class action judgments, should be carefully scrutinised. Proposed reforms should be evaluated to ensure that by superficially enhancing access to justice, the reforms do not surrender currently exempt assets to a system that ultimately denies justice by exploiting the 'blackmail' of oppressive aggregation. Persons doing business in the global marketplace should consider these risks before prematurely endorsing uniform legal principles and dispute resolution procedures. Otherwise, what are now perceived as global opportunities may translate into global liabilities, liabilities assessed by American juries and judges in remote fora that may prove utterly insensitive to foreign cultures.

International class actions in other nations

In 1999, the European Commission issued a 'Green Paper' that solicited input regarding possible amendments to the European Union's Product Liability Directive.[79] One of the major questions raised by the Green Paper was whether the Directive should provide for class actions or other types of 'group actions' as special measures to 'improve access to justice' by persons injured by defective products in

---

'pain and suffering' award that was 'for Europeans, an unbelievably high amount': Schlosser, 'Lectures', 47. The possible enforcement of thousands of such awards from an enforceable American mass tort judgment creates a palpable 'judicial blackmail' scenario.
79 See Green Paper, *Liability for Defective Products*, COM (1999) 396 final (European Commission, 28 July 1999).

Europe.[80] Although the European Commission recently decided not to issue a formal 'White Paper' at this time (pending further study),[81] the storm of controversy raised by this suggestion continues to rage. Many member states are considering 'access to justice' problems and are proposing and implementing their own 'solutions'. As a result, the EU currently resembles a 'patchwork quilt' of varying class and group action laws and initiatives.[82]

Even if a 'harmonised' class action principle is never promulgated, the selective adoption of American-style class action rules by individual nations, such as those in the EU, threatens a barrage of 'forum shopping' by litigants and counsel who seek to create 'transnational' class actions. Since most EU member states do not recognise the doctrine of *forum non conveniens*, and since those states are also obliged to enforce judgments rendered by the courts of sister EU nations, the enactment of class action rules by any member state arguably enables class action practice by the citizens of all member states within the borders of a single forum. Such a development is already imminent in Scandinavia, where a Swedish proposal, in the guise of promoting greater access to justice by large groups of injured parties, threatens all

---

80 *Ibid.*, 31–3.
81 See Report from the Commission, *On the Application of Directive 85/374 on Liability for Defective Products*, COM (2000) 893 final (European Commission, 31 January 2001), 27: 'At this stage, there is no indication that action concerning access to justice specifically with regard to product liability cases would be appropriate.'
82 *Ibid.*, 26–7. The Report summarises the present situation as follows: 'In Portugal, popular legal action exists whereby the Public Prosecutor's Office and consumers' organisations can intervene in cases of injury to private individuals ... In Austria, civil procedural rules allow the victim to pass on his/her liability claim to a consumers' association ... In Belgium, plaintiffs with similar but separate claims can institute proceedings before the same court and then ask the court to handle their claims at the same hearing, without joining them ... In Greece, legal action by consumer groups is possible ... In Denmark, the rules on legal proceedings allow popular legal actions to be brought in all consumer-related areas ... In France, legislation exists which enables consumer organisations to defend the civil interests of consumers. This does not, however, include actions for compensation for a group of injured persons. Consequently, there are no actions similar to the "class actions" in the United States ... In Germany, in the event of a series of accidents, there is a "trial action" which will subsequently form the basis of compensation between industry and the injured persons ... In Ireland, the rules of court provide a procedure whereby one or more persons having the same interest in a single claim may bring or defend the claim on the behalf of all of those interested ... In Italy, consumers' associations can defend consumers' interests, but cannot act on behalf of injured persons ... In Finland, a few years previously, the question of popular legal actions had been examined. The consumer ombudsman can assist individuals before the court; the trial costs can be covered entirely by a special budgetary fund ... In the Netherlands, multi-party legal action is possible under the Group Actions Act from May 1994 ... In Spain, consumers' associations can bring a legal action on behalf of one of their members. An amendment of the rules on court proceedings will make it possible to bring joint actions, as from January 2001 ... In Sweden, rules concerning popular legal actions are being considered, and a proposal might be put forward in the future ... In the United Kingdom, multi-party actions can be brought in the courts in England and Wales under a rule of civil procedure on group litigation. Under this procedure one or more individuals can act in a representative capacity and bring proceedings on behalf of others where they have the same interest.'

of the evils inherent in the American class action experience on a 'trans-European' scale.

Certain Scandinavian civil code countries, such as Sweden and Finland, appear to be more favourably disposed towards the American class action model, at least in consumer cases where large numbers of persons with small claims aggregate their claims to rectify a wrong that might otherwise go unredressed. In Sweden, for example, work has proceeded on a class action Act since at least June 1999, and a revised statute is expected to be introduced in 2001. The Act's supporters believe that the social and legal differences between Sweden and the USA provide adequate safeguards against abuse and the 'blackmail' effect of aggregating mass claims against defendants.[83] The proposed Swedish Act incorporates most of the major components of Federal Rule 23, but requires only 'common issues', not a predominance of such issues, and allows the class action to proceed without a formal certification.[84]

Although it appears that the Swedish Act may be enacted, its opponents stress several important objections. For example, it appears that the Swedish statute will permit class counsel to enter into fee agreements that enhance their compensation if they prevail, agreements that, although subject to court approval, strongly resemble 'contingent fees'.[85] The opponents are concerned that these entrepreneurial incentives plant the same seeds of abuse that ultimately produced the class action abuse in America. More importantly, the opponents stress that the Swedish Act, if passed, will burden Swedish courts with countless class actions filed under Swedish procedure against non-resident defendants by classes that include non-resident plaintiffs. In other words, they claim the Swedish Act creates the peril of the 'trans-European' class action in which the courts of one member country assume jurisdiction over controversies that involve and affect citizens throughout the continent.[86]

This scenario may be a real danger. For many years, the trend in Europe has been to expand the scope of jurisdiction over foreign parties.[87] The risks are compounded by Article 22 of the Lugano Convention, which grants jurisdiction over controversies affecting different states to the court in which the first action is filed.[88]

83 See generally R. Nordh, A Short Presentation of the Swedish Proposal for Group Actions (2001) 11 *Duke J Comp & Int'l L* 381. See also P. H. Lindblom, 'Individual Litigation and Mass Justice: a Swedish Perspective and Proposal on Group Actions in Civil Procedure' (1997) 45 *Am J Comp L* 805.
84 *Ibid.*
85 The Swedish proposal refers to these arrangements as 'risk agreements': *ibid.* See van Dunne, 'Class Actions', 5: 'Agreements with counsel in class action litigation resembling the American contingency fee system, subject to approval, are permitted.' See also Faulk, 'The International Class Action', 327; Lindblom, 'Individual Litigation', 826.
86 See generally Faulk, 'International Class Action', 327.
87 See J. Fitzpatrick, 'The Lugano Convention and Western European Integration: a Comparative Analysis of Jurisdiction and Judgments in Europe and the United States' (1993) 8 *Conn J Int'l L* 695, 726–7.
88 Convention on Jurisdiction and Enforcement of Judgments in Civil and Commercial Matters, Done at Lugano, OJ 1988 No. L 319, 16 September 1988, p. 9. The Lugano Convention was developed to extend the 'full faith and credit' system of the Brussels Convention on

Recognition and enforcement of judgments rendered by EU member states is comparable to the regime applicable to 'sister state judgments' under the 'Full Faith and Credit' clause of the US Constitution.[89] Judgments within the scope of the Convention are recognised and enforced throughout the EU, and review of the merits of the judgment is explicitly precluded.[90] Indeed, judgments rendered in signatory states to the Lugano Convention have more 'full faith and credit' in 'sister states' than judgments rendered in different American states because, under the Convention, 'the jurisdiction of the Court in which the judgment was given may not be reviewed'.[91]

Arguably, if a class action is filed in Sweden under the proposed Swedish Act, the Swedish court could acquire complete jurisdiction over the controversy, thereby disenfranchising individual plaintiffs who may prefer to sue elsewhere. This situation would be a strong incentive for 'forum shoppers'. As a general rule, the Conventions governing jurisdiction and enforcement of judgments in Europe do not distinguish between EU and non-EU plaintiffs. Any plaintiff, regardless of domicile, can bring an action in any member state's courts so long as the Convention's jurisdictional provisions are satisfied, and judgments rendered in those actions will be enforced throughout the EU.[92] The risk of extraterritorial class actions is further heightened in view of the trend to expand the 'long arms' of European courts through 'exorbitant jurisdiction'[93] and because European courts typically

Jurisdiction and Enforcement of Judgments to European countries that are not yet members of the EU: see Convention on Jurisdiction and Enforcement of Judgments in Civil and Commercial Matters, Done at Brussels, OJ 1983 No. C. 97, 27 September 1968, p. 1 (consolidated reprint in OJ 1998, No C27). In turn, the Brussels Convention arose from a provision in the Treaty of Rome, which created the European Economic Community, which motivated member states to facilitate the formalities for mutual recognition and enforcement of judicial judgments: see Treaty Establishing the European Economic Community, Done at Rome, 25 March 1957, article 220, 298 UNTS 11, 1973 Gr Brit TS No 1 (Cmd 5179-II), in Treaties Establishing the European Communities (EU Official Pub Off 1987).

89 See D. L. Woodward, 'Reciprocal Recognition and Enforcement of Civil Judgments in the United States, the United Kingdom, and the European Economic Community' (1983) 8 *North Carolina Journal of International Law and Commercial Regulation* 299, 316; A.T. von Mehren, 'Recognition and Enforcement of Sister State Judgments: Reflections on General Theory and Current Practice in the European Economic Community and the United States' (1981) 81 *Colum L Rev* 1044, 1045–51.

90 See von Mehren, 'Recognition'. There are a number of exceptions to this general rule, but only the 'public policy' exception appears arguably applicable.

91 Brussels Convention, Art. 28, para. 3.

92 See Fitzpatrick, 'The Lugano Convention', 727 n. 151; M. Kerr, 'The EEC Judgments Convention: Some Repercussions beyond the EEC' (1996) 4 *Europarecht* 353.

93 'Exorbitant' jurisdiction can be defined as an assertion of jurisdiction that is not generally accepted under international legal principles, and is generally analogous to the US Supreme Court's insistence on reasonableness and minimum contacts as a basis for personal jurisdiction: Fitzpatrick, 'The Lugano Convention', 723 n. 137. In so far as EU domiciliaries are concerned, judgments based upon 'exorbitant' jurisdiction are not enforceable. However, those same judgments are expressly enforceable against non-EC defendants: *ibid.*, 724–5. See also Schlosser, 'Lectures', 22.

do not recognise the doctrine of *forum non conveniens*.[94] Indeed, the standards for asserting jurisdiction over non-EU domiciliaries are so much broader than those governing EU citizens that they have been termed 'discriminatory',[95] and a civil law court in Sweden (or in any other civil law nation) is obliged to entertain an international class action against non-EU citizens if its jurisdiction is established.[96]

There are serious and unresolved questions regarding whether one EU member state could refuse to enforce another member state's class action judgment under any of the Lugano Convention's exceptions. Depending on the forum state's attitudes towards aggregation of claims, attitudes that are, to say the least, currently in flux, such a judgment may or may not be contrary to the forum state's 'public policy'.[97] Even then, the public policy test may not be applied to rules relating to jurisdiction,[98] and depending upon how the issue is cast, the enforceability of an extraterritorial class action may be deemed a jurisdictional question. Moreover, since the forum state must evaluate recognition based upon the same findings of fact upon which the original court determined its jurisdiction, there is generally no opportunity to build a different factual record.[99] The problem is compounded further because, in the EU, such a class action judgment must be enforced even if it is not a final decree. A judgment that is provisional or preliminary may be enforced even though it may be subjected to modification or appellate review in the originating state.[100] Although such enforcement may be relatively harmless when traditional legal principles are concerned, enforcement of provisional class action judgments precludes the development of experience necessary for a 'mature' evaluation of the controversy. As a result, the EU enforcement procedure unwittingly facilitates one of the very evils that produced class action abuse in the United States.[101]

Perhaps the greatest problem raised by the Lugano Convention concerns its impact on non-EU domiciliaries sued in EU courts. If the defendant is not domiciled

---

94 See Fitzpatrick, 'The Lugano Convention', 750 concluding that the doctrine is precluded by the Jurisdiction and Judgments Conventions. See also Schlosser, 'Lectures'. The doctrine of *forum non conveniens* was developed to mitigate the effects of unfair assertions of jurisdiction when the defendant's contacts were relatively slight and the inconvenience of the forum was great: *Dow Chemical Company v. Alfaro*, 786 SW 2d 674, 676–7 (Tex 1990), cert. denied, 111 S Ct 671 (1991) (discussing the origins of the doctrine). The doctrine was not recognised in civil law nations because they typically rejected the 'transient' jurisdiction which *forum non conveniens* was designed to remedy: Fitzpatrick, 'The Lugano Convention', 721 n. 124.

95 See Schlosser, 'Lectures'. All civil law systems have provisions creating jurisdiction over defendants neither residing within the jurisdiction nor having sufficient contact with the court's district that would normally allow specific jurisdiction to be exercised. All these provisions may be characterised as provisions discriminating against foreigners.

96 See Schlosser, 'Lectures', 20: 'A [civil law] court having jurisdiction is committed to exercise it, because it is a public service entrusted to it by statute. A German or French judge would find it very awkward if he had any discretionary power to decline jurisdiction.'

97 See Lugano Convention, Art. 27(1).   98 *Ibid.*, Art. 28, para. 3.

99 *Ibid.* See also Fitzpatrick, 'The Lugano Convention', 705 n. 43.

100 See Schlosser, 'Lectures', 30.

101 See herein for a discussion on the role of 'maturity' in mass tort litigation.

in Europe, there is no uniform jurisdictional test. Instead, the domestic law of the forum state determines jurisdiction. The import of this rule is startling for non-EU defendants sued, for example, under Sweden's proposed class action rule. For such a defendant, there is no jurisdictional requirement for the recognition and enforcement of class action judgments, so long as the judgment originates from a member state's courts.[102] Thus, even if a member state found that enforcement against a non-EU defendant was against its own public policy, the court would be obliged to enforce the judgment. Thus, the greatest risk from the Swedish proposal is posed to non-EU defendants who are, to say the least, placed in a 'precarious situation'.[103] In its own way, therefore, Sweden and other adventurous EU member states may truly become 'Courthouses for the World' for class actions against foreign defendants over which they assert jurisdiction.

Conclusion

Class action abuse is a problem that may never be solved satisfactorily. Massive abuses still occur under current rules in the United States, and the reforms to correct the abuses are neither completely enacted nor necessarily sufficient. The diverse attitudes of American State courts create significant opportunities for 'forum shopping' by enterprising plaintiffs' counsel, and gigantic judgments that are precluded by one State's laws are perfectly permissible in other jurisdictions. Although some common law nations, such as Australia and Canada, have embraced and even liberalised American class action jurisprudence, others, such as the United Kingdom, have rejected the concept in favour of more conservative 'group action' procedures. To say the least, the future of class actions in the common law nations remains controversial. As long as the controversy persists, and as long as abuses are permissible, the American paradigm is clearly unsuitable for wholesale export to foreign legal systems.

In view of this uncertainty, it is reasonable for civil law nations to approach the issue with caution. In liberal social democracies where litigation is not valued as

---

102 See Fitzpatrick, 'The Lugano Convention', 722 n. 132; von Mehren, 'Recognition', 1058.
103 See M. Bogdan, 'The "Common Market" for Judgments: the Extension of the EEC Jurisdiction and Enforcement Treaty to Nonmember Countries' (1990) 9 St Louis U Pub L Rev 113, 129. Taken to its extreme, the scope of EU member states' jurisdiction over non-EU domiciliaries doing business on the Internet in the global economy is arguably unlimited. Such an argument raises vast concerns that are far beyond the scope of this article, but that must be considered before enacting class action procedures in the EU. See J. L. Goldsmith, 'Against Cyberanarchy' (1998) 65 U Chi L Rev 1199, 1217–18: 'Under standard assumptions about cyberspace architecture, persons can upload or transmit information knowing that it could reach any and all jurisdictions, but not knowing which particular jurisdiction it might reach. Can every state where those transmissions appear assert specific personal jurisdiction over the agent of the information under the purposeful availment and reasonableness tests?'

a social tool, the necessity of class relief is questionable. For those societies, pervasive regulation and active enforcement by public authorities is typically sufficient to resolve mass controversies, especially when private claims may be annexed to the proceeding and resolved in an ancillary manner. Moreover, civil law traditions, which distrust judicial independence and discourage judicial creativity, are neither conceptually nor culturally suited to exercise the discretion necessary to administer the American class device. Without such a discretionary tradition, inflexible aggregate enforcement will almost certainly magnify the impact of substantive laws far beyond anything envisioned by parliamentary drafters, and the absence of *stare decisis* will preclude consistent implementation of safeguards necessary to prevent abuse. These problems suggest that civil law nations considering collective liability paradigms should eschew the American model in favour of devices more compatible with their unique traditions, such as the more conservative 'group actions'.

The international legal community's infatuation with American class actions masks their most serious evil, namely, the potential extraterritorial impact of their abuses on foreign defendants. Already, as the Holocaust class actions have shown, the threat of American 'judicial blackmail' has coerced not only businesses, but also sovereign states, into gigantic settlements. The willingness of some foreign courts to enforce substantial American tort judgments and the movement towards international treaties mandating international enforcement of American decrees threatens unprecedented judicial imperialism. Furthermore, the selective enactment of American-style class action principles by EU member states threatens not only 'trans-European' class actions against EU domiciliaries, but also global class actions against non-EU defendants who are embraced by the expanding (and discriminatory) reach of EU jurisdiction.

Considering these complications, we must remember that the goal of promoting increased 'access to justice' is not achieved by promoting access alone. Any system of collective litigation must not only enhance accessibility, but also must ensure the reliable and efficient dispensation of justice to all participating parties. Although 'justice' may be a relatively abstract term in some academic circles, and although it may seem an idealistic goal when administrative reforms are discussed, we must never forget that, to the individual, whether plaintiff or defendant, it is the only legitimate objective. To the extent aggregation systems fail to appreciate completely an individual's grievances, and to the extent such systems unduly influence defendants to resolve disputes economically, rather than on their merits, such systems deny justice and pervert the fundamental goals of civilised jurisprudence. The potential for perversion will be exponentially enhanced if demonstrably defective devices, such as American class actions, are given extraterritorial dignity or, even worse, grafted onto rigid international systems that are culturally incapable of preventing abuse. Caution, careful deliberations and a thorough appreciation of cultural differences are therefore essential lest by risking Armageddon, we gain not justice, but merely results.

Appendix: proposed amendments to Fed R. Civ. P. 23

In a jointly-authored paper,[104] this author proposed that Rule 23(b)(3)(A) be amended, as emphasised, to require consideration of:

> The interests of members of the class in individually controlling the prosecution or defense of separate actions, *with attention to the nature of the claims asserted by or against the class members, and the type of relief sought, including an evaluation of the amounts in controversy sought by or against individual class members.*

In order to preclude 'judicial economy' reasoning to certify classes without an adequate litigation history, this author proposed that Rule 23(b)(3)(B) be amended, again as emphasised, to mandate specific review of:

> The extent and nature of any litigation concerning the controversy already commenced by or against members of the class, *with attention to the experience gained through prior trials of individual claims, the number of those trials, the extent to which the resulting judgments have been reviewed on appeal, and the results of those appeals.*

To ensure that variations in state law are adequately evaluated in multijurisdictional class actions, to make certain that courts permit adequate discovery for case evaluation, and to require consideration of the procedural impact of class certification in the context of an actual trial, the author proposed that Rule 23(b)(3)(D) be amended to require consideration of:

> The difficulties likely to be encountered in the management of a class action, including:
>
> i. the nature and extent of discovery necessary to evaluate the claims asserted by or against the members of the class;
> ii. the manner in which the claims asserted by or against a certified class will be tried; and
> iii. variations of state law underlying the claims asserted by or against the members of the class in actions that seek class certification for individual claims arising under the laws of more than one state. In such cases, the burden shall be upon the party seeking class certification to demonstrate that the burdens and complexities of state law variations do not render the case unmanageable as a class action.

This author also proposed that Rule 26 be amended to incorporate, as an element of certification, a test, akin to preliminary injunction analysis, that 'balances the probable outcome on the merits against the burdens imposed by class certification'.[105]

---

104 Faulk and Colbert, 'Reforming an Abusive System', 249–50.   105 *Ibid.*, 250

Part VI
Conflict of laws issues

14 Adapting international private law rules for electronic consumer contracts

LORNA E. GILLIES

Introduction

The role of international private law is often regarded as being 'derived from a desire to do justice'[1] for parties involved in cross-border disputes. The onset of electronic commerce and the increasing prevalence of electronic contracts pose new challenges for international private law. Entering into a contract by electronic means enables parties who are domiciled (or have a place of business) in different jurisdictions to use the Internet or e-mail for the purchase and sale of goods and services or a combination of both.[2] Whilst issues of privacy and security are undoubtedly of extreme importance to consumers when conducting their transactions online,[3] other aspects of the electronic consumer contract are just as important. From an international private law perspective, rules of jurisdiction and the law to be applied to online consumer contracts have been the subject of considerable debate.

International private law and electronic commerce

In a paper published in 1997, Vaughan Black asserted that international private law need only be considered in one-off cases when cross-border matters

The assistance of the Clark Foundation for Legal Education is gratefully acknowledged.
1 A. E. Anton, *Private International Law* (2nd edn, Edinburgh: W. Green & Sons, 1990), 1. See also P. M. North and J. J. Fawcett, *Cheshire and North's Private International Law* (13th edn, London: Butterworths, 1999), 5.
2 See L. Davies, 'Contract Formation on the Internet: Shattering a Few Myths' in L. Edwards and C. Waelde (eds.), *Law and the Internet: Regulating Cyberspace* (Oxford: Hart Publishing, 1997); A. D. Murray, 'Entering into Contracts Electronically: the Real WWW' in L. Edwards and C. Waelde (eds.), *Law and the Internet: a Framework for Electronic Commerce* (2nd edn, Oxford: Hart Publishing, 2000), explaining how e-mail and the Internet are used in contract formation.
3 See C. Gethin and S. Gribble, 'Cyber Rules for Consumer Protection Urgently Needed Says International Federation', Consumers International Press Release (6 September 1999), www.consumersinternational.org/news/pressreleases/electronic060999.html; L. Enos, 'Consumer Watchdog Unveils Net Conduct Code', *Ecommercetimes* (25 October 2000), http://www.ecommercetimes.com/perl/story/4636.html.

arise.[4] Given today's globalisation of markets and finance, combined with increased co-operation between governments internationally, cross-border cases are by no means exceptional.[5] Rules and principles of international private law need to be considered more often, especially if parties to a contract have not agreed which law is to apply to that contract, or if aspects of their agreement are in dispute. The use of the Internet as a means of advertising, promoting and selling goods and services has contributed to the globalisation of consumer contracts.

As every country has its own rules of jurisdiction and choice of law, the implementation of such rules becomes very important in cross-border disputes. Jurisdiction is inherently territorial. Different jurisdiction rules apply depending on the domicile of the parties involved and the subject matter of the proceedings. Rules of personal jurisdiction enable proceedings to be raised against an individual who is domiciled or an organisation that has a place of business (or perhaps a branch or agency) in the jurisdiction.

This essay will focus on issues of personal jurisdiction pertaining to electronic consumer contracts. Rules of international private law are of increasing significance to electronic consumer contracts. First, it is right that parties know which jurisdiction and what applicable law will govern their contract in the event of a dispute. Secondly, knowledge of the jurisdiction and applicable law is crucial for consumers as they are usually regarded as the weaker party in consumer contracts. Issues of consumers' access to justice arise as a result. In particular, consumers are often unaware of their legal rights and how these can be enforced in cross-border contracts. Thirdly, the inherent nature of advertising and selling online has resulted in competing offline interests between businesses and consumers. International private law rules are no less significant for businesses advertising and contracting online. Businesses could (reasonably) be required to know the jurisdiction and applicable law rules where every real or potential consumer is domiciled. Consumers, on the other hand, could increasingly be expected to accept the jurisdiction or applicable law clauses in their contracts, invariably favouring the businesses' jurisdictions. International private law ought to be capable of providing consistent rules of jurisdiction and choice of law despite these competing interests.

Consumer contracts in electronic commerce

Existing rules of jurisdiction for consumer contracts have now been adapted for electronic consumer contracts by the European Union. Given that

4 V. Black, 'Consumer Protection in the Conflict of Laws: Canada, the United States and Europe' in I. Ramsay (ed.), *Consumer Law in the Global Economy, National and International Dimensions* (Aldershot: Dartmouth, 1997), 210.
5 See J. H. A. Van Loon, 'The Increasing Significance of International Co-operation for the Unification of Private International Law' in Th. M. De Boer (ed.), *Forty Years on: The Evolution of Post War Private International Law in Europe* (Deventer: Kluwer Law International, 1990), 101, 122.

consumers are being encouraged to make purchases of goods and services over the Internet whilst the number of electronic transactions increases, such rules are necessary.[6] This essay will examine the rules of jurisdiction and choice of law adopted in Europe so far, evaluate the implications of these rules, and assess whether they will be of benefit to the consumer purchasing online, thereby facilitating the consumer's access to justice in the event of a dispute. The recently approved Brussels 1 Regulation, the E-Commerce Directive,[7] the Distance Selling Directive, and the proposals for the replacement of the Convention on Contractual Obligations in Europe will be considered.[8]   ·

However, adapting existing rules of jurisdiction and choice of law for electronic consumer contracts should not be confined to Europe. The essay will therefore contrast European Community initiatives with some of the measures taken in the United States, where courts have used a variety of tests to determine whether jurisdiction or the applicable law has been established in online cases. Those tests include 'minimum contacts', 'fair play and substantial justice' and 'substantial connection' to the forum. The rules should be applied to online contracts in the same way that rules of jurisdiction and applicable laws are applied to consumer contracts conducted offline.[9]

Access to efficient justice is an important factor in the development of cross-border rules for transactions utilising new technologies. As stated earlier, international private law rules have implications for consumers if they are to continue to contract for goods and services over the Internet.[10] Accordingly, principles of international private law should be adapted globally to facilitate the relevance of international private law to electronic consumer contracts, as well as consumers' access to justice. Recent efforts made by the European Union, the US courts and the Federal Trade Commission contribute to providing a certain degree of protection for consumers. In addition to international private law rules, alternative dispute resolution systems ('ADR') may provide other means for consumers to seek redress in

6 See OECD, *Dismantling the Barriers to Global Electronic Commerce* (Paris: OECD, 1997), www.oecd.org//dsti/sti/it/ec/prod/DISMANTL.HTM; and the OECD's Workshop, 'Consumers in the Online Marketplace: OECD Workshop on the Guidelines: One Year Later' (Berlin: Federal Ministry of Economics and Technology, 13–14 March 2001), www.oecd.org/dsti/sti/it/consumer/index.htm. Copyright OECD.
7 Directive 2000/31/EC of the European Parliament and of the Council of 8 June 2000 on certain legal aspects of information society services, in particular electronic commerce, in the Internal Market OJ 2000 No. L178 ('E-Commerce Directive').
8 At the time of writing, proposals to replace the Rome Convention have not yet been published.
9 See Enos, 'Consumer Watchdog'.
10 This essay is confined to consideration of rules of jurisdiction and choice of law for contractual disputes in a consumer contract. Rules of jurisdiction and choice of law for tortious/delictual claims are beyond its scope. Equally, whilst issues of recognition and enforcement *per se* will not be examined, such matters are important when an electronic consumer contract is in dispute. Consumers' ability to enforce their rights and be granted remedies is crucial to the continued development of both international private law and consumer protection laws. Issues of recognition and enforcement will become increasingly important as the number of electronic consumer contract disputes increases.

the event of a dispute. Whilst such schemes are to be welcomed, they should not replace substantive jurisdiction and choice of law rules for consumers purchasing goods and services online. As the OECD has recommended:[11] 'The same level of protection provided by the laws and practices that apply to commerce off-line should be afforded to consumers participating in commercial activities through the use of the global networks.'

The medium used by the parties to contract with each other should not determine the rights and rules available to them. In addition, rules of jurisdiction and choice of law must facilitate the recognition and enforcement of a judgment. The harmonisation of international private law rules[12] is therefore essential. Nevertheless, a realistic solution for consumers to benefit fully from access to justice when contracting online could ultimately be the combined application of harmonised international private law rules and the use of ADR (or ODR[13]) systems, but as an 'alternative' to recognising and enforcing judgments obtained by such rules.

International private law rules for electronic consumer contracts – European initiatives

Jurisdiction rules for electronic consumer contracts

The Brussels 1 Regulation is a Community instrument that replaced the Brussels Convention on Jurisdiction and Recognition of Foreign Judgments[14] from March 2002.[15] The Regulation has implications for electronic commerce and consumers. The most contentious rules of jurisdiction replaced by the Regulation relate to consumer contracts. In Europe, the Brussels 1 Regulation now modifies existing rules of jurisdiction for consumer contracts, including those conducted electronically. The Regulation's new rules and their potential impact for electronic consumer contracts conducted over the Internet will now be considered.

11 OECD Recommendation DSTI/CP(98)4 (2001).
12 Van Loon, 'Increasing Significance', 101 ff.
13 See documents of the Conference jointly hosted by the OECD, The Hague Conference on Private International Law and the International Chamber of Commerce, 'Building Trust in the Online Environment: Business-to-Consumer Dispute Resolution' (The Hague, December 2000, copyright OECD), www.oecd.org/dsti/sti/it/secur/act/Online.trust/documents.htm.
14 See K. Regan, 'EU OK's E-Commerce Dispute Law', *Ecommercetimes* (1 December 2000), www.ecommercetimes.com/perl/story/5635.html. The Regulation was approved on 30 November 2000 and is published as the 'Council Regulation (EC) No 44/2001 of 22 December 2000 on jurisdiction and the recognition and enforcement of judgments in civil and commercial matters' OJ 2001 No. L12, p. 1 ('Brussels 1 Regulation').
15 Article 76, Brussels 1 Regulation, 16.

Electronic commerce in the European Union

In the last five years, the European Union has pursued several initiatives to address electronic commerce issues, most notably the Directives on Distance Selling[16] and Electronic Commerce.[17] The latter Directive does not seek to introduce new rules of international private law, whilst the former Directive provides limited applicable law for contracts with consumers conducted at a distance. The replacement of the Brussels Convention makes provision for rules of jurisdiction in electronic consumer contracts.

The basis for developing rules of jurisdiction for civil matters in Europe

The Brussels 1 Regulation aims to provide for the free movement of judgments in civil and commercial matters in terms of the European Union's *acquis communautaire*.[18] The *acquis* extends to facilitating co-operation in civil and commercial matters throughout the European Union. The revision of the Brussels Convention is one measure taken in terms of Title IV of the Treaty of Amsterdam, for Justice and Home Affairs matters. The Treaty of Amsterdam extended the European Union's (internal) competencies by transferring matters from the Third Pillar to the First Pillar. As Beaumont reports, the measures provided under the new Article 65 EC 'for the field of judicial cooperation in civil matters having cross-border implications insofar as necessary for the proper functioning of the internal market' include:[19]

a. improving and simplifying: ...
   - the recognition and enforcement of decisions in civil and commercial cases, including decisions in extra judicial cases;
b. promoting the compatibility of the rules applicable in the member States concerning the conflict of laws and jurisdiction;

The Preamble of the Brussels 1 Regulation states that a 'Community legal instrument' was required to achieve the objective that rules of jurisdiction and enforcement of judgments would be dealt with consistently throughout the European Union.[20] The shift in emphasis from a Convention to a Community Regulation is

---

16 European Parliament, Directive 97/7/EC of the European Parliament and of the Council of 20 May 1997 on the Protection of Consumers in Respect of Distance Contracts ('Directive on Distance Selling'), OJ 1997 No. L0007.

17 E-Commerce Directive, n. 7 above.

18 Preamble of the Amended proposal for a Council Regulation on Jurisdiction and the Recognition and Enforcement of Judgments in Civil and Commercial matters (presented by the Commission pursuant to Article 250 (2) of the EC-Treaty), Recital 5.

19 OJ 1997 No. C340, p. 203. See P. R. Beaumont, 'European Court of Justice and Jurisdiction and Enforcement of Judgments in Civil and Commercial Matters' (1999) 48 *ICLQ* 223, 225.

20 *Ibid.*

significant. Basedow has suggested that the European Union should seek to 'communitarise' or 'harmonise' substantive and procedural rules of its Member States in accordance with increased competences post-Treaty of Amsterdam.[21] International private law is one area in which harmonisation of civil law is sought. Basedow also maintains that measures taken for communitarisation will enable the European Union to make collective representation with EU member states at the international level, whilst at the same time enabling the objective of the Internal Market's 'proper functioning' to be upheld.[22]

It is submitted that the effects of the Community's new competence are now beginning to emerge, internally and externally. The effect of communitarisation is demonstrated by the harmonisation of international private law rules for civil and commercial matters throughout the European Community. The Brussels 1 Regulation must be considered against the backdrop of Article 65 EC and the Community's objective to provide regulation of the internal market.

European rules of jurisdiction and choice of law for electronic contracts, especially those for consumer contracts, will have implications for the global nature of electronic commerce. In Europe, the application of jurisdiction and choice of law rules at the national level depends upon rules approved and adopted by the European Union collectively. Article 65 EC makes express reference to international private law, despite the statement in the last Report on the draft Regulation stipulating that the Regulation will be 'legislating for the Internal Market'.[23]

The external competence of the European Union will be demonstrated by the way in which the European Union contributes towards negotiations for global measures in electronic commerce. The European Union's role in the development of jurisdiction and choice of law rules for electronic commerce is significant, especially for the future application of international private law rules within the European Union. This is demonstrated in the latter case by member states' relations and ability to negotiate with other states (where the Brussels 1 Regulation will not apply) globally for agreement on jurisdiction and choice of law rules. The application and effect of communitarisation and the increase in the European Community's competences ought to be closely monitored. The implications of this will be remarked upon later.

21 See J. Basedow, 'The Communitarisation of the Conflict of Laws under the Treaty of Amsterdam' (2000) 37 *Common Market Law Reports* 687; C. T. Kotuby, Jr, 'External Competence of the European Community in the Hague Conference on Private International Law: Community Harmonization and Worldwide Unification' [2001] *Netherlands International Law Review* 1; and O. Remien, 'European Private International Law, The European Community and Its Emerging Area of Freedom, Security and Justice' (2001) 38 *Common Market Law Reports* 53.
22 Basedow, 'The Communitarisation of the Conflict of Laws', 703. See also Kotuby, 'External Competence', 6.
23 Committee on Legal Affairs and the Internal Market, 'Report on the Proposal for a Council Regulation on Jurisdiction and the Recognition and Enforcement of Judgements in Civil and Commercial Matters' (COM (1999) 348 C5–0169/1999 1999/0154(CNS)) 18 September 2000 at Justification for Amendment 11, Recital 4i.

The Brussels 1 Regulation's rules of jurisdiction for civil and commercial matters

Consumer protection, and by implication international private law, rules are challenging for businesses if such rules enable consumers to raise court proceedings in their own jurisdiction:[24] 'Consumer protection issues are particularly tricky for online merchants, since they routinely provide for jurisdiction of the courts at the consumer's domicile and for the application of his or her national law.'

This difficulty had to be dealt with during the negotiations to replace the Brussels Convention.[25] After much national consultation, the following new rules were approved.

Special jurisdiction for contracts under Article 5.

Article 5 of the new Regulation states, *inter alia*, that in matters relating to a contract, a person domiciled in a member state can be sued in the courts of the place of performance of the obligation in question.[26] The new Regulation clarifies the meaning of place of performance depending upon whether that performance is for goods or services. Article 5(1)(b) provides that, for the sale of goods, 'the place of performance of the obligation in question shall be... the place in a Member State where, under the contract, the goods were delivered or should have been delivered'. For services, the Regulation states that it is 'the place in a Member State where, under the contract, the services were provided or should have been provided'. This appears straightforward enough. Article 5(1)(c) states that subparagraph (a) wil l apply if subparagraph (b) does not. Whilst it is to be welcomed that the European Union has sought to distinguish between the place of performance of goods and services, the definition for place of performance of digital goods or services capable of being purchased online has yet to be tested.

Exclusive jurisdiction over consumer contracts in Articles 15–17.

The new Regulation contains the following provisions for consumer contracts, including contracts concluded online:[27]

Article 15

1. In matters relating to a contract concluded by a person, the consumer, for a purpose which can be regarded as being outside his trade or profession,

---

24 R. Auf der Mar, 'Internet-Enabled Distribution Models' [1999] *International Business Laywer* 264.
25 See Committee on Legal Affairs and the Internal Market, 'Draft Report on the Proposal for a Council Regulation (EC) on Jurisdiction and the Recognition and Enforcement of Judgments in Civil and Commercial Matters' (COM(1999) 348 final 'C5–0169/1999' 1999/0154 (CNS)), 3 March 2000; 'Report on the Proposal for a Council Regulation on Jurisdiction and the Recognition and Enforcement of Judgements in Civil and Commercial Matters'.
26 Brussels 1 Regulation, 4.   27 Brussels 1 Regulation, 6–7.

jurisdiction shall be determined by this Section, without prejudice to Article 4 and point 5 of Article 5, if:

a. it is a contract for the sale of goods on instalment credit terms; or
b. it is a contract for a loan repayable by instalments, or for any other form of credit, made to finance the sale of goods; or
c. in all other cases, the contract has been concluded with a person who pursues commercial or professional activities in the Member State of the consumer's domicile or, by any means, directs such activities to that Member State or to several States including that Member State, and the contract falls within the scope of such activities.

2. Where the consumer enters into a contract with a party who is not domiciled in the Member State but has a branch, agency or other establishment in one of the Member States, that party shall, in disputes arising out of the operations of the branch, agency or other establishment, be deemed to be domiciled in that State.
3. This Section shall not apply to a contract of transport other than a contract which, for an inclusive price, provides for a combination of travel and accommodation.

Article 16

1. A consumer may bring proceedings against the other party to a contract either in the courts of the Member State in which that party is domiciled or in the courts for the place where the consumer is domiciled.
2. Proceedings may be brought against a consumer by the other party to the contract only in the courts of the Member State in which the consumer is domiciled.
3. This Article shall not affect the right to bring a counter-claim in the court in which, in accordance with this Section, the original claim is pending.

Article 17
The provisions of this Section may be departed from only by an agreement:

1. which is entered into after the dispute has arisen; or
2. which allows the consumer to bring proceedings in courts other than those indicated in this Section; or
3. which is entered into by the consumer and the other party to the contract, both of whom are at the time of conclusion of the contract domiciled or habitually resident in the same Member State, and which confers jurisdiction on the courts of that Member State, provided that such an agreement is not contrary to the law of that Member State.

Article 15(1)(a) and (b) define the consumer contract. The types of consumer contracts remain those for the sale of goods on instalment credit terms or for loans to supply goods. Importantly, Article 15(1)(c) may have implications for consumer contracts concluded over the Internet. Jurisdiction will be established if by 'any means' businesses 'direct' their professional or commercial activities to the consumer's domicile or other states including 'individual Member States'. Businesses located in or with a branch in Europe[28] using the Internet to promote and sell goods or services to consumers domiciled in a member state will have to consider the implications of the new Regulation's provisions, particularly what is meant by 'directs such activities'. Whilst the phrase 'any means' is very wide, it will be the manner and extent to which a business with a branch or agency domiciled in Europe is deemed to have directed its activities to a consumer that will determine jurisdiction under this section. The general rule that a consumer is entitled to sue a business either in the business's or the consumer's jurisdiction is retained in Article 16.

What is a 'branch, agency or other establishment' in the context of electronic commerce?

A consumer can only sue a business under the provisions of the Brussels Convention if the business is domiciled in Europe. However, if the business has a branch, agency or other establishment in Europe, then the consumer can sue under the Convention, and in due course the Regulation, where that branch is situated. Businesses need to use servers for their websites to be accessed on the Internet. An interesting question is whether a Web or host server located in a member state will be deemed to be a 'branch, agency or other establishment' of a business. Schu does not view a Web server as such. In a comparison of European and US jurisdictions, he maintains that the physical location of a server is irrelevant to a contract.[29]

The European Court will probably be requested in the future to give an autonomous definition of what is meant by 'other establishment' in the context of electronic commerce. Web servers are often located in different jurisdictions from businesses using them for websites. Despite the new Regulation, the present position is by no means clear on the issue of Web servers and whether jurisdiction can be established in the place where they are located. It may be asked why the drafters of the Regulation did not take the opportunity to clarify this important and relevant matter. Nevertheless, the E-Commerce Directive states that 'the place of establishment of a company providing services via an Internet website is not the place at which the technology supporting its website is located.'[30]

Accordingly, it is submitted that the location of a server will not establish jurisdiction. The Web server is a conduit of information, similar to a telephone or a facsimile machine. It needs information input from the owner or operator of the website for the website to be available and useful to third parties, including consumers.

---

28 *Brenner and Noller* v. *Dean Witter Reynolds* C-318/93, [1994] ECR I-4275.
29 R. Schu, 'The Applicable Law to Consumer Contracts Made over the Internet: Consumer Protection through Private International Law?' (1997) 5 *International Journal of Law and Information Technology* 192, 204, 207, and particularly, 221–2.
30 E-Commerce Directive.

That information may well come from another server or servers. In any event, it is submitted that for the consumer, the location of a Web server is of secondary importance to the content of a website. Indeed, if jurisdiction could be established, difficulties will arise if more than one server transmits the website's content. For consumers to be able to sue businesses in their own jurisdictions, what is important is whether the owner of the website is actively or passively directing its activities to consumers, in terms of Article 15(1)(c). The extent of a website's activity might fall in between these two recognised parameters.[31]

As stated earlier, the server's location does not appear to have concerned those who proposed the Brussels 1 Regulation. The Regulation makes clear that it is where the activities on a website are *directed to* (as opposed to where the website and its activities or information *come from*) that will enable jurisdiction to be established in the case of electronic consumer contracts. Given the labyrinth of networks that make up the Internet and the effort that would be required to establish where a server or servers may be located, this appears to be the most sensible approach. Indeed, there are practical difficulties in identifying the location of servers. Several servers could be used cumulatively and the rule establishing jurisdiction could be thwarted by 'online forum shopping'.

The debate on the position of Web servers will no doubt continue in Europe until a case raises this point. The consumers' perception of a website, whether they regard websites as targeting them in their own jurisdictions, and the language used, may have to be taken into account.

The impact of the new provisions for consumers contracting online

The European Community has consistently sought to ensure that the protection of the consumer as the 'weaker party' under the EC Treaty is maintained in future Community instruments.[32] The Brussels 1 Regulation exemplifies this objective, as consumers can raise proceedings in their own jurisdiction, or can be sued only in their own jurisdictions in terms of the new Article 16.

The impact of this provision on businesses is now clear. In order to take advantage of advertising and selling to consumers across borders in Europe, businesses domiciled or having a branch, agency or other establishment in Europe will be required to comply with the jurisdiction and applicable laws of each of the European Union's member states. Small and medium-sized businesses, those businesses that have been encouraged to take advantage of online advertising, might be dissuaded

31 B. K. Epps discusses US Supreme and Federal Court cases on this point in '*Maritz, Inc., v. Cybergold, Inc.*: The Expansion of Personal Jurisdiction in the Modern Age of Internet Advertising' (1997) 32 *Ga L Rev* 237, 255 ff.
32 See Committee of Legal Affairs and the Internal Market, 'Draft Report', at 'Justification for Amendment 10', 'Recital 4h' (new), referring to the relationship between Articles 3(f), 65 and 95(3) EC.

from doing so with the introduction of the new Regulation. Nevertheless, the distinction between an active and a passive website must be considered. This distinction has been considered in numerous US cases. The European Commission's interpretation of 'active' and 'passive' sales[33] in its 'Guidelines for Vertical Restraints' provides an indication as to how such sales are regarded (albeit in terms of competition law rules) by the European Community. The Guidelines refer to Article 4(b) of the Block Exemption Regulation. Essentially, the Commission concludes that 'the use of the Internet is not considered a form of active sales into such territories or customer groups, since it is a reasonable way to reach every customer.'[34]

Interestingly, the European Commission regards as passive selling the situation where a customer views a website that leads to contact with the seller. The Commission goes as far as to say that the language of a website 'plays normally no role in that respect'.[35] Whilst these statements may be useful, the Guidelines define active and passive sales in relation to targeting goods for sale to *customers or groups of customers in a specific area ('territory') of another business*, hence the relevance to competition law. There is no requirement to distinguish groups of customers and territories attributed to businesses for international private law. Nevertheless, such guidance could be repeated, or addressed in the context of jurisdiction rules under Article 15(3) of the Brussels 1 Regulation.

European initiatives for electronic commerce and the information society interaction with international private law

The European Union has introduced a number of Directives to address legal issues arising from the increased use of information technology services throughout the Community. How these Directives might interact with the Community's jurisdiction and choice of law rules for consumer contracts will be considered.

The E-Commerce Directive

The E-Commerce Directive came into force on 8 June 2000, and allows for the regulation of information society providers by subjecting them to their own state's regulatory regimes, where they exist. This concept is known as the 'country of origin principle'. Recital 23 in the Preamble of the Directive specifies that the Directive will not seek to make provision for rules of international private law nor affect existing rules. At the time of its inception, opposing views were expressed as to whether the proposals for the Brussels Regulation (where jurisdiction for consumer contracts was drafted on the basis of the 'country of destination principle') would clash with the new Directive.[36] However, it is widely

---

33 See European Commission, 'Guidelines for Vertical Restraints' OJ 2000 No. C291/1, 12 ff.
34 *Ibid.*   35 *Ibid.*
36 See S. Dutson, 'E-Commerce European Union Transnational E-Commerce' (2000) 16 *Computer Law and Security Report* 105, 106.

believed that the bases of jurisdiction for the Directive and the Regulation are different.[37]

The proposals for the Brussels 1 Regulation were drafted to provide that in consumer contracts the consumer's domicile is the basis of jurisdiction. Stone[38] and Dutson[39] appear to agree that the bases of jurisdiction for the Directive and the Regulation are different and are therefore not likely to conflict with each other. They maintain that the Brussels Regulation provided rules of *personal* jurisdiction, whereas the Directive's basis of jurisdiction is in relation to the *subject matter*. It is submitted that this relates to the *nature* of these two pieces of Community legislation. The E-Commerce Directive is a public law instrument, essentially providing a framework for member states to regulate the providers of information society services in their jurisdiction. The Brussels Regulation, as the Brussels Convention before it, provides private (in the sense of cross-border) international law rules for individuals, and in particular consumers.

Therefore, it seems that any concern that the Directive and Regulation will clash is unwarranted. Indeed, as Stone points out, Article 3 of the Directive does not seek to limit or restrict international private law's provisions for consumer protection.[40] This view is reiterated here. In private litigation involving consumers there is little scope for conflict. Accordingly, the European Union's aim in seeking to provide rules of jurisdiction for consumer contracts as well as harmonisation of international private law rules is facilitated. At the same time, for matters outwith the remit of personal jurisdiction, the European Union's preference for the 'country of origin principle' to be applied by its member states (in the regulation of service providers' conduct within member states' territory, for example) is maintained.

European initiatives for choice of law principles for electronic consumer contracts

In Europe, proposals for the replacement of the Convention on the Law Applicable to Contractual Obligations ('the Rome Convention') are awaited. It is anticipated that the Rome Convention will be replaced by a Community instrument, in terms of the European Community's Justice and Home Affairs' *acquis* and the five-year action plan for Justice and Home Affairs Matters.

37 Dutson, 'E-Commerce'. See also P. Stone, 'Internet Consumer Contracts and European Private International Law' (2000) 9 *Information and Communications Technology Law* 5; P. S. Atiyah, J. N. Adams and H. MacQueen, *The Sale of Goods* (10th edn, Harlow: Longman, 2001), 57.

38 Stone, 'Internet Consumer Contracts'.

39 Dutson, 'E-Commerce'.

40 Stone, 'Internet Consumer Contracts', 16. See also G. Pearce and N. Platten, 'Promoting the Information Society: the EU Directive on Electronic Commerce' (2000) 6 *European Law Journal* 363, 374–8.

The Rome Convention harmonised international private law rules for contracts between parties domiciled in Europe. Such harmonisation demonstrated one of the objectives of the original member states of the European Economic Community by virtue of Article 220 of the Treaty.[41] The Rome Convention contains important choice of law provisions for consumer contracts in Europe. However, as with jurisdiction matters, the question of how the applicable law for an electronic consumer contract is determined is not confined to Europe. The applicable law is significant to consumers generally, as it determines which law will govern their contracts and any dispute arising from them. Such concerns are compounded when consumers contract over the Internet with businesses in distant jurisdictions. In any re-evaluation of choice of law rules for electronic consumer contracts to facilitate consumers' access to justice, consumers ought still to be able to agree the applicable law of the contract or rely on the laws of their domicile or habitual residence where no agreement has taken place, or one is made purporting to limit or restrict the use of the laws of the consumer's domicile.

Choice of law rules for consumer contracts in the Rome Convention

For contracts in general, Article 3 of the Convention allows the parties freedom to choose the applicable law, whilst Article 4 determines what the applicable law will be in the absence of such a choice. In the latter case, the applicable law is determined by the place to which the contract is most closely connected. Article 5 provides rules for 'certain consumer contracts'. If the parties to a consumer contract have agreed a choice of law clause, Article 5(2) maintains that the consumer should not be deprived of the consumer protection laws of his or her habitual residence. This ensures that businesses cannot take advantage of either Article 3 or Article 4.

If using the Internet to buy goods and services is similar to using a telephone or facsimile, then applicable law rules should not be inherently different from those used for offline contracts. Accordingly, in the same way that the Brussels 1 Regulation has sought to clarify rules of jurisdiction for consumer contracts conducted over the Internet, any proposals to replace the Rome Convention must seek the same clarification. The global nature of the Internet and difficulties in ascertaining the true location of the parties often render it difficult to ascertain the applicable law of an electronic consumer contract. Unlike the telephone or facsimile, it is possible for parties to an electronic contract to manipulate technology and to hide their true identity from the other party. Accordingly, there ought to be clear, consistent and, preferably, global choice of law rules to ensure consistency in the application of choice of law principles for electronic consumer contracts whether an agreement exists or not.

---

41 For further discussion, see I. F. Fletcher, *Conflict of Laws and European Community Law* (Amsterdam: North Holland Publishing Company, 1982), chaps. 2, 5.

The Distance Selling Directive

The Distance Selling Directive[42] also provides specific applicable law rules for contracts concluded at a distance (including the Internet in terms of Article 2(4)). Article 12(2) ensures that the consumer will not be deprived of protection from the choice of law rules of a non-member state if in the circumstances the contract is more closely connected with that state. Such a rule appears to have been introduced to prevent the choice of law of a non-member state being imposed upon the consumer, possibly rendering the Directive inapplicable. Accordingly, the 'most close connection' test continues to determine choice of law for contracts concluded over the Internet.

It is anticipated that any EU proposals to determine the applicable law for electronic consumer contracts will be as important and as fiercely debated between businesses and consumer organisations as the proposals for the Brussels 1 Regulation were. The replacement of the Rome Convention should make express reference to those activities directed at consumers, including websites. It is useful to consider what Giuliano and Lagarde stated in their report on the Rome Convention:[43]

> Thus the trader must have done certain acts such as advertising in the press, or on radio or television, or in the cinema or by catalogue aimed specifically at that country or he must have made business proposals individually through a middleman or by canvassing.

The form of advertising referred to by Giuliano and Lagarde is probably passive advertising, that is advertising on billboards or in newspapers. By contrast, websites can actively or passively advertise to consumers. Websites enable businesses to 'target' potential customers no matter where those consumers are domiciled. It is the extent to which websites target consumers that ought to be considered when drafting international private law rules for electronic consumer contracts.

Accordingly, the same questions that have arisen as a result of Article 15(2) of the Brussels Regulation will have to be reconsidered if proposals to replace the Rome Convention refer to the test 'in any way ... directs such activities to consumers' as a means of targeting consumers. Essentially, the question to be asked is the extent to which a website is deemed to be targeting consumers in their own jurisdiction. The answer to this question will depend upon how Article 15(2) of the Brussels 1 Regulation is interpreted, as well as the nature and extent of website activity. Nevertheless, proposals to replace the Rome Convention will apply only to defendants (i.e., businesses and their branches) located within the member states of the European Community. Given the Community's *acquis* in Justice and Home Affairs, proposals

---

42 Directive on Distance Selling, OJ 1997 No. L0007.
43 Report on the Rome Convention by M. Giuliano and P. Lagarde (1980) OJ C282/1, 24, also referred to in C. G. J. Morse, 'Consumer Contracts, Employment Contracts and the Rome Convention' (1992) 41 *ICLQ* 1, 6–7.

for a 'Rome Regulation' will need to be complementary to the Brussels 1 Regulation, the E-Commerce Directive,[44] and the future potential of electronic commerce in Europe generally. Inevitably, such measures will go only some way to addressing global access to justice required by consumers who are contracting online.

In 1992, Morse wrote that 'the practical impact of Article 5 in the United Kingdom is difficult to assess, if only because the international aspects of consumer contracts have so far presented few practical problems. This may change.'[45] The consistent growth of electronic consumer contracts has brought the significance of choice of law rules to the fore. The Rome Convention was not prepared with electronic consumer contracts in mind. Proposals to establish the applicable law for electronic consumer contracts throughout the European Union ought to be sufficiently flexible to include all electronic consumer contracts, and not simply 'certain consumer contracts' as in the present Rome Convention. Consumers can now order 'electronic' goods and services online. Therefore, proposals to replace the Rome Convention should include reference to the provision of electronic goods or services, particularly if those goods or services are capable of being provided to consumers outwith their habitual residence. This is presently excluded under Article 5(4) of the Convention. Jaffey's[46] assertion that the consumer ought to be allowed to 'consult' his or her own law first in the event of a dispute should not be affected by the type and nature of goods or services purchased. Choice of law rules need to be clear and consistent regardless of the medium used and the type of good or service purchased by the consumer. Such a requirement is even more prevalent for electronic consumer contracts between parties domiciled in Europe.

The global impact of the European Union's initiatives

Both Endeshaw[47] and Burnstein regard global measures as necessary for Internet regulation. Indeed, Burnstein states:[48]

> Nations must be willing to relinquish some measure of sovereignty in exchange for the benefits of the Internet, and ultimately nations should not allow national laws and local regulations to obstruct the thriving global Internet.

The conflict between national consumer protection laws, private international laws and the (apparent) 'virtual' borderless nature of electronic commerce must

---

44 See Pearce and Platten, 'Promoting the Information Society', 377.
45 Morse, 'Consumer Contracts', 11.
46 A. J. E. Jaffey, *Topics in Choice of Law* (London: British Institute of International and Comparative Law, 1996), 51.
47 A. Endeshaw, 'The Proper Law for Electronic Commerce' (1998) 1 *International Journal of Law and Information Technology* 5, 10.
48 M. Burnstein, 'A Global Network in a Compartmentalised Legal Environment' in K. Boele-Woelki and C. Kessedjian (eds.), *Internet Law: which Court Decides, which Law Applies?* (The Hague: Kluwer Law International, 1998), 34.

be addressed. Consumers' access to justice will not benefit if different national (i.e., international private) laws and procedures regulate electronic commerce. If this issue is not addressed, the incidence of forum shopping by businesses will increase. Businesses would be increasingly likely to 'target' their activities towards countries with jurisdiction and choice of law rules less favourable to the consumer. If access to justice is the right of every consumer contracting on the Internet, measures to harmonise international private law rules must be taken at the international level. It is widely recognised that the Brussels 1 Regulation represents the communitarisation of international private law rules throughout Europe. However, this Regulation is not adequate in addressing the global nature of electronic consumer contracts and the disputes that undoubtedly will arise from them.

An overview of international private law rules for electronic consumer contracts in the United States

Numerous recent cases at both State and federal levels have considered issues of jurisdiction and choice of law in disputes concerning electronic commerce. Rather than attempt an extensive and detailed examination of every decision on the issues of jurisdiction and choice of law, the general rules for jurisdiction and choice of law will be explained, and a few of the pertinent issues emerging from the US case law will then be considered. The implications these cases might have for the future regulation of electronic consumer contracts will be briefly discussed.

Framework of international private law in the United States

Principles of personal jurisdiction

The test of establishing cross-border personal jurisdiction in the United States outlined in *International Shoe Co.* v. *State of Washington*[49] is well known. In that case, jurisdiction over a defendant not resident in the forum could be established provided that a State's long-arm statute did not conflict with the due process requirement of the Fourteenth Amendment of the US Constitution, or contravene 'notions of fair play and substantial justice'.[50] The test of due process is only satisfied if the test of 'minimum contact' with the forum has been met.

The test of minimum contact was affirmed in *World-Wide Volkswagen Corp.* v. *Woodson*.[51] In that case, minimum contact was established by a defendant who made contact with another jurisdiction for the purposes of selling software from that

---

49 326 US 310 (1945).   50 *Ibid.*, 316.   51 444 US 286 (1980).

jurisdiction. That decision possibly developed from an older Supreme Court decision which confirmed that the degree of contact a defendant had with the forum meant 'he should reasonably anticipate being haled into court there'.[52] The second 'fair play' test has been subjected to far greater analysis than the minimum contact test, and as Abramson suggests, the 'fair play' test 'continues to develop independently from the minimum contacts enquiry'.[53] Where appropriate, States have also used their own long-arm statutes to assert jurisdiction. In the absence of specific national (or international) guidance for electronic commerce, US courts have had to apply these tests to determine if jurisdiction has been established in a cross-border matter where the parties contract over the Internet. The developments and to some extent the limitations of these tests have been demonstrated in the case law where an electronic contract is in dispute.

Choice of law principles

In 1971 the *Restatement (Second) (Conflict of Laws)* introduced the 'most significant relationship' test for international private law (conflict of laws) for contracts.[54] Each State has applied the *Restatement (Second)* to a greater or lesser extent.[55] The *Restatement (Second)* replaced the rules for choice of law in the original *Restatement*, which determined choice of law from the place where the performance occurred. In terms of Section 187 of the *Restatement (Second)*, an agreement on the applicable law is likely to be upheld by the courts if such agreement demonstrates what the parties have reasonably agreed. Clearly, in the case of a consumer, whether inequality of bargaining power affected the applicable law chosen would have to be considered. Such inequality is compounded when a consumer enters into a contract with a business over the Internet.

As with issues of jurisdiction for electronic commerce, it has been for the courts to examine whether the existing choice of law rules for offline transactions can be extended or adapted to determine the applicable law for online contracts. Most of the case law analysis on the matter of personal jurisdiction has questioned if the due process clause could be extended so as to include the economic activities carried out by a party not located in the forum. This would apply to the case of a consumer domiciled in the United States who accesses and orders goods from a business's website where that business's premises are not located in the same State as the consumer, or even in the United States.

---

52 *Ibid.*, 297.
53 L. Abramson, 'Clarifying "Fair Play and Substantial Justice": How the Courts Apply the Supreme Court Standard for Personal Jurisdiction' (1991) 18 *Hastings Const L Q* 441, 469.
54 E. F. Scoles, P. Hay, P. J. Borchers and S. C. Symeonides, *Conflict of Laws* (3rd edn, St. Paul, Minnesota: West Group, 2000), 58.
55 See P. Hay, *An Introduction to US Law* (2nd edn, Salem, New Hampshire: Butterworths, 1991), 128.

Developments in international private law rules for electronic commerce in the United States

Unlike the European Union approach, where there has been little or no case law, US courts have considered the application of existing principles of jurisdiction and choice of law in the context of electronic commerce. The approaches of Europe and the USA in determining jurisdiction and choice of law rules demonstrate how such rules can be developed in different ways. Many cases in the USA have considered jurisdiction and choice of law issues in respect of intellectual property rights, trademarks and domain name infringements, as well as contractual disputes (involving consumers or otherwise).

Several US authors have expressed concerns that jurisdiction should not be established wherever a website is capable of being viewed, i.e., worldwide jurisdictional reach.[56] The previous US Administration's view was that regulation of electronic commerce was necessary, probably by a combination of government and self-regulatory measures. In the meantime, what the cases in the USA have sought to do is to ensure that the rules of jurisdiction and choice of law briefly explained above can apply or 'adapt'[57] to electronic commerce matters in the absence of specific legislative measures.

International private law and electronic commerce in the United States: some issues emerging for consumer contracts

The domicile of the parties in an electronic contract links traditional territorially based jurisdiction concepts and the Internet. However, some of the key issues demonstrated by a number of US cases illustrate the need for the adoption of specific legislative rules for electronic commerce activity and contracts. Accordingly, the following issues will be considered: the jurisdictional reach of active and passive websites; the effect of economic activity within the forum state; whether jurisdiction can be established where a website is physically located; and whether jurisdiction and choice of law rules should extend to goods or services purchased by a consumer over the Internet if those goods or services were not received by the consumer in their domicile or habitual residence. These issues are common to electronic commerce cases in the USA and will become prevalent elsewhere. The issues demonstrate the need for specific legislative provisions at the appropriate level to strengthen electronic commerce, international private laws and consumer protection rules.

56 See Epps, '*Maritz*'; D. L. Stott, 'Personal Jurisdiction in Cyberspace: the Constitutional Boundary of Minimum Contacts Limited to a Web Site' (1997) 15 *John Marshall Journal of Computer and Information Law* 819, 840; S. Puathasnanon, 'Cyberspace and Personal Jurisdiction: the Problem of Using Internet Contacts to Establish Minimum Contacts' (1998) *Loy LA L Rev* 691.
57 See R. Rochlin, 'Cyberspace, International Shoe and the Changing Context for Personal Jurisdiction' (2000) *Conn L R* 32: 653, 654.

The distinction between active and passive websites

A number of cases in the United States have examined whether the content and activities of a website are sufficient to establish jurisdiction in the State where website activity is directed. This has obvious implications for the consumer. If the website directs its activities in the consumer's jurisdiction, should jurisdiction be established where the consumer is domiciled? Establishing jurisdiction at the consumer's domicile would clearly be advantageous to the consumer, who is more likely to know the rules and procedures of his or her own jurisdiction, or at least be able to identify them more quickly than if the relevant jurisdiction was, for example, where the business is located. Equally, most consumers will be unable to fund the cost of pursuing a case abroad.

Zippo Manufacturing Co. v. *Zippo Dot Com, Inc.*[58] illustrates the way in which personal jurisdiction is capable of being established by the activity of a website. In *Zippo*, the court demonstrated the way in which the activity of a website could establish jurisdiction in another forum. The court classified website activity as being either active, or passive, or neither active nor passive. The court held that the plaintiff's activity constituted activity in the forum. As the plaintiff's website enabled him to contract with a party in another jurisdiction, jurisdiction was established where that other party was domiciled.

Before the *Zippo* case, cases such as *CompuServe Inc.* v. *Patterson*,[59] *Inset Systems, Inc.* v. *Instruction Set, Inc.*[60] and *Maritz, Inc.* v. *Cybergold, Inc.*[61] demonstrated how US courts determined personal jurisdiction from the activities of a website. Indeed, in *Maritz*, it was held that the website was neither active nor passive, even though viewers were able to add their names to a mailing list on the site. This might therefore apply to many websites that provide a similar service. In *Maritz*, the court upheld the important test of 'fairness', and jurisdiction was held to be established. In each of these cases, the general issue was whether the website in issue constituted an advertisement, and whether jurisdiction could be established where the plaintiff was situated. By contrast, *Bensusan Restaurant Corp.* v. *King*[62] demonstrated that the passive website is one that is simply an information provider, similar to an advertisement on a billboard or newspaper.

As Epps explains,[63] the facts in the *Maritz* case fell between the active and passive spectrum of website activity. Jurisdiction is established as if the website was an 'active' site, subject to a fairness test. In referring to the *Maritz* case, Epps maintains that the Supreme Court extended the reach of personal jurisdiction by considering the activities of such websites. Many websites do not 'interact' with those browsing them. Such sites may provide facilities for those browsing to register as little as their name or e-mail address with the site for future information or special offers.[64]

---

58 952 F Supp 1119 (W. D. Pa. 1997). 59 89 F 3d 1257 (6th Cir. 1996).
60 937 F Supp 161 (D. Conn. 1996). 61 947 F Supp 1328 (E. D. Mo. 1996).
62 937 F Supp 295 (S. D. N. Y. 1996). 63 Epps, 'Maritz'.
64 An example of 'a user [being able to] exchange information with the host computer': Epps, 'Maritz', 255.

Potentially, many other similar websites could fall into this category. This is one of the reasons why Epps, and others,[65] criticise the decision in *Maritz*. Essentially, this case illustrates the similarities that can be drawn between the content and activities of websites and advertising. Epps, however, points out that the court in *Maritz* should have considered such an analogy.[66] Epps maintains that the court went too far in extending personal jurisdiction[67] because it failed to consider the relationship between website content and advertising. Nevertheless, Epps contends that *Maritz* will 'continue to influence many courts and commentators in their reasoning and their findings'.[68]

Despite emerging views from the courts concerning the continued benefit of the active/passive website distinction,[69] future legislation ought to address the legal impact of advertising when determining if jurisdiction can be established from the activities of a website. On that point, developments in Europe will be observed with interest. If websites are to be regarded as advertising to consumers, then the question is whether such sites should establish jurisdiction wherever they are capable of being viewed by consumers anywhere, or whether the courts should look to the nature of the website's activities, the consumers targeted on the basis of that activity, and the level of interaction between the consumer and the website.

Economic activities in the forum: the effects of acting within the forum state

The second issue to be considered is whether website activity constitutes economic activity within the forum state, or constitutes acting within the forum state, and is thereby sufficient to establish jurisdiction in that state. The point is developed by Scoles *et al.* who ask whether 'a foreign business entity has purposefully produced effects in the forum state of such significance that it is not manifestly unfair to require him to resolve a resulting legal dispute in this state'.[70] In other words, does targeting a consumer with the result that the consumer purchases goods or services from a business's website mean that that business is subject to the jurisdiction and domestic rules of the consumer's domicile?

The jurisdictional effect of economic activity within the forum was expressed in *McGhee* v. *International Life Ins. Co*, where the court asserted that 'it is sufficient for purposes of due process that the suit was based upon a contract which had

---

65 See, e.g., the Comment by C. McWhinney, S. Wooden, J. McKown, J. Ryan and J. Green, 'The "Sliding Scale" of Personal Jurisdiction via the Internet' (2000) *Stan Tech L Rev* 1, stlr.stanford.edu/STLR/Events/personal.jurisdiction/index.html.
66 In his paper, Epps refers to 'globally and nationally distributed magazines' as such an analogy: '*Maritz*', 266, 268.
67 *Ibid.*, 269–79.   68 *Ibid.*, 279.
69 See Michael Geist's views on his website, http://aixl.uottawa.ca/-geist/framset.html; and also the decision in *Digital Control* v. *Boretronics*, 2001 US Dist. LEXIS 14600, where the Federal Court held that the test was not sufficient for courts to determine jurisdiction.
70 Scoles, Hay, Borchers and Symeonides, *Conflict of Laws*, 308 in 2nd edn.

a substantial connection with that state'.[71] The issue to be resolved is whether there is a 'substantial connection' to the forum in order to assert jurisdiction, and how such a substantial connection is defined. Minimum contact in the jurisdiction is required, provided 'additional activities'[72] are directed within the stream of commerce. Such a requirement has, according to Stott, helped to distinguish between active and passive websites. He maintains that if additional activity demonstrates that a website has entered the 'stream of commerce' in line with the decision in *Asahi Metal Industry Co. Ltd* v. *Superior Court*,[73] then personal jurisdiction ought to be upheld.[74]

Jurisdiction established where a website server is located

The question whether a website's location can confer jurisdiction has yet to be determined in Europe. The view stated above is that it should not be possible for jurisdiction to be conferred where the Web server is located. To do so would certainly lead to forum shopping. It would enable a server to be located in a jurisdiction less favourable to the consumer, or it would result in practical difficulties if more than one server were used to send the website's information.

The position of a Web server was considered in *Amberson Holdings LLC* v. *Westside Story Newspaper*.[75] Following this case, it is doubtful whether US jurisdiction could be established on the basis of a server's location. In *Amberson*, the court held that personal jurisdiction could not be found under the *International Shoe* minimum contact test. This case demonstrates the likelihood of difficulties in satisfying the minimum contact and fair play and substantial justice tests for jurisdiction on the basis of where a server is located. Given the nature and difficulties in ascertaining what server(s) a website uses, this is hardly surprising.

Distinction between goods and services received in the consumer's domicile or elsewhere

The distinction between the situation where goods and services are received in the consumer's domicile or elsewhere is an important one in the context of electronic consumer contracts, particularly in the absence of a stipulated choice of law. Section 188 of the *Restatement (Second)* provides that it is the local law of the state having the most significant relationship to the transaction that shall determine the applicable law of the dispute. From the consumer's point of view, it is not important whether the contract exists and applies in cyberspace. What is important is that the consumer may have to resort to another set of laws, which may or may not be in

---

71 355 US 220, 223 (1957) per Black J.
72 Stott, 'Personal Jurisdiction', 840, citing both the *Maritz* case and *Asahi Metal Industry Co. Ltd* v. *Superior Court*, 480 US 102 (1987).
73 *Ibid.*   74 Stott, 'Personal Jurisdiction', 853.
75 110 F Supp. 2d 332 (2000), discussed in R. J. Peach, 'Dot-com's Host Server in NJ Isn't a Foothold for Jurisdiction' (2000) 161 *New Jersey Law Journal* 875.

his or her favour. Essentially, the issue here is whether it would be reasonable for a consumer to be able to sue a business for goods or services that the consumer did not receive in his or her domicile. Provided that the contract is a consumer contract for the sale of goods or for the provision of credit for the purchase of goods, jurisdiction and choice of law rules should continue to favour the consumer no matter where the goods are delivered.

The United States has sought to address electronic commerce issues by creating a framework for electronic commerce and by questioning and applying the use and development of existing jurisdiction and choice of law principles. This provides a valuable insight into how rules of international private law for electronic consumer contracts can be developed further. The United States is pursuing a regulatory framework for the adoption of appropriate jurisdiction and choice of law rules. The Federal Trade Commission has advocated a global solution to consumer protection[76] and has also considered alternative methods by which consumers should seek redress of their disputes online. Nevertheless, precisely what rules will be implemented in any regulatory framework remains to be seen. The US case law demonstrates an urgent need for more precise or particularised jurisdiction and choice of law rules for electronic consumer contracts. If international private law rules are to be capable of being applied to facilitate the harmonisation, or at least consistency, of decisions, such rules are desirable.

Conclusion

> Nations must be willing to relinquish some measure of sovereignty in exchange for the benefits of the Internet, and ultimately nations should not allow national laws and local regulations to obstruct the thriving global Internet.[77]

Given that the problems of jurisdiction and choice of law in electronic commerce are inherently global, the appropriate level at which rules are developed ought to be considered. Ensuring access to justice for consumers, no matter where they are domiciled and no matter where the businesses with which they deal are situated, is crucial to maintaining consumer confidence in and the continued growth of business by electronic means. Consumers ought to have a reasonable expectation of their rights and duties when they make purchases online and to know where they can enforce these rights. The issue whether global, regional or national legislative measures are required for electronic consumer contracts remains a live one. Developments in the European Union and the United States illustrate the extent to

76 See Atiyah, Adams and MacQueen, *The Sale of Goods*, 58–9.
77 Burnstein, 'A Global Network', 34. Endeshaw supports the requirement for global regulation: 'The Proper Law', 10.

which regional initiatives have influenced the continued development of international private law rules.

There is a strong argument for 'global' (either multinational or multi-regional) measures to be used to create appropriate legislative structures for the 'information society' generally.[78] Whilst this would appear to benefit the consumer, the viability of global consumer protection rules for electronic consumer contracts will continue to be debated. This is perhaps where international private law could be harmonised globally in order to facilitate uniform application of jurisdiction and choice of law principles. Rather than creating new rules, international private law should be capable of adapting present offline rules for transactions that take place online. The global application of this notion is an extension of Foss and Bygrave's[79] 'online/offline' paradigm. It may also encourage other regional organisations or bodies to formulate international private law rules in conjunction with larger organisations such as the OECD and WIPO, as well as the Hague Conference on Private International Law.

It has been seen that the European Union has sought to address the implications of electronic commerce at a regional level. This step clarifies existing rules of jurisdiction for online consumer transactions. However, to a large extent the Brussels Regulation does not apply to parties domiciled outside Europe. The European Union has included in its Justice and Home Affairs Framework for an assessment of the Brussels Regulation five years after its implementation,[80] although it is doubtful whether this will allow a reasonable time for such an assessment.

The role of the Hague Conference on Private International Law

The role of international organisations such as the Hague Conference on Private International Law should also be considered. Indeed, this is evident from Secretary-General Hans Van Loon's recent article in *Forum du Droit International* where he indicated the changing nature of the Hague Conference's relationship (and those of its members) with the European Union and its member states, many of which are themselves members of the Hague Conference.[81] The Hague Conference is presently drafting a worldwide Judgments Convention. It remains to be seen

---

78 See M. Docherty and R. Fletcher, 'Responding to the Legal Problems of Electronic Commerce' (2000) 5 *Communications Law* 2, 3, advocating a global solution and maintaining that whatever system is used to regulate the Internet, 'it should not produce over-regulation'. See also K. W. Grewlich, *Governance in 'Cyberspace'. Access and Public Interest in Global Communications* (The Hague: Kluwer Law International, 1999).

79 M. Foss and L. A. Bygrave, 'International Consumer Purchases through the Internet: Jurisdictional Issues Pursuant to European Law' (2000) 8 *International Journal of Law and Information Technology* 99.

80 Brussels 1 Regulation, Preamble 28, 3.

81 H. Van Loon, 'Globalisation and the Hague Conference on Private International Law' (2000) 2 *Forum du droit international* 230. See also Kotuby, 'External Competence'.

what role the proposed Convention will have and the extent to which it will impact upon enforceable rules of jurisdiction for electronic consumer contracts. However, Van Loon's article suggests that the European Union will exercise its 'external competence' in the negotiations for the worldwide Judgments Convention, and that in the not too distant future the European Union may well become a member of the Hague Conference in its own right.[82]

International private law principles need to be developed for electronic commerce at both international and regional levels, a point reiterated by Van Loon.[83]

From the international private law perspective, the continued development of rules and procedures for jurisdiction, choice of law and recognition and enforcement, will have to be considered by other countries and other regional economic areas. How the Hague Conference's proposed worldwide Judgments Convention will work in practice alongside regional instruments such as the Brussels 1 Regulation (together with the Rome Convention and in due course its replacement), and what involvement the European Union and its member states will have in its negotiation, remains to be seen.[84]

Kotuby maintains that the European Union will contribute to the continuing negotiations of the Hague's proposed Convention in conjunction with EU member states. He explains that the European Community does have external competence on international matters if such matters are 'inextricably linked to an internal Treaty objective'.[85] However, it is the member states that have the knowledge and experience of negotiating with organisations such as the Hague Conference and implementing such instruments. This is feasible, given that any Convention would ultimately be applied in the contracting states to the Convention.

Nevertheless, there are major concerns about the Hague Conference's proposed worldwide Convention in relation to consumer contracts. Consumer contracts are given no separate treatment from ordinary 'business to business' contracts in the latest draft proposals.[86] Further, the most recent proposed Convention purports to

---

82 Van Loon, 'Globalization', 234.   83 *Ibid.*
84 Several authors considered the issue of European Union competency and the extent of member states' future involvement in the Hague Convention negotiations and the notion of external competence: Basedow, 'Communitarisation of Conflict of Laws'; P. Beaumont, 'A United Kingdom Perspective on the Proposed Hague Judgments Convention' (1998) 24 *Brook J Int'l L* 75; R. Dehousse, 'European Institutional Architecture after Amsterdam: Parliamentary System or Regulatory Structure?' (1998) 35 *CMLR* 595, 598; J. Israël, 'Conflicts of Law and the EC after Amsterdam: a Change for the Worse?' (2000) 7 *Maastricht Journal* 81; Kotuby, 'External Competence'; I. Pernice, 'Multilevel Constitutionalism and the Treaty of Amsterdam: European Constitution-Making Revisited?' (1999) 36 *Common Market Law Reports* 703, 705; Remien, 'European Private International Law'; A. Von Bogdandy, 'The Legal Case for Unity: the European Union as a Single Organisation with a Single Legal System' (1999) 36 *Common Market Law Reports* 887, 894; N. Walker, 'Justice and Home Affairs' (1998) 47 *ICLQ* 231, 232.
85 Opinion 1/76 [1977] ECR 741, cited in Kotuby, 'External Competence', 3 ff.
86 Article 7 of The Hague's proposed Convention on Jurisdiction and Foreign Judgments in Commercial Matters. The latest draft of the proposed Convention is dated June 2001 and was produced after informal meetings held in Washington (December 2000), Geneva (February 2001),

limit Article 7 to contracts for 'private use or consumption' (Article 7(1)) provided the other party to the contract is a business. Significantly, businesses will not be subject to Article 7 if they can demonstrate that they would not have entered into a contract had they known that the other party was a consumer. How businesses can reasonably satisfy this requirement remains to be seen. The proposals no longer appear to favour the consumer as they can, at present, be 'opted out of' by countries that accede to the Convention. In any event, the proposals have failed to capture the support of certain countries, including the United States. Indeed, following the outcome of the meeting to be held in January 2002, the Convention could be further limited in scope or even be abandoned.

The European Union has led the development of international private law rules for electronic consumer contracts. The response of other jurisdictions, in particular the United States, to the electronic consumer contract rules in the new Brussels 1 Regulation is awaited. There is a continuing need for global co-operation in the development of applicable law rules for electronic consumer contracts. The role of international private law must be to provide for coherent and compatible rules of jurisdiction and choice of law for electronic commerce, including consumer contracts, in the form of harmonised rules and procedures. International and regional consumer organisations ought to have a significant role in the formulation and monitoring of appropriate rules for electronic consumer contracts.

Modified rules of jurisdiction for electronic consumer contracts will shortly come into force within the European Union. In due course, European choice of law rules will follow. Whether this addresses the requirement for principles for electronic consumer contracts is debatable. The effect of the Brussels 1 Regulation, and the outcome of the Hague Conference's proposals, should also be carefully monitored if consumers are to be provided with access to justice enabling their contractual disputes to be determined by clear, consistent and harmonised rules.

Ottawa (February–March 2001, where the proposals for consumer contracts were considered) and Edinburgh (April 2001), as well as the first Diplomatic Meeting at The Hague in June 2001. In August 2002, the Hague Conference released a position paper on the proposals limiting their scope to rules for, *inter alia*, choice of court: see http://www.hcch.net.

15 Waving goodbye to conflict of laws? Recent developments in European Union consumer law

AXEL HALFMEIER

Introduction

It is a widely held view that the law with respect to electronic commerce and consumer protection across national borders is in a state of chaos. It is whispered in the hallways of law schools that the Internet has brought about a new world which is expanding rapidly and forcing a myriad of jurisdictional and conflict of laws problems on us. Law students ask their teachers why they do not teach them 'Internet law'. Governmental bureaucracies claim that there is great legal uncertainty, which hinders the growth of electronic commerce. A typical example of this position is the argument of the European Commission as to why it felt that a Directive on electronic commerce was necessary:[1]

> The development of information society services within the Community is
> hampered by a number of legal obstacles to the proper functioning of the
> internal market which make less attractive the exercise of the freedom of
> establishment and the freedom to provide services; these obstacles arise from
> divergences in legislation and from the legal uncertainty as to which national
> rules apply to such services; in the absence of coordination and adjustment of
> legislation in the relevant areas, obstacles might be justified in the light of the
> case-law of the Court of Justice of the European Communities; legal
> uncertainty exists with regard to the extent to which Member States may
> control services originating from another Member State.

These assumptions rest on weak foundations. Consumer transactions through the Internet are still not very common, at least not in the European Union. The reason for this cannot be a legal uncertainty felt by consumers, since such uncertainty has not prevented masses of European consumers in the past from entering into doubtful transactions. One example is the notorious time-sharing contracts concluded by German consumers regarding real estate on the Canary Islands with

---

1 Directive 2000/31/EC of the European Parliament and of the Council of 8 June 2000 on certain legal aspects of information society services, in particular electronic commerce, in the internal market ('the E-Commerce Directive') OJ 2000 No. L178/1, recital 5.

choice of law clauses pointing towards the law of the Isle of Man.[2] It is a reasonable assumption that most of these time-sharing customers were less than familiar with the contract law of the Isle of Man, if they knew the location of this island at all! Legal certainty therefore is not necessarily a prerequisite for economic success.

With regard to the legal problems of international electronic commerce, it seems at first glance that they would greatly enhance the importance of conflict of laws rules, since these are the legal tools that are at hand to regulate cross-border conflicts. It was even claimed by a German conflicts of law scholar that private international law is the 'Archimedean point of the Internet',[3] in the sense that, because the Internet is an international medium, all questions would in the end come down to the issue of the applicable national law, a question cherished by private international law scholars.

But again, this assumption may turn out not to be the complete answer. Conflict rules are the typical medium through which nation states adjust the competing regulatory interests among themselves. These rules are based on the assumption that national law is the basic legal instrument.[4] In a case involving several nations, the problem is seen as being to decide which nation's law should apply to the case at hand. As nation states lose their regulatory power, these basic concepts of private international law are also on the retreat. This at least seems to be the consequence of recent developments in European consumer protection law which will be discussed in this essay. They show that there are new mechanisms of European Union law that supplement or even replace traditional private international law doctrine. Is it time to wave goodbye to conflict of laws?

In the area of consumer law, these developments affect the protection of the individual consumer entering into a cross-border contract (discussed in the following section), and the protection of consumer interests against unfair trade practices such as in advertising (discussed below at pp. 395–402).

2 Strangely enough, these 'Canary Islands Cases' have been an important part of the German private international law discussion: see, e.g., BGH (German Federal Court), judgment of 19 March 1997, 135 BGHZ 124.
3 See T. Hoeren, *Rechtsfragen des Internets* (Cologne: RWS Kommunikationsforum, 1998), n. 392.
4 '[Private international law] builds on the axiom that there are orders outside the own state which are to be accepted as law . . . It says when to apply the private law of the own state or of a foreign state': G. Kegel and K. Schurig, *Internationales Privatrecht* (8th edn, Munich: Beck, 2000), 5, 16. Likewise, one of the traditional French textbooks on private international law starts in its first sentence with the concept of the nation state: 'Le droit interne envisage la société juridiquement constituée sous la forme d'un État . . . Mais des relations s'établissent par la force des choses entre les différents groupements *constitués en États*': H. Battifol and P. Lagarde, *Droit international privé* (8th edn, Paris: Libr. Générale de Droit et de Jurisprudence, 1993), Vol. I, 12 (emphasis added).

Consumer contracts

Jurisdiction

Although the question of jurisdiction must carefully be distinguished from the question of applicable law, it still deserves closer examination in the context of consumer contracts. In practice, it may often be easier to persuade a judge to apply the forum state's law than to apply a foreign law. This phenomenon is known in German discussions as *Heimwärtsstreben*.[5] Jurisdiction rules will also determine to a large extent whether consumer cases are litigated at all, since the consumer will usually hesitate to start litigation and even more so in a foreign forum. In the eyes of the European Union institutions, the consumer is therefore considered to be the 'weaker party'[6] with regard to litigation abroad.

According to this approach, Article 13 of the Brussels Convention of 1968 on Jurisdiction and Enforcement of Judgments in Civil and Commercial Matters[7] gives the consumer the choice of jurisdiction between his or her home courts and the courts of the supplier's place of business. If the professional supplier wants to sue the consumer, he or she can only do so at the consumer's home forum (Brussels Convention, Article 14). A prior forum selection to the disadvantage of the consumer, for example, in the general terms of the contract, is not considered to be binding (Article 15). These rules, however, apply only to certain special consumer contracts or contracts concluded under specific circumstances (Article 13).

It is not necessary to elaborate on these restrictions, since they have fallen away to a large extent on 1 March 2002 when the new EC Regulation 44/2001[8] entered into force. With this regulation, the jurisdictional rules inside the European Union, except for Denmark, which has declared certain reservations to the Amsterdam Treaty and therefore is not affected by Regulation 44/2001, become Community Law instead of ordinary international law as they used to be under the Brussels Convention. The change of legal source for these rules may not be of much relevance in practice, but it could mean that changing these rules in the future may become easier because such changes no longer need to be ratified by national legislatures, but can be ordered solely from Brussels.

Regulation 44/2001 also contains some material changes compared to the Brussels Convention. Consumers' access to justice will be improved, since most of the specific conditions under which the consumer protection rules of the Brussels Convention apply will fall away. Under Regulation 44/2001, Article 15(1), the jurisdictional consumer protection rules apply to most cross-border consumer contracts:

---

5 See J. Kropholler, *Internationales Privatrecht* (4th edn, Tübingen: Mohr Siebeck, 2001), 42.
6 Council Regulation (EC) 44/2001 of 22 December 2000 on jurisdiction and the recognition and enforcement of judgments in civil and commercial matters: OJ 2001 No. L12/1 recital 12.
7 Reprinted with later amendments in 1998 OJ, C 27/1.   8 See n. 6 above.

In matters relating to a contract concluded by a person, the consumer, for a purpose which can be regarded as being outside his trade or profession, jurisdiction shall be determined by this Section, without prejudice to Article 4 and point 5 of Article 5, if:

a. it is a contract for the sale of goods on instalment credit terms; or
b. it is a contract for a loan repayable by instalments, or for any other form of credit, made to finance the sale of goods; or
c. in all other cases, the contract has been concluded with a person who pursues commercial or professional activities in the Member State of the consumer's domicile or, by any means, directs such activities to that Member State or to several States including that Member State, and the contract falls within the scope of such activities.

While it seems unclear under what conditions an offer of goods or services on the Internet will be 'directed to several states' in the sense of the aforementioned rule, once a contract with a consumer is concluded, the first alternative of Article 15(1)(c) is fulfilled. The supplier has then 'pursued commercial activities' in the consumer's state of domicile by contracting with that consumer, although one may think of restricting this to cases in which the supplier knew of the consumer's domicile. Once a cross-border consumer transaction is made, through the Internet for example, the consumer can only be sued in his or her home territory and has the option of bringing action there himself or herself.

It must be noted, however, that these extensive consumer protection rules apply to their full extent only with regard to suppliers that have their business seat inside the European Union, or that act through a subsidiary or branch office there. If the supplier acts from outside the European Union, neither the Brussels Convention nor Regulation 44/2001 apply (Article 4(1) of both instruments). In those cases, domestic rules apply with regard to the jurisdiction of the consumer's home forum. At least in Germany, these domestic procedural rules do not necessarily give the consumer access to his or her home forum in a contract case, unless the defendant supplier has assets in Germany, or unless the place of performance of the obligation that has allegedly been breached is in Germany. If German law governed the contract, the seller's obligations are to be fulfilled at his or her place of business, not at the consumer's residence, so that a German court would not have jurisdiction to determine a claim based on these obligations.[9]

The 1999 draft of the Hague Convention on global jurisdiction rules contains a provision on consumer contracts[10] that is very similar to that in Regulation

9 See § 29 ZPO (Code of Civil Procedure); R. Patzina in A. Belz and G. Lüke (eds.), *Münchener Kommentar zur Zivilprozessordnung* (2nd edn, Munich: Beck, 2000), § 29, n. 19.
10 Hague Conference on Private International Law, Preliminary Draft Convention on Jurisdiction and Foreign Judgments in Civil and Commercial Matters, Art. 7, reads: '(1) A plaintiff who concluded a contract for a purpose which is outside its trade or profession, hereafter designated

44/2001, but it is unclear whether and when the work on this Convention will be finished. The US delegation has raised several objections to this draft of the Hague Convention, particularly to the proposed consumer protection rule. The American representative stated that this rule has raised a 'storm of controversy in the electronic commerce world'.[11]

Why this storm broke out is not quite clear. If the intention of US electronic commerce businesses is to force forum selection clauses on consumers through the small print of their business terms, as some unofficial statements suggest, this strategy seems rather old-fashioned and neither fair nor transparent. Even though US courts apparently enforce derogating forum-selection clauses in consumer contracts, this seems limited to domestic cases. In the leading case on forum-selection clauses in consumer contracts, the US Supreme Court stated that it is reasonable for a holiday cruise operator to organise a central place for litigation through its business terms and not unreasonable to expect a US plaintiff to travel to another State of the United States in order to sue the cruise operator.[12] This argument cannot easily be transferred to an international case where, for example, an American consumer plaintiff would be forced to sue overseas if the forum-selection clause were to be enforced. It is doubtful whether American courts would refuse to provide a forum for the consumer in such a case.[13] In the aforementioned cruiseline decision, the US Supreme Court noted: 'It bears emphasis that forum-selection clauses contained in form... contracts are subject to judicial scrutiny for fundamental fairness.'[14]

as the consumer, may bring a claim in the courts of the State in which it is habitually resident, if (a) the conclusion of the contract on which the claim is based is related to trade or professional activities that the defendant has engaged in or directed to that State, in particular in soliciting business through means of publicity, and (b) the consumer has taken the steps necessary for the conclusion of the contract in that State. (2) A claim against the consumer may only be brought by a person who entered into the contract in the course of its trade or profession before the courts of the State of the habitual residence of the consumer.' See www.hcch.net/e/conventions/draft36e.html.

11 J. D. Kovar, Letter of 22 February 2000 to the Hague Conference on Private International Law [2000] DAJV (German-American Lawyers' Association) Newsletter 44, 45. The diplomatic conference held at The Hague in June 2001 could not resolve these differences. The summary on the outcome of this conference reports several different proposals regarding consumer contract cases, only to add that there is 'no consensus in respect of any of them': ftp://hcch.net/doc/jdgm2001drafte.doc. See Art. 7, n. 43. Further negotiations have been postponed until well into 2002.

12 Carnival Cruise Lines, Inc. v. Shute, 499 US 585 (1991).

13 An American commentary on Shute ambiguously says that public policy reasons against enforcement of the exclusive selection of a foreign forum may 'loom larger in the international setting' than in the interstate setting: E. Scoles and P. Hay, Conflict of Laws (2nd edn, St. Paul, Minn.: West Publishing, 1992), 369. Even in the landmark decision on the enforcement of forum-selection clauses in the USA, the Supreme Court already speaks critically of the 'remote alien forum' and speculates that the 'selection of a remote forum to apply differing foreign law to an essentially American controversy might contravene an important public policy of the forum': M/S Bremen v. Zapata Off-Shore Co, 407 US 1, 17 (1972).

14 Carnival Cruise Lines, Inc. v. Shute, 499 US 585, 595 (1991).

Furthermore, any e-commerce supplier today must already face the possibility of being sued by its customers in courts all over the world, depending on local procedural rules which often do not enforce forum-selection clauses contained in consumer contracts.[15] The European Court of Justice has held that a forum-selection clause contained in a standard form contract is invalid under the Unfair Contract Terms Directive 93/13/EEC, even in a domestic setting.[16] Taking the perspective of European suppliers who do business with US consumers, they will often be under US jurisdiction according to 'long-arm statutes' and the somewhat vague rules on 'doing business' there.[17] The Hague draft may have considerable drawbacks, but at least the consumer protection rule seems to be a sensible and clear harmonisation. Nevertheless, it must for the moment be acknowledged that this project has reached an impasse and that its future is uncertain.[18]

A preliminary conclusion is that consumer protection rules regarding jurisdiction inside the European Union are well ordered and easily accessible with the Brussels Convention, and with Regulation 44/2001 as its successor. The realm of jurisdictional uncertainty begins where the consumer ventures beyond the European Union's borders by way of the Internet.

Active and passive consumers

The situation is more complex with regard to the selection of the applicable substantive law. Ambitious academic projects designed to create a uniform

---

15 Under the German Code of Civil Procedure, forum-selection clauses in international consumer contracts are only enforceable if they are concluded in writing, which will rarely be the case in electronic commerce. See § 38 (2) ZPO and R. Bork in F. Stein and M. Jonas (eds.), *Kommentar zur Zivilprozessordnung* (21st edn, Tübingen, Mohr: 1993), § 38 II n. 14–19.

16 Cases C-240/98 to C-244/98, judgment of 27 June 2000 (*Océano*), [2000] ECR I-4941, para. 24.

17 This will, according to the classic case of *International Shoe Co.* v. *State of Washington*, 326 US 310 (1945), depend on the extent of that corporation's economic activities in the USA. With regard to e-commerce, the US courts tend to distinguish between 'active' commerce through the Internet, which provides sufficient grounds for personal jurisdiction, and only 'passive' websites that do not give rise to personal jurisdiction over their author. See *Bensusan Restaurant Corp.* v. *King*, 937 F Supp 295, 301 (SDNY 1996), where a 'passive' website offering only information was not considered sufficient to establish jurisdiction. On the other hand, 'if the defendant enters into contracts with residents of [the forum state] that involve the knowing and repeated transmission of computer files', jurisdiction is established: *Zippo Manufacturing Company* v. *Zippo Dot Com, Inc.*, 952 F Supp. 1119, 1124 (W.D. Pa. 1996); cf. *CompuServe Inc.* v. *Patterson*, 89 F 3d 1257 (6th Cir. 1996). The reference to the transmission of computer files is due to the specifics of these cases. Contracts regarding the sale of goods or provision of services with customers in the forum state should also provide jurisdiction, since the US Supreme Court has clearly said that a physical presence in the forum state is not necessary, and that business transacted with the forum state through mail or telecommunication is sufficient: *Burger King Corp.* v. *Rudzewicz*, 471 US 462, 476 (1985).

18 See A.T. von Mehren, 'The Hague Jurisdiction and Enforcement Convention Project Faces an Impasse: a Diagnosis and Guidelines for a Cure' [2000] *Praxis des internationalen Privat- und Verfahrensrechts* 465.

substantive 'European private law' are well under way but are still many years away from a stage at which they could seriously be considered for legislative action. On the contrary, some member states on the Continent are implementing large-scale reforms of their own domestic private law codes, for example the new Civil Code of the Netherlands,[19] and the structural revision of the law of obligations in the German Civil Code that was recently adopted by the German Parliament.[20]

Therefore, harmonisation of private law in the European Union has run mainly on two distinct but parallel tracks. One is the piecemeal harmonisation through specific EC Directives that have to be implemented by national legislation. Regarding consumer law, this piecemeal work has covered various areas including door-to-door selling,[21] distance selling,[22] unfair terms in general contract terms[23] and, recently, the sale of consumer goods.[24] The other track of harmonisation is the idea that international decisional harmony, meaning that 'the same substantive law would be applied irrespective of where the proceedings were brought',[25] could be achieved through uniform conflicts rules. These have been in force in the area of contract law for several years by virtue of the Rome Convention on the Law Applicable to Contractual Obligations of 1980.[26]

In its Article 5, the Rome Convention codifies the idea that the consumer should always be able to rely on the mandatory substantive rules of the domestic law of his or her home country regardless of any choice of law clauses in the consumer contract, the assumption being that the consumer would be familiar with that law. However, Article 5 applies this principle only to certain contracts concluded under specific circumstances, especially if:

> in that [the consumer's home] country, the conclusion of the contract was preceded by a specific invitation addressed to him or by advertising, and he [the consumer] had taken in that country all the steps necessary on his part for the conclusion of the contract...

The purpose of this provision as it was understood during the drafting of the Rome Convention is to protect the 'passive' consumer who reacts to an offer or advertisement directed at him, but not the 'active' consumer who actively seeks out offers in

---

19 The 'Nieuw Burgerlijk Wetboek' has been in force in the Netherlands since 1992.
20 *Bundesgesetzblatt I*, (2002), 42.
21 Council Directive 85/577/EEC of 20 December 1985 to protect the consumer in respect of contracts negotiated away from business premises, OJ 1985 No. L372/31.
22 Directive 97/7/EC of the European Parliament and of the Council of 20 May 1997 on the protection of consumers in respect of distance contracts, OJ 1997 No. L144/19.
23 Council Directive 93/13/EEC of 5 April 1993 on unfair terms in consumer contracts, OJ 1993 No. L95/29.
24 Directive 99/44/EC of the European Parliament and of the Council of 25 May 1999 on certain aspects of the sale of consumer goods and associated guarantees, OJ 1999 No. L171/12.
25 L. Collins *et al.* (eds.), *Dicey and Morris on the Conflict of Laws* (13th edn, London: Sweet and Maxwell, 2000), para. 32–012.
26 Reprinted in OJ 1998 No. C27/34.

foreign countries.[27] With regard to the medium of the Internet, it may be hard to establish whether the consumer only reacted to an advertisement or whether she actively searched the Internet for a good bargain from a foreign supplier. The distinction between passive and active consumers does 'not really make any sense in the context of a system which may enable the Website to be accessed from most parts of the world'.[28] This gave rise to some scholarly controversies regarding the application of Article 5 in e-commerce cases.[29]

Case law on this problem is, at least in Germany, not yet available. It can be speculated that there are simply very few e-commerce consumer disputes that reach even lower first instance courts. One reason for this could be that prepayment by the consumer through a credit card is common, if not standard, in such transactions. This is generally a sensible way to make use of the efficiency advantages of e-commerce, especially in cross-border transactions. Should a conflict arise, however, the consumer is adequately protected only if he or she has the possibility of cancelling the payment to the credit card company. Therefore, conflicts between the supplier and the consumer will usually turn into conflicts between the consumer and the credit card company as to the possibility of a charge back under the credit card contract. This will rarely pose any conflict of laws questions, since the credit card customer usually has his or her credit card contract with his or her home bank or with a subsidiary or branch office of the credit card company in the customer's home country. Consumer protection regarding e-commerce therefore depends mainly on how the credit card contract is treated, and not on conflict of laws rules.

The EU plans to revise the Rome Convention to bring it more in line with other Community instruments,[30] such as new Regulation 44/2001. It would make sense to co-ordinate the provisions on consumer protection in the area of jurisdiction with those in private international law. A group of eminent conflicts scholars has already suggested new wording for parts of the Rome Convention. Their proposal would apply the consumer's home law to all contracts between a consumer and a supplier that are concluded and executed across borders, and would no longer distinguish between active and passive consumers.[31]

27 See M. Giuliano and P. Lagarde, Report on the Rome Convention, OJ 1980 No. C282/1, 24; European Consumer Law Group, 'Jurisdiction and Applicable Law in Cross-Border Consumer Complaints', DG XXIV, ECLG/157/98 (29 April 1998).
28 Collins *et al.*, *Dicey and Morris*, para. 33–011.
29 For the German discussion, see P. Mankowski, 'Das Internet im Internationalen Vertrags- und Deliktsrecht' (1999) 63 *Rabels Zeitschrift für ausländisches und internationales Privatrecht* 234; A. Heldrich in O. Palandt (ed.), *Bürgerliches Gesetzbuch* (60th edn, Munich: Beck, 2001), Art. 29 EGBGB, para. 5.
30 Action Plan of the Council and of the Commission on how best to implement the provisions of the Treaty of Amsterdam on an area of freedom, security and justice, OJ 1999 No. C19/1.
31 European Group for International Private Law, 'Proposals for a Revision of the European Convention on Contractual Obligations' [2001] *Praxis des internationalen Privat- und Verfahrensrechts* 64. The relevant part of the proposal reads: 'La loi applicable . . . ne peut priver le consommateur

The *Ingmar* case: mistake or revolution?

However, the conflict of laws rules contained in the Rome Convention may become less important in the light of a recent decision by the European Court of Justice. Even though *Ingmar GB Ltd.* v. *Eaton Leonard Technologies, Inc.*[32] is not a consumer law case, it has important implications for consumer protection throughout the European Union. Ingmar was a British company which acted as a commercial agent in the United Kingdom for Eaton Technologies, based in California. The agency contract was terminated, and Ingmar demanded certain payments relating to this termination. Under EC Directive 86/653,[33] Ingmar would have been entitled to such compensatory payments, but the agency contract was governed by Californian law by virtue of a choice of law clause. The European Court of Justice decided that regardless of the national law governing the agency contract, the relevant provisions of Directive 86/653 must still be applied to any commercial agent carrying out his or her activities inside the European Union.[34]

How does this ruling conform with the conflict of laws rules of the Rome Convention? These rules give the parties to a contract the freedom to choose the law governing the contract (Rome Convention, Article 3(1)), and the validity of the choice of law clause was not placed in question here. Therefore, Californian law should apply according to the Rome Convention.

As is often the case with European Court of Justice rulings, things become clearer by looking at the opinion of the Advocate General. He referred to the Rome Convention, Article 7(2), which reads:

> Nothing in this Convention shall restrict the application of the rules of the law of the forum in a situation where they are mandatory irrespective of the law otherwise applicable to the contract.

In view of this provision, Advocate General Léger argued that the Directive on commercial agents states that the parties cannot derogate from certain of its provisions, including those relevant to the case at hand. He therefore regarded these provisions as rules of a mandatory nature in the sense of the Rome Convention, Article 7(2).[35]

This reasoning, however, does not conform with most of the traditional conflict of laws theory. The concept of mandatory rules of the forum as embodied in

---

de la protection que lui assurent les dispositions impératives de la loi du pays dans lequel il a sa résidence habituelle au moment de la conclusion du contrat, à moins que le fournisseur établisse qu'il ignorait le pays de cette résidence du fait du consommateur.'

32 ECJ, Case C-381/98, judgment of 9 November 2000; [2001] 1 CMLR 9.

33 Council Directive 86/653/EEC of 18 December 1986 on the co-ordination of the laws of the Member States relating to self-employed commercial agents, OJ 1986 No. L382/17.

34 ECJ, Case C-381/98, judgment of 9 November 2000; [2001] 1 CMLR 9, para. 25.

35 *Ibid.*, Opinion of Advocate General Léger, para. A88.

the Rome Convention is quite narrow. Not every rule that is mandatory, in the sense that the parties cannot contract out of it, is at the same time considered to be mandatory in the international sense as envisaged by the Rome Convention, Article 7(2).[36] Under the Rome Convention, and under traditional private international law doctrine, not all mandatory substantive contract law of the forum state is applicable in a cross-border case. This becomes clear if one looks at the special conflict rules contained in the Rome Convention regarding consumer cases (the above-cited Article 5) as well as employment law cases (Article 6). It is typical for consumer law and employment law that its rules cannot be contracted out of, because their very existence is based on the idea of the protection of the party who is typically too weak to have his or her interests adequately reflected in the contract. If all of these norms were mandatory regardless of the applicable law, Articles 5 and 6 of the Rome Convention would be largely useless.

Therefore, it is generally accepted that Article 7(2) of the Rome Convention does not refer to all mandatory rules, but only to those that are mandatory in an international sense, that is, those that are applicable without reference to the governing law even in cross-border cases.[37] One German scholar aptly speaks of Article 7(2) as referring to 'super-mandatory rules' which are to be distinguished from ordinary mandatory rules.[38] What are these 'super-mandatory rules'? It is clear that they include legal rules that are extremely vital to the interests of the forum state, such as rules on currency limitations, rules against trading with the enemy, and other rules of a politically sensitive nature.[39]

But the scope of Article 7(2) of the Rome Convention is less clear where the forum state's interests become more indirect. What about the interest of the forum state in having its citizens or residents protected in consumer or employment relations? In these areas, it is controversial as to whether these state interests are enough to regard the respective rules as super-mandatory,[40] or whether it should be said that in general these rules primarily protect individual consumers' interests and therefore cannot all be regarded as super-mandatory rules.[41] The latter seems to be the

36 U. Magnus in Staudinger, *Bürgerliches Gesetzbuch* (13th edn, Berlin: Sellier de Gruyter, 2000), Art. 34 EGBGB, para. 51; cf. Collins *et al.*, *Dicey and Morris*, paras. 1–049–1–050, distinguishing between statutes that are applicable only to contracts governed by British law and those that are applied regardless of the rules of the conflict of laws.
37 French scholars usually speak of *lois de police*, but add that the mandatory character must also exist with regard to cross-border cases. The rule in question must be 'du caractère "internationalement impératif"': B. Audit, *Droit international privé* (Paris: Economica, 1991), para. 816.
38 Magnus in Staudinger, *Bürgerliches Gesetzbuch*, para. 12.
39 *Ibid.*, paras. 68–9. Super-mandatory rules are those that should be applied to all cases decided before domestic courts in the interest of society as a whole, owing to their character as 'Eingriffsakte' (state intervention).
40 See B. von Hoffmann in H.T. Soergel (10), *Bürgerliches Gesetzbuch* (12th edn, Stuttgart: Kolhammer, 1996), Art. 34, EGBGB para. 4: 'In the welfare state, it is hard to draw the border between the public good and the balancing of private interests.'
41 See Magnus in Staudinger, *Bürgerliches Gesetzbuch*, para 71.

widely accepted position, in Germany at least, so that the realm of application of Article 7(2) of the Rome Convention remains limited. The German Federal Court stated in one of the Canary Islands cases that German rules on door-to-door selling enacted to implement the EC Directive on this subject could only be applied if the conditions of Article 5 of the Rome Convention (i.e., the 'passive' consumer model) were met, since otherwise Article 5 would be circumvented.[42]

This means that domestic law implementing EC Directives was not considered to be super-mandatory solely by virtue of its European heritage, but only if the specific Directive orders such super-mandatory application.[43] But in the *Ingmar* case, the relevant Directive did not contain any explicit language on its application regarding cross-border cases. Advocate General Léger and the European Court of Justice therefore relied on a very general argument in order to establish the relevant provisions' super-mandatory nature: the objective of those provisions was in their opinion not only to protect commercial agents, but also to secure the 'operation of undistorted competition in the internal market' and therefore those provisions must not be circumvented by 'the simple expedient of a choice-of-law clause'.[44]

This reasoning is broad enough to cover many other EC Directives, especially those regarding consumer protection. As in the Directive on commercial agents, the consumer protection Directives not only seek to protect the individual consumer, but also aim at establishing uniform conditions of competition in the internal market of the European Union.

Looking at the relevance of the *Ingmar* decision in this respect, two possible paths are open. First, *Ingmar* was more or less a mistake by the court because it did not appreciate fully the distinction between ordinary mandatory rules and super-mandatory rules in the sense of Article 7(2) of the Rome Convention. The decision will then remain isolated, and will have effect only in the specific area of commercial agents acting in the European Union for principals from outside the Union.

On the other hand, one could also take *Ingmar* seriously and transfer the reasoning to the field of consumer protection, as some commentators have suggested.[45] This would mean that all of the EC Directives regarding consumer protection are to

---

42 BGH, judgment of 19 March 1997, 135 BGHZ 124, 136.
43 See Magnus in Staudinger, *Bürgerliches Gesetzbuch*, paras 41–2. See also the draft for an EC Directive regarding financial services which in its Art. 11(3) explicitly orders its super-mandatory application: 'Consumers may not be deprived of the protection granted by this Directive when the law governing the contract is that of a country that does not belong to the European Community, when the consumer is resident on the territory of a Member State of the European Community and when the contract has a close link with the Community.' (Commission Proposal of 23 July 1999, COM (99) 385 final (EC document no. 599PC0385).)
44 *Ingmar GB Ltd. v. Eaton Leonard Technologies, Inc.* ECJ, Case C-381/98, judgment of 9 November 2000; [2001] 1 CMLR 9, paras. 24–5.
45 See N. Reich, 'Comment on *Ingmar*' [2001] *Europäische Zeitschrift für Wirtschaftsrecht* 51; L. Bernardeau, 'Droit communautaire et lois de police' (2001) I *La semaine juridique* 328.

be considered as super-mandatory rules in the sense of Article 7(2) so that a uniform minimum level of consumer protection would always exist before European courts regardless of conflict of laws rules. The discussion around Article 5 of the Rome Convention would lose much of its significance because many areas of consumer protection are now covered by EC Directives.

Ingmar could therefore lead to a victory of EC legislation over the traditional private international law approach as it is embodied in the Rome Convention. This may be regrettable, since it replaces the well-ordered system of the Rome Convention with the bureaucratic piecemeal approach of EC Directives, but it also would have considerable advantages both for consumers in the European Union as well as for businesses dealing with them. The consumer would have the certainty that a minimum standard would be applied regardless of the supplier's place of business and regardless of choice of law clauses contained in the small print of consumer contracts. Businesses could tailor their activities to the uniform European Union standard in consumer protection without having to research several national laws and attempting to comply with all of them. The uniform standard set in Brussels would replace to a large extent the complicated interplay between the Rome Convention and national consumer protection legislation.

Non-contractual consumer protection law

Market regulation by nation states

Consumer protection rules are not only contained in contract law rules, but also in other private law rules in many European states, such as, in Germany, provisions on unfair advertising or other unfair trading practices.[46] While most cases involving these rules used to involve domestic parties, there is an increasing tendency to apply such law to cross-border situations, especially in electronic commerce, where marketing activities are often directed towards the whole European common market. The enforcement of this part of consumer law in many European countries is the task of consumer associations or state-funded or quasi-official institutions. The implementation of EC Directive 98/27 on cross-border injunctions[47] has made it easier to bring such claims in cross-border situations, but this Directive does not cover the question of the applicable law in such situations.

The starting point in answering this question is the private international law of the member state where the suit is brought. Since non-contractual consumer

---

46 Gesetz gegen den unlauteren Wettbewerb § 1 and 3.
47 Directive 98/27/EC of the European Parliament and of the Council of 19 May 1998 on injunctions for the protection of consumers' interests, OJ 1998 No. L166/51.

protection law must be qualified as part of the law of torts in a general sense, the conflict of laws rules regarding torts will apply. This area has not been harmonised within the European Union, since the Rome Convention only applies to contractual obligations. Therefore, domestic conflict of laws rules apply, which rules usually follow the principle that the nation state may regulate the commercial activity that affects that nation's market.[48] In Germany, for example, cross-border advertising will be governed by the law of the marketplace.[49] This rule has been developed by the German Federal Court for all tort claims involving unfair competition. Such claims shall be subject to the law of the place 'where the competition interests of the competitors come into conflict'.[50] Therefore, any e-commerce services or advertisements affecting the German market are to be judged by German law regardless of their origin.

A similar approach has been proposed for a 'Rome II Convention' (or EC Regulation), which would harmonise the international private law in the field of non-contractual obligations. In cases of alleged unfair competition, this proposal would apply the law of the country in which the market affected by the relevant act of competition is located.[51] Under these traditional conflict rules, the nation states therefore retain the right to apply domestic law to all economic activities that affect the domestic market, say, for example, advertisements in internationally distributed newspapers or on the Internet. This general regulatory power regarding economic activities on its own territory is part of the basic concept of a nation state. According to this concept, and thus under the traditional private international law rules, it is of no relevance whether the economic activity that is in dispute is legal in the country where it originates.

With respect to the affected economic actor, such regulation by the market state does not seem unfair, since one may legitimately demand from this actor that he or she play by the rules of the market that he or she does business in. This fairness idea also seems to be at the core of the US rules on jurisdiction: whoever 'purposefully avails [him]self of the privilege of conducting activities in the forum state, thus invoking the benefits and protection of its laws',[52] should also bear the consequences and play by that state's economic rules.

48 See O. Remien, 'European Private International Law, the European Community and its Emerging Area of Freedom, Security and Justice' (2001) 38 *CML Rev* 53, 68, noting that in unfair competition or advertising cases 'there is a clear tendency to take the law of the market concerned'.
49 See A. Lüderitz in H.T. Soergel (10), *Bürgerliches Gesetzbuch* (12th edn, Stuttgart: Kolhammer, 1996), Art. 38 EGBGB, para. 18, n. 20.
50 BGH, decision of 30 June 1961, 35 BGHZ 329, 333. For an overview of German private international law regarding unfair competition, see Sack, 'Das internationale Wettbewerbs- und Immaterialgüterrecht nach der EGBGB-Novelle' [2000] *Wettbewerb in Recht und Praxis* 269.
51 Art. 4(b) of the 'Proposition pour une convention européenne sur la loi applicable aux obligations non contractuelles' [1999] *Praxis des internationalen Privat- und Verfahrensrechts* 286, 287.
52 *Hanson v. Denckla*, 357 US 235 (1958).

Influence of European law

The traditional pre-eminence of national regulation is called into question by the delegation of authority away from the nation state to international and regional authorities, in particular, in Europe, to the European Union.[53] The European Union's programme consists in establishing a free internal market in the Union without any limitations set by national regulatory interests. This political and economic programme was elevated to a legal principle in the *Cassis* decision[54] by the European Court of Justice, and national regulation was degraded to an exception to the rule. The basic rule is that every member state of the Union must accept the results of its sister states' regulation with effect even for its own territory.[55] A national regulation of cross-border economic activities inside the Union is possible only under certain conditions that are prescribed in the EU Treaty and in the European Court of Justice's case law.

Basic liberties of the EU Treaty

In order to secure the functioning of the internal market, the EU Treaty guarantees certain basic liberties for the benefit of all economic actors. With regard to consumer law, the most important liberties are the free movement of goods and services inside the Union (EU Treaty, Articles 28 and 49). Keeping in mind the example of unfair advertising, the order of a national court prohibiting certain advertisements has to be regarded as a restriction on these liberties. The free movement of goods is restricted where the circulation of a news magazine containing the incriminated advertisement would be prohibited. If similar prohibitions were to affect electronic media, especially any offers or advertisements on the Internet, they would be considered as restrictions on the freedom to provide services, since Article 49 of the EU Treaty protects all commercial media activity.[56] This includes all offers that are made free of charge for the recipient, as is often the case on the Internet, but which are still produced with a commercial intention,[57] for example, to profit from the sale of advertising space or to improve a company's public image.

---

53 For a more detailed analysis of European Union law and of the E-Commerce Directive's implications in the field of tort law, see A. Halfmeier, 'Vom Cassislikör zur E-Commerce-Richtlinie: auf dem Weg zu einem europäischen Mediendeliktsrecht' (2001) *Zeitschrift für europäisches Privatrecht* 837.
54 ECJ, Case 120/78, judgment of 20 February 1979, [1979] ECR 649.
55 Regarding the implications of this rule for private international law from a German perspective, see J. Basedow, 'Der kollisionsrechtliche Gehalt der Produktfreiheiten im europäischen Binnenmarkt: favor offerentis' (1995) 59 *Rabels Zeitschrift für ausländisches und internationales Privatrecht* 1.
56 With respect to television programmes, see ECJ, Case 155/73, judgment of 30 April 1974 (*Sacchi*), [1974] ECR 409.
57 See ECJ, Case 36/74, judgment of 12 December 1974 (*Walrave*), [1974] ECR 1405; ECJ, Case 352/85, judgment of 26 April 1988 (*Bond van Adverteerders*), [1988] ECR 2085.

There has been a complicated discussion following the European Court's *Keck* decision,[58] regarding the distinction between product-related restrictions, which are subject to the European Court's review, and those restrictions that merely regulate certain modalities of sale, which the European Court has said it will not review. This culminated in the distinction that advertisements that are printed on the product package are protected by the liberties of the EU Treaty, but this may not be so for the same advertisement printed in a newspaper.[59] This discussion will not be rehearsed here, since it loses much of its importance with respect to electronic commerce. Every limitation on the content of e-commerce activities coming from another member state will be a restriction on the free movement of services, since it will restrict the offer of this service. The European Court has said this explicitly with regard to print media. Every prohibition regarding the content of a magazine that is sold across borders is a restriction on the publisher's freedom to circulate goods.[60]

These basic liberties guaranteed by the EU are not unlimited. Starting with the *Cassis* decision, the European Court has developed standards of review regarding national restrictions on the basic liberties of the EU Treaty. The court employs a reasonableness test that is similar to the review of legislative acts by courts where such review is possible, for example by the German Constitutional Court. As a first step of the test, a legitimate goal has to be identified that could be furthered by the restriction in question. Secondly, the European Court will ask whether the national restriction is suitable and necessary to achieve this goal.[61]

National rules of consumer protection and against unfair competition have been accepted by the court as pursuing legitimate goals, as early as in the *Cassis* decision itself.[62] The decisive question is whether certain national consumer law rules are suitable and necessary in the eyes of the court. The answer to this question will not be determined by these concepts, but rather by the values and preferences that are put into the legal terms by the judges. In view of this lack of predictability regarding questions of necessity, it is argued by some writers that the member states should have some leeway in their own decisions regarding the necessity of specific rules, which should not be replaced by the European Court's own assessments.[63]

58 Cases C-267/91 and C-268/91, judgment of 24 November 1993, [1993] ECR I-6097. On the consequences of this decision, see N. Reich, 'Europe's Economic Constitution or a New Look on Keck' (1999) 19 *Oxford Journal of Legal Studies* 337.
59 See ECJ, Case C-470/93, judgment of 6 July 1995 (*Mars*), [1995] ECR I-1923.
60 See ECJ, Case C-368/95, judgment of 26 June 1997 (*Familiapress*), [1997] ECR I-3689.
61 Typical applications of this two-step test can be found in, e.g., ECJ, Case C-55/94, judgment of 30 November 1995 (*Gebhard*), [1995] ECR I-4165; ECJ, Case C-19/92, judgment of 31 March 1993 (*Kraus*), [1993] ECR I-1663; ECJ, Case 274/87, judgment of 2 February 1989 (*Meat Products*), [1989] ECR 229.
62 ECJ, Case 120/78, judgment of 20 February 1979, [1979] ECR 649, para. 8.
63 A. Epiney in C. Calliess and M. Ruffert, EUV/EGV, Art. 30 EGV para. 46 (1999).

The European Court, however, does not show any such deference to the member states' preferences. It uses its own standard of necessity, especially with respect to consumer protection issues. The German courts have used the model of a rather simple-minded consumer for a long time, a consumer who had to be protected by the government by paternalistic rules (for example, to pick a very controversial case, against beer containing anything other than hops, yeast, malt and water). The European Court follows a different consumer model, and bases its decisions on the assumption that consumers should usually be protected by the provision of information on the products, and not by prohibitions of certain products (as long as they are not dangerous). This model yields different results regarding the necessity of certain regulations.[64]

The European Human Rights Convention

A further source for uniform European standards in this area is the European Human Rights Convention which is interpreted by a separate judicial body, the European Court of Human Rights in Strasbourg. Every restriction on the content of electronic media will be a restriction on the freedom of expression as it is guaranteed in Article 10(1) of the Convention. This provision applies not only to political expressions, but also to commercial expressions, such as advertising or other media content,[65] although the standards of review may be different for different types of expression.

According to Article 10(2) of the Convention, restrictions on expression are allowed in so far as they are 'necessary in a democratic society'. Again, we face here the problem of different national traditions and values, and this problem is approached in the case law of the Strasbourg Court with the term of a 'margin of appreciation' that could in certain cases be left to the member states of the Convention. However, recent decisions of the Strasbourg Court regarding freedom of expression show that this margin may be rather thin and that the court is self-confident enough to set its own uniform standards.[66] While the case law of the court cannot be discussed in

---

64 See, e.g., ECJ, Case 178/84, judgment of 12 March 1987 (*Beer Purity*), [1987] ECR 1227 (German prohibition of certain beer contents violates free movement of goods); ECJ, Case 120/78, judgment of 20 February 1979 (*cassis*), [1979] ECR 649 (information on lower alcohol content of French liquor is sufficient to protect the consumer); ECJ, Case C-368/95, judgment of 26 June 1997 (*Familiapress*), [1997] ECR I-3689 (consumer will notice that the size of an advertisement is not necessarily connected to the size of the product). On a closer examination, the real problem in these and other cases is not the empirical question of how the consumer actually behaves, but the judgment on which consumer behaviour is worthy of protection by the law. For Germany, see N. Reich, *Europäisches Verbraucherrecht* (3rd edn, Baden-Baden: Nomos, 1996), 133; S. Niemöller, *Das Verbraucherleitbild in der deutschen und europäischen Rechtsprechung* (Munich: Beck, 1999), review by N. Reich, (2000) 164 *Zeitschrift für das gesamte Handelsrecht und Wirtschaftsrecht* 433.

65 ECHR, judgment of 20 November 1989, (1990) 12 EHRR 161 (Market Intern).

66 See ECHR, judgment of 1 July 1997, [1999] *Neue Juristische Wochenschrift* 1321 (*Oberschlick*); ECHR, judgment of 21 January 1999, [1999] *Neue Juristische Wochenschrift* 1315 (*Fressoz et Roire*).

depth here,[67] it provides an additional source for the development of uniform standards in unfair advertising and other media-related consumer protection issues.

Although the Human Rights Convention is not formally connected to the European Union, it is nevertheless very relevant for European Union law. Since the Treaty of Maastricht, it is explicitly stated in Article 6(2) of the EU Treaty that the rights contained in the Human Rights Convention shall be respected by the European Union. This had been accepted earlier by the European Court of Justice, so that, in effect, any media-related restriction on the free movement of goods or services must be justified not only according to EU Treaty law, but also according to Article 10 of the Human Rights Convention.[68]

Even though national consumer protection rules will be applied to advertising and other marketing activities according to private international law, they must therefore be justified under uniform European standards. The regulating power of the nation states is clearly reduced in the field of consumer law, and the traditional conflicts rule pointing towards domestic law loses much of its importance.

This result corresponds with the European Union's programme of reducing the differences between national legal orders in order to open up the internal market. The review of economic regulation according to a uniform European standard follows the *Cassis* rationale. National legal traditions and peculiarities are scrutinised under a uniform logic of necessity, levelling out differences according to rational criteria.[69] While private international law only chooses between national laws, but generally accepts their differences, the European influences sketched above substantially alter national law and gradually replace them with new and truly European standards.

The E-Commerce Directive

General approach

Although the effects described above arise already under EU 'primary' law, meaning the law of the EU Treaty, the authorities in Brussels deemed it necessary that issues of electronic commerce should be addressed by specific secondary law in order to remove the alleged legal uncertainties.[70]

---

67 More details regarding advertising can be found in G. Nolte, 'Werbefreiheit und europäische Menschenrechtskonvention' (1999) 63 *Rabels Zeitschrift für ausländisches und internationales Privatrecht* 507; R. Kulms, 'Werbung: Geschützte Meinungsäußerung oder unlauterer Wettbewerb?' (1999) 63 *Rabels Zeitschrift für ausländisches und internationales Privatrecht* 520.

68 ECJ, Case C-368/95, judgment of 26 June 1997 (*Familiapress*), [1997] ECR I-3689; ECJ, Case C-260/89, judgment of 18 June 1991 (*ERT*), [1991] ECR I-2925.

69 Cf. C. Joerges, 'Die Europäisierung des Privatrechts als Rationalisierungsprozeß und als Streit der Disziplinen' [1995] *Zeitschrift für Europäisches Privatrecht* 181; H.W. Micklitz, 'Perspektiven eines europäischen Privatrechts' [1998] *Zeitschrift für europäisches Privatrecht* 253.

70 See n. 1 above.

The E-Commerce Directive had to be implemented by the member states by January 2002. It applies to 'information society services', which encompasses all commercial Internet activities.[71] However, certain important fields, such as data protection and intellectual property issues, are explicitly excluded from its scope of application and will continue to be governed by their own specific rules.

The basic concept of the E-Commerce Directive is that Internet activities shall only be regulated by that Member State in which the supplier of these services has its place of business. The choice of this place inside the European Union may therefore be important in the future for the possible content of an Internet service. This place of business cannot be created simply by technical equipment in a certain country, but is determined by the location of the people who in fact decide on the content of the service.[72]

The country of origin of the service is supposed to regulate the service according to its own rules, and the receiving country in principle may no longer exercise any regulatory power. Article 3 of the E-Commerce Directive reads:

1. Each Member State shall ensure that the information society services provided by a service provider established on its territory comply with the national provisions applicable in the Member State in question which fall within the co-ordinated field.
2. Member States may not, for reasons falling within the co-ordinated field, restrict the freedom to provide information society services from another Member State.
3. . . .
4. Member States may take measures to derogate from paragraph 2 in respect of a given information society service if the following conditions are fulfilled:
   a. the measures shall be:
      i. necessary for one of the following reasons:
         – public policy, in particular the prevention, investigation, detection and prosecution of criminal offences, including the protection of minors and the fight against any incitement to hatred on grounds of race, sex, religion or nationality, and violations of human dignity concerning individual persons,
         – the protection of public health,
         – public security, including the safeguarding of national security and defence,
         – the protection of consumers, including investors;

---

71 Art. 2(a) of the E-Commerce Directive points to the definition included in Directive 98/34/EC as amended by Directive 98/48/EC, OJ 1998 No. L217, p. 18, which defines 'information society services' as all services rendered electronically on individual demand without physical meeting of the parties.

72 See the similar questions with regard to the EC's TV Directive: ECJ, Case C-56/96, judgment of 5 June 1997 (VT 4), [1997] ECR I-3143.

      ii. taken against a given information society service which prejudices the objectives referred to in point (i) or which presents a serious and grave risk of prejudice to those objectives;

      iii. proportionate to those objectives;

   b. before taking the measures in question and without prejudice to court proceedings, including preliminary proceedings and acts carried out in the framework of a criminal investigation, the Member State has:

      – asked the Member State referred to in paragraph 1 to take measures and the latter did not take such measures, or they were inadequate,

      – notified the Commission and the Member State referred to in paragraph 1 of its intention to take such measures.

5. Member States may, in the case of urgency, derogate from the conditions stipulated in paragraph 4 (b). Where this is the case, the measures shall be notified in the shortest possible time to the Commission and to the Member State referred to in paragraph 1, indicating the reasons for which the Member State considers that there is urgency.

6. Without prejudice to the Member State's possibility of proceeding with the measures in question, the Commission shall examine the compatibility of the notified measures with Community law in the shortest possible time; where it comes to the conclusion that the measure is incompatible with Community law, the Commission shall ask the Member State in question to refrain from taking any proposed measures or urgently to put an end to the measures in question.

Looking at paragraphs (1) and (2) of this Article, the remaining regulatory competence of the member states depends on the extent of the 'coordinated field'. This term has caused problems already in the EC TV Directive, whereby TV programmes are to be regulated only by their country of origin as far as the field co-ordinated by the Directive is concerned. However, the European Court decided with regard to the TV Directive that the co-ordinated field does not cover all rules relevant to the content of TV programmes, especially not general rules on unfair advertising. The Swedish Consumer Ombudsman was therefore allowed to proceed in Sweden with an action against unfair advertising in a TV programme that originated in the United Kingdom.[73]

   In the E-Commerce Directive, these uncertainties regarding the scope of the co-ordinated field are eliminated by a broad definition of the co-ordinated field. According to Article 2(h)(i) of the E-Commerce Directive, it consists of all requirements with which the service provider has to comply in respect of the pursuit of the activity of an information society service, in particular 'requirements regarding the quality or content of the service including those applicable to advertising'. Contrary

---

73 ECJ, Cases C-34/95, C-35/95 and C-36/95, judgment of 9 July 1997 (*De Agostini*), [1997] ECR I-3843.

to the TV Directive, the E-Commerce Directive therefore generally rules out any regulation by the receiving country regarding the content of the service. This includes not only administrative regulations, but also restrictions imposed by courts based on private law, such as laws on unfair competition or consumer protection.[74]

How does this relate to the operation of private international law? The E-Commerce Directive purports in its Article 1(4) not to 'establish additional rules on private international law nor does it deal with the jurisdiction of Courts'. This sibylline language leaves us with two possible interpretations. If it means what it literally says, namely that all decisions by national courts resulting from the application of existing rules of private international law would be reconcilable with the Directive, then the Directive would never achieve its goal of eliminating legal uncertainties arising from the application of differing national laws. As described above, the existing private international law rules in the area of advertising and unfair competition point towards the law of the marketplace and therefore to the different national laws of the member states if a marketing activity is directed at the whole internal market. This literal interpretation would defeat the Directive's purpose and cannot be seriously considered.[75]

The Directive's language therefore must be interpreted in accordance with its purpose, meaning that private international law rules as such may remain untouched, but their results must be measured against the Directive and must be reduced to the limit compatible with the Directive.[76] This procedure would also conform with Recital 23 of the Directive, which states that the applicable law determined by conflict rules 'must not restrict the freedom to provide information society services as established in this Directive'. The German implementation of the E-Commerce Directive follows this interpretation. It states that, in respect of e-commerce services from other EU member states, restrictive domestic rules are to be applied only under the conditions of Article 3(4) of the Directive.[77]

Even though the Directive does not establish new private international law rules, it severely weakens the existing private international law since its results will be acceptable under EU law only under the limiting conditions laid down in the Directive.

---

74 This is reflected especially in the E-Commerce Directive, recital 25, which states that 'national courts, including civil courts, dealing with private law disputes can take measures to derogate from the freedom to provide information society services in conformity with conditions established in this Directive'. The last part of this sentence means that an injunction against unfair advertising would be possible only under the conditions laid down in the Directive.

75 With respect to the drafts of the E-Commerce Directive, see P. Mankowski, 'Internet und internationales Wettbewerbsrecht' [1999] *Gewerblicher Rechtsschutz und Urheberrecht International* 909, 913. The Directive would not make sense if it could be circumvented through private international law rules.

76 See H. Schack, 'Internationale Urheber-, Marken- und Wettbewerbsrechtsverletzungen im Internet' [2000] *Multimedia und Recht* 59, 63.

77 Teledienstegesetz § 4(5), 2001 Bundesgesetzblatt I 3721.

The country-of-origin principle

Some German writers have suggested that the E-Commerce Directive creates a country-of-origin principle, in the sense that private law claims based on activities falling under the Directive would always be governed by the law of the country of origin of that activity.[78] Some even claim that this principle would include the application of the private international law of the country of origin, meaning that the applicable substantive law would depend on a series of conflicts rules, possibly resulting in the application of the substantive law of the marketplace.[79] This latter opinion is untenable, since it completely conflicts with the purpose of the Directive, which aims to clarify applicable rules and not to complicate matters through the application of a series of national conflict rules.[80]

But even the general idea of a country-of-origin principle in the Directive is flawed. The Directive does not order the receiving states to apply the substantive law of the country of origin of the service, but it generally forbids any restriction imposed by the receiving state (see Article 3(2) cited above). However, as in general EU law, a service provider should not be able to rely on this protective rule if he or she does not even meet the requirements imposed by his or her home country's law.[81]

The review of a claim against a service falling under the scope of the E-Commerce Directive must therefore follow this procedure. First, the governing law is determined according to existing conflicts rules. This will usually lead to domestic substantive law, if the case relates to an activity affecting the domestic market. If the activity is lawful under these domestic substantive rules, there can be no claim against the service provider at all. The Directive therefore contains a most-favourable-law principle rather than a country-of-origin principle.[82]

Only if the activity is unlawful under domestic substantive rules and the claim against the service provider would exist, must it then be determined whether this would also be the case in the country of origin, in which case the restriction to be imposed by the domestic court would be possible according to the principle stated above.[83] If the applicable law of the receiving state provides for a restriction

---

78 See G. Spindler, 'E-Commerce in Europa' [2000] *Multimedia und Recht* Supplement 7/2000, 4, 9; N. Dethloff, 'Europäisches Kollisionsrecht des unlauteren Wettbewerbs' [2000] *Juristenzeitung* 179, 180; P. Mankowski, 'Das Herkunftslandprinzip als internationales Privatrecht der e-commerce-Richtlinie' (2001) 100 *Zeitschrift für vergleichende Rechtswissenschaft* 137, 179, proposing a new private international law rule as an implementation of the E-Commerce Directive.

79 See Spindler, 'E-Commerce'.   80 See Mankowski, 'Das Herkunftslandprinzip', 152.

81 For this general principle, see ECJ, Case 120/78, judgment of 20 February 1979 (*Cassis*), [1979] ECR 649; N. Reich, 'Rechtsprobleme grenzüberschreitender irreführender Werbung im Binnenmarkt' (1992) 56 *Rabels Zeitschrift für ausländisches und internationales Privatrecht* 444, 492.

82 For this distinction regarding EU Treaty law, see Basedow, 'Der Kollisionsrechtliche Gehalt der Produktfreiheiten', 15.

83 T. Bodewig, 'Elektronischer Geschäftsverkehr und unlauterer Wettbewerb' [2000] *Gewerblicher Rechtsschutz und Urheberrecht International* 475, 480.

that would not exist in the country of origin, such a stricter national regulation is only possible under the conditions set out in Article 3(4) of the E-Commerce Directive, as cited above. These conditions are of both a substantive and a procedural nature.

With regard to the substantive conditions under which stricter national regulation is possible, Article 3(4)(a) contains a catalogue of legitimate goals, including consumer protection, and states that the national measure in question must be necessary to achieve these goals. This concept is basically the same as the concept used by the European Court in its review of national restrictions on the basic liberties of the EU Treaty. The same substantive criteria regarding the necessity of consumer protection measures or measures against unfair competition must be applied here.[84]

The procedural conditions laid out in Article 3(4)(b) seem rather problematic, especially with respect to judicial proceedings which often need to be quick in order to be effective. The wording 'without prejudice to court proceedings' in this paragraph should be interpreted in the sense that the existing procedural rules of the member states will not be altered. Injunctions or other preliminary measures may therefore be granted without going into the cumbersome notification procedure described in Article 3(4)(b). This special procedure can apply only for administrative restrictions planned by the member states' governmental authorities, not for civil court proceedings.[85]

With regard to restrictions on e-commerce services in the interests of consumer protection, the E-Commerce Directive therefore does not change much when compared with the existing EU Treaty law. Such restrictions are possible, but they must be justified on rational grounds of necessity according to the *Cassis* doctrine. A country-of-origin principle in the sense of a new conflicts rule does not exist.

Conclusion

The chaos described in the introduction to this essay could be ameliorated slightly, but private international law does not remain untouched by political and economic developments. In the field of consumer contracts, as well as in non-

---

84 An identical 'pattern of review' regarding the EU Treaty basic liberties and E-Commerce Directive Art. 3(4) is also seen by E. Jayme and C. Kohler, 'Europäisches Kollisionsrecht 2000: interlokales Privatrecht oder universelles Gemeinschaftsrecht?' [2000] *Praxis des internationalen Privat- und Verfahrensrechts* 454, 455. Cf. Mankowski, 'Das Herkunftslandprinzip', 171, claiming that the E-Commerce Directive's conditions for national measures are stricter than those under EU Treaty law.

85 Cf. E. Crabit, 'La directive sur le commerce électronique le projet Méditerranée' [2000] *Revue du droit de l'Union européenne* 749, 790, arguing that notification procedures must be followed even in court proceedings as long as possible.

contractual consumer protection law, traditional conflicts rules still exist, but are often blotted out by substantive EU rules.

Although one cannot wave goodbye to private international law, one has to reconsider its operation. The *Ingmar* case shows that the scope of *lois de police* thought to be narrow under traditional doctrine may expand to cover many areas of EU legislation. The E-Commerce Directive highlights the existing principles of EU law under which domestic rules, although theoretically applicable by virtue of private international law, must often be scrutinised according to substantive European standards of rationality and necessity.

Both of these tendencies will contribute to a uniform European standard of consumer protection which will follow the logic of rationality founded with *Cassis*. This uniform standard will be developed not only by the EU legislature, but also by the European courts, both the Human Rights Court in Strasbourg and the European Court of Justice in Luxemburg, through their case law. It may call into question many national rules and national idiosyncrasies, but there will certainly not be any 'race to the bottom'[86] regarding cross-border consumer protection in Europe.

---

86 Cf. Mankowski, 'Das Herkunftslandprinzip', 158, warning of the race to the bottom and 'Delawarisation'.

Index

Printed in the United States
By Bookmasters